Central Europe in the High Middle Ages

This groundbreaking comparative history of the early centuries of Bohemia, Hungary and Poland sets the development of each polity in the context of the central European region as a whole. Focusing on the origins of the realms and their development in the eleventh and twelfth centuries, the book concludes with the thirteenth century when significant changes in social and economic structures occurred. The book presents a series of thematic chapters on every aspect of the early history of the region covering political, religious, economic, social and cultural developments, including an investigation of origin myths that questions traditional national narratives. It also explores the ways in which west European patterns were appropriated and adapted through the local initiatives of rulers, nobles and ecclesiastics in central Europe. An ideal introduction to the essential themes in medieval central European history, the book sheds important new light on regional similarities and differences.

NORA BEREND is Senior Lecturer in the Faculty of History at the University of Cambridge, and Fellow of St Catharine's College, Cambridge. Her previous publications include *At the Gate of Christendom: Jews, Muslims and 'Pagans' in Medieval Hungary* (c. *1000*–c. *1300*) (Cambridge, 2001), for which she received the Royal Historical Society's Gladstone Prize in 2002, and *Christianization and the Rise of Christian Monarchy: Scandinavia, Central Europe and Rus'* c. *900–1200* (as editor, Cambridge, 2007).

PRZEMYSŁAW URBAŃCZYK is Professor at the Cardinal Wyszyński University in Warsaw and in the Institute of Archaeology and Ethnology, Polish Academy of Sciences. He specializes in the medieval archaeology and history of Poland, East Central Europe, Scandinavia and the north Atlantic islands. His previous publications include *Zdobywcy północnego Atlantyku* (Conquerors of the North Atlantic) (2004) and *Trudne początki Polski* (Poland's Difficult Origins) (2008), which won the Klio prize for best history book of the year.

PRZEMYSŁAW WISZEWSKI is Professor at the University of Wrocław, Department of Historical and Pedagogical Sciences. He specializes in comparative regional history, with a special emphasis on borderlands, from the tenth to the twentieth centuries. His previous publications include *Domus Bolezlai: Values and Social Identity in Dynastic Traditions of Medieval Poland* (c. *966–1138*) (2010), the Polish edition of which was honoured with the Prize of the Ministry of Science.

# CENTRAL EUROPE IN THE HIGH MIDDLE AGES

## BOHEMIA, HUNGARY AND POLAND

### *c.* 900–*c.* 1300

NORA BEREND,
PRZEMYSŁAW URBAŃCZYK AND
PRZEMYSŁAW WISZEWSKI

**CAMBRIDGE**
**UNIVERSITY PRESS**

University Printing House, Cambridge CB2 8BS, United Kingdom

Published in the United States of America by Cambridge University Press, New York

Cambridge University Press is part of the University of Cambridge.

It furthers the University's mission by disseminating knowledge in the pursuit of education, learning, and research at the highest international levels of excellence.

www.cambridge.org
Information on this title: www.cambridge.org/9780521786959



First published 2013

Printed in the United Kingdom by Butler Tanner and Dennis Ltd

*A catalogue record for this publication is available from the British Library*

*Library of Congress Cataloguing in Publication data*
Berend, Nora.
Central Europe in the high Middle Ages : Bohemia, Hungary and Poland c.900–c.1300 / Nora Berend, Przemysław Urbańczyk and Przemysław Wiszewski.
p. cm.
Includes bibliographical references.
ISBN 978-0-521-78156-5 – ISBN 978-0-521-78695-9 (pbk.)
1. Europe, Central – History – To 1500. 2. Bohemia (Czech Republic) – History – To 1526. 3. Hungary – History – 896-1301. 4. Poland – History – To 1572. I. Urbanczyk, Przemyslaw. II. Wiszewski, Przemyslaw. III. Title.
DAW1046.B47 2013
943.000902–dc23
2013013357

ISBN 978-0-521-78156-5 Hardback
ISBN 978-0-521-78695-9 Paperback

# CONTENTS

# NOTE AND ACKNOWLEDGEMENTS

Przemysław Urbańczyk and Przemysław Wiszewski wrote the sections on Bohemia and Poland; Nora Berend wrote the Introduction and the sections on Hungary. The availability of the source material has led to some imbalances in the discussion of themes and areas.

Central European names often have many alternative spellings in the medieval texts, and yet another modern form reconstructed by scholars. We signal various versions in the first instance, and then use the modern vernacular form. Similarly, central European town names, except some of those generally familiar to English-speakers, are used in the vernacular, with the modern names in parentheses if they are different. Regions and geographical names are given in English to facilitate reading, with local variants in parentheses in the first instance where needed. Eastern, Western and Central Europe as well as Eastern and Western are capitalized when they refer to concepts or to the political division of Europe after the Second World War, but are used in the lower case when they refer to relative geographical position in the pre-modern world.

Nora Berend wishes to thank László Veszprémy, Béla Zsolt Szakács, Walter Pohl, Jonathan Shepard, Teresa Shawcross and László Koszta for their comments and bibliographical suggestions. The authors would like to thank the copy-editor, Karen Anderson Howes, for her excellent work.

# MAPS

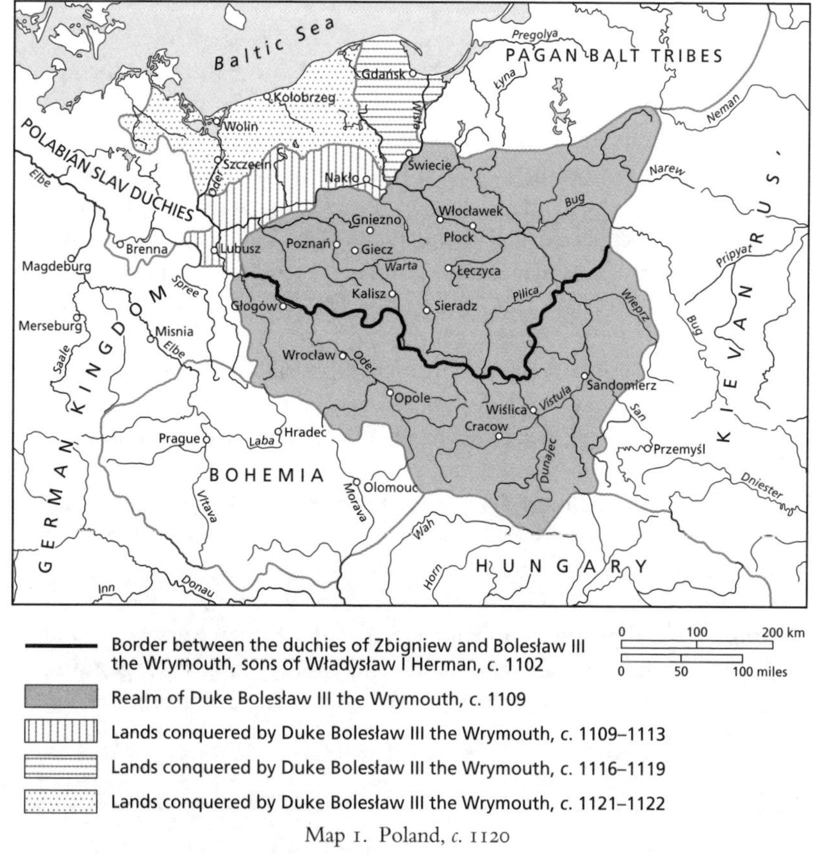


Map 1. Poland, *c.* 1120

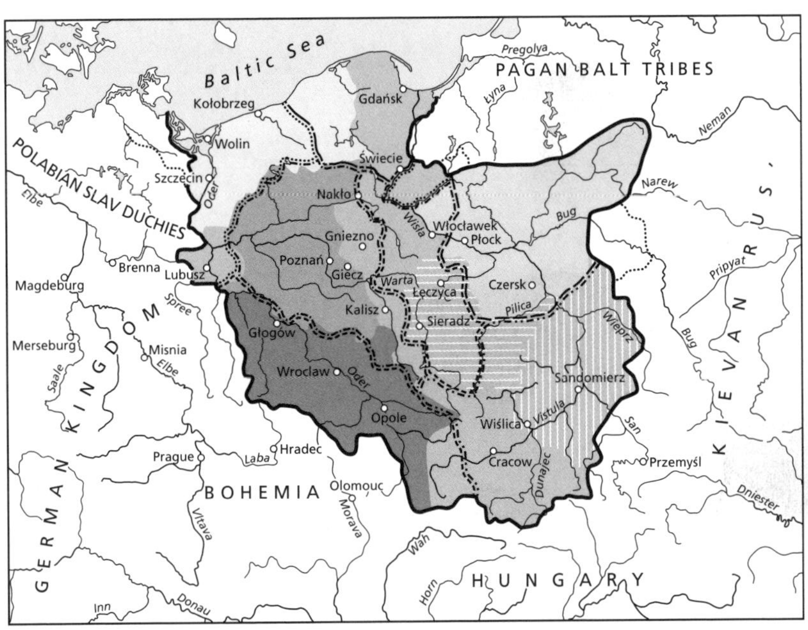


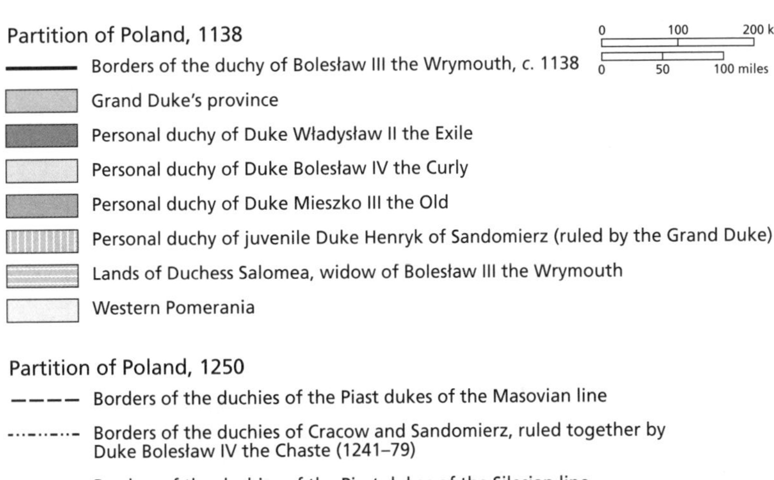

## Partition of Poland, 1138

0 100 200 km
0 50 100 miles

- Borders of the duchy of Bolesław III the Wrymouth, *c.* 1138
- Grand Duke's province
- Personal duchy of Duke Władysław II the Exile
- Personal duchy of Duke Bolesław IV the Curly
- Personal duchy of Duke Mieszko III the Old
- Personal duchy of juvenile Duke Henryk of Sandomierz (ruled by the Grand Duke)
- Lands of Duchess Salomea, widow of Bolesław III the Wrymouth
- Western Pomerania

## Partition of Poland, 1250

- Borders of the duchies of the Piast dukes of the Masovian line
- Borders of the duchies of Cracow and Sandomierz, ruled together by Duke Bolesław IV the Chaste (1241–79)
- Borders of the duchies of the Piast dukes of the Silesian line
- Borders of the duchies of the Piast dukes of the Greater Poland line
- Borders of Gdańsk–Pomerania
- Borders of lands lost by the Piasts after 1138

Map 2. The partition of Poland in 1138 and 1250

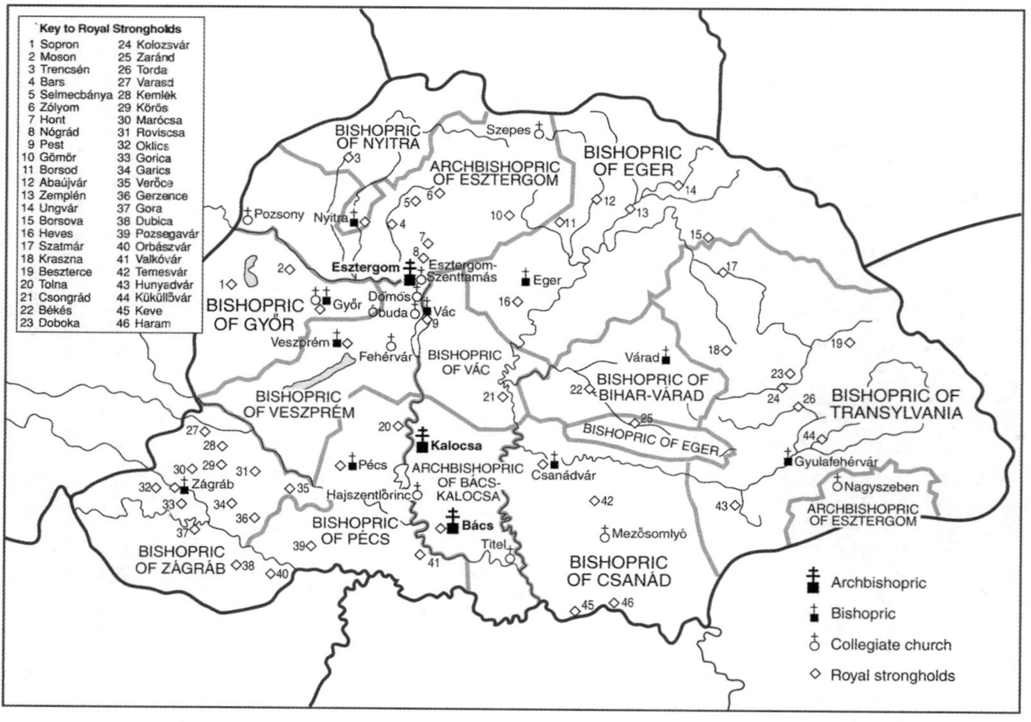


Map 3. The Kingdom of Hungary in the twelfth century

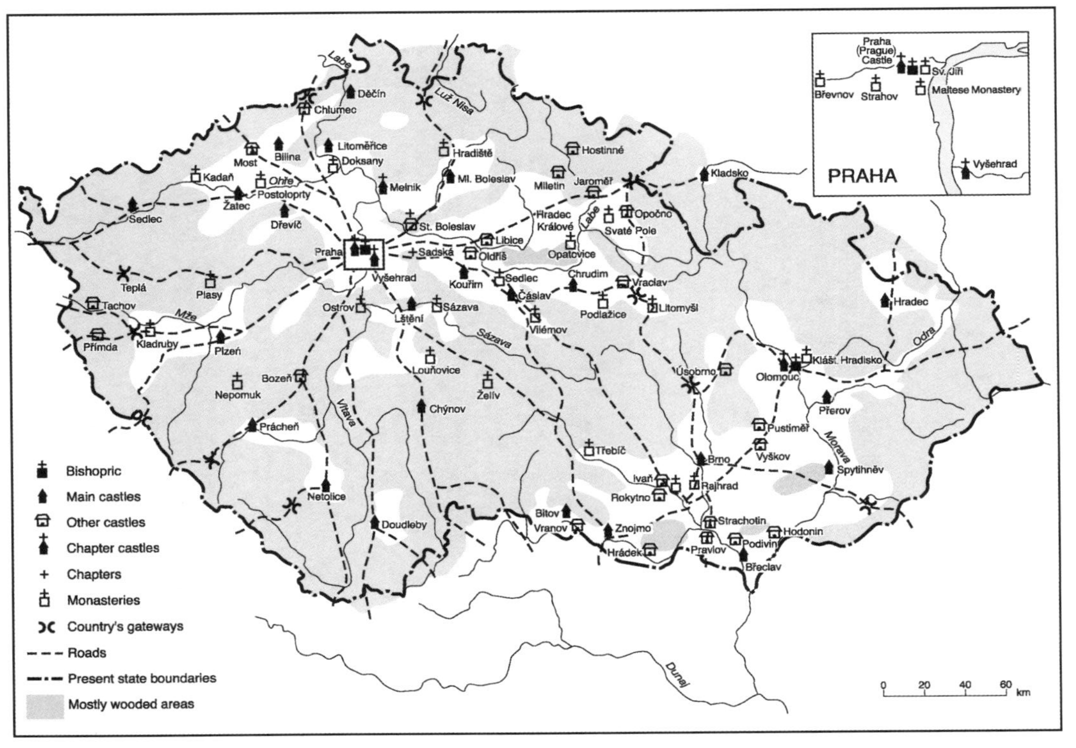


Map 4. Czech lands in the first half of the twelfth century (after Z. Boháč)

# I

# INTRODUCTION: DID CENTRAL EUROPE EXIST IN THE MIDDLE AGES?

## THE CONCEPT OF CENTRAL EUROPE

'It is time that some scholarly institute of ours . . . decides, in the end, which historical region we live in: Western Europe or Eastern Europe; Central Europe or Central-Eastern Europe; Carpathian Europe or the Danubian area; or elsewhere.'[1] This irritated outburst highlights the difficulties of determining whether Central Europe exists, and if so, where, even in modern times. Because the concept of Central Europe is a modern rather than a medieval one, it is necessary to look at its origin, meanings and implications in modern history before discussing its relevance to the Middle Ages.

Searching for a definition reveals a multitude of divergent ones. Based on claims of common identity, history or culture, 'Central Europe' at its narrowest can include the so-called Visegrád group (initially Czechoslovakia, Hungary and Poland, but since the 'velvet divorce', the Czech Republic, Hungary, Poland and Slovakia), but alternatively it can mean these countries and some or all of the following: Austria, Germany, Liechtenstein, Slovenia, Switzerland, Croatia, Romania, Serbia and Ukraine. The reason for such discrepancy, apart from the historically changing borders of various states, is that the criteria which determine inclusion in 'Central Europe' vary widely. They can be cultural, political,

[1] Tibor Baráth, '"Kárpát-Európa" vagy "Kelet-Európa"' (1940), in Iván T. Berend, ed., *Helyünk Európában*, 2 vols., 2nd edn (Budapest, 1986), vol. I, 506–8 (see 508).

socio-economic, historical or a combination of these, and past- or present-oriented.

For example, Central Europe has been defined as the area of German cultural influence; the area closest to and under the strongest Western influence; the area of the Habsburg Empire; the area of the Polish-Lithuanian commonwealth; the area whose eastern limits correspond to the eastern frontiers of medieval kingdoms, in turn corresponding to the frontier between Catholic West and Orthodox East; the area where East and West meet; the easternmost area that has a Western cultural orientation; a cultural zone; the countries that joined the EU in 2004 or are on track to join; a community of destinies in times of crisis alone; and an area shaped by a whole host of historical developments. The historically changing meaning of Central Europe has also been emphasized.[2] No more or less precise is the recent United Nations definition of 'a cultural region called Central Europe', based on eight factors including aspects of religious, cultural, social, economic and political development, many of them in a comparative perspective with Western, South-Eastern, Eastern, Southern and Northern Europe.[3] Other definitions focus on modes of self-perception and include multiculturality and multilingualism,

[2] Lonnie R. Johnson, *Central Europe: Enemies, Neighbors, Friends* (New York and Oxford, 1996), 3–12; Georges Castellan, *Histoire des peuples de l'Europe centrale* (Paris, 1994); Chantal Delsol, Michel Maslowski and Joanna Nowicki, eds., *Mythes et symboles politiques en Europe centrale* (Paris, 2002); Peter J. Katzenstein, ed., *Mitteleuropa: Between Europe and Germany* (Providence, RI, 1997); André Sellier and Jean Sellier, *Atlas des peuples d'Europe centrale*, new edn (Paris, 1995); Ferenc L. Lendvai, *Közép-Európa-koncepciók* (Budapest, 1997); Mária Ormos, *Közép-Európa: Volt? Van? Lesz?* (Budapest, 2007), 9–21; Gérard Beauprêtre, ed., *L'Europe centrale, réalité, mythe, enjeu, XVIIIe–XIXe siècles* (Warsaw, 1991); 'Europe centrale. Mitteleuropa', *Revue germanique internationale* 1 (1994) (entire issue, and especially Krzysztof Pomian, 'L'Europe centrale: essais de définition', 11–23); Jacques Le Rider, *La Mitteleuropa* (Paris, 1994); George Schöpflin and Nancy Wood, eds., *In Search of Central Europe* (Cambridge, 1989); 'Central Europe: ten years after', issue 6, 1 (1999), *European Review of History/Revue Européenne d'Histoire*; Robin Okey, 'Central Europe/Eastern Europe: behind the definitions', *Past and Present* 137 (1992), 102–33; Przemysław Urbańczyk, ed., *Origins of Central Europe* (Warsaw, 1997); Ferenc Fehér, 'On making Central Europe', *Eastern European Politics and Societies* 3, 3 (1989), 412–47.

[3] Peter Jordan, 'A subdivision of Europe into larger regions by cultural criteria', United Nations Group of Experts on Geographical Names, Working Paper no. 48, 23rd session, Vienna, 28 March–4 April 2006, unstats.un.org./unsd/geoinfo/gegn23wp48.pdf (accessed 7 Jan. 2010).

the area of coffee-house culture, strudel and spritzer, marked by Ashkenazi Jewish culture, seen by some as the principal representative of a Central European culture. Even 'love of poetry, idealism and cynicism' have been cited as defining characteristics of the region.[4]

Historically, *Mitteleuropa* was significant among such designations. Sometimes this is translated as Middle Europe. It usually refers to the areas under strong German cultural influence prior to the First World War, and can thus be invoked as a region with – at least in many respects – a common culture, although the area it designates can be the region between the Rhine and the Vistula or the much larger zone between the Rhine and the Dnieper. The term also has a geographical meaning, but is no more objective or precise than 'Central Europe'; there never existed one sole concept of *Mitteleuropa*.[5]

In case it would seem that the obviously 'right' solution is for the term 'Central Europe' to cover the geographical centre of Europe, it is necessary to emphasize – as has been demonstrated many times – that definitions of 'geographical' subregions of Europe have very little to do with geography. Moreover, there is in fact absolutely no consensus about *where* the geographical centre of Europe is. That in itself depends on how one defines the borders of Europe, notably whether islands are included or not. Therefore many places lay claim to being Europe's centre, including places in Austria, Lithuania, Hungary, Slovakia, Estonia and Belarus. These places go as far west as Frauenkirchen, Austria, at 47°50'N 16°55'E, and as far east as Purnuškės in Lithuania, at 54°54'N 25°19'E. One calculation even

[4] Examples include: Ormos, *Közép-Európa*, 10, 269; Le Rider, *Mitteleuropa*, 75–91; Johnson, *Central Europe*, 6; Philip Longworth, *The Making of Eastern Europe: From Prehistory to Postcommunism*, 2nd rev. edn (London, 1997), 5–6; Czesław Miłosz, 'Central European attitudes', in *Cross-Currents: A Yearbook of Central European Culture* 5 (1986), 101–8, repr. Schöpflin and Wood, eds., *In Search*, 116–24; Jacques Rupnik, 'Central Europe or Mitteleuropa?', in Stephen R. Graubard, ed., *Eastern Europe . . . Central Europe . . . Europe* (Boulder, CO, 1991), 233–65, esp. 235–8.

[5] Frank Hadler, 'Mitteleuropa – "Zwischeneuropa" – Ostmitteleuropa. Reflexionen über eine europäische Geschichtsregion im 19. und 20. Jh.', *Geisteswissenschaftliches Zentrum für Geschichte und Kultur Ostmitteleuropas Berichte und Beiträge* (1996), 34–63; Richard G. Plaschka, Horst Haselsteiner, Arnold Suppan, Anna M. Drabek and Brigitta Zaar, eds., *Mitteleuropa-Konzeptionen in der ersten Hälfte des 20. Jahrhundert* (Vienna, 1995); Le Rider, *Mitteleuropa*; Peter Bugge, 'The use of the Middle: Mitteleuropa vs Střední Evropa', *European Review of History – Revue Européenne d'Histoire* 6, 1 (1999), 15–35. Egon Schwarz, 'Central Europe – What it is and what it is not', in Schöpflin and Wood, eds., *In Search*, 143–56, lists many older works.

locates Europe's centre in southern Norway, 60°00'N 07°30'E. One cannot unambiguously and factually determine what exact area 'Central Europe' should contain, based on geography.[6]

To make matters even more complicated, the terminology itself is debated, some scholars preferring Eastern Europe, rather than Central Europe, for the countries under investigation in this book, with yet others choosing East-Central, Central-Eastern or other designations. Some, notably István Bibó, used Eastern Europe to indicate the three states of Czechoslovakia, Hungary and Poland.[7] More often, however, Eastern Europe includes in one category everything east of the Rivers Elbe and Saale, thus encompassing a much larger area than treated in this book (including East German and Austrian, Czech, Slovak, Hungarian, Polish, Lithuanian, Romanian, Ukrainian, Belarusian, Russian, Bulgarian, Croat and Serb lands).[8] Eastern Europe has also been characterized in historical geography as a march-land or shatterbelt territory, where independent antagonistic powers emerged, and where conflicting great power interests, impulses and influences from East and West clashed, a region that cannot be unified either in itself or as part of one of the contending powers.[9]

East-Centre Europe, East-Central Europe, Central-Eastern Europe and the German *Ostmitteleuropa* (since 1918) have all been proposed as designations of the whole area between the Baltic, Adriatic, Aegean and Black Seas in the broadest definition, or for the area between Germany and Russia, or just for the countries treated in this book. (Thus the terms can cover only Czech and Slovak lands, Hungary and Poland, or also Romania, Slovenia, Croatia, Albania, Austria, Bosnia and so on.) The extent of the

[6] E.g. Okey, 'Central Europe', 103–4; László Péter, 'Central Europe and its reading into the past', *European Review of History – Revue Européenne d'Histoire* 6, 1 (1999), 101–11, on 101: 'The nationality of the map-maker rather than some principles of geography determine the location of "Central Europe".'

[7] István Bibó, 'A Kelet-Európai kisállamok nyomorúsága' (1946), in Bibó, *Válogatott Tanulmányok*, ed. Endre Nagy and István Vida, 4 vols. (Budapest, 1986–90), vol. II, 185–265; French tr. *Misère des petits états d'Europe de l'Est* (Paris, 1986, 2nd edn 1993).

[8] E.g. Longworth, *Making of Eastern Europe*; Robert Bideleux and Ian Jeffries, *A History of Eastern Europe: Crisis and Change*, 2nd edn (London, 2007); various authors, 'Historiography of the countries of Eastern Europe', *American Historical Review* 97, 4 (1992), 1011–1117, includes Poland, Czechoslovakia, Hungary, Romania, Yugoslavia and Bulgaria.

[9] David Turnock, *The Making of Eastern Europe: From the Earliest Times to 1815* (London and New York, 1988).

territory included in the definition partly depends on the period which serves as its basis. For example, if the designation is based on the later medieval kingdoms of Bohemia, Poland-Lithuania and Hungary, that, in modern terms, translates to the Czech Republic, Slovakia, Hungary, Poland, Lithuania, Belarus, Ukraine, Croatia and Transylvania (i.e. part of Romania). For the purposes of this book, it is important to point out that the union of Poland-Lithuania happened much later than the period we cover, and the eastern areas were not part of the kingdom of Poland.

The terminology, itself suggestive of a 'middle' position, is often linked to the characterization of the area as lands in between, where East and West meet, a meeting conceived of in a variety of ways (for example, in one formulation the region is a 'child of the West who later married the East', while elsewhere it is a mixture of Eastern and Western).[10] *Westmitteleuropa* is much rarer, designating

[10] Quotation from George H. Hodos, *The East-Central European Region: An Historical Outline* (Westport, CT, and London, 1999), 19; Oskar Halecki, *Borderlands of Western Civilization: A History of East Central Europe* (New York, 1952, 2nd edn ed. by Andrew L. Simon, Safety Harbor, FL, [2000?]); Jerzy Kłoczowski, *L'Europe du Centre-Est dans l'historiographie des pays de la région* (Lublin, 1995); Kłoczowski *et al.*, *East-Central Europe's Position within Europe: Between East and West* (Lublin, 2004); Kłoczowski, with Hubert Łaszkiewicz, eds., *East-Central Europe in European History: Themes and Debates* (Lublin, 2009); Klaus Zernack, 'Zum Problem der nationalen Identität in Ostmitteleuropa', in Helmut Berding, ed., *Nationales Bewußtsein und kollektive Identität* (Frankfurt am Main, 1994), 176–88; Jacques Rupnik, 'In search of East-Central Europe: ten years after', in *Central and Southeastern Europe in Transition: Perspectives on Success and Failure Since 1989*, ed. Hall Gardner (Westport, CT, 2000), 5–19; Paul Robert Magocsi, *Historical Atlas of East Central Europe* (Seattle, 1993); Alan Palmer, *The Lands Between: A History of East-Central Europe since the Congress of Vienna* (London, 1970); Werner Conze, *Ostmitteleuropa von der Spätantike bis zum 18. Jahrhundert* (Munich, 1992); Piotr S. Wandycz, *The Price of Freedom: A History of East Central Europe from the Middle Ages to the Present* (London and New York, 1992); Anna Adamska and Marco Mostert, eds., *The Development of Literate Mentalities in East Central Europe* (Turnhout, 2004); Piotr Górecki and Nancy Van Deusen, eds., *Central and Eastern Europe in the Middle Ages: A Cultural History* (London and New York, 2009), who use the two terms in the title, and 'East Central Europe' in the introduction and conclusion, focusing on the three kingdoms of Bohemia, Hungary and Poland; J. W. Sedlar, *East Central Europe in the Middle Ages, 1000–1500* (Seattle, 1994), and the whole series of which it is a part, *A History of East Central Europe*, edited by Peter F. Sugar and Donald W. Treadgold (Seattle, 1974–); Florin Curta, ed., *East Central and Eastern Europe in the Early Middle Ages* (Ann Arbor, 2005); Natalia Aleksiun *et al.*, eds., *Histoire de l'Europe du Centre-Est* (Paris, 2004); Rudolf Jaworski, 'Ostmitteleuropa. Zur Tauglichkeit und Akzeptanz eines historischen

the area of German economic, social and cultural influence, a symbiosis with German culture, and is used sometimes for Bohemia.[11] The term *Zwischeneuropa*, implying a region open to be dominated by neighbouring great powers, appeared in the early twentieth century but was not widely adopted. Along with *Europe médiane*, it is also sometimes used instead of Central or East-Central Europe by those who see the in-between status of these countries as their main characteristic.[12] A few other terms have been coined by medievalists for the countries covered in this book, such as 'younger Europe', 'newcomers' to Europe or 'third Europe'.[13] The same areas, therefore, can be designated by a variety of different names, sometimes as synonyms, other times as carriers of a distinct meaning, while the same term can mean a different area for each scholar.

All students of history know that terminological debates can be infertile. In this case, however, it is very pertinent to ask 'what's in a name'.[14] Regional and national identity as seen from inside and as imposed from outside are at stake. The two, in the modern period, can be radically different from each other. The diversity of terms and seeming word-games relate to political and other interests, and to questions of identity. Thus, the origin of the concept of *Mitteleuropa* is strongly linked to German economic and political interests, and hence been rejected by many as a disguise or justification for German domination. The term had sporadic seventeenth-century precedents, and was used in the early nineteenth century as a geographic label. It quickly acquired economic and political significance with Friedrich List in the first half of the nineteenth century. *Mitteleuropa* was

Hilfsbegriffs', in Winfried Eberhard, Hans Lemberg, Heinz-Dieter Heimann and Robert Luft, eds., *Westmitteleuropa Ostmitteleuropa. Vergleiche und Beziehungen. Festschrift für Ferdinand Seibt zum 65. Gesburtstag* (Munich, 1992), 37–45; Ferdinand Seibt, 'Zwischen Ost und West. Versuch einer Ortsbestimmung,' in Seibt, ed., *Die böhmischen Länder zwischen Ost und West. Festschrift für Karl Bosl zum 75. Geburtstag* (Munich and Vienna, 1983), 1–16.

11 Eberhard, *et al.*, eds., *Westmitteleuropa*, ultimately going back to Halecki.

12 Otto Forst de Battaglia, *Zwischeneuropa. Von der Ostsee bis zur Adria* (Frankfurt am Main, 1954).

13 Jerzy Kłoczowski, *Młodsza Europa. Europa Środkowo-Wschodnia w kręgu cywilizacji chrześcijańskiej średniowiecza* (Warsaw, 1998); Jan M. Piskorski, 'After Occidentalism: the Third Europe writes its own history', in Piskorski, ed., *Historiographical Approaches to Medieval Colonization of East Central Europe* (Boulder, CO, 2002); Aleksander Gieysztor, *L'Europe nouvelle autour de l'an mil: la papauté, l'Empire et les 'nouveaux venus'* (Rome, 1997).

14 Wandycz, *Price of Freedom*, uses this as the title of his Introduction, 1.

connected to a role Germany envisioned for itself in Europe, namely a desire for economic and political expansion and hegemony, sometimes linked to a German self-representation as the 'middle', that is, centre, of Europe. German unification was seen as a first step to uniting Europe or parts of Europe from the 'centre' (Germany), especially from the middle of the nineteenth century. Although France, Belgium, the Netherlands and Scandinavian countries were also often included among regions to be brought under German economic and political dominance, eastern and south-eastern areas of Europe were thought by many to be 'natural' spheres of German influence, civilizing mission and cultural hegemony.

Diverse proponents of the *Mitteleuropa* concept before the First World War meant different regions by this term. An economic association, the Mitteleuropäischer Wirtschaftsverein, was founded in 1904 in Berlin, but the real father and popularizer of the concept was Friedrich Naumann, who called for the establishment of an economic federation centring on Germany and Austria-Hungary, with the voluntary adhesion of smaller states.[15] Although he did not advocate domination by force, unlike many others who referred to *Mitteleuropa*, his ideas have been interpreted variously as the forerunner of the concept of a more democratic federation, or as a proposal simply for a different form of German domination. By the time of the First World War, *Mitteleuropa* and its translation in local languages was used by many not only in Western Europe, but also in the region itself. After the end of the First World War, the new or newly re-emerging states of Czechoslovakia, Hungary and Poland came to be the focal point of the concept. Both British and French power politics had a role for Central Europe, and a French *Europe centrale* idea emerged (although in a geographical sense the term was used already in the middle of the nineteenth century) as a means of counter-balancing German power – an attempt that failed.

German plans for a German-led Central Europe did not disappear during the period between the two world wars. With Hitler gaining power, trade agreements with various central and east European countries were put in place in 1934. Nazi Germany associated German *Lebensraum* with *Mitteleuropa* and turned it into a 'natural' sphere of expansion towards Russia (as early as the nineteenth century some authors used the term in a context of German superiority). This

[15] *Mitteleuropa* (Berlin, 1915).

compromised the term in the eyes of many German-speakers (who now prefer *Ostmitteleuropa* or *Zentraleuropa*), as well as in the eyes of people affected by Nazi policies of expansion. Others, however, reclaimed the term as a scholarly concept on par with terms such as Central Europe or *Ostmitteleuropa*.[16]

Eastern Europe as a designation for the countries covered in this book is no less loaded or more objective a term. As Larry Wolff has shown, this 'Eastern Europe' was created by West Europeans during the era of the Enlightenment, as a barbaric and exotic complement to their own civilized countries.[17] During the eighteenth century, the traditional north–south divide (Italy as the land of civilization, the north as the land of the uncouth barbarians) was replaced by a new east–west division. The imagery of the 'barbarians' itself was partly borrowed from earlier times – when it was used to describe northerners – but was now applied to 'Eastern Europeans'. Such images were created as a counterpoint to what the philosophers and travellers of the west saw as their own culture. Real observation was often clouded by preconceptions, fantasy and desire, and the resulting construction of 'Eastern Europe' was not based on a factual analysis, even if it included elements of reality. Many components of this construct were perpetuated by the ideology of the 'iron curtain' and applied to the Soviet bloc.

Political events strongly influenced the changing denomination of the region, the acceptance or rejection of the term 'Eastern Europe', in the twentieth century. Historians from the region (notably Oskar Halecki) initiated the creation of a section dedicated to the history of

[16] Le Rider, *Mitteleuropa*; Hans-Dietrich Schultz and Wolfgang Natter, 'Imagining *Mitteleuropa*: conceptualisations of "its" space in and outside German geography', *European Review of History – Revue Européenne d'Histoire* 10, 2 (2003), 273–92; Piskorski, ed., *Historiographical Approaches*; Schwarz, 'Central Europe'; Stefan Troebst, 'Introduction: what's in a historical region? A Teutonic perspective', *European Review of History – Revue Européenne d'Histoire* 10, 2 (2003), 173–88; Rudolf Jaworski, 'Zentraleuropa – Mitteleuropa – Ostmitteleuropa. Zur Definitionsproblematik einer historischen Großregion', *newsletter MODERNE* 2, 1 (1999), 2–4. Local uses include e.g. Arnold Dániel, 'A középeurópai vámunió és a magyar közgazdaság' (1915), and Zsigmond Kunfi, 'Középeurópa' (1916), the latter rejecting the attempts to build a Central European union as imperialist: both appear in I. Berend, ed., *Helyünk Európában*, vol. I, 55–62, 63–83, respectively.

[17] Larry Wolff, *Inventing Eastern Europe: The Map of Civilization on the Mind of the Enlightenment* (Stanford, 1994).

'Eastern Europe' at the International Historical Congress of 1923 in Brussels, which was subsequently established.[18] The term's meaning changed radically after the Second World War, when Eastern Europe became the almost exclusive name for the area, designating the whole Soviet bloc. The name itself was understood by some as a type of historical legitimization of Soviet dominance over the region, by labelling Russia and all the countries of the bloc as one historical region, although émigrés (notably Halecki) played a key role in militating against the terminology of a unified Eastern Europe. Such dissenters succeeded only in the 1980s, when other emigrants from the region (among them Milan Kundera, Czesław Miłosz and György Konrád) and dissidents within it (including Václav Havel and Adam Michnik) reintroduced Central Europe into political terminology as a way of distancing themselves and their countries from the Soviet Union and insisting on ties to the West, thereby questioning the status quo. Many local people resented and rejected the term 'Eastern Europe' as pejorative, defining themselves as inhabitants of Central Europe, culturally belonging to the West. At the same time, in Germany and Austria an increasing number of writers and conferences addressed the issue of Central Europe (*Mitteleuropa*) as a project in different ways, from political to cultural and anti-political. Thus Central Europe was coming back into vogue and readopted by Westerners, to emerge again strongly by 1989, linked to the influence of expatriates and dissidents, but also to internal intellectual developments in Western Europe.[19]

[18] G. Des Marez and F.-L. Ganshof, eds., *Compte rendu du Ve Congrès International des Sciences Historiques Bruxelles 1923* (Brussels, 1923), 409. O. Halecki's paper militating for the significance of the eastern half of Europe for the history of Europe as a whole, 'L'histoire de l'Europe orientale: sa division en époques, son milieu géographique et ses problèmes fondamentaux', is published in full in *La Pologne au Ve Congrès International des Sciences Historiques, Bruxelles 1923* (Warsaw, 1924), 73–94. Here he was already arguing that part of eastern Europe was western in civilization. In his later work he preferred a clear distinction between eastern Europe and his two Central Europes; for more on this, see below. See also Jaroslav Bidlo, 'Was ist die osteuropäische Geschichte? (Deren Inhalt und Perioden)', in *VIIe Congrès International des Sciences Historiques. Résumés des Communications présentées au Congrès, Varsovie 1933* (Warsaw, 1933), vol. II, 197–207.

[19] Milan Kundera (on Russia kidnapping Central Europe), 'The tragedy of Central Europe', *New York Review of Books*, 26 April 1984, is political and rhetorical rather than historical. Le Rider, *Mitteleuropa*, ch. 9; Timothy Garton Ash, 'Does Central Europe exist?', *New York Review of Books*, 9 October 1986, 45–52, repr. in Schöpflin and Wood, eds., *In Search*, 191–215; Francesco M. Cataluccio, 'In

Similarly, East-Central Europe (French *Centre-Est*), pioneered by emigrants from the region, has been used by locals in a bid not just to assert the independence of their countries, but also to investigate the past in that framework. Paternity of the term 'East-Central Europe' as an alternative to the German orientation of the term *Mitteleuropa* has been attributed to Tomáš Masaryk, designating the lands between Russia and Germany. On a conceptual level, he did argue for the role of the small nations between Russia and Germany in a new Europe, but he did not call them by this term; rather, he used 'Eastern Europe', 'small nations', 'non-German nations in the East'. Between the world wars, such a subdivision appeared, for example in the title of the journal *Archivum Europae Centro-Orientalis* from 1935. From the 1940s, Halecki introduced the term in historical studies. After the Second World War, scholars originating in the region itself – although at first usually emigrants – increasingly used this term, which then (usually excluding Germany and Russia) became widespread both in the region itself and in Western scholarship.

Pre-1989 East-Central Europe (Czechoslovakia, Hungary, Poland) as one historical region (although with varying boundaries over time) was defined as the most troubled region of the Soviet bloc, distinguished by recurrent crises, a reformist communism, the most vigorous dissident culture and revolts. The view that East Central Europe is not just a construct, but reality, a historical and

Search of Lost Europe', Introduction in Bronisław Geremek, *The Common Roots of Europe* (Cambridge, 1996), 1–16; Sven Papcke and Werner Weidenfeld, eds., *Traumland Mitteleuropa? Beiträge zu einer aktuellen Kontroverse* (Darmstadt, 1988); Ormos, *Közép-Európa*, 245–68; Timothy Garton Ash, 'Mitteleuropa?', in Graubard, ed., *Eastern Europe*, 1–21; Jacques Rupnik, 'Central Europe or Mitteleuropa?', in Graubard, ed., *Eastern Europe*, 233–65; Miroslav Kusý, 'We, Central-European East Europeans', in Schöpflin and Wood, eds., *In Search*, 91–6; Schöpflin's introduction in Schöpflin and Wood, eds., *In Search*, esp. 17–19; Sellier and Sellier, *Atlas des peuples d'Europe Centrale*, 7: 'depuis 1989, on ne parle plus d'Europe de l'"Est" mais – á nouveau – d'Europe "centrale"; Tony Judt, 'The rediscovery of Central Europe', in Graubard, ed., *Eastern Europe*, 23–58; Czesław Miłosz, 'Looking for a center: on the poetry of Central Europe', George Konrad, 'Letter from Budapest' 'Milan Kundera interview' with Alan Finkielkraut, Roman Szporluk, 'Defining "Central Europe": power, politics and culture', and Jan Triska, 'East Europe? West Europe? Both? Neither?', all in *Cross Currents: A Yearbook of Central European Culture* 1 (1982), 1–11, 12–14, 15–29, 30–8, 39–44; Krishan Kumar, 'The 1989 revolutions and the idea of Europe', *Political Studies* 40 (1992), 439–61.

cultural region based on common structural phenomena, is upheld in some German scholarship. Others maintain that East Central Europe, like all spatial organization, is an interpretation, a result of historians arranging past realities in terms of space, which in fact is not determined by geography or past history. After traditional German *Ostforschung* was discredited, its strong institutional framework served as the basis for a reorientation towards new research in East Central Europe. The Fédération des instituts de l'Europe du Centre-Est, a non-governmental organization founded in 1992, fosters collaboration among historians of the region. The term has also been favoured by some Westerners.[20] A shift even from East Central Europe to Central Europe, however, has been noted since 2000, with the 'East' increasingly seen as pejorative. At the same time, the equivalent term in German scholarship, *Ostmitteleuropa*, has been challenged by demonstrating its roots in German political interests in the area between the two world wars.[21]

[20] Paternity is attributed to Masaryk: Robert Bideleux and Ian Jeffries, *A History of Eastern Europe: Crisis and Change,* 1st edn (London, 1998), 12; and Curta, 'Introduction', in Curta, ed., *East Central and Eastern Europe,* 1–2; but see Szporluk, 'Defining "Central Europe"', 30–2; Thomas G. Masaryk, *The New Europe: The Slav Standpoint* (London, 1918); Johann P. Arnason, 'Introduction: demarcating East Central Europe', In *European Journal of Social Theory* 8, 4 (Nov. 2005), 387–400; Gottfried Schramm, 'Ein Rundgespräch über "Ostmitteleuropa". vom sinnvollen Umgang mit einem Konzept für unsere Zunft', *Jahrbücher für Geschichte Osteuropas* 48 (2000), 119–22; Joachim Bahlcke, 'Ostmitteleuropa', in Harald Roth, ed., *Studienhandbuch östliches Europa,* vol. I, *Geschichte Ostmittel- und Südosteuropas* (Cologne, 1999), 59–72; Hans-Dietrich Schultz, 'Räume sind nicht, Räume werden gemacht. Zur Genese "Mitteleuropas" in der deutschen Geographie', *Europa Regional* 5 (1997), 2–14; Jürgen Kocka, 'Das östliche Mitteleuropa als Herausforderung für eine vergleichende Geschichte Europas', *Zeitschrift für Ostmitteleuropa-Forschung* 49 (2000), 159–74; Wandycz, *Price of Freedom,* 1 (arguing that the term 'East Central Europe' is arbitrary); Charles Gati, 'East-Central Europe: the morning after,' *Foreign Affairs* 69, 5 (1990), 129–45; Jerzy Kłoczowski, ed., *Historia Europy Środkowo-Wschodniej,* 2 vols. (Lublin, 2000); Michael G. Müller, 'West European perspectives on the history of East Central Europe: traditions and current trends', in Katarzyna Karaskiewicz, ed., *Polska-Niemcy-Europa: księga jubileuszowa z okazji siedemdziesiątej rocznicy urodzin Profesora Jerzego Holzera* (Warsaw, 2000), 411–20; Maciej Janowski, 'Pitfalls and opportunities: the concept of East-Central Europe as a tool of historical analysis', *European Review of History – Revue européenne d'Histoire* 6, 1 (1999), 91–100; many of the articles in *Cross Currents* 1 (1982), listed in n. 19.

[21] One example is Paul Robert Magocsi, whose *Historical Atlas of East-Central Europe* (1993) became *Historical Atlas of Central Europe* (Seattle, 2002); Troebst, 'Introduction: what's in a historical region', esp. 173–6, 180.

Some scholars rejected these terms and upheld 'Central Europe' or 'Eastern Europe' as the only viable notion.[22]

Modern history provides examples not only of resistance to an imposed East European identity, but also of attempts to create a 'Central Europe' from within the region itself. Ideas of a co-operation or federation between the countries themselves, as an alternative to domination by a great power from the outside, have surfaced, and failed, a number of times in the nineteenth and twentieth centuries. Poles, Hungarians, Czechs, Slovaks, Croats and Slovenes (but also Serbs, Romanians and others not included in the focus of our book) all conceived federative projects, including in the nineteenth century Adam Jerzy Czartoryski, Stanisław Staszic, František Palacký, Pavel Josef Safarik, Miklós Wesselényi, László Teleki and many others. The plans comprised sometimes only Slavic countries with or without Russia, and at other times all the 'small nations', including Hungary. Some wanted the protectorate of one or other great power, others an independent federation. They usually centred on the nation of the plan's author as the leader of the confederation or union. During the First World War, such plans proliferated: famously, Tomáš Masaryk and Eduard Beneš, Józef Piłsudski and Béla Kun all formulated federative plans that failed. Economic co-operation was initiated in the 1920s through various institutions and plans, continuing in the early 1930s. But by 1936, Milan Hodža's plan for economic co-operation among the Danubian countries was met with polite refusal in all of them except Austria. During the war, those developing plans for a new Central Europe were almost exclusively emigrant politicians and thinkers, among them Beneš and Hodža, Władysław Sikorski and Oszkár Jászi (who had already presented a federative plan in 1918), with a brief period (1945–8) of hope in realizing some federative solution. After 1948, with the formation of the Soviet bloc, federative ideas and indeed the terminology of Central Europe disappeared.

It was not just political protest or the repudiation of an externally imposed identity that motivated those living in the area to define

[22] Hugh Seton-Watson opposing Halecki concluded that these countries should be called 'Central Europe', while the editors of the book he published his article in opted for 'Eastern Europe': 'Is there an East Central Europe?', in Sylva Sinanian, István Deák and Peter C. Ludz, eds., *Eastern Europe in the 1970s* (New York, 1972), 3–12; Emil Niederhauser, *Kelet-Európa története* (Budapest, 2001), supported 'Eastern Europe'.

their belonging and identity through a regional name. A local search for identity (itself politicized) also contributed to this process. The scholars who were among the earliest proponents and analysers of a separate regional identity, such as Oskar Halecki and Jenő Szűcs were influenced by political events, notably the formation and continued existence of the Soviet bloc, but also expressed the local intellectual grappling with the question of historical identity-formation.

A long line of intellectuals participated in this quest for identity, especially in Hungary. Poets and novelists as well as scholars have written since the beginning of the twentieth century about Hungary's place, in between East and West, querying its belonging to either or both. This search for an identity is expressed in the title of a collection of many of these writings from 1905 to 1983, *Our Place in Europe.*[23] The articles and essays in the collection demonstrate both the diversity of views and the passions evoked by the quest for identity. Some Hungarians view themselves as followers of West European models; others, on the contrary, emphasize belonging to the East and the need to nurture their Eastern characteristics. Hungary is seen by some as the last bastion of Western Christendom against attacking Eastern barbarians; and by others as a third, separate region, a region where neighbouring civilizations clash or which holds the key to a balance of power. To be a bridge or to lead expansion and subjugate others have both been proposed as a consequence of in-between status.

This summary shows that local intellectuals by no means all upheld Hungary's Western orientation. Some militated for Hungary's place in Western Europe, others in Central or some type of in-between Europe (using a variety of related terms) and yet others in Eastern Europe. Among the earliest images is the 'ferry-boat country',[24] a mobile area constantly moving between East and West, a definition that recurs on a conceptual level throughout the twentieth century. Heated debates focused on whether East-Central, or Central-Eastern Europe was the correct designation for Hungary's place. Whether directly engaging with politics or not, ultimately a political motivation lurks behind the variety of self-designations.

[23] I. Berend, ed., *Helyünk Európában*. Another collection debating the notion of Central European identity, including some articles by Hungarians as well as translations of pieces by T. Garton Ash and others is *Kell-e nekünk Közép-Európa? Századvég* special issue (1989).

[24] Endre Ady, 'Morituri' (1905), reproduced in I. Berend, ed., *Helyünk Európában*, vol. I, 45–7.

The diversity of identity within the supposed Central European region is even more striking if we compare Czech, Hungarian and Polish views on the matter. There is no cultural unity, no common feeling of belonging to Central Europe, despite some assertions to the contrary. A Hungarian may be nostalgic for the 'good old days' of the Austro-Hungarian monarchy, but a Pole will certainly not long for a period when Poland was divided into three parts.[25] Moreover, Czech and Polish views on their identity often radically diverge. Many Poles have emphasized the Eastern roots of their culture, while Czechs have often been interested in their cultural connection to German areas, have tried to appropriate the concept of Central Europe and have staunchly argued for a West European identity.[26] Only in the run-up to 1989 did a – politicized – view of belonging to Western Europe (or Europe) prevail; otherwise no single identity has ever characterized the region.

The validity of the method of regional subdivisions in itself has been challenged. Some scholars reject any attempt to designate regions and insist on the differences between each country that render any regionalization ultimately false. Some object to the inherent 'othering' implied in regional subdivision, one (or more) subdivision(s) being compared against another (in this case, Western Europe) taken as the standard, assuming an 'essentialised, global difference' between the two. 'Is East Central Europe . . . interesting because it is . . . comprehensible in the same terms in which we understand the European continent in its entirety? . . . Or, is [it] . . . interesting because . . . [it] is in some global or perhaps even essential sense, different from the continent in its entirety . . . ?'[27] Others argue that despite undoubted differences between and even within countries, there are fundamental similarities in historical development (features, tendencies, processes) that suffice to make regional designations such as Central and Eastern Europe

[25] Pomian, 'L'Europe centrale', at 17, against cultural definition 15–17.

[26] Judt, 'The rediscovery of Central Europe', 47; Martin Schulze Wessel, 'Die Mitte liegt westwärts. Mitteleuropa in tschechisher Diskussion', *Bohemia. Zeitschrift für Geschichte und Kultur der böhmischer Länder* 29, 2 (1988), 325–44; Hans-Werner Rautenberg, ed., *Traum oder Trauma? Der polnische Beitrag zur Mitteleuropa-Diskussion (1985–1990)* (Marburg, 1991); Bugge, 'The use of the Middle'.

[27] Piotr Górecki and Nancy Van Deusen, 'Toward a new cultural history of East Central Europe?', in Górecki and Van Deusen, eds., *Central and Eastern Europe*, 192–212; see 205–6; Wolfgang Schmale, 'Die Europäizität Ostmitteleuropas', *Jahrbuch für Europäische Geschichte* 4 (2003), 189–214, at 195, similarly posed the problem that the term 'East Central Europe' possibly limits understanding; Schwarz, 'Central Europe', is also sceptical.

meaningful. Such disagreements are the stuff of writing history. While the critics are right in arguing against 'othering', this does not disqualify the regional approach to history.

Regional history need not essentialize. Rather, it can facilitate the recognition of similarities on a larger scale, and allow us to step outside national frameworks. Such regional subdivision can serve as a 'heuristic concept for comparative analysis in order to identify transnational structures common to a constructed meta-region', without forgetting that it is a construct for comparative purposes.[28] Regional subdivision may rest on political assumptions or aims; scholars may forget that a particular historical region as a construct goes back to specific political interests and debates. One must be aware of the implications of such politically based arguments. Yet that does not mean that regional similarities in historical development cannot exist in reality. Because of the separate yet often blurred use of historical regions in politics, the media, the public sphere and mental mapping, and in the humanities and scholarship, a conscious definition of one's terms is necessary. Some historians argue for the indistinguishable nature of political discourse and historical concepts, while others believe that the two can be disentangled, and that historical regions can be useful tools for historians.[29]

From the previous discussion it is clear that there is not one 'correct' designation, nor one 'true' way of subdividing Europe. Every subdivision of space is ultimately socially and culturally constructed, even if factual evidence can be garnered in support of each one. Depending on one's focus and criteria, divergent subdivisions are equally justifiable. Both in terminology and in encompassing smaller or larger areas into one meaningful unit, several, equally valid approaches coexist. The historical subdivision of space is ultimately a question of historical interpretation.[30] One must keep in mind Jürgen Kocka's questions: whether the regional designation

[28] Troebst, 'Introduction: what's in a historical region', 177–8.

[29] Troebst, 'Introduction: What's in a historical region'. The point was specifically made for Central Europe by Alexei Miller, 'Central Europe: a tool for historians or a political concept?', *European Review of History – Revue européenne d'Histoire* 6, 1 (1999), 85–9, and Janowski, 'Pitfalls and opportunities', while Péter, 'Central Europe and its reading into the past', argues that Central Europe is related only to political aspirations, did not exist in the past and is a reductionist device with no real analytic value. See Ormos, *Közép-Európa*, 17, on a solely political meaning.

[30] E.g. Jordan, 'A subdivision of Europe'; Schultz, 'Räume sind nicht'.

signals an internal perspective or a view from outside; and whether it is a history-based scholarly term or a present-focused political one.[31]

## MEDIEVAL CENTRAL EUROPE?

Modern historians who designate Central Europe (or Eastern Europe or East-Central Europe and so on) as a separate region of Europe contrast it to other European regions, usually to Western Europe. The significant historical similarities on the basis of which Central Europe has been described as one region relate primarily to modern history and economic development, often labelled as backwardness. These include the region becoming a raw-material and food-supplying area to the West in the early modern period; its primarily agricultural economy with a late (twentieth-century) industrialization; the continued importance of the nobility and especially the gentry well into the modern period; the lack, weakness or foreign origin of the middle class; a nation-building process that happened later and was more drawn out than in the West; and long fights for an independent nation-state. This characterization of Central Europe has often been used together with the terminology of centre and periphery, informed by economic theories, reminding us that 'Eastern Europe' was not the only periphery of 'Western Europe'. In fact, the westernmost parts of 'Western Europe', such as Portugal and Iceland, are also peripheries in this scheme.[32] This terminology does not apply to the centuries under study here. Although the region's polities joined Latin Christendom later than Western Europe's, one might argue for medieval socio-economic backwardness or political peripherality only through a teleological view of the Middle Ages (containing the

[31] Kocka, 'Das östliche Mitteleuropa'.

[32] Iván T. Berend, *History Derailed: Central and Eastern Europe in the Long Nineteenth Century* (Berkeley, 2003); Iván T. Berend, *Decades of Crisis: Central and Eastern Europe Before World War II* (Berkeley, 1998); Iván T. Berend, *Central and Eastern Europe 1944–1993: Detour from the Periphery to the Periphery* (Cambridge, 1996); Iván T. Berend, *From the Soviet Bloc to the European Union: The Economic and Social Transformation of Central and Eastern Europe* (Cambridge, 2009); Peter F. Sugar, ed., *Eastern European Nationalism in the Twentieth Century* (Washington, DC, 1995); Hodos, *The East-Central European Region*; Longworth, *Making of Eastern Europe*; Bideleux and Jeffries, *A History of Eastern Europe*, 2nd edn.

inevitable roots of modern backwardness), and not on the basis of the medieval evidence itself.

It would be easy to argue that Central Europe did not exist in the Middle Ages. No medieval concept of either Central or Eastern Europe was formulated. Geographical notions of west and east were in use, but in no way corresponded to modern ideas. When the three realms discussed in this book are mentioned in contemporary medieval texts, they appear as individual units. Many descriptions in these texts resonate with later stereotypes about Central (or Eastern) Europe, backwardness and lack of civilization. This is no wonder, because medieval stereotypes influenced the emergence of the modern ones. Yet there is a misleading convergence as well. What to a casual reader today may be a depiction of 'backwardness' in fact had a different meaning at the time. Medieval western depictions of Bohemia, Hungary and Poland are not simple accounts of facts. Their authors were most often from German lands whose rulers and societies were the neighbours of, and in intensive contact with, the polities they depicted. Their texts were in the service of particular aims and often used set images. Medieval depictions have their own flavour as well: in order to denigrate, they emphasize the barbarity and impiety of the population. Thus stereotypes about people predated ideas about regional identity.

Thus, for example, Thietmar of Merseburg between 1013 and 1018 wrote of the Hungarians as alien folk: they represented God's vengeance.[33] He emphasized that at Quedlinburg at Easter, on the emperor's order, dukes of the Poles and Czechs and emissaries from other Slavs, Greeks, Beneventans, Hungarians, Bulgarians and Danes gathered. Thietmar thus boasted of the territorial extent of imperial power.[34] Lack of piety, cruelty, falsehood and other vices and behaviour contrary to that expected from Christian rulers and their subjects crop up in descriptions of Bohemia and Poland.[35] Thietmar reluctantly praised István I, but immediately moderated that by highlighting the less than Christian behaviour of his parents, particularly his mother, who is shown as both unwomanly and impious.[36] All this

[33] Robert Holtzmann, ed., *Thietmari Merseburgensis episcopi chronicon*, MGH, Scriptores rerum Germanicarum (henceforth SRG) n.s. 9 (Berlin, 1935), bk II, chap. 7, pp. 46, 47 (2 versions).

[34] Thietmar of Merseburg II. 31, pp. 76, 77.

[35] e.g. Thietmar of Merseburg VI. 99, pp. 390–3; VII. 10, pp. 408–11.

[36] Thietmar of Merseburg VIII. 4, pp. 496–9.

because Thietmar judged neighbouring rulers by their relationship to the emperor: he was favourable only in instances when they recognized and contributed to increasing imperial power. In comparison, Rodulfus Glaber and Guibert of Nogent, who had no political interest in the area, gave much more neutral or positive descriptions of the Hungarians after that people's conversion, and the former extolled István I's merits.[37]

A *locus classicus* of medieval descriptions of others, delightful natural features coupled to an uncivilized population, is applied by Otto of Freising to the Hungarians. The country 'seems like the paradise of God' but contrasted with 'the barbarous nature of its people'. 'One seems justified in blaming fortune, or rather in marveling at divine patience, that has exposed so delightful a land to such ... monsters of men.'[38] Such descriptions are also typical in texts about the eastern Baltic shores to justify conquest.[39] The Poles are likewise branded as ferocious, barbarous and lacking fidelity to their princes.[40] These are not objective accounts, but fit into Otto's overall aim to demonstrate how Frederick Barbarossa restored 'the right order of the world'.[41] Other western descriptions also have to be understood in their context. For example, Bartholomew (Bartholomaeus Anglicus) in the middle of the thirteenth century mentioned cities in his description of European realms corresponding in part to their importance in his (and his sources') scheme: the more important the realm, the more cities they are noted to have.[42] Others referred to

[37] John France, ed. and tr., *Rodulfi Glabri Historiarum Libri Qvinqve. Rodulfus Glaber The Five Books of Histories*, Oxford Medieval Texts (Oxford, 1989), bk 3, chap. 2, p. 96; bk 5, chaps. 17, 23, pp. 240, 246–8; Guibert de Nogent, *Dei Gesta per Francos*, ed. R. B. C. Huygens, Corpus Christianorum Continuatio Mediaeualis 127A (Turnhout, 1996), bk 2, chap. 8, pp. 121–2.

[38] G. Waitz, ed., *Ottonis et Rahewini Gesta Friderici I. imperatoris*, MGH SRG (Hanover, 1912), bk 1, chap. xxxii, pp. 49–50; Eng. tr. *Otto of Freising and his continuator, Rahewin, The deeds of Frederick Barbarossa*, tr. by Charles Christopher Mierow (Toronto, 1994), 65–6. I changed the translation of 'talibus hominum monstris tam delectabilem exposuit terram,' because 'caricatures of men' is unjustifiably tame.

[39] Marek Tamm, 'A new World into old words: the eastern Baltic region and the cultural geography of medieval Europe', in Alan V. Murray, ed., *The Clash of Cultures on the Medieval Baltic Frontier* (Farnham, 2009), 11–35, esp. 25.

[40] Waitz, ed., *Ottonis et Rahewini Gesta*, bk 3, chap. 1, p. 167.

[41] Sverre Bagge, 'Ideas and narrative in Otto of Freising's Gesta Frederici', *Journal of Medieval History* 22, 4 (1996), 345–77.

[42] Peter Biller, *The Measure of Multitude: Population in Medieval Thought* (Oxford, 2000), 223–5.

information from Central Europe only in a piecemeal way, when these were relevant to their own history, and the transmission of the material rather than inherent significance often determined inclusion.[43]

Members of the medieval polities of Central Europe themselves did not see their own countries as forming one region. Many ties of marriage, alliance and escape into exile to a neighbouring polity, as well as enmity, war and conquest, criss-crossed the medieval history of these polities, which I do not intend to detail here. Sources from the region sometimes speak of friendship and alliances binding two of the countries. Thus, Cosmas of Prague several times referred to the old friendship between the rulers of Czechs and Hungarians (referring to the latter with the archaizing *rex Pannonicus*), and also to the catastrophic results of breaking such a friendship.[44] The relations between Czechs and Poles, however, are more often depicted as hostile, often ascribed to alleged Polish deceit, but other times to a Czech show of force.[45] Such enmity is also recorded by Poland's first chronicler, Gallus Anonymous, who blames the deceitfulness of the Czechs.[46] Cosmas also approvingly describes Czechs joining a German punitive expedition against Poland.[47]

Yet a medieval form of regionalism appeared in some contemporary sources and political actions: a desire for conquest and lordship over the three realms – without a conscious conceptual formulation of belonging to one area. Gallus Anonymous celebrated Bolesław the Brave's brief conquest of Bohemia (1003–4) and defeats of the Hungarians.[48] Czech dukes' pretension over Hungary and Poland

[43] Zsuzsanna Reed Papp, 'Perceptions of Eastern Europe: Peoples, Kingdoms and Region in Thirteenth- and Fourteenth-Century English Sources', unpublished Ph.D. dissertation, University of Leeds, 2009.

[44] *Cosmae pragensis chronica boemorum*, ed. Bertold Bretholz, MGH SRG, n.s. 2 (Berlin, 1923), e.g. bk II, chap. 41, p. 146; bk. II 48, p. 155; III. 9, p. 169; III.42, pp. 215–17; Eng. tr. Lisa Wolverton, Cosmas of Prague, *The Chronicle of the Czechs* (Washington, DC, 2009).

[45] Cosmas e.g. I.34, pp. 60–2; II.2, pp. 82–4; III.1, pp. 161–2; III.22, pp. 189–90.

[46] *Gesta Principum Polonorum: The Deeds of the Princes of the Poles*, ed., tr. and notes Paul W. Knoll and Frank Schaer, corrected reprint (Budapest, 2007), bk I, chap. 24, pp. 90–2; II.4, p. 124; III.23, pp. 260–8.

[47] Cosmas III.27, p. 195.

[48] *Gesta Principum Polonorum* I.6, pp. 30–2.

emerged in the period: Duke Břetislav in 1038 subjugated Poland and planned to do the same with Hungary.[49] Vratislav was set above Bohemia and Poland by Emperor Henry IV.[50] Such plans materialized briefly in the personal union of the three polities under Václav (László V; Wacław) III Přemysl (1305–6), while some other kings reigned simultaneously over two of the three realms at various times. A similar, albeit negative, image of regional belonging emerges from another of Cosmas's stories: civil war in Bohemia caused rejoicing in Hungary and Poland, safe from Czech attack.[51] In 1335, a meeting of the three kings of Bohemia, Hungary and Poland was the first conscious effort at three-way collaboration in the region. Not even rulers uniting the three realms formulated a concept of Central Europe.

If the concept of Central Europe is a modern historical one, and if even in the modern period it cannot lay claim to being an exclusive framework for the countries in question, is it justified to treat the histories of medieval Bohemia, Hungary and Poland together? One may even concede the reality of a *Mitteleuropa* in Habsburg times, but query the existence of any such meaningful entity before that period. Indeed, most studies only focus on modern differences between Western and Central Europe; and several explicitly posit a divergence between them starting some time in the early modern or modern period. The two most significant such analyses are István Bibó's and Zsigmond Pál Pach's. Bibó distinguished East European 'small states' as having a common path of development from the eighteenth century, which diverged from Western Europe in a negative way. He tied this divergence not to these states' inherent backwardness or character, but to a historical cul-de-sac he identified in the creation of the Habsburg Empire, leading to the lack of 'normal' nation-state development. Subsequently, existing nations had to create states, which led to the unresolvable problems of border disputes, lack of democracy, anti-minority policies and all the 'misery' of the region.[52]

Pach, analysing economic development, saw a crucial change from the end of the fifteenth century: whereas before this the progressive evening out of west and east European economic development was bringing these areas closer to each other, from then, eastern European development started to diverge, leading to ever greater differentiation between the two areas. He identified the main cause of divergent

[49] Cosmas II.13, p. 101 (1055). [50] Cosmas II.37, p. 135, in 1086.
[51] Cosmas III.20, p. 185. [52] Bibó, 'A Kelet-Európai kisállamok'.

developments as economic. He argued that, during the period between the end of the fifteenth and the seventeenth centuries, the shifting of western trade routes to the Atlantic was not simply a result of geographic discoveries, but of the changing economic structures, which led to a concomittant transformation in Central and Eastern Europe. The latter became the agricultural periphery of an industrializing West, producing raw materials and food for the West and buying Western industrial products. In the newly forming world economy not the colonies, but Central and Eastern Europe played this role first.[53] Some scholars try to find the tenuous roots of later divergence already in the beginnings, the Middle Ages (see below), but there is a fairly general consensus that the gap, if it existed, was minimal in the later Middle Ages. Is it not more justified to suggest a regional development in Bohemia, Hungary and Poland (under whatever name) only for the modern period, then, as most aspects identified as regional characteristics developed after the Middle Ages?

In order to answer that question, we need to look more closely at modern historians' claims about what 'made' medieval Central Europe a historical region. I should like to distinguish between superficial or facile contrasts between the medieval history of Western and Central Europe that sometimes one finds on the one hand, and analyses by medievalists or those drawing on detailed medieval research on the other hand. A few examples of the former will suffice:[54] Central Europe is characterized as a part of Western Christianity where Caesaropapist and Islamic influences diluted Western value systems, and introduced new elements. The division between God and Caesar was less fully established than in the West (represented by Canossa, the emperor's penance to the pope). Proof for this is the fate of Central European ecclesiastics, such as St Stanisław (of Szczepanów) and John of Nepomuk (Jan Nepomucký). Their murder by the order of kings would demonstrate the weight of secular power over the spiritual. What about Thomas Becket, whose story would by this criterion make England part of Central Europe?

[53] Zsigmond Pál Pach (first formulated in 1960 at the XI World Historical Congress), in 'A nemzetközi kereskedelmi útvonalak XV–XVII. századi áthelyeződésének kérdéséhez', *Századok* 102, 5–6 (1968), 863–81, Eng. tr. 'The shifting of international trade routes in the fifteenth–seventeenth centuries,' *Acta Historica Academiae Scientiarum Hungariae* 14, 3–4 (1968), 287–321; Immanuel Wallerstein's similar explanation is in *The Modern World System*, 2 vols. (London, 1974, 1980).

[54] Schöpflin and Wood, eds., *In Search*, 19–20.

What about Bolesław II the Bold, who lost his throne and had to go into exile and do penance for the murder of Stanisław? Indeed, what about Canossa itself, since in the end Henry invaded Rome. The pope escaped only thanks to his Norman allies and died in exile while Henry imposed his own choice as pope. Other assertions focus on the late absorption of Central Europe into the Western cultural sphere: Western institutions (universities, Gothic, feudalism, etc.) were adopted, but the local political, economic and cultural context differed from the western one, and so these institutions were either transformed or remained alien in Central Europe. This leads to a definition of Central Europe as transitional, transmittory and liminal. What about the peculiarities of Italian Gothic, compared to French Gothic? What about the difference between universities that were corporations of students, such as Bologna, and those that were corporations of masters, such as Paris? What about English 'bastard feudalism', not to mention the concept of 'feudalism' itself, sharply criticized in scholarship? Comparisons between actual Central European phenomena and schematic models of West European (or sometimes Russian) developments will never lead to historical understanding. Most of Western Europe does not fit such models either.

Scholarly analyses by medievalists do not lead to a uniform response about the characteristics, if any, of medieval Central Europe. Some scholars choose to treat a much larger historical region as one unit, with more or less justification. They can be as minimalist as Jean Sedlar, who grouped together Czechs, Slovaks, Hungarians, Poles, Romanians, Yugoslavs, Albanians, Bulgarians and Greeks as East Central Europe. Nothing more defines this historical region than diversity, with no uniform character or culture, many different ethnic groups and languages, but a similar experience in modern times.

On the other hand, the definition of Eastern Europe can be as detailed as Philip Longworth's, who lists scores of common elements for a region that includes Europe east of Germany.[55] He sees crucial political, cultural and economic differences between Eastern and Western Europe from the time of the emergence of states, and claims that common characteristics define Eastern Europe, with its history having a strong bearing on its development. He posits that the basic division and difference between Western and Eastern Europe go back

[55] Sedlar, *East Central Europe*; Longworth, *Making of Eastern Europe*, chs. 10–11.

to Constantine who established eastern Rome, while the barbarians conquered the west. From Charlemagne, the western ruler arrogated both the imperial title and the designation 'Europe' for the West. The Schism symbolized and confirmed the significant differences between East and West. For the medieval period he cites the following regional features distinguishing Eastern Europe: subsistence economy, the difference of Byzantium and the Latins, German settlement and German law, with its effect on commerce and urbanization, the Mongol invasion which orientalized, an institutional development different from the West, especially a lack of centralization, and strong centrifugal tendencies, manifest for example in the division of Poland. Cultural differences, notably a different alphabet and literatures, were also significant and generated incomprehension and hatred. Western crusades against Byzantium and Prussia epitomize these differences. The importance of oral customary law (except in Byzantium itself, where Roman law was preserved) in contrast to Norman common law (which was valid for an entire state overcoming local divisions), the lack of absolutism, uniformity, feudalism and Western-style urbanization are key regional characteristics. So is the Orthodox Church which defers to and depends on secular power and has no autonomy. In the East, a wider gap exists between the sovereign and the subject. Spiritual and political power are indivisible; in other words, there is no church–state division. Greek, Latin (that is, Roman) and German Christianity competed to convert the barbarians of this Eastern region. Eastern Europe adopted Western and Byzantine institutions, but in the course of transfer, institutions changed their nature. His conclusion, explicitly polemical against Czesław Miłosz, is that Eastern Europe was not Western in culture and Easternized by force, but that Western immigration was largely responsible for Western influence.[56]

There are obvious problems with this characterization of Eastern Europe as a historical region in the Middle Ages. Leaving aside specifics concerning Byzantium and Kievan Rus' that would not be accepted by specialists, I shall focus on how the characteristics of this East European region fit medieval Bohemia-Moravia, Hungary and Poland. It is obvious that the perspective is a Russian/Byzantine one, subsuming a wider region, but which often in fact does not fit these three realms (for the sake of brevity, designated as 'Central Europe'

[56] Longworth, *Making of Eastern Europe*, 328.

henceforth). The difference between Byzantium and the Latins is obviously not relevant to Central Europe in this way; the Mongol invasion did not orientalize the region; the Orthodox Church played a very small role in Central Europe: all these issues are discussed in detail in the following chapters. A few times, Longworth distinguishes as East-Central Europe the three countries, notably discussing German influence there separately. But this line of analysis remains too superficial to justify the grouping together of these countries as one historical region. Other characteristics given for Eastern Europe remain problematic. For example, choosing the lack of centralization and strong centrifugal tendencies ignores political anarchy in western Europe, emerging and disappearing states such as Burgundy, or the many divisions of the Iberian polities. The emphasis on the importance of oral customary law does not account for early written legislation in Central Europe, especially Hungary.

Can there be a meaningfully constructed region of Bohemia-Moravia, Hungary and Poland for scholars of the Middle Ages? It is significant that medievalists were instrumental in starting to define the countries under investigation here as a separate historical region (whether under the term 'Central Europe', 'East-Central Europe' or the 'third Europe' does not matter for our purposes), and these arguments also left a lasting mark on the discussion about the characteristics of medieval Central Europe. From the middle of the twentieth century, scholars started to identify common elements in the medieval history of the three Central European countries. Francis Dvornik, Oskar Halecki and Jenő Szűcs investigated the historical origins of the region. None of these works were divorced from then current politics. Dvornik and Halecki tried to prove that Central Europe was unjustly seen as 'Eastern', while Szűcs sought the roots of modern Central Europe's situation in the Middle Ages.

Dvornik argued that Central Europe, and particularly first Moravia, then Bohemia, and finally eleventh-century Kievan Rus' could have been a bridge between East and West, and avoided a split between them by channelling Eastern influences to the West, and then Western ones to the East, acting as an intermediary between Byzantium and the West. The only period when a synthesis of Eastern and Western was close to being achieved, was during the Middle Ages between about the ninth and early twelfth centuries; it was 'Europe's lost opportunity'. The culprits for him were the Franks, from Charlemagne on, and German emperors with a few exceptions.

German eastward colonization and later the rise of imperial power in Russia posed the two threats to Central Europe. He also bemoaned that Czechs and Poles failed to fuse into a single nation, despite several brief attempts at union. He found a common link between central European states in Christianity and Western traditions.[57]

In two pioneering books, Oskar Halecki opposed the terminology and concept of Eastern Europe and the then-current idea that Europe was really only Western Europe.[58] He subdivided Europe into four regions: Western, West Central, East Central and Eastern Europe. Although in The *Limits and Division of European History*, he stressed common political structures within medieval Europe, he also laid out his vision of the inner dualism of Central Europe, between a western Germanic and an eastern section, defined as the lands between Scandinavia, Germany, Italy and the Soviet Union. He called this area East Central Europe (arguing against the denomination Central-Eastern Europe, which, he says, would mean the central part of Eastern Europe, hence something entirely different). He emphasized the dynamic within central Europe, the diverse peoples of the eastern areas having to defend themselves against German threat and dominance. He also raised an issue that has been debated ever since, not least by Polish historians: whether the northern- and easternmost lands (the Baltic areas, Ruthenia, Ukraine), which were part of the Polish state at its largest extent, belong to East Central Europe or not. In *Borderlands of Western Civilization*, he elaborated the concept of East Central Europe, the lands between Sweden, Germany, Italy, and Turkey and Russia. They became the borderlands of western civilization, with the latter's spread. The book provides a chronological history of the region, its *Leitmotif* being the development of individual national cultures in connection with Western Europe, but repeatedly submerged by neighbouring empires. He restated the argument about the four regions of Europe and deplored the neglect East Central Europe has suffered in history writing.

[57] Francis Dvornik, 'Western and Eastern traditions of Central Europe', *Review of Politics* 9 (1947), 463–81; Dvornik, *The Making of Central and Eastern Europe* (London, 1949), quotation from 240.

[58] Oskar Halecki, *The Limits and Divisions of European History* (London and New York, 1950), esp. 125–41, for Central-Eastern Europe 127; Halecki, *Borderlands of Western Civilization*.

Jenő Szűcs elaborated on the characteristics of medieval Central-Eastern Europe (the name he preferred for Bohemia, Hungary and Poland).[59] According to him, the area was the eastern border of the Carolingian Empire, in a period when the *Occidens* (West) was defined in distinction to Byzantium and the Mediterranean. Only later did the notion of Western *Europe* (not the same as the West) develop, and only after that time did historical regions of Europe emerge, from *c.* 1000. Around the same time, another border appeared: along the Lower Danube and eastern Carpathians, and up to the Baltic in the thirteenth century. Everything west of this was called *Europa Occidens* or *Occidentalis* already between 1100 and 1200. Because the main framework was *Christianitas*, and the key medieval East–West division was between Roman and Byzantine Christianity, Central Europe and Scandinavia were called Western Europe in the Middle Ages.

According to Szűcs, Central-Eastern Europe was the recipient of influences from both west and east, created by the first expansion of the West. Through conversion, Bohemia, Hungary and Poland became part of Christendom, that is, the West, as the two were coextensive at the time. Although the three new polities became part of the same civilization as the West, structure and civilization were not the same. Rus', although it converted to Byzantine Christianity and thus in civilization was part of the East, in state and other structures was closer to Bohemia, Hungary and Poland than to Byzantium. In all four, royal power was much stronger than in the West, and states were built from 'followers', rather than on varied groups with their own liberties. After *c.* 1200 this structurally similar Eastern Europe quickly disintegrated. Rus' was conquered by the Mongols, while Bohemia, Hungary and Poland integrated more structural elements from the West, so that Central-Eastern Europe was no longer simply 'civilizationally' Western. These included the heavy plough, a new agricultural system, urbanization, noble and urban liberties, the unification of the peasantry, the first parliaments and written contracts. Yet this integration happened through quick, compressed development, as opposed to gradual Western processes. Therefore, although based on Western models, Central-Eastern

[59] Jenő Szűcs, 'Vázlat Európa három történeti régiójáról', *Történelmi Szemle* 3 (1981), 313–59, Eng. tr. 'The three historical regions of Europe: an outline', *Acta Historica Academiae Scientiarum Hungariae* 29 (1983), 131–84.

European developments were anorganic, resulting in hybrid forms, or remained incomplete, and often necessitated reforms from above. Examples include the lack of local chivalric culture; *familiaritas* instead of vassalage, which did not include the conditional donation of land; parliaments consisting of nobles and ecclesiastics, without burghers. Romanesque and Gothic art, autonomous cities, corporate liberties and other Western innovations occurred in a less dense pattern in German areas and even less densely in Central Europe; they did not occur at all east of Hungary and Poland. Local specificities in structures made East-Central Europe a region already distinct in the Middle Ages. In 1500, the economic divergence reproduced the Elbe–Leitha border of the Carolingian Empire, as did the iron curtain later. Early modern and modern catastrophes were not causes of divergence but results of structural differences which determined responses to world historical challenges.

Other scholars have emphasized some of these, or a variety of different elements as distinctive to medieval Central Europe.[60] Drawing out some common elements that recur in many books, as well as results of studies with a more specialized focus, I should like to highlight some of the problems inherent in these approaches, as well as some of the real similarities that emerge. Older scholarship insisted on a backwardness from the beginning, sometimes associated to alleged 'Slavic' characteristics such as the inability to form states without outside assistance – ideas that clearly signal the period and intellectual currents of the times that gave birth to them. Without the negative bias, Central Europe was – and sometimes still is – equated with Slavs, in the scholarship of Slavic countries, which saw Hungarians as intruders in the region. The belated start (the emergence of polities and Christianization in the period between the late ninth and early eleventh century when established

[60] Aleksiun *et al.*, eds., *Histoire de l'Europe du Centre-Est*; Arnason, 'Introduction'; Gieysztor, *L'Europe nouvelle*; Johnson, *Central Europe*; Castellan, *Histoire des peuples de l'Europe centrale*; Delsol, *et al.*, eds., *Mythes et symboles politiques*; Longworth, *Making of Eastern Europe*; Urbańczyk, ed., *Origins of Central Europe*; Conze, *Ostmitteleuropa*; Wandycz, *Price of Freedom*; Péter Váczy, 'A középkori Kelet-Európa', in Bálint Hóman, Gyula Szekfű and Károly Kerényi, eds., *Egyetemes történet*, vol. II, *A középkor története* (Budapest, 1936), chap. 5, 673–80, and many of the other works listed above that devote sections to the medieval history of the region. A very political argument is in Gábor Klaniczay, 'Medieval Central Europe: an invention or a discovery?', *in The Paradoxes of Unintended Consequences*, ed. Lord Dahrendorf *et al.* (Budapest, 2000), 251–64.

Christian western neighbours already existed) is mentioned as a characteristic of the region, but sometimes also as a more or less inevitable cause of its backwardness. One should keep in mind that most European polities developed in that period: there was no France or Castile before that. Is it not a mirage, or the successful construct of nineteenth-century national history, to see more continuity between parts of the Carolingian Empire and the Capetian kingdom of France, for example, than between Slavic client rulers of the Carolingians and the kingdom of Bohemia? The customary reference to 'old foundations' in the western cases needs to be questioned in terms of the actual content of continuities in political or social structures, invariably found to be myths rather than realities (e.g. between Visigothic Spain and medieval Castile or Aragon, or between the time of Clovis and the Capetians).

Some scholars point out the narrowing or complete closure of the original 'gap' between the West and Central Europe over the course of the Middle Ages, until divergent developments of the late fifteenth century disrupted the balance. Others, on the contrary, insist on significant structural differences even during those first five centuries. Linked to the later start is the adoption of models and norms from the more developed West (and, although less frequently mentioned, also from the more developed East, Byzantium). Central European rulers at first relied on immigrant clerics, and borrowed ecclesiastical and royal institutions, literacy and administrative organizations from western Europe, with primarily ecclesiastical influences from Orthodox Christendom also affecting Moravia-Bohemia and Hungary. The new realms adapted what they borrowed to local needs and developed their own varieties of, for example, liturgy, and local saints. Many scholars emphasize the multiplicity of influences, often in a general way as 'eastern' and 'western', or 'Byzantine' and 'Latin', but sometimes more specifically, for example, tracing the influence of missionaries or the adoption of liturgy from particular areas. Steppe or nomadic impact and influence are also highlighted, especially for Hungary, in which the kingdom resembled other sedentary neighbours of nomads, for example, in the Balkans, Russian areas or Georgia.[61]

Whereas the tracing of specific influences obviously does contribute to characterizing a region, two important caveats need to be made.

[61] Peter B. Golden, 'Nomads and Their Sedentary Neighbors in Pre-Činggisid Eurasia', *Archivum Eurasiae Medii Aevi* 7 (1987–91), 41–81; Nora Berend, *At the Gate of Christendom: Jews, Muslims and 'Pagans' in Medieval Hungary, c. 1000–c. 1300*

First, while we can often be certain about contacts, *how* certain influences came into play in the medieval period is an extremely complicated and sometimes unresolvable issue; witness on-going debates about the source of influences in architectural forms, or in the Christianization of certain countries. Second, the *fact* of influences from more than one area in itself is often seen as defining Central Europe's in-between status, and receives explanatory significance in models of backwardness or as part of what was peculiar to or even 'wrong' with Central Europe. This, however, is not tenable; outside influences are no specificity of Central Europe. The same is true of Iberia and Scandinavia, but also of the 'core' itself. Was not medieval England the recipient of Celtic, Anglo-Saxon and Norman influences, and the medieval 'West' itself of Roman and Germanic ones?

Some scholars insist on the significance of eastern influences,[62] but more commonly, in slightly varied form, the emphasis is on the predominance of western links, models and influences, with a slight inflection due to eastern influences. Thus, for example, while early Byzantine influences in conversion to Christianity in Moravia and Hungary, and to a lesser extent Bohemia, are acknowledged, the fact that these areas joined Latin Christendom is used to prove the overwhelming importance of western influence and adoption of western models, because to do otherwise would be to 'admit' belonging to 'the East', equated to something negative and shameful. Explanatory frameworks, therefore, often guide conclusions about influences, when in fact the scholarly assessment of the combination of influences is not conclusive. One example will highlight how difficult it is in fact to determine the relative weight of certain influences: the question of Byzantine influences in Hungary. When political reasons in the 1950s and 1960s especially favoured an eastern orientation, many elements of Hungarian medieval culture were identified as Byzantine, whereas later, when proving a western orientation came to the fore, the same elements were reclassified as proving western influence. Art historians supposed Byzantine influence on building styles in Hungary, which are now identified as Italian

(Cambridge, 2001); Florin Curta and Roman Kovalev, eds., *Other Europe in the Middle Ages: Avars, Bulgars, Khazars and Cumans* (Leiden, 2008); István Zimonyi, 'The nomadic factor in mediaeval European history', *Acta Orientalia Academiae Scientiarum Hungaricae* 58, 1 (2005), 33–40.

62 Apart from Dvornik, notably Dimitri Obolensky, *The Byzantine Commonwealth: Eastern Europe 500–1453*, 2nd edn (London, 2000).

instead. We can identify Greek monasteries, although some affiliations are disputed; but whether the introduction of certain saints or elements of the liturgy can be accounted for through Byzantine influence or the Ottonian empire is still debated. How much Byzantine influence there is, and *what* it consists of, is an open question requiring further research.

While for some the later start and consequent borrowing of institutions in themselves are signs of backwardness (that these areas in the Middle Ages were not innovators, initiators of new structures, means that they lagged behind), more commonly, not simply the adoption but the adaptation of western institutions and models is seen as the cause of problems. According to the scholar's viewpoint, adaptation can mean change that is inevitable when ideas or institutions are transplanted to a different context; or it can amount to mutilation, distortion, shallow adaptation (Szűcs) or autochthon 'original characteristics' (Makkai).[63] It can be branded as peripheral, continuing archaic western practices. Local specificities can also be interpreted in the light of national pride as a refusal to borrow certain elements. Being a specific cultural zone of the west can carry positive or negative connotations. Usually, a variety of deficiencies, missing elements compared to western Europe are highlighted, such as a lack of Roman and Carolingian background (or late, superficial attachment to these zones, since parts of what much later became Hungary – Pannonia – and Romania – Dacia – were in the Roman Empire), lack of feudalism and lack of urbanization.

The perspective of modern scholars reflecting on these issues has been ultimately to explain either modern economic backwardness and/or the lack of modern democratic freedoms. The two main ways of doing this have been either to postulate a breaking point, a period when Central European divergence started; or to claim a development different from Western Europe and therefore 'doomed' from the very beginning. Again, one has to be particularly careful not to compare a schematic model of Western developments, which never existed in fact, with real developments in Central Europe. This is particularly true of 'feudalism', which is an umbrella term for a

[63] László Makkai, 'Les caractères originaux de l'histoire économique et sociale de l'Europe orientale pendant le Moyen Age', *Acta Historica Academiae Scientiarum Hungaricae* 16, 3–4 (1970), 261–87; for a different version, see Makkai, 'Feudalizmus és az eredeti jellegzetességek Európában', *Történelmi Szemle* 1 (1976), 257–77.

wide variety of phenomena, with no consistent institutional content even in one country, let alone 'the West': the modalities and existence of landed tenure in particular varied widely. Moreover, such comparisons present a homogenizing image of 'the West' as the cradle of all new institutions and structures. Yet western monasticism was born in Italy and adopted in the other western countries as well, while Gothic was born in France and went through a whole series of adaptations locally in the west as it spread, and so on. Neither 'the West' nor 'the East' can be typologized in an essentializing manner: the development of Germany differed from that of France which differed from that of England and Italy. The Balkans developed differently from Rus', and the Byzantine Empire was not a uniform entity. Many of the purported 'differences' therefore are in fact produced by a comparison between a detailed knowledge of one or more Central European countries and a schematic model of Western Europe.

Moreover, the underlying idea that whatever was unlike Western Europe was a sign of backwardness and failure, and that medieval differences are the direct causes of modern problems needs to be proven rather than assumed. If we take the central areas of the old Carolingian Empire as the norm, other regions naturally had a 'belated' or otherwise aberrant development. This, however, is not very helpful in explaining the history of non-Western European countries. Switzerland developed even later than Central Europe, and in a unique manner, yet this did not cause backwardness. As Marc Bloch has pointed out, origins do not explain everything, nor predetermine all subsequent development. Also, as the signs in a Chinese ice-cream store in New York remind us, 'normal' depends on our viewpoint: 'flavors: lychee, mango, red bean. Exotic flavors: vanilla, chocolate, strawberry'. The success of Western Europe in the modern age of course needs to be analysed (although not in this book), but perhaps not in terms of the belatedness or backwardness of other areas from the beginning. Some scholars have even suggested that it may be Western Europe's 'abnormal' development that needs to be explained.[64] Therefore we should not look at medieval Central Europe as the predetermined cradle of undemocratic and economically backward modern states, nor try to prove that back then, the

[64] E.g. Longworth, *Making of Eastern Europe*, in his conclusion; Joachim Henning, 'Ways of life in Eastern and Western Europe during the early Middle Ages: which way was "normal"?', in Curta, ed., *East Central and Eastern Europe*, 41–59.

region was the same as 'the West'; but try to understand medieval developments in their own context.

Other scholars seek to grasp the specificity of medieval Central Europe by identifying the 'presence and interaction with the local peoples of Germans and Jews'.[65] German colonization and Jewish settlement, or in more general terms the diversity of peoples and languages, are often seen as its characteristic trait. For the Middle Ages, ethnic and linguistic diversity was the norm rather than the exception everywhere in Europe, and Jews were present in medieval Europe as a whole. Yet there are two elements truly characteristic of Central Europe: peaceful western immigration in a more organized manner, and the presence of a very wide variety of different groups, particularly in Hungary and Poland. Western immigration included Walloons, Italians, French and others, but Germans were both numerically the most significant and the focus of modern scholarship for generations.

Central Europe's close ties to German areas and strong German influence there feature frequently among the region's historical co-ordinates. But German settlement is a particularly contentious part of Central Europe's history, in light of Nazi ideas of *Lebensraum* and the consequent expulsions of Germans after the Second World War. The significance of German settlement and its role in Central Europe were initially formulated from a German perspective. For example, F. Naumann posited the continuity of German eastward settlement between the twelfth and nineteenth centuries, from medieval settlers to the Habsburgs. Others even saw German eastward colonization from the twelfth century on as creating Central Europe. The fallacy of such a position, the discontinuities and diverse forms of German settlement, rather than one continuous movement of *Ostsiedlung*, has been demonstrated. Much scholarly energy has been spent on debating the role of medieval German settlers in Central Europe. Germans as the carriers of civilization to Central Europe from the perspective of German scholarship clashed with Germans as brutal oppressors, planting the seeds of later ethnic conflict, from the

[65] Quotation from Wandycz, *Price of Freedom*, 9. Cf. Bahlcke, 'Ostmitteleuropa'. Of the voluminous literature on Germans in the region see e.g. K. Bosl *et al.*, eds., *Eastern and Western Europe in the Middle Ages* (London, 1970); Charles Higounet, *Les Allemands en Europe centrale et orientale au Moyen Âge* (Paris, 1989); Piskorski, ed., *Historiographical Approaches*, which is an excellent guide to earlier scholarship; Le Rider, *Mitteleuropa*, 17–24.

perspective of local Central European scholarship. This dynamic determined much of the subsequent literature, even when it tried to move away from such stances. For example, K. Bosl and others published a volume dedicated to Eastern and Western Europe in the Middle Ages, which focused in fact on Slavs and Germans, arguing against seeing them as locked in eternal fight.[66] Some scholarly studies from early on, however, understood the dynamics of the interaction between locals and Germans through the prism of medieval realities rather than modern concerns. Rulers and elites invited peasants and townsmen and offered them favourable conditions to settle, in contrast to the Baltic areas (where Germans as well as others waged crusades and conquered territories). This was not a unified 'German movement'. How much novelty German settlers introduced, their influence on as well as acculturation to locals, continues to be contested.

Some specificities of medieval Hungary and Poland can be conceptualized in terms of frontiers. This should not be used in a way to subsume all warfare (characteristic of the whole of Europe) or to account for all the developments in these areas. More narrowly focused, however, this approach can enrich our understanding of these countries' past. At the meeting points of the western Christian and the 'pagan' world, raids and immigration from the latter, and resulting policies and even the formulation of royal ideology are distinctive features of Hungary and Poland. The cleric of a medieval king, Béla IV of Hungary, wrote of his realm in the middle of the thirteenth century as the 'gate of Christendom'. This position also partly accounts for the greater variety of populations that were found in these medieval kingdoms than elsewhere: western and eastern immigrants, including a diversity of western Europeans, Jews, Armenians, various Turkic nomads and Muslims.

More specialized studies have focused on a closer analysis of certain Central European developments and institutions. These include the delayed introduction of writing (in Latin, but in Bohemia also in Old Church Slavonic) and 'service settlements'.[67] These villages of peasants and craftsmen who provided for the needs of the elite have long been thought to occur in these three polities alone, but

[66] Bosl *et al.*, eds., *Eastern and Western Europe in the Middle Ages*.

[67] Adamska and Mostert, eds., *The Development of Literate Mentalities*; Florin Curta, 'The archaeology of early medieval service settlements in Eastern Europe', in Górecki and Van Deusen, eds., *Central and Eastern Europe*, 30–41.

twelfth-century German and tenth- and early eleventh-century Bulgarian analogies led to the questioning of this institution as peculiarly Central European.

Some historians, however, choose to emphasize a common European culture. In *The Limits and Divisions of European History*, Halecki posited a common political structure, and cultural and religious tradition between Western and Eastern Europe in the Middle Ages, the development of a sharp dualism starting only with the latter's conquest by empires. He emphasized that Eastern Europe was no less European than Western Europe, and opposed definitions of European civilization as Western. Rather, Europe for him was a distinct community of all nations, and a variety of peoples, with a Greco-Roman heritage and the deep influence of Christianity. He saw the making of European civilization as a longer process, not tied to one starting date. B. Geremek focused on common elements, Europe as one community, with its own culture and Poland's connectedness to this whole.[68] These include a common Latin culture and Catholic Church, a network of authority, with decisions taken in Rome affecting Poland, and Poland having an important role in the realization of papal and imperial policies. This universalistic community is also reflected in a common consciousness, the local horizon of small groups serving as the model for the large scale: *christianitas* provided a religious and political structure, with the bond of Christian community manifest, for example, in the collective consciousness against the Mongol threat. Yet even Geremek wrote about local 'peculiarities' within this common framework: the export of western models to Poland, but their weak penetration, the development and impact of indigenous culture on the foreign elite culture. Several historians, however, have highlighted how these areas were not simply passive recipients. The joining of these new parts had profound consequences for the 'old' or 'core' areas as well, truly 'making' Europe, or resulting in the 'Europeanization of Europe'.[69]

If we move away from trying to ascertain the extent to which Central Europe differed from an essentialized 'West' (or 'East'),

[68] Halecki, *The Limits and Divisions of European History*; Geremek, *The Common Roots of Europe*. Both link to modern politicized contexts, as described above.

[69] Robert Bartlett, *The Making of Europe: Conquest, Colonization and Cultural Change 950–1350* (Princeton, 1993); Piskorski, 'After Occidentalism', 19; Gieysztor, *L'Europe nouvelle*.

because no such West and East in fact existed, then we can dispense with a defensive or combative stance about whether Central Europe was backward, or western, 'normal' or 'peculiar'. 'West' and 'East' themselves consisted of very different areas with a variety of local cultures, all of which were a balance between features common to Latin Christendom, or even more broadly defined areas such as Christendom, and local 'peculiarities'.

The work of generations of scholars has traced what was indeed similar in this constructed historical region in the Middle Ages. Some of these features in turn were similar to other areas; notably, regional similarities exist with Kievan Rus' and Scandinavia.[70] Christianization and the formation of polities were interlinked: in all three of our polities, local rulers emerged who centralized power and introduced Christianity. In this they resemble the three Scandinavian countries Denmark, Norway and Sweden. These polities were organized by local elites and, Christianized later than west European countries, became part of Latin Christendom (similar polities under their own elites emerged in the Orthodox world as well, such as Rus' and Bulgaria). They became the easternmost part of Latin Christendom. In all three, royal centres and ecclesiastical centres were interlinked in the first centuries: royal fortifications were the places where the first churches were built. Ecclesiastical and royal administrative systems also overlapped initially. They incorporated influences from, and formed political ties to, the German and Byzantine Empires (including alliances and hostility); such ties were also exploited to consolidate power against internal rivals. (German influence was also important in southern Scandinavia.) Bohemian influence in Poland and Bohemian and Polish influence in Hungary were crucial at the beginnings of the Christian polities. They borrowed ecclesiastical and royal institutions, practices of government, literacy and artistic forms from established neighbours to the west and the east. None used literacy prior to the introduction of Christianity (with the insignificant exception of runes,

[70] Jonathan Shepard, 'Conversions and regimes compared: the Rus' and the Poles, ca. 1000', and Márta Font, 'Missions, conversions and power legitimization in East Central Europe at the turn of the first millennium', both in Curta, ed., *East Central and Eastern Europe*, 254–82, 283–95; Márta F. Font, *A keresztény nagyhatalmak vonzásában: Közép- és Kelet-Európa a 10–12. században* (Budapest, 2005), German tr. *Im Spannungsfeld der christlichen Großmächte. Mittel- und Osteuropa im 10.–12. Jahrhundert* (Herne, 2008); Nora Berend, ed., *Christianization and the Rise of Christian Monarchy: Scandinavia, Central Europe and Rus'* c. *900–1200* (Cambridge, 2007).

used by part of Hungary's population, but only for words or short inscriptions). In all three monasticism was introduced by the rulers, and monks played a part in Christianization. All three were recipients of a significant influx of immigration by elites, peasants and burghers. Urbanization that started during these centuries benefited from the immigrants' legal status and from local economic and social developments. Hungary and Poland were also influenced by non-Christian civilizations, with diverging social and political organization (in some ways this resembled the Iberian peninsula, where centuries of interaction between Christians and Muslims included warfare as well as borrowing). All three were affected by the Mongol invasion of the middle of the thirteenth century, but neither was conquered for a longer period. A mixture of borrowing, adaptation and local traditions created these realms, which in its specifics was different in each case, as explored in the chapters to follow, but which, as a process, resembled that in other medieval polities.

Some significant differences between the three polities should not be forgotten. These included political structures in two ways: different levels of political fragmentation and the existence or absence of a royal title. Hungary was a kingdom, but neither Poland nor Bohemia had a king for most of the period. The royal title in itself, however, was not a sign of greater power. Bohemian dukes were usually as powerful as kings, and the effective power of many a Polish ruler did not depend on their title. Internal divisions and fragmentation had more of an impact on the ruler's power. Bohemia and Hungary remained more or less unified, although at times Hungarian kings had to cede substantial powers to other members of the dynasty, while Poland underwent a long period of fragmentation. Bohemia was also part of the German Empire, while the other two polities were not, but there was no imperial intervention in internal Bohemian matters; therefore in reality this difference was less significant than it may seem. Reliance on imperial help by members of the dynasty against internal rivals at times characterized not just Bohemia but also Hungary and Poland. The real difference lay in that Bohemia's inclusion in the Empire fostered Bohemian involvement in the affairs of the Empire, and notably from the thirteenth century recurrent attempts by Bohemian rulers to become emperor. Cultural differences existed as well, such as the influence of Old Church Slavonic in Moravia and Bohemia.

Western 'scholarly neglect' of Central (or East-Central) Europe has featured prominently among local complaints. Many writers noted with regret or bitterness that, except for specialists, western historians neglected to incorporate the region in their studies, because, even in the early 1990s, it was simply thought of as 'a medley of troublesome nationalities with unpronounceable names', neither exotic nor familiar enough.[71] Yet this evaluation no longer reflects the state of scholarship, which, indeed, started to change in the early 1990s. Scholarly treatments of medieval history increasingly break through the traditional geo-political divide. Apart from the proliferation of scholarly studies on numerous thematic aspects of medieval history which incorporate these countries, recent studies of medieval Europe such as Robert Bartlett's, as well as textbooks, such as William Chester Jordan's and Malcolm Barber's, include these areas.[72] That 'medieval studies' includes all of Europe has recently even been expressed on the cover of Ashgate's 2010 catalogue, which features a photo of Prague.

It would be easy to argue that Central Europe did not exist in the Middle Ages, either in terminology or in the consciousness and identity of its inhabitants. Although this book does not claim the existence of Central Europe as an essential unit of European history, let alone as a conscious identity of the countries in question in the Middle Ages, it does argue that, despite differences, enough significant similarities existed in political, socio-economic and cultural terms to warrant examining the early history of this region together, in a comparative perspective. The non-existence of a concept in the period itself does not disqualify modern historians' analyses; contemporaries may not have seen parallels that historians do.

We do not lay claim to any exclusively correct terminology for the region: 'Central Europe' is one of the many possible names. It is also a term historians created, rather than one they borrowed from the period under investigation. We use it as a short-hand for the medieval polities of Bohemia-Moravia, Hungary and Poland between their beginnings and the end of the thirteenth century; these incorporated some modern territories that today are not part of Central Europe in some categorizations, for example, Croatia from

[71] Wandycz, *Price of Freedom*, 1.

[72] Bartlett, *The Making of Europe*; William Chester Jordan, *Europe in the High Middle Ages* (London, 2001, 2002); Malcolm Barber, *The Two Cities: Medieval Europe 1050–1320*, 2nd edn (London, 2004).

the beginning of the twelfth century, today's Slovakia (which was not called Slovakia in the Middle Ages) and Transylvania. Various alternative terms could be used to denote Bohemia-Moravia, Hungary and Poland, such as Eastern Europe, Central-Eastern Europe or East-Central Europe. We find the composite terms cumbersome, and 'Eastern Europe' misleading as it tends to suggest a broader historical region than just these three polities. We do not wish to take a stand in modern political debates on terminology, however, where the stake is a politicized historical identity, to determine whether these countries belong to 'the East' or 'the West'. We are using 'Central Europe' in a value-neutral way, not trying to imply superiority over more eastern areas or a gradation of development by west, central and eastern. We do not suggest any of the following through the use of this term: belated development, backwardness, an inherent 'abnormality' of development; a fundamental similarity to 'the West'; a sphere of German civilization; an in-between status. We are also attempting to evacuate value-judgements inherent in proving that these countries belonged to Western civilization. Nor are we trying to isolate the region through the use of this term from 'the East'. We do suggest that in the medieval period, after their inception, these polities were integral parts of Latin Christendom. That, however, should not be taken to carry political meanings for the present.

The lack of objective criteria to define regional subdivisions means that many different subdivisions are possible and equally valid, depending on the choice of time period and of structural elements that are seen as significant. Therefore different authors' solutions will diverge. It is possible to construct a smaller or larger historical region; therefore Central Europe could be studied as part of an even larger area, or broken down into smaller component parts. It could be considered, as we have done in a previous book,[73] to be one historical region with Scandinavia when looking at Christianization and the formation of polities. Historically, one could also reserve the term for the Habsburg Empire, or the periods in which local people formulated their own identity in terms of a 'Central Europe'. Our approach is based on one possible subdivision, one possible way of interpreting historical processes. We are not the first to suggest a regional approach for these three

[73] Berend, ed., *Christianization and the Rise of Christian Monarchy*.

countries, to move beyond 'parochial, isolated, self-centered' national histories.[74] Without arguing that these countries constituted one unit in the medieval period, it is instructive to study the parallels as well as the differences in their development in a more systematic manner. In some ways, there were more historical similarities within the 'Central Europe' we examine here in the early centuries of the countries' development than in some subsequent historical periods.[75] We wish to explore these not as a prelude to modern times, but in their own context.

This book focuses on the formative period of the region, the origin of the polities and their development in the eleventh and twelfth centuries, with a concluding chapter on the thirteenth century, when, while some of the trends of the previous two centuries continued, significant changes began to reshape the area.

[74] For the quotation, see Wandycz, *Price of Freedom*, xi. Comparative books include, on tenth–eleventh and eleventh–twelfth-century Bohemia-Moravia, Hungary, Poland and Rus': Dvornik, *Making of Central and Eastern Europe*; Font, *Im Spannungsfeld der christlichen Großmächte*. Michael Borgolte, 'Vor dem Ende der Nationalgeschichten? Chancen und Hindernisse für eine Geschichte Europas im Mittelalter', *Historische Zeitschrift* 272, 3 (2001), 561–96, argues for a truly European medieval history to replace national approaches.

[75] A historical region may only exist in a particular time period: Klaus Zernack, 'Das Zeitalter der nordischen Kriege von 1558 bis 1809 als frühneuzeitliche Geschichtsepoche', *Zeitschrift für historische Forschung* 1 (1974), 55–79.

# 2

# THE HISTORY OF THE REGION AND THE QUESTION OF ORIGINS

The new polities of central Europe did not develop in a vacuum. Though sources are scarce, we have some knowledge of populations and political units prior to the development of Bohemia-Moravia, Hungary and Poland. A brief description of these is in order, to understand the complex heritage of the early societies. The new dynasties in each case created origin myths, some of which were later elaborated further. In modern times, the question of origins became highly politicized; it is therefore important to discuss the historical basis of these ideas of origins.

## EARLY HISTORY OF THE REGION

### *Carpathian basin*

Various populations and power centres existed in the Carpathian basin prior to the development of the kingdom of Hungary. Human remains go back to the lower Palaeolithic period: the oldest settlement (Vértesszőlős) is thought to be about 350,000 years old. Archaeologists have found human remains, tools and settlements of hunters from the Middle and Upper Palaeolithic in a number of sites. The area became more densely inhabited in the Neolithic age, supported by a mixture of agriculture, animal raising and fishing. People had permanent settlements and made ceramics. From this period on, different archaeological cultures followed each other, sometimes linked to immigration and conquest. Modern scholars gave these populations names based on the names of towns or villages near which their remains were found (such as the Nagyrév culture in the Early Bronze Age) or based on archaeological characteristics in burial or other aspects of their culture (e.g. the Tumulus culture of the Late Bronze Age). Their ethnic identification has sometimes been attempted but remains controversial or impossible to substantiate. Metallurgy and fortified centres appeared.[1]

In the fourth century BCE Celts (La Tène culture) arrived in the region of the Danube. From roughly the same period, Greek and later Roman written sources also provide some information (although it is not necessarily reliable) on the peoples of the Carpathian basin. The Celts migrated in different waves from different areas, attested in the diversity of finds. They conquered the local populations of the regions west and north of the Danube, while most of the eastern territories of the Carpathian basin were not subjugated. In the second century BCE, Roman sources listed Scordisci (southern areas of the Carpathian basin), Taurisci (in the south-western areas), Boii (in the northern areas) and Daci (in the east, in what later became Transylvania). Loose military and political organization characterized these populations. In the first century BCE Roman sources mention many regional groups; the area was inhabited by a mixed population of Celtic and Illyrian groups.[2]

Starting in 15 BCE, during the last phase of the expansion of the Roman Empire, the Romans gradually conquered the lands west of the Danube and around the Lower Danube. The conquered lands were first attached to Illyricum province. Pannonian resistance to the conquerors hindered Roman progress: the most significant uprising, starting in 6 CE, was a Pannonian–Dalmatian revolt. Roman diplomacy and the tactics of laying waste the land succeeded in splitting the rebels and quashing the rebellion. The province of Pannonia was created by the subdivision of Illyricum probably during the reign of Emperor Tiberius (14–37). The whole area west of the Danube (Transdanubia) had become part of the Roman Empire by the middle of the century.

1 Zsolt Visy, ed., *Hungarian Archaeology at the Turn of the Millennium* (Budapest, 2003), 77–191, with a substantial bibliography.

2 *Ibid.*, 192–202; Miklós Szabó, *Les celtes de l'Est: le Second Âge du Fer dans la cuvette des Karpates* (Paris, 1992); Szabó, *The Celtic Heritage in Hungary* (Budapest, 1971).

After Trajan's victory over the Dacians in 106, the Roman province of Dacia was established (although it did not cover the entire Dacian territory). Immigration was actively encouraged, while the local population was partly sold into slavery to other areas, partly subjugated. Dacia was part of the Roman Empire until 271, when Roman legions withdrew due to Goth attacks. Roman rule in Pannonia lasted longer, and led to some degree of Romanization and Christianization. The province was divided into Lower and Upper Pannonia at the beginning of the second century, and subdivided into more administrative units later. Towns were founded and roads built; trade networks flourished. Immigrants arrived in significant numbers.

Local populations adopted Romanized burial rites, bought and copied Italian artefacts and adopted Roman names. The senatorial aristocracy of the Empire, however, saw the population of the Danubian parts as only superficially Roman, uneducated and crude, and resented their military significance, which increased as Pannonian legions played a crucial part in defending Italian areas against 'barbarian' military attacks. Christianity spread in Pannonia from the third century on (although some scholars date the Christianization of Sirmium (Sremska Mitrovica in present-day Serbia) from much earlier), first in some of the towns. Several Christian martyrs of the early fourth century, such as Demetrius, who subsequently enjoyed a widespread cult, were killed in Pannonia. Christianity, which continued to be a religion of urban populations, started to be more widespread in Pannonia after the 320s; its earliest archaeological remains come from the fourth century.[3]

A variety of 'barbarian' military groupings dominated the areas east of the Danube from the first century CE. Although their attacks periodically targeted Pannonia throughout its existence, it was in the late fourth century that invaders started to have a significant impact on Roman Pannonia. Emperor Valens suffered a crushing defeat by an army made up of Goths and Alans, and died in battle

[3] András Mócsy, *Pannonia and Upper Moesia: A History of the Middle Danube Province of the Roman Empire* (London and Boston, 1974); Visy, ed., *Hungarian Archaeology*, 203–61; Dorottya Gáspár, *Christianity in Roman Pannonia: An Evaluation of Early Christian Finds and Sites from Hungary*, BAR International Series 1010 (Oxford, 2002); Endre Tóth, 'Das Christentum in Pannonien bis zum 7. Jahrhundert nach den archäologischen Zeugnissen', in Egon Boshof and Hartmut Wolff, eds., *Das Christentum im Bairischen Raum von den Anfängen bis ins 11. Jahrhundert* (Cologne, 1994), 241–72.

near Hadrianopolis (Adrianople) in 378. The following year, Goths, Alans and Huns raided Pannonia from the Balkans. Unable to oppose them, the Romans accepted them as allies and settled them in the province. In the following decades, various warrior groups moved through the region; the area of Pannonia under effective Roman rule was shrinking. The process culminated in the arrival of the main armies of the Huns under their ruler Ruga. By 437 Roman rule ceased in all parts of Pannonia.[4]

Local Romanized populations survived the collapse of imperial rule, but controversy surrounds the nature and longevity of this continuity. In trying to gauge the impact and continuity of Romanization, scholars have distinguished between different strata of society, and also between a continuity of settlements, of the Church and of the economy and technology. It is thought that most of the Romanized Christians left Pannonia during the fifth century. The last vestiges of the Romanized elites probably survived into the sixth century, because until then there is data on refugees (fleeing from attacks or migrations) from the area; the last such emigration recorded is that of the inhabitants of Sirmium to Dalmatian towns at the end of the sixth century. It seems that Romanized elites either emigrated or lost their social standing.

The institution that provided a continued framework for a Romanized population for a while after the collapse of Roman rule was the Christian Church. After the beginning of the fifth century, however, few bishops of Pannonian churches are recorded, and two bishops in the late sixth century are mentioned as having fled their dioceses. Germanic peoples settling in the Carpathian basin were Arians, who used existing ecclesiastical buildings without maintaining Roman ecclesiastical structures. Some of the Roman roads, buildings and walls survived, sometimes even to this day. During the fifth century and in later periods, some of these buildings and roads were

[4] Mark B. Shchukin, *Rome and the Barbarians in Central and Eastern Europe First Century BC–First Century AD*, BAR International Series 542 (Oxford, 1989); Visy, ed., *Hungarian Archaeology*, 263–80; László Várady, *Das letzte Jahrhundert Pannoniens (376–476)* (Amsterdam, 1969); Walter Goffart, *Barbarian Tides: The Migration Age and the Later Roman Empire* (Philadelphia, 2006); Herwig Wolfram, *The Roman Empire and Its Germanic Peoples* (Berkeley and Los Angeles, 1997), 35–101; Guy Halsall, *Barbarian Migrations and the Roman West, 376–568* (Cambridge, 2007), 201–9, 242–54; Edward James, ed., *Europe's Barbarians, AD 200–600* (Harlow, 2009), esp. 67–75, 95–101.

reconstructed and reused, and Roman roads and towns influenced medieval trade and settlement patterns. Such technological continuity, however, did not mean that linguistic or cultural continuity persisted over the following centuries. The one exception, where the continuity of a Romanized Christian population (which survived even the Avar conquest) is proposed by archaeologists until at least the seventh century, is the western fringe of Pannonia province, the only area where Roman toponyms survived. A large Christian community lived at Keszthely-Fenékpuszta (Valcum), where an early Christian basilica, built between the end of the fifth century and the middle of the sixth, was rebuilt *c.* 600 and destroyed around 630.[5]

With the Goth-Alan-Hun settlement in Pannonia in 379/80 began the long period of the 'barbarian' control over the Carpathian basin, with the influx of a series of groups. First establishing themselves in the area between the Black and Caspian Seas, the Huns gradually moved west, and by around 410 the ruler and main armies lived on the plains of the Carpathian basin. They were the allies of Aëtius, the increasingly powerful military commander of the Western Roman Empire. In 434 Bleda and his younger brother Attila became the leaders of the Huns. They conducted successful diplomatic negotiations with the Eastern Roman Empire, receiving annual gifts and other privileges. They also led campaigns, with great successes in the Middle Danube and Morava River Valley. Probably in 445, Attila became the sole ruler of the Huns after Bleda's death (according to a Roman account, Bleda was assassinated on Attila's orders). Attila established a short-lived empire centring on the Carpathian basin. Sometimes taking tribute from both the Eastern and Western Roman Empires and sometimes fighting them, Attila led his armies deep into the Balkans, Gaul and Italy, destroying many cities. Legends about him had started to develop already during his lifetime. His reign was seen as divinely ordained, with an aim to rule over the world. His personal centralized power in fact led to the collapse of Hun power after his death in 453. Both internal rivalries and external enemies put an end to Hun rule, and the Huns were dispersed and disappeared from the Carpathian basin.[6]

[5] Visy, ed., *Hungarian Archaeology*, 289–91; Tóth, 'Das Christentum', 257–60; Gáspár, *Christianity*, 53–8.

[6] Christopher Kelly, *Attila the Hun: Barbarian Terror and the Fall of the Roman Empire* (London, 2009); Visy, ed., *Hungarian Archaeology*, 284–7; Wolfram, *The Roman Empire*, 123–44.

In the 450s, Ostrogoths obtained Pannonia, settled there either by the Huns or through an alliance with the Eastern Roman emperor. The rest of the Carpathian basin was inhabited by Sarmatians and Germanic groups. In 473, the Ostrogoths left. Prolonged warfare and frequent changes in the balance of power brought parts of the Carpathian basin under the rule of a variety of warrior groupings, including Gepids and Langobards over the next hundred years.[7]

### *The Bohemian basin and the Morava and Dyja Valleys with adjacent territories (later Bohemia and Moravia)*

The first traces of human inhabitants in the Czech Valley were dated to the oldest Palaeolitic era (2.5 million–750,000 BCE). The oldest stone tools were found on the Zlatý Kopec (Golden Hill) near Přezletice. Various stone tools have been found in other locations also: Beroun-Dalnice, Suchodol, Čakovice. Several places inhabited by *Homo erectus* (*ergaster*) from the period of the dominance of Acheulean tools (750,000–250,000 BCE) were found during excavations in Písečný Vrch, Bečov (both in the Czech Valley) and Stránská Skala (Moravia). The first artefacts linked to the activity of *Homo sapiens sapiens* were dated between 40,000 and 12,000 BCE. The most famous of these were finds of settlement and burial areas in Moravia (Předmostí u Přerova, Dolní Věstonice, Pavlov, Petřkovice, 30,000–25,000 BCE).

Palaeolithic hunters left not only their tools but also elements of their symbolic culture, among them small statues traditionally called Venus and representations of animals made of mammoth tusks. As a result of worsening climatic conditions, during the period 20,000–15,000 BCE population density became sparse. That changed *c.* 5500–4900 BCE. From this period artefacts of Western Linear Pottery have been found in Bohemia and Moravia. The number of inhabitants started growing with the spread of new agricultural techniques *c.* 3500–2000 BCE (the wheel, the lister or sulky plough, cattle breeding). From that time, finds belonging to a large number of different archaeological cultures were identified in Bohemia and

[7] Visy, ed., *Hungarian Archaeology*, 283–301; Peter Heather, *Goths and Romans, 332–489* (Oxford, 1991), 225–93; Heather, *The Goths* (Oxford, 1996), 116–23, 151–61; Florin Curta, *Southeastern Europe in the Middle Ages* (Cambridge, 2006), ch. 1; Wolfram, *The Roman Empire*, 140, 194–9, 279, 281–5.

Moravia. Widespread European cultural formations were present (Globular Amphora Culture, Corded Ware Culture, Bell-Beaker Culture) as well as more regional cultures (Lengyel Culture). Some archaeologists argue that although some elements of material culture changed as a result of cultural exchange with the West, structures more important for social identity (for example, burial rites, symbolic culture, settlement areas etc.) developed constantly based on local circumstances without visible breaks or deep changes (this was possibly the case of the passage from Corded Ware Culture to Bell-Beaker Culture). From the Neolithic era rondel enclosures survive, built *c.* 4900–4200 BCE by people of Moravian Painted Ceramic Culture. Their function is debatable; most archaeologists argued that they were places of cult.[8]

Since *c.* 2000 BCE bronze metallurgy was known in the Czech Valley. Ore-mining and metallurgy led to the differentiation of social status, and to specialization in occupations related to crafts. Czech archaeologists argued that hierarchically organized societies with sun cults existed, with a 'nobility' on top, whose members had burials with expensive furnishing. As before, a wide range of cultures is well attested, among them, the Unetice Culture, widely known in Europe, and two local cultures for Bohemia and Moravia: the Veteřov-Mad'arovce Culture and Knovíz Culture with elements of cannibalism in the latter. With the start of the Iron Age (*c.* 800 BCE), archaeological finds become more homogeneous and belong to the Halstatt Culture, widespread in Europe, although with characteristic local variants (Halstatt Tumulus Culture, Bylany Culture).

Celts arrived in the Czech Valley in the second half of the fifth century BCE. From the Celtic tribal name 'Boii' the land was called 'Boiohemum'. Apart from the Boii, the most influential Celtic tribe was the Volcae Tectosagi, who lived in Moravia. Both tribes, together with Danubian Celts, controlled trade between the Mediterranean

[8] *Space in Prehistoric Bohemia*, ed. Evžen Nestupný (Prague, 1998); J. Kopacz and Lubomír Šebela, 'Moravia at the turn of Stone and Bronze Ages in the light of stone material', in *A Turning of Ages: Jubilee Book Dedicated to Professor Jan Machnik on His Seventieth Anniversary* (Cracow, 2000), 313–35; E. Nestupný, 'Community areas of prehistoric farmers in Bohemia', *Antiquitas* 65 (1991), 326–31; Jan Turek and Jaroslav Peška, 'Bell Beaker settlement pattern in Bohemia and Moravia', in *Bell Beakers Today: Pottery, People, Culture, Symbols in Prehistoric Europe. Proceedings of the International Colloquium, Riva del Garda (Trento, Italy), 11–16 May 1998*, ed. Franco Nicolis (Trento, 2001), 411–28.

world and the Germans. From the middle of the second century BCE until 50 BCE Bohemian and Moravian Celts migrated towards the south-west, fighting with the Romans, and ultimately settled down in Gaul. Their place was taken by Germans, Marcomans with their famous king Marobud (35 BCE–37 CE). Although part of the tribe wandered towards Rome during the first century, they lived in Bohemia until the middle of the fifth century. Besides artefacts characteristic of German culture, elements of Przeworsk Culture, developed in what today are the southern regions of Poland, were identified. They are dated to the second century in Bohemia and to much earlier times, *c.* 50 BCE, in Moravia.

The fifth century was the time of great population mobility. Germans left Bohemia and Moravia, partly with Alans and Vandals *c.* 406, partly with Marcomans through 450. In Moravia, after the Hun raids, populations with a culture characteristic of Danubian territories settled. The German tribe of Heruli lived in southern areas of Moravia, but they were defeated and absorbed at the beginning of the sixth century by Longobards. In the Bohemian basin from the beginning of the fifth century members of the so-called Vinařice formation dominated, whose culture had many elements in common with that of the Huns (for example, burials of warriors with horses). At the end of the fifth century and beginning of the sixth centuries Longobards arrived through the Laba Valley in Bohemia and settled down in the south of the region. Soon, around the middle of the sixth century, they moved farther south, towards the Danube and Rome. Then the time of the Slavs began.[9]

### *The lands between the Carpathian Mountains, the Baltic Sea and the Oder and Bug Rivers (later Poland)*

The first stone tools and settlement traces related to the activity of *Homo erectus* on the territory of what today is Poland appeared in 500,000 (Trzebnica) and 440,000–370,000 (Rusko) BCE. Inhabitants

[9] *Pravěké dějiny Čech*, ed. R. Pleiner and A. Rybová (Prague, 1978), is outdated. The most comprehensive and reliable synthesis is *Archeologie pravěkých Čech*, vols. I–VIII (II, Slavomil Vencl and Jan Fridrich, *Paleolit a mezolit*; III, Ivan Pavlů and Marie Zápotocká, *Neolit*; IV, Miroslav Dobeš, Evžen Neustupný, Jan Turek and Milan Zápotocký, *Eneolit*; V, Luboš Jiráň, *Doba bronzová*; VI, Natalie Venclová and Petr Drda, *Doba halštatská*; VII, Natalie Venclová and Petr Drda and *Doba laténská*; VIII, Vladimír Salač and Eduard Droberjar, *Doba římská a stěhování národů*) (Prague, 2007–8).

of the southern parts of Poland used stone tools typical of the eastern zone of the Acheulean Culture. After the period of glaciation, *Homo neandertalis* arrived. The first location with their characteristic stone tools is in Racibórz-Studzienna, dated to 220,000 BCE. In several other locations in southern Poland archaeologists have excavated not only tools but also remains of fireplaces and traces of hunting activity. In the Paradise Cavern (Jaskinia Raj) 300 reindeer antlers were found. Archaeologists argue that they were used to build a fence against wild animals in front of the cave entrance. During the cave excavations pigments supposedly used for body paintings were also found (70,000–60,000 BCE). The *Neandertalis* settlement lasted in the lands of Poland until the next glaciation (42,000–40,000 BCE).

After the end of the glaciation (*c.* 40,000 BCE) the first groups of *Homo sapiens sapiens* appeared alongside the remaining *Homo neandertalis* settlement. From 10,000 BCE inhabitants lived as hunters and gatherers in small groups, and produced tools of stone and horn. Larger groups of hunters appeared as the climate changed, starting in the eastern and central parts on wide grasslands and tundra territories. As a consequence of climate change, reindeer wandered through the land. From 5400 BCE a relatively stable settlement organization (wooden long houses instead of leather huts, in settlements inhabitated by a population of 40–100 people) appeared, along with traces of agriculture and animal breeding (including cattle, sheep, goats and pigs), which weakened the role of hunting and gathering. Their material culture was that of Western Linear Pottery. Settlement of this type started on the southern border of Poland, in Silesia and Lesser Poland *c.* 5,400 BCE and then expanded towards Greater Poland and Kuyavia, finally crossing the Rivers Bug and San. Around 4900–4800 BCE people using elements of Lengyel Culture appeared on the southern borders of Poland. Researchers believe that they arrived from the Carpathian basin. Their cultural patterns resemble those known from Bohemia and Moravia, including the building of rondel settlements and using cultic artefacts similar to Bohemian ones.

The Eneolithic era began in Poland *c.* 4100/3800 BCE when the first copper tools were made. New technologies spread over Polish lands until 3200/3000 BCE. The most characteristic material culture of the period was that of the Funnel Beaker Culture. Apart from ochre- and flint-mining and bronze metallurgy, the use of wheels in the economy and four-wheeled cattle-drawn carriages were also among technological novelties. The differentiation of functions between settlements was typical of the period. Cultic rituals were developed. On the territory of what is today Kuyavia, megalithic constructions with burials were built. With time cultural differentiation among regions started; the influence of other cultures and economic practices (e.g., people of the Globular Amphora Culture who were mostly shepherds) sped up the process. Around 2300 BCE bearers of the Únětice Culture appeared in southern Poland and the Bronze Age started. Apart from tools and cultic artefacts, a growing number of weapons made of bronze changed the patterns of social life. When Lusatian Culture dominated (*c.* 1550–500 BCE), strongly fortified settlements were built all over the land under its influence. Bronze jewellery became increasingly popular. From 800 BCE, iron was used by Lusatian Culture people, although iron metallurgy did not exist. Trade and subsequent contacts with the Halstatt Culture changed the Lusatian Culture. Different regional cultural groups emerged, among other places, in Silesia, Greater Poland, Pomerania and south-eastern Poland. They differed mainly in pottery and iron adornments, but also in the characteristics of their strongholds (location, strength of fortification, number and size of large, wooden houses inside the stronghold). Scythian raids in *c.* 520–450 BCE destroyed what at the time was the wealthiest Silesian group of the Lusatian Culture. But other branches of the culture continued to exist and evolve.

During the fourth century BCE the Lusatian Culture disappeared. It was replaced by the Pomeranian Culture in the northern and central provinces of later Poland and the La Tène Culture in the southern regions. Artefacts related to the La Tène Culture from the borderlands between Silesia and Lesser Poland suggest strong contacts with the Boii tribe inhabiting the Czech Valley. The Celtic culture in Lesser Poland was also influenced by the local Przeworsk Culture. The latter developed in the third century BCE and lasted until the middle of the fifth century CE. It shaped the life of people living in southern and central parts of Poland. Beginning in the first century Germanic tribes of Vandals and Burgunds inhabited southern regions of Poland, accepting the patterns of Przeworsk Culture. In Eastern Pomerania, tribes of Goths and Gepids settled during the first century, developing the Wielbark Culture. Goths conquered Kuyavia, Greater Poland and Moravia, wandering towards the south and ending their migration at the Black Sea. Soon Gepid tribes went the same direction. After the Hun invasion in the last quarter of the fourth century, the majority – but not all – of Germanic settlers left the territory of Poland. Their place would be taken by Slavs.[10]

## THE AVAR EMPIRE

The Avars, a military confederation made up of many different separate groups, were the next rulers of the region.[11] Although generations of scholars have tried to establish the ethnic make-up of the Avars, Walter Pohl summarized the futility of such an undertaking: 'we only know that they carried an ancient, very prestigious name . . . and we may assume that they were a very mixed group of warriors'.[12] The Avars fled from Central Asia when more powerful warriors conquered the steppe, and entered into an agreement with the Roman emperor Justinian to serve the Empire in return for payment. On the basis of the wealth provided by Roman payments, and military victories over various nomad groups, Khagan Bayan and his successors built up and maintained their military following, and gained supremacy over the various nomad groups on the steppes north of the Black Sea.

From a position of strength, and unable to move south of the Danube because of Byzantine opposition, the Avars allied with the Lombards, defeated the Gepids and conquered the Carpathian basin in 568. The Avars ravaged the Balkan lands of the Byzantine Empire, and captured Sirmium. They were paid an annual tribute in gold to ensure the peace, and at times fought in the employ of Byzantium. The khagan and a small elite ruled the Avar Khaganate. There was no 'ethnic' base to this polity; the groups included under the designation

[10] *Pradzieje i wczesne średniowiecze Małopolski: przewodnik po wystawie, katalog zabytków/ Prehistory and Early Middle Ages of Little Poland: Exhibition Guide and Catalogue*, ed. Jacek Rydzewski (Cracow, 2005); *Pradzieje Wielkopolski od epoki kamienia do średniowiecza*, ed. Michał Kobusiewicz (Poznań, 2008); *Pradzieje ziem polskich*, ed. Jerzy Kmieciński, vol. I, *Od paleolitu do środkowego okresu lateńskiego*, part 1, *Epoka kamienia*, part 2, *Epoka brązu i początki epoki żelaza* (Warsaw, 1989).

[11] Walter Pohl, *Die Awaren. Ein Steppenvolk in Mitteleuropa, 567–822 n. Chr.* (Munich, 1988); Visy ed., *Hungarian Archaeology*, 302–12; Curta, *Southeastern Europe*, 61–9, 75–81, 90–6; M. B. Szőke, 'The question of continuity in the Carpathian Basin of the ninth century AD', *Antaeus* 19–20 (1990–1), 145–57.

[12] Walter Pohl, 'Conceptions of ethnicity in early medieval studies', in Lester K. Little and Barbara H. Rosenwein, eds., *Debating the Middle Ages: Issues and Readings* (Malden, 1998), 15–24 (at 19).

'Avar' changed over time. The Slav presence in the Carpathian basin also became significant during the Avar period.

Avar military fortunes waned after their failed campaign against Constantinople in 626. Civil wars followed, and in the end, Bulgars and Slavs, until then subject to Avar rule, created separate power centres, although the Avar power centre continued to exist between the Middle Danube and Tisza Rivers, attested by richly furnished graves. Based on changes in archaeological finds, some scholars argued for a major immigration of new peoples (according to one view, Hungarians; see below) fleeing from the Khazars *c.* 670, and the creation of a new political and cultural entity in the Late Avar period from the beginning of the eighth century. Others, however, more convincingly, argue that internal change rather than the presence of new ethnic groups is behind the distinctive archaeological finds. Thus archaeologists have suggested the increasing sedentarization and growing polarization of society.

In the 790s, Frankish military offensives, consequent Avar in-fighting and finally Frankish and Bulgar military victories led to the collapse of Avar power. According to one view, the remnants of the Avars continued to occupy the lands east of the Tisza, and eventually merged into the population under Hungarian dominion in the tenth century. The inhabitants of the territories of the Avar Empire were certainly not all physically wiped out with that Empire's collapse, but Avar identity was linked to the Khaganate.

With the political failure of the Avar Empire around 800, the name 'Avar' disappeared from the sources in just over two decades. The western part of the previous Avar Empire was incorporated into the military frontier system (marches) of the Carolingian Empire, while south-eastern areas of the defunct realm became part of the Bulgar Khanate. The exact chronology and extent of Bulgar rule is debated, but during the ninth century the Khanate incorporated eastern areas (later southern Transylvania) of the Carpathian basin. According to some scholars even a part of the Great Plains was included in the Khanate, but there is no contemporary supporting evidence for this.[13]

[13] Curta, *Southeastern Europe*, 161, 178; Csaba Szalontai, 'Bolgárok a 9. századi Kárpát-medencében?', in Szabolcs Felföldi and Balázs Sinkovics, eds., *Nomád népvándorlások, magyar honfoglalás* (Budapest, 2001), 106–29.

## THE EARLY SLAVS

The network of polities that existed across eastern and central Europe by the end of the first millennium emerged after several centuries of dynamic demographic, ethnic and political change. From the tenth century onwards the region is relatively well described in the surviving written sources, but our knowledge of the earlier period remains fragmentary. Little written evidence exists, and archaeologists struggle to convert a vast amount of excavated data into a historical narrative. Any attempt to construct a coherent picture of events before 900 must rely on some speculation.

In the sixth and seventh centuries Byzantine observers of the central European area recorded the presence of *Sklavinoi*[14] in that region. Slavic material culture is first discerned by archaeologists at the same time: this new *ethnos* replaced those cultures that are traditionally identified with the Germanic peoples. No sources offer specific data to help explain the mechanisms behind this change in material cultures.

Such uncertainty allows space for contradictory interpretations, which typically reflect changes in the geo-political context of the modern central European nations.[15] This is especially the case in Poland. Proponents of the so-called autochthonic theory suggest that the early Slavs were direct heirs of the earlier central European populations, which underwent substantial cultural transformation during the migration period. Those who subscribe to the so-called allochthonic theory argue that the first Slavs were migrants from the south-east of the continent, who settled lands that had been earlier deserted by Germanic inhabitants. The two factions agree only that no unambiguous archaeological evidence exists for the presence of Slavs before the middle of the sixth century.[16]

Any attempt to reconcile these contradictory positions is hindered by a lack of written records, problems with the chronology of

[14] Jordanes, *Romana et Getica*, MGH 1 (Berlin, 1882), 35.

[15] P. Urbańczyk, 'Political circumstances reflected in post-war Polish archaeology', *Public Archaeology* 1 (2000), 49–56.

[16] Gerard Labuda, *Słowiańszczyzna starożytna i wczesnosredniowieczna* (Poznań, 1998), 11–19; Witold Mańczak, 'Czy słowiański Biskupin to naukowa legenda?', *Slavia Antiqua* 38 (1997), 191–4 (here 194); Z. Gołąb, *O pochodzeniu Słowian w świetle faktów językowych* (Kraków 2004/1992), 363–6 (original publication: *The Origins of the Slavs: A Linguist's View* (Columbus, OH, 1992)).

linguistic developments and the difficulties of ethnic associations in archaeological finds. The rapid expansion of Slavdom cannot be explained by referring only to cultural categories or to demography. Several recent studies employ a range of methods to reconstruct the complex process of a new, emerging ethnicity, but remain a source of debate.[17]

These controversies do not disguise the remarkable success of early Slavic culture and language, which expanded over two hundred years across a vast area of Europe – from the Dnieper to the Alps, from the Balkans to the Baltic Sea. The inhabitants of this region either brought with them, or developed locally, an egalitarian social structure; an unspecialized economic system; a simple material culture that was characterized by few types of arms and little jewellery; and a 'single' language. They brought an unprecedented uniformity to lands that had previously shown a high degree of cultural difference. People were making undifferentiated pottery, living in small sunken houses built either in rows or in a haphazard manner, and they were burying their dead by cremating them and placing the remains in simple pits accompanied by very few or no furnishings.

This cultural or ethnic revolution coincided almost exactly with a period of political domination by the Avars who, having invaded the Carpathian basin in 568, achieved political dominance over the region for almost two hundred and fifty years. Therefore the highly militarized nomads and sedentary agriculturalists could have established a system of collaboration that had taken shape already during the time of the Avars' presence in the east European steppe zone. The new empire, ruled from the centre located in the plains area, might have achieved stability by simultaneously supplying the militarized nomads with food and large numbers of untrained soldiers, and the agriculturalists with security and long-term stability. The expectations of the two groups allowed the radically different political-economic models to complement one another, which resulted in a beneficial

[17] Pohl, *Die Awaren*, 94–127; P. Urbańczyk, *Władza i polityka we wczesnym średniowieczu* (Wrocław, 2000), 134–9; W. Pohl, 'Początki Słowian: kilka spostrzeżeń historycznych', in *Nie-Słowianie o początkach Słowian*, ed. P. Urbańczyk (Poznań, 2006), 11–26 (here 21–5); Paul Barford, *The Early Slavs* (London, 2001); Sebastian Brather, *Archäologie der westlichen Slawen. Siedlung, Wirtschaft und Gesellschaft im früh- und hochmittelalterlichen Ostmitteleuropa* (Berlin, 2001); F. Curta, *The Making of the Slavs: History and Archaeology of the Lower Danube Region c. 500–700* (Cambridge, 2001).

and durable coexistence. This system was enforced by the steppe warriors who, while fewer in number, politically dominated the agriculturalists.[18]

There are no direct sources which allow us to study early Avar–Slavic relations, although some inferences may be drawn from Byzantine sources. Of particular interest is the only case of a joint Byzantine–Avar military action in 578.[19] It was directed against the Slavs who lived east of the Carpathian Mountains. The Avars aimed at forcing Slavic chieftain Daurentios to acknowledge Khagan Bayan's suzerainty and to pay an annual tribute. No battle was necessary; a demonstration of military superiority was enough to persuade the Slavs, who took refuge in the woods.[20] Avar–Slavic relations centred not on territorial subordination but on prestige and regular contributions. The Slavs who fulfilled these expectations could live with relative freedom and be assured of military protection against external threats.

The only recorded case of a successful revolt against the Avars took place in 623, somewhere between the Alps and the Sudeten Mountains. A charismatic Frankish 'merchant', Samo, led 'sons of Huns [that is, Avars] and Slavic women' against both the Avars and the Franks in 626 and 631, creating an independent enclave that is misleadingly referred to as 'Samo's kingdom'. Despite the historiographical declarations of its might and large extent, there is no historical or archaeological evidence that sheds light on the precise location or size of a short-lived experiment, which did not survive the death of its leader in 658. No memory of that event survived in later Slavic records, and there are no accounts of any other successful military mobilizations.[21]

This may be explained by long-term advantages of co-operation with the nomads. Owing to a simple and self-sufficient economy that

[18] P. Urbańczyk, 'Foreign leaders in early Slavic societies', in *Integration und Herrschaft. Ethnische Identitäten und Soziale Organisation im Frühmittelalter*, ed. W. Pohl and M. Diesenberger (Vienna, 2002), 215–67; P. Brown, *The Rise of Western Christendom* (Cambridge, 1996), 126.

[19] Georgios Kardaras, 'The Byzantine–Avar cooperations against the Slavs (578)', in *Zborník na počesť*, ed. Jozefa Hošša and J. Zabojník (Bratislava, 2006), 31–3.

[20] *Menander Protector. Historiae Fragmenta*, tr., ed. by R. C. Blockley (Liverpool, 1985), frag. 21, 193–5.

[21] Patrick J. Geary, *The Myth of Nations: The Medieval Origins of Europe* (Princeton, 2002).

easily adapted to varied geographical conditions, as well as to the military protection of the Avars, the Slavs permanently settled a large part of Europe. They would continue to thrive after the defeat and subsequent implosion of the nomadic empire; at the beginning of the ninth century they could consider themselves the sole lords over a quarter of the continent. With the final defeat of the Avars at the turn of the ninth century, an aggressive Frankish Empire and the politically indifferent Slavic masses faced each other along an axis from the North Sea to the Adriatic. At the same time, both the Empire and unco-ordinated groups of Slavs were able to expand successfully in other directions. Charlemagne's empire occupied an area stretching from the Pyrenees to the Elbe and from the North Sea to Rome; the Slavs took lands from the Dnieper to the Elbe and from the Baltic Sea to the Balkans. While the Franks acquired their share of the continent with the sword, the Slavs expanded by enlarging their settlement area and cultural influence. Slavic oral traditions lack the heroic ethnogenetic legends that were so familiar to the Germanic peoples. Separate processes led to two distinct organizational and cultural formations that were stable enough to dominate the history of a large part of the continent over the following centuries.

A gradual centralization of power took place among the Western Slavs, that is, those Slavs who lived north of the Middle Danube and west of the Bug River. The earliest evidence for political consolidation can be found in the Moravian zone, which had mixed traditions and an Avaro-Slavic elite that is sometimes associated with the so-called Blatnice–Mikulčice style, best known for its characteristic jewellery.[22] The syncretism of this material culture may indicate that some of the nomads underwent gradual agrarization when mixing with the Slavs who lived north of the Hungarian plain. That the Avars disappeared as a political grouping and indeed as a culturally distinct group from the contemporary chronicles may indicate a rapid 'Slavicization' by means of a process similar to that which took place in the late ninth century, when the nomadic Bulgars gave way to a new Slavic polity that retained the Bulgars' ethnic name and some elements of their vocabulary. The Avars' legacy probably contributed to the sudden rise to prominence of the Moravians, who were the

[22] M. Profantová, 'Blatnicko-mikulčický horizont v Čechách: současný stav a problémy', in Krzysztof Wachowski, ed. *Śląsk i Czechy a kultura wielkomorawska* (Wrocław, 1997), 85–94.

Avars' closest neighbours. They had not been mentioned in the *Divisio imperii* announced by Louis the Pious in 817 but already five years later the Frankish Annals record some Moravians who came to Frankfurt among other envoys of 'Eastern Slavs' ('orientalium Sclavorum') with gifts for the emperor.[23]

## THE SLAVS AND THE CARPATHIAN BASIN IN THE NINTH CENTURY: 'GREAT MORAVIA'

Frankish rulers tried to ensure their control over the central Danubian basin through both the creation of marches at the edges of the Empire, and the recognition or installation of client dukes in more distant areas. A variety of Slavic, and according to some scholars, Bulgar-Turkic peoples gained political significance in the Carpathian basin. Several Slavic dukes, who were at the same time Frankish clients and leaders of war bands, emerged over separate principalities. Their relations with the Carolingians were invariably tumultuous: while often benefiting from Frankish backing to gain power, they equally frequently rebelled against Frankish domination and tried to create independent power centres and stop payments to the Franks. Thus Carolingian rulers repeatedly intervened over the course of the ninth century, trying to establish more loyal client dukes in the various principalities.

Already in 818, one of the dukes, Liudewit, on the Sava river, in Lower Pannonia, revolted, and Carolingian expeditions were sent to quash the rebellion over a period of several years. In the aftermath of this revolt, to ensure Frankish domination more effectively, the eastern marches were reorganized in the years around 830. According to some historians, the main impetus for the reorganization came from Bulgar victories in the region, according to others, from Frankish in-fighting. Louis the German established the Slavic ruler Pribina (or Priwina, d. 861), who swore fidelity to him, in Lower Pannonia, from Lake Balaton to the confluence of the Drava (Drau) and the Danube (*c.* 838). According to some, Pribina's seat had been previously in Nitra (today in Slovakia), until 833 when the Moravian ruler Mojmír (Moimír, before 833–46) expelled him and conquered his lands, but others dispute this and suggest another Pannonian area as

[23] *Annales regni Francorum,* ed. F. Kurze, MGH, Series Scriptores (henceforth SS) 6 (Hanover, 1985), a. 822.

Pribina's previous seat. Between losing that and receiving his new seat from Louis, Pribina was involved in local power struggles. Baptized some years previously on Louis's orders, Pribina introduced Christianity to his lands. He and his son Kocel (or Chezil, *c.* 861–870s) had their centre at Mosaburg (Zalavár, Moosburg). Whether they were counts over a Frankish border county or client rulers of the Franks beyond the Frankish march is unresolved. The territory came under the rule of Arnulf of Carinthia after either Kocel's death or his removal *c.* 874.[24]

The Moravians appear in the sources in 822. The Slav Mojmír created a new centre of power, 'Great Moravia'. The name 'Great Moravia' ('Megale Moravia') occurs only in Constantine Porphyrogenitus's (913–59) *De administrando imperio*, and has been variously interpreted as meaning 'further away' geographically from the Byzantine perspective, or 'old', that is, 'former', no longer in existence (because Constantine wrote about Great Moravia after it ceased to exist).[25] Modern nationalist interpretations of the name as an empire have been completely discredited by scholarship.

The location where this newly prominent polity lay is usually understood to be north of the Danube, with its central areas on the two sides of the Morava River. This view has been challenged by some historians. They advanced arguments in favour of a location south of the Danube in Pannonia and near the southern Morava River, but many of these have been effectively countered.[26] Both

[24] Visy, ed., *Hungarian Archaeology*, 312–17; Eric J. Goldberg, *Struggle for Empire: Kingship and Conflict under Louis the German 817–876* (Ithaca and London, 2006), 83–5; 'The Land of Nitra', in Alfried Wieczorek and Hans-Martin Hinz, eds., *Europe's Centre around AD 1000: Catalogue* (Stuttgart, 2000), 51–4; Herwig Wolfram, *Grenzen und Räume. Geschichte Österreichs vor seiner Entstehung, 378–907* (Vienna, 1995) (also relevant for the following section).

[25] Constantine Porphyrogenitus, *De administrando imperio*, ed. Gyula Moravcsik, tr. R. J. H. Jenkins, new rev. edn (Washington, DC, 1967), chap. 13, pp. 64–5, chap. 38, pp. 172–3, chap. 40, pp. 176–7. See also chap. 41, pp. 180–1 (Moravia).

[26] Imre Boba, *Moravia's History Reconsidered: A Reinterpretation of Medieval Sources* (The Hague, 1971); Charles R. Bowlus, *Franks, Moravians, and Magyars: The Struggle for the Middle Danube 788–907* (Philadelphia, 1995); Martin Eggers, *Das 'Großmährische Reich'. Realität oder Fiktion? Eine Neuinterpretation der Quellen zur Geschichte des mittleren Donauraumes im 9. Jahrhundert* (Stuttgart, 1995); see also Curta, *Southeastern Europe*, 127, n. 39. For a summary of counter-arguments, see Herwig Wolfram, 'Moravien – Mähren oder nicht?,' in *Svätopluk 894–1994*, ed. Richard Marsina and Alexander Ruttkay (Nitra, 1997), 235–45.

Sirmium (Sremska Mitrovica) and Marosvár (Csanád, modern Cenad in Romania) have been proposed as the centre of a southern Moravia. Some even claim the existence of two Moravias, one north of the Danube and the other east of it and on the Lower Danube from the southern Morava River to the Drina.[27] The archaeological evidence, however, backs the northern thesis: strongholds appearing around 800 such as Mikulčice and Staré Město, objects proving Carolingian influence, as well as a strong warrior culture, combined with objects associated to the Byzantine form of Christianity. Although it has been suggested that the appearance of these forts was a result of Moravia's north-west expansion from a southern power base, the archaeological evidence of the southern areas does not support the existence of a strong centre of power there in the ninth century. The interpretation of the written evidence provided by Frankish sources continues to be debated.[28]

Throughout its existence, Great Moravia was in an uneasy relationship with the Eastern Franks.[29] Frankish rulers repeatedly intervened in Moravia, but Moravian rulers were also powerful enough to help East Frankish rebels. Mojmír's conflict with Louis the German ended in the former's expulsion; Louis installed Mojmír's nephew, Rostislav (Rastislav, Rastiz), as ruler in 846. After a tumultuous rule during which he opposed Louis several times, including backing Louis's son Carloman in a revolt against his father, Rostislav was captured and blinded, and his own nephew, Svatopluk (Zwentibald, d. 894), who had already ruled his own principality and swore loyalty to Carloman, was installed; Svatopluk then united the previously separate duchies (*c.* 871). Under his rule, Moravia reached its apogee. Years of warfare with the Franks ended in 874 (the peace in Forchheim) with Frankish recognition of Svatopluk.

[27] For example, Toru Senga, 'La situation géographique de la Grande-Moravie et les Hongrois conquérants', *Jahrbücher für Geschichte Osteuropas* n.s. 30, 4 (1982), 533–40; Bowlus, *Franks, Moravians*, 11–12.

[28] Recently archaeologists as well as historians have contributed to this debate in the special issue of *Early Medieval Europe* 17, 3 (2009), with a list of previous articles on the topic.

[29] Bowlus, *Franks, Moravians*; Dušan Třeštík *et al.*, 'Moravia', in Alfried Wieczorek and Hans-Martin Hinz, eds., *Europe's Centre around AD 1000: Handbook* (Stuttgart, 2000), 191–214; on finds, see 'Great Moravia: an early Slav polity', in Wieczorek and Hinz, eds., *Europe's Centre: Catalogue*, 65–71.

Military hostility with the Eastern Franks (involvement in war against margraves) continued to alternate with periods of peace. Svatopluk controlled, at the height of his power in the second half of the 880s, most of the central Danubian basin. Nonetheless, the exact territories under Svatopluk's rule and the period during which he had effective control over them are debated, even discounting the claim of proponents of the southern Moravia thesis, that southern territories were the core areas of his realm and that he expanded north of the Danube, conquering Nitra after 871. Some scholars argue that Svatopluk (or even Rostislav) conquered the southern areas, including all or part of Pannonia. Others warn against conceiving of Moravia as a state with core areas or clear-cut boundaries, as it never achieved that level of development. Sometime before 890, Svatopluk gained the royal title. Already towards the end of Svatopluk's life in 892, Arnulf (877–99), after consolidating his position as East Frankish king, and relying on Hungarian warriors, started a successful attack against Moravia. After Svatopluk's death, internal rivalry as well as attacks from the outside weakened Moravia further. In 906, Hungarian military victory put an end to the Moravian polity, which was divided between the Hungarians, the Ostmark and the Bohemians.

Christianity was reintroduced to Pannonia and Moravia in the ninth century. The few local Christian communities that survived until the 630s do not seem to have continued beyond that time. Frankish overlordship and influence included the spread of the Latin form of Christianity to Pannonia. The diocese of Salzburg (archdiocese from 798), whose missionary work Pribina had encouraged, and the bishopric of Passau claimed ecclesiastical rights over the territory. No independent ecclesiastical structure was established. From the time of Pribina, rulers as well as landowners established many churches, as in Zalavár. Four of these have been excavated, one wooden and three stone churches. One, later the church of the Benedictine monastery of St Adorján, was built in the middle of the ninth century at the seat of Pribina and Kocel. Christian cemeteries, one of them showing continuity of use between the ninth century and the Árpád age, have also been found. Moravia under Mojmír turned to the Eastern Frankish Empire, and the Moravians were baptized in 831 by clergy from the bishopric of Passau, suffragan of Salzburg. Nevertheless, archaeological evidence shows that the pagan sanctuary in the main Moravian stronghold, Mikulčice, continued in uninterrupted use. Elsewhere, archaeological evidence also points to a parallel existence of pagan cult sites and Christian churches. Several contemporary authors reproached the Moravians for continuing pre-Christian practices. Ecclesiastically, Moravia was subject to the bishop of Passau, who sent missions there. But then Rostislav requested teachers from Byzantium *c.* 862; his aims according to some scholars were political, to establish independence from the Franks. This turn to Byzantium is prominent in the argument for a southern Moravian polity, but it is not decisive, both because the lands the missionaries traversed to get to Moravia in the north were not under firm Frankish control, and no prohibition existed against clerics from Byantium proselytizing in western lands.

The brothers Constantine (Cyril) and Methodius were dispatched to Moravia (863). They were to train pupils who could be ordained priests. To facilitate this teaching, the brothers used the local language. They created a new script that eventually came to be called Glagolitic, and translated religious texts into Old Church Slavonic, a literary language probably based on the Macedonian dialect. After a few years, the brothers went to Rome, to the pope, whence Methodius returned by papal commission to Kocel's court in Pannonia. In 869 at Kocel's request to elevate Methodius to episcopal rank, Pope Hadrian II consecrated him archbishop of Sirmium (with authority over the realms of Rostislav, Svatopluk and Kocel). In 870, however, Methodius, whose archbishopric threatened the ecclesiastical jurisdiction of Salzburg, was taken captive by the Franks and imprisoned.

To prove the ecclesiastical claims of the archbishopric of Salzburg against such contestation, the *Conversio Bagoariorum et Carantanorum*, written *c.* 870 extolled the archbishopric's missionary successes in the area. Due to Svatopluk's victories over the Franks, and pressure from the newly elected Pope John VIII, Methodius was released and reinstated in 874 as metropolitan of Pannonia. Proponents of the southern location of Moravia see a correspondence between Methodius's archbishopric and Svatopluk's realm, the former reinforcing the ruler's independence. Those upholding Moravia's northern location hypothesize that the pope transferred Methodius's title to Svatopluk's realm north of the Danube, or argue that the see of Sirmium was used in reference to an ancient archdiocese in order to buttress Methodius's rights against Salzburg, without concern for political geography. Although Methodius gained papal approval, the resistance of Bavarian bishops, notably Wiching (his own suffragan and bishop of Nitra), continued. After Methodius's death in 885 even his disciples were forced to leave Moravia, and the use of Slavonic liturgy was forbidden.[30]

## HUNGARIAN 'PRE-HISTORY' OR 'ETHNOGENESIS'?

Traditional histories give an account of the emergence and migration of the Hungarians going back to the first millennium BCE. This story, however, lacks a firm basis in evidence. National historiographies created the story of origins, tracing a people back to its supposed cradle, from which it migrated while retaining its ethnicity intact. It is now widely accepted that such stories are more akin to myth-making than to history-writing. The growing criticism of the methodology of automatically equating types of finds with ethnic groups, and of the attempt to identify fixed ethnicity behind early medieval terminology has led to a re-evaluation of much of the history of the early Middle Ages.[31]

Written sources provide evidence only from around the middle of the ninth century, apart from fanciful guesswork that certain ethnonyms or even rulers that appear in earlier written evidence refer to the Hungarians (just to give some examples: Strabo's *Ugroi* or a people that appear in Byzantine, Muslim and Armenian sources as *Saviroi*, Jordanes's Hunugurs of the steppe in the middle of the sixth century, and a ruler called Mouageris who is mentioned by a Byzantine source for the year 527).[32] The Hungarians' self-designation, Magyar, seems to be first attested by Muslim sources of the ninth century.

[30] Fritz Lošek, ed., *Die Conversio Bagoariorum et Carantanorum und der Brief des Erzbischofs Theotmar von Salzburg*, MGH Studien und Texte (Hanover, 1997); Herwig Wolfram, *Salzburg, Bayern, Österreich. Die Conversio Bagoariorum et Carantanorum und die Quellen ihrer Zeit* (Vienna and Munich, 1995); Wolfram, *Conversio Bagoariorum et Carantanorum. Das Weissbuch der Salzburger Kirche über die Erfolgreiche Mission in Karantanien und Pannonien* (Vienna and Cologne, 1979); Petr Sommer, Dušan Třeštík, Josef Žemlička and Zoë Opačić, 'Bohemia and Moravia', in N. Berend, ed., *Christianization and the Rise of Christian Monarchy*, 214–62; see 214–17, 219–25; Béla Miklós Szőke, 'The Carolingian Civitas Mosapurc (Zalavár)', in Wieczorek and Hinz, eds., *Europe's Centre: Handbook*, 140–2; 'Christianisation', in Wieczorek and Hinz, eds., *Europe's Centre: Catalogue*, 72–7.

[31] E.g. Walter Pohl and Helmut Reimitz, *Strategies of Distinction: The Construction of Ethnic Communities, 300–800* (Leiden, 1998); Andrew Gillett, ed., *On Barbarian Identity: Critical Approaches to Ethnicity in the Early Middle Ages* (Turnhout, 2002), with a detailed bibliography of earlier literature; Pohl, 'Conceptions of ethnicity'.

[32] Gyula Kristó, *Hungarian History in the Ninth Century* (Szeged, 1996), 7–14.

What is usually called 'Hungarian pre-history', that is, the history of the 'ancient Hungarians' up to their arrival in the Carpathian basin, is thus a tenuous construct based on linguistics, folklore analogies, archaeology and later written evidence. None of these, however, can offer certainties; on the contrary, often hypotheses from one discipline are joined to hypotheses from another to reach 'firm' conclusions. The underlying framework is a Romantic nationalist one. It is based on the premise that the Hungarians, as a people, existed for about two thousand years before their arrival and settlement in the Carpathian basin. As much recent work has demonstrated for a variety of peoples of early medieval Europe, the formation of a people is not the same as the continuity of bloodlines; early medieval 'ethnicity' was based on political affiliation and not genetics.[33]

Substituting ethnogenesis for 'Hungarian pre-history' at least underlines that the formation of the people was a process. One should beware, however, of simply using 'ethnogenesis' instead of 'pre-history' to designate the same idea, that is, that some core group, the 'ancient Hungarians' have existed for almost two thousand years before they migrated from the east and settled in the Carpathian basin. Nor do I wish to use 'ethnogenesis' to refer to any particular theory or imply any particular content, form or procedure in the formation of a people. The process can also be designated as one of Hungarian identity-formation. My main point is that the 'Hungarians' did not exist as a discrete ethnic group or people for hundreds, let alone thousands, of years prior to their settlement in the Carpathian basin. Through processes we cannot adequately grasp for a lack of sources, Hungarians as a people emerged by the ninth century, although not as a rigidly defined, closed group: many other ethnically and linguistically divergent peoples were subsequently incorporated and became part of 'the Hungarian people'.[34]

[33] From the growing literature especially relevant for non-Germanic 'ethnogenesis', see Gillett, *On Barbarian Identity*; Geary, *The Myth of Nations*; Curta, *The Making of the Slavs*; Ildar Garipzanov, Patrick Geary and Przemysław Urbańczyk, eds., *Franks, Northmen, and Slavs: Identities and State Formation in Early Medieval Europe* (Turnhout, 2008).

[34] For a criticism of ethnogenesis theory used for the Germanic peoples of the early Middle Ages, see Charles R. Bowlus, 'Ethnogenesis: the tyranny of a concept', in Gillett, ed., *On Barbarian Identity*, 241–56. On terminology, see Walter Pohl, 'Archaeology of identity: introduction', in Pohl and Mathias Mehofer, eds., *Archaeology of Identity / Archäologie der identität* (Vienna, 2010), 9–23.

The traditional approach to the origin of the Hungarians as a people is tied to linguistics. Linguists classify Hungarian as part of the Ugric language group within the Uralic language family. The emancipation of the Hungarian language (and thus, according to many scholars, of the Hungarian people) from the Finno-Ugric group supposedly happened in the first half of the first millennium BCE. According to this line of thought, the Hungarians, after detaching themselves from the other Finno-Permic and Ugric (Khanty and Mansi) groups, came under the influence of Turkic peoples of the steppe, which resulted, among other things, in linguistic borrowings. An equally old counter-thesis held that the Hungarians were Turkic in origin, like many other peoples of the steppe. Both views garnered ideological support: late nineteenth- and early twentieth-century nationalists found an association with peoples 'smelling of fish' demeaning, and warrior rather than fishing–gathering ancestors more desirable, while to be related to peoples in the Soviet Union was advantageous when Hungary was part of the Soviet bloc. Debates about origins, tied to national pride, far from being dead among Hungarians, are flourishing again, increasingly independently of scientific considerations.

Linguists used to suppose the existence of a Uralo-Altaic family of languages. From the second half of the twentieth century, many linguists rejected the viability of an Altaic group, or the relationship between Uralic and Altaic. Others then revived the notion of a language group including these or even more languages. The question revolves around determining the genetic relationship between languages versus influence and borrowing. Recently, a linguist with no nationalist feelings at stake concluded that correlations between Hungarian and Ugric/Finnic languages are no stronger than between Hungarian and Turkic languages; linguistic correlations span a wide Eurasiatic area. Her conclusion, that there is no Uralic language family, has had a sharply critical reception among linguists.[35]

[35] Angela Marcantonio, *The Uralic Language Family: Facts, Myths and Statistics* (Oxford, 2002); Marcantonio, 'What is the linguistic evidence to support the Uralic theory or theories?', *Linguistica Uralica* 40, 1 (2004), 40–5. Reviews of her book can be found in, e.g., Ante Aikio, 'Angela Marcantonio, *The Uralic Language Family: Facts, Myths and Statistics*', *Word – Journal of the International Linguistic Association* (2003), issue 3, 401–12; Merlijn De Smit, 'Angela Marcantonio, *The Uralic Language Family: Facts, Myths and Statistics*', *Linguistica Uralica* 39, 1 (2003), 57–67; Marianne Bakró-Nagy, 'Az írástudók felelőssége: Angela Marcantonio, *The Uralic Language Family: Facts, Myths and Statistics*', *Nyelvtudományi Közlemények* 100

Traditional accounts, then, trace the emergence of the Hungarians from the Uralic group and their migration. Usually they situate the original 'homeland' (*Urheimat*) of the Uralic group on the eastern side of the Ural Mountains. From this conglomeration of peoples 'the ancient Hungarians' supposedly moved away to a new area and thus appeared as a separate people. This emergence of the Hungarians from other Finno-Ugric groups is localized south of the east Uralian *Urheimat*: by some in the area around the confluence of the Rivers Volga and Kama, by others east of the Ural River (north of the Caspian Sea and Lake Aral). The Hungarians then migrated westwards, while some people joined them and others were detached. Scholars have speculated about the route and chronology of their migrations, about the ethnogenesis of the Hungarians and their social and political structure, with widely varied results.[36] Although it has already been convincingly argued that a 'Hungarian people' existed only from the eighth or ninth centuries, many Hungarian scholars claim that such a people emerged much earlier, even as early as 1000 BCE.[37]

Linguists have identified Iranian, Turkic and Slavic influences (borrowing, and the development of common structures due to lengthy periods of coexistence) on the Hungarian language. Linguistic analysis also provided the basis for arguments about ancient vocabulary and the time periods when certain loan-words entered the language. These, in turn, were the foundation for opinions about the

(2003), 46–63. See also László Kovács and László Veszprémy, eds., *Honfoglalás és nyelvészet* (Budapest, 1997); Enikő Szíj, 'Research on the prehistory of the Hungarians and Finno-Ugric Studies', and László Honti, 'Research on the prehistory of the Hungarian language', both with extensive bibliographies, in Balázs Gusztáv Mende, ed., *Research on the Prehistory of the Hungarians: A Review*, Varia Archaeologica Hungarica 18 (Budapest, 2005), 115–56, 157–69.

36 Antal Bartha, *A magyar nép őstörténete* (Budapest, 1988); András Róna-Tas, *Hungarians and Europe in the Early Middle Ages: An Introduction to Early Hungarian History* (Budapest, 1999), chs. 6–7; Gyula Kristó, *A Kárpát-medence és a magyarság régmúltja (1301-ig)* (Szeged, 1993), 41–74; Kristó, *Hungarian History in the Ninth Century*; István Zimonyi, 'The state of the research on the prehistory of the Hungarians: historiography (Oriental sources, history of the steppe)', in Mende, ed., *Research on the Prehistory of the Hungarians*, 87–102. Short comments by István Vásáry and Ferenc Makk can be found in Mende, *Research on the Prehistory of the Hungarians*, 103–9, 111–14; see also István Vásáry, *Magyar őshazák és magyar őstörténészek* (Budapest, 2008). Voluminous earlier literature can be found in these works.

37 For the eighth to ninth centuries, see Jenő Szűcs, *A magyar nemzeti tudat kialakulása* (Szeged, 1992). For early dating, see Róna-Tas, *Hungarians and Europe*, 319; Gábor Vékony, *Magyar őstörténet – magyar honfoglalás* (Budapest, 2002), 92–3.

location of the 'ancient Hungarians' in certain periods, and their economic practices and religious beliefs. To draw conclusions from linguistics alone about historical processes is problematic. Often, linguistic developments cannot be dated with certainty. Linguists themselves have revised the dating of Turkic influences on the Hungarian language several times over the past hundred years. In turn, such datings are used to determine the geographical location of the 'ancient Hungarians' in the corresponding period. One example illustrates the impact of the revision of dating: based on traditional dating, in the late fifth and sixth centuries, the Hungarians moved from the Volga–Kama region to the Caucasian area; upon reclassifying the Khazar language as Bulgar-Turk, however, Hungarians could be localized in that period in any area from the Volga to the Black Sea.[38]

Moreover, although some scholars emphasize that, owing to the fluidity of group formations, linguistic reconstruction ('ancient Hungarian') does not mean that an 'ancient Hungarian people' was the direct precursor of the historical Hungarians, this distinction between historical linguistics and ethnohistory often got lost. Ethnography, providing analogies from Finno-Ugric or Turkic folklore and generalizations about the typology of development (towards increasingly complex social and economic structures) supplemented linguistic arguments, but these do not provide secure evidence. The only certainty that has emerged is that Hungarian-speakers merged with many other groups by the ninth century.

Archaeology similarly offers no certainties. The inherent difficulties of the ethnic identification of archaeological material is by now well known. No archaeological finds can be securely identified as 'Hungarian' in any of the areas of the supposed Hungarian migrations, and archaeological interpretations are often debated. Much of the excavated material from the supposed Hungarian homelands is obviously not connected to the Hungarians. Some finds and archaeological cultures were attributed to proto-Hungarians, only for the identification to be questioned again. The method of trying to identify earlier steppe finds as Hungarian based on tenth-century Carpathian finds has been criticized. Steppe finds that resemble

[38] Károly Czeglédy, *Magyar őstörténeti tanulmányok* (Budapest, 1985), 156–63; Lajos Ligeti, *A magyar nyelv török kapcsolatai a honfoglalás előtt és az Árpád-korban* (Budapest, 1986); on the Khazar language, see 475–89.

tenth-century finds from the Carpathian basin used to be dated to a period before the tenth century and classified as 'Hungarian', but according to more recent datings, the steppe and Carpathian basin finds are contemporary, suggesting a typology unconnected to ethnic links.

Certain features, such as partial horse burials, used to be thought of as 'Hungarian', but it has been proven that other steppe peoples used similar burial styles. Archaeologists have increasingly uncovered broad regional similarities between Hungarian ornaments of the conquest age in the Carpathian basin and Bulgar material; the Hungarian finds have ties much closer to the Bulgar finds than to the eastern ones. A Mediterranean rather than independent 'Eastern Steppe' style characterizes the first generations of Hungarians in the Carpathian basin: this points to the Black Sea region (whether Crimea, or the Lower Danube cannot be determined).[39] Finally, while some see DNA analysis as the solution to Hungarian pre-history, biological anthropologists have emphasized the hypothetical nature of conclusions about Hungarian ethnogenesis based on the analysis of human remains.[40]

Medieval authors had their own ideas about Hungarian 'pre-history', which provided the basis for the development in

[39] On various theories about an ancient Hungarian homeland, see János Makkay, 'The secondary homeland of the proto-Hungarians in Western Siberia', in Mende, ed., *Research on the Prehistory of the Hungarians*, 369–91; Róna-Tas, *Hungarians and Europe*, 116–40; but see Péter Langó, 'Archaeological research on the conquering Hungarians: a review', in Mende, ed., *Research on the Prehistory of the Hungarians*, 175–340, esp. 175–9. For an example of an older synthesis, see István Fodor, *Vázlatok a finnugor őstörténet régészetéből* (Budapest, 1973). See also Péter Langó, 'A Kárpát-medence X. századi lelethorizontjának bulgáriai vonatkozásai, néhány kiemelt példa alapján', in Gábor Fancsalszky *et al.*, *Avarok, bolgárok, magyarok* (Budapest, 2009), 34–46; Csanád Bálint, 'Zwischen Orient und Europa. Die "Steppenfixierung" in der Frühmittelalterarchäologie', in Joachim Henning, ed., *Zwischen Byzanz und Abendland. Pliska, der östliche Balkanraum und Europa im Spiegel der Frühmittelalterarchäologie* (Frankfurt am Main, 1999), 13–16; Bálint, 'A 9. századi magyarság régészeti hagyatéka', in László Kovács, ed., *Honfoglalás és régészet* (Budapest, 1994), 39–46; Bálint, *Die Archäologie der Steppe* (Vienna and Cologne, 1989). Some recent summaries on the history and problems of ethnic identification in archaeology include Curta, *The Making of the Slavs*, 24–34; Mats Roslund, *Guests in the House: Cultural Transmission between Slavs and Scandinavians 900–1300 AD* (Leiden, 2007), 86–128.

[40] Gyula Farkas, 'Biological anthropology/human biology and the prehistory of Hungarians', in Mende, ed., *Research on the Prehistory of the Hungarians*, 9–32; Csanád Bálint, 'A contribution to research on ethnicity: a view from and on the east', in Pohl and Mehofer, eds., *Archaeology of Identity*, 145–82.

modern scholarship of the story of a long migration. Hungarian chronicles record origin myths, which may in some cases be based on oral tradition, reworked by erudite medieval authors; and may in other cases be entirely medieval constructions. These include the story of descent and migration from Scythia, a miraculous stag leading the brothers Hunor and Magor to new lands.[41] The dynasty's own origin myth was probably the birth of Álmos, the ancestor of the Árpád dynasty, from the union of the woman Emese and a *turul* (perhaps a falcon); the Christian chronicler reworked this to present it as a dream rather than an actual union.[42] Metal discs depicting an eagle or *turul* and objects decorated with stags and eagles characteristic of conquest-age art have been interpreted as representations of animal ancestors.[43]

The Hungarian Anonymous *c.* 1200 and the Hungarian Chronicle composition which survives in its present form from the fourteenth century depict the long migration of the Hungarians. The anonymous author talks about the Scythia–Etyl–Suzdal–Dnieper–Galicia–Havaserdő route. Etyl could signify the Don or the Volga. The Chronicle has the Hungarians migrating from Scythia through the lands of the Pechenegs, 'white Cumans', Suzdal, Kiev and Transylvania. These accounts are usually understood as in some way reflecting the memory of migrations. Work on other, similar migration stories, however, highlighted the importance of symbolic geography in these descriptions as well as of the biblical model. These authors created a link between migration and the forming of a people, from barbarism to civilization. These stories were erudite

41 Aemilius [Emil] Jakubovich, ed., *P. Magistri, qui Anonymus dicitur, Gesta Hungarorum*, in Imre Szentpétery, ed., *Scriptores Rerum Hungaricarum* (henceforth *SRH*), vol. I (Budapest, 1937, repr. Budapest, 1999), 13–117, see 34–7; Alexander [Sándor] Domanovszky, ed., *Simonis de Kéza, Gesta Hungarorum*, in *SRH*, vol. I, 129–94; László Veszprémy and Frank Schaer, ed. and tr., *Simonis de Kéza Gesta Hungarorum – Simon of Kéza, The Deeds of the Hungarians* (Budapest, 1999), 12–14; Alexander [Sándor] Domanovszky, ed., *Chronici Hungarici compositio saeculi XIV*, in *SRH*, vol. I, 217–505 (288–9); György Györffy, *Krónikáink és a magyar őstörténet. Régi kérdések – új válaszok* (Budapest, 1993); Imre Katona, 'A magyar honfoglalás mondaköre', in László Kovács and Attila Paládi-Kovács, eds., *Honfoglalás és néprajz* (Budapest, 1997), 267–73.

42 *P. Magistri*, 38.

43 Fodor, *Ancient Hungarians*, 32–3. They are often called totems, but a convincing counter-argument is made by Gábor Vargyas, 'A "magyarok totemizmusa" nyomában', in Kovács and Paládi-Kovács, eds., *Honfoglalás és néprajz*, 323–31.

and constructed, based on ideas from classical antiquity and the Bible; one cannot suppose *a priori* that they reflect actual events.[44] Given the relatively late composition of the Hungarian texts, a large array of literary models was also already at the service of the authors, which suggested the need for a faraway homeland and a story of migrations.

Such *origo gentis* accounts served the political aims of a particular group. They became foundations for an identity, rather than reflecting an already existing ethnic identity of a whole people. The Hungarian origin myth stories have the same characteristics as those of the Goths, Lombards and others:[45] an already existing, identifiable people migrating, encountering enemies on the way, each battle showing the valour of the people and their cohesion. They have both an eponymous founder and chieftains during the migration. In the course of the migration, they acquire civilization and Christianity. Their installation in their current home is proof of their tenacity and bravery. There is also variation between different versions of the story in terms of the route of migration, names and other details. The medieval narratives about Hungarians should no more be taken as encapsulating folk traditions of real migrations than the other learned medieval texts.

A medieval text exists which may seem to contradict such a conclusion, and to confirm the Hungarian migration stories. This is a text by the Dominican friar Ricardus, written in Hungary and claiming to be an account based on Friar Julian's oral narrative about his journey.[46] According to this text, Dominicans from Hungary read in the *Gesta* of the Hungarians how the Hungarians who went out from their original homeland under seven leaders were converted under St István (Stephen, 997–1038), while those who stayed behind remained pagans. Therefore they searched for years to find and convert the pagan Hungarians, because they had no idea where they

[44] Walter Goffart, *The Narrators of Barbarian History (AD 550–800): Jordanes, Gregory of Tours, Bede, and Paul the Deacon*, 2nd edn (Notre Dame, IN, 2005); Magali Coumert, *Origines des peuples: les récits du Haut Moyen Âge occidental (550–850)* (Paris, 2007).

[45] Coumert, *Origines des peuples*, esp. 503–52.

[46] Heinrich Dörrie, *Drei Texte zur Geschichte der Ungarn und Mongolen: Die Missionsreisen des fr. Iulianus O.P. ins Ural-Gebiet (1234/5) und nach Rußland (1237) und der Bericht des Erzbischofs Peter über die Tartaren*, Nachrichten der Akademie der Wissenschaften in Göttingen aus dem Jahre 1956. Philologisch-Historische Klasse (Göttingen, 1956), 131–62.

were. A friar finally found them and told his brothers, who organized a mission. Modern scholars date this to about 1235. Only one, Julian, made it to 'Great Bulgaria' (interpreted as Volga Bulgaria) after months of hardship. There he met a Hungarian woman living in one of the towns and, following her instructions, found the pagan Hungarians on the River 'Ethyl'.

He could communicate with them because they spoke Hungarian, and they were eager to hear him preach the faith. Julian, however, was worried that if the pagan populations between the kingdom of Hungary and the pagan Hungarians heard about the conversion, they would close the way between the two Hungarian populations in order to prevent the subjugation of the peoples in between; and that, if he died, there would be no one to complete the task. Therefore he returned to Hungary to gather more friars. He returned by way of the Mordvani, Rus' and Poland. A somewhat later letter by Julian himself describes a journey (dated to 1237), when he reached the eastern edge of Rus' and was told about the Mongol destruction of the lands of the pagan Hungarians and Bulgars.[47] He also refers to brothers going to Magna Hungaria before him, who encountered in the frontier regions of Suzdal some pagan Hungarians who had fled from the Mongols and were willing to convert. The ruler of Suzdal was angered by this attempt at evangelizaton and expelled the friars; although they tried to persist, they did not get any further. Julian and his companions also returned to Hungary. The rest of the letter focuses on the Mongols.

Some scholars argue that Julian made two journeys, the first to the Volga, described in the account by Ricardus, and the second, during which he could no longer return to Magna Hungaria, depicted in his own letter. They see Ricardus's text as further proof of the migration of the Hungarians. Several problems are ignored to uphold such a claim. To begin with the least of them, 'Etil' was used as the name of the Volga, but also of other rivers. Notably, Emperor Constantine Porphyrogenitus described the place where the Hungarians migrated from, and which in his own times (the middle of the tenth century) were inhabited by Pechenegs, as Etelköz. This name form in Hungarian signifies a territory between two rivers. The other rivers Constantine mentioned in his narrative about the area have been identified as the Dnieper, Bug, Dniester, Prut and Szeret. Etelköz has been variously identified as the

47 Dörrie, *Drei Texte*, 162–82.

area between the Don and Lower Danube; between the Dnieper and Lower Danube; and between the Bug and Lower Danube. Therefore Julian's 'Etil' may or may not be the Volga; Ricardus's geography is vague enough to allow multiple interpretations.

More significantly, the supposed description of the 'pagan Hungarians' consists of the greatest stereotypes western Christian sources had applied to the Hungarians of the ninth and tenth centuries, which a literate author of the thirteenth century would have known well: they eat horse-meat, drink blood and fight well. Moreover, the account written by Ricardus, based theoretically on Julian's oral report, has been questioned: its most ardent critics think the whole text is an imaginary account, based on Julian's own letter, and Julian made only one trip, never reaching Magna Hungaria. Julian himself does not say anything about the language the pagan Hungarians spoke, nor does he talk about reaching their land. Significantly, the contemporary Alberic of Trois-Fontaines recorded what would correspond to Julian's supposed 'second' journey, but had no knowledge of the 'first': according to his Chronicle, four Dominicans travelled from Hungary to 'old' (Magna) Hungaria in 1237 (to get news of whether the Mongols wanted to attack Hungary), but the Mongols had already invaded it.[48] Other thirteenth-century friars who travelled east after Julian, such as Johannes of Plano Carpini and William of Rubruq identified Bashkiria as Magna Hungaria, referring to information from Dominicans. This may refer to Ricardus's account, but does not prove the veracity of its contents. Even those who accept the authenticity of the first journey emphasize that Ricardus's narrative is not precise in many of its details.[49]

That Hungarian-speaking groups lived somewhere north of the Black Sea in the early thirteenth century is not impossible, but does

[48] Alberic's Chronica recorded events until 1241 and he died *c.* 1252: *Albrici monachi Triumfontium Chronicon*, ed. Paulus Scheffer-Boichorst, MGH Scriptores 23 (Hanover, 1874), 631–950 (at 942).

[49] György Györffy, *Julianus barát és Napkelet fölfedezése* (Budapest, 1986, repr. Budapest, 2002). According to Sinor, Ricardus elaborated the account of the same voyage Julian described: Denis Sinor, 'Un voyageur du treizième siècle: le Dominicain Julien de Hongrie', in *Inner Asia and Its Contacts with Medieval Europe* (London, 1977), no. XI, and 'Les relations entre les Mongols et l'Europe jusqu'à la mort d'Arghoun et de Béla IV', in *Inner Asia and its contacts*, no. X; István Zimonyi, 'Julianus', in Gyula Kristó, Pál Engel and Ferenc Makk, *Korai Magyar Történeti Lexikon: 9.–14. század* (Budapest, 1994) (henceforth *KMTL*).

not tell us anything about pre-ninth-century history; that in the ninth century Hungarian-speakers did indeed live in that region is known from many other sources. None of the medieval texts gives a trustworthy account of the location of a supposed ancient Hungarian homeland. Hungarian-speakers in the east were much more likely the descendants of those whom Constantine Porphyrogenitus's informant described as moving east when the other Hungarians moved west (see below): therefore not remnants in an ancient homeland, but descendants of ninth-century migrants.

The Hungarians appear in the written sources around the middle of the ninth century, but much uncertainty remains in our knowledge of the specific details of their history.[50] Hungarian historians tried to reconstruct the history of the period prior to the move to the Carpathian basin using brief ninth-century references in Latin and Muslim sources, as well as Constantine Porphyrogenitus's longer, but problematic, description from the middle of the tenth century.[51] According to Constantine, the Hungarians lived in an area near Khazaria, called Levedia after the name of their voivode, and lived and fought together with the Khazars for three years. The voivode had a Khazar wife, and the Khazar ruler was instrumental in the election of the first overall leader, who was to obey the ruler.[52] Arab and Persian sources that described the Hungarians *c.* 870 did not discuss their relations to the Khazars – except Ibn Rusta's remark that the Khazars used to dig trenches to protect themselves against the Hungarians – indicating that they lived separately.[53]

50 Some authors mention the 830s as the first appearance of written evidence. This, however, refers to a single text mentioning a group at the Lower Danube, who may be the Hungarians; the dating of the episodes is uncertain, and the text in which these occur is from the tenth century: István Zimonyi, 'Préhistoire Hongroise: méthodes de recherche et vue d'ensemble', in Sándor Csernus and Klára Korompay, eds., *Les Hongrois et l'Europe: conquête et intégration* (Paris and Szeged, 1999), 29–43 (see 41); Kristó, *Hungarian History in the Ninth Century*, 15–17. After that, it is from the 860s that contemporary sources start to give information on the Hungarians.

51 Overviews can be found in e.g. Kristó, *Hungarian History in the Ninth Century*; Antal Bartha, *Hungarian Society in the Ninth and Tenth centuries* (Budapest, 1975).

52 Constantine Porphyrogenitus, *De administrando imperio*, chap. 38, pp. 170–3.

53 István Zimonyi, *Muszlim források a honfoglalás előtti magyarokról: a Ǧayhānī – hagyomány magyar fejezete* (Budapest, 2005), 34–49, lists all the textual variations, Arab edn and Hungarian tr. (German tr., *Muslimische Quellen über die Ungarn vor der Landnahme. Das ungarische Kapitel der Ǧaihânî-Tradition* (Herne, 2006)).

Exactly when and for how long the Hungarians were under Khazar political domination is an open question: scholarly opinions range from 20–30 to more than 200 years of living under Khazar dominion.[54] The information Constantine transmitted (based on Hungarian informants) does indicate that the Hungarians were subject to the Khazars, providing military service to the khagan; it was not long before their settlement in the Carpathian basin that the Hungarians became independent of Khazar rule. According to Constantine, they left the empire together with some groups that rebelled against the Khazars, the Kabars (or Kavars).[55]

Constantine related that after a war between Kangar-Pechenegs and the Hungarians living in Levedia, one group of the latter moved east towards Persia, and the rest, under Levedi, moved west, to Etel Kouzou (Etelköz); according to another interpretation the emperor did not suggest Hungarian migration, but rather that eastern and western parts of their areas were separated by the incoming Pechenegs. The location of the territories mentioned by Constantine has been debated: modern scholars situated Levedia between the Dnieper and Don, the Don and Donets, the Volga and Don, the Don and Kuban, the Kodyma and Ingul, and the Etelköz area between rivers identified above. According to one view, the two names designate the same territory.[56] The identification of populations, such as the Kangar-Pechenegs, and places rests on hypotheses and, although some may be more plausible than others, ultimately the only certainty is that in the ninth century the Hungarians were present north of the Black Sea, and moved west as a result of attacks.[57]

[54] Sándor László Tóth, 'Szövetség vagy vazallitás? (Megjegyzések a magyar–kazár kapcsolatokhoz)', in *Magyaroknak eleiről: ünnepi tanulmányok a hatvan esztendős Makk Ferenc tiszteletére*, ed. Ferenc Piti (Szeged, 2000), 637–54; Zimonyi, *Muszlim források*, 250–9; Peter B. Golden, 'Irano-Turcica: the Khazar sacral kingship revisited', *Acta Orientalia Academiae Scientiarum Hungaricae* 60, 2 (2007), 161–94 (see 180–2, 187).

[55] Whoever the Kabars were, the derivation of their name is debated: Sándor László Tóth, 'Kabarok', in *KMTL*; Zoltán Kordé, 'Kabars, Sicules et Petchenègues: les Hongrois et les auxiliaires militaires,' in Csernus and Korompay, eds., *Les Hongrois et l'Europe*, 231–9.

[56] István Zimonyi, 'Etelköz' and 'Levedia', in *KMTL*; Sándor László Tóth, *Levediától a Kárpát-medencéig* (Szeged, 1998).

[57] There are many debates on the interpretation of Constantine's text: cf. Moravcsik's edition; János Harmatta, 'Konstantinos Porphyrogennetos magyar vonatkozású művei', in László Kovács and László Veszprémy, eds., *A Honfoglaláskor írott forrásai*

Archaeologists have debated the dating and identification of a variety of finds east of the Carpathian basin, but the only consensus is the need for more thorough research methodologies and a comparison and review of the material now in a number of separate states. Some graves in today's Romania and Ukraine are seen as remains of the Hungarians of the Etelköz.[58]

Hungarians are mentioned in the areas north of the Black Sea to the Lower Danube region several times during the later ninth century, although some of the identifications are debated.[59] Arab and Persian sources situate the Hungarians around 870 as neighbours of the Bulgars along the lower Danube, and of the Pechenegs and Khazars along the River 'Atil' (perhaps Don). King Louis the German in 860 wrote about the 'uuangariorum marcha', and some scholars suggested that this refers to the Onogurs, or to the Hungarians who were already living in the region; the expression however need not concern either, but instead may be based on German etymology.[60] Around 861, Cyril met Hungarian raiders in the Crimean peninsula. An oft-cited episode from *The Life of Methodius* concerns the meeting between Methodius and a possible 'king of Hungary' (korolju ougъrьskomou) who came to the lands of the Danube. It is variously interpreted as a meeting during the former's trip to or from Constantinople *c.* 882, or as a meeting between Svatopluk (whom Methodius accompanied) and Charles III in 884; some scholars see this as a reference to the Hungarians, whereas others argue it has nothing to do with them.[61]

Hungarian warriors penetrated into the Carpathian basin several times from 862. Theotmar's letter shows that groups of Hungarians were active around the Middle Danube, fighting sometimes for the

(Budapest, 1996), 105–11; István Kapitánffy, *Hungaro-Byzantina: bizánc és a görögség középkori magyarországi forrásokban* (Budapest, 2003), 139–44.

58 László Kovács, 'Remarks on the archaeological remains of the ninth–tenth century Hungarians', in Mende, *Research on the Prehistory of the Hungarians*, 351–68 (351–7); and on archaeology, n. 39 in this chapter; István Bóna, *A magyarok és Európa a 9–10. században* (Budapest, 2000), 17–20.

59 Bóna, *A magyarok és Európa*, 9–16.

60 Pál Engel, *The Realm of St Stephen: A History of Medieval Hungary 895–1526* (London, 2001), 6; István Bóna, 'Wangarok', in *KMTL*.

61 'The Life of Methodius', in Marvin Kantor, *Medieval Slavic Lives of Saints and Princes* (Ann Arbor, 1983), 125; p. 138, n. 76, identifies him as Charles III (the Fat). See Péter Király, 'A Konstantín-és Metód-legenda magyar részletei', in Kovács and Veszprémy, eds., *A honfoglaláskor írott forrásai*, 113–18; Bowlus, *Franks, Moravians*, 215; Curta, *Southeastern Europe*, 129 (which does not take into account Bowlus and Kantor's identification).

Franks, then for the Moravians, and on their own account by 900. According to the *Annales Bertiniani*, they attacked Louis the German's realm in 862. Other conflicts with the Hungarians are cited in Carolingian sources in the 880s.[62] They appeared on the side of Arnulf of Carinthia, the East Frankish king against the Moravians in 892.[63] Medieval authors and modern scholarship concur that, in the following years, Arnulf continued his alliance with the Hungarians to further his own aims: destroy Moravia and gain imperial coronation.[64] This was the beginning of what turned out to be the Hungarian conquest of and settlement in the Carpathian basin.

Modern and medieval myths surround the settlement of the Hungarians in the territory that became the kingdom of Hungary. The traditional term used in Hungarian historiography, *honfoglalás*, literally 'the occupation of the homeland' (even the German *Landnahme* does not accurately convey the Hungarian connotation, let alone the English 'conquest') signals the modern conceptualization of this settlement. Nationalist historiography enshrined the story of the brave warriors taking a new land destined to be the homeland of the Hungarians, tying this conquest to the year 895, or more broadly to the period 895–902. The millenial celebrations of 1896 created and popularized images that determined the view of the Hungarian settlement for generations of Hungarians, not least the monumental statue of the seven tribal chieftains as they arrive on horseback (Budapest, Hősök tere).[65]

The nineteenth-century view of the arrival of the population is in turn based on medieval texts. No contemporary Hungarian descriptions exist. The Hungarian Chronicle composition, which was probably begun in the late eleventh or early twelfth century,

[62] Lošek, ed., *Die Conversio Bagoariorum et Carantanorum und der Brief des Erzbischofs Theotmar*; Félix Grat, Jeanne Vielliard and Suzanne Clémencet, eds., *Annales Bertiniani (Les Annales de Saint-Bertin)* (Paris, 1964); Janet L. Nelson, tr. and annotated, *The Annals of St-Bertin* (Manchester, 1991), 102; Bowlus, *Franks, Moravians*, 237–9 (also raided St Gall: Bowlus, *Franks, Moravians*, 236).

[63] *Annales Fuldenses*, ed. Fridericus Kurze, *MGH SRG* (Hanover, 1891), a. 892, p. 121; Timothy Reuter, tr. and annotated, *The Annals of Fulda* (Manchester, 1992), 123–4; Bowlus, *Franks, Moravians*, 224–34.

[64] Bowlus, *Franks, Moravians*, 235–6, listing the medieval texts of Widukind and Liutprand, 370, n. 2.

[65] Ildikó Matolcsy *et al.*, eds., *Az ezredév* (Budapest, 1979).

but took its final (surviving) form in the fourteenth, includes a mythic version of an attack by eagles which preceded the Hungarian entry into Pannonia, the election of seven captains and the conquest of Svatopluk's realm.[66] The Hungarian Anonymous (probably writing at the end of the twelfth or beginning of the thirteenth century) developed the legendary version of these events that then became the basis for modern national histories. He invented a series of battles against various opponents, and gave a detailed fictitous description of the taking of the land.[67]

Two medieval myths offered an overall explanation for the settlement of the Hungarians. One, the elements of which are present in several of the chronicles, described the captains of the population deciding to settle after finding a land whose description evokes an earthly paradise. The account was also influenced by the biblical story of God leading Israel to the Promised Land. The Hungarians employed a ruse by sending a beautiful white horse with gilded accoutrements to the local ruler in exchange for a handful of earth, grass and a little water, informing him after the transaction was completed that he had in fact ceded his land through the ceremony; the Hungarians then defeated the ruler and occupied the land.[68] Modern scholarship found the basis of this story in the oath-taking ceremony of nomads which was linked to the making of alliances.[69] Another, thirteenth-century myth which made the Hungarians the relatives of the Huns, presented the settlement as a reconquest of the Hungarians' heritage, that is, the land that had belonged to the Huns and now rightfully belonged to the Hungarians.[70]

Relying on this story, and interpreting archaeological evidence tendentiously, one modern scholar alleged that there was indeed a dual Hungarian conquest.[71] Drawing on earlier ideas concerning the identification of various ethnonyms with the Hungarians, he claimed that Hungarians first moved into these areas around 670, and the late-ninth-century second wave of conquerors found them settled in the Carpathian basin. Attractive to nationalists, such a thesis would

[66] *Chronici Hungarici*, 286–90. [67] *P. Magistri*. [68] *Chronici Hungarici*, 288–9.

[69] Hansgerd Göckenjan, 'Eid und Vertrag bei den altaischen Völkern', *Ural-Altaische Jahrbücher* n.s. 16 (1999–2000), 11–31.

[70] *Simonis de Kéza*, in *SRH*, vol. I, 143–65; in Veszprémy and Schaer, *Simon of Kéza*, 15–81.

[71] Gyula László, *A 'kettős honfoglalás'* (Budapest, 1978).

'prove' a Hungarian 'historical right' to the land. Variations of the idea resurface from time to time, such as Hungarians settling *c.* 680, leaving (around 800), and then returning to the Carpathian basin *c.* 895, but both the original thesis and its later versions have been convincingly refuted.[72]

Events of the Hungarian conquest appear in a variety of western and Byzantine sources. Regino of Prüm recorded everything he knew of the Hungarians, compressing the story between the years 889 and 901: their leaving Scythia, expelled by the stronger Pechenegs, their defeat of the Moravians and raids into Lombardy.[73] The mid-tenth-century account by the Byzantine emperor Constantine Porphyrogenitus relates that Hungarians settled on lands later occupied by the Pechenegs, but then Symeon of Bulgaria, whom the Hungarians had previously defeated, allied with the Pechenegs to destroy the Hungarians. The Pechenegs attacked while the Hungarian army was away, and destroyed the land and the families who had stayed behind. The returning Hungarians, seeing this, wiped out Great Moravia, ruled by Svatopluk, and conquered the land.[74] Individual military events are referred to in a number of other sources.

The process of conquest and settlement has been reconstructed by historians in the main, but several points remain debated.[75] As Arnulf's allies, Hungarians continued to attack Moravia, which progressively disintegrated. This was probably interrupted by a peace treaty in 894

[72] Imre Boba, 'A twofold conquest of Hungary or "Secundus ingressus"', *Ungarn-Jahrbuch* 12 (1982–3), 23–41. For criticism, see Visy, ed., *Hungarian Archaeology*, 302–7; Bálint, *Die Archäologie der Steppe*, 233–5.

[73] *Reginonis abbatis Prumiensis Chronicon*, ed. Fridericus Kurze, MGH SRG (Hanover, 1890), 1–153 (at 131–3, 143, 148). On sources from German lands, see Hansgerd Göckenjan, 'Die Landnahme der Ungarn aus der Sicht der zeitgenössischen ostfränkisch-deutschen Quellen', in *Ungarn, Türken und Mongolen. Kleine Schriften von Hansgerd Göckenjan*, ed. Michael Knüppel and Eberhard Winkler (Wiesbaden, 2007), 297–314.

[74] Constantine Porphyrogenitus, *De administrando imperio*, chap. 38, pp. 172–3; chap. 40, pp. 174–7.

[75] Bowlus, *Franks, Moravians*, 235–67; Gyula Kristó, ed., *A honfoglalás korának írott forrásai* (Szeged, 1995), a collection of sources in translation with detailed commentary; Fodor, ed., *Ancient Hungarians*, 15–18; Róna-Tas, *Hungarians and Europe*, 332–8; Gyula Kristó, *Levedi törzsszövetségétől Szent István államáig* (Budapest, 1980); István Erdélyi, *A magyar honfoglalás és előzményei* (Budapest, 2002); Bóna, *A magyarok és Európa*, 25–35; Gyula Kristó, 'La conquête hongroise: réalité et tradition', in Csernus and Korompay, eds., *Les Hongrois et l'Europe*, 137–48.

(some scholars believe this was the historical basis of the 'white horse' legend). Then, it is thought at Arnulf's instigation, they raided northern Italy for several years. The Byzantine emperor also sent emissaries to their chiefs at the Lower Danube, to help him against Symeon of Bulgaria (894). Probably in Symeon's employ, while the main army was away, the Pechenegs inflicted a defeat on the remaining Hungarians in their settlement area, and occupied those lands. After Arnulf's death, the Hungarians also raided Bavaria in 900. Although Moravia was disintegrating, the people still mounted a successful defence against the Hungarians in 902. Around the same time, Bavarians invited and assasinated one of the Hungarian military leaders, 'Chussol'. Hungarians then returned briefly to Italy, this time to help Berengar. In 906 they attacked Saxony and the following year defeated the Bavarians, which guaranteed Hungarian domination of these lands up to the Enns.

The reasons for the population movement are based on guesswork rather than hard facts. It is possible that, after the Pechenegs inflicted a defeat on the Hungarians, the latter fled into the lands that became their permanent base. It is also possible that the conquest was much more gradual, and was linked to the complex web of alliances and hostilities in the region, in which the Hungarians were military actors. Thus historians debate whether the conquest was the outcome of military pressure and defeat, or was planned. While traditionally the conquest was tied to 895–6, following the *Annals of Fulda*'s dating of a major defeat inflicted on the Hungarians, historians now tend to see the conquest as taking a longer period, roughly between 892 and 907, although they disagree over the precise dating.

Some historians suggest that the conquest of Transylvania and the plains regions around the River Tisza (the north-eastern Carpathian basin) by the Hungarians occurred prior to and separately from their moving out of Etelköz as a result of the defeat by the Pechenegs, by 892. Cemeteries in the territory of what are today Poland and Ukraine (e.g. Przemyśl, Sudova Vyshnya, Krilos) have been interpreted as those of Hungarian military outposts, guarding the newly conquered areas.[76] Different views exist about the direction of the conquest. Some suggest that Transylvania and the Hungarian plain were conquered first. Others suggest that the Hungarians entered from the north-east, took only the Upper Tisza region at first, and then

[76] Fodor, ed., *Ancient Hungarians*, 16, 437–48.

extended their rule to other parts of the Carpathian basin, including Transylvania. The conquest was extended through war to the trans-Danubian (western) areas (Pannonia) – previously under Eastern Frankish control – from about 900, definitely secured by 907.

The 'Hungarians' who arrived in the Carpathian basin at the end of the ninth century were themselves not homogeneous: a Hungarian-speaking population moved in probably together with Turkic-speakers.[77] The population of the newly conquered lands also consisted of many different groups. A heterogeneous mixture of peoples then merged and became 'Hungarians'. The make-up and fate of the local population have been debated, notably the question of continuity between pre- and post-conquest populations. Scholars have disagreed over the size of the local population of Slavs, their exact areas of settlement and whether this local population included Avars and Bulgars. It is also an open question whether people descended from the Avars had by then been assimilated to the Slavs, and if so to what degree. Local inhabitants of the conquered lands, people who descended from the population of the Avar Empire (it is not known what they were called) and Slavs (probably different Slavic groups, but not corresponding to more modern Slav peoples, since that differentiation had not developed yet), eventually merged with the Hungarian population, adopting the language of the conquerors. Perhaps a similar process incorporated the Bulgars in the south-eastern part of the Carpathian basin. Debates over the relative size of local populations, particularly the Slavs found in the Carpathian basin and the Hungarians, had political overtones. Older historiography used the argument that, because the Slavs assimilated linguistically, their population must have been significantly smaller than the conquering Hungarians. Others argue that assimilation was in the direction of the group exercizing political power, and suggest the Slavic population was originally much larger.[78]

[77] Lóránd Benkő, 'La situation linguistique des Hongrois de la conquête et ce qui en résulte,' in Csernus and Korompay, eds., *Les Hongrois et l'Europe*, 121–36.

[78] István Kniezsa, 'Magyarország népei a XI-ik században', in Jusztinián Serédi, ed., *Emlékkönyv Szent István király halálának kilencszázadik évfordulóján,* 3 vols. (Budapest, 1938), vol. II, 365–472, esp. 454–5; György Györffy, 'Magyarország népessége a honfoglalástól a XIV. század közepéig', in József Kovacsics, ed., *Magyarország történeti demográfiája* (Budapest, 1963), 45–62; Gyula Kristó, 'Die Bevölkerungszahl Ungarns in der Arpadenzeit', in *Historische Demographie Ungarns (896–1996)*, ed.

Historians have expressed different opinions on whether the Hungarians were nomads or semi-nomads prior to and at the time of their settlement in the Carpathian basin. Based on descriptions of their raiding, as well as the textual tradition of Ǧayhānī which describes the Hungarians moving with their tents according to the changing seasons, many scholars supposed a nomadism that would exclude any agricultural activity. Against this view, linguistic arguments were used to suggest the knowledge of certain types of agricultural activities, objects and animals. Opinions are still divided on whether the Hungarians were settled agriculturalists who also raised animals; nomads who knew some elements of agricultural cultivation; or had Slavs under their rule who were agriculturalists and paid tribute. The debate is partially over definitions of 'semi-nomad', as some scholars claim that the practice of agriculture is incompatible with nomadism, while others express the opposite opinion.

Currently, scholarly views tend towards the idea that in the pre-conquest period Hungarians mixed nomadism and agriculture, whether this is characterized as nomadic or semi-nomadic. Settlement in the Carpathian basin was fast: archaeologists have uncovered a settlement pattern that was dense already in the tenth century. Although the Hungarian plain area of over 100,000 km$^2$ is often mentioned as an ideal place for the continuation of steppe nomadism, before the nineteenth-century regulation of the rivers, much of this area was a swamp or was flooded for at least parts of each year. Animal-raising could not be based on long-distance migrations, but the area was suitable for raising animals in a more sedentary way, moving the animals away from and back to the river: over the summer, floodplains dried out, providing pasture.[79]

Gyula Kristó, Pál Engel and András Kubinyi (Herne, 2007), 9–56; Kinga Éry, 'A Kárpát-medence embertani képe a honfoglalás korában', in Kovács, ed., *Honfoglalás és régészet*, 217–25 (see 225); Katalin Fehértói, 'Árpád-kori személyneveink összetétele', www.nytud.hu/NMNyK/eloadas/fehertoi.rtf (accessed 7 May 2009); Márta Font, 'Hongrois et Slaves à l'époque Arpadienne', in Csernus and Korompay, eds., *Les Hongrois et l'Europe*, 171–99; Béla Miklós Szőke, 'Political, cultural and ethnic conditions in the Carpathian basin at the time of the Magyar conquest', in Wieczorek and Hinz, eds., *Europe's Centre: Handbook*, 137–9; Erwin Gáll, 'Burial customs and the question of tenth-century populations in the Transylvanian basin', *Acta Archaeologica Carpathica* 14 (2010), 271–314. On the continuity of local populations and later immigration, see Chapter 5.

79 Fodor, ed., *Ancient Hungarians*, 27–30; György Györffy, 'Waren die landnehmenden Ungarn Nomaden oder Halbnomaden?', in *Die Nomaden in Geschichte und*

Hungarian political organization, if Constantine Porphyrogenitus is to be believed, initially consisted of a number of voivodes, headed by a 'first voivode'. At the instigation of the Khazar khagan, as a means of organizing this subordinated loose confederation, a ruler was elected.[80] Arab and Persian sources describing the Hungarians of the late ninth century mention a k.nd.h (kende or kündü) and a ğ.l.h. (gyula), the first either as king or nominal ruler, the second as military leader. The terminology together with the story of the killing of Álmos just before the Hungarians' entry into Pannonia, found in the Hungarian chronicle tradition, has been used to argue that the Hungarians adopted a Khazar-style dual kingship of a sacral and a military leader. Defeat or old age, signs of the weakening of his supernatural abilities, led to the ritual sacrifice of the sacral king. Whether sacral kingship or, as the alternative interpretation suggests, a political organization where power was shared between a (non-sacral) ruler and a military commander, it seems this political structure was changing. Western sources of the end of the ninth and beginning of the tenth centuries mention one leader (designating him as *rex* or *dux*), as did the Byzantine emperor Leo VI at the end of the ninth century (although he copied much of the information provided by Emperor Maurikios in his *Strategikon* of *c.* 600). Constantine Porphyrogenitus by the middle of the tenth century described a different organization again, under many leaders (see next chapter). To what extent the divergent descriptions reflect divergent, changing realities, or the viewpoints and perhaps misunderstandings of the authors, is impossible to determine.[81]

Written sources refer to the cruelty and bestiality of the Hungarians. Such descriptions (the Hungarians eating raw meat and drinking blood, tearing out the heart of their victims and eating it) are part of set *topoi*. However, some of the sources also give an account of Hungarian military equipment and tactics. Overall, ninth-century

*Gegenwart. Beiträge zu einem internationalen Nomadismus-Symposium am 11. und 12. Dezember 1975 im Museum für Völkerkunde*, ed. Rolf Krusche (Leipzig, 1981), 223–5; Gyula Kristó, 'A honfoglaló magyarok életmódjáról', *Századok* 129, 1 (1995), 3–62; Visy, ed., *Hungarian Archaeology*, 326–8; several articles in Kovács and Paládi-Kovács, eds., *Honfoglalás és néprajz*. On the meaning of nomadism, see A. M. Khazanov, *Nomads and the Outside World* (Cambridge, 1983).

80 Constantine Porphyrogenitus, *De administrando imperio*, chap. 38, pp. 170–3.

81 György Györffy, 'Dual kingship and the seven chieftains of the Hungarians in the era of the conquest and the raids', *Acta Orientalia Academiae Scientiarum Hungaricae* 47 (1994), 87–104; Róna-Tas, *Hungarians and Europe*, 341–54; Kristó, *Hungarian History in the Ninth Century*, 159–73; Golden, 'Irano-Turkica'.

Hungarian military activity is the best-known and least controversial aspect of Hungarian history of that period: they conducted raids for booty, and were available for hire, fighting in several wars in the employ of regional powers. For example, in the second half of the ninth century, they attacked the Eastern Franks several times, as well as Slav neighbours. According to Muslim authors, they sold Slav captives as slaves. As described above, Hungarians made an alliance with Arnulf of Carinthia. They also had a role in Byzantine strategy. Emperor Leo VI's *Tactica* implies that the Tourkoi (Hungarians) are the only possible useful ally against Bulgarians. The emperor composed the work from the mid 890s, drawing on Emperor Maurikios's *Strategikon* of *c.* 600, but through a process of selection and rewriting. Alone, the work cannot be a reliable basis of information, but in this case there is much supplementary information that shows Byzantine employment of Hungarian warriors. Hungarians helped defeat the Bulgarians in 895, and it is even possible that they were bodyguards at Constantinople at the end of the ninth century. The Hungarians also had an important place in Byzantine attempts to form a coalition against Symeon of Bulgaria in the early tenth century. The tenth-century raids (after their settlement in the Carpathian basin) were simply a continuation of ninth-century patterns.[82]

It is certain that the old historiographic construct, the Hungarian people that emerged several thousand years ago and migrated to settle finally in the Carpathian basin, is untenable. We should conceptualize ethnogenesis not as the migration of the Hungarians, but rather as a series of contacts and amalgamations between different loosely defined groups, as a result of which a people emerged. We have solid evidence about the Hungarians only in much closer proximity to their final settlement area than the supposed Uralic homeland, and from the ninth century on. A new military and political formation was created at least partly through

[82] Hansgerd Göckenjan, 'A német évkönyvek híradásai a magyar honfoglalásról', Kornél Szovák, 'Az itáliai kútfők' and István Elter, 'A magyar kalandozáskor arab forrásai', all in Kovács and Veszprémy, eds., *A honfoglaláskor írott forrásai*, 131–41, 163–72, 173–80, respectively; Sándor László Tóth, 'Les incursions des Magyars en Europe', in Csernus and Korompay, eds., *Les Hongrois et l'Europe*, 201–22, with an extensive bibliography; Zimonyi, *Muszlim források*, 34–5, 38–49; Jonathan Shepard, 'Byzantine writers on the Hungarians in the ninth and tenth centuries', *Annual of Medieval Studies at CEU* 10 (2004), 97–123; Ferenc Makk, 'Kalandozások', in *KMTL*.

Khazar influence. The Hungarians as a people (whatever the history of the language itself) emerged, as far as it is possible to ascertain, in the early ninth century. As in other steppe warrior societies (which are better documented from later periods), the organizational principle was more likely military than ethnic. The 'Hungarians' thus incorporated a diverse mixture of what we would call 'ethnic groups'. They inhabited the Black Sea steppes in the ninth century, and were involved in military activities around the Lower Danube and eventually in the Carpathian basin. As so many other confederations, they too were displaced from these areas, and conquered the central Danubian basin. After their settlement, in the tenth century, social and political changes started to transform the conquerors.

## THE BEGINNINGS OF BOHEMIA

With the fall of Great Moravia, the first Slavic political and ecclesiastical experiment came to an end. There are no surviving written sources for the period that immediately followed. Archaeological finds suggest the collapse of political administration and ecclesiastical infrastructure. A return to the 'old beliefs' is implied by the sacrificial site that was located on the ruins of a church in Pohansko.[83] Yet some historians suggest that local centres were sustained by the Moravian aristocracy.[84]

After 906, the lands of modern Slovakia, Moravia and Bohemia came completely under the influence of western/Latin civilization and of the Roman Church, even if some traditions of the Slavonic liturgy survived in isolated enclaves. But some elements of the Great Moravian legacy may be traced in the subsequent history of the region, such as the tradition of building round churches. The most prominent examples among numerous constructions are the royal foundations of St Vitus's rotunda at the Prague Castle and the rotunda of St Gereon on the Royal Castle of Wawel Hill, Cracow. The Bohemians also 'inherited' the Slavic name for a church (*kostel*) and, most likely, the Slavonic script that had been invented by St Constantine-Cyril.

The concentration of political power in the Bohemian basin was slower and achieved through a different process than it had been in Great Moravia. The region, surrounded by mountain belts, encompasses the whole of the Vltava and the uppermost Elbe water

[83] Sommer *et al.*, 'Bohemia and Moravia', 216.

[84] Idzi Panic, *Ostatnie lata Wielkich Moraw* (Katowice, 2003), 195–6.

systems. Fertile soils and a mild climate offer favourable conditions for agriculture. The symbolic centre of the area is marked by the sacred mountain, Řip.[85] From the sixth and seventh centuries, this land was inhabited by Slavs who were identified in the Frankish sources as *Boemani/Beehaimi*.[86] The discussion on their original 'tribal' subdivision and on the pre-state history of these peoples has a very weak source base. However, according to Bohemian historiography, the main tribe were Čechs, who lived in the centre of the region and later gained the upper hand over their neighbours.

Apart from Čechs, at least two other tribal organizations played a significant role in the early medieval political history of the Czech Valley. One of them was a political body created, according to some historians, on the territory of Czech Croats, in northern parts of the valley, with their main stronghold in Stará Kouřim and fortress in Libice. A second organization is believed to have existed along the middle course of the River Ohřa, the so-called Lučané (the name of the alleged tribe) duchy with its central stronghold Rubín near Podbořan. Elites of these organizations were able to compete with the Přemyslids during the first half of the tenth century, striving to dominate the whole Czech Valley. In the end, the latter won. Přemyslids at first bound to themselves only the most influential members of elites of competing polities. But finally they conquered their territories and attached them to the Czech–Přemyslid realm (*c.* 935–50). After 950 the only territory that was quasi-independent from Přemyslid rulers was the duchy of the magnate called Slavnik, with its central stronghold Libice. If it survived it was because of the protection of Frankish kings Henry I (919–36) and Otto I (936–73). Nevertheless, although Slavnik could accentuate Croatian traditions as a foundation of his duchy, he had to accept the suzerainty of the Prague ruler, Boleslav I the Cruel (Ukrutný, 935–67/72).[87]

85 D. Třeštík, *Mýty kmene Čechů: tři studie ke 'starým pověstem českým'* (Prague, 2003), 76.

86 As noted above, their name came from the Celtic *Boii*, who settled in the area of later Bohemia *c.* fourth century BC.

87 Marzena Matla, *Pierwsi Przemyślidzi i ich państwo (od X do połowy XI wieku): ekspansja terytorialna i jej polityczne uwarunkowania* (Poznań, 2008); Jan Mařík, 'The Slavniks and Saxony', in *Der Wandel um 1000. Beiträge der Sektion zur Slavischen Frühgeschichte der 18. Jahrestagung des Mittel- und Ostdeutschen Verbandes für Altertumsforschung in Greifswald, 23. bis 27. März 2009*, ed. Felix Biermann, Thomas Kersting and Anne Klammt (Greifswald, 2011), 191–7; Jiří Sláma, 'Přemyslids and Slavnikids', in Wieczorek and Hinz, eds., *Europe's Centre: Handbook*, 282–3.

We know very little concerning the socio-political development of Bohemia because the handful of external sources that survive record only events connected to the activities of elites. They refer generally to 'the Bohemians', led by *duces*; we do not learn about this group's economic base or political legitimacy or whom they represented. The *Annales Fuldenses* records fourteen such dukes in 845, but provides no information on their names or origins. Writing several years later, the so-called Bavarian Geographer mentioned *Fraganeo*.[88] These 'people of Prague' boasted 'forty *civitates*', but no subdivisions are mentioned and the meaning of this name has been endlessly debated.[89]

Frankish rulers readily intervened in Bohemia. Multiple accounts in Frankish sources (for 791, 805, 817 and 822) indicate a loose subordination of the region, sustained by casual military action. In 805, Charlemagne himself invaded Bohemia and killed 'ducem eorum nomine Lechonem',[90] who was most likely a politically ambitious leader of the local Avaro-Slavic elite. Such small-scale interventions did not halt the hierarchization, centralization and militarization of power relations in Bohemia, which was stimulated by the example of more organized neighbours to both the west and the east. Frankish sources offer a reasonable, if very fragmented, insight into the gradual centralization of political power that must have resulted from the vigorous competition between leading families.

Thus, in 845, we learn of fourteen Bohemian *duces* who arrived at Louis the German's court in Regensburg/Ratisbon and asked to be baptized.[91] Despite this attempt to ease relations with the powerful Eastern Franks, the king launched a series of attacks against his eastern neighbors,[92] resulting in an enforced tribute from the Bohemians. In 869, the Bohemians supported an East Frankish expedition which overturned Rostislav's reign in Great Moravia. His successor Svatopluk initiated a more aggressive strategy towards his western neighbours, who were soon subordinated. In 872, five or six 'dukes' tried to impede Karloman's military expedition.[93] One of them was Gorivei/Bořivoj (852/5–888/9), the historic founder of the Přemyslid

[88] *Descriptio civitatum et regionum ad septentrionalem plagam Danubii*, ed. Fritz Losek, MGH Studien und Texte, 15 (Hanover, 1997).

[89] Jerzy Nalepa and J. Fraganeo, *Słownik starozytności słowianskich*, vol. II (Wrocław, 1964), 66.

[90] *Annales regni Francorum* a. 805.

[91] *Annales Fuldenses* a. 845.

[92] *Annales Fuldenses* a. 846, 849, 857.

[93] *Annales Fuldenses* a. 845.

dynasty.[94] The history of his family is recorded in numerous legends of St Václav, and in the *Chronicle of the Bohemians* written during the early twelfth century by Cosmas of Prague. We learn that, in 874 or 884, Bořivoj was allegedly baptized together with his wife and his retinue by the Moravian archbishop Methodius.[95] It is possible that he might also have built the first Bohemian church of St Clement in his fort of Levý Hradec.[96] It was believed that he built another church in Prague on the site of a former pagan temple, which he dedicated to the Virgin Mary.

In 895, the Frankish sources recorded two Bohemian *primores* – Vitislav along with Bořivoj's oldest son Spytihněv (?–*c.* 905/915) – paying homage to King Arnulf in Regensburg as representatives of all Bohemian dukes.[97] This could have been an attempt to capitalize on the weakening of Great Moravia after Svatopluk's death one year earlier and the ensuing succession crisis, both of which served to undermine a power that might otherwise have counterbalanced the political strength of the East Franks. In that same year, Bohemia was subordinated to the Regensburg archdiocese. In 897, the dukes again went to the king seeking protection against the aggressive policy of Svatopluk's sons as they tried to regain control over Bohemia. The subsequent collapse of Great Moravia left a geo-political vacuum in the region that was effectively filled by the ambitious Bohemian rulers. The regional centre of political power moved from Mikulčice to Prague, which was more or less controlled by its mighty East Frankish neighbour. Thus, the price for Bohemia's increasing independence from their eastern neighbours was a growing dependence on their western neighbours. This was clearly demonstrated when the Bavarian margrave Liutpold used the title 'duke of Bohemians'.

Some sources name Spytihněv as the first Christian ruler of Bohemia; he was praised for abandoning idolatry and for baptizing all his people.[98] Conversion was strongly promoted by his mother, Duchess Ludmila, who sent invitations to Bavarian priests delegated by the bishop of Regensburg.

94 This identification of the original Bohemian dynasty is a product of the historiography of the nineteenth century.

95 Cosmas I.14. The work is available in an English translation: Cosmas of Prague, *The Chronicle of the Czechs*, tr. and ed. Wolverton.

96 E.g. Ivan Borkovský and Levý Hradec, *Nejstarší sídlo Přemyslovců* (Prague, 1965), 50.

97 *Annales Fuldenses* a. 895.

98 *Passio s. Vencezlai incipiens verbis Crescente fide christiana. Recensio bavarica*, ed. J. Emmler, Fontes Rerum Bohemicarum (henceforth FRB) I (Prague, 1878), 183–91 (here ch. 1).

This series of accounts offers an insight into the slow consolidation of power, as well as the elimination of political competition, which took place over approximately seventy years and which found expression in the steadily diminishing number of leaders who represented Bohemians at foreign courts. The challenge for overall domination ended in 921 when Wenceslas/Václav (921–35) – later canonized – Bořivoj's grandson, effectively monopolized political power in the centre of the Bohemian basin and adopted the position of sole ruler.

## BEFORE POLAND

We know even less about political developments in the lands north of the Carpathian and Sudeten Mountains. These areas were so distant that they attracted hardly any attention from the Frankish chroniclers. Einhard's remark that Charlemagne subordinated 'omnes barbaras ac feras nationes, quae inter Rhenum ac Visulam [Vistula] fluvios oceanumque ac Danubium positae' is not very informative.[99]

From the early ninth century, a process of concentrating local power may be inferred from the raising of monumental mounds in south-eastern parts of today's Poland.[100] Investment in visibly impressive topographic features may indicate the emergence of political elites who symbolically demonstrated their status and mobilized followers to collective action.[101] In this way, the tensions that arose from the growing discrepancy between an egalitarian ideology and the stratification of society could have been eased by reference to the traditional, albeit magnified, cultural symbol of the grave-mound.[102] It seems that Jan Długosz, a fifteenth-century Polish historian, correctly stressed the importance of this material symbol, which attracted the eyes of even the distant onlooker: 'the barrow . . . [that the] sons of Krakus . . . raised to such a height . . . [that it would] dominate all the hills around'.[103]

99 *Einhard: The Life of Charlemagne,* tr. Samuel Epes Turner (New York, 1880), I.16.

100 Recently Kazimierz Radwański ('Wielkie kopce krakowskie i próba uściślenia ich chronologii', *Rocznik Krakowski* 69 (2003), 5–23; here 22) dated them to the middle of the ninth to the early tenth century.

101 E.g. Lotte Hedeager, *Iron Age Societies: From Tribe to State in Northern Europe, 500 BC to AD 700* (Oxford, 1992), 291.

102 Leszek Słupecki ('Monumentalne kopce Krakusa i Wandy pod Krakowem', in *Studia zdziejów cywilizacji* (Warsaw, 1998), 62–5) prefers to view them in the context of a pagan reaction against an expanding Christianity.

103 Jan Długosz, *Roczniki czyli kroniki sławego Królestwa Polskiego* (Warsaw, 1961), 189–90.

The phenomenon of raising monumental mounds to signal the dominant position of elites was transient and strictly regional; it would give way in the middle of the ninth century to a new form of material expression: the building of impressive earth-and-wood strongholds across the vast lands between the Baltic and the mountainous belt. The strongholds are clear markers for the centres of local communities, whose leaders were ready to invest in building fortified centres in order to manifest their political ambitions.

The only source which may be used to study the early political development of the 'Polish' lands is a two-page report written shortly before 850 for Louis the German.[104] This mysterious document lists a series of supposed West Slavic tribes and estimates their military power:[105]

> Prissani, ciuitates LXX. Velunzani, ciuitates LXX. [ . . . ] Vuislane. Sleenzane, ciuitates XV. Lunsici ciuitates XXX. Dadosesani ciuitates XX, Milzane, ciuitates XXX. Besunzane, ciuitates II. Verizane, ciuitates X. Fraganeo, ciuitates XL. Lupiglaa, ciuitates XXX. Opolini, ciuitates XX. Golensizi, ciuitates V.

Some of these 'ethnonyms' are confirmed by much later sources, such as the *Sleenzane*[106] and the *Dadosesani*;[107] others are identified through lexical similarities with various geographical names; a few remain cryptic (for example, *Lupiglaa*).[108]

To these problems we may add the chaotic sense of geography and the completely unreliable figures for the *civitates*,[109] which are thought to have functioned as secondary centres. This document demonstrates the ignorance of the East Frankish court concerning political circumstances

[104] W. H. Fritze 'Geographus Bavarus', *Lexikon des Mittelalters* (Munich), vol. IV (1999), 1269–70 (here 1270).

[105] *Descriptio civitatum*, traditionally refered to as the 'Bavarian Geographer'. A less ethnically charged name was suggested: 'Ostfrankische Völkertafel' (Fritze, 'Geographus', 1270).

[106] *Silenzi* by Thietmar of Merseburg (VI. 57) and *Zlasane* in the 'Document of Prague' of 1083: *Die Urkunden Heinrichs IV*, part 2, ed. Dietrich von Gladiss, Monumenta Germanie Historica, Diplomata 4, Die Urkunden der deutsche Könige und Kaiser, 6 (Hanover, 1959), no. 390, p. 517.

[107] *Diedesizi/Diedesi* by Thietmar (IV.45; VI.57; VII.20) and *Dedosize* in the 'Document of Prague'.

[108] P. Urbanczyk, 'Slavic and Christian identities during the transition to the Polish statehood', in Garipzanov *et al.*, eds., '*Franks, Northmen and Slavs*, 205–22.

[109] E.g. *civitates CCCC aut eo amplius* of the *Glopeani* mentioned in the second part of the 'Bavarian Geographer'.

east of the Oder River. External observers at the time were aware that, in the middle of the ninth century, west of the Oder and north of the Sudeten Mountains, there had emerged certain ethno-political units, but their character, territorial extent and organizational stability remain unknown.

The concept of 'tribe', commonly applied in Polish historiography, is unhelpful in exploring the ethnopolitical division of the area. Before the emergence of the Piast realm, we are left with inferences from anthropological principles, supported by archaeological data. Archaeological evidence points to the growth of human organizational potential from the middle of the ninth century onwards, as indicated by the trend in building fortified centres. The oldest Slavic strongholds, apart from having a military and/or settlement function, would hold symbolic meaning for local societies as centres of power, reinforced by religious rituals.[110] However, they are also indicators that local societies or their elites were able to mobilize their members or followers for common goals. Thus strongholds functioned as the symbolic nodes of social geography. They indicated the division of a network of agricultural settlements into separate units concentrated around fortified sites of power.[111]

A short statement, included in the hagiography of St Methodius, remains the only written record for political developments north of the Carpathians in the second half of the ninth century. According to its author, a 'mighty duke in *Vislech*' harassed the Christians (the Moravians), but was finally captured and forcibly baptized between 874 and 880.[112] This solitary sentence captured the imagination of Polish historians to such a degree that they eventually conceived of a

110 For further discussion, see Przemysław Urbańczyk, 'Wczesna urbanizacja ziem polskich', in *Civitas et villa: miasto i wieś w średniowiecznej Europie środkowej*, ed. Cezary Buśko *et al.* (Wrocław and Prague, 2002), 37–47; Z. Kobyliński, 'Early medieval hillforts in Polish lands in the sixth to the eighth centuries: problems of origins, function, and spatial organization', in *From the Baltic to the Black Sea*, ed. D. Austin and L. Alcock (Boston, 1990), 147–56; M. Dulinicz, 'Miejsca, które rodzą władzę (najstarsze grody słowiańskie na wschód od Wisły)', in *Człowiek, sacrum, środowisko: miejsca kultu we wczesnym średniowieczu*, ed. S. Moździoch (Wrocław, 2000), 85–98.

111 Martin O. H. Carver, 'Town and anti-town in the first millennium Europe', in *Archeologia w teorii i w praktyce*, ed. A. Buko and P. Urbańczyk (Warsaw, 2000), 373–96.

112 Spisy dawne skarbca i biblioteki kapitulnej krakowskiej, ed. August Bielowski, Monumenta Poloniae Historica, vol. 1 (Lwów, 1864) (henceforth MPH I), 107.

'state of Vislane', whose ruler supposedly competed with Svatopluk's Great Moravia and initiated a process of state-formation in the southern part of what today is Poland. Archaeologists tried to support this idea, searching for the Vislane tribe's 'capital' in the village of Wiślica, where a small church and presumed baptismal font were eagerly dated to the early tenth century.[113] These interpretations were later proved wrong when detailed analyses showed that the 'baptismal font' was a natural feature; that the church was built in the eleventh century; and that a political centre in Wiślica developed only during the eleventh and twelfth centuries.

This does not mean that Great Moravia held no influence over areas of southern Poland. The proximity of this Slavic, Christian power could have resulted in the earlier appearance of strongholds in Lesser Poland (Małopolska),[114] while the large deposit of axe-like iron ingots excavated from the centre of Cracow suggests a shared cultural zone. In Silesia, the stone facades of some strongholds and the spread of imports from the south allow us to demonstrate the close contacts between the two regions. This, however, cannot justify drawing the northern frontier of Great Moravia across Lesser Poland and Silesia (Śląsk), which has been attempted by some historians[115] and archaeologists.[116]

[113] Włodzimierz Antoniewicz, 'Znaczenie odkryć w Wiślicy', *Silesia Antiqua* 10 (1968), 105–15 (here 106 and 114).

[114] E.g. Jan Gancarski, 'The early medieval stronghold at Trzcinica in the district of Jasło: preliminary research results', in Z. Woźniak and J. Gancarski, eds. *Polonia Minor medii aevi: studia ofiarowane Panu Profesorowi Andrzejowi Żakiemu w osiemdziesiątą rocznicę urodzin* (Cracow and Krosno, 2003), 165–80 (here 174).

[115] E.g. Henryk Łowmiański, *Początki Polski*, vol. IV (Warsaw, 1970), 356f.; Lech Tyszkiewicz, 'Die slawische Burgenorganisation und ihre Umgestaltung in das mittelalterliche Kastellaneisystem Oberschlesiens', in T. Wünsch, ed., *Stadtgeschichte Oberschlesiens. Studien zur städtischen Entwicklung und Kultur einer ostmitteleuropäischen Region vom Mittelalter bis zum Vorabend der Industrialisierung* (Berlin, 1995), 9–24 (here 15); and Tyszkiewicz, 'Warunki polityczne włączenia Śląska do państwa Piastów', in *Śląsk około roku 1000*, ed. M. Młynarska-Kaletynowa and E. Małachowicz (Wrocław, 2000), 73–88 (here 75).

[116] E.g. Krzysztof Wachowski, 'Śląsk a Wielkie Morawy i Czechy: aktualne dylematy historyka i archeologa', in *Viae historicae: Księga jubileuszowa dedykowana profesorowi Lechowi Tyszkiewiczowi w siedemdziesiątą rocznicę urodzin*, ed. M. Goliński and S. Rosik (Wrocław, 2001), 167–77 (here 172), and 'Śląsk około roku 1000', in *Polska na przełomie I i II tysiąclecia*, ed. S. Skibiński (Poznań, 2001), 325–34 (here 325); Kazimierz Jaworski, 'Wczesnośredniowieczne grodziska plemienne w Sudetach' *Archeologia Żywa* 2 (36) (2006), 56–64 (here 64).

Indeed, a map of the early strongholds does not reveal any particular concentration of fortified centres in this region. It shows instead a division of the Polish lands into a poorly organized eastern territory, where strongholds were scarce, and a western territory, including Silesia, Greater Poland (Wielkopolska, Polonia Maior) and Pomerania (Pomorze), which was filled with numerous fortified sites.[117] It is interesting to note in this earlier period that Greater Poland, where the first territorial polity had emerged by the middle of the ninth century, had not earlier boasted a high density of settlements, a high number of strongholds or an extraordinary richness of burials. Nor did it attract an inflow of Arabic silver, which in the ninth century clearly concentrated around the strategic estuaries of the Oder and Vistula.[118]

Thus while in the centre of the Bohemian basin the newly Christianized *duces Bohemorum* gained overall political control, north of the mountainous belt the situation remained fluid. Neither historians nor archaeologists have identified any leader with aspirations to build a stable territorial organization.

## PEOPLE AND DYNASTIES

In all three polities, the beginnings of dynastic power are shrouded in medieval myths and chroniclers' elaborations. Ethnonyms and dynastic geneologies are products of medieval efforts to grapple with the problem of origins.

### *Bohemians*

The chronology and origin of the choronym and ethnonym applied to the Czechs (*Čech*) is problematic. In Bohemian historiography, a nationalist vision has tended to dominate the debate: 'it was Czechs who laid the foundations for early statehood and not their rulers, the Přemyslids'. Consequently Czechia is considered 'one of the few early

[117] Map 169 in Zofia Kurnatowska, 'Fortifications and the rise of tribal aristocracy among the Slavs in the period before the foundation of the Polish state', in Wieczorek and Hinz, ed., Europe's Centre: Handbook, 169–71.

[118] Map 2 in Sebastian Brather, 'Frühmittelalterliche Dirham-Schatzfunde in Europa. Probleme ihrer wirtschafts-geschichtlichen Interpretation aus archäologische Perspektive', *Zeitschrift für Archäologie des Mittelalters* 23/4 (1996), 73–153.

medieval states that developed from one *gens*'.[119] Although sources written in the ninth and tenth centuries clearly show the political differentiation of the Bohemian basin with several political units ruled by their own 'dukes', historians have argued about the exact character of these polities. Some medievalists believed that they were a result of evolution among different Slavic tribes living in the basin. For these researchers, the Czech tribe was one among many, and it came to dominate the others only gradually, mostly through military expansion and close co-operation with the East Frankish realm.[120]

Others suggested that there was only one *gens* in the Bohemian basin. According to them, the different names in the sources simply described local political organisations of the same tribe, as for example 'groups of strongholds'. The same tribe was able to group and regroup according to political circumstances, but their existence did not rely on ethnic difference from the 'Czech' tribe. Finally Dušan Třeštík argued that tribes in the plural did not exist in the Bohemian basin in the ninth century, and that the polities mentioned in the sources were simply different Bohemian duchies. He argued that dukes known from the sources who ruled different areas were a testimony of the presence of a multilateral political structure in the Bohemian basin. Nevertheless, these 'duchies' were all descendants of the bigger and older community, the Czech tribe. Therefore they shared one language, a social structure and customs, which made the Přemyslids' conquest and unification easier.[121] Although at first sight it is tempting to classify these theories as anachronistic and/or nationalistic, no other, more plausible theory exists nowadays. The only hope is that archaeological excavations and their fast publications and analysis allow researchers to verify the alleged homogeneous elements of culture and social structure of the inhabitants of the Bohemian basin before Boleslav I the Cruel's reign. In addition, the application of anthropological approaches might result in a theory more coherent with modern visions of ethnogenesis and the state-formation process.[122]

119 D. Třeštík, *Počátky Přemyslovců: wstup Čechů do dějin (530–935)* (Prague, 1997), 17.

120 Rudolf Turek, *Die frühmittelalterlichen Stämmgebiete in Böhmen* (Prague, 1957).

121 D. Třeštík, 'České kmeny: historie a skutečnost jedné koncepce', *Studia Maedievalia Pragensia* 1 (1988), 129–43.

122 Matla-Kozłowska, *Pierwsi Przemyślidzi i ich państwo*, 16–17.

According to the commonly accepted theory the ethnonym 'Czech' derives from the earliest period of Slavic settlement in the Bohemian basin. It is true that written sources testify to the presence of the term 'Čechs' only in the late tenth-century legend of St Václav.[123] Therefore, it may be suggested that the ethnonym *Čechy*, just like the ethnonym *Poloni* explored below, was a product of the respective ruling houses, which followed in the general trend of applying precise names to early medieval Christian realms and their inhabitants.[124] The problem is that using Latin in communication for official purposes, both external observers and elites of the Přemyslid polity called ducal subjects 'Boemi'. This learned term of antique roots was commonly present in both the oldest hagiographical and historiographical sources and ducal charters. It is no doubt that rulers accepted it as the official name of their people. Theoretically, if they wanted to 'invent a name' for the people and the polity, they did not need to create a new one. It existed before and after the Přemyslids. The dynasty might only popularize a kind of Slavic version of that. But this was not what happened. Both names were used in parallel from the beginning of the state-formation process, 'Bohemi' in Latin, 'Čechs' in the vernacular. This does not necessarily mean that a big tribe of 'Čechs' populated the whole Bohemian basin in the ninth century. It only proves that the term had strong social acceptance, strong enough for ensuring the name's survival despite the pressure of the Latin name. It is possible that the dynasty popularized the Slavic name, which at the beginning was connected with a smaller social group (the direct subjects of Přemyslids?) and only after the dukes' expansion came to describe the society of all inhabitants of the basin. But it looks highly improbable that the dynasty 'invented' the name in terms of an artificial construction. More plausible may be that it was borrowed from the social reality of the ninth century and used by rulers and their entourages to create the fiction of the common origins of Přemyslid subjects, fiction that had its roots in past reality but was retold, rewritten according to the dukes' needs.

As in the Polish context, however, the etymology of the name used by the Přemyslids to identify their subordinates is unclear. At least

123 *Sborník staroslovanských literárních památek o sv. Václavu a sv. Ludmile*, ed. J. Vajs (Prague, 1929), 14 (Vratislav, the father of Václav, lived 'v Čechách') and 36 (Glagolitic version, he lived 'v Česěch').

124 *The Naming of Medieval States*, ed. P. Urbanczyk (in preparation).

sixty possible explanations of its meaning were proposed and no single one prevailed.[125] According to some research, this testifies to the antiquity of the name's origin. The word lost its direct meaning for users, as was the fate of many other names of tribes originating from the times of the common Slavic past, the times before the expansion of the sixth and seventh centuries (for example, Chorvats, Doulebs, Obodrits, Serbs). Later, medieval chroniclers provided their readers with a simple rationalization: the name of 'patria' and the people was derived from the name of the people's father: 'Boemus'[126] or 'Čech'.[127] In this way the name, both in Latin and the vernacular, deprived of its original meaning, was revealed to be quite useful to certify the closeness of the Czech past to wider, biblical and antique patterns.

A Bohemian dynastic genealogy was first recorded in the second half of the tenth century. A monk called Christian, allegedly a member of the Přemyslid dynasty, wrote the life and passion of Sts Ludmila and Václav. In his work he included a short history of the dynasty. Built of many common *topoi*, it is a vivid testimony of the tendency towards unification of local tradition and Christian learned culture. As the founders of the dynasty, he named Přemysl and his wife Libuše. During the time of a deadly plague the tribe, which until this time had no ruler and inhabited no town, called Přemysl as a righteous man to be duke. When he agreed, the plague vanished and history began. Although Přemysl was a pagan, he was also the man chosen by God to be a just ruler, whose rule brought peace and happiness for the people. The anecdote recalled for contemporary readers or listeners a basic truth: the faiths of the Czech people were bound with the history of the dynasty. Christian did not enumerate all the rulers between Přemysl and the period of Christianization, although he mentioned that there were many of them. He focused on the role played by the dynasty and the people in the conversion. Only members of the Přemyslid dynasty, Bořivoj, Vratislav and especially Vacláv, were active propagators of the true faith. Only the foreign, extraneous members – as Drahomira, wife of Vratislav from a pagan, Slavic

125 V. T. Kolomijec, 'Etimologija etnonima "čech"', *Slavia: Časopis pro slovanskou filologii*, 52 (1983), 290–5.

126 Cosmas I.2, p. 7.

127 *Kronika tak řečeného Dalimila*, ed. Marie Bláhová (Prague and Litomysl, 2002), ch. 2, p. 13.

dynasty – dared to oppose Christianity and even started a rebellion against the just, Christian duke Václav. Regardless of who was responsible for the revolt, all fighting against God's will had to be punished. That was the case when the Czech people expelled the Christian duke Bořivoj and made one of the magnates, called Stroimir, its false ruler. Bořivoj with the help of God and the Moravian duke Svatopluk defeated him and took over the throne. Conflicts inside the dynasty had more complicated consequences. Václav's younger brother, Boleslav I the Cruel, at first rebelled with his mother against Václav. Defeated, for many years he co-operated with his brother. Yet at the end, not without being conscious of his guilt, he allowed his servants to kill his brother. Christian stressed the responsibility of Boleslav but also suggested that he played his own role in God's plan. Václav, protector of the poor and the church, duke and friend of King Henry I, had to die as a martyr in order to be the perfect Christian ruler and saint.[128]

Christian did not bother to picture or even suggest the long and great history of the dynasty before Václav. He focused on the implementation of Christian patterns of social roles for rulers and the populace to the history of the Czech people. His work clearly testifies that the Přemyslids were chosen by God to rule Czechs but also Moravians, that their people should obey them not only as just rulers but also – in Václav's case – as dukes of almost royal majesty commonly acknowledged.

A more complicated vision of the beginnings of the Přemyslid dynasty was proposed in the early twelfth century by Cosmas, dean of Prague cathedral. In his 'Chronica Boemorum' he listed a complete chain of pagan rulers' names reigning between Přemysl (Premizl) and Bořivoj, the first Christian duke. After Přemysl they were Nezamysl,

[128] *Legenda Christiani. Vita et passio sancti Venceslai et sancte Ludmile ave eius*, ed. Jaroslav Ludvíkovský (Prague, 1978); František Graus, 'Kirchliche und heidnische (magische) Komponenten der Stellung der Přemysliden. Přemyslidensage und Wenzelsideologie', in *Siedlung und Verfassung Böhmens in der Frühzeit*, ed. František Graus and H. Ludat (Wiesbaden, 1968), 148–65; Jiří Hošna, *Druhý život svateho Václava* (Prague, 1997); Agnieszka Kuźmiuk-Ciekanowska, *Święty i historia. Dynastia Przemyślidów i jej bohaterowie w dziele mnicha Krystiana* (Cracow, 2007), 105–29, 169–207; Jaroslav Ludvíkovský, 'La legende du prince: laboureur Přemysl et sa version primitive chez le moine Christian', in *Charisteria Thaddeo Sinko* (Warsaw, 1951), 151–68; D. Třeštík, 'Deset tezí o Kristiánově legendě', *Folia Historica Bohemica* 10 (1980), 7–38.

Mnata, Voyn, Vnislau, Crezomizl and Gostivit.[129] All were supposedly sole rulers of the *Čechs*. Just as in other Slavic royal genealogies, a figure was appointed from among simple farmers to initiate a family of the highest status, here, Přemysl 'the Ploughman'.[130] The list is commonly considered unreliable but it allows us to look more closely at local Czech traditions – at least some of them – connected with the dynasty. Although *Legenda Christiani* analysed above mentioned Přemysl and his wife Libuše as founders of the dynasty, Cosmas went far beyond the short statements present in Christian's work. He stressed the role of Libuše, daughter of Krok (Crocco). The latter, in hard times of internal conflicts among members of the tribe after the end of the golden era of beginnings, was one of the *potentes* and commonly acknowledged as a just judge and mediator. His authority was accepted gradually by all Czechs, and he was also connected with the supernatural sphere. All of his three daughters had special powers. Kazi and Tethka were active in the sphere of human health and nature; their names well known and venerated by Cosmas' contemporaries. The youngest daughter, Libuše (Lubossa), was a prophetess. After her father's death, the people acknowledged that she would inherit his authority as the wisest among the three sisters. But soon her counsellors and the whole people agreed that they needed a man to rule over them. This man was seen by her in a prophetic vision. Led by clues provided by her, representatives of the Czechs found the future man outside the tribe – the humble ploughman Přemysl (*Premizl*). The story in many aspects was similar to biblical and classical models, although enriched with elements of local beliefs and folklore, which made it easier to accept for readers and listeners the whole concept of genesis of dynastic power. And such a concept had very real consequences. Libuše was not keen to establish a man at her side and warned the people about the consequences of making someone a duke: they would obey him without any objection, he would assign their place in society without consulting them, and above all he would have all of them and all of their things in his power ('vos et omnia vestra erunt eius in potestate').[131] That was the simplest and shortest definition of how the Přemyslids' idea of how ducal power was perceived by the political elites of their realm.[132]

129 Cosmas I.9, p. 21. 130 Cosmas I.4–9. 131 Cosmas I.5, p. 14.

132 Marie Bláhová, 'Stát a vláda státu v pojetí kronikáře Kosmy', in *Średniowiecze polskie i powszechne*, ed. Idzi Panic, vol. II (Katowice, 2002), 115–37.

By placing it at the root of the union between the dynasty and the people, Cosmas stressed that these rights of rulers were not defined simply in a decisive historical moment, the moment of building everlasting matrices of social life. We should add that these matrices were dictated by the founding couple. After their marriage, Libuše and Přemysl created not only a set of laws establishing the social order of Czechs but also the capital of their reign, the city of Prague.[133] The chronicler also focused the readers' attention on the fact that people's obligation towards rulers were not forced by violence used in the name of a ruler, but commonly, freely and consciously accepted by all members of society. Czech elites must be aware that, after the decisive moment of announcing the people's will of choosing a man for Libuše as a duke, they were obliged by forces stronger than their will to serve him and his descendants for ever: 'huius proles postera hac in omni terra in eternum regnabit et ultra'.[134]

The political context of this story, written in times of revolts and civil wars between proponents of candidates to the Prague throne, is clear. It is less clear why Cosmas, unlike Christian, inserted into his chronicle additional details describing the history of the dynasty, which at first sight had no special, additional value for the major narrative meaning. Two main elements may be distinguished: first, the description of local customs, beliefs and traditions; and, second, the list of names of forgotten or fictive rulers between the legendary eponymous Přemysl and the first historical member of the dynasty, the Christian duke Bořivoj (first mentioned in sources in 872, d. 888–91). In the first case Cosmas's work is vivid proof of how deeply in the Czech elite's consciousness the past and present of all Czechs was intertwined with the dynasty's faiths. The second was inevitable in times when the older a dynasty was, the more highly it was evaluated by its subjects and neighbours. Pagan rulers, descendants of Přemysl, were useful in Cosmas's vision of Czech history only as milestones – signs of the long-lasting reign of the dynasty. He added nothing more to the dynastical list than names of succeeding rulers. As he said openly: there is nothing that should be said about them directly, as they were pagans.[135]

133 Cosmas I.9, pp. 18–19. See also Martin Nodl, 'Kosmův mýtus o počátcích práv a zákonů kmene Čechů a jeho pozdější transformace', in *Limity a možnosti historického poznání: sborník z cyklu přednášek*, ed. Martin Elbel (Olomouc, 2008), 125–34.

134 Cosmas I.5, p. 15.

135 Cosmas I.9, p. 21.

It is especially interesting that Cosmas did not use antique or biblical heroes to bind their histories with the dynasty's past. Local traditions of both supernatural and almost 'democratic' and 'constitutional' roots of dynastic power seem completely adequate for establishing the foundations for a joint history of the Czechs and Přemyslids, even if they were radically changed during their retelling by a Christian monk.[136]

## *Poles*

Identifying the Piasts' political background must remain equally speculative. It is commonly accepted in Polish historiography that Mieszko I (before 963–92) ruled the tribe of *Polanie*, who subsequently gave their name to the kingdom of Poland. This simple evolutionary vision is severely undermined by a lack of evidence.[137] Instead, the surviving sources suggest that the earliest names of the realm (*Polonia*) and its inhabitants (*Poloni*) appeared in reliable

[136] Dušan Třeštík, *Kosmova kronika: studie k počátkům českého dějepisectví a politického myšlení* (Prague, 1968), had revolutionary consequences for the interpretation of Cosmas's chronicle by Czech medievalists as a work in its shape, content, structure and meaning conditioned by a chronicler's broadly defined social enviroment. Against a vast comparative background, the meaning of Cosmas's vision of Czech origins was analysed by Jacek Banaszkiewicz (see for example his 'Slavische Sagen de origine gentis (Al-Masudi, Nestor, Kadłubek, Kosmas): dioskurische Matrizen der Überlieferungen', *Maedievalia Historica Bohemica*, 3 (1993), 29–58). The same structural approach to Cosmas's chronicle and its stories of pagan times was applied by Vladimír Korbusický, *Báje, mýty, legendy: najstarší české pověsti v kontextu evropské kultury* (Prague, 1997), although results of his analyses have been strongly criticized by Czech historians.

Antique and biblical *topoi* and themes in Cosmas's work have recently been analysed by Josef Sadílek, *Kosmovy stare pověsti ve světle dobových pramenů (antické a biblické motywy)* (Prague, 1997). Czesław Deptuła was interested in the same elements, but he focused on the vision of the birth of Czech society where Cosmas applied biblical narrative patterns to local traditions: *Galla Anonima mit genezy Polski: studium z historiozofii i hermeneutyki symboli dziejopisarstwa średniowiecznego* (Lublin, 2000, 2nd edn; 1st edn, Lublin, 1990), 171–219. The question of oral tradition used by the chronicler has recently been analysed by Marie Bláhová, 'Verschriftliche Mündlichkeit in der Böhmischen Chronik des Domherrn Cosmas von Prag', in Adamska and Mostert, eds., *The Development of Literate Mentalities*, 323–42.

[137] Przemysław Urbańczyk, 'Who named Poland?', in *Mittelalter – Eines oder viele?*, ed. S. Moździoch, W. Mrozowicz and S. Rosik (Wrocław, 2010), 167–82.

accounts at around the same time, *c.* 1000. It was at this point that the subjects of Mieszko I's son, Bolesław, were called *Palani*,[138] *Poliani*,[139] *Polani*[140] or *Poleni*,[141] while Bolesław himself was known as *PRINCE [P]S POLONIE*, according to coins struck after 1003.[142] The appearance of this vocabulary across a series of sources produced in Italy, Saxony, Hungary and Poland may indicate a spreading knowledge among western elites of the existence of Bolesław I the Brave (992–1025), Emperor Otto III's most important ally on the eastern border of the Empire as well as a promoter of the cult of St Adalbert (Vojtěch, Wojciech) of Prague. Alternatively, it may reveal a decision to choose a suitable name for both the state and its inhabitants, legitimized by royal confirmation in 1025.[143]

Even more problematic was the term *Lechitae*, which were first mentioned by Master Vincent in the early thirteenth century. Apparently, this 'ethnonym' was the product of a tendency to provide etymological explanations. Therefore, we ought to question the long-standing opinion that, 'among the eastern Lechitae, the tribe of Polanie played the leading role and gave the state its name'.[144] We are left with the cryptic accounts offered by Constantine Porphyrogenitus, who mentioned *Ditzike*,[145] and Widukind of Corvey, who wrote *c.* 973 about '*Misacam regem, cuius potestatis erant Sclavi qui dicuntur Licicaviki*.'[146] These might represent the first attempts by external observers to attach a name to the power that had suddenly emerged in the middle of the south Baltic plains. Nevertheless, we do not know if the followers of Mieszko I identified themselves with any

[138] *Sancti Adalberti martyris vita prior,* 25, ed. Georgius H. Pertz, MGH, Scriptores, 4 (Hanover, 1841), 575–95.

[139] *Annales Hildesheimenses*, ed. Georg Waitz (Hanover, 1878) (MGH, Scriptores rerum Germanicarum in usum scholarum, 8) s.a. 1003 25.

[140] *Sancti Adalberti martyris vita altera*, 21, 23, 25 and 30, ed. Georgius H. Pertz, MGH, Scriptores, 4, 595–612.

[141] Thietmar of Merseburg III.55.

[142] Stanisław Suchodolski, *Początki mennictwa w Europie Środkowej, Wschodniej i Północnej* (Wrocław, 1971), 108.

[143] See detailed discussion in P. Urbańczyk, *Trudne początki Polski* (Wrocław, 2008), ch. 12.

[144] Łowmiański, *Początki Polski*, vol. V, 406 and 422.

[145] Constantine Porphyrogenitus, *De administrando imperio*, 33.

[146] *Widukindi monachi Corbeiensis rerum gestarum saxonicarum*, ed. Paul Hirsch, MGH, Scriptores rerum Germanicarum in usum scholarum, 60 (Hanover, 1935), III.66, 141.

specific name. No study has offered a convincing explanation of these two cryptic names, which have no direct parallels at all in historical traditions.

The chronology of building fortified centres between 920/30 and 940/50 proves that the establishment of a stable military and economic infrastructure was initiated by Mieszko's predecessor, most probably his father, traditionally called Semomysl. Mighty earth-and-wood strongholds in Bnin, Giecz, Gniezno, Grzybowo, Ostrów Lednicki, Poznań and Smarzewo – uniformly designed and constructed with the use of characteristic 'hooks' – mark an area of around 5,000 km$^2$, which was used as a springboard for swift expansion. This process was accompanied by the burning of many older strongholds in the second half of the tenth century and their replacement with newer models.

The origin of the Piast dynasty that went on to rule Poland until the late fourteenth century is uncertain. Unlike the Přemyslids, no hagiographical or annalistic sources written in the tenth and eleventh centuries give any information about the family background that reached beyond Mieszko I and his Christian wives. The first wider account comes from the early twelfth-century *Cronicae et gesta ducum sive principum Poloniae*, written by the itinerant monk traditionally recognized as 'Anonymous Gallus'.[147] His story about pre-Christian times consists of three short chapters that briefly list Mieszko's four predecessors (Piast, Siemowit, Lestek and Semomysl) and outline their deeds in very little detail.[148] There has been endless discussion concerning the factual reliability of this list, which cannot be proven without any earlier or contemporary sources mentioning Mieszko's I predecessors.[149] As was the case of the Přemyslid Bořivoj I's predecessors, the whole list may be fictive but that does not exclude the source from a historian's interest. Anonymous's story – just as the works of Christian and Cosmas – lets us delve into local, Polish traditions concerning the beginning of Poles and their polity. In comparison with Cosmas's story, Anonymous's version of the dynasty's political begininngs shows several deep differences. It is

147 The chronicler came from the Italian monastery in Lido according to Tomasz Jasiński, *O pochodzeniu Galla Anonima* (Cracow, 2008), 54.

148 *Galli Anonymi Cronicae et gesta ducum sive principum Poloniae*, ed. K. Maleczyński, MPH, n.s., 2 (Cracow, 1952), I.1–3.

149 Przemysław Wiszewski, 'At the beginnings of the piast dynastic tradition: the ancestors of mieszko in the "Chronicle" of Gallus Anonymus', *Quaestiones Medii Aevi Novae* 9 (2004), 153–82.

striking that, unlike the Czechs, the eponymous founder of the dynasty was not a ruler. Like Přemysl, Piast was a simple farmer, a ploughman of the duke. But unlike the mythical founder of the Czech ruling dynasty, not he but his son, Siemowit, became a duke elected by God and the people. Nevertheless, Piast was affected by supernatural powers, when two anonymous wanderers prophesied his family's social elevation. That glory would be achieved thanks to Piast's virtue of hospitality. According to Anonymous's account, the Piast dynasty was not the first that ruled the Poles. Its members were not responsible for pronouncing laws or creating a capital city. All those elements existed before Siemowit came to power. Anonymous drew quite a vivid picture of Piast's deeds as humble and poor, but of the man as a generous member of society, in contrast to the mighty duke Popiel. But the act of taking power by Siemowit was just mentioned as the result of God's election. Like Cosmas, Anonymous was not willing to delve into the pagan past of the dynasty, but unlike the Czech historiographer he went beyond listing names of three rulers preceding Mieszko I, the first Christian – and historical – Piast ruler.

The scarce information about their deeds together with the story about Piast's honest behaviour inclined historians to point out elements in Anonymous's story which might be recognized as vestiges of a Polish version of a universal Indo-European scheme of *origo gentis*. According to the most elaborate and plausible construction, Piast and his wife played the role of heroes of the third (in G. Dumézil's system) function: providers of food and hospitality, earthly peace and opulence for the community. Their descendants were carriers of (1) the first function: Siemowit as a model organizer and administrator of the state; (2) the second function: Siemowit as brave warrior and Lestek as the warrior and conqueror; (3) the third function: Siemomysł, who especially made the name of the family famous but in a context of courtly fame and earthly splendour.[150] Proponents of such an approach saw in Anonymous's story about the beginning of the dynasty patterns deeply rooted in the past and in a shared Indo-European or at least Slavic culture.

[150] Jacek Banaszkiewicz, *Podanie o Piaście i Popielu: studium porównawcze nad wczesnośredniowiecznymi tradycjami dynastycznymi*, 2nd edn (Warsaw, 2010), 104–42, esp. 121–3.

Other researchers tried to harmonize Anonymous's account with basic structures of medieval Christian culture and vision of beginnings present there. They saw the story as a kind of metaphor preparing readers by the story about the first beginning of the Polish history (the meeting of Piast and the wanderers) for the second, real beginning: the Christianization of Mieszko and his people. The clear division between the pagan and Christian past of the Poles is also clearly visible here, as it was in the history of Jews in the times of the Old and New Testaments. The story of Piast and his pagan descendants was about natural virtues backed up by God's will, the latter decisive for the elevation and happiness of both dynasty and its people. The whole account had nothing in common with real pagan times of the Poles. Rather, it was the story of proving God's goodwill for the dynasty from the beginning of its reign over the Poles.[151] The story about the pre-Christian times of the dynasty in the context of Anonymous's chronicle proved the deep connection of the Piast family with God and the people. Only the unanimous consent of both sides made Siemowit a duke. It also predefined roles played by the rulers in Christian times. Like their predecessors, they had to be the administrators and guardians of the social life of their people, and mighty warriors and conquerors in relations with neighbours. The long and glorious past of the Piast family has its value here, as in Cosmas's chronicle in relation to the Přemyslid past, but even more important was the idea that each ruling member of the dynasty was a virtuous duke caring for his people but also for the family tradition. The pagan history of the Piast dynasty presented by Anonymous also included the faiths of Popiel, the ruler of Gniezno and direct predecessor of Siemowit. His deeds and especially his tragic end were a kind of general warning: rulers who did not obey God's and the people's law and customs must be punished and lose their power. That would happen not via human rebellion but via nature's action towards a sinner. In that also the story of Anonymous differs from Cosmas's version of the beginnings of the Přemyslids. The latter were *ex definitione* just and everlasting rulers. Anonymous suggested that the power is right only when exercised under the laws. The ruler who broke them was a public enemy.[152]

[151] Deptuła, *Galla Anonima mit genezy Polski*.

[152] Przemysław Wiszewski, *Domus Bolezlai: Values and Social Identity in Dynastic Traditions of Medieval Poland (c. 966–1138)* (Leiden and Boston, 2010), 157–77.

In the early thirteenth century, Master Vincent wrote a new version of the 'history of the Poles', in which he introduced numerous biblical and Greco-Romano motifs. He supplemented the list of the Piast dynasty's predecessors with a series of alleged rulers, some even forming new dynasties (as for example the so-called *Grakchides*). These dukes were all connected to Lesser Poland, which at the time of Poland's feudal partition was competing with Greater Poland for supremacy. In this context, the chronicler sought to balance the role of the archdiocesan see Gniezno, seen by Anonymous as the first capital of Poland, by presenting Cracow as an even more ancient political centre. In fact, there is no archaeological evidence of any building activity at the royal Wawel Hill in Cracow before the late tenth century at the earliest.[153] As with Anonymous's list, we also find no confirmation of the names introduced by Master Vincent in the pre-Christian history of Poland. The goal of the chronicler was to make Polish history longer, comparable with the ancient histories of Greeks and Romans, even intertwined with them. He also wrote a proper 'origo gentis Polonorum', which the chronicle of Anonymous lacked, with the duke Grakch/Krak as the founder of the laws and the capital of the country (Cracow). As for the rulers, Vincent stressed even more than Anonymous the role of a Piast duke as a man appointed by God, natural lord (*domini naturales*) of the Poles. Without them at the top of the social order nothing would go well for Poles: they would be robbed by neighbours and their land would be ruined. But at the same time he also stressed that the duke was constantly watched and censored by his *potentes*, members of the elite. For him the Piast dynasty had been chosen to rule the land, but were not the only ones to have a just claim to do so. His detailed picture of its predecessors proved that other families might replace the Piasts. But only when the latter died out completely would their possible heirs be elected by God and acknowledged by the people's elite.[154]

[153] Andrzej Kukliński, 'Spór wokół datowania wczesnośredniowiecznego wału obronnego na Wawelu w Krakowie', in Woźniak and Gancarski, eds., *Polonia Minor medii aevi*, 419–41.

[154] Jacek Banaszkiewicz, *Polskie dzieje bajeczne mistrza Wincentego Kadłubka* (Wrocław, 2002).

## *Magyars*

Medieval authors used a wide variety of names for the Hungarians.[155] Some of these were probably based on self-designation, while others were existing names applied to the Hungarians, either as a learned construction, or due to some perceived similarities between the Hungarians and the original bearers of a given name. Byzantine sources used Tourkoi, Turks, because Hungarian military strategies and forms of life recalled those of Turkic peoples already known to Byzantine authors. This name for Hungarians (and the country name Tourkia) continued in use over centuries. Arabic and Persian sources sometimes use Turk, but most often (al-)m.ǧġ.rīya (interpreted as maǧġarīya) or m.ǧf.rīya, maǰġar or its variations, sometimes bāšgirt and its variations, which may be a confusion between the name of Bashkirs and Magyars, or a name by which another people (according to one view, the Volga Bulgars) designated the Magyars. The (al-)m.ǧġ.rīya form according to some scholars derived from the self-identification 'Magyar'.

Latin sources use ungar(us), hungar(us), sometimes with fanciful etymologies from the word 'hunger' (which was plausible in a German context), although the term ultimately derives from the name 'Onogur'. This was an existing ethnonym ('Ten Arrows') of Turkic nomadic people, who according to some scholars were part of the Bulgar confederation. The name designated populations living around the Danube prior to the Hungarian settlement. Some claimed that 'Onogurs' were in fact Hungarians who had arrived in the Carpathian basin already in the seventh century; but a much more likely explanation is that the existing name was applied probably by Slavs to a new group, the Hungarians, when they appeared in the region. Such a process was a common one, when a newly arrived group received its name from previous inhabitants of a territory, or from a group with similar characteristics. The Latin form of the name was then adopted by many others to designate Hungarians, becoming the basis for modern ethnonyms as well. Occasionally, other designations appear in some sources, including *savartoi asphaloi*, Hun, Scythian and other ancient ethnonyms applied to the Hungarians.

[155] Kovács and Veszprémy, eds., *Honfoglalás és nyelvészet*, with further bibliography; Zimonyi, *Muszlim források*, 50–4; Árpád Berta, 'Die chasarische Benennung der Ungarn', in Christa Fragner and Klaus Schwarz, eds., *Festgabe an Josef Matuz. Osmanistik – Turkologie – Diplomatik* (Berlin, 1992), 7–11.

The self-designation Magyar crops up in the forms *moger*, *mager* from the twelfth century on.

The Hungarians' two different names from distinct roots (Magyar, Hungarus) prompted many linguistic explanations. Already *c.* 1200, the Hungarian Anonymous noted that his people was called 'Moger' after Magog, from whom the Árpád dynasty descended; and after the castle of Hung (Hunguar) where the conquerors first entered and stayed for a while, the warriors came to be known as 'Hunguaros'.[156] Although his etymologies were wrong on both counts, the dual denomination of Magyar and the forms in western languages, such as Hungarian, continued to interest scholars throughout the centuries. Linguistic explanations of the term 'Magyar' vary radically, tied to conceptions of Hungarian 'pre-history'. Traditionally, the ethnonym has been derived from two words: mańća, the self-designation of Hungarian, Mansi (Vogul) and Khanty (Ostyak) people, meaning 'man', and the Finno-Ugric -er, which also meant 'man'. The two were joined when the meaning of the first word was already obscure, or when two population groups merged and created a new ethnonym from their respective names. Other explanations derive -er from a Turkic or Indo-European root. Finally, some argue that Magyar is not a composite word but derives in its entirety from an Indo-European root, 'manu-'; or a Turkic term meaning 'central place', designating the leading Hungarian tribe.[157]

Hungarian scholars traditionally designate the settlers as the Magyar (Hungarian) tribal confederation based on Constantine's evidence and later texts. The name may be misleading in more ways than one. The group clearly contained Turkic-speakers as well as Hungarian-speakers and was not ethnically homogeneous.[158] The concept of tribes has now fallen out of favour in scholarship, and the idea of self-contained political units under their own leader and with their

[156] *P. Magistri*, 33, 35, 37. Later, Simon of Kéza used the eponymous Mogor and the Hung river: *Simonis de Kéza*, in *SRH*, 144, 165; in Veszprémy and Schaer, ed. and tr., *Simon of Kéza*, 14–15, 78–9.

[157] János Gulya, 'A magyarok önelnevezésének eredete', in Kovács and Veszprémy, eds., *Honfoglalás és nyelvészet*, 85–97; Kristó, *Hungarian History in the Ninth Century*, 57–70; Árpád Berta, 'Le système des noms de tribus hongroises d'origine Turke', in Csernus and Korompay, eds., *Les Hongrois et l'Europe*, 45–59.

[158] Lóránd Benkő, 'La situation linguistique des Hongrois de la conquête et ce qui en résulte', and Árpád Berta, 'Le systéme des noms de tribus d'origine Turke', in Csernus and Korompay, eds., *Les Hongrois et l'Europe*, 121–36, 45–59, respectively.

own territories has been relinquished by scholars writing on many other early medieval peoples. Recent scholarship also questions the traditional view of Hungarian tribes as ethnic and territorial units. Constantine Porphyrogenitus's term, *genea*, has been translated as 'clans' or 'tribes', but the term lacks absolute precision and Constantine used it in rather flexible ways.[159] He clearly designated groupings within the people of the 'Turks' (Hungarians) and probably implied blood relations within each group; but whether he referred to extended family units or military groupings based on imaginary blood ties is an open question. Equally, to what extent his text reflected contemporary reality among the Hungarians, and how extensively it was coloured by Byzantine ideas about nomads, cannot be ascertained.

Constantine Porphyrogenitus recorded the names of these *geneas*: Kabars, Nyeki, Megyeri, Kürtügyermatu, Tarján, Jeneh, Keri and Keszi (as reconstructed in scholarship based on the Greek forms). Placenames based on the same names are known from the Carpathian basin in large numbers (more than 300 instances) in the eleventh century and later. Several attempts to reconstruct the settlement patterns of the Hungarians based on such evidence failed: the toponyms do not relate to any straightforward settlement pattern, because all of them are scattered over most of the territory.[160]

Military and political leadership has been reconstructed in a number of different ways. Later texts indicate seven military leaders of the conquest period. Ibn Ḥayyān in the eleventh century, drawing on earlier works, wrote that the Hungarians in the tenth century had seven military leaders; the reconstructions of their names, provided by him in Arabic, are debated.[161] Anonymous, at the beginning of the thirteenth century, who also wrote of seven leaders of the conquerors, invented completely different names for them. Constantine Porphyrogenitus also described the leaders of the 'clans' as military ones, not political heads. He related that the Hungarians did not obey

[159] I thank Jonathan Shepard and Teresa Shawcross for their help with Constantine's text.

[160] György Györffy, 'A magyar törzsek és törzsi helynevek', in Kovács and Veszprémy, eds., *Honfoglalás és nyelvészet*, 221–34; Sándor László Tóth, 'A honfoglaló magyar törzsek szállásterületei', in György Pálfi, Gyula L. Farkas and Erika Molnár, eds., *Honfoglaló magyarság Árpádkori magyarság: antropológia – régészet – történelem* (Szeged, 1996), 17–22.

[161] Elter, 'A magyar kalandozáskor arab forrásai'.

their princes in every respect, but simply had an agreement to fight together 'at the rivers' wherever war erupted.

Constantine's account also suggests a hierarchical leadership composed of several different individuals. The 'first head', a paramount leader, was a prince from the Árpád dynasty (which subsequently ruled the kingdom of Hungary until 1301). Two other leaders held judicial functions, which are not described in detail: the *gylas* (*gyula*), who was more senior, and the *karchas* (*horcha*). Finally, each clan had its own prince (*archon*). The title *gyula* (*jila*) is also attested in Muslim sources, but as designating a military leader. The idea that a military leader and a judge (or two judges) were at the head of the people, however, may be due to the application of a Byzantine administrative model, rather than a reflection of Hungarian reality.

The bias of the emperor's informant may have led to the exaggeration of the role of the Árpád family. Analysing narrative accounts of the settlement, Gyula Kristó rejected the role of Árpád as a military leader, since his name is never mentioned in western sources. Instead, he proposed that Árpád was the sacral king. He relied on the Hungarian Chronicle's account concerning the murder of Álmos (Árpád's father) before the entry of the Hungarians to their new homeland, interpreting it as the reflection of an inefficient sacral king's ritual sacrifice. The military leader, *gyula*, according to Kristó, was Kusal (whose name appears in medieval texts as Curzan, Kusanés, Chussol, Cussal and so on), who played a prominent military role in the battles of the 890s, according to western and Byzantine sources. Other hypotheses feature Kusal as a member of the dynasty, perhaps Árpád's younger brother, as *horcha*, the leader of the Kabars, or as one of the chieftains.[162] The nature and origin of the power of the paramount ruler from the Árpád family must remain guesswork. He did not seem to possess supreme power in every respect. A member of the family certainly had such a position by the middle of the tenth century, though not necessarily earlier.

What has been described as a tribal confederation was a group of people of different ethnic and linguistic backgrounds, held together by military leaders and warfare. The precise internal organization of these groups cannot be reconstructed. Whatever the form of political

[162] Gyula Kristó, *Honfoglaló fejedelmek: Árpád és Kurszán* (Szeged, 1993); Kristó, *Hungarian History in the Ninth Century*, 159–73; Róna-Tas, *Hungarians and Europe*, 344–5.

organization was in the first half of the tenth century, it is impossible to know exactly when and how it disintegrated. When political structures are described again, in the late tenth and early eleventh centuries, a number of independent territorial leaders are mentioned, but no confederation made up of several groups. The nature and chronology of political transformation during the tenth century are obscure. Equally, the extent to which political organization from the late tenth century changed previous political structures is unclear, due to the paucity of sources on the earlier times. A multiplicity of leaders gave way to sole royal power, although the beginnings of that process cannot be traced due to a lack of evidence. The nature of many of the changes remains hypothetical. If a dual kingship of sacral and military kings ever existed, it came to an end during the tenth century. Several local leaders, who may have emerged due to their military prowess or were perhaps the heads of powerful extended families, held power, at some point recognizing the Árpád dynasty as providing a paramount ruler.

Several historians assumed that chieftains had their own fortified local centres in the tenth century. According to György Györffy's hypothesis, the tenth-century elite continued nomadic seasonal migration within the Carpathian basin. Each chieftain had a winter and a summer settlement centre along a main river, and moved between these two seats. No corroborating evidence has been discovered: archaeological excavations have failed to find any evidence of such seats. Early earth-and-wood forts started to be excavated in the late nineteenth century. Although there were various hypotheses about the tenth-century origins of some of them as local centres of chieftains, none of the archaeologically excavated strongholds can be dated definitely to the tenth century. According to current opinion, they were more likely to have been built during the eleventh century, although there is no absolute archaeological proof for dating the beginnings of these constructions. According to some archaeologists, cemeteries of castle warriors started to appear in the eleventh century, although this has been questioned. In the case of Borsod, a tenth-century settlement was found which was not surrounded by an earthen wall, with a fortification built on its burned remains in the eleventh century. In some cases, the eleventh-century fort was built directly on the fifth-century Roman walls. In the case of Zalavár (Mosaburg), a ninth-century stronghold was the seat of a Slav ruler; in the eleventh century, it was once again used as a political and ecclesiastical centre. No evidence proves the existence of tenth-century fortified power centres, although the picture may change with the excavation of new earthen forts and improved dating methods.[163]

Historians have also speculated about possible continuities between a presumed 'nomadic state' and the new 'Christian state' of the eleventh century.[164] Any attempt to reconstruct the characteristics of this hypothetical 'nomadic state', however, is based purely on analogies and guesswork, and the data we do have show a rupture in the political organization. The construction of strongholds with the cemeteries of the warriors attached to these strongholds seems to have started from the beginning of the eleventh century. Political-administrative divisions (counties), minting and ecclesiastical organization were all introduced in the early eleventh century and represent a radical departure from previous structures. Political continuity from pre-Christian to Christian times lay in the dynasty itself, whose power was not simply maintained but increased via Christianization.

The Árpád dynasty seems to have held some type of supreme power, even if the exact nature of their power – military leaders, sacral kings or paramount rulers among many chiefs – is debated, and its origins obscure. According to Constantine (chapter 38), and most probably based on oral information from one of Árpád's descendants, Termacsu, who visited Constantinople in the middle of the tenth century, while the Tourkoi ('Turks') had had voivodes, they did not have a ruler over them, until the Khazar khagan decided to elevate one of the voivodes, Levedias, as *archon*, so that he would obey the Khazars thereafter. Levedias declined the offer, and suggested instead having another voivode, Álmos, or his son, Árpád, elevated to the position that required obedience to the khagan. The khagan's envoys therefore returned to the Tourkoi, and the people preferred Árpád to his father, respecting him for his wisdom and military abilities alike. This may be an attempt by Constantine's informant to deny the legitimacy of any claim from Álmos's other descendants. Árpád was

[163] György Györffy, 'A honfoglaló magyarok települési rendjéről', *Archaeologiai Értesítő* 97 (1970), 191–242; István Bóna, *Az Árpádok korai várai*, 2nd edn (Debrecen, 1998); Fodor, *Ancient Hungarians*, 57–61; Visy, ed., *Hungarian archaeology*, 328–31; Mária Wolf, 'The hillfort of Borsod', in Wieczorek and Hinz, eds., *Europe's Centre: Handbook*, 387–8.

[164] Gyula Kristó, *A magyar állam megszületése* (Szeged, 1995).

therefore elevated on a shield as *archon*. Whereas before him the Tourkoi had no princes (*archons*), from the time of his elevation, *archons* always came from among his family. It should be noted, however, that Constantine also used the term '*archon*' for the leaders of each *genea* in chapter 40, where Árpád is not the only *archon*, simply the first or paramount chief. Termacsu was a member of the dynasty, and it may be argued that he provided information biased in favour of his line. The emphasis on Árpád's valour and the perpetual nature of dynastic leadership does indeed fit into that framework, but the description of the elevation is curious, since the narrative highlights readiness to be subjected to the khagan as a prerequisite for Árpád's designation for the post. Later medieval Hungarian chroniclers described succession within the dynasty by primogeniture, while many scholars suggest that originally seniority (the eldest capable male of the lineage) was the norm, until Géza and István changed the rules.

# 3

# THE FORMATION OF POLITIES AND CHRISTIANIZATION

The tenth and eleventh centuries were a period of transition, a time when Christian polities emerged. Leaders increased their power at the expense of various rivals and Christianity penetrated the region, ultimately turning it into part of Latin Christendom. In all three areas, new polities formed under the leadership of a local elite, which became the basis of the medieval kingdoms. The reinforcement and extension of rulers' power were intertwined with Christianization. Internal rivalries as well as relationships with neighbours – the East Frankish Kingdom (later the Ottonian Empire) in particular, but also other neighbouring territories where Christianization and the development of a polity had already started – had a significant impact on this process. Hungarians raided while Bohemians and Poles were sedentary. Nonetheless, all had contacts with Frankish/Ottonian society and were influenced by it. All three Ottonian emperors intervened frequently in political developments beyond their eastern frontier and, while they could pose a threat to their neighbours, they were also a powerful model of kingship for contemporary rulers. The dynasties of the three polities were frequently bound together by common political interests or by military conflicts. Their relations were dynamic and sometimes unpredictable, despite attempts to regulate them through pragmatic marriage strategies.

The role of Otto III (983–1002) in the creation of the new polities is debated. According to some historians, he left unfinished his ambitious plans to create a union of Christian states as a rival to Byzantium. Others see him as reacting to local rulers' initiatives. During the last two years of his reign, Otto III established friendly relations along his eastern frontiers, stretching from the Baltic Sea to the Adriatic. According to one view, this was a peaceful strategy intended to produce a friendly buffer zone along the Empire's eastern borders. Whatever the reasons, Poland, Hungary and the Venetian Republic, under Pietro II Orseolo, all benefited: Bolesław and István received independent archbishoprics; István was officially crowned; and the doge was freed from annual tribute. Symbolic of this co-operation, the 'imperial' name, Otto, was given to the sons of all three leaders.[1]

The Bohemian case was different. The Bohemian Church had existed for many years and had always been subordinated, first to Passau, later Regensburg and finally Mainz. One suspects that there would have been vigorous opposition from Archbishop Willigis of Mainz, for whom the Bohemian bishopric was a valuable source of income and prestige. Therefore it is implausible that the creation of an archbishopric of Prague was intended in 1000.[2]

Autonomous Christian polities developed in central Europe, unlike, for example, in the Baltic region, where Christianization was linked to conquest and subjugation in many areas. In all three polities, Christianization was inseparable from the strengthening of one ruler at the expense of his rivals. In Bohemia, this process took place earlier than in Poland and Hungary. The territorialization of dynastic power was a process rather than a single event. Territories under the rule of each dynasty were consolidated gradually.

## CHRISTIANIZATION AND ITS LINKS TO POLITICAL FORMATIONS

Christianization did not happen in a vacuum, but there is very limited information on previous beliefs and practices in all three areas. Local dynasties relied on the new religion in the building of political power.

1 Urbańczyk, *Trudne początki Polski*, 266.

2 E.g. Johannes Fried, *Otto III. und Boleslav Chrobry. Das Widmungsbild des Aachener Evangeliars, der 'Akt von Gnesen' und das frühe polnische und ungarische Königtum* (Stuttgart, 1989), ch. III.2, and D. Třeštík, 'Von Svatopluk zu Bolesław Chrobry. Die Entstehung Mitteleuropas aus der Kraft des Tatsächlichen und aus einer Idee', in *The Neighbours of Poland in the Tenth Century*, ed. P. Urbańczyk (Warsaw, 2000), 111–146 (here 142).

## Pre-Christian Slav beliefs

We know almost nothing about the religious beliefs or rituals observed by people who lived on either side of the Carpathian and Sudeten Mountains. For Bohemia, we find only very late references to an observed folk tradition of reverence for 'holy groves'.[3] Most of the discoveries of so-called cult sites are not convincing.[4] Thus, just as in Poland, reliance on studies of burial customs directs discussion.

In Bohemia, from the late eighth century onwards, the archaeological evidence suggests a gradual shift from cremation ritual to inhumation. Although the expansion of Christianity surely increased the pace of this change, the early appearance of skeleton graves and the very slow disappearance of cremations mean that changing burial rituals cannot be attributed solely to Christianization. The transition to burying unburnt dead bodies might have taken place as part of a general trend, perceived across larger areas of Europe.[5] In addition, grave goods may be misleading, as attested by the Carolingian liturgical chalice found in a ninth-century 'princely' burial in Kolin.[6] In Poland, the same transition to inhumation took place much later, in the very late tenth or even in the eleventh century; throughout the ninth century, all graves contained only burnt bones.

Linguists observed that the oldest Slavic lexicon included no notion of temples, statues or priests, which has been used to suggest that early Slavs were unaware of such forms of religious expression.[7] However, the lack of an exclusive sacral terminology cannot be used to deny the existence of cultic objects and buildings among the early Slavs; they were just not clearly separated from everyday life. There were pagan sanctuaries in the natural world that were connected (really or symbolically) with the zone of the *anaecumene*.[8] Here sacred groves, waters, mountains and stones appeared. It is unsurprising that the

[3] Cosmas II.1.

[4] See particular entries in the *Encyklopedie slovanskýh bohů a mýtů* by N. Profantova and M. Profant (Prague, 2000).

[5] Ivo Štefan, 'Zmìna pohřebniho ritu v raném středovìku jako archeologický a kulturnì-antropologický problem', *Archeologicke Rozhledy* 59 (2007), 805–36.

[6] M. Lutovský, 'Kolínský knížeci hrob', *Sborník Národního muzea v Praze: Řada A – Historie* 48 (1994), 37–76.

[7] L. Moszyński, *Die vorchristliche Religion der Slaven im Lichte der slawischen Sprachwissenschaft* (Cologne, Weimar and Vienna, 1992), 115–17.

[8] L. Słupecki, *Slavonic Pagan Sanctuaries* (Warsaw, 1994), 229–38.

concentration of cults around such features, devoid of physical constructions, should be hardly traceable through archaeology.[9]

## *The Christianization of Bohemia*

Christianity was introduced into the Bohemian basin in the second half of the ninth century through Great Moravian influences, but the Christianization of Bohemian elites started with the ruler's support no sooner than the tenth century. Originally the Christianization of Bohemia was overseen by the bishopric of Passau. In 895, however, the missionary agenda fell under the direct control of Regensburg, whose bishop, Tuto, established the archpresbyteriate in Prague.[10] These early connections are made plain by the Czech version of the Lord's Prayer – still in use today – which must have been translated from the early ninth-century Old High German text.[11] After its possible beginnings under Spytihněv, Christianity was established in Bohemia in the tenth century.

The acceptance of Christianity even at the highest level did not proceed without reverses. Vratislav (905/15–21), seeking anti-Frankish allies, married the Havelan/Stodoran princess Drahomira, who was later accused of stubbornly remaining pagan and resisting German domination.[12] With Vratislav's death, the infant Václav (921–35) inherited the throne. His mother Drahomira gained a prominent voice in Bohemia, allowing her to expel all priests from the country. Legends also accuse her of killing her pro-Christian mother-in-law, Ludmila, which likely provoked a retaliatory expedition from the Bavarian duke Arnulf in 922.[13] Affiliation to the German Church was confirmed by Duke Václav's decision to build a large rotunda church in Prague, devoted to the Ludolfings' patron, St Vitus.[14] Drahomira persuaded her younger son, Boleslav, to kill Václav in

[9] On Slavic religion(s), see P. Urbańczyk and S. Rosik 'The Kingdom of Poland', in N. Berend, ed., *Christianization and the Rise of Christian Monarchy*, 273–9.

[10] Sommer *et al.*, 'Bohemia and Moravia', 218.

[11] J. Cibulka, 'Επιούσιος – nasoštьnyi – quotidianus – vezdejší', *Slavia* 25 (1956), 406–15.

[12] Cosmas I.15.

[13] C. Lübke, Regesten *zur Geschichte der Slawen an Elbe und Oder (vom Jahr 900 an)*, vols. I-V (Berlin, 1984–8), vol. II, *Regesten 900–983* (Berlin, 1985), no. 19 (32–33).

[14] According to a later account, Henryk I gave Václav the arm relic of St Vitus: see Třeštík, *Pocátky Přemyslovců: vstup Čechů*, 411–13.

Stará Boleslav on 28 September 935. This act may be interpreted as an attempt to restore the old faith, and to achieve political independence for the principality. Yet Boleslav I the Cruel harnessed Christianity to his efforts to consolidate his authority. He promoted his murdered brother to sainthood, which sanctified the family's claims to the throne and furnished Bohemia with a holy patron. The Bohemian Church, however, did not gain independence, but remained a part of the Regensburg diocese until 974.

The only indication that Boleslav tried to change the status quo comes from a dubious story reported by Cosmas in the early twelfth century. The chronicler suggested that, already in 967, Pope John XIII had agreed to establish a bishopric in Prague (for Bohemia),[15] and the Emperor Otto I accepted as bishop a priest called Dětmar (Thietmar, Dietmar) who was proposed by Duke Boleslav.[16] The pope's agreement was ascribed to the persuasive power of Boleslav's I daughter, Mlada-Maria, abbess of the first Benedictine monastery in Bohemia. But it was the duke who had been successful in gaining acceptance of the emperor.

The results of the process of Christianization should be evaluated carefully, especially in relation to people of lower social status. Bishop Wolfgang of Regensburg in 974 had allegedly reproached the Czechs concerning their lack of knowledge about the 'orthodox religion'.[17] Archaeological finds suggest that certain elements of pagan burial rituals survived in Bohemia long into the eleventh century.[18] This is supported by official condemnation in 1039 by Břetislav I (1034–55) of the practice of burying bodies outside 'the cemeteries of the faithful', in the woods.[19]

At the beginning of the twelfth century, the chronicler Cosmas of Prague wrote that many Czechs were *semipagani* rather than *christiani*. He related also deeds of Duke Břetislav II (1092–1100), who – according to Cosmas – in 1092 'lucos sive arbores, quas in multis locis colebat vulgus [. . .] extirpavit [. . .]'. The duke prohibited also 'Item et supersticiosas instituciones, quas villani, adhuc semipagani in pentecosten tertia sive quarta feria observabant, offerentes libamina super fontes mactabant

15 Cosmas I.22. 16 Cosmas I.23.

17 *Othloni Vita sancti Wolfkangi episcopi*, chap. 29, ed. G. Waitz, MGH SS, vol. 4 (Hanover, 1981).

18 Z. Krumphanzlová, 'Der Ritus der slawischen Skelttfriedhöfe der mittleren und jüngeren Burgwallzeit in Böhmen', *Památky Archeologické* 57 (1966), 277–327.

19 Cosmas II.4.

victimas et demonibus immolabant, item sepulturas [...] fiebant in silvis et in campis.'[20] After two centuries of the formal dominance of Christianity, the basic structure of the popular belief system seemed untouched. The chronicler was rather conscious of that. His picture of 'pagan' Czech rituals observed before Christianization was vastly similar to what he wrote about the end of the eleventh century, and what probably reflected his view of his contemporaries: 'multi villani velut pagani hic latices seu ignes colit, iste lucos et arbores aut lapides adorat, ille montibus sive collibus litat, alius, que ipse fecit, idola surda et muda rogat et orat, ut domum suam et se ipsum regant'.[21]

We can assume that the Christianization of Czech elites was completed at the beginning of the eleventh century. The cult of Duke Václav (907–35) as the patron saint of the state, apparent since the second half of the tenth century, can be seen as the sign of a successful fusion of the political interests of the dynasty with Christian ideology. This does not mean that even the behaviour and customs of members of the Czech elite were fully informed by Christian values. Even clergymen had problems transforming their own habits into a form acceptable for people more strictly observing the Roman vision of the Christian life. When the bishop of Prague, Vojtěch-Adalbert, tried to persuade his subordinates – both secular and religious – to change their lives according to more evangelical ideals (forbidding selling Christian slaves to pagans and Jews, and marriage to more than one lawful wife, breaking the right of asylum in a church, etc.), they refused and he left his bishopric twice, in 988 and 994. Only long after his death did Duke Břetislav I in 1039 connect Vojtěch-Adalbert's cult with his own politics. After conquering Poland, he transferred the body of the bishop from his grave in Gniezno to Prague as another patron saint of the Czech realm. Perhaps the translation had a political subtext, as an argument for the creation of an archbishopric in Prague, but that failed. Afterwards the first and most important patron saint St Václav, was still strongly emphasized in the dynastic propaganda of power, and his cult developed further, especially from the second half of the eleventh century.[22]

20 Cosmas III.1, 161.

21 *Ibid.*, 10; Petr Sommer, 'Heidnische und christiliche Normen im Konflikt. Die Vorstellungswelt der böhmischen Gesellschaft im frühen Mittelalter', in *Prozesse der Normbildung und Normveränderung im mittelalterlichen Europa*, ed. Doris Ruhe and Karl-Heinz Spieß (Stuttgart, 2000), 161–86.

22 Further literature includes Sommer *et al.*, 'Bohemia and Moravia'; Petr Sommer, Dušan Třeštík, Josef Žemlička and Eva Doležalová, 'The Christianisation of

Christian institutions were implanted from the tenth century. By 976 Bohemia received its own bishopric located in Prague. The new diocese was incorporated into the Mainz archbishopric, which was ruled by Chancellor Willigis. In January 976 Dětmar, the first bishop of Prague, was consecrated.[23] A monk probably sent from the monastery of Corvey, he apparently spoke Slavonic.[24] Later sources reveal that Dětmar's first duties included the consecration of a series of churches already built and awaiting official recognition.[25]

It is difficult to provide conclusive arguments about the administrative organization of the early Bohemian Church. Historians maintain that since the beginning of the tenth century a network of wooden churches was built in the most important ducal strongholds across the Bohemian basin. They point at the central part of the basin as the territorial core of the Christianization process. That is in accordance with their supposition that the whole process was directly connected to the Přemyslid rulers' exercise of ducal power. For the latter, Christianity was another tool to strengthen the cohesion of their polity and domination over the conquered, still pagan elites in other parts of the basin. Boleslav I the Cruel was believed to have built twenty new churches during his reign. Yet we have no evidence of the remains of any wooden church from early Bohemia, not to mention any stone church from the tenth-century Přemyslid realm outside the capital. Of course, they had to exist during the missionary period and after the creation of the bishopric in Prague. But one should be careful not to multiply their number and to point out their exact location before the year 1000.

As for the clergy of this period, researchers believed that priests came mainly from Bavaria until 975, when Bohemia was under the patronage of Regensburg. After the bishopric's establishment and its subordination to the the archbishopric of Mainz, most of the itinerant clergy came from Saxony and Swabia. We know that priests of local origin appeared in the Czech Church in the eleventh century. Before the year 1000 only a few Czech clergymen could have existed, and they were trained, in Regensburg at least until 975. Based on the idea that Duke Boleslav built so many churches, historians suggested that the number of priests in these times reached one hundred (at least five

Bohemia and Moravia', *Annual of Medieval Studies at CEU Budapest* 13 (2007), 153–63.

[23] J. Sobiesiak, *Bolesław II Przemyślida: dynasta i jego państwo* (Cracow, 2006), 181.

[24] Cosmas I.23. [25] Cosmas I.24.

priests in every church). That, however, is purely guesswork and rather too optimistic.[26]

The first monasteries were firmly connected to ducal power. Boleslav II the Pious (Pobožný, 972–99) funded the Benedictine nuns' abbey in Prague and initiated the foundation process of the Benedictine abbey in Ostrov, which was completed *c.* 1000 by his son, Duke Boleslav III. The Ostrov monastery was settled by monks from Niederaltaich Abbey. Apart from dukes, the bishop of Prague, Vojtěch-Adalbert (982–96), took an active part in introducing monasticism and founded the Benedictine abbey in Břevnov, to which he invited monks from one of the most prestigious Italian abbeys located on Rome's Aventine Hill. Their activity in Bohemia was disrupted when Duke Boleslav II murdered the bishop's family, the Slavnikids (Slavnikovci), destroyed their seat (the stronghold Libice) and forced the monks to leave the monastery. Its existence was renewed in the middle of the eleventh century when the duke settled Benedictine monks from Niederaltaich once again in Břevnov. At that time all major monasteries in Bohemia were subordinated to the power of the duke. The origins and early status of the abbey in Sázava are unclear. It was first mentioned as the monastery of Benedictine monks living according to the traditions of the Slavonic Church. Many historians argued that neither the existence of an orthodox church in the Bohemian basin, nor the persistence of an orthodox liturgy was possible in the tenth or first half of the eleventh century. Whatever the character of the abbey, in 1092 the monks following Slavonic traditions were expelled and Benedictine monks from Břevnov were settled. The first Benedictine abbey in Moravia originated no earlier than in 1045 in Rajhrad, probably as the foundation of Duke Ota I the Beautiful (Sličný, 1061–87) and his wife, the Hungarian princess Eufemia. Until the middle of the eleventh century all monastic buildings, churches included, were built of wood and were of modest size. It is hard to suggest that they played a serious role in mass conversion or the propagation of the faith.[27]

26 Petr Sommer, 'Der beginnende böhmische Staat und seine Heiligen', *Questiones Medii Aevii Novae* 14 (2009), 41–54; Sommer, 'Die gegenwärtige tschechische kirchliche Archäologie', in *Kirchenarchäologie heute. Fragestellungen – Methoden – Ergebnisse*, ed. Niklot Krohn (Darmstadt, 2010), 544–60.

27 Walter K. Hanak, 'Saint Procopius, the Sázava monastery and the Byzantine–Slavonic legacy: some reconsiderations', *Byzantina et Slavica Cracoviensia* 1 (1991), 71–80; Vacláv Hunacek, 'Ostrov zwischen Břevnov und Sázava', in *Boleslav II. Der*

## The Christianization of the Poles

Processes of power concentration must have occurred north of the Sudeten Mountains. Our only means for reconstructing these are archaeological data, since the written records suggest a realm appearing *ex nihilo* in 963, under Mieszko I. Yet Mieszko was not the first, or only, contributor to a centralized power structure. Archaeological finds indicate that a core territorial domain was established in the first half of the tenth century in Greater Poland. A previously marginal area became densely settled and strongholds appeared; in the second quarter of the tenth century, these were built on a unified model in Bnin, Giecz, Gniezno, Grzybowo, Ostrów Lednicki, Poznań and Smarzewo.[28] Around the middle of the tenth century, many former strongholds surrounding this core territory were burnt and replaced with new military and administrative centres.[29] Thus, archaeological data allow an insight into the process of establishing a stable polity, as well as of this polity's subsequent expansion.

The Bohemian and Polish dynasties joined forces for the first time in 965, that is, shortly after King Otto I (936–73) was pronounced emperor (in 962) and after Margrave Gero had decided to subordinate Lusatia. According to tradition, Mieszko I demanded the hand of Boleslav I's daughter, Dobrava (in Polish, Dobrawa). The arrogance of the peripheral pagan ruler, who sought a marriage with 'a good Christian' princess in Prague, has left a rather negative impression in

*Tschechische Staat um Jahr 1000. Internationales Symposium, Praha 9.–10. Februar 1999*, ed. Petr Sommer (Prague, 2001), 463–80; Dana Koutná-Karg, 'Die Anfänge des Klosters Břevnov', in *Tausend Jahre Benediktiner in den Klöstern Břevnov, Braunau und Rohr*, ed. Johannes Hoffman (St Ottilien, 1993), 219–30; Petr Sommer, 'Sázava und böhmische Klöster des 11. Jahrhunderts', in *Der heilige Prokop, Böhmen und Mitteleuropa. Internationales Symposium Benešov–Sázava 24.–26. September 2003*, ed. Petr Sommer (Prague, 2005), 151–71; Dušan Třeštík, 'Slavische Liturgie und Schrifttum in Böhmen des 10. Jahrhunderts. Vorstellungen und Wirklichkeit', in *Der heilige Prokop, Böhmen und Mitteleuropa*, 205–36; Martin Wihoda, 'Das Sázava Kloster in ideologischen Koordinaten der böhmischen Geschichte des 11. Jahrhunderts', in *Der heilige Prokop, Böhmen und Mitteleuropa*, 257–71.

28 The strongholds of Giecz and Ostrów Lednicki had roots in the ninth century; see Zofia Kurnatowska, 'Ostrów Lednicki in the early Middle Ages', in *Polish Lands at the Turn of the First and the Second Millennium*, ed. P. Urbańczyk (Warsaw, 2004), 167–84; Kurnatowska, 'The stronghold in Gniezno in the light of older and more recent studies', in *Polish lands at the turn of the first and the second millennium*, 185–206.

29 Z. Kurnatowska and S. Kurnatowski, 'Parę uwag o odmiennościach kulturowych Małopolski (widzianych od północy)', in Woźniak and Gancarski, eds., *Polonia Minor medii aevi*, 165–80 (here 174).

the Bohemian tradition. Cosmas even tried to ridicule Dobrava by saying that despite her age she wore 'a maiden's wreath'.[30] The Bohemian duke's acceptance may be understood better in light of other sources that refer to this early period. According to Widukind of Corvey, 'King' *Misaca* had already fought the invading army of the Saxon fugitive Wichmann Billung the Younger in 963.[31] Thus the marriage may have been triggered by the expansion strategy of Margrave Gero, which was threatening for both west Slavic realms.[32]

The Jewish merchant-traveller, Ibrāhīm ibn Ya'qūb al-Turtushi wrote of Mieszko – *Mashaqqah* – 'the king of the north', who was said to move around his domain with an ever-present retinue of 3,000 armed horsemen.[33] Not without reason did both Ibrāhīm and Widukind refer to Mieszko I as 'king'. They stressed his military power as a tool for sustaining his dominant status over possible rivals. We do not know how the members of his mounted military elite were recruited. Archaeological evidence indicates that they were armed in a similar fashion to Scandinavians: these men were perhaps hired Viking warriors rather than representatives of the local population.[34] Alternative explanations suggest that Mieszko I had purchased or copied arms which were considered the best available at the time. His prosperity has been revealed by the discovery of silver deposits from the middle of the tenth century, concentrated in Greater Poland.[35] The economic development of the region is further confirmed by numerous discoveries of scales and weights, which indicate the growing frequency of trading transactions.[36]

The decision of Mieszko I to marry Dobrava in 965 placed him firmly at the centre of the political stage, alongside his Bohemian father-in-law. A year later his official baptism, and that of his close supporters, confirmed his place among central European rulers acknowledged by Christian powers. The sudden appearance of a

[30] Cosmas I.27. Some historians suspect that she had been married before.

[31] Widukind III.66.

[32] H. Ludat, *An Elbe und Oder von das Jahr 1000* (Cologne and Vienna, 1971), 35.

[33] Dmitrij Mishin, 'Ibrahim ibn-Ya'qub al-Turtushi's account of the Slavs from the middle of the tenth century', *Annual of Medieval Studies at the CEU, 1994–1995* (1996), 184–99.

[34] Michał Kara, 'Z badań nad składem etnicznym, organizacją i dyslokacją drużyny pierwszych Piastów', *Kronika Wielkopolska* 3, 62 (1993), 33–47.

[35] Brather, 'Frühmittelalterliche Dirham-Schatzfunde', Abb. 4, p. 191.

[36] *Ibid.*, Abb. 7.

new, potentially dangerous enemy must have alarmed Otto I, who *c.* 965 was said to have collected tribute, 'up to the river Warta'.[37] Yet already in 967 Mieszko I was considered the *amicus imperatoris* at Otto's I court.[38] This rising status may have been due not only to Mieszko's baptism, but also to his decisive victory in that same year over the rebel Wichmann Billung and his Veletian allies.[39] Mieszko's baptism was most likely intended, in part, to reinforce his power by adding to it a new ideological dimension. The process of constructing a new collective identity was based on self-recognition as a Christian realm and was accelerated by frequent military conflicts, especially when there was a necessity to act in common.

In 968, Mieszko I received his own bishop, Jordan. His official status is unknown, although his function is clear: he was a missionary ever present at the ruler's side.[40] Jordan was not subject to any metropolitan see, and according to several historians he acted as an 'episcopus immediate subiectus sedis apostolicae'.[41] Such an institution was unknown at the time, however, and that Jordan was the only holder of such a title in Europe seems unlikely. Most probably he acted as a missionary bishop. Perhaps after several years he or his successor, Unger, was recognized as the bishop of a more or less stable diocese with its seat in Poznań and a territory covering the whole Piast realm until 1000.

In this early period, the Polish Church was under a powerful southern influence. Bohemian clergy would have arrived in Poland in 965 together with the Bohemian princess, Dobrava. That Christianity came to Poland from Bohemia is confirmed by linguistic studies, which show that the earliest Polish Christian vocabulary might have been mediated by the orthodox Slavic rite, introduced during the Great Moravian period by Cyril and Methodius. Thus, the

37 Thietmar of Merseburg II.29: '*usque in Vurta fluvium*'.

38 Widukind III.69.

39 Widukind III.69.

40 Gerard Labuda, 'Zjazd i synod gnieźnieński roku 1000 w nowym oświetleniu historiograficznym', in D. A. Sikorski and A. M. Wyrwa, eds., *Cognitioni gestorum* (Poznań, 2006), 166.

41 Anzelm Weiss, *Biskupstwa bezpośrednio zależne od Rzymu w średniowiecznej Europie* (Lublin, 1992), recently criticized by Dariusz A. Sikorski, *Kościół w Polsce za Mieszka I i Bolesława Chrobrego: rozważania nad granicami poznania historycznego* (Poznań, 2010), 159–66, who claimed that Jordan was a bishop of an except bishopric, as were several bishoprics in Italy and Gaul. Suggestions that Jordan was subordinated to one of the German archbishoprics, probably Mainz, lack any historical confirmation.

Polish Church may have inherited elements of the Great Moravian experiment when adjusting the Slavic language to the needs of the new religion.[42] These contacts could have been renewed around the turn of the millennium when the Bohemian-born archbishop Radim-Gaudentius (Radzim-Gandenty) was put at the head of the Polish Church.

By March 1000, Otto III for the first time in imperial history crossed the frontier of his realm into Poland, not as the commander of an invading army, but as a friend and donor.[43] According to the available sources, Otto's prime intention was to pray at the burial site of the martyred Vojtěch-Adalbert in Gniezno, which he visited *orationis et reconciliationis gratia*. He brought with him a copy of the imperial *lancea Regis* (the so-called lance of St Mauritius),[44] golden altar panels and Radim-Gaudentius, the brother of Vojtěch-Adalbert, now the saint's 'personal archbishop'.

During the meeting in Gniezno in 1000 between Emperor Otto III and Duke Bolesław I the Brave (Chrobry, 992–1025), and despite some controversy involving the old Polish bishop Unger, a Polish Church province was created, with its archiepiscopal see in Gniezno; Radim-Gaudentius was the first archbishop. To him were subordinated bishops of Kołobrzeg (Reinbern), Wrocław (Jan) and Kraków (Poppo); these dioceses at that time had no precise boundaries.[45] Although the creation of the province was the result of a papal privilege, superiors of the Magdeburg archbishopric did not accept the new situation. That led to several conflicts for supremacy over the Polish Church until 1130, when the Piast duke Bolesław III the Wrymouth (Krzywousty, 1102–38) received confirmation of its independence.[46] Otto III also granted Bolesław I the prerogative to

[42] Urbańczyk, *Trudne początki Polski.*

[43] For a detailed analysis, see Roman Michałowski, *Zjazd gnieźnieński: religijne przesłanki powstania arcybiskupstwa gnieźnieńskiego* (Wrocław, 2005), and P. Urbańczyk, *Trudne początki Polski*, ch. 11.

[44] *Galli Anonymi Cronicae* I.6. Otto's gift is in the cathedral treasury of Cracow; the original imperial lance is exhibited in the Schatzkammer of the Hofburg in Vienna.

[45] For more details, see Urbanczyk and Rosik, 'Poland', 284.

[46] Roman Michałowski, 'Christianisation of political culture in Poland in the tenth and the early eleventh century', in *Political Culture in Central Europe (Tenth–Twentieth Century), vol. 1, Middle Ages and Early Modern Era*, ed. Halina Manikowska and Jaroslav Pánek (Prague, 2005), 31–40; Gerard Labuda, 'Die Gründung der Metropolitanorganisation der polnischen Kirche auf der Synode in Gnesen am 9. Und 10. März 1000', *Acta Poloniae Historica* 84 (2001), 5–30; Jerzy Strzelczyk, 'Die

nominate new bishops and freed him from paying tribute to the Empire.[47] However, despite the arguments advanced by some Polish historians, there is no proof of any formal royal coronation. Otto III left Poland with an arm of St Vojtěch-Adalbert, the constituent parts of which he would later use to found monastic foundations in Aachen, Rome, Reichenau, Esztergom and Pereum, near Ravenna.[48]

Although establishing the province was an important step in stabilizing the social position and increasing the scope of influence of Christianity among the ruler's subjects, it did not mean that all or even the majority of these subjects accepted the Christian faith. Despite the optimistic assessments of the Christian chroniclers, it is difficult to estimate how rapidly a new Christian identity promoted by the Piasts was fully accepted among their people. The origin of the clergy who, until the eleventh century, were all immigrants from Bohemia, Germany and Italy, may have hindered the process of conversion. Its slow pace among commoners subject to the ruler is confirmed by Thietmar who, at the beginning of the eleventh century, described the harsh methods applied by Bolesław the Brave to enforce the observance of fasts and to uproot adultery.[49] Since there are no cemeteries or even single graves that would indicate an acceptance of Christian eschatology in Poland before the very late tenth century, archaeologists suggest that there were hindrances to the non-elites accepting new identities.[50] In eastern Poland openly 'pagan' burial customs, such as cremation, survived even until the thirteenth century. In general, the Christianization of the masses in Poland began

Bedeutung der Gründung des Erzbitums Gnesen und die Schaffung einer kirchlichen Organisation für die Ausformung einer "kirchlichen Kulturlandschaft"', Siedlungsforschung 20 (2002), 41–64; *Polen und Deutschland vor 1000 Jahren. Die Berliner Tagung über den 'Akt von Gnesen'*, ed. Michael Borgolte (Berlin, 2002).

47 Thietmar of Merseburg IV.45.

48 T. Dunin-Wąsowicz, 'Najstarsi polscy święci: Izaak, Mateusz i Krystyn', in *Kościół, kultura, społeczeństwo: studia z dziejów średniowiecza i czasów nowożytnych*, ed. S. Bylina *et al.* (Warsaw, 2000), 35–47.

49 Thietmar of Merseburg, VIII.2; Roman Michałowski, 'The nine-week Lent in Boleslaus the Brave's Poland: a study of the first Piasts' "Religious Policy"', *Acta Poloniae Historica* 89 (2004), 5–50.

50 E.g. Helena Zoll-Adamikowa, 'Zum Beginn der Köperbestattung bei den Westslawen', in *Rom und Byzanz im Norden. Mission und Glaubenswechsel im Ostseeraum während des 8.–14. Jahrhunderts*, vol. II, ed. Michael Müller-Wille (Mainz and Stuttgart, 1998), 227–38.

some time before the middle of the twelfth century with the development of a network of parish churches and monasteries.[51]

Bolesław the Brave initiated a lay and ecclesiastical infrastructure. He and his son directed the building of stone chapels, churches and palaces.[52] Besides smaller churches, they completed great cathedrals in Poznań and Gniezno. Bolesław also ordered that *palatia* be built in Ostrów Lednicki, Giecz and Przemyśl, which were designed according to a single 'Ottonian' model as simple rectangular palaces with adjacent round chapels.[53] Yet the number of churches known from written and archaeological sources is meagre, no more than twenty to thirty for the entire polity until the death of Bolesław I. Only one monastery of proven existence, the Benedictine hermits' abbey in Meseritz (Międzyrzecz), functioned during these times. Perhaps one more monastery, in Łęczyca, settled with monks from Břevnov and founded by Radim-Gaudentius, was active, but its origin and fate are not clear. The relative weakness of Christianity in the Piast realm became apparent during fights after the death of Mieszko II (1025–34) (see below). When Kazimierz (Casimir) the Restorer (Odnowiciel, 1034–58) reconquered his land he had to rebuild the Church entirely. Only his son Bolesław II the Bold (Śmiały, 1058–79) succeeded in rebuilding the organization in a shape roughly resembling the Church of Bolesław I. The new cathedral in Gniezno was finished not earlier than during the reign of his brother, Władysław I Herman (1079–1102). During this time dukes established three Benedictine abbeys: in Tyniec (*c.* 1044), Mogilno (*c.* 1060) and Lubiń (*c.* 1076). Even during the reign of Bolesław III the Wrymouth Poland was seen as the land whose inhabitants should be regularly instructed in the Christian faith and whose clergy had too much work with the basic religious education of the Piasts' subjects to take part in any serious missionary movement. Whether that was true is less important than that it was an

[51] Urbańczyk and Rosik, 'Poland', 263–300.

[52] A chronology of the oldest forms of Polish architecture has been debated. More precise dating is possible through the accelerator dating of organic particles contained in original gypsum and lime mortars (AMS dating). See P. Urbańczyk, 'Akceleratorowa chronologia najstarszej architektury murowanej w Polsce', in *Architektura romańska w Polsce: nowe odkrycia i interpretacje*', ed. T. Janiak (Gniezno, 2009), 33–49.

[53] Urbanczyk and Rosik, 'Poland', 296–7. Very similar buildings were discovered in the imperial *Pfalz* of Werla and in Esztergom, Hungary.

opinion acceptable for others: the Poles at the beginning of the twelfth century were still in need of their own priests' missionary work.[54]

Nonetheless, the difference in the depth of the Christianization of the Piasts' realm between the tenth–first half of the eleventh century and the twelfth century was significant. The number of monasteries grew quickly in the twelfth century. They soon started to be erected by wealthy families of knights, not just dukes. Local churches were also founded by knights on their estates already in the first half of the twelfth century. Although the regular network of parishes was built no earlier than in the first half of the thirteenth century, non-Christian burials slowly disappeared. Traditional rites survived and in the eyes of the clergy sometimes did not differ much from pagan rituals or polluted Christian feasts. Yet Christianity ceased to be an exclusively court ideology, as it was in the tenth and first decades of the eleventh century. It both fitted into and shaped the social order on a broader scale. Of symbolic character were two facts: the royal coronation of Bolesław II the Bold in 1076 acknowledged by the pope and against the emperor's will, and the magnates' rebellion three years later against the king when he sentenced to death for treason Bishop Stanisław of Cracow, a member of the local elite. For all actors in these dramatic events, Christianity was a common language of political symbols, not only a set of abstract, moral values taught by priests scattered across the vast land. From the last quarter of the eleventh century, Christianity – for the elites of the Piast realm, but also for a growing number of common subjects – began to serve as the framework for the perception of the world as well as for social and political activities.[55]

[54] Roman Michałowski, 'La christianisation de la Pologne aux Xe–XIIe siècles', in *Clovis. Histoire et memoire. Actes du Colloque International d'Histoire de Reims du 19 au 25 septembre 1996*, ed. Michel Rouche (Paris, 1997), vol. II, 419–34.

[55] Roman Michałowski, 'Christianization of the Piast monarchy in the tenth and eleventh centuries', *Acta Poloniae Historica* 101 (2010), 5–35; Marek Derwich, 'Les deux fondations de l'abbaye de Lubiń dans le cadre de l'implantation de monachisme bénédictin en Pologne (moitié de XIe – fin du XIIe siècle)', *Le Moyen Âge* 108 (2002), 9–24; Przemysław Nowak, 'Die polnische Kirchenprovinz Gnesen und die Kurie im 12. Jahrhundert', in *Römisches Zentrum und kirchliches Peripherie. Das universale Papstum als Bezugspunkt der Kirchen von den Reformpäpsten bis zu Innozenz III.*, ed. Jochem Johrendt (Berlin, 2008), 191–206.

## *Magyars: settlement, traditional beliefs and Christianization*

After their entry into the Carpathian basin, the Hungarians continued their traditional ways in some respects, for example raiding, while other features of their life changed gradually, such as the development of permanent settlement. About a century later, major transformations led to the emergence of the Christian kingdom of Hungary.

As described in Chapter 2, debates surround the question of Hungarian nomadism at the time of their entry into the Carpathian basin. Archaeological excavations attest to the foundation of stable settlements after the conquest; these may have initially served as winter bases but rapidly turned into permanent villages with houses, which were in areas where the soil was suitable for cultivation. The population engaged in agriculture as well as raising livestock. By the tenth century, the inhabitants of the villages were also already making pottery and establishing iron-works.[56] Family structures, whether society consisted of clans (extended families) or also of nuclear families, are equally debated; the evidence about social and family structures comes from burial patterns, which can be interpreted in a number of ways. Tenth-century burials also provide rich evidence of pre-Christian material culture (clothing, weapons and jewellery).[57]

Grave goods show the divisions between the elite, powerful and wealthy clans with the *ur* (eventually designating lords) at their head, and commoners (*ín*). Cemeteries with poor grave goods used to be thought to belong to the local Slavic population, but are now seen as those of commoners, including Hungarians. Solitary graves of the clan leaders, and of female members of the family, furnished with exceptionally rich grave goods, were separate from communal cemeteries, although sometimes they included servants. The military elite or retinues of leaders, often buried in cemeteries of their nuclear family, are also distinguished by their richly furnished graves. Archaeologists now see 'extended family cemeteries' of fifteen to twenty-five graves as the exception rather than the rule, and burials in smaller, nuclear

[56] Fodor, *Ancient Hungarians*, 27–30, 57–64, 415–36; Visy, ed., *Hungarian Archaeology*, 326–32; Kovács and Paládi-Kovács, *Honfoglalás és néprajz*; György Györffy, *Wirtschaft und Gesellschaft der Ungarn um die Jahrtausendwende* (Budapest and Vienna, 1983). For an overview between conquest and Christianization, see Róna-Tas, *Hungarians and Europe*, 339–71.

[57] Fodor, *Ancient Hungarians*, 65–414; Visy, ed., *Hungarian Archaeology*, 338–43; Kovács and Paládi-Kovács, *Honfoglalás és néprajz*; Kovács, *Honfoglalás és régészet*.

family groups as the norm among commoners in village communities. Some of these cemeteries show a continuity of population, while others were discontinued or used by a different population after the tenth century.

An important sign of status was the leather belt decorated with mounts. Other archaeological signs of wealth and status include sabretaches with mounts or metal plaques, ornamented bow cases, weapons and harnesses and, primarily in female graves, jewellery and gold and silver ornaments on dresses. The use of such status symbols was restricted to members of families providing the ruler's retinue and the military elite, although who exactly was entitled to use which type of status symbol is debated. Riding was important not just for the warriors but for all members of society, and horse accoutrements including saddles and stirrups were adapted to different needs (those of warriors, women and children). Ornaments on clothing and remains that allow the reconstruction of clothing have been excavated in substantial numbers. Both men and women wore caftans and soft-soled felt boots. Men wore wide trousers and pointed caps. Women's hair was richly ornamented with rings holding braids in place, pearls and metal ornaments. They also wore a variety of jewels, bracelets and earrings. Hair-rings were also worn by men.

After their installation in the Carpathian basin, the Hungarians continued the military activities that in the ninth century had already been a crucial constituent of their political and economic life, to some extent similarly to the Vikings. Raiding formed the basis of the elite's wealth and power, and their military service was available for hire. Hungarian scholarship has called the raids conducted after the Hungarians' arrival in their new territory *kalandozások*, which can be rendered as 'going on adventures'. Although some Hungarian historians formulated a variety of hypotheses about the raids' motivations as a desire for settlement in western Europe, or for securing the new areas of settlement, or even as a political tool, these raids instead clearly fit into the same framework as Viking and later steppe nomad raids: raiding settled neighbours for plunder provided wealth and loyal military followers. These raids were extensions of ninth-century raiding, and at least initially occurred very frequently, perhaps every year, in various directions. Their targets were frequently German areas, but also Italy, French lands, Burgundy and even Lérida on the Iberian peninsula. In the tenth century, they raided Bulgaria and Byzantium as well. Historians no longer interpret raiding as the centrally organized activity of all warriors together, but instead as the actions of separate armies under their own military leaders.[58]

The weapons used in these raids are well attested from grave finds: primarily bows and arrows, which could be shot to a distance of 200–250 m, and could reach a specific target within 60–70 m. Sabres were used by only some of the warriors (of the 140 finds so far, 51 come from the Upper Tisza region; the others probably come from the graves of community leaders), with the use of double-edged swords increasing from the late tenth century. Axes and lances were also found in some graves. According to Muslim sources, 20,000 horsemen obeyed the military leader, the *jila*. They attacked the Slavs, selling their captives into slavery.[59] Due to the lack of sources, not much is known about the raids against Slavs, but raids against western lands which started in the late ninth century are much better documented. Hungarians raided for plunder and captives, resorting to great brutality. They gained a reputation for ferocity because of these raids, and were widely feared among their settled neighbours, as attested especially by monastic chronicles.

Yet modern scholarship has shown that their impact on the west was not as serious as once believed. The Hungarians also had to modify their style of warfare, and began to use infantry from subject peoples, who were, however, difficult to control. During the tenth century, the raiders increasingly extorted protection payments from populations eager to avoid being plundered. Captives were initially sold into slavery then, in the tenth century, increasingly ransomed immediately.

Settled neighbours also used Hungarian armies in their own service.[60] Bavarians, Byzantines, Franks and Lombards (in northern Italy)

[58] Kristó, *A magyar állam megszületése*, 277–97; Bóna, *A magyarok és Európa*, 29–32, 36–40, 43–65; János B. Szabó, *A honfoglalóktól a huszárokig: a középkori magyar könnyűlovasságról* (Budapest, 2010), 39–105; Sándor László Tóth, 'Les incursions des Magyars en Europe', in Csernus and Korompay, eds., *Les Hongrois et l'Europe*, 201–22; Ferenc Makk, 'The Magyar raids', and István Bóna, 'Hungarian military tactics in the raids on Europe', both in Wieczorek and Hinz, eds., *Europe's Centre: Handbook*, 143–4 and 145–9 respectively; *Medieval Warfare and Military Technology: An Encyclopedia*, ed. Clifford J. Rogers (Oxford, 2010), vol. II, 284–6.

[59] István Zimonyi, 'A 9. századi magyarokra vonatkozó arab források: a Dzsajhánihagyomány', and István Nyitrai, 'A magyar őstörténet perzsa nyelvű forrásai', in Kovács and Veszprémy, eds., *A honfoglaláskor*, 49–59 and 61–76 respectively; Zimonyi, *Muslimische Quellen*.

[60] Bowlus, *Franks, Moravians*, 244–5, 253–4; Shepard, 'Byzantine writers'; Panagiotes T. Antonopoulos, 'Byzantium, the Magyar raids and their consequences', *Byzantinoslavica* 54 (1993), 254–67.

paid to employ Hungarians in military ventures. Citing a few examples suffices to demonstrate the nature of such engagements. Byzantines employed them against the Bulgarians in 895 and continued to maintain contacts with Hungarians in the first two decades of the tenth century against the same, while calling on their services again in 935 against the Lombards. The Frankish emperor Arnulf employed them against Berengar I in 899, who in turn relied on them to defeat both Rudolf of Burgundy in 922 and the rebellious Pavia in 924. Their last such engagement was on the side of Svyatoslav of Kiev in his campaigns to create a power centre on the Lower Danube (in Bulgarian areas) in 969–71.

The survival of raiding depended on the inability of the surrounding populations to defend themselves. As the Ottonians and Byzantines consolidated their power, they were able to confront the raiding armies. In any case, the seeming invincibility of the Hungarians, a notion expressed in some medieval and modern works, is untenable; even before 955, they suffered several defeats. As modern scholars have demonstrated, Hungarian mounted archers were not superior to western heavy-armed warriors in close combat. Indeed, they could be at a distinct disadvantage, for arrows were not particularly useful in such battles.

Major defeats at Riade (933) and near Augsburg (955) inflicted by German rulers, and at Arcadiopolis (970) by Byzantines, forced the cessation of Hungarian raids and contributed to the reorganization of society. The most famous of these events was the battle near Augsburg in 955. It is often called the battle of Lechfeld, although the battle did not take place on the open plain of the Lech River. The aftermath of the battle itself was especially disastrous for the raiders, when the retreating army was trapped by floods and more or less destroyed by forces positioned in forts on river crossings.[61]

Evidence for the political organization of the Hungarians at the time of their settlement in the Capathian basin mainly comes from the Byzantine emperor Constantine Porphyrogenitus, who collected data on potential enemies and allies in his *De administrando imperio* composed *c.* 948–52. By this time, Hungarians (usually called *Tourkoi* in Byzantine sources of the period) both caused concern at Constantinople because of their recurring raids against Byzantium

[61] Charles R. Bowlus, *The Battle of Lechfeld and Its Aftermath, August 955: The End of the Age of Migrations in the Latin West* (Aldershot, 2006).

between 934 and 970 (with the Pechenegs providing a possible counterweight), and were seen as possibly useful allies against Symeon of Bulgaria. Yet – as has been convincingly argued – by exiling the court official dealing with the Hungarians, Constantine found himself in sudden need of information. He thus gathered all available data on the Hungarians, hence the lengthy treatment, but also the problematic nature of his evidence: it is often impossible to tell how reliable and precise Constantine's 'facts' are.[62] The emperor drew heavily on earlier written sources, which described the situation before and in the early tenth century. His contemporary information seems to have come from local informants who provided partial and probably biased reports: possibly Kabars in the eastern parts of the Hungarian settlement areas, about whom he wrote at length, and Hungarian leaders visiting Constantinople: the *gyla*, Boultzous (in Hungarian Bulcsú) and Termatzous (in Hungarian Termacsu). This last, or someone in his entourage is thought to have provided the material about Árpád's descendants. Geographically, Constantine had detailed knowledge only of eastern parts of the Hungarian territories. Politically, he emphasized the role of Árpád and his family, who took control of some areas after settlement in the Carpathian basin, according to one view in the Upper Tisza region (see below), but more probably west of the Danube, which was their base in the better-attested eleventh century.

The Árpáds gradually extended their power over the lands of the other leaders. This process was not without power struggles. During the tenth century, several leaders oriented towards the Byzantine Empire. In the middle of the tenth century (*c.* 948), first Bulcsú, the *karchas*, then the *gyula* or Gyula,[63] and perhaps Termacsu converted in Constantinople. These baptisms were linked to diplomacy; the emperor Constantine Porphyrogenitus was Bulcsú's godfather, and

[62] Constantine Porphyrogenitus, De administrando imperio, chaps. 38–40, pp. 170–9; Dimitri Obolensky, *The Byzantine Commonwealth: Eastern Europe 500–1453* (London, 1971, repr. 2000), 153–8; Kristó, *Hungarian History in the Ninth Century*, 97–106; Shepard, 'Byzantine writers'; Sándor László Tóth, 'The territories of the Hungarian tribal federation around 950 (some observations on Constantine VII's "Tourkia")', in *Byzanz und Ostmitteleuropa 950–1453. Beiträge zu einer table-ronde des XIX International Congress of Byzantine Studies, Copenhagen 1996*, ed. Günter Prinzig and Maciej Salamon (Wiesbaden, 1999), 23–33.

[63] Skylitzes uses this as a personal name, Constantine as a title; for analysis, see Lóránd Benkő, *Az ómagyar nyelv tanúságtétele* (Budapest, 2002), 17–51.

also granted him and Gyula money and the title of *patrikios*. Giving gifts and honours to barbarians, sometimes linked to their conversion, was a well-known Byzantine diplomatic tool. According to Ioannes Skylitzes, whose narrative presents the story of these conversions (he drew from earlier sources, including some that are no longer extant), Bulcsú only feigned his conversion and continued his raids against Byzantium, until, when raiding against the Franks (955), he was captured and executed on the orders of Otto I.[64] Gyula, however, was sincere and even took a monk, Hierotheos (whom the patriarch consecrated to be bishop of Tourkia), back with him to his lands. Whether these lands were in Transylvania or east of the Tisza River on the Hungarian plain is debated.[65] Hierotheos converted many people, according to the text, although the extent to which the population was converted under him and his successors is impossible to measure. From the early eleventh century, Byzantine lists record the metropolitanate of Tourkia, and the seals of bishops of Tourkia survive from the eleventh century.

The location of archaeological finds of liturgical and other objects of Byzantine origin have been used to determine the area of Byzantine influence, especially finds of Byzantine reliquary pectoral crosses. However, it is not always possible to distinguish between commerce and conversion as the ultimate cause of the presence of such goods. Objects of Byzantine origin are concentrated in the Tisza region and the Banat area. Finds of Byzantine reliquary pectoral crosses come from eastern Hungary (particularly the areas between the Rivers Körös and Maros), north-eastern Trans-Danubia (between Veszprém and Esztergom), scattered east of the northern section of the Tisza, and a few between the Danube and Tisza. Whether these crosses were used by a Christianized population or as amulets or jewellery is debated. Some of these finds were in tenth-century cemeteries; others were found in cemeteries that continued into the eleventh century. Byzantine earrings and other jewellery, as well as

[64] *Ioannis Scylitzae Synopsis Historiarum*, ed. Hans Thurn, Corpus Fontium Historiae Byzantinae 5 (New York and Berlin, 1973), 239; Greek text and Hung. tr. with notes in Gyula Moravcsik, *Az Árpád-kori magyar történelem bizánci forrásai* (Budapest, 1988), 84–6.

[65] The matter is further complicated by the fact that some scholars use Transylvania as a technical term for medieval Transylvania, while others use it more loosely for a larger area, which includes the Banat, Maramureş and Crişana regions of present-day Romania.

coins, found especially along the Tisza between the Maros and the Körös Rivers, have been interpreted as a sign of trade, probably of salt, from the middle of the tenth century onwards between local potentates in these areas and Byzantium, which supposedly also served to stabilize relations and avoid raids.[66]

The Árpáds initially participated in this eastern orientation; a member of the dynasty, Termacsu, one of Árpád's great-grandsons, whose uncle Falicsi was paramount ruler at the time, as noted, visited Constantinople with Bulcsú *c.* 948, and received the title 'friend' (*phílos*) of the emperor.[67] Afterwards, however, perhaps linked to the need to establish a firmer power base through contacts with a regional power where the family had no rivals, the Árpáds turned to the west instead. The first period when firmer evidence is available is during the reign of Géza (Geise, Gevitza *c.* 970–97). He seems to have initiated a process of transformation, which led both to Christianization according to its Latin form and to a sole ruler holding more power and effective leadership.

In Hungary, Christianization and the building of royal power went hand in hand. Archaeological evidence is interpreted by some scholars as a sign of late tenth-century political disruption. In the region of the Upper Tisza, cemeteries of the first half of the tenth century show a

[66] István Baán, 'The Metropolitanate of Tourkia: the organization of the Byzantine Church in Hungary in the Middle Ages', in *Byzanz und Ostmitteleuropa*, 45–53; Paul Stephenson, *Byzantium's Balkan Frontier: A Political Study of the Northern Balkans, 900–1204* (Cambridge, 2000), 38–45; Katerina Hornicková, 'Byzantine reliquary pectoral crosses in Central Europe', MA thesis, Central European University, 1998; Hornicková, 'The Byzantine reliquary pectoral crosses in Central Europe', *Byzantinoslavica* 60, 1 (1999), 213–50; Imre Szatmári, 'Bizánci típusú ereklyetartó mellkeresztek Békés és Csongréd megyében', *Studia Archaeologica* 1 (1995), 219–254.

[67] Wieczorek and Hinz, eds., *Europe's Centre Handbook*, 361–72. The genealogy according to Constantine is:

Árpád
/

| / | / | \ | \ | |
|---|---|---|---|---|
| Tarkacsu | Jeleg | Jutocsa | Zoltán | |
| / | / | / | / | |
| Teveli | Ezeleg | Falicsi | Taksony | [from unknown father: Tasi] |
| / | | | | |
| Termacsu | | | | |

different pattern from other areas, as well as a discontinuity between the first and the second half of the century. In the earlier half of the tenth century, they contain a very high percentage of male graves, and these include more weapons and signs of rank (ornamented belts and sabretaches, weapons and horse accoutrements) than cemeteries elsewhere. One possible interpretation is that the cemeteries belonged to artificially organized groups of elite warriors, perhaps the military retinue of the ruler. Others see these as cemeteries of the most powerful clans whose power was subsequently broken by Géza. In either case, it is possible to link the disruption in the life of these communities to a change in political power.[68]

Géza's role is debated: some historians attribute to him not only the early steps in strengthening the Árpád dynasty's power at the expense of other chieftains, but also the foundation of the first bishopric and the first Benedictine abbey. Prior to Géza, various sources in the ninth and tenth centuries mentioned a number of different types of rulers over the Hungarians – *kündü*; *gyula*; voivode; *archon* – and often explicitly described several leaders at the same time, at most under a notional overall paramount ruler. Géza, however, was designated as *senior magnus*, *dux* or even *rex*, clearly setting him above other powerful men. His power seems to have been very different from that of his predecessors. He initiated the introduction of Christianity in his territories. The narrative sources mention Géza's strict and cruel rule. Thietmar of Merseburg specifically emphasized his confrontation with some of his subjects, presumably from the elite, who refused to accept Christianity.[69]

A lack of sources prevents the full exploration of local beliefs prior to Christianization.[70] All the material used as evidence for traditional

[68] Fodor, *Ancient Hungarians*, 125–208; Visy, ed., *Hungarian Archaeology*, 341.

[69] Gyula Kristó, 'Géza fejedelem megítélése', in László Veszprémy, ed., *Szent István és az államalapítás* (Budapest, 2002), 369–80; Nora Berend, József Laszlovszky and Béla Zsolt Szakács, 'The kingdom of Hungary', in N. Berend, ed., *Christianization and the Rise of Christian Monarchy*, 341–2; Thietmar of Merseburg VIII.4 (at 444); *Legenda S. Stephani regis minor*, ed. Emma Bartoniek, in *Scriptores Rerum Hungaricarum*, ed. Imre Szentpétery, 2 vols. (Budapest, 1937–8, repr. 1999), vol. II, 393–400 (here 394).

[70] Róna-Tas, *Hungarians and Europe*, 364–70; Visy, ed., *Hungarian Archaeology*, 333–7; Fodor, *Ancient Hungarians*, 31–5; László Szegfű, 'Le monde spirituel des Hongrois païens', in Csernus and Korompay, eds., *Les Hongrois et l'Europe*, 103–20; Éva Pócs, 'A magyar mitológia és Európa', in Kovács and Paládi-Kovács, eds., *Honfoglalás és néprajz*, 309–22.

beliefs is problematic. Archaeological material is difficult to interpret; ethnographic parallels are of dubious relevance; the few written references are often by hostile writers, either by later Christian authors mirroring their prejudices or by contemporaries who repeat stereotypes. Medieval Christian chronicles refer to earlier forms of oral traditions, such as epic poems about the military deeds of heroes, and laments, but barely quote or paraphrase these, and none survives. The Hungarian Anonymous explicitly belittles such traditions.[71] Scholarly consensus used to hold that the population held animistic-shamanistic beliefs. The existence of shamanism among the Hungarians, however, has recently been questioned. These arguments in the main are that the *táltos*, attested in Hungary, did not have the full characteristics of a shaman, and no evidence of these beliefs exists prior to the early modern period. Instead of a pre-Christian survival, such folk beliefs may be of more recent origin.

Scholars have suggested the existence of other beliefs and practices based mainly on folklore, linguistic evidence, a few contemporary narratives and the prohibitions found in early Christian sources. These include recourse to healers; animistic practices; the cult of ancestors and the belief that kin groups descended from an animal ancestor; cult at holy springs and trees; and beliefs in various spirits, and in two souls, one of which continues after death. Muslim as well as Christian sources that describe the Hungarians before their conversion to Christianity mention that they worshipped forces of nature. A probably late tenth-century Muslim text claimed they made burnt offerings to a god of the heavens.[72]

Hungarians followed some of the common practices among nomadic steppe populations. For example, it seems that they took oaths on dogs, where the dog was cut in half to symbolize the fate of the oath-breaker. Widukind reported such an event, but misunderstood the significance of the dog; he thought that it was in order to humiliate the

[71] *P. Magistri*, 33–4; Loránd Benkő, 'Anonymus élő nyelvi forrásai', in Kovács and Veszprémy, eds., *A honfoglaláskor*, 221–47 (here 225–9).

[72] Zimonyi, 'A 9. századi magyarokra vonatkozó arab források', 55; Nyitrai, 'A magyar őstörténet perzsa nyelvű forrásai', 72; István Zimonyi, 'Egy új muszlim forrás a Kárpát-medencében élő magyarokról', in Szabolcs Felföldi and Balázs Sinkovics, eds., *Nomád népvándorlások, magyar honfoglalás* (Budapest, 2001), 88–96.

Hungarians that their old allies threw a dog in front of them, when in fact they were renouncing the alliance.[73]

Neither archaeological evidence nor written sources indicate the existence of cult buildings. Natural sites such as holy groves, mentioned in Christian texts, may have served as cult places in pre-Christian practice, but left no trace. Archaeology is richest in providing evidence about burials.[74] Thousands of graves have been excavated, and objects and decorations on such objects have served as the basis for various conclusions about pre-Christian beliefs as well. It is, however, important to emphasize that the interpretation of various finds is hypothetical, and many aspects of the belief system cannot be fully understood. Horse burial is one example of the limits of interpreting archaeological evidence. Partial horse burials, of the whole skin with the head and legs still included, as well as symbolic horse burials (the burial of a harness or accoutrements), are well attested. They clearly signalled social status: all horse burials were linked to the wealthy elite. Thus they were found either in solitary graves, or only in the graves of the leaders of communities within cemeteries, and never in those of commoners. The choice of one or other form of horse burial, however, was not linked to the wealth of the buried person, and varies even within the same cemeteries. None of the hypothetical interpretations for variations of this practice can be substantiated. It is therefore not known why partial or symbolic horse burial was preferred in any given burial. A later Christian chronicle mentioned the eating of horseflesh as a pagan custom, and it has been argued that the parts of the horses not buried in the graves were consumed at a burial feast.[75] No evidence of the burial of entire horses – practiced by steppe peoples – exists among the Hungarians.

In general, burial practices demonstrate significant variations. Burials in coffins are not unknown, although the majority of corpses were rolled in textiles or mats. A great diversity occurs in the types of food provided for the deceased, and the way in which it was placed in the grave, indicating a belief in some form of afterlife. According to

[73] Widukind, I.38, p. 56; Göckenjan, 'Eid und Vertrag'; N. Berend, *At the Gate of Christendom*, 98–9; cf. Theotmar's letter in Lošek, ed., *Die Conversio Bagoariorum et Carantanorum und der Brief des Erzbischofs Theotmar*, 148.

[74] See Fodor, *Ancient Hungarians*, 31–43, for a summary, and most of the volume itself on individual sites; Visy, ed., *Hungarian Archaeology*, 338–43; N. Berend *et al.*, 'The kingdom of Hungary', 320–2.

[75] *Chronici Hungarici*, 338.

some archaeologists at least part of the trepanations on skulls in graves indicate a belief in a soul that left the body after death, while others identify it as a purely medical practice. A range of evidence is interpreted to suggest widespread fear of the dead that led to divergent methods of protection. These included placing silver plates on the eyes and mouth, tying up corpses and in some cases the mutilation of corpses. These various means most probably were intended to prevent the souls of the dead from returning to harm the living. In some cases, however, the silver eye and mouth pieces on the face-cloth are thought to have been intended to help show the soul the way to the other world. The dead themselves needed to be protected; at least this is the interpretation given to sharp objects (axes, knives, scythes) placed in the graves.

Although according to some hypotheses, Hungarians had extensive contacts with Christianity already prior to their arrival in the Carpathian basin, these cannot be substantiated. The first evidence of significant contact is linked to the conversions of the middle of the tenth century in Byzantium, with no evidence of extensive contacts with Christianity by the population within the area that later became Hungary prior to the late tenth century. The textual evidence of early contacts is tenuous. In some cases, there is no certainty that the people mentioned under a variety of names in the sources are indeed Hungarians. In the more securely identifiable cases, the accounts suggest mostly hostile encounters. Linguistic evidence, of Slavic, including Bulgar-Slav influence in Christian terminology in Hungarian, cannot be precisely dated, nor is it conclusive in pinpointing the area of transmission. Those supposing either early Christianization or early knowledge of Christianity without mass conversion claim that these loan-words entered Hungarian before the conquest, but they may equally have been adopted afterwards. At the end of the ninth century, the Byzantine emperor Leo VI referred to the Hungarians as pagans. The only material evidence relating to religious contacts is a sabretache plate (of Tiszabezdéd), which includes a Greek cross, found in a grave including horse burial according to the pre-Christian rite. The dating of the object is inconclusive; it is not certain that it originates from the period before the Hungarian settlement, and in any case cannot be taken as evidence of widespread Christian influences.[76]

[76] N. Berend *et al.*, 'The kingdom of Hungary', 325–6; Károly Mesterházy, 'A honfoglaló magyarok hitvilága és a monoteizmus', *Acta Musei de János Arany Nominati* 7 (1992), 89–120.

Local Christian populations existed in the Carpathian basin prior to the Hungarian conquest: Carolingian Christianization in the area is well attested. The continuity of some of the pre-conquest population has been demonstrated through the study of burials, the continuous production of certain artefacts such as pottery before and after the conquest, and the survival of Slavic toponyms in Hungary. The influence of Great Moravian Christianity has also been supposed. There is no firm evidence, however, of such local influences leading to widespread acceptance of Latin Christianity among the conquerors. Tenth-century burials show no clear sign of extensive contacts with Christianity (apart from the Byzantine pectoral crosses described earlier). The analysis of objects of trade show that Christian objects constituted a very small segment of imported goods and even these may not have been used as Christian cult objects among the Hungarians. Archaeological excavations of Christian cemeteries and church-building do not offer proof of Christianization prior to the end of the tenth and early eleventh centuries. Various earlier Christian buildings were rebuilt in the eleventh century: in some of these perhaps there was a continuity of cult; in other cases the stones of presumably ruined earlier churches were reused in the construction of new churches in the eleventh century.[77]

Some scholars claim that the Hungarian ruler Taksony initiated the Latin orientation of the dynasty before the 970s, but this is based on a far-fetched interpretation of one sentence in Liudprand's account. More certainly, however, the first western missionary attempts are recorded just before and around 972, although many of these are known from a single vague mention. They include envoys supposedly sent by the pope, by the emperor and by ecclesiastics of German lands. Some, such as Bishop Piligrim of Passau, certainly exaggerated the success of the mission. Piligrim claimed that about 5,000 people converted from the elite and that, as a result of the mission, Christian slaves were allowed to practise their religion. He also recounted that pagans and Christians coexisted peacefully. One cannot take his evidence at face value, however. He was both influenced by literary models and had his own agenda. He may have relied on a biblical *topos* from Isiah, and he was influenced by the Venerable Bede. He also wished to further his ecclesiastical aims of 're-establishing' 'his'

[77] N. Berend *et al.*, 'The kingdom of Hungary', 326–7.

suffragan sees, including Pannonia (which became western Hungary) as heir to Lorch (Lauriacum), in opposition to the archbishop of Salzburg. Others paint a picture of utter failure.[78]

It is clear from several independent sources that the ruler Géza converted to Christianity with his household and started the conversion of the elite, although several controversies surround this initiative which cannot be resolved for lack of data. It is not certain who baptized Géza: Bishop Prunwart of Sankt-Gallen is the likeliest, given that the information (although without giving Géza's name) comes from a monastic necrology. Some scholars instead favour Bishop Bruno of Augsburg (before his elevation to his see) or Adalbert of Prague, but the evidence rests on late and unreliable sources. It is not known whether Géza was baptized together with his son, Hungary's first Christian king István, or whether István was baptized later. István's year of birth is unknown, as is the date of the baptisms, but because Thietmar of Merseburg recorded what is supposed to be István's previous pagan name, Waic (Vajk), scholars have argued that he cannot have been baptized as an infant. It is also uncertain why missionaries initially arrived in Hungary. German sources mention Hungarian envoys present at the imperial court in Quedlinburg at Easter 973; it is usually supposed that these envoys asked for missionaries, but no explicit evidence is available. The motivation of Géza is also debated. Perhaps he feared a German–Byzantine rapprochement; perhaps he was influenced by the discussion concerning the establishment of the bishopric of Prague. Thietmar of Merseburg records a story which, if true, highlights Géza's syncretistic understanding of his new faith: an ecclesiastic at Géza's court reproached him for sacrificing to pagan gods after his conversion, to which Géza responded that it brought him wealth and power.[79]

[78] Liudprand, *Liber de Ottone rege*, ed. Albert Bauer and Reinhold Rau, Fontes ad Historiam Aevi Saxonici Illustrandam, Ausgewählte Quellen zur deutschen Geschichte des Mittelalters 8 (Darmstadt, 1971), 496–523, chap. 6, at 502; Piligrim, [Letter to Pope Benedict VI *c.* 973–4], in *Codex diplomaticus et epistolaris Slovaciae*, ed. Richard Marsina, vol. I (Bratislava, 1971), no. 44, at 42–3; N. Berend *et al.*, 'The kingdom of Hungary', 328–30.

[79] Thietmar of Merseburg IV.59 (at 174), VIII.4 (at 444); N. Berend *et al.*, 'The kingdom of Hungary', 329–31; Csanád Bálint, 'Quedlinburg. Der erste Schritt der Ungarn nach Europa und dessen Vorgeschichte. Sackgassen, Fallen, Wahlmöglichkeiten', in *Der Hoftag in Quedlinburg 973. Von den historischen Wurzeln zum Neuen Europa*, ed. Andreas Ranft (Berlin, 2006), 29–35.

## CONSOLIDATION

In all three polities, internal consolidation was a complex process, tied to the establishment of institutional structures, but also linked to the building of – sometimes ephemeral, sometimes more stable – alliances, the elimination of rivals and power struggles between neighbours. Rulers positioned themselves in the context of neighbouring polities, the Ottonian Empire and Byzantium.

### *Bohemia*

Boleslav I consolidated his power over Bohemia through war and alliances. He subordinated all the lands within the Bohemian basin. Echoes of this struggle are found in Widukind's report concerning the defeat of a certain *subregulus*;[80] this may be read in light of the burning of numerous local strongholds, which archaeological finds substantiate.[81] A brutal internal policy centring on the physical elimination of political opponents gained Boleslav I the nickname 'the Cruel'. He constructed the stronghold in Prague (the Hrad) and installed a network of garrisons which ensured a close surveillance of local leaders. Perhaps only around the north-eastern territory with the main stronghold of Libice did there survive a semi-independent principality, ruled by Duke Slavnik.[82] He may have maintained his position due both to his supposed blood ties with the Prague dynasty[83] and to an appeal to older, tribal tradition of independent political organization of the region. Another possible reason was suggested by Bruno of Querfurt, the hagiographer of Slavnik's son Vojtěch-Adalbert, who wrote that Slavnik was a 'very close relative' of the Saxon Ludolfingian dynasty.[84]

80 Widukind I.35.

81 J. Sláma, 'K počátkům hradské organizace v Čechách', in *Typologie raně feudálních slovanských států* (Prague, 1987), 175–90 (here 182).

82 Archaeological excavations revealed the cross-cultural character of a tribal centre (then ducal residence) in Libice: see Jarmila Justová, 'Kontakty zlické Libice s avarsko-slovanským, karolinským a velkomoravským kulturním okruhem', *Sborník Národního Muzea v Praze. Řada A – Historie* 39, 1–2 (1985), 23–31; Justová, 'The bailey of the ducal residence at Libice-nad-Cidlinou and its hinterland', in *Archeology in Bohemia 1986–1990* (Prague, 1991), 140–5.

83 Třeštík, *Počátky Přemyslovců*, 354, 422.

84 *S. Adalberti Pragensis episcopi et martyris vita altera auctore Brunoni Querfurtensi*, ed. Jadwiga Karwasińska, MPH n.s., 4/2 (Warsaw, 1969), 1–69 (21).

Boleslav I attempted to counterbalance the growing political power of Germany under Henry I by tightening Bohemia's traditional relations with Bavaria, leading to a long-standing alliance. Boleslav continued his father's policy of strategic co-operation with the Polabian Slavs, which lasted for more than two centuries. He also tried to take advantage of German–Hungarian conflicts, and allowed the Magyar plunderers to pass freely as they made their way to Thuringia and further west. Nonetheless, he was forced to accept the suzerainty of Otto I in 950, and resume tribute payments. Bohemian assistance was provided to the German king to defeat the Magyars at Lechfeld in 955.[85] Bohemia fell under the permanent control of the Empire, albeit indirectly. Boleslav also capitalized on the defeat of the Magyars to extend his territory into Moravia and the territory of present-day western Slovakia. Historiographical traditions both in Poland and in Bohemia claim that he also subordinated parts of Silesia and Lesser Poland, based on Ibrāhīm ibn Ya'qūb's claim that *Fraga* and *Cracoa* were the two main centres of Boleslav I. Some historians see this as a continuation of a longer process whereby the Cracow area was brought under subordination, beginning with the reign of Svatopluk of Great Moravia in the late ninth century. None of these hypotheses has yet been corroborated by reliable historical or archaeological evidence; one may conclude similarly about the supposed subordination of south Polish Silesia, first by Great Moravia and later by Bohemia.[86] It is more likely that Silesia and Lesser Poland acted as typical 'buffer/border zones' until the late tenth century. Recently Polish medievalists, mainly archaeologists, have raised doubts on the basis of a lack of archaeological finds even over a vast range of Boleslav's conquests and his long-lasting reign over Silesia and Lesser Poland.[87] The vision of a more or less centralized state, the 'Reich' built by Boleslav I offered by traditional Czech

[85] Widukind III.44.

[86] There is a discussion in P. Urbańczyk, 'Politická příslušnost Slezka v desátém století v nejnovější polské historiografii', in *Dějiny ve věku nejistot: sborník k příležitosti 70. narozenin Dušana Třeštíka*, ed. Jan Klápště, Eva Plešková and Josef Žemlička (Prague, 2003), 292–304.

[87] Andrzej Buko, 'Małopolska czeska i Małopolska polańska', in *Ziemie polskie w X wieku i ich znaczenie w kształtowaniu się nowej mapy Europy*, ed. Henryk Samsonowicz (Cracow, 2000), 150–2; Sławomir Moździoch, 'Slezsko v 10. století', in *Přemyslovský stát kolem roku 1000: na pamét' knížete Boleslava II*, ed. J. polanský, Jiři Slama and Dušan Třeštík (Prague, 2000), 222–4.

historiography,[88] is less plausible than modern historians' attempts to show that Boleslav I's Přemyslid *regnum* in the Bohemian basin was surrounded by a broad tributary zone across which strategic strongholds functioned as military outposts.[89]

Boleslav I the Cruel, and later his son Boleslav II the Pious, sustained friendly relations with the Empire while using every occasion to enlarge the margin of their political independence. Boleslav II alternated between allegiance to the German ruler (for example, attending the imperial Easter *Hoftag* in Quedlinburg in 973,[90] and later acknowledging Otto II's succession) and support of the claims of the Bavarian duke Henry the Quarrelsome (after the death of Otto I in 973, after the defeated Henry sought refuge at Boleslav II's court in 975, and after the death of Otto II in 982).[91] He acted in keeping with a traditional Přemyslid strategy to lever power in Bavaria as a counterbalance to the overwhelming Saxon pressure. This could entail warfare; Otto II invaded Bohemia more than once,[92] and Boleslav II launched several counter-attacks. Such conflict was brought to an end at Easter 986, when Boleslav II (together with Henry the Quarrelsome and Mieszko I) visited the young King Otto III at the imperial *Hoftag* in Quedlinburg. In 987 he married Emma, a cousin of the Bavarian dukes.

The Bohemian Church became a source of new contestation. Boleslav II nominated Vojtěch-Adalbert of the Slavnikid family to

[88] The hypothesis is rooted in the nineteenth-century creation of the modern Czech national consciousness via the works of Fantišek Palacký (1798–1876), as one can read in his monumental series *Dějiny narody českého v Čechách a na Moravě dle původních pramenů*, vol. I, 2nd edn (Prague, 1930), 141–4. Nowadays most leading Czech medievalists agree with a model of a strongly controlled ducal administrative state created by Boleslav I as a result of his military expansion; see Třeštik, 'Von Swatopluk zu Bolesław Chrobry', 127–30; Josef Žemlička, 'Expanze, krize a obnova Čech v letech 935–1055', *Český Časopis Historický* 93 (1995), 205–21 (here 208–9); Třeštík, 'Das Reich der böhmischen Boleslavs und die Krise an der Jahrtausendwende. Zur Charakteristik der frühen Staaten in Mitteleuropa', *Archeologické Rozhledy* 47 (1995), 267–78; or even Jiří Sláma, 'Český kníže Boleslav II', in *Přemyslovský stát kolem roku 1000*, 14.

[89] J. Žemlička, *Čechy v době knižeci (1034–1198)* (Prague, 1997), 40.

[90] Thietmar of Merseburg II.31.

[91] Sobiesiak, *Bolesław II Przemyślida.*

[92] Thietmar of Merseburg III.7.

the bishop's seat in 982.[93] Vojtěch-Adalbert turned out to be a zealous advocate of Christian doctrine and he expected both the Bohemian clergy and the aristocracy to observe the highest moral standards. He also interfered with princely judicial prerogatives.[94] Finally, he provoked an open conflict with Boleslav II.[95] There is some suggestion, too, that he offered support to his own family as they sought to establish a stable political niche between the Přemyslid and Piast states. His oldest brother, Sobeslav, even issued a coin bearing the highly provocative title *DUX*.[96] The bishop also struck his own coins, challenging the ducal monopoly. During the winter of 988, Vojtěch-Adalbert suddenly left his diocese, and later asked for asylum in Rome. In 992, a synod in Rome, led by Pope John XV, ordered Vojtěch-Adalbert to resume his episcopal duties in Bohemia.[97] Yet in late 994, he returned to Rome. Boleslav II seized the Slavnikids' dynastic seat on 28 September 995, murdering four brothers together with their families. He eradicated the semi-independent enclave of Sobeslav, who sought asylum at the Piast court. Boleslav II removed the last challenge to his domination within the Bohemian basin, and also secured access to the silver mines of Kutná Hora. When Pope Gregory V allowed Vojtěch-Adalbert to choose missionary duties instead of returning to his seat,[98] Boleslav II placed first his own brother Christian, a former monk of Regensburg, on the diocesan throne in Prague,[99] and then Thiadag/Dydak, a monk of the Corvey monastery.[100]

Events at the turn of the century demonstrated the need for elites to support a duke, and the limits on ducal power. Boleslav III the Red-haired (Ryšavý, 999–1002 and 1003–4) attempted to secure the throne for his daughter and her husband, and therefore had his brother, Jaromir, castrated, and tried to strangle another brother, Oldřich/Udalrik. As a result, they took refuge at the Bavarian court with their mother, Princess Emma. Soon the duke had set Bishop

93 According to Sobiesiak, *Boleslaw II Przemyślida*, ch. 2, Vojtěch-Adalbert was elected against the will of the duke.

94 *S. Adalberti Pragensis episcopi et martyris vita prior*, ed. Jadwiga Karwasińska, MPH s.n., IV/1 (Warsaw, 1962) (henceforth Vita I), 1–84 at 10.

95 Vita I.12.

96 J. Hašková, 'Slavnikovci v historické výpovédi svých minci', *Archeologicke Rozhledy* 47 (1995), 225–30.

97 Vita I.15. 98 Vita I.22. 99 Cosmas I.30.

100 Thietmar of Merseburg VII.56–8.

Thiadag of Bohemia against him too; Thiadag escaped to Meissen in order to request help from Margrave Ekkehard.[101] The Bohemian nobles expelled the duke and offered power to a certain Vladyvoj (1002–3), probably a relative of the Přemyslids. This resulted in Vladyvoj's decision to accept Bohemia as an imperial fief from the German king, Henry II.[102] When Vladyvoj died, Bolesław the Brave intervened to support the deposed duke. Boleslav III regained the throne and enacted bloody revenge, killing many of his opponents, including his own son-in-law. Opposed to Boleslav III, the Bohemian nobles offered the throne of Prague to Bolesław the Brave (1003).[103] For a short period, Bohemia and Poland formed a personal union.

But Bolesław refused to accept Henry II's request to swear the traditional allegiance of the Bohemian rulers.[104] In addition, earlier he had invaded the regions of Meissen and upper Saxony.[105] Already by February 1004, King Henry II had led an unsuccessful retaliatory expedition to Milzen. In August of that same year, the mutilated Jaromir (1004–12, 1033–4) joined a direct attack on Bohemia.[106] Taken by surprise and deserted by his Bohemian supporters, Bolesław fled Prague. Power returned to the Přemyslids, who sought for ways of strengthening their control. Duke Oldřich (1012–33) used a new form of sacral legitimation of ducal power. One of his coins bore the inscription: *ODALRICUS DUX / REGNET IN PRAGA SANCTA*.[107] Such legitimation had no effect: in 1033, Oldřich was expelled. Henry III ordered a tripartite division of the country among Oldřich, his brother Jaromir (who had ruled from 1004 to 1012) and Oldřich's son, Břetislav. When Oldřich died in November of 1033 and Jaromir was killed, Břetislav I (1034–55) inherited the throne and consolidated his power in both Bohemia and Moravia. To strengthen his position among Czechs and his neighbours, in 1038–9 Břetislav launched an expedition into the Piast lands. He seized the seats of bishoprics in Wrocław, Poznań and Gniezno before returning to Prague. Silesia was incorporated into the Bohemian polity. Besides the usual plundering, Břetislav took the relics of St Vojtěch-Adalbert, his brother Archbishop Radim-Gaudentius and the 'Five Martyr

101 Thietmar of Merseburg V.22–3.

102 J. Žemlička, *Rod Přemyslovců na rozhrani 10. a 11. stoleti* (Prague, 2000), 272.

103 Thietmar of Merseburg V.29–30.

104 Thietmar of Merseburg V.31.

105 Thietmar of Merseburg V.36.

106 Thietmar of Merseburg VI.10.

107 J. Hásková, *Česká mince doby románské* (Cheb, 1975).

Brothers' from Gniezno. St Vojtěch-Adalbert was reburied in the St Vitus rotunda in Prague, perhaps in a bid for an archbishopric. If that was Břetislav's aim, he did not succeed.

Břetislav had twice ignored reminders of the tribute due to the empire from Bohemia and Moravia, with the addition of new tribute owed from Silesia. In June 1040, two German armies invaded Bohemia from Saxony and Bavaria; Břetislav resisted, reinforced with a Hungarian contingent. In the end, his occupation of Silesia was acknowledged. Despite Břetislav I's promise to deliver the tribute personally, the German king Henry III (1039–56) launched a new expedition against Bohemia in 1041, and eventually the duke capitulated. Břetislav I walked barefoot through Regensburg wearing a penitentiary sack and begging for pardon, which was duly granted.[108] He again swore allegiance and held on to Silesia. He also promised to support a planned war against Hungary, which he fulfilled a year later.

Břetislav's activity was the high point of Přemyslid strategy to consolidate power. His military efficiency gained him the Czechs' political – and military – support; he strove for both political and ideological (transferring saints' relics from Gniezno to Prague) domination over neighbours, displayed to contemporaries in an ostentatious manner (the solemn ducal entrance to Prague and procession at the same time with spoils taken from Poland and relics from Gniezno, well remembered by posterity); aimed at a relatively independent position in relation to the Empire. Underneath lay the common problem of all Přemyslid rulers: competition within the family, often used against dukes by their enemies. The only way to stay in charge was to gain solid authority among the nobility and lesser warriors (see Chapter 5).

Břetislav I failed in his attempts to rule without imperial supervision and dominate his northern neighbour. But as a result of his and his predecessors' deeds, the Bohemian polity was acknowledged commonly as a powerful, stable and separate socio-political organism. Strong relations to the Empire did not evolve in annexation of the realm. And although Bolesław I the Brave c. 1000 dominated his Bohemian neighbours both politically and ideologically, they survived as a separate polity on the central European political stage.

[108] *Annales Altahenses Maiores*, ed. E. Von Oetele MGH SRG, 20 (Hanover, 1891), 795–6.

## *Poland*

Mieszko I initially followed a strategy similar to that of the Bohemian duke towards the Ottonian empire, switching allegiance between the ruler and the Bavarian duke Henry the Quarrelsome. Mieszko I may have been acting in solidarity with his Bohemian brother-in-law, but he too stood to benefit from limiting the increases in Saxon power. In 982, however, Bohemian–Polish co-operation lasted only a short while: Mieszko I soon became a supporter of the widowed Empress Theophano, who fought for the claims of her infant son Otto III. Mieszko's subsequent loyal co-operation with the empire is best demonstrated by his participation in the German invasions into Bohemia in 985–6.[109]

To stabilise his political position Mieszko relied extensively on marriage alliances. After the death of Dobrava, in 980 he married Oda, the daughter of Dietrich/Teoderich, margrave of the Northern March. Between 980 and 984, Mieszko I gave his daughter Sventoslava-Gunhild/Sigrid in marriage to the still-pagan Swedish ruler Erik Sägersal (?–995). His son Bolesław Chrobry married in 984 a daughter of the Meissen Margrave Rikdag and in 986/987 a Hungarian princess (both were sent home), and finally the south Sorabian princess, Emnild.

In the late 980s Mieszko gained control over Cracow and most of Lesser Poland; he supposedly subordinated Wrocław along with the larger part of Silesia, all the while defending his territorial gains against Bohemian counter-action. He also controlled Western and Eastern Pomerania along with their ports at Szczecin and Gdańsk. At the end of his life, consolidation may have been threatened by rivalry between his sons from two different marriages. After Mieszko I's death his younger sons were expelled with their mother Oda by the victorious son of Dobrava, Bolesław the Brave.[110] The latter tried to establish privileged relations with elites of Bohemia. Early in 997, Vojtěch-Adalbert arrived in Poland together with his half-brother Radim-Gaudentius.[111] Their older brother Sobeslav had found asylum there in 995. Thus Bolesław the Brave hosted at his court three surviving Slavnikid brothers. He even promoted the Czech duke and saint,

[109] *Annales Hildesheimenses* a. 985, 986. [110] Thietmar of Merseburg IV.58.

[111] *S. Adalberti Pragensis episcopi et martyris vita altera auctore Brunoni Querfurtensi*, ed. Jadwiga Karwasińska, MPH s.n., 4/2 (Warsaw, 1969) (henceforth Vita II), 1–69 (at 19).

his maternal great-uncle Václav, to the position of first patron of his own state. One of his first coins bore the inscription: *VENCIEZLAVUS.*[112] Like his father, Bolesław was keen in his policy of strengthening relations with all his powerful neighbours. His sister, the wife of the Swedish king Erik, Sventoslava-Gunhild, after the death of her first husband married Sven Forkbeard, the king of Denmark. Bolesław's close associations with Scandinavia find clear evidence in the parallel production of coins minted in Norway, Denmark, Sweden and Poland. According to numismatic analysis, Bolesław the Brave, Sven Forkbeard, Olav Trygvason and Olaf Skötkonung all issued their first coins of similar appearance and content around the year 995.

Bolesław's greatest accomplishment occurred in 1000, when he achieved the elevation of his political status to the rank of the highest imperial aristocracy, the abolition of the obligation to pay tribute to the emperor and the creation of a complete church province with archdiocese and four bishoprics whose territories covered his realm. He was then not just another mighty ruler at the eastern border of the Empire: he had become a full member of Christendom's political elite, stabilizing the eastern borders of the imperial zone of interests. His position was contested by imperial aristocracy from the very beginning. The archbishops of Magdeburg never accepted the independence of the Polish Church.[113] Bishop Thietmar of Merseburg expressed his doubts about the legality of Otto III's decision.[114] After the death of Otto III his situation became more complicated, but even then Bolesław the Brave may have entertained ideas of creating a unified Polish–Bohemian polity. He accepted the throne of Prague at the demand of Bohemian nobles (1003–4). The experiment, however, was short-lived: as a result of conflict with Henry II, Bolesław had to flee Prague in 1004.[115]

The conflict had just begun and the stakes were high for Bolesław: maintaining his newly achieved status or being degraded to the position of dependent ruler, as his father had been shortly after 963.

[112] Stanisław Suchodolski, *Początki mennictwa w Europie Środkowej, Wschodniej i Północnej* (Wrocław, 1971), Fig. 83.

[113] P. Urbańczyk, 'Paliusz Gaudentego', in *Viae historicae: księga jubileuszowa dedykowana Profesorowi Lechowi A. Tyszkiewiczowi*, ed. M. Goliński and S. Rosik (Wrocław, 2001a), 242–60; also Urbańczyk, *Trudne początki Polski*, ch. 12.

[114] Thietmar of Merseburg IV.45 (*ut spero legitime*).

[115] Thietmar of Merseburg VI.14.

After the first period of long wars in a formal agreement adopted in February 1013 at Magdeburg, the Polish duke was permitted to rule over Lusatia and Milzen, as a formal vassal of the German king.[116] The agreement was sealed by the marriage of Bolesław the Brave's son and heir Mieszko to Richeza, the niece of the late Otto III. Yet this did not mean a stable peace between the Polish and German rulers. In February 1014 Bolesław refused to provide military support for the king's expedition to Italy.[117] He also ignored the invitation to the Easter *Hoftag* at Quedlinburg in 1015, which provoked war with the emperor.[118] After heavy fighting, the emperor was forced to retreat and to sign a new peace in Bautzen/Budziszyn on 30 January 1018, in which Bolesław's rights over Milzen, Lusatia and Moravia were again acknowledged. This treaty was strengthened with the duke's marriage to the late margrave Ekkehard's daughter, Oda.[119] As a result, Bolesław intervened in Rus', after Grand Duke Yaroslav imprisoned Bolesław the Brave's son-in-law, Svyatopolk, in 1018.[120] Bolesław seized Kiev and placed Svyatopolk on the throne of the grand dukes.[121] He also regained control over eastern Lesser Poland, which had been held by Rus' since 981.

Bolesław's participation in a series of prolonged wars from which he emerged victorious suggests that his military force was effectively organized. Without doubt, his standing inside his realm relied on efficient military skills and the ability to provide his elite with goods, ensuring their privileged position. He also created a system of ducal seats in the western style (*palatia*) which accentuated his unique position in society. In addition, his coinage seem to indicate that its primary function was as a symbolic demonstration of his status as Christian monarch. In the end, Bolesław achieved the royal title (1025), which after his sudden death was taken over by his son, Mieszko II (also 1025).[122] The latter was not so successful as his

[116] *Die Annales Quedlinburgenses*, ed. Martina Giese, MGH, Scriptores rerum germanicarum in usum scholarum separatim editi, 72 (Hanover, 2004), a. 1013.

[117] Thietmar of Merseburg VI.92.

[118] Thietmar of Merseburg VII.21–3; VII.59–64.

[119] Thietmar of Merseburg VIII.1. [120] Thietmar of Merseburg VII.65.

[121] *The Russian Primary Chronicle: the Laurentian Text*, tr. and ed. Samuel Hazzard Cross and Olgerd P. Sherbowitz-Wetzor (Cambridge, 1953), p. 132, a. 6526 (1018).

[122] *Annales Quedlinburgenses* a. 1025; Wipo, *Gesta Chuonradi imperatoris*, ed. H. Bresslau, Die Werke Wipos, MGH SRG, 61 (1915), pp. 3–62, IX.

father but his ways of consolidating power and gaining authority among neighbours were almost the same as his father's. Up to the final (and lost) war of 1031 he was even on better terms with the imperial aristocracy. In the Empire, some despised him as a usurper or praised him as an ideal Christian king, but all treated his realm as a stable political entity and him as the important political player.

### *Hungary*

Géza's son István continued the process of concentrating power in the hands of a sole ruler, and was crowned king in 1000/1. At times it is impossible to disentangle István's real power from later legend. Under his successors, he was soon venerated as the founder of the kingdom, and was canonized in 1083. Throughout the Middle Ages, when individuals or groups wished to prove their entitlement to possessions or rights, they often attributed the original grant to István. In many such cases, there is historical proof of the substantially later origin of the privileges or possessions claimed. In the modern age, István became the founder of the Hungarian state, and was used for nationalist causes, notably claiming that all of István's realm rightfully belonged to the modern Hungarian state. Nor has the political utility of the first king declined in contemporary Hungary: the government moved the 'Holy Crown of Hungary', which used to be identified (certainly erroneously, as detailed below) as István's crown, into the parliament building as a symbol of the Hungarian state in 2000.

Scraping away such accretions, one can rectify the picture to some extent. Instead of creating the 'Hungarian state' with fully fledged territorial and administrative paraphernalia, István extended his personal power as much as he could, sometimes through brutal means. He founded dioceses, though not the ten traditionally attributed to him. He started the creation of counties, but did not leave a fully formed network of counties covering the whole kingdom at his death. He issued legislation and charters, had coins minted, probably introduced the tithe and gained recognition as the king of Hungary. It is important to remember, however, that his successors continued and modified many of these beginnings. What remains impossible to tell is the extent to which many of the earliest medieval sources we have already distort the picture: both chronicle and hagiographical accounts were composed at a time (late eleventh and early twelfth centuries) when Hungary's kings László (Ladislas) and Kálmán (Coloman) were defining and defending their own positions against both pope and emperor. It is therefore impossible to verify in many instances to what extent and how the texts composed at the time reinterpreted István's reign and various actions, in order to construct a historical memory that would serve contemporary rulers.[123]

The dynasty's conversion to Christianity contributed in important ways to royal power, giving access to personnel (warriors and ecclesiastics from the west who provided expertise and introduced forms of governance and institutions) and to models that could be followed (such as administrative territorial divisions or the use of writing). István was also recognized as a Christian king, and even praised for his Christian piety and for the help he provided to pilgrims travelling to Jerusalem through his kingdom.

István went much further than his father in destroying traditional political structures. Through his marriage to the Bavarian Gisela, sister of Henry II (later the emperor), he was able to garner military support from German lands: narrative sources name various knights in István's army. István used his military force to break the power of rival local leaders. The first of these, according to the Hungarian Chronicle, was Koppány, who contested his right to the succession, trying to marry the widowed Sarolt, István's mother. Apparently he invoked the traditional pattern of succession after Géza's death: that a suitable older male member of the lineage rather than the son (István) should succeed the ruler. According to the unverifiable account, Koppány was defeated in battle and quartered; his body parts were sent to various cities for public display.

Others, relatives or not, who did not pose such a direct challenge, also became the target of István's wars. The exact reconstruction of the events is an open question, but the historicity of István's building of power through military means is not. Problems surround the dating of some of the events, and some elements are debatable (for example, the identification of Gyula as István's uncle Procui, mentioned by Thietmar of Merseburg as driven from his lands, or the historical truth

[123] László Veszprémy, 'The invented eleventh century of Hungary', in *The Neighbours of Poland in the Eleventh Century*, ed. Przemysław Urbańczyk (Warsaw, 2002), 137–54; Veszprémy, ed., *Szent István és az államalapítás*; N. Berend *et al.*, 'The kingdom of Hungary'; György Györffy, *King Saint Stephen of Hungary* (Highland Lakes, NJ, 1994). The last three items provide detailed information on all other aspects of István's reign dicussed below.

behind the Ajtony story). István defeated his maternal uncle, Gyula, in 1003. That he was a *de facto* autonomous ruler who was subjugated is suggested by the terminology of the *Annales Hildesheimenses*, which called Gyula *rex* and his territory *regnum*.[124] The exact location of his territory within Transylvania has been disputed.[125] If, as supposed, this Gyula descended from the one who converted to Byzantine Christianity in the middle of the tenth century, he may also have been Christian, but there is no clear evidence of his ancestry and of either Gyula's religious adhesion. One source claimed that Gyula's *regnum* was converted by István, while later Hungarian sources described Gyula as pagan, resisting conversion to Christianity.[126] It may be that Christianization took off only after conquest in the area, but it is equally possible that later sources distorted reality, portraying all István's enemies as having a religious motive in their opposition to a holy king.

Medieval sources describe István's victory over Ajtony (Achtum), a convert to Byzantine Christianity.[127] Modern scholars date the event to either 1008, or just before 1030. Legendary accretions, notably on the details of the war against Ajtony, do not necessarily discredit the kernel of the story, although our knowledge is on no more certain grounds than with most other events described in this chapter. Ajtony's links to Byzantium were not exclusively religious; the hagiographical text, the *Legenda Maior* of St Gerard, which may be based on eleventh-century material, and which is the main source for his story, explicitly describes Ajtony as politically dependent on the Empire. The Hungarian Chronicle also describes István's victory over Keán: according to some historians this is an erroneous rendering of the war against the ruler of Bulgaria, according to others, Keán was an independent Bulgarian territorial ruler in Transylvania, and yet others

[124] *Annales Hildesheimenses*, a. 1003, 29 (also copied in *Annales Altahenses Maiores* a. 1003, at 16).

[125] Benkő, *Az ómagyar nyelv*, 35–41; Florin Curta, 'Transylvania around AD 1000', in *Europe around the Year 1000*, ed. Przemysław Urbańczyk (Warsaw, 2001), 141–65.

[126] *Annales Hildesheimenses* a. 1003, 29; *P. magistri* 65; *Chronici Hungarici*, 314–15.

[127] *P. Magistri*, 50, 89–90; *Legenda Sancti Gerhardi episcopi*, ed. Emericus Madzsar, in *SRH*, vol. II, 461–506 (at 487, 489–92); see Benkő, *Az ómagyar nyelv*, 100–105, on the linguistic development of the Turkic name Achtum to the Hungarian form found in toponyms, Ajton/Ajtony. Curta, 'Transylvania around AD 1000', rejects the story as completely fabricated, but without a full knowledge of the secondary literature.

admit that nothing definite can be known concerning him, not even whether he existed.[128] The territories of the vanquished enemies were incorporated into the realm. Therefore the subjugation of territorial lords, whether Christian or pagan, was a means of increasing royal power.

Other opponents were disposed of as well: István's relative Vazul was blinded and his sons were exiled to eliminate them as potential rivals to the throne after the death of István's son and heir Imre (Emeric, d.1031). Conspirators who were discovered plotting to assassinate the king were mutilated.[129] Although narrative sources written after István's canonization usually portray his enemies as pagans or as inspired by the devil, what was at stake was the process of extending territorial power, and eventually creating sole rulership, with the ruler designating his successor.

István's coronation as king was both a culmination and a symbol of his success in this undertaking. The coronation did not so much confer power on him as demonstrate both internally and externally that he had reached the apogee of power, which at the time was conceived of as kingship. His father Géza was already called *rex* (king) in recognition of his real power in some contemporary sources, although he was never crowned; similarly, István's power was acknowledged, rather than created, by the coronation. Controversy surrounds the details of his coronation, in conjunction with the elevation of the Polish ruler and the creation of the independent Hungarian and Polish archbishoprics of Esztergom and Gniezno. The role of Emperor Otto III has been much disputed: whether he initiated a grandiose plan for a new Christian empire in which these rulers would gain their position, or simply reacted to local demands.[130] In any case, the role of Pope Sylvester II was more limited, contrary to the widespread idea that he sent István his crown. That story was invented by Hartvic, who wrote a *vita* (saint's life) of István *c.* 1100, for particular political purposes connected to the context of his own times. It vindicated independence from both the

[128] *Chronici Hungarici*, 315.

[129] *Legenda S. Stephani regis minor*, 399; *Chronici Hungarici*, 313–14, 320 (attributing the deed to Queen Gisela's order).

[130] Fried, *Otto III und Boleslaw Chrobry*; Gerd Althoff, *Otto III* (University Park, PA, 2003); Gieysztor, *L'Europe nouvelle autour de l'an Mil*; articles in Wieczorek and Hinz, eds., *Europe's Centre: Handbook*, 481–539.

Empire and the papacy and buttressed royal rights over the Church, justified by divine command given to the pope to send a crown, and the assertion – found objectionable by Innocent III – that István ruled by both laws. Thietmar of Merseburg described the coronation as a result of the emperor's favour and encouragement. This was even used to argue that the emperor encouraged the pope to send a crown, something that has no basis in fact.[131] Indeed, Hartvic's main source, the *Legenda Maior* of István, mentions only a papal blessing prior to the coronation. Even Pope Gregory VII, who argued that Hungary was subject to the Holy See because it was offered to St Peter by King István, said nothing of a papal crown sent to the first king of the realm, although it would have been a crucial proof for his argument.[132]

The regalia that exist today mostly survive from later periods, although the so-called coronation mantle was indeed made under István's reign, but as a chasuble rather than a royal mantle. The lance, which was clearly a significant element of the royal regalia at this time, appearing on one of the first coins with the inscription 'lancea regis' as well as on István's portrait on the chasuble, was probably a copy of the imperial lance given to the king by the emperor, as in the Polish case. It disappeared, and was never replaced, after Henry III's victory over King Samuel Aba (1044); Henry sent the regalia including the lance to Rome. The existing crown, first called 'holy crown' in the middle of the thirteenth century, is made up of two separate parts, the so-called Greek and Latin crowns. The Greek crown dates from the mid

[131] *Legenda S. Stephani regis ab Hartvico episcopo conscripta*, ed. Emma Bartoniek, in *SRH*, ed. Imre Szentpétery, vol. II, 401–40 (at 413–14); Eng. tr. with introduction Nora Berend, 'Hartvic, *Life of King Stephen of Hungary*', in *Medieval Hagiography: An Anthology*, ed. Thomas Head (New York, 2000), 375–98; Gábor Thoroczkay, 'Anmerkungen zur Frage der Entstehungszeit der Hartvik-Legende des Stephan des Heiligen', *Specimina nova: Pars prima, sectio mediaevalis* 1 (2001), 107–31; Thietmar of Merseburg IV.59 (at 174); e.g. Gyula Kristó, *Szent István király* (Budapest, 2001), 52–8.

[132] *Legenda S. Stephani regis maior*, ed. Emma Bartoniek, in *SRH*, ed. Imre Szentpétery, vol. II, 377–92 (at 384); Franz-Josef Schmale, ed., *Gregorii papae VII Epistolae Selectae*, Fontes litem de Investitura Illustrantes, Ausgewählte Quellen zur deutschen Geschichte des Mittelalters 12a (Darmstadt, 1978), 110, no. 33, and Erich L. E. Caspar, ed., *Das Register Gregors VII*, MGH Epistolae Selectae (Berlin, 1920), II, 13, p. 145; László Veszprémy, 'The Holy Crown of Saint Stephen', in Attila Zsoldos, ed., *Saint Stephen and His Country. A Newborn Kingdom in Central Europe: Hungary* (Budapest, 2001), 95–110; N. Berend *et al.*, 'The kingdom of Hungary', 343.

1070s based on the rulers represented on it (King Géza I of Hungary, 1074–7, and Emperor Michael VII, 1071–8). It has been suggested that it was adapted from an already existing crown in Byzantium before being sent as a gift to Géza himself as a sign of his subordination to the emperor or, according to others, to his wife, who was Byzantine. The 'Latin crown' was in fact not a crown in itself (what object it comes from has not been established, although hypotheses abound); it became the cruciform upper part of the existing crown, with Latin inscriptions and the portraits of apostles. Many scholars advocated a late twelfth–early thirteenth-century date, but recent argument is in favour of its redating to the first half of the eleventh century, based on its epigraphy. The construction of the present crown from these two parts is usually thought to have occurred during the reign of Béla III (1172–96). Scholarly debates as well as unfounded speculations continue to surround the origin of the crown. The sceptre is now usually dated to the early eleventh century, based on its similarity to sceptres of Emperor Henry II and Rudolf III of Burgundy from that period. The existing sword and orb are late medieval.[133]

István exercised royal power through administrative means as well. A variety of innovations linked to governance, administrative territorial division, ecclesiastical organization, written legislation and charters were introduced, probably through immigrant clerics. The division of lands into districts around forts ('castles') and into counties was initiated during István's reign (or, according to some historians, earlier). Royal lands were organised into castle districts (*várispánság*) around a system of strongholds under a royal representative (*ispán*, *comes*). These strongholds were not very large; they were not meant to shelter the population of the whole surrounding territory. Most earthen forts that have been excavated to date were built using the same structure and technique: wooden structures were built into the

[133] Endre Tóth and Károly Szelényi, *The Holy Crown of Hungary: Kings and Coronations* (Budapest, 1999); Éva Kovács and Zsuzsa Lovag, *The Hungarian Crown and Other Regalia*, 2nd edn (Budapest, 1988); Veszprémy, 'The Holy Crown of Saint Stephen'; Ernő Marosi, 'La "couronne latine"', *Acta historiae artium Academiae Scientiarum Hungaricae* 43 (2002), 72–82; János M. Bak, 'Holy Lance, Holy Crown, Holy Dexter: sanctity of insignia in medieval East Central Europe', in Bak, *Studying Medieval Rulers and Their Subjects* (Farnham, 2010), no. VI, 56–65; Tibor Kovács and István Bardoly, eds., *The Coronation Mantle of the Hungarian Kings* (Budapest, 2005).

earthen rampart. The outer side of the wall was steep, the inner side sloped. A few cases showed that a wooden palisade was placed on top of the earthen wall. The contemporary term was *castrum* or *civitas*, vernacular *vár*. The uniformity of techniques and need for manpower to construct such forts led scholars to suppose that the forts were built according to royal orders. The archaeological dating of these strongholds may be possible with more precision in the future: no absolute proof exists that they date from István's reign. Although they may well date from the early eleventh century, some may go back to earlier periods. Whereas some of these forts were the seats of counties established by the king, the function of some of the others is unknown.[134]

Counties (*comitatus*, *megye*), administrative territorial divisions, were put in place around strongholds where the *ispán*s had military and judicial roles. The surrounding territory was organized and brought under the control of the *comes* residing in the stronghold, although not every stronghold functioned as such a central place. The borders of the county territories were recorded with great precision from early on. Not all the land was organized in this way, however, nor was there a symmetrical pattern applied throughout; the distance between strongholds varied greatly, and so did the size of counties. According to one view, some early large counties were tribal territories of chieftains whose power survived at least until the reign of István.[135] It is usually supposed that István based this organization on Frankish examples transmitted through his contacts with the empire, whence ecclesiastics and warriors came to Hungary, transporting ideas of territorial organization. Because of the adoption of Slavic terminology in Hungarian (*megye* – county; *ispán* – 'count', royal representative), scholars have debated whether this organization predated the Hungarians' arrival and was adopted by them, or whether the local population transmitted a terminology that subsequently came to designate new realities (e.g. the original meaning of *megye* was border, but its new meaning within the kingdom was a unit of administrative

[134] Bóna, *Az Árpádok korai várai*; István Bóna, 'Várak Szent István korában', in Veszprémy, ed., *Szent István*, 296–301; Visy, ed., *Hungarian Archaeology*, 328–31; Fodor, *Ancient Hungarians*, 57–61.

[135] Attila Zsoldos, 'A megyeszervezés kezdetei a Magyar királyságban: az óriás és az átlagos nagyságú megyék kérdéséhez', in *A Veszprém megyei levéltár kiadványai* 22 (Veszprém, 2010), 299–318.

territorial organization). The latter explanation is favoured in Hungarian scholarship.

The first mentions of *comitatus* organization from the early years of the eleventh century (1002–9) refer to the western parts of the realm, the areas under the control of István. Historians have advanced two widely divergent explanations concerning the system of land divisions and, within each, have provided several alternative interpretations on questions of detail. According to one, István I created two separate organizations: the system of castle districts (*várispánság*, *comitatus*) and the system of counties (*megye*, *provincia*). The first was the military, the second the civil organizational division of territories. Some of the lands of a castle district could lie in one county and others in another: they were not under the jurisdiction of the county *ispán*, but the castle *ispán*. According to another explanation, only one system of territorial divisions existed, combining military and civil functions; castle district (*várispánság*) and county were either synonyms, or the castle district was a smaller subdivision within the county. A revised version of the first explanation claims that the districts of royal castle lands (*várispánság*) on the one hand, and the county – which included the royal lands as well as other, ecclesiastical and lay estates – on the other hand, were closely linked to each other at the time of István I, but gradually grew more distinct. According to this view, initially the same royal stronghold (with its royal representative, the *ispán*), which was the centre of the castle district, also served as the centre of the county, and both castle district and county could be called *comitatus*. Each county included at least one castle district, but a castle district contained not only lands within the county, but also some lands outside it, and could exist independently of counties. Royal counties did not have a separate officialdom from the castle district; the castle district's *ispán*, his deputies and his officers governed the counties as well. According to recent views, about thirty counties existed by the time of István's death. The process of county-formation continued over three centuries.[136]

[136] Gyula Kristó, *A vármegyék kialakulása Magyarországon* (Budapest, 1988); several articles in Veszprémy, ed., *Szent István*, 420–81; articles in Wieczorek and Hinz, eds., *Europe's Centre: Handbook*, 373–93; Gyula Kristó, 'Die Entstehung der Komitatsorganisation unter Stephan der Heiligen', *Études historiques hongroises* 1 (1990), 13–25.

The counties at first also developed jointly with ecclesiastical territorial organization. It is likely that initially the territorial organization of bishoprics corresponded to that of the counties. The stronghold that was the *ispán*'s seat also housed a church and, according to the legislation, its priest was to co-operate with the *ispán* in enforcing Christian observance. Many of these priests eventually became archdeacons, whose function was administrative. Later, this territorial correspondence ceased, as both counties and ecclesiastical divisions (bishoprics and archdeaconries) proliferated and the territorial extent of many counties changed.

Although according to some historians the first bishopric (Veszprém) was founded by Géza, it was István who established at least all other early dioceses, and more probably all early ones including Veszprém. In the first years of the eleventh century, the bishoprics of Győr and Veszprém and the archbishopric of Esztergom provided the ecclesiastical structure of lands under the rule of the dynasty. That they were all west of the Danube shows that this was the only area where the Árpáds' rule was stable from the beginning. In the territories that István attached to his lands as king, he also established the dioceses of Transylvania, Pécs, Kalocsa, Eger and Csanád. Other dioceses were established from the middle of the eleventh century by István's successors. István probably established the bishop's tithe, although the relevant decree attributed to him may be a later interpolation in the surviving texts. Incontrovertible evidence of the tithe's existence comes only from the second half of the eleventh century.[137]

The establishment of Greek and Latin monasticism – the foundation of the Benedictine monastery of Pannonhalma, and the convent of nuns in Veszprémvölgy (which was probably Greek) – is attributed by some to Géza and others to István. István certainly founded all the other earliest Benedictine monasteries at Pécsvárad, Zalavár, Bakonybél, Somlóvásárhely and Zobor, and perhaps founded or gave donations to communities of Greek monks (Szávaszentdemeter, Pentele). Other Greek monasteries were founded by local potentates. Later in the

[137] Gábor Thorockay, 'The dioceses and bishops of Saint Stephen', in Zsoldos, ed., *Saint Stephen*, 49–68; articles in Wieczorek and Hinz, eds., *Europe's Centre: Handbook*, 394–426, on Christianization; László Koszta, 'L'organisation de l'Église chrétienne en Hongrie', in Csernus and Korompay, eds., *Les Hongrois et l'Europe*, 293–311.

eleventh century royal foundations of both Benedictine and Greek monasteries continued.[138]

The building of royal seats and monumental expressions of royal power such as churches were central to rulership. Some are known from narrative sources but none survives from the earliest period of kingship. Part of a chapel belonging to the royal palace of Fehérvár (later Székesfehérvár) used to be thought to have been built during István's reign, but even that has now been redated to a later period. The royal basilica at Fehérvár was the most important ecclesiastical building linked to the new royal power. It became the burial church of István and his son Imre, and subsequently other kings, and housed the regalia. Yet the basilica constructed during István's reign does not survive in its original form. The sarcophagus of István, recarved from a Roman sarcophagus, perhaps not for his burial in 1038 but for his canonization in 1083, displays Christian symbolism.[139]

Scholars often emphasize that, while medieval coins were practical objects for economic purposes, their imagery and inscriptions also conveyed symbolic significance. The minting of coins was a royal monopoly in Hungary, and started with the silver deniers of István. Two types are known from his reign, containing Christian and royal symbolism. The first carried the inscription 'LANCEA REGIS' with an arm holding a lance, and 'REGIA CIVITAS' with what has been variously interpreted as a church or a crown on the reverse. The later type is inscribed 'STEPHANUS REX' and 'REGIA CIVITAS' with crosses. Thus the coins could also be a vehicle of royal power. Given their similarity to Bavarian coinage, these coins are thought to be influenced by the Bavarian types, perhaps through the activity of Bavarian minters in Hungary. Minting, mining, customs duties, the sale of salt, and fines stipulated by legislation provided royal revenues, supplementing those from the extensive royal lands.[140]

138 Imre Takács, ed., *Mons Sacer 996–1996: Pannonhalma 1000 éve*, 3 vols. (Pannonhalma, 1996); Takács, ed., *Paradisum plantavit: Bencés monostorok a középkori Magyarországon Benedictine Monasteries in Medieval Hungary* (Pannonhalma, 2001); Beatrix F. Romhányi, *Kolostorok és társaskáptalanok a középkori Magyarországon* (Budapest, 2000).

139 Articles in Wieczorek and Hinz, eds., *Europe's Centre: Handbook*, 394–426.

140 László Kovács, *A kora-Árpád-kori magyar pénzverésről: érmetani és régészeti tanulmányok a Kárpát-medence I. (Szent) István és II. (Vak) Béla uralkodása közötti időszakának (1000–1141) érméiről*, Varia Archaeologica Hungarica 7 (Budapest,

The use of writing in governance both had practical value and could be a form of royal display. A very limited literacy in runic script existed among probably only a part of the population before Christianization. István, however, introduced Latin literacy in the service of royal government. The first known charter, dated 1002, and three others are generally accepted as originally dating from the reign of István: these are donations or foundations, and survived in later interpolated copies. Based on the analysis of the style of these charters, scholars identified a scribe from the imperial chancery of Otto III who may be responsible for the production of the charters of István; he seems to have moved to Hungary and imported the usages of the imperial chancery. Early charters were issued to ecclesiastical institutions, which benefited from the donations registered in writing. Subsequently, many individuals and groups attempted to derive their rights from the first king, even forging charters to prove this. A king's mirror, the so-called *Admonitions* of István, was written most probably by a foreign cleric during the king's reign, for his son Imre. It focused on the king's duties and the main aspects of royal power, including the role of the church.[141]

Written legislation, a significant innovation, was also introduced during István's reign.[142] Moreover, earlier and more extensive legislation survives from Hungary than from most of the other polities of central Europe and Scandinavia where new Christian rulers were centralizing power. The surviving texts, however, are not the same as the original legislation. Only later copies of the laws exist, and they each contain a somewhat different text. The earliest manuscript is the late twelfth-century *Admont Codex*, which contains two books of laws, divided into fifty chapters (thirty-five and fifteen chapters), without any mention of István's name. Nine fifteenth- and sixteenth-century

1997); László Kovács, 'Coinage and other forms of currency in Hungary', in Wieczorek and Hinz, eds., *Europe's Centre: Handbook*, 125–6.

[141] György Györffy, *Diplomata Hungariae Antiquissima, vol. I, 1000–1131* (Budapest, 1992); Gábor Thorockay, 'La storiografia del Diploma di Pannonhalma di Santo Stefano', in *Mille anni di storia dell'arciabbazia di Pannonhalma*, eds. József Pál and Ádám Somorjai (Rome, 1997), 39–82; Előd Nemerkényi, *Latin Classics in Medieval Hungary: Eleventh Century* (Budapest, 2004), ch. 3.

[142] János M. Bak, György Bónis and James Ross Sweeney, eds. and trs., *The Laws of the Medieval Kingdom of Hungary*, vol. I, *1000–1301* (Bakersfield, CA, 1989), the laws of István at 1–11; Monika Jánosi, *Törvényalkotás a korai Árpád-korban* (Szeged, 1996); Gábor Hamza, 'Les lois de Saint Étienne et l'Europe', in Gábor Hamza, ed., *Sanctus Stephanus et Europa* (Budapest, 1991), 15–23.

codices contain the *Admonitions* as the first book of the laws, and fifty-five chapters as the second. Two chapters (bk I, 16 and 21) can be found only in the *Admont Codex*; six (bk I, 48–53) only in the later manuscripts. At least some if not all of these six are probably later interpolations, most likely from the twelfth century, given the similarity of the texts to King Kálmán's laws. The two manuscript versions might also represent two different eleventh–twelfth-century redactions; that is, a new redaction of the first book might have been prepared during Kálmán's reign.

The composition of the laws has been debated: some historians claim that the two books of laws currently existing were promulgated in this format during István's reign, one issued early in the reign, the second *c.* 1030–8. Others argue that the legislation was in fact issued piecemeal over the course of the reign, but was then collected: the first composition before 1038; the other, incorporating decrees that were not included in the first book, after István's death, perhaps during the reign of András I (Endre, Andrew; 1046–60). The second argument is more convincing, given the fact that within each law-book there are contradictory regulations. The legislation encompassed Christianization, issues of social order and various civil and criminal matters, from servitude to murder. It also included explicit protection for the person and goods of the king: nobody was to deprive the king of his goods, warriors and servants; if somebody sought to kill the king or betray the kingdom, the punishment was death.

Extensive parts of the legislation issued during István's reign, and those of his successors, concerned the introduction of Christianity and the eradication of previous practices.[143] István's laws stipulated the acceptance of Christianity by the entire population. The infrastructure of churches was to be put in place. Ten villages were to build a church and give animals and servants to it; the king provided vestments and altarcloths, while the bishop supplied priests and books. Little is known of the reality of church-building programmes: it is impossible to tell how many such churches came into being during István's reign. István's legislation emphasized adherence to a set of requirements, stipulating punishments for the infringement of Christian observance. Thus, numerous decrees protected the celebration of Sundays and feastdays. The oxen, horses or tools of those

[143] For a detailed analysis and further bibliography on the rest of this section, see N. Berend *et al.*, 'The kingdom of Hungary'.

working on Sunday were to be confiscated. All were to attend church on Sunday except those guarding the fire; those who did not were to be punished by beating and the shaving off of their hair. Those who disturbed the divine service by murmuring and not paying attention were to receive punishment according to their social rank. Those of higher rank (*maiores*) were to be expelled in disgrace; those of lesser rank (*minores et vulgares*) were to be bound in the narthex of the church and beaten, and their hair was to be shaved off. Fasting was obligatory on Friday and during Ember days; those who ate meat were to be imprisoned for a week, fasting. Deathbed confession was of paramount importance, and those unwilling to confess their sins were to be buried as infidels without divine service and alms. Relatives, if they failed to call a priest to attend the dying, were themselves to be punished. Ecclesiastical and royal power jointly oversaw Christian observance. The bishop judged according to the canons those negligent in their observance in the first instance; those who objected were to be judged in this manner seven times, and then handed over to royal judgement, as the king was ultimately the defender of Christianity. Punishments for various other crimes, such as murder and taking a false oath, also included a component taken from Christian practices, fasting.

In order to create a religious monopoly for Christian priests, others who called on supernatural powers were condemned: *strigae* (witches) were to fast in the first instance; the second time they were branded and the third, handed over to secular judges. *Malefici* (practitioners of black magic) were to be handed over to the family of those they had harmed; divination was punished by whipping.

Christianization entailed changes not simply in religious observance but also in social practices. Some social customs, especially those concerning marriage and sexual conduct, also became the target of Christian laws, as widely attested from other newly converted areas as well. In Hungary, these included the abduction and rape of women, fornication, adultery and the repudiation of one's wife. Christian regulation also struck at an important aspect of pre-Christian identity, by turning the traditional hairstyle (which entailed shaving off the hair at the top of the head) into a sign of humiliation for the non-observance of Christianity: the shaving off of hair was a punishment for non-attendance at church on Sunday, for disturbing the divine services by murmuring in the case of commoners and for fornication.

The dynasty's conversion was a turning point, after which royal power effectively backed the conversion of the entire population. This top-down process of populations converting in the wake of royal baptism was characteristic of many early medieval conversions. Christianization, which started under Géza, intensified during István's reign, with his full support, and Christianity became the official religion of the realm. István employed various means to Christianize his subjects. Bruno of Querfurt and Adémar de Chabannes both mentioned that István Christianized the 'black Hungarians' by force after he defeated them.[144] Missions continued, though it seems not without encountering resistance: contemporary sources mention that a missionary was wounded. Monks participated in Christianizing the population. As shown by the legislation, expectation focused on conformity in behaviour and practice, which was consistent with early medieval Christianity. The *Legenda Maior* of St Gerard, which may or may not include reliable information from the eleventh century, describes baptism coming first, and the teaching of Christian precepts afterwards.[145]

The personnel and materials needed in this early period were imported from abroad. Ecclesiastics were almost exclusively immigrants in the first few decades of the eleventh century, including bishops and monks, from German lands, the Italian peninsula and elsewhere. They also brought books and liturgy to Hungary; liturgical manuscripts show influences from southern German, Lotharingian, northern Italian and other lands (see Chapter 6).

## REVOLTS

Religious change and the centralization of power did not go unchallenged. In Poland and Hungary, rebellions sought to overturn both trends. In Bohemia, both Christianity and rulership had been consolidated earlier.

[144] Bruno of Querfurt, *Epistola Brunonis ad Henricum regem*, ed. Jadwiga Karwasińska, MPH n.s., 4/3 (Warsaw, 1973), 97–106 at 100; *Ademari Cabannensis Chronicon*, ed. Pascale Bourgain, Richard Landes and Georges Pon, Corpus Christianorum Continuatio Mediaeualis 129 (Turnhout, 1999), III.33 (at 155). The identification of the 'black Hungarians' is debated.

[145] *Legenda S. Gerhardi episcopi*, 494.

## *Poland*

Mieszko II (1025–34) was crowned (probably with his father's crown) on 25 December 1025, which was viewed as an usurpation by the new German king and emperor, Conrad II (1024–39).[146] There was also imminent danger for the new monarch from the unresolved claims by his brothers. The older of the two, Bezprim, escaped to Rus', while the younger, Otto, found asylum in Germany; both were eager to claim their share of political power. Through rivarly for the throne and external war, central power disintegrated in Poland in the early 1030s. Mieszko II launched an expedition to Saxony in 1028 with the purpose of encouraging internal German opposition. The emperor retaliated, representing the rights of the expelled Otto, Mieszko's younger brother. This initially brought little success but Mieszko's situation became hopeless when, in 1031, he was attacked simultaneously from three directions: at the eastern fringe of Lesser Poland, Grand Duke Ylaroslav the Wise regained for Rus' the so-called Red Strongholds (*Grody Czerwienskie*); in the south, Oldřich's son Břetislav expanded his control; and to the west Conrad II permanently removed Lusatia and Milzen from Polish control. The emperor also offered support to Mieszko II's older brother, Bezprim (1031–2), who took the throne as the deposed king sought refuge in Bohemia, where he was castrated.[147] The Polish queen Richeza with her infant son Kazimierz found refuge among her relatives in Germany. Bezprim swore allegiance to the emperor and sent his brother's royal insignia to Germany.

In the spring of 1032, Bezprim was killed by rebel nobles who recalled Mieszko II.[148] The German reaction was to force Mieszko to relinquish his royal title and accept a form of co-rule between his younger brother, Otto, and their cousin, Dietrich. Mieszko resumed sole power in 1033, but he himself died in May 1034 after bringing his son back to Poland. Kazimierz the Restorer (1034–58; in exile after his fathers death until 1039) inherited the throne. The growing opposition of nobles resulted in 1034 in the expulsion of Kazimierz. This provoked a period of political chaos. Central power disintegrated and

[146] E.g. *Annales Magdeburgenses*, ed. G.H. Pertz, Monumenta Germaniae Historica, Series Scriptores, vol. 16 (Hanover, 1859), 105–96 a. 1025 and 1030; *Annales Hildesheimenses* a. 1028 and 1030.

[147] *Annales Hildesheimenses* a. 1031; *Galli Anonymi Cronicae* I.17.

[148] *Annales Hildesheimenses* a. 1032.

a pagan reaction resulted in the destruction of a substantial part of the ecclesiastical infrastructure in Silesia, Greater Poland and northern parts of Lesser Poland.

The struggle resulted in the collapse of both ducal and church administration. In the twelfth-century chronicle of Anonymous the vivid account is contained of servants killing their lords and of wild animals taking up residence in the archiepiscopal cathedral at Gniezno.[149] Some researchers argue that there is also archaeological evidence for the collapse of the infrastructure of the rulers' power and anti-Christian sentiment: the remains of a pagan temple discovered in Wrocław. According to them it was built in the winter of 1032–3, atop the destroyed rampart of the royal and episcopal stronghold. Some years later the site was methodically levelled and covered with soil before the stronghold was rebuilt.[150] This interpretation is based on one plank excavated in Wrocław; its top was carved in a form known from the wooden fences of structures from Polabia identified by archaeologists as pagan temples (Gross Raden).

In 1039, Kazimierz the Restorer started the restoration of central power. He swore allegiance to Emperor Conrad II, who in return supported him with five hundred warriors. The duke concentrated on reconsolidating the monarchy, although with support of new elites rather than the members of old, rebellious one. Using marital bonds as strategy to pacify and strengthen relations with Rus' and Hungary, Kazimierz stabilized his internal but also external political position. With the help of Rus', the duke defeated the Masovian ruler, Maslav, who was supported by the pagan Pomeranians, and in 1047 reconquered this province. His next move was to regain control over Silesia, which was subordinated to the control of the Czech duke Břetislav I. He succeeded in 1050, although the German king Henry III ordered him in 1054 to pay tribute from the province for the Czech rulers (300 pounds of silver and 30 pounds of gold).

Engagements in the south led Kazimierz to locate his headquarters in the southern province of Lesser Poland, which had not suffered from the pagan rebellion. His main seat was now in Cracow, where he temporarily located the Polish ecclesiastical centre and where

149 *Galli Anonymi Cronicae*, I.19.

150 Sławomir Mozdzioch, 'Archeologiczne ślady kultu pogańskiego na Śląsku wczesnośredniowiecznym', in Moździoch, ed., *Człowiek, sacrum, środowisko: miejsca kultu we wczesnym średniowieczu* (Wrocław, 2000), 155–93 (here 176–87).

Bishop Aaron, who had been the first abbot of the Benedictine abbey at Tyniec, arrived around the year 1046 following his consecration at Cologne.[151] The period of rebellion and then rebuilding brought deep changes in the power structure and social order of the Piast realm (see Chapter 5). Although the Piast realm and Polish Church survived, the period of the dynasty's domination in northern Central Europe had gone, although dreams of invincible Piast power remained.

## *Hungary*

Just as religious and political transformation were interlinked, so was resistance to these profound changes. From the early days of István's reign, sources emphasized the rebels' traditional (pagan) identity and adherence to the traditions of their fathers. The most significant rebellion broke out after the first king's death. As all of István's sons had predeceased him, he appointed his nephew (his sister's son), Peter Orseolo (r. 1038–41, 1044–6). His cousin Vazul (the son of Géza's brother) seems to have aspired to the throne; he was blinded, but his sons, who fled into exile, eventually did gain the crown, aided by popular revolt against Peter. Before that, hostility to Peter led to the election of Samuel Aba (1041–4), according to modern historians either a nephew or son-in-law of István. Peter regained the throne briefly with the military backing of Emperor Henry III, but was deposed again by a popular revolt which broke out in 1046; people returned to 'the custom of the pagans'. The Hungarian Chronicle, which is the main source for the rebellion, survives in a fourteenth-century text, which incorporates earlier redactions. How much of this account comes from a near-contemporary author and how much is later revision is debatable. The specific customs listed by the Hungarian Chronicle were idolatry, eating horseflesh, recourse to 'magicians' and fortune-tellers, and shaving the top of the head and separating their hair in three tresses in the pagan manner. The rebels also wished to eradicate the Christian structures put in place by István: they killed ecclesiastics, destroyed churches and abolished tithes. Their aim combined the

[151] For suggestions about his Irish origin, see J. Strzelczyk, *Iroszkoci w kulturze europejskiej* (Warsaw, 1987), 419–22.

eradication of Christianity and that of strong individual royal power: Peter was blinded, according to contemporary accounts written outside Hungary.

The leader of the rebellion, Vata, was a territorial lord probably in eastern Hungary; he may have been a pagan who never converted or, according to the chronicle, he may have returned to paganism. He probably wished to maintain his separate power. He was the first to offer himself to the 'demons'. The rebels recalled Vazul's sons, András, a Christian, probably baptized in Kiev, and Levente (a pagan), who were pretenders to the throne from another branch of the dynasty. After their return they permitted pagan practices, but when András was crowned king, he put an end to paganism, allegedly decreeing the death penalty for pagan practices (his legislation does not survive). Levente, who according to the chronicle would have favoured paganism, died and was buried according to pagan custom. The chronicle also records another rebellion in 1060–1, with people demanding the right to live according to the pagan rites of their fathers, kill ecclesiastics and destroy churches. The rebellion was rapidly quashed by the king. According to one interpretation, this was a rebellion by impoverished freemen.[152]

These revolts could not restore the status quo that preceded Christianization and the development of royal power. In the Hungarian case, the change in political as well as religious institutions was radical. Sole rulership replaced a variety of territorial and other leaders. Immigrant ecclesiastics and imported ecclesiastical institutions were introduced, and local religious specialists were condemned and eliminated. Both the building of royal power and the organization of Christian society continued in the second half of the eleventh century.

In all three polities, Christianity was made compulsory from above by the ruler, parallel to the centralization of power in the hands of one dynasty. In the course of this dual process of religious and political change, rulers relied on external allies and force to some extent. In all three realms, Christian polities under one dynasty were established and consolidated.

[152] *Chronici Hungarici*, 337–44, 359–60; Gyula Kristó, 'Megjegyzések az ún. "pogánylázadások" kora történetéhez', *Acta Universitatis Szegediensis de Attila József Nominatae. Acta Historica* 18 (1965), 1–57.

# 4

# POLITICAL LIFE AND GOVERNMENT, c. 1050–c. 1200

After the emergence of new Christian polities, the history of the three central European countries diverged in terms of their politics. Poland and Hungary were independent realms; Bohemia-Moravia became part of the Holy Roman Empire. Each polity was affected by territorial subdivision to some extent, above all Poland, which fragmented into principalities. Hungarian rulers held a royal title continuously, whereas some Bohemian and Polish rulers were styled kings, and others dukes.[1] Yet some structures of governance, for example, the strongholds and districts organized around them, were similar in all three realms.

In the late 1970s, Dušan Třeštík and Barbara Krzemieńska developed a model describing the emergence and organization of central European states in the tenth through the twelfth centuries. They argued for striking similarities in the organization of social, political and economic life in Bohemia, Poland and Hungary. According to them, the ruler had almost absolute power based on the warrior elite, who were dependent on him and served as his bodyguard, and who until the twelfth century did not own land. The ruler retained almost exclusive control over land and the peasants who farmed it, and allocated part of the revenues to members of the elite. The territorial organization of state administration was based on the system of strongholds and their respective districts. (Chapter 5 discusses the social and economic implications of the model.) This model of the development

[1] For a comparative history, see Font, *Im Spannungsfeld der christlichen Großmächte*.

of central European states in the eleventh and twelfth centuries informed studies on all three polities published from the 1970s through the 1990s. Today, however, it is being questioned.

## SUCCESSION AND TERRITORIAL DIVISION

Succession was a key problem in all three realms and was often contested. Seniority and the succession of the ruler's eldest son were the two most frequently employed patterns, but neither came to be firmly accepted by all. In addition, permanent or more or less temporary territorial subdivisions of power existed.

### *Bohemia*

The transmission of ducal power among Přemyslids was fairly straightforward from the time of Bohemia's Christianization until the reign of Břetislav I. After the reigning duke's death his oldest relative was accepted by the magnates as his successor. With only two or three living relatives who qualified in each generation, struggles for power were infrequent and of short duration. The situation changed radically after the middle of the eleventh century, when Břetislav I left five ambitious adult sons. From that time, the Přemyslid dynasty had several branches.

According to some historians, and based on information about the so-called Testament of Břetislav I in the work of Cosmas of Prague, Břetislav sought to implement the so-called *seniorátní (stařešinsky) řád* ('the law of seniority') to avoid succession crises. Shortly before his death, he allegedly instructed magnates that the oldest of his five sons, Spytihněv II (1055–61), should become supreme ruler over all Přemyslid lands, both Bohemia and Moravia, with his seat in Prague. Břetislav prepared Spytihněv to play this leading role by making him governor of Moravia and bestowing upon him the ducal rights to issue coins and build strongholds. Three of his four brothers gained power over parts of Moravia (the future duchies of Brno, Olomouc, Znojmo), but were to be subject to their oldest brother's power.[2] After a supreme duke's death, his place was to be taken by his oldest relative.[3] This would safeguard an indivisible territory under the rule of the eldest, while his younger brothers would acquire smaller domains on the condition that they accepted the seniority of the duke of Prague.

[2] The fourth, Jaromír, became bishop of Prague. [3] Cosmas II.13, p. 102.

This model of inheritance, however, was not new in Bohemian history, and the idea of the testament suggested by Cosmas was in fact a *post factum* explanation for problems concerning the transmission of supreme power among numerous relatives after Břetislav I's death. The latter during his reign, not in his last will, divided Moravia among his sons, which again was nothing new. He himself had been established as the governor of Moravia during the reign of his father, before he came to rule all Přemyslid lands. But after his death, over the next few decades, Moravia became permanently divided into hereditary duchies of Břetislav's sons' descendants, without their being excluded from succession to the Prague seat.[4]

Cosmas's narrative suggests the growing role of elites in the process of succession. Břetislav I supposedly entrusted magnates as guardians of his will, to prevent his sons and descendants from breaking the law of succession by seniority. It is hard to tell if in practice the influence of the nobility, who controlled warriors located in ducal strongholds throughout the country, disrupted peaceful succession or if that effect was due to the ambitions of Přemyslids to rule alone over Bohemia and Moravia, as their predecessors had. A series of feuds developed after Spytihněv II had forced his mother, Judith, who tried to protect her younger sons, to escape to Hungary. He himself turned against his younger brothers, attacked their Moravian domains before 1058, deposed them from their seats and united the Přemyslid heritage. He also bound to himself Moravian magnates shortly after his succession through an oath of allegiance.

Vratislav II (1061–92) ascended the senior duke's throne at Prague according to seniority. His younger brothers received their political share: Konrad of Brünn western Moravia along with its capital, Brno, and Ota (Otta) the Beautiful (Sličný, 1061–87) eastern Moravia, with its centre at Olomouc.[5] Jaromir-Gebhard was to become bishop of

[4] The only biography of Břetislav I is Barbara L. Krzemieńska, *Břetislav I. Čechy a středni Evropa v prvé polovině XI století* (Prague, 1999).

[5] On succession rules established after the death of Břetislav I, with a special emphasis on Moravia, see Martin Wihoda, 'Testament knížete Břetislava', in *Saga moravskych Přemyslovcu: zivot na Morave od XI. do pocatku XIV. stoleti. Sbornik a katalog vystavy poradane Vlastivednym muzeem v Olomouci a Muzeem mesta Brna k 700. vyroci tragicke smrti Vaclava III., posledniho ceskeho krale z dynastie Přemyslovcu. Olomouc, Přemyslovsky palac, 20. dubna az 6. srpna 2006, Brno, Hrad Spilberk, 14. zari 2006 az 21. ledna 2007*, ed. Renata Fikova (Olomouc, 2006), 33–50.

Prague but Vratislav tried to install his own candidate.[6] War with his younger brothers forced him to accept Jaromir's rights. Spytihněv II's only son, Friedrich (Svatobor), remained as a courtier at his uncle Vratislav II's court.

Although Vratislav II was crowned in 1086, the end of his reign was overshadowed by a growing succession crisis. According to seniority, the next in line to inherit were the king's brothers – Konrád and Ota – whose political support came from their Moravian fiefs. Vratislav II, however, favoured his own sons. The oldest, Břetislav, received land with its capital in the stronghold Hradecko, on the eastern borders of Bohemia. One of his younger sons, Boleslav, born to his third wife, the Polish princess Sventoslava/Svatava, received control of Olomouc after the death of Vratislav II's younger brother, Ota (1087). This triggered open conflict. Ota's widow Euphemia and their two sons – Svatopluk and Ota the Black – sought assistance at the court of her brother-in-law, Konrád, at Brno. This provoked a retaliatory attack by the king in 1091, which was at first supported by Břetislav. After Břetislav abandoned the royal army,[7] Vratislav agreed to a truce. Shortly before his death, Vratislav II followed the rule of seniority and appointed Konrád as his legal successor.

On Vratislav II's death (1092), Konrád took the throne, but when he in turn died shortly afterwards, Břetislav II was elected. Once again the law of seniority was respected. But Břetislav tried to establish a new pattern for succession: supreme power over Bohemia was to be held only by descendants of Vratislav II. As Břetislav's only son was four years old, he appointed his oldest half-brother, Bořivoj, as his heir, stipulating that Bořivoj secure succession for Břetislav's son. When he died during a fight with Moravian relatives two days prior to Christmas in 1100, Bořivoj II took power; the hereditary law of succession seemingly prevailed. Yet a series of civil wars between Přemyslids meant that only military predominance secured the right to the throne. Initially Bořivoj II was successful against the eldest Přemyslid, Oldřich of Brno, but was then expelled in 1107 by Svatopluk, Oldřich's younger brother. Svatopluk appointed as his successor Vladislav, Bořivoj's younger brother, claiming the unworthiness of both Bořivoj and Oldřich for the throne. Instead of a principle of seniority or heredity, such legitimation of succession favoured moral rights (*idoneitas*). In reality, however, when Svatopluk

[6] Cosmas II.18. [7] Cosmas II.39.

was killed in 1109 during an expedition to Poland, warriors elected Ota the Black, prince of Moravia, as duke, while the bishop of Prague and part of the elite acclaimed Vladislav. Bořivoj retained his claims. All candidates sought acceptance from the German king Henry V, but his decisions had restricted impact. Fighting continued, and the power to create dukes was vested not in the 'Czech people', but in swords and the intervention of neighbours. When after a period of civil wars among pretenders the Czech elites gave the throne to Sobeslav I, the last living son of King Vratislav II, this represented succession neither by seniority nor by heredity.

Sobeslav I (1125–40) had to contend with his cousin, Ota the Black of Moravia, the eldest living Přemyslid, whom he removed from Olomouc. Ota gained the military support of the new German king Lothar III in 1126. Sobeslav I defeated the invaders at the battle of Chlumec, where Ota himself was killed. After the victory Sobeslav tried to strengthen his position as sole ruler: he expelled Moravian dukes from Brno and Znojmo, and forced other members of the dynasty to stay at his court. After he broke the magnates' opposition, he appointed new rulers to the Moravian duchies, and even thought about passing the throne to one of them, Konrád of Znojmo. But near the end of his life he persuaded the German king Conrad to approve the succession of Sobeslav's young son, Vladislav. The future duke took the pendant from the king's hands as a sign of taking power over Bohemia as a fief. This was an obvious breach of the law of seniority because there were several older Přemyslids living. The duke called 'all' the nobles to Sadska where they were made to swear allegiance to his young heir. Despite these measures, after Sobeslav's death in February 1140, the nobles broke their oath by refusing to elect his son and chosen heir, Vladislav.[8]

After disputes the nobles elected one of the youngest Přemyslids, another Vladislav, the son of the late duke Vladislav I. His election represented the free decision of the 'duke-makers', as a middle ground between two arguing factions, and as an attempt to elevate a ruler who would be weak and easy to guide. Vladislav II's refusal to give his electors a larger share in ruling the Prague duchy provoked a rebellion in 1142, and the offer of the throne to Konrád of Znojmo. The rebels won the battle at Vysoké and attacked Prague, prompting the duke to

[8] Vratislav Vaníček, *Soběslav I. Přemyslovci v kontextu evropských dějin v letech 1092–1140* (Prague, 2007), 118–63, 226–95.

seek military support from the German court of Conrad III. The siege of Prague was broken and the rebels retreated to Moravia. Violent quarrels continued, but Vladislav II's position as ruler was secured. It was further strengthened through co-operation in numerous expeditions of German kings as well as through acquisition of a royal title. According to an imperial privilege for Vladislav, permission to wear the royal crown was granted to all his 'successores'. Vladislav II and his allies claimed that this established hereditary royal dignity in Vladislav's family and thus cancelled the law of seniority and the magnates' right to choose a ruler. Yet the royal dignity of Vladislav diminished neither the rights of other Přemyslids to rule the three duchies in Moravia – Brno, Olomouc and Znojmo – nor their conviction about the continued validity of the principle of seniority.[9]

Vladislav II abdicated in favour of his oldest son Bedřich in 1172. Yet Emperor Frederick Barbarossa did not accept hereditary succession: in 1173 he deposed Bedřich during a meeting in Hermsdorf, and chose Oldřich, Soběslav I's son and King Vratislav II's grandson, to rule over Bohemia. The new duke first accepted the dignity, but then abdicated in favour of his older brother, Soběslav II (1173–8). Thus the 'royal branch' of the Přemyslids was still holding power, but the seniority principle was applied to their members, while Přemyslids from the Moravian lines were excluded from succession to the Prague throne.

All this did not prevent further political upheavals, which turned the political life of Bohemia into sheer power play without any clear rules other than that the strongest contender would win. In 1178 Barbarossa, disappointed by the lack of active military aid from Soběslav, deposed him and restored Bedřich, son of Vladislav II, to power, starting another series of civil wars in Bohemia. In 1182 Bedřich was expelled from the country and Czech magnates offered supreme power over Bohemia to Konrád II Ota of Znojmo, and he accepted. Yet due to Barbarossa's intervention, Bohemian magnates were forced to accept Bedřich once again. Konrád, however, ruled all of Moravia, if not formally then effectively independent of the duke of Prague. He even started using the title of Moravian margrave and

[9] Michal Mašek, Petr Sommer and Josef Žemlička, *Vladislav II. Druhý král z Přemyslova rodu. K 850. výročí jeho korunovace* (Prague, 2009).

claimed that he took power over Moravia directly from the hands of the emperor, not as a favour of the Prague duke.[10]

In 1189 after Bedřich's death Konrád II Ota took the Prague throne almost without dispute (excepting the duchess-widow Agnes) and immediately gave up his margrave title. On at least one occasion, he clearly expressed that as the Bohemian duke he could not also be margrave ('Boemorum dux quondam marchio Morauie'). When Konrád died without offspring during the Sicilian raid of Henry VI in 1191, the throne went according to his last will to the oldest member of the dynasty, Duke Václav, Soběslav II's brother. The seniority principle had no authority, and in 1192 Přemysl, Vladislav II's son, deposed Václav with the help of Prague's Bishop Jindřich (Henry). His rule over Bohemia was based exclusively on military power and mighty allies. His position was guaranteed by Emperor Barbarossa's decision: Přemysl Otakar (Odocarus) would rule over Bohemia, and his brother Vladislav Jindřich (Henry) as margrave over Moravia, clearly subordinated to the duke of Prague. The dominant position of the emperor in the successions of Prague's dukes was never more obvious than in 1193, when Barbarossa deposed Přemysl Otakar, and instead installed Bishop Jindřich as duke, breaking all local principles of succession.[11]

When Jindřich died in 1197 Bohemian magnates elected Vladislav. From the beginning his brother, Přemysl Otakar, tried to depose him, and after a series of fights Vladislav returned to Moravia, leaving Bohemia and honorary superiority over the whole Přemyslid state in the hands of Přemysl. The latter acquired the royal crown from the German king Otto IV Welf in 1198. He succeeded in ensuring exclusive heredity of the throne for his sons in 1212 when Emperor Frederick II included that principle in the Golden Bull. From that time, supreme power – if not the royal title – was hereditary in the direct line of Přemysl Otakar's descendants.[12]

[10] *Letopis Jarlocha, opata kláštera milevského*, in FRB, 2, ed. J. Emler (Prague, 1874), 481; Jiří Kejř, 'Böhmen und das Reich unter Friedrich I', in *Friedrich Barbarossa. Handlungsspielräume und Wirkungsweisen des staufischen Kaisers*, ed. Arnold Haverkamp (Sigmaringen, 1992), 241–89.

[11] On political fights over the Prague throne between 1037 and 1193 and their socio-economic background, see Lisa Wolverton, *Hastening toward Prague: Power and Society in the Medieval Czech Lands* (Philadelphia, 2001).

[12] Kejr, 'Böhmen und das Reich unter Friedrich I'; Kejr, 'Böhmen zur Zeit Friedrich Barbarossas', in *Kaiser Friedrich Barbarossa. Landesausbau – Aspekte seiner Politik – Wirkung*, eds. Bernhard Töpfer and Evamaria Engel (Weimar, 1994), 101–13. On

### *Poland*

Although no specific source described the rules of succession in the early Piast state, one can conclude from the course of events that two principles were in conflict. On the one hand, all male members of the ruling duke's immediate family could be regarded as co-rulers. At least this was expressed in the so-called *Dagome iudex* register: Duke Mieszko (called here 'Dagome iudex') together with his wife and their sons ruled the 'civitas Schinesghe', giving it to St Peter. It is striking that Bolesław, Mieszko's eldest son, was not mentioned. It seems a duke's sons had the right to rule only if the duke appointed them. On the other hand, the oldest male offspring of a deceased duke had priority for the succession at least in reality if not according to legal tradition. As clear rules were lacking, the fights for power between relatives started soon after the death of the ruler (in the case of Mieszko I) or when his political position weakened (Mieszko II, Bolesław II the Bold). When after the long period of crisis Kazimierz the Restorer regained power, he may have taken measures to avert any trouble caused by a lack of clear regulation on the question of succession. The surviving sources do not question the direct succession of the eldest Kazimierz's son, Bolesław II the Bold, and they make no mention of any resistance from Władysław Herman or any other relative. Władysław Herman's well-documented dedication to Mazovia suggests that this province had been allocated to him much earlier, perhaps in his father's will. It is possible that the province was administered personally by him but under the close surveillance of his brother. It is unclear whether Władysław participated in the rebellion against his brother in 1079. He certainly succeeded him as ruling duke, although until Bolesław's death the latter was referred to as 'king'. However, Władysław Herman tended to ally with the expelled king's opponents. This is clearly indicated by his two marriages, both to women called Judith: the first in 1080 to a daughter of the Bohemian duke Vratislav II; the second in 1088 to Henry IV's sister and recent widow of King Salamon (Solomon) of Hungary. These marriages connected him to the monarchs who had once fought against Bolesław II. Nonetheless, in official communications with his subjects and neighbours he stressed the continuity of rule, and

the Golden Bull, see Martin Wihoda, *Zlatá bulla sicilská: podivuhodný příběh ve vrstvách paměti* (Prague, 2006).

even the rights of succession of Bolesław II's male offspring. Both of them, however, predeceased him, not necessarily by natural deaths.[13]

Władysław Herman had two sons. His oldest son, Zbigniew, was born from a woman who in clerical eyes was not his lawful wife. Bolesław and his last wife, Judith of Swabia, tried to deprive him from the right of succession and made him a priest. Yet the elites regarded him as the rightful heir, and magnates rebelled against Władysław, kidnapped Zbigniew from the monastery of Quedlinburg and installed him as duke in 1093. At first his father publicly accepted his succession rights. Three years later, however, Władysław defeated Zbigniew at Gopło Lake and imprisoned him. Zbigniew was pardoned in 1097 and joined forces with his younger half-brother Bolesław (son of Władysław and his second wife, Judith of Bohemia) and after two civil wars they forced their ageing father in 1099–1100 to divide his realm into three parts: Bolesław received the whole of the southern belt, including Silesia, as well as being granted some control over Lesser Poland; Zbigniew ruled in central Greater Poland and Kuyavia; and Władysław Herman was allowed to keep hold of his preferred region of Mazovia, from where he formally controlled the entire territory as 'senior duke'.

At his death in 1102, according to Władysław Herman's will, his sons divided the realm into two parts: Zbigniew (1102–7) took the northern provinces of Greater Poland, Kuyavia and Mazovia, while Bolesław III the Wrymouth assumed control of Silesia and Lesser Poland in the south. Zbigniew, the older brother, was destined to hold supreme power over Bolesław, who did not however accept subordination. It seems that the two brothers' realms were effectively independent from one another and coexisted for five years. Finally, in 1106, Bolesław III captured Greater Poland with no visible resistance from Zbigniew, who retreated to Mazovia. In early 1107 Zbigniew accepted the inferior status of vassal in a reunited realm. Yet he was expelled in early 1108, and when he returned to Poland with the formal approval of Bolesław, he was accused of treachery, blinded and possibly put to death in the ducal prison.[14]

[13] Tadeusz Grudziński, *Boleslaus the Bold and Bishop Stanislaus: The Story of a Conflict* (Warsaw, 1985); Gerard Labuda, *Mieszko II król Polski (1025–1034): czas przełomu w dziejach państwa polskiego*, 2nd edn (Poznań, 2008).

[14] Zbigniew Dalewski, *Ritual and Politic: Writing the History of a Dynastic Conflict in Medieval Poland* (Leiden, 2008); Dalewski, 'Begräbnis des Herrschers. Ritual und Streit um die Thronfolge in Polen des früheren Mittelalters', *Frühmittelalterliche*

If the first condition for succession during the tenth and eleventh centuries was being the son of a ruling duke, and the second was being the oldest among brothers, the most important criterion in the twelfth century became the support of the elites and neighbours during the inevitable conflict for power. Bolesław III, having experienced the long series of civil wars and the intervention of the German king Henry V, who intervened for Zbigniew, introduced a system of succession aimed at satisfying numerous claimants to power while maintaining the essential unity of the country. He may have been inspired by the practical example of Bohemia and Rus'. No official documents exist recording the details of Bolesław's proposed system. A much later bull issued by Pope Innocent III in 1210, however, explains that senior status in the country should be allocated to the man who is 'the oldest in the whole family' (*de toto genere maior*) and not necessarily to the oldest son of the ruling duke.

Bolesław III's attempt to introduce the seniority principle in succession also meant that the differentiation of political power was introduced. Younger dukes controlled their principalities (whether these were hereditary from the beginning or only came to be so after several decades is still debated), and a 'senior duke' who, in addition to his own principality, also administered a centrally located territory with Cracow and the Pomeranian fiefs. The senior duke's sphere of power was ill defined and changeable, although traditionally historians thought it was his responsibility to exercise control over aspects of government pertinent to the country as a whole, including: diplomacy; waging war; the nomination of archbishop and governors to strategic strongholds (*voievoda*); settling conflicts between provincial princes; and minting coins.

It is not easy to determine precisely how Poland was divided when Bolesław III died on 28 October 1138, since two of his sons were too young to assume power: eight-year-old Henryk and a newborn infant, Kazimierz II. Władysław II, Bolesław IV and Mieszko III the Old (Stary, 1138–1202) received Silesia, Mazovia and Greater Poland respectively. The oldest, Władysław II the Exile (Wygnaniec, 1138–46), the only son of his father's first, Rus'ian wife, became the senior duke. A peaceful coexistence with his brothers did not last for very

*Studien* 43 (2009), 327–48; Dalewski, 'Um 1055: Was Herrscher taten, wenn sie viele Söhne hatten – zum Beispiel im Osten Europas', in *Die Macht des Königs. Herrschaft in Europa vom Frühmittelalter bis in die Neuzeit*, ed. Bernhard Jüssen (Munich, 2005), 125–37.

long. To force acceptance of his superior authority in 1142, Władysław II defeated his half-brothers with the help of a Rus' contingent. The peace was mediated by the widowed duchess Salomea, Bolesław III's second wife. At her death in 1144, conflict started again. The senior duke once more marched against his half-brothers and in 1146 had surrounded Mieszko at Poznań, capital of Greater Poland. Archbishop of Gniezno, Jakub of Żnin, declared an anathema on Władysław II, which helped to turn the war to the advantage of the junior brothers. Their combined armies defeated their half-brother and forced him into exile. The victors did not dismantle the system of the 'seniorate'. The next eldest, Bolesław IV the Curly (Kędzierzavvy, 1146–73), sat on the senior duke's throne. When Władysław II the Exile died in 1159, the senior position of Bolesław IV was legalized, although his troubles did not end. Władysław's two sons inherited their father's claims to Silesia and enjoyed Emperor Frederick I Barbarossa's support. Due to imperial pressure, in 1163 Bolesław the Curly allowed them to return and take control over Silesia.

At first, succession went smoothly. After Bolesław IV's death, in 1173 Mieszko III the Old, the eldest member of the dynasty, became senior duke. But he was deposed from the throne of Lesser Poland in 1177 by a rebellion of knightly elites and his younger brother, Kazimierz the Just (Sprawiedliwy, 1177–94). Kazimierz obviously broke with the legal tradition of the seniorate. This was accepted by the Polish archbishop and bishops during a summit at Łęczyca in 1180 in exchange for ducal liberties for the Church. When Kazimierz II died in 1194, Mieszko III tried again to take power in Cracow. Magnates of Lesser Poland headed by the bishop of Cracow instead accepted the hereditary succession of Kazimierz's minor sons Leszek and Konrad. But in 1198 one of the factions competing in Cracow recalled Mieszko III once more, and his status as senior duke was accepted. Mieszko III's death in 1202 did not mean the end of the seniority system, at least in theory. A papal bull of 1210 restored it and the throne in Cracow was taken by the oldest Piast, Mieszko I Tanglefoot of Opole (Plątonogi, duke 1163–1211). But his reign was short and after his death there were no more opportunities to maintain the integrity of the country based on the seniority principle. Poland became divided between an increasing number of individuals from several branches of the Piast dynasty ruling in Silesia, Greater and Lesser Poland, Mazovia and – later – Kuyavia. All were competing with one another to subordinate the largest possible territories, and to build stable dominance over their relatives. Hegemony based on military and political dominance replaced the old seniority principle.[15]

## *Hungary*

In Hungary, the institution of kingship and a single realm survived throughout the medieval period, yet this seeming continuity hides rifts that were often divisive.[16] It was widely accepted that rulers came from one dynasty, but that still left great scope for contestation, as no rules regulated the specific order of succession. The centuries following István's reign were thus rife with rivalries. István himself, after the death of his last remaining son and heir, appointed his nephew Peter Orseolo; the revolts against his rule were described in Chapter 3. Thereafter, although not every succession was disputed, most were. Thus András I wished his son Salamon to succeed him, while András's own brother Béla, who was the supposed heir until Salamon's birth in 1053, wanted the crown for himself. When András had the child Salamon crowned, Béla first fled to Poland, but then returned and defeated his brother András who died of his wounds; Béla I ruled from 1060 to 1063. In the following generations, rivalry between András's and Béla's descendants was perpetuated. With the backing of German armies, Salamon (who had been living in the margraviate of Austria) took the throne in 1063, after Béla was mortally injured by the baldachin of the throne, which collapsed on him just before the battle.

15 Zbigniew Dalewski, 'Ritual im Wandel. Herzogserhebungen der polnischen Herrscher um die Wende vom 12. zum 13. Jahrhundert', in *Ritualisierung politischen Willensbildung. Polen und Deutschland im hohen und späten Mittelalter*, ed. Wojciech Fałkowski (Wiesbaden, 2010), 79–100. See Benedykt Zientara, *Heinrich der Bärtige und seine Zeit. Politik und Gesellschaft im mittelalterlichen Schlesien* (Munich, 2002), for the late twelfth- and thirteenth-century political activity of the Piast dukes.

16 The most detailed political history is still György Székely and Antal Bartha, eds., *Magyarország története: előzmények és magyar történet 1242-ig*, 2 vols: (Budapest, 1984). For useful overviews, see Engel, *Realm of St Stephen*; Gyula Kristó, *Histoire de la Hongrie médiévale: le temps des Arpads*, tr. Chantal Philippe (Rennes, 2001); Gyula Kristó and Ferenc Makk, *Die Ersten Könige Ungarns. Die Herrscher der Arpadendynastie*, tr. Tibor Schäfer (Herne, 1999). Z. Kosztolnyik's works are utterly unreliable. Works on individual rulers, indicated in the following notes, are relevant to all aspects of their reign.

Béla I's sons, Géza, László and Lampert, went to Poland. Géza then returned to Hungary with Polish troops, and a compromise solution was reached: he received a share of the realm (the duchy), while Salamon ruled as king (1064–74). But in 1074 Salamon, with German troops, attacked Géza, who, with his brother László, received military help from Moravia and defeated Salamon. After Géza (1074–7), his brother László I (Ladislas) ruled (1077–95). Salamon tried unsuccessfully to regain the throne, was imprisoned for a while and finally probably died in the Balkans fighting against the Byzantines. Popular legend, however, turned him into a repentant hermit who ended his saintly life in Pula (Istria).

Succession after László's death was disputed by his two nephews, Álmos (who was the younger) and Kálmán.[17] The latter had perhaps been destined for an ecclesiastical career, his contemporaries extolled his learning, and according to some scholars, following a later chronicle text, he was a bishop before taking the throne with papal approval. Whether László himself designated Kálmán to be his successor cannot be ascertained. Once Kálmán (1095–1116) ascended the throne, Álmos rebelled against him numerous times, drawing on German and Polish help. Finally Kálmán had Álmos and his son Béla blinded in 1113, perhaps inspired by the Polish Bolesław III the Wrymouth who had had his own rebellious brother Zbigniew blinded in the previous year. After an uncontested transition of power, following Kálmán's death, to his son István II (Stephen; 1116–31), during the latter's reign discontented nobles elected a *comes* Bors and Ivan as king.[18] The episode was abortive and short, and debates surround the identity of the protagonists.

From István II, who had no sons, the royal title went to his blind cousin Béla II (1131–41), who had many supporters in the entourage of István II. His ascent was not smooth; two months passed between István II's death and Béla's coronation, but the sources provide no details about the events. A new pretender emerged, Boris, a son of Kálmán's second wife Euphemia, who had been repudiated before giving birth; this was due to adultery according to the chronicle written under the reigning king whom Boris tried to unseat, but he is not designated as a bastard in contemporary western sources.

[17] Márta Font, *Koloman the Learned, King of Hungary* (Szeged, 2001).

[18] John Tuzson, *István II (1116 – 1131): A Chapter in Medieval Hungarian History* (Boulder, CO, 2002).

He tried to gain the throne several times, culminating in armed attacks in 1132 with Polish and Rus' armies, and in 1146 with German mercenary troops, although he was ultimately unsuccessful. Béla's eldest son Géza II followed him on the throne (1141–62). His younger brother István was probably the candidate of the internal opposition in the last years of Géza's reign, but failed to gain enough external support to dethrone Géza. After Géza's death, however, internal rivalry once again unseated the next king, Géza's eldest son István III (Stephen; 1162, 1163–72), after a few weeks. Géza's brother László II (Ladislas) became king in 1162, followed after László's death in 1163 by another brother, István IV (Stephen), who had the backing of Byzantine troops. István III in his turn invaded and expelled István IV. When he died without children, the crown passed to his brother Béla III (1172–96).

Béla III took power relying on his own retinue, Byzantine support and the backing of some of István III's supporters as well as opponents; in all, he had the loyalty of a significant part of the lay elites.[19] Yet he did not take power unopposed; his younger brother Géza had his own supporters, and Béla imprisoned him in 1173/4; Géza was eventually freed and tried to gain Czech and German support, but failed and was imprisoned again. Finally he went into exile in Byzantium. Béla himself ensured the succession by first crowning his son Imre (Emeric) king (1182), and then appointing him duke of Slavonia (1194), while leaving forts, estates and money to his younger son András. Although Imre took the throne unopposed in 1196, the following year his younger brother attacked him with the aid of the Austrian duke. Hostilities initiated by András recurred during Imre's reign.

Often, two clashing models of succession led to rivalry.[20] Brothers of ruling kings retained the idea of their rights through seniority, while kings generally wanted their son to inherit. Several princes with equally good claims could also contest succession when there was no direct descendant of the previous king, and brothers vied with each other for the crown. Primogeniture came to be accepted generally as the principle governing succession only at the end of the

[19] Gyula Kristó and Ferenc Makk, eds., *III. Béla emlékezete* (Budapest, 1981).

[20] Márta F. Font, 'Krone und Schwert. Die Anerkennung des Herrschaftsrechts in Mittel- und Osteuropa', in *East Central Europe at the Turn of the first and second Millennia*, ed. Vincent Múcska (Bratislava, 2002), 9–36.

twelfth century. As in so many other kingdoms, continuity of rule within one dynasty, therefore, did not mean uncontested succession.

One attempt at a solution was the establishment of the duchy (*ducatus*).[21] András I created the duchy for his brother Béla *c.* 1048, giving him the ducal title together with eastern parts of the realm (east of the Tisza River) and the Nitra region. Some historians have speculated that the origin of this institution lay in the political organization of the conquering Hungarians, with the heir to the throne being the leader of warrior groupings organized from associated non-Hungarian peoples. Others suggest that there was a territorial division between Géza and Koppány in the tenth century, which was a precursor to the duchy. Yet another assumption is that the heir to the throne always held the duchy. The sources used for these claims are medieval, but written much later (sometimes centuries later) than the purported events. In some cases, modern explanations hinge on tenuous or unsubstantiated interpretations of a word or a phrase. Independent territorial rulers certainly existed before, but it is much more convincing to see the origins of the institution of the duchy itself in the middle of the eleventh century, before which it is not documented. The establishment of the duchy amounted to the division of authority within the realm. The duchy comprised about one-third of the realm, although it was not one contiguous territory; its two centres were Bihar and Nitra. Whether the duchy existed continuously from the middle of the eleventh century is debated. It may not have been in use between 1060 and 1063. In 1064 Salamon gave it to Béla's son Géza. Géza, in turn, when he became king, bestowed it on his own brother László. When László I became king, he possibly gave part of the duchy, Bihar, to his younger brother Lampert. Kálmán appointed his own brother Álmos, but eventually dismantled the institution itself when he decided to deprive the always rebellious Álmos of the title in 1107. The duchy was briefly revived by László II in 1162. He gave it to his brother István IV, who held it for a few months before ascending the throne on László's death.

Another, and eventually preferred, solution to neutralize possible rivals to the throne was to appoint members of the dynasty as the head of newly conquered or annexed territories, which in any case were governed separately. László I gave a royal title to his nephew Álmos (son of Géza I) over a part of Croatia in 1091. From the early twelfth

[21] Gyula Kristó, *A XI. századi hercegség története Magyarországon* (Budapest, 1974).

century, when the duchy as a separate territory disappeared, Croatia and Dalmatia were assigned to be ruled by princes. Such separate government could be given to a younger brother, but also to the heir to the throne: in 1114, Kálmán made his young son and heir István king of Croatia and Dalmatia. In 1137, the future László II was duke of Bosnia. István III's younger brother Béla (the future Béla III) was duke of Croatia and Dalmatia (1161–3), while Imre filled the position in 1194–6. Imre's younger brother András (II) became duke of Croatia and Dalmatia towards the end of 1198, and added Rama and Hum (in modern Bosnia-Herzegovina) to his lands in the same year through conquest. Neither these, nor the thirteenth-century cases when royal princes were at the head of Slavonia, Transylvania, Bosnia and occasionally other territories such as Styria, represented continuously existing institutions; appointments were linked to the actualities of political power.

The separately governed lands did not always have a member of the royal family at their head. The separate administration of Croatia under a *ban* is discussed below. Transylvania became part of the kingdom of Hungary, but its governance changed over time. Little is known of its eleventh-century history, and it seems that settlement from western parts of the kingdom continued during that period. A target of Pecheneg and Cuman raids in the late eleventh century, the region was organized into separate administrative areas. In the north, one of the highest dignitaries of the realm exercized power: the *ispán* of Szolnok county, which centred on Szolnok but extended to Dés (Dej, Romania). Further south, eventually the counties of Doboka, Kolozs and Torda developed. The southernmost area, from the River Maros (Mureş) to the southern Carpathians, was organized under another royal official, although when this happened is controversial. Some historians accept the fourteenth-century chronicle's claim that Zoltán, a relative of István I, was prince of Transylvania at the beginning of the eleventh century. This, however, has no historical basis. The earliest *princeps*, Mercurius, is attested in the early twelfth century, but whether his title represents an office or designates a local potentate is debated. Territorial rule here developed under the *ispán* of county Fehér with its centre at Gyulafehérvár (Alba Iulia, Romania). From the late twelfth century, the royal dignitary in power was called voivode, and by the early thirteenth century the offices of voivode and the *ispán* of Gyulafehérvár were held by the same person. During the thirteenth century, several counties were established, but from

1263 the voivode's authority extended to the whole of Transylvania, and he also held the office of the *ispán* of Szolnok. The voivode had a military role (especially in defence of the frontier) and administrative tasks. Transylvania was under separate governance but did not have territorial or legal autonomy.[22]

## ROYAL POWER AND THE COURT

### *Bohemia*

At first Bohemian rulers were generally dukes (*duces*). The first ruler to receive royal dignity from the emperor was Vratislav II (1085/6). It was a personal favour for the loyal associate of Emperor Henry IV. Royal dignity did not change Vratislav's position in Bohemia, but it is possible that he used it to legitimize his pretensions to superiority over the Polish duchy of Władysław Herman as 'rex Boemorum et Polonorum'. This royal title was not hereditary. His successors were all called dukes until the royal coronation of Vladislav II (1158). In the latter's case, royal dignity was a personal privilege too, granted by Emperor Frederick I Barbarossa in recognition of faithful military service. After Vladislav's abdication (1172) one must wait thirty years for the next Bohemian king.

In 1203 Přemysl Otakar I received the crown from the German king Otto IV Welf. In recognition of his position in the Empire and

[22] László Makkai and András Mócsy, eds., *History of Transylvania*, vol. I (Boulder, CO, 2001); Béla Köpeczi, ed., *History of Transylvania* (Budapest, 1994); Gyula Kristó, 'Die Stellung Siebenbürgens innerhalb des Königreichs Ungarn im früheren Mittelalter', in *Mediaevalia Transilvanica* 7/8 (2004), 53–60; Gyula Kristó, *Early Transylvania (895–1324)* (Budapest, 2003); Ioan Marian Tiplic, *Transylvania in the Early Middle Ages (Seventh–Thirteenth Century)* (Gundelsheim, 2006); Curta, *Southeastern Europe*, 350–7; Ioan-Aurel Pop, *Romanians and Hungarians from the Ninth to the Fourteenth Century: The Genesis of the Transylvanian Medieval States* (Cluj-Napoca, 1996). The highly politicized debate on the primacy of Hungarian or Romanian settlement in Transylvania will not be discussed here; on the Hungarian view, see for example Gyula Kristó, *Nichtungarische Völker im mittelalterichen Ungarn* (Herne, 2008), 210–41, and on the Romanian, Ştefan Pascu, *A History of Transylvania* (Detroit, 1982). For summaries of key differences, see e.g. Holly Case, *Between States: The Transylvanian Question and the European Idea during World War II* (Stanford, 2009); Balázs Trencsényi, Dragoş Petrescu, Cristina Petrescu, Constantin Iordachi and Zoltán Kántor, eds., *Nation-Building and Contested Identities* (Budapest and Iaşi, 2001) and at mek.niif.hu/06000/06046/06046.pdf (for a summary of historiography, see 309–14).

his co-operation with the imperial court, Emperor Frederick II Stauf in 1212 granted him a privilege guaranteeing the royal title to all his successors, although their subordination to emperors remained. A hereditary royal crown did not change the ruler's power in Bohemia, with one important exception: Přemysl Otakar I obtained the magnates' consent that only members of his family were entitled to inherit the royal title. All other members of the dynasty would only rule in Moravian duchies or have high positions at the Prague court.[23]

From the second half of the eleventh century, titles used by the Bohemian rulers referred to their rule over people or territory. Each ruler could use both forms of the title in the same period, for example 'W[ratislaus] Boemiorum inclytus dux' and 'Wratizlaus, Boemie dux'.[24] Perhaps because of the number of different territories potentially ruled by the duke of Prague (Bohemia, Moravia, sometimes Silesia, Lusatia, and regions of Austria and Bavaria) an emphasis on power over people was more common. One should remember, however, that to be duke of the 'Boemi' meant above all control over knightly elites: magnates and warriors, rather than simple rights to the land. Thus King Vladislav II's royal seal displayed the title: 'WLADISLAUS DEI GRATIA BOEMORUM REX'. Claiming supreme power over the Piast duke Władysław Herman, Vladislav II was called by the archbishop of Mainz 'rex Boloniorum' (1085, 1088). This strange form was a result of a fusion of two ethnonyms: 'Boemi' and 'Poloni'. Cosmas of Prague called him 'Wratizlaus rex tam Boemicus quam Polonicus'.[25]

The titulature of Moravian rulers was more varied. In the second half of the eleventh century Ota of Olomouc mysteriously referred to 'Otto dei gracia id, quo est' (1078).[26] From the beginning of the twelfth century names of territories were used: 'Otto II dux

[23] Martin Wihoda, 'První ceská království', in *Stát, státnost a rituály Přemyslovského veku problémy, názory, otázky: sborník príspevku z konference konané dne 18. října 2005 v Brne*, ed. Martin Wihoda (Brno, 2006), 67–99.

[24] *CDB I, Codex diplomaticus et epistolaris Regni Bohemiae*, ed. Georg Friedrich, (Prague, 1904–7) (henceforth *CDB*), vol. I, no. 124, p. 130; I, no. 60, p. 62; no. 62, p. 63; no. 64, p. 67; no. 66, p. 69. Other examples can be found in *CDB* I, no. 83, p. 89; no. 108, p. 110; no. 111, p. 112; no. 292, p. 261.

[25] *CDB* I, no. 84, p. 90; no 90, p. 97; see Martin Wihoda, 'Between the emperor and the pope: A traumatic century of Czech history', in *The Neighbours of Poland in the Eleventh Century*, 128–9.

[26] *CDB* I, no. 79, p. 83.

Moraviae' (after 18 February 1126), or 'Wratizlaus, Otto, Cunradus duces Moravienses' (the charter of the papal legate Guido, 1143).[27] In the second half of the twelfth century, perhaps as an imitation of Bohemian ducal titles, the name of their people appeared: 'Oldricus dei gratia Morauorum dux' (1174).[28] At the same time, more specific descriptions concerning the ruled land were used: 'Fridericus dux Olomucensis provintie' (1169), 'Conradus princeps de Znogen' (1177).[29]

Throughout the eleventh and twelfth centuries Bohemian rulers claimed the protection and benevolence of God in their title, both in charters and on ducal seals through the stereotypical formula: 'Dei gratia dux Boemorum/Boemie'. Narrative sources contained a more developed image of the sacral aspect of Bohemian ducal power. Some historians maintain that contemporaries expressed through this the idea of 'rex imago Dei'. Yet medieval sources scarcely provide evidence of such a complicated ideological message. It is present, perhaps, in narratives emphasizing the goodwill of God for the Přemyslids, expressed in instant action on their behalf when they were in danger. One of the first narrative sources written in Bohemia, the so-called Legenda Christiani – composed at the turn of the tenth and eleventh centuries by the anonymous monk Christian, possibly a member of the ducal dynasty – contains a story that during a war between Duke St Václav of Prague and the ruler of Kouřim, the duke challenged his opponent to a duel to avoid shedding the blood of Bohemian wariors. The duke of Kouřim, however, renounced hostilities and accepted Václav's supreme power, because he saw a sign of the Holy Cross on Václav: he declared that it was impossible to fight someone who received such a vivid testimony of God's love.[30] The direct protection of God was supplemented by the support of two Bohemian saints: Václav and Vojtěch-Adalbert. Cosmas of Prague wrote that Czech knights repelled the troops of the Polish duke Bolesław I the Brave from Prague in 1002 only with the help of St Václav. He was also the saint who was credited with preventing a civil war between King Vratislav II and his son Břetislav in 1091.[31] Supernatural protection made the rulers of

[27] *CDB* I, no. 110, p. 111; no. 135, p. 137.
[28] *CDB* I, no. 270, p. 238.
[29] *CDB* I, no. 247, p. 218; no. 280, p. 247.
[30] *Legenda Christiani*, 100–2.
[31] Cosmas pp. 64, 154–5.

Prague the most important intermediaries between the Creator and Czech people.

Official sources referred to the sacral character of Přemyslid power to argue that only members of the dynasty could obtain ducal power. In the first half of the twelfth century it was evident that rulers of the Czechs should originate only from the Přemyslid family. But that was not so obvious at the beginning of the eleventh century. In 1001 the Piast duke Bolesław I took power in Prague with the assent of the majority of the local elite. Although he lost it the following year, Piast rulers maintained control over Moravia until *c.* 1034. This was possible because contemporaries attributed more significance to the the will of the 'people' (i.e. assembly of warriors) than to hereditary rights in the possession of power. Their support was decisive during succession wars. One of the most spectacular confirmations of the role played by magnates as watchmen of the political order is Cosmas's description of the circumstances of Břetislav I issuing his last will. When the dying duke finished presenting the seniority principle of succession, he emphasized that magnates gathered around him would have to monitor his sons and relatives to obey these rules. Members of the elite were the key to a lawful succession. Přemyslids themselves had to be monitored by the people.

Yet such a reality did not deny – at least in the ducal court's propaganda – the sacral origin of the power held by the dynasty. The *Legenda Christiani* included a short description of the beginning of Czech history. Like animals, Czechs simply wandered the Earth. Affected by plague, they turned to a prophetess for help. She responded through divination. Following it they created the city of Prague and elected as a ruler Přemysl, who married the prophetess. The plague ended and Czechs 'ex sobole eius [i.e. Premizli] rectores seu duces preposuere sibi'.[32] This story was a synthesis of the ideological grounds of ducal power. On the one hand the origin of dynastic power had a sacral character derived from the revelation of God's will. On the other hand the manifestation of this will was impossible without the active co-operation of the Czechs. Their free will was decisive in the acceptance of Přemysl's descendants as Czech rulers. God's will, the hereditary principle limited to the Přemyslid dynasty and the decisive role of the Czech people were

[32] *Legenda Christiani*, p. 18.

presented as a coherent whole. This story – based on a common European tradition of *origo potestatis* – encapsuled the ideal vision of political order in Czech society in the eleventh and twelfth centuries.

In the eleventh century the role of the Prague dukes in Czech society was still based on a traditional perception of social roles with the duke as the guardian of tradition and social order, and of social obligations in particular. The duke alone – at least formally – was entitled to judge whether the actions of his subjects, nobles and commoners alike, had been consistent with pertinent norms and to punish them for transgressions. This did not imply that he was totally free to shape the social order. He had to take into consideration the constant scrutiny and appraisal by the aristocrats (*primates terre*) and nobles (*populus*) of his fitness for exercising authority. Any sign of weakness or departure from the prescribed role could bring upon him their mutiny, and his exile and occasionally mutilation at the hand of his victorious rival and close relative. Perhaps the ruler's acknowledged need regularly to reconfirm his resolve to hold on to power underlay the acts of bloody vengeance directed against individuals and families perceived as internal foes. In extreme cases, this led to the extinction of entire family lines and their households, servants and associates: the Slavnikids in 995 and the Vršovci clan in 1108. According to contemporary chroniclers, during the carnage of the entire 'house' of Vršovci, ordered by Duke Svatopluk, some 3,000 people were slain in Bohemia and Moravia. Although many judged the duke's actions to be cruel and unjust, nobody dared oppose his decision.

In the early eleventh century, the workings of central authority were formed by the tradition of ducal rule harking back to the ninth century. Přemyslid dukes relied on their closest companions and followers. It is doubtful that the duke gave them court offices during the first half of the eleventh century. The first traces of court officials appear in the second half of the eleventh century; their introduction was probably an echo of the 'imitatio imperii', copying imperial customs in court organization. The distribution of court offices became the most important tool used by dukes to influence the political sentiments of the elites. These dignities were connected to revenues flowing both directly from the duke's treasury and from landed estates given by the duke as beneficia. Ducal liberty in office distribution was, apart from the threat of uncontrolled violence against rebellious members of the Czech people, the key to obtaining elites' obedience and support.

Court offices held by lay nobles are attested relatively early, from the late eleventh and early twelfth centuries. Initially, the most important was that of the palatine (*palatinus*), who was responsible for leading warriors during the absence of a ruler, but the office quickly disappeared. In the twelfth century, his duties were performed by the bailiff (*camerarius, summus camerarius*) and the castellan (*castellanus*) of Prague. The marshal (*marsalcus*) was another influential figure. Already in the first half of the twelfth century, the master of the horses (*agazo*), judge (*iudex, iudex curie*), bailiff, cup-bearer (*pincerna*), *dapifer* and master of the hunt (*venator, summus curie ducis venator*) appeared in the duke's inner circle. With the exception of the judge, who was responsible for holding the tribunal at court, their duties were defined by the ruler of the moment. The chancellor (*cancellarius*) prepared ducal charters and co-ordinated diplomacy. From the second half of the twelfth century, the bailiff's position began to increase in significance. Among the lower dignitaries, the most important positions were held by the *supanus*, the head of the ducal administration in a province, and the *castellanus*, governing administrative units below the provincial level.

Making a written record of common law and confirming it with a ducal privilege limited the duke's power over the political elite. In 1189, Konrád II Ota as duke of Znojmo regulated the powers of principal court offices, claiming these were rooted in the past. The bailiff (*camerarius*) was responsible for collecting taxes and court-imposed fines for the ducal treasury, while the castellan (*castellanus*) would represent the ruler before the local community and accompany the judge (*iudex*) in performing judiciary duties. The court could convene in the presence of other knights, and not only noblemen but also freemen could appear before it. This demonstrates that in the second half of the twelfth century the authority of the duke and consequently of his representatives became limited not only with regard to the high nobility. Nobles played a growing role in establishing and maintaining public order. Scholars are in agreement that the model of hierarchy of offices and the nobles' role in the judiciary system was characteristic of the second half of the twelfth century. With the passage of time, the ducal offices' hierarchy became increasingly specific, closely connected with local tradition, legal order and needs of the ruler.

## Poland

The royal crown was seldom worn; each crowned Piast wore it only for a short time. Bolesław I was crowned in 1025 and died the same year; Mieszko II reigned as king between 1025 and 1031. The next Piast to be king, Bolesław II the Bold, was crowned in 1076, but was expelled from the country in 1079. Like his namesake in 1025, he also received a crown from the pope. According to tradition, Bolesław II's crown was held in the treasury of Cracow cathedral. The next Piast to wear the royal crown was Przemysł II, crowned in 1295 and murdered in 1296. For eleventh-century Piast rulers, royal coronation perhaps had a great significance for their status abroad, but no source suggests that their position within the realm changed in comparison with all other Piast rulers who bore only the ducal title.[33]

Piasts and their wives used both the people and the territory they ruled over in their titulature. Titles incorporating the name of the territory ('Salomea ducissa Polonie', 1143)[34] were used less frequently in charters than those referring to the name of subjected people (for example 'invictissimus dux polonorum Wladizlaus', in the inventory of the vault of Cracow cathedral, 1101).[35] Titles emphasizing the territorial scope of the rulers' power dominated after the division of the Piast realm after 1138. Bolesław I the Tall (Wysoki), duke of Silesia (1163–1201), in a charter (1175) described his and his father's position as connected with ruled territories: 'Bolezlaus dux Zlesie filius... principis Wladyzlai maximi ducis Zlesie et Cracovie'.[36] At the same time the term 'Polonia' changed its meaning. Although it could still refer to the whole Piast realm as before, more often it signified the territory of Greater Poland. Duke Mieszko III the Old of Greater Poland was called in his charters 'Mescho dei gracia dux Polonie' (1145, 1173, 1181, 1186, 1188).[37] But when he wanted to emphasize that he was the senior and supreme duke of the whole of Poland, he was named 'Misico divina favente clemencia dux tocius Polonie'.[38] His opponent, Duke Kazimierz the Just, ruler of Cracow but also

[33] Zbigniew Dalewski, '"Vivat princeps in eternum": sacrality of ducal power in Poland in the earlier Middle Ages', in *Monotheistic Kingship: The Medieval Variants*, ed. Aziz Al-Azmeh (Budapest, 2004), 215–30.

[34] *Kodeks dyplomatyczny Wielkopolski / Codex Diplomaticus Maioris Poloniae*, vol. I, ed. Ignacy Zakrzewski (Poznań, 1877) (henceforth *KDWp* I), no. 9.

[35] *KDWp* I, no. 4; MPH I, pp. 376, 517 (the example cited in the text).

[36] *KDWp* I, no. 21. [37] *KDWp* I, nos. 10–11, 20, 26–8. [38] *KDWp* I, no. 22.

hegemon of the whole dynasty, used 'Kazimerus dux Polonie' (1178) in his charters. He was designated in the same way in a papal bull (1180),[39] even though he never ruled Greater Poland. Thus the difference in the meaning of the word 'Polonia' in the titles of rulers can be specified only within their political context.

As the Piast realm was founded (in the beginning exclusively and later largely) on the strength of the ruling duke's warriors, in the tenth and eleventh centuries no other aristocratic families are attested either competing with or supporting the Piasts. Moreover, we know very little about court offices in Poland before the end of the eleventh century. The court and administration system of Władysław Herman discussed in detail by Gallus Anonymous do not appear complex. The top position was held by the palatine Sieciech who was the duke's principal adviser and acted as his deputy during military campaigns, but his influence was perceived as exceptional and inappropriate. It was emphasized that the supreme power should have rested with the duke, fully and exclusively, and he should not have ceded it to anyone. Alongside the palatine, the office of *comes* is mentioned: its holders acted as provincial governors or commanders of principal strongholds. *Vastaldiones* are mentioned as the duke's representatives at a lower level and with more limited powers.

The ruler's immediate circle remains elusive. Its members' position relative to the ruler was not very strong, yet at the same time the ruler had to have recourse to their co-operation, advice and aid. The chronicle of Anonymous suggests that in the twelfth century Polish elites expected the ruler to listen to their advice, although the final decision had to be his alone. His advisers were depicted monitoring the implementation of their ruler's decision. The ruler was not allowed to change his expressed will without consultation with his advisers.

Insofar as we can reconstruct them, conflicts between Piasts and powerful nobles mostly concerned inheritance after the ruler's death (see above), and drastic violations of traditional social norms. In 1079, King Bolesław II the Bold was deposed following his sentencing for treachery and the execution of Stanisław, bishop of Kraków. In 1149, the blinding of the palatine Piotr Włost accelerated the fall and expulsion of Władysław II the Exile. It is noteworthy that, although Bolesław III the Wrymouth had the palatine Skarbimir blinded for his

[39] *KDWp* I, nos. 23, 25.

alleged conspiracy against the duke (1136), the latter soon made peace with him, apparently aware of the possible consequences. In the twelfth century, the Piast rulers' political decisions were influenced by public opinion or, more precisely, the opinion of the magnates. When Otto, bishop of Bamberg, asked Bolesław the Wrymouth to forgo vengeance against the Pomeranians who had invaded his land, he refused so as not to lose authority in the eyes of his subjects, relenting only after the Pomeranian duke's public act of penance.

By the second half of the eleventh century, dukes could no longer rule disregarding the entitlements of two privileged groups: the members of their inner circle of advisers and warriors (the so-called *druzhina*; see below) and prelates of the Church. In the course of the twelfth century, the tendency towards limiting the power of Polish dukes via the rights of the nobles, warriors (knights) and clergy intensified. The first liberty for the Church issued in the late twelfth century introduced written rules to be honoured by the duke. Soon, charters of immunity were issued for knights and settlers in newly founded villages, and in the thirteenth century for towns as well. A new model of ducal power was based on co-operation between dukes and both secular and ecclesiastical elites. This new system of power distribution was derived from a combination of the territorialization of ducal power and the fixing in writing of the rights of separate social groups. The duke ruled over territories, but people were subject less to his will and more to laws. Different social groups (clergy, warriors, peasants etc.) who had been living according to traditions and local laws strove for recognition by the ruler and the fixing of their rights in writing. The process started around 1170 and was accelerated by the political struggle between dukes. Socio-political changes gained momentum due to the economic reforms introduced in Silesia by Bolesław the Tall. The real fruits of the transformation became visible in the second half of the thirteenth and in the fourteenth century.[40]

## *Hungary*

Hungarian kingship was based on personal prowess, the co-operation of the elite, landed possessions, a variety of revenues, an increasing

[40] Sławomir Gawlas, 'Fürstenherrschaft, Geldwirtschaft und Landesausbau. Zum mittelalterlichen Moderniesierungsprozess im piastischen Polen', in *Rechtsstadtgründungen im mittelalterlichen Polen*, ed. Eduard Mühle (Cologne, 2011), 13–76.

organization of governance through established institutions, and warfare. The kings' personal role was not negligible, for example as military leader or the creator of good compromises. Yet one should beware of the pitfalls of drawing wide-ranging conclusions from the alleged personal qualities of individual rulers. This has been a standard procedure in the historiography of Hungary (as well as in other national historiographies). Such an enterprise, however, is not simply futile, but misleading, because the narrative descriptions on which they are based are provided by the Hungarian Chronicles, which reflect the political concerns of the times when they were composed, rather than the true characteristics of the people described; moreover, what survives has been heavily reworked. One example illustrates the problem well. Kálmán was described in an extremely negative light: puny, cunning, hairy, one-eyed, hunch-backed, lame and lisping. He shed innocent blood in having Álmos and Béla blinded, and was punished for it by an early death. Ultimately inspired by biblical imagery (Leviticus 21:17–23) taken up in canon law, and medieval ideas about physiognomy, this is clearly not a realistic portrayal. Yet other descriptions seem more believable, such as the cruelty and youthful insouciance of István II, Kálmán's son, leading his warriors into unnecessary and unproductive wars; yet this description was just as much the outcome of textual revision by an author inimical to the Kálmán branch of the dynasty. The two fourteenth-century versions of the Hungarian Chronicle which include the details cited above are the result of the revision of an earlier chronicle, a revision occasioned by the ascension of the Álmos branch of the dynasty to the throne, and carried out during the reign of either Géza II (1141–62) or István III (1162–72). As the then ruling kings descended from Álmos's son Béla II, who had been blinded by King Kálmán, the chronicler retrospectively delegitimized Kálmán and his son through such depictions. The characterization of kings in the chronicle therefore is not a sound basis for historical judgements.[41]

[41] *Chronici Hungarici*, 421, 430, 434–7, 442. Eng. tr. and facsimile, Dezső Dercsényi, ed., *The Hungarian Illuminated Chronicle* (Budapest, 1969); for an analysis of the images, see László Veszprémy, Tünde Wehli and József Hapák, *The Book of the Illuminated Chronicle* (Budapest, 2009). See also Kornél Szovák, 'L'historiographie hongroise à l'époque arpadienne', in Csernus and Korompay, eds., *Les Hongrois et l'Europe*, 375–84.

Legitimizing their rule was a key concern for the rulers. Papal or imperial backing could play a role, but was not essential: Géza I, who seized power in 1074 from the crowned king Salamon, was treated by both Pope Gregory VII and King Henry IV of Germany as a usurper, yet retained power as the latter two were engaged in conflict with each other. Coronation by the archbishop of Esztergom became necessary sometime before 1172; the archbishop's right in this respect was confirmed by Pope Innocent III in 1212. Yet this was not an unsurmountable obstacle for those who failed to gain such coronation during the twelfth century. As discussed in detail in Chapter 6, Archbishop Lukács (Lucas) refused to crown László II and István IV as usurpers, yet they were crowned by the archbishop of Kalocsa. Lukács also refused to crown Béla III; he too received the crown from the archbishop of Kalocsa.[42]

History-writing and building projects also contributed to royal legitimization. Not only the portraits of rulers, but also ideas of royal legitimacy themselves changed in the course of the revisions of the chronicle. According to modern historians, two different forms of legitimization were invoked in two separate rewritings of the text. In order to legitimize the Álmos branch of the dynasty, the primacy of *legitimitas* through inheritance and coronation was propounded in the middle of the twelfth century. Then a late twelfth- or early thirteenth-century reworking emphasized idoneity – suitability and personal valour – as the basis of rulership, because of the circumstances of Béla III's coronation (1172–96), which were not according to the usual custom.[43]

Novel forms of legitimization were also introduced over time. László I suffered from a 'legitimacy deficit' and in 1083 organized the canonization of István I, his son Imre, two hermits and the martyred bishop Gerard (Gellért), to emphasize the holy origins of the dynasty and of the Christian realm. Similarly motivated at least in

[42] Erik Fügedi, 'A magyar király koronázásának rendje a középkorban', in *Eszmetörténeti Tanulmányok a magyar középkorról*, ed. György Székely (Budapest, 1984), 255–73; Erik Fügedi, 'Coronation in medieval Hungary', in Fügedi, *Kings, Bishops, Nobles and Burghers in Medieval Hungary*, ed. János M. Bak (London, 1986), 159–89.

[43] József Gerics, *Legkorábbi gesta-szerkesztéseink keletkezésrendjének problémái*, Értekezések a történeti tudományok köréből n.s. 22 (Budapest, 1961), 88–112; Gyula Kristó, 'Legitimitás és idoneitás: adalékok Árpád-kori eszmetörténetünkhöz', *Századok* 108 (1974), 585–621.

part by political considerations, Béla III in 1192 achieved the canonization of László I. This supported the idea of legitimate rulership through idoneity: Béla's coronation by the archbishop of Kalocsa appeared more acceptable in the perspective of László's canonization because it sanctified a ruler who had deprived the crowned king Salamon of the throne. Probably more importantly, the canonization also had to do with Béla III's aspirations connected to the crusades. In the developing cult of chivalry, László was transformed into a holy knight, in the service of God. He became the most popular Hungarian saint: a chivalrous hero, an ideal knight and allegedly the elected leader of the first crusade (although in fact he died prior to the papal call for the crusade).[44]

Royal titles were initially somewhat fluid but used the name of the people: István used 'Ungrorum rex' and 'Pannoniorum rex'; his successors kept both (with variations such as 'Hungarorum rex') and by the end of the eleventh century shifted to the territorial designation 'Ungarie rex'. This territorial designation may have existed from the beginning, but the evidence is not conclusive. Two of István's charters already indicate a territory rather than a people, but one survives in a thirteenth-century transcript and therefore the royal title may have been updated according to formulas then current; the other is a Greek charter and may follow the Byzantine model of territorial designation ('krales Hungarias') rather than translating a practice existing in Hungary. In the twelfth century, kings routinely added the names of new territories, over which they maintained some claim, to their title.[45]

Royal authority has often been seen as near-absolute, relying on Otto of Freising's statements. He claimed that the Hungarians 'all render such obedience to their prince that every man regards it as wrong, I will not say to enrage him by open contradiction, but even to annoy him by secret whisperings', and asserted that the will of the

[44] Gábor Klaniczay, *Holy Rulers and Blessed Princesses: Dynastic Cults in Medieval Central Europe*, tr. Éva Pálmai (Cambridge, 2002), 173–94; László Veszprémy, '*Dux et praeceptor Hierosoliminatorum*. König Ladislaus (László) als imaginärer Kreuzritter', in *The Man of Many Devices, Who Wandered Full Many Ways . . . : Festschrift in Honor of János M. Bak*, ed. Balázs Nagy and Marcell Sebők (Budapest, 1999), 470–7.

[45] Györffy, *Diplomata Hungariae*; Imre Szentpétery and Iván Borsa, eds., *Regesta regum stirpis Arpadianae critico-diplomatica / Az Árpád-házi királyok okleveleinek kritikai jegyzéke*, 4 vols. (Budapest, 1923–87).

prince alone was enough to determine punishment, replacing formal sentencing, and that all obeyed his call to arms.[46] Otto also describes the Hungarians as barbarians with no real houses and no developed system of government. To accept this description as a statement of fact does not take into account the context: as Sverre Bagge's analysis has shown, the function of each part of Otto's text needs to be understood in light of his overall argument. The tyrannical form of government and barbarian character of the inhabitants of Hungary are juxtaposed to the anarchy of the Italians, whose barbarian origin is modified by Roman culture. Both represent deviations from 'proper respect for rank and social hierarchy', represented by the Germans.[47] Otto's depiction therefore should not be taken as reality; indeed, other pieces of evidence contradict it.

The Hungarian kings' power was far from absolute. Brute force was part of ensuring royal power, but never for long or as the sole means of rulership. Even in its most spectacular instances, such force also depended on the loyalty of at least part of the elite. Notably, after Béla II's ascent, in 1131 and in the following year during the pretender Boris's attack, the king's followers massacred many members of the elite, who were held responsible for the blinding of Béla and his father, or were suspected adherents of Boris. This was possible only because the king had a sufficient number of loyal men among the nobles. Much information survives on elite families supporting the king; it is clear that kings were unable to survive without such support. This is most clearly demonstrated by the fate of various pretenders: only those who had the backing of key figures within the realm could gain real, lasting power.

Members of the elite were also at the royal court and filled various court offices. The royal court developed throughout the period. Two dignitaries are documented at István's court: the count palatine and the commander of the bodyguard. Over the next two centuries, the increasing appearance of a variety of dignitaries in the documents probably reflects the gradual emergence of new offices at the court: the marshal (*magister agazonum*, *lovászmester*); head of the heralds and guard (*magister praeconum*, *ajtónállómester*); and from

[46] Waitz, ed., *Ottonis et Rahewini Gesta*, bk I xxxii (xxxi) at 50–1; Mierow, *Otto of Freising*, 67.

[47] Sverre Bagge, 'Ideas and narrative in Otto of Freising's *Gesta Frederici*', *Journal of Medieval History* 22, 4 (1996), 359–60.

the middle of the twelfth century, butler (*magister pincernarum, pohárnokmester*), steward (*magister dapiferorum, asztalnokmester*) and chamberlain, overseeing economic matters (*magister cubiculariorum*, from 1214 *magister tavernicorum, tárnokmester*). The count palatine (*comes palatinus; nádor*, probably from Slavic *dvor*, court) was the head of the royal court. He oversaw the *udvarnokok* (*udvornici*, royal serving people), and was responsible for gathering the revenues of the king. He also commanded the warriors attached to royal lands. With the appearance during István II's reign (1116–31) of the *curialis comes*, who was appointed as the head of the royal court in charge of its people and revenues, the office of the palatine increasingly developed as that of judge and second in the realm after the king. In the thirteenth century, he was the ruler's deputy in the latter's absence from the realm.[48] A list of dignitaries started to be added to charters in 1171, but became a consistent and standard feature of charters only from 1192. The royal chapel was the centre of literacy. In the twelfth century, notaries wrote the charters, and the head of the chapel community (*comes capellae*, an ecclesiastic) sealed them with the royal seal. Finally, the chancery became a separate institution during Béla III's reign.[49]

## ROYAL AUTHORITY AND THE EMERGENCE OF THE NOBILITY

According to the model developed by Třeštík and Krzemieńska, the genesis of the knightly estate in both Bohemia and Poland was related to the so-called *druzhina*, a group of warriors forming the duke's inner circle, attested in the second half of the tenth century. Commanding his *druzhina*, who were fully dependent on him, the duke was able to

48 Vilmos Frankl, *A nádori és országbírói hivatal eredete és hatáskörének történeti fejlődése* (Pest, 1863); Iván Bertényi, 'Zur Gerichtsstätigkeit des Palatinus und des Landesrichters (Judex Curiae Regiae) in Ungarn im XIV. Jahrhundert', *Annales Universitatis Scientiarum Budapestinensis de Rolando Eötvös Nominatae* 7 (1965), 29–42; Erik Fügedi, *Ispánok, bárók, kiskirályok* (Budapest, 1986), 46–52.

49 András Kubinyi, 'Königliche Kanzlei und Hofkapelle in Ungarn um die Mitte des 12. Jahrhunderts', in Herwig Ebner, ed., *Festschrift Friedrich Hausmann* (Graz, 1977), 299–324; György Györffy, 'Die ungarischen Königsurkunden bis 1200', *Typologie der Königsurkunden. Kolloquium der Commission Internationale de Diplomatique in Olmütz 30.8.–3.9.1992*, ed. Jan Bistrický (Olomouc, 1998), 259–70.

subdue and control the inhabitants of the territory which would form the nucleus of a more permanent state organization. The existence of such a community of warriors supporting the duke and closely bound to him in tenth-century Poland is attested by Ibrāhīm ibn Ya'qūb.

### *Bohemia*

This model has been questioned by Czech scholars. Contrary to the ruler's allegedly unconstrained power until the end of the twelfth century, evidence suggests that already by the middle of the eleventh century the duke could rule with the support of just the most powerful members of his immediate circle. In Moravia and probably in Bohemia in the eleventh century numerous groups of warriors existed who possessed their estates. Their dependence on a ruler's will was much weaker than traditionally believed. They were connected with a ruler but not as dependants, more as allies bound by oaths of fidelity and by the acceptance of conditions of service previously announced by a ruler. According to Cosmas of Prague, Duke Břetislav I in 1055 obliged the nobles to supervise the implementation of succession principles. Admittedly, Cosmas's record of the event dates to the first quarter of the twelfth century, which coincides with the earliest references to 'district courts'.

Until Přemysl Otakar I made royal dignity hereditary in his family, all dukes were elected by members of the knightly elite, who acted according to their own interests. Warriors and their leaders were duke-makers in Bohemia, next to the emperor, and each ruler had to consider his actions in that light. The nobles as representatives of the people, rather than either the people as a whole or the clergy, legitimized the authority of the *dux Bohemorum*.

Even during the lifetime of a duke, the magnates' and warriors' political sympathy waxed and waned. Warriors could serve one duke or another and often broke their oaths of fidelity. The infidelity of the Bohemian aristocracy was almost proverbial at twelfth-century Přemyslid courts. A duke, even if he took power with the emperor's aid, would not rule long without the consent of his warriors. As a reward for the most important or faithful nobles, dukes in the twelfth century distributed court offices. Usually a new duke did not wait for the death or resignation of a former holder of an office, nor did they normally create new posts in the twelfth century. Therefore, almost each new face on the throne provoked a total exchange of courtly elites.[50]

Knightly factions unhappy with a ruler were ready to support any member of the dynasty who could gather enough warriors to fight for the Prague throne. And, after each turnover, hostility between factions escalated. Dukes who took power more than once returned to Prague to avenge harm caused by noble traitors or supporters of the previous ruler. All this caused not only permanent political instability, but also made fights between contestants for power more deadly. Every member of the elite had something to lose and, if his preferred candidate for rulership were defeated, a noble suffered in consequence. Thus the only choice for nobles and warriors during the civil war was to fight to the death or to change sides quickly and join the possible winners. Losers did not expect mercy. During the entire twelfth century dukes were conscious of the unreliability of Bohemian magnates and warriors and tried to bind them to themselves more effectively in different ways. Svatopluk II, after years of fighting for the throne, remembering the ease with which his mighty supporters had fled from him, created a new group of potential officials, called *milites secundi ordini*. They originated mostly from younger descendants of nobles and warriors of lower social standing. They were all *homines novi* but without a chance to maintain their newly achieved status when the ruler changed even if they changed their loyalties to the new ruler.

Much earlier than previously thought, already in the eleventh century, and by the late eleventh–early twelfth century at the latest, the elite – *comites*, *proceres*, *primates*, *milites primi ordini* – were set apart from ordinary warriors (*milites*). It seems convincing that in the second half of the eleventh century members of the warrior elite played the role of leaders and representatives for ordinary warriors. Usually a ruler communicated with and influenced his warriors indirectly, with the help of these privileged members of the group. When Spytihněv took power in Prague in 1055, he worried about the fidelity of Moravian rulers, his brothers. Therefore he asked Moravian nobles, listed by name, to take the vow of fidelity. When they refused, he defeated them with his own warriors, and took their 'arms and horses'.

50 Libor Jan, 'K pocátkum ceské šlechty: družina, beneficium, pozemkové vlastnictví', in *Šlechta, moc a reprezentace ve stredoveku*, ed. Martin Nodl and Martin Wihoda (Prague, 2007), 45–52.

Apparently, external signs of status indicated the membership of *proceres* in a warrior group, but their social role was that of local leaders rather than ordinary warriors.

In theory all warriors were equal in terms of law, yet the *militi primi et secundi ordinis* in reality played quite different roles in society. The higher echelon formed a narrow elite of both local and state importance. The second group consisted of simple warriors, socially dominant over the peasants, but their members had no political importance as individuals. The future knightly estate most likely evolved from both groups of the elite whose role as an autonomous political subject probably dates to the late eleventh century. The group's members had a relatively independent economic status. They also had a provincial assembly representing their interests. Functionaries were not arbitrarily chosen by the ruler. From the second half of the eleventh century, court offices, although not hereditary, would be generally held by members of several families forming Bohemia's top elite, who retained their position for generations. Two equally important factors in keeping such a position were, first, the will of the ruler and, second, coming from a family which for generations had participated in deciding the realm's politics.[51]

On the one hand Bohemian *milites* and especially magnates played a decisive role in dukes gaining and holding power in the eleventh and twelfth centuries. But, on the other hand, they depended on the duke, who led simple warriors to Poland or Italy to gain riches and glory. It was a duke who distributed offices together with revenues connected to them. Service to a duke, fighting for him and monitoring his fidelity to Czech tradition were important elements of the noble ethos. The thirteenth century brought a fundamental shift in the emancipation of the nobles from under the power of Bohemian kings. A network of fortified stone castles, serving as residences of high nobles and centres of their vast estates, reflected the influence of western chivalrous culture and signalled the emergence of the knightly estate modelled on the west European pattern in the thirteenth century. At the same time rulers freed themselves from dependence on their warriors. Succession became hereditary, giving a new position to the king. The ruler also gained military independance: colonization, the mining industry and

[51] Vratislav Vanícek, 'Sociální mentalita ceské šlechty: urozenost, rytírství, reprezentace. (Obecné souvislosti, pojetí družiny, "modernizacní" trend)', in *Šlechta, moc a reprezentace ve stredoveku*, 141–88.

town foundations enabled a duke to contract with mercenaries instead of relying on traditionally gathered warriors. The latter were still important both for political stability and for the royal army. But the process of a growing independence of the two main parties in society from each other had begun.[52]

## *Poland*

Traditional explanations of the warrior elite's origin in the Piast realm were based on two presumptions. First, members of the ducal druzhina were in tenth and first half of the eleventh century strictly and totally dependent on a ruler. Second, their independence started not earlier than during the rule of Kazimierz the Restorer, during the long and costly process of restoration of ducal authority and political structures after the crisis in the 1030s.

It is difficult to estimate the size of the duke's *druzhina* at the beginning of the eleventh century either in absolute numbers or as a proportion of the given country's population. Some scholars refer to Gallus Anonymous's account of Poland under Bolesław I the Brave and argue that Piast's *druzhina* consisted of more than 1,000 warriors. But this seems unlikely. Archaeological excavations of early medieval cemeteries have revealed few burials of warriors with expensive equipment, which suggests otherwise. The source of the *druzhina*'s strength and influence lay not in their numbers but in their connection to the duke as well as their costly (and thus exclusive) equipment and military training, which enabled them to keep under control the population subjected by the ruler.

His closest supporters – governors of provinces and army commanders in his absence (*comites*) – and top officials were recruited from among the duke's warriors. On the one hand, the hypotheses that this group partially recruited from the former tribal aristocracy subdued in the tenth century and then absorbed into the Piast apparatus of power cannot be totally rejected. On the other hand, the scale of destruction inflicted upon tribal strongholds in the process of the

[52] Vratislav Vaniček, 'Šlechta a český stát za vlády Přemyslovcu: k formování ideologie české šlechty od 11. do počatku 14. století', *Folia Historica Bohemica* 12 (1988), 65–107; Martin Vichoda, 'Snemy Cechu', in *Šlechta v promenách veku*, ed. Tomáš Knoz and Jan Dvorák (Brno, 2011), 17–37; Libor Jan, *Ćeska moravská šlechta ve 13. a 14. stoleti: otazky zrodu a kontinuity* (Brno, 2011), 38–62.

formation of the polity, revealed by archaeological excavations, suggests that Mieszko I had not been interested in maintaining traditional signs of the local aristocracy's domination. It seems most likely that the narrow power elite in the state of Mieszko I and his successors emerged through a process of synthesis. Initially, loyal tribal aristocrats could be among the duke's trusted followers but in the eleventh century close ties with the ruler became essential.

Kazimierz the Restorer, during the violent power struggle following the crisis of the 1030s, removed, perhaps even physically eliminated, the members of the elite who had been active under Bolesław I and Mieszko II and instead relied on new people, who owed their position and loyalty exclusively to him. By the second half of the eleventh century, this forced rotation at the top of the power structure, resulting in the emergence of a narrow circle closely bound to the ruler and fully dependent upon him. By the century's end, a group of high nobles partially independent of the duke began to evolve as well. Few of them were rich enough to emulate the duke in the splendour of their endowments to the Church. Nonetheless, their privileged position incited the envy of their fellow nobles, and even of the ruler himself, which occasionally resulted in violent actions taken against prominent aristocrats. This in turn led to crises engulfing the entire realm, like the war of Zbigniew and Bolesław III against Władysław Herman and his palatine Sieciech.

In an attempt to ease the financial burden on the ruler, and being well acquainted with the German system, Kazimierz probably started to supply his aristocracy with land as fiefs in return for military service.[53] If not Kazimierz the Restorer, then his successors allowed warriors to gather land and form quite large estates. Indeed, unlike in Bohemia, the first accounts of knightly private property in Poland start relatively late, from the end of the eleventh and beginning of the twelfth century. Landowning strengthened the political independence of nobles. As a result, Władysław Herman was seen by contemporaries as dependent on the support of the aristocracy to sustain his position. The political weakness of the duke afforded an important role to his close aide, the palatine, Sieciech. His own political ambitions served to extend the role of the monarch's closest ally, which is testified by the unusual issuing of coins bearing his name

[53] Jerzy Wyrozumski, *Dzieje Polski piastowskiej (VIII w.–1370)* (Cracow, 1999), 111.

(*ZETEH*).[54] This became possible only when the old system of military organization transformed into one in which former warriors were more politicians, allies of a ruler, than soldiers. They still fought, but the time of strong control over warriors and elites was almost gone at the beginning of the twelfth century, if it ever existed.[55]

From the late eleventh century we see the split of warrior status into two categories. The senior ones formed a group of the duke's influential advisers and office-holders. They participated in decisions in the matters of the realm and their importance grew during the period of the fragmentation of Poland after 1138. At least from the late eleventh century, they accumulated estates securing the family's position even after the death of its prominent member. In the twelfth century, the largest estates comprised dozens of villages. In the second half of the twelfth century, with the ruler's revenues from military campaigns reduced, the high nobility began to focus on acquiring landholdings. Their Church foundations endowed with landed estates provide the earliest evidence of the existence of large *latifundia*. The other group within the elite consisted of young warriors who were the most combat-worthy element in the ruler's army.

Alongside the mounted warriors of the *druzhina*, peasants would be called to arms on foot or on horseback, and they formed the bulk of the ducal army in the twelfth century. Likewise, armed servants in retinues of Polish clergymen were very likely also peasants. It must be emphasized, however, that already in 1136 the papal bull issued for the archbishopric of Gniezno mentioned *milites* among its subjects. Castle warriors ensured the stronghold's defence and also went on military campaigns with the duke. They probably did not occupy themselves with farming but were supplied with the necessary provisions and craft goods from service villages of the castle estate. On the other hand, they were not part of the *druzhina* and had no chance ever to join it.

[54] Stanisław Suchodolski, 'Czy monety palatyna Sieciecha świadczą o jego dążeniu do przejęcia władzy w Polsce?', in *Causa creandi: o pragmatyce źródła historycznego*, ed. Stanisław Rosik and Przemysław Wiszewski (Wrocław, 2006), 365–75.

[55] Tadeusz Wasilewski, 'Poland's administrative structure in early Piast times: castra ruled by comites as centres of provinces and territorial administration', *Acta Poloniae Historica* 44 (1981), 5–31; Karol Modzelewski, '*Comites, principes, nobiles:* the structure of the ruling class as reflected in the terminology used by Gallus Anonymous', in *The Polish Nobility in the Middle Ages: Anthology*, ed. Antoni Gąsiorowski (Wrocław, 1984), 177–206.

In the second half of the twelfth century, the knightly estate gradually emerged. With the provincial fragmentation of Poland split between the sons of Bolesław the Wrymouth following his death, local dynasties ruled over their respective provinces and, in order to secure fidelity, transferred land on a large scale to members of their entourage and nobles. In the course of the thirteenth century, this process resulted in the establishment of a provincial aristocracy and a group of mounted warriors subscribing to the western chivalrous ethos and subsisting primarily on revenues generated by their landholdings.[56]

### *Hungary*

Royal armies consisted of the land-holding nobility, castle-warriors (*várjobbágy*) provided by the castle districts, who were bound to the service of the king, warriors of the ecclesiastical lands, and various eastern and western settler groups who depended on the king. From the eleventh century, the latter included western knights, eastern nomads (primarily Pechenegs in the early centuries), Székely (whose origin and identity have been hotly debated) and Muslims. Not only were royal armies made up of a number of different groups, but these constituents also brought a variety of military techniques: westerners fought as heavy cavalry, in western-style armour and arms, while the nomads, Székely and Muslims did so as light cavalry with bows and arrows. Several pieces of evidence demonstrate the recurrent need to draw more warriors into the army. Thus, Kálmán was keen to regulate the number and type of warriors that *ispán*s sent to the royal army depending on the level of income from freemen: with a revenue of over 100 *pensae*, one man with armour; with a revenue between 40 and 100 *pensae*, one man without armour. Géza II actively recruited Muslim soldiers from the east. Western knights were also actively recruited by many rulers. This trend continued in the thirteenth century.[57]

[56] Tomasz Jurek, 'Geneza szlachty polskiej', in *Šlechta, moc a reprezentace ve stredoveku*, 63–140.

[57] Attila Zsoldos, 'The first centuries of Hungarian military organization', in *A Millennium of Hungarian Military History*, ed. László Veszprémy and Béla K. Király (Boulder, CO, 2002), 3–25. For Kálmán's regulation, see Bak *et al.*, eds., *Laws*, p. 29, c. 40. See also Szabó, *A honfoglalóktól*; N. Berend, *At the Gate of Christendom*, 140–2.

The emergent power of the nobility in the period was tied to their warrior status as well as to their role in politics.[58] Foreign and local nobles both formed a part of the elite and held large estates. German warriors first entered in the entourage of Queen Gisela, and both Germans and others arrived in the kingdom throughout the period.[59] Nobles who arrived in the entourage of the new queens and settled at court could sometimes play a significant political role: Beloš, the brother of Queen Helena (Jelena; Béla II's queen), was regent during the minority of her son Géza II. One example illustrates the continuities and discontinuities of the elite's power. Of those holding high offices under István III, several, such as Ampod and Dénes, supported Béla III immediately upon his entry to Hungary, and continued to hold similar high offices during his reign (palatine and *ban* in the former case, county *ispán* of Bács in the latter). Others opposed him and dropped out of the ranks of high officials.

The local elite together with the newcomers were crucial to governing the realm. They not only filled court offices, but also provided the representatives of the king at the head of the counties (called 'count', *ispán*, from the southern Slav *župan*; *comes*) and in royal fortresses (castle- or *várispán*), and thus held the most important non-ecclesiastical offices. The royal council consisted of those who held high office, the upper sections of the lay and ecclesiastical elite, *ispán*s and bishops. The king consulted them on, and needed their consent about, internal and external matters. Members of the council could also prompt royal actions, for example royal donations to ecclesiastical institutions. All members of the council probably never gathered together. Twelfth-century charters contain witness lists of those actually present at various royal decisions: they invariably come from among such high officials, but never include all of them. Nobles also emulated the ruler in starting to have recourse to written instruments. The earliest non-royal charters were both issued by nobles: Otto in 1061 and Peter around 1067, to give donations to

58 Fügedi, *Ispánok, bárók.*

59 Erik Fügedi and János Bak, 'Foreign knights and clerks in early medieval Hungary', in Nora Berend, ed., *The Expansion of Central Europe in the Middle Ages* (Farnham, 2013), 319–32; Nora Berend, 'Noms et origines des immigrants nobles en Hongrie (XIIIe siècle): la liste des *advenae* entre mythe et réalités', in *Anthroponymie et déplacements dans la Chrétienté médiévale*, ed. Monique Bourin and Pascual Martínez Sopena (Madrid, 2010), 247–64.

their monasteries.[60] King Béla III, whose power was much more secure than that of his predecessors, started the novelty of donating whole counties to members of the lay elite, which eventually contributed to a major shift in power. Important though the elite were as counsellors and supporters of the king, during the eleventh and twelfth centuries they did not gain independent power in their own right, a situation that changed in the thirteenth century.

The first two centuries of the Hungarian kingdom witnessed many power struggles between claimants to the throne and more or less successful attempts to establish separate territorial bases of authority. Many kings aimed at consolidating their power, but some spent virtually their entire reign trying to achieve this. Other rulers left a significant mark on legislation or institutions of government. The nobility's rise as a significant political player began during the period, but it was only in the thirteenth century that changes tipped the balance in favour of noble over royal power.

## CENTRES OF POWER, FORTS AND ADMINISTRATION

### *Bohemia*

At the end of the tenth and beginning of the eleventh centuries the Přemyslids lost control over lands north of the Carpathians (with centres in Cracow and Wrocław), and their domination over Moravian magnates weakened. Přemyslid rulers tried to emulate imperial rituals of power but they had to adapt them to local traditions, which was difficult in a weakened and divided realm. The complex political situation was reflected in the geography of power. Prague was the capital city from the late tenth century, but it was the ducal fortress of Vyšehrad that remained the symbolic seat of supreme power. Allegedly, already in the eleventh century it was protected by stone walls, which set it apart from other ducal residences. It served as the ducal treasury, state prison and seat of the Chapter of Vyšehrad, a privileged ecclesiastical foundation. Prague would attain a similar

[60] Györffy, *Diplomata Hungariae*, no. 50/II, pp. 170–4; no. 58, 182–5; László Solymosi, 'Die Entwicklung der Schriftlichkeit im Königreich Ungarn vom 11. bis zum 13. Jahrhundert', in *Schriftkultur zwischen Donau und Adria bis zum 13. Jahrhundert: Akten der Akademie Friesach 'Stadt und Kultur im Mittelalter', Friesach (Kärnten), 11.–15. September 2002*, ed. Reinhard Härtel (Klagenfurt, 2008), 483–526.

status of Bohemia's symbolic centre when its stone walls were erected *c.* 1138.

According to the chronicler known as the canon of Vyšehrad, Duke Soběslav I 'metropolis Bohemiae Pragam more Latinarum civitatum coepit renovari'. This did not entail any change to the legal framework regulating community life but the city's architectural form subsequently altered and the number of church foundations grew. By the middle of the twelfth century, the ruler of Bohemia wanted his capital to resemble – physically and symbolically – the western cities he was familiar with. In the twelfth century, the capitals of duchies dependent on the Prague ruler, particularly in Moravia, often aspired to the status of a power seat comparable to Vyšehrad or Prague and dominated systems of strongholds (turned into *castellanies* by the twelfth century at the latest). Some strongholds also comprised a ducal residence and served to accommodate the itinerant ducal court: in the Bohemian basin, Žatec, Chrudim, Starou Boleslav, Plzeň and Hradec Králové among others. In Moravia governors of such strongholds represented the local duke rather than the ruler from Prague. They did not necessarily contribute to the state's integration.

According to traditional historiography, Břetislav I developed a uniform administration in Bohemia-Moravia in the eleventh century, based on ducal strongholds, whose governors were responsible for keeping social order and providing military support. The roots of a regular network of strongholds reached deep into the tenth century. Initially, the governor of a ducal stronghold was called a *comes* (tenth–eleventh centuries), and *castellanus* only from the twelfth century. They controlled the inhabitants of each stronghold's administrative district, in particular administering justice and overseeing the collection of dues and tributes. During the eleventh and twelfth centuries officials of lower rank emerged as well, taking over judicial and tax-related duties (see Chapter 5).[61]

Recently, historians have argued that this hypothetical administrative system was based on false presumptions. Its proponents transferred

[61] A summary of traditional views, and an original conceptualization of the Czech duchy ruled by an 'itinerant duke' based on Vyšehrad and Prague, and a topography of power organized accordingly, can be found in Andrzej Pleszczyński, 'Miejsca władzy w Czechach w X-XII wieku. Zarys modely przestrzennego centrum wczesnośredniowiecznej wspólnoty, jego geneza i charakter ideowy', in *Sedes regni principales. Materiały z konferencji. Sandomierz 20–21 października 1997*, ed. Barbara Trelińska (Sandomierz, 1999), 81–94.

the Carolingian administrative system to Great Moravia and the Přemyslid monarchy. According to critics of the traditional explanation, the ducal administration of the whole land was divided into two sections: the duke's private property on the one hand, and land under his power but not in his direct property on the other. The dukes' own landed property was administered through a network of manors (*curiae*), sometimes but not necessarily connected to castellan strongholds. The *villicus*, an official at the head of a manor, was responsible for the economy of ducal estates. His position and that of an official administering justice over ducal subjects was independent of the *castellanus*. The latter, as ducal representative, was responsible only for maintaining good relations with local magnates or wider elites. According to this view, in parallel with the network of castellan strongholds, a complex system of ducal manors existed, of no political or administrative but simply economic significance. They were the middle level in the administration of ducal landed property. Below the manors were single villages belonging to a duke.[62]

### *Poland*

Compared to the Přemyslids, the Piast realm comprised a larger number of territories that had a geographic, political and historic potential to become separate regions. Simultaneously, the pressure for centralization was stronger for an extended period of time. The subsequent provincial fragmentation of Poland after 1138, when each province was ruled by its own branch of the ducal dynasty, fostered the idea of hereditary rule of local dukes and a relative equality within the lineage which appeared later and in much stronger measure than in Bohemia.

From the middle of the tenth century to the end of the twelfth, the perception of the Piast geography of power by members of the dynasty and its subjects changed significantly. According to the *Dagome iudex*, Mieszko I's realm was described as 'civitas Schinesghe cum pertinentiis'.[63] The central point, *civitas Schinesghe*, is commonly

[62] Libor Jan, *Vaclav II. a struktury panovnické moci* (Brno, 2006), 13–37, 59–75, 163–222; Jan, 'Hereditas, výsluha, kastelánie: nekolik poznámek k terminologii a metodologii soucasné historiografie premyslovského období', *Časopis Matice Moravske*, 128 (2009), 461–72.

[63] Victor Wolf von Glanvell, *Die Kanonessammlung des Kardinals Deusdedit, vol. 1, Die Kanonessammlung selbst* (Aalen, 1967) (repr., Paderborn, 1905), lib. III, cap. 199, p. 359, lines 11–12. See Przemysław Wiszewski, 'Dagome iudex et Ote senatrix: on the

seen as 'the state of Gniezno', surrounded by the peripheral provinces. The inner boundaries of *pertinentia* and *civitas* are not attested in the sources. The charter did not contain any information about the number or general character of *pertinentia*. It is simply a term derived probably from contemporary Italian chancery practice, describing the territory of Italian *civitates*. The realm's ecclesiastical organization and its division into dioceses in 1000 (see Chapter 3) is a strong argument for the existence of administrative provinces.

Even if the period after the middle of the eleventh century was relatively stable as far as political geography is concerned, the general pattern of administrative divisions provided the framework for significant changes observed after 1138. During the time of Poland's feudal partition (1138–*c.* 1295), the number of main power centres – centres of separate duchies – proliferated. But the process started not earlier than the last quarter of the twelfth century. Since 1138, the main places of ducal power remained Cracow, Płock, Poznań and Wrocław, capitals of ancient administrative units. Very shortly after 1138 Cracow was perceived as the most important stronghold in Poland. Controlling it was commonly accepted to confer supreme authority over the other Piast dukes. During the 1170s and 1180s, Kalisz, Opole, Sandomierz and Racibórz were established as the central places of new duchies. The number of duchies' centres increased steadily and in the thirteenth century between twenty and thirty such places existed at the same time.

Researchers also constructed a hierarchy of Piast ducal strongholds. Traditionally the cities of Gniezno, Poznań and Cracow were mentioned as the most important strongholds until the middle of the twelfth century. Archaeologists have recently identified several other strongholds which seem to have been of an equal or similar rank (see Chapter 3). The network of highest-ranking strongholds was evidently not stable. Its changing nature is even more obvious when we focus on archaeological data. During the reign of Mieszko I the biggest and most fortified and – therefore seen as the main – strongholds of Greater Poland were Gniezno, Poznań, Giecz and

place of the Polish ruler in the aristocratic circle of the Holy Roman Empire at the close of the tenth century', in *Potestas et communitas. Interdisziplinäre Beiträge zu Wesen und Darstellung von Herrschaftsverhältnissen im Mittelalter östlich der Elbe / Interdisciplinary Studies of the Constitution and Demonstration of Power Relations in the Middle Ages East of the Elbe*, ed. Aleksander Paroń, Sébastien Rossignol, Bartłomiej Sz. Szmoniewski and Grisza Vercamer (Wrocław and Warsaw, 2010), 111–23.

Ostrów Lednicki. Bolesław I and Mieszko II constructed a network of new 'central places of power' on the borderlands of their rule. The scheme changed after the great crisis in the 1030s. After that, dukes concentrated their attention on the ducal seats in a few of the central strongholds (Cracow at first, then Poznań, Gniezno, Wrocław and Płock). In the first half of the eleventh century, the Piasts created new 'sites of power' to suit their political needs to serve as administrative centres and impress through monumental ecclesiastical and residential structures.[64] In the eleventh century a stronghold's importance was not connected with its place in the Church administration, but first of all with the military and administrative role it played for rulers. Some strongholds would serve as the ruler's temporary residences. The presence of a church and/or ducal palace (as in Giecz, Gniezno, Ostrów Lednicki and Poznań) could be a factor contributing to the centre's bigger size, but most strongholds were small fortified places with the primary function of controlling the subject population.

At least by the twelfth century, the Piast realm was divided into several lands, each with its capital in the most important stronghold (*sedes regni principales*), whose network was not totally stable until the end of the century. These units were called provinces (*provinciae*) and their heads were ducal *comites* living in cities (*civitates*). Alongside them appeared ducal officials called *vastaldiones*. Some historians argued that they were independent from the power of ducal *comites* and administered estates belonging to a ruler. Most probably both terms – *comes* and *vastaldus* – described the same office. In Anonymous's chronicle, both offices were mentioned in parallel.[65]

Changes in power structures affected administrative structures in the eleventh century. The system of strongholds evolved: even those regarded as the principal ones in the first half of the eleventh century were sometimes abandoned as continuing wars destroyed the local settlement structure. Shifting administrative concerns or changes in the targets of individual rulers' expansion plans resulted in the flourishing of some centres and the demise of others. Stabilization came only with the change in the function of strongholds. From the late eleventh and in the twelfth century, strongholds were transformed into castellanies, seats of the duke's representative (*comes*, *castellanus*). Their military role, once dominant, lost some of its former

[64] For further literature, see Wiszewski, *Domus Bolezlai*, 435–50.

[65] *Galli Anonymi Cronicae*, 65.

importance, replaced by administrative, judicial, cultural and economic functions as the centres of handicrafts, trade and exchange. At the beginning of the twelfth century offices related to strongholds first appeared in sources next to heads of local ducal administration (*comites*). The Anonymous chronicler mentioned in the first quarter of the twelfth century that ducal dues were collected and distributed by ducal men called 'villici ac vicedomini'.[66] We do not know much about them; they were under the control of the ducal court's officials and their activity was concentrated in ducal strongholds (*civitates*). The formation of the stable system of castellanies was a prolonged process which continued at least through the middle of the twelfth century. From the late twelfth century, chartered towns, a new form of settlement, started to take over their functions.[67]

## *Hungary*

From the eleventh century, two seats founded by Géza and István emerged as key centres of royal power: Esztergom and Fehérvár. Esztergom developed as an administrative centre, which was also the seat of the archbishopric; it was at a strategically as well as economically significant location on the Danube, controlling mercantile and military access. Fehérvár was a sacral centre with the royal basilica that housed the regalia as well as the graves of István and Imre. From the beginning of the twelfth century Hungary's kings were buried there, although this custom was not binding during the following century, and some royal burials occurred elsewhere. A yearly law-day was held here on the feast of István I by the king or his delegate, the *palatinus comes* (*nádor*). In the thirteenth century, the provost (head of the cathedral chapter) was usually the vice-chancellor of the royal chancery. These two seats were developed by successive kings not only as centres of royal power, but also as statements of prestige. They combined a royal residence and a church building. Royal residences were built in stone, so the building material itself distinguished them from the usual earth-and-wood constructions. During the eleventh and twelfth centuries, Castle Hill in Esztergom housed the largest

[66] *Galli Anonymi Cronicae*, 34.

[67] On eleventh–twelfth century topography of power, see Tadeusz Wasilewski, 'Sedes regni principales i sedes regni państwa polskiego jako ośrodki wojskowe, administracyjne i gospodarcze w XI i XII wieku', in *Sedes regni principales*, 57–66.

building complex of the realm including a royal palace, archiepiscopal palace, cathedral and chapter-house. After a fire, Béla III had the palace as well as the cathedral at Esztergom rebuilt in early Gothic style by French masons; he introduced architectural forms that were in step with the latest fashion and until then had been unknown in Hungary. Veszprém was probably the queens' seat, where the cathedral benefited from donations by queens, who were also buried there. The bishop of Veszprém had the right to crown the queen.[68]

The administrative subdivision of the lands of the realm, the origins of which were discussed in Chapter 3, continued over the course of the eleventh and twelfth centuries. By the end of the twelfth century, sources mention seventy-two or seventy-eight *comitatus*, which some historians interpret as referring to counties, and others as designating castle districts. The organization of royal castle districts was fundamental for royal power. The castle district provided warriors for the royal army: the so-called castle warriors (*várjobbágyok*). Their main obligation apart from participation in the army was office-holding, and they lived off the revenue of the castle lands assigned to them, although their person and property ultimately belonged to the king. Each castle mustered its own contingent of warriors. The *ispán* was the military leader of the castle district, taking its troops to war under his banner (according to other historians who do not distinguish between castle district and county, but see them as synonyms, the military contingents and leadership were provided at county level). Forts (called *castra*, sing. *castrum*, castles, from the twelfth century) were mainly of earth-and-wood construction. Roman ruins were also reused in many places. In the first half of the thirteenth century, many castle lands were donated to nobles. After the middle of the thirteenth century, when old-style forts ceased to provide efficient defence, the royal castle organization collapsed and ceased to exist.[69]

Counties (*megyék*, sing. *megye*) multiplied in the eleventh and twelfth centuries, by subdivision as well as by the creation of new counties. According to a very hypothetic calculation, their number

[68] Julianna Altmann *et al.*, *Medium Regni: Medieval Hungarian Royal Seats* (Budapest, 1999); Visy, ed., *Hungarian Archaeology*, 348–53; László Gerevich, ed., *Towns in Medieval Hungary* (Boulder, CO, 1990), 26–35, 54–95.

[69] Kristó, *Vármegyék*, 100–207; Attila Zsoldos, *A szent király szabadjai: Fejezetek a várjobbágyság történetéből* (Budapest, 1999); Zsoldos, 'The first centuries of Hungarian military organization'.

may have doubled between the reign of István and the middle of the twelfth century; new counties continued to emerge thereafter. The county of the eleventh and twelfth centuries continued to be the basic unit of administration and taxation (and also, according to those historians who do not distinguish between castle districts and counties, of military organization). Royal officials (*ispán*s, counts) were at the head of counties, but it seems that during the eleventh and twelfth centuries there was no firm association between an *ispán* and one particular county. Even in the thirteenth century, the *ispán* of one county might perform official functions, such as inducting people into the possession of their estates, in another county. Several individuals were the *ispán* of more than one county at any one time, delegating their power to a *curialis comes* (*udvarispán*) in each county. *Ispán*s held their office from the king, and this office was not hereditary in principle. The revenues from fines and tolls were divided in a two-to-one ratio between the king and the *ispán* according to Otto of Freising. Revenues in kind were consumed by the royal court during its *iter* in the counties. *Ispán*s exercised their judicial authority over the inhabitants of the county, with the exception of those who had immunity. At the same time, *ispán*s were also important lay landholders in their own right. For example, information survives on the extent of the private holdings of one county *ispán*: in 1171, Benedek, *comes* of Veszprém, had twelve estates.[70]

The counties in the frontier zones had their own organization. The term 'march' (*marchia*) was sometimes used, according to the German model, and the organization itself has features of the Carolingian one. The *gyepű* (*indagines*) was supposed to hinder enemies from penetrating the kingdom: where marshes or forests did not already make the land unpassable, ditches, hedges and piles of logs blocked their advance. The populations of royal and ecclesiastical lands provided the workforce to create these. 'Gates', entry points, were defended by forts; legislation on controlling exports is partly modelled on Carolingian law. Insufficient data exist to determine the exact extent to which the *gyepű* surrounded the inhabited areas of the realm. Beyond this defensive system, the *gyepűelve* was a large stretch of mostly uninhabited land. The frontier areas were defended by groups of warriors settled in these regions (often light mounted

[70] Kristó, *Vármegyék*; see also Attila Zsoldos's articles on the development of individual counties (in Hungarian): vm.mtmt.hu (under his name).

archers such as Turkic Pechenegs) and guards from the castle organization, who patrolled their areas and sent news to the king: 'if a report of importance should reach the borderland, the count will send two messengers with four war horses to the king'. Toponyms such as 'guard' and 'archer' are understood to indicate settlements of such borderguards.[71]

## LAW

### *Bohemia*

Legal organization in Bohemia was in many ways similar to Poland but was not without its differences. Diverse norms of common law scattered around the area started to be recorded in writing in ducal charters only by the late twelfth century. The first written codification of traditional law appeared when Duke Konrád II Ota in 1189, after uniting Moravia and Bohemia under his rule, published his *statuta*. Historians have argued that this does not represent a codification of common Czech laws, because the statutes used a legal framework existing in Moravia. Nevertheless and although the norms were influenced by Roman law vocabulary they allow a partial knowledge of the traditional legal norms of the Přemyslid realm.

Assemblies of a duke and his subjects (*colloquia*) in Bohemia were more regularly summoned and perhaps from much earlier than in Piast lands. Two dates for 'conventions of all the Czech' were mentioned in sources: days of St Vitus (15 June) and St Václav (28 September). It was also possible to call together smaller conventions during the whole year and according to immediate needs. It was during these meetings not only that proclamations of new laws or validations of estate transactions took place but here also criminal cases were judged. Nowadays some historians argue that these assemblies of a ruler and elites of nobles – of variable size – were responsible for a dynamic process of criminal and civil law-making. They say that law, in the form of case law, was

[71] Hansgerd Göckenjan, *Hilfsvölker und Grenzwächter im Mittelalterlichen Ungarn* (Wiesbaden, 1972); Zoltán Kordé, 'Kabars, Sicules et Petchenègues: les Hongrois et les auxiliaires militaires', in Csernus and Korompay, eds., *Les Hongrois et l'Europe*, 231–9; Attila Zsoldos, 'Confinium és marchia: az Árpád-kori határvédelem néhány intézményéről', *Századok* 134 (2000), 99–116; Timothy Reuter, *Germany in the Early Middle Ages, c. 800–1056* (Harlow, 1991), 79. For the quotation, see Bak *et al.*, eds., *Laws*, p. 28 c. 36.

created between the eleventh and thirteenth centuries not by dukes, but by nobles under the honorary presidency of the ruler. Rulers were subject to this law like any other Czech noble. Such assemblies were also suitable places for the reconciliation of feuding parties. Yet this was not evident in cases of quarrels between noble families. The right to vengeance without recourse to a court was respected in Bohemia until the end of the twelfth century. The law of the land (*ius terre*) was based on the traditional rights of nobles. It took time to change their habits under the influence of more formal concepts of law.[72]

The Czech legal system in the twelfth century was dominated by the vision of the ruler as limited by an obligation to execute law in a manner controlled by the people or at least the elite. The assembly could be presided over by the duke but he would not determine its decisions: on the contrary, he was obliged to accept them. The ruler's declaration of deference to the assembly of nobles, however, is first documented in the second half of the twelfth century.[73]

Judicial assemblies were organized around four times a year, and even for the not so numerous Czech elite it was impossible to present during these assemblies all those cases that had to be judged. Therefore, less important questions were solved at the ducal court or by an official (*iudex curie*) appointed by the duke. Sentences issued by them were treated as verdicts by the ducal court. These trials took place at the ruler's place of residence (*curia ducis*).[74] Some historians suggest that a ruler himself could solve cases, but others have pointed out that from the twelfth century a duke had to have the agreement of representatives of the elite (*nobiles seniores Bohemie*), who always accompanied him during trials. It is controversial whether such close control of magnates was an eleventh-century reality, or whether it appeared in the twelfth century as the outcome of the change in the balance of power.[75]

A duke, who was the supreme judge of his realm's elites, intervened only in cases dealing with elites, nobles and clergymen. To those

[72] Jan, *Václav II*, 213–15.

[73] Libor Jan, 'Zrod zemského soudu v Čechách', in *Kultura prawna w Europie środkowej*, ed. Antoni Barciak (Katowice, 2006), 74–84.

[74] Zdeněk Šimeček, 'K charakteristice středověkých kolokvi, v Čechách', *Český Časopis Historocký* 18[68], 6 (1970), 593–601 (here 594–595).

[75] Jan, *Václav II*, 212, n. 191.

occupying lower positions in the social hierarchy, the commander of the local stronghold, later the castellan, represented the ruler's will while the punishment for transgressions would be decided by the court seated at the stronghold (*hradsky sud*), in which key positions were held by the duke's representatives. However, no sources attest the remit of such courts and, according to one hypothesis, as they comprised members of the local elite, they would decide only criminal cases and in accordance with common law. On the other hand, some scholars argue that the assembly of nobles, the so-called district court, which convened for judiciary (and other) purposes, functioned as early as the eleventh century. Lower courts are mentioned for the first time in laws issued by Břetislav I in 1039, but the reliability of these so-called Gniezno laws is disputable. They were mentioned only by the chronicler Cosmas of Prague more than one hundred years later. Nevertheless, in the twelfth century lower courts functioned, with castellans or – according to the apocryphal law of Břetislav I – archpriests as their head. Later a judge (*iudex*) was nominated by dukes to organize and preside over this basic level of the legal system. The role of lower courts in early medieval Bohemia and their relation to a ruler's power remain debated.

Civil cases and some minor criminal cases continued to be judged by local representatives, men of widely accepted authority, or settled after discussions between families. Ducal slaves and peasants were judged by the *villicus*, the manager of the ducal estate where they lived, according to local *ius terre*, but in specific cases they had recourse to laws in force in other parts of the realm or even (in the thirteenth century) to chartered towns' law. Colonization in the twelfth and thirteenth forced rulers to issue liberties acknowledging specific laws for settlers, new villages and chartered towns with their legal autonomy.

### *Poland*

We know very little about common law on the territory of Poland. No collection of written norms has been reconstructed. The very existence of some unified 'Polish law' in the early eleventh century is unlikely. Rather, there existed a set of local customs and norms. Individual rulers tried to impose new norms from above, but this was difficult. The troubled adoption of Christianity provides a telling example.

The multiplicity of local norms meant flexibility. It also secured the continuity of local communities without contesting supreme authority which was the guarantor of the continuation of traditional norms in exchange for certain concessions. It is striking that, unlike in the Přemyslid and Árpád polities, there is no evidence of any widely accepted codification of even basic rights of Piast rulers and their officials in the thirteenth century, let alone earlier. Some historians have suggested that no generally acknowledged set of duties that subjects owed to a ruler existed. They argue that legal uniformization, although not yet a codification, started under the influence of western court and administrative culture, especially that known from the Empire. Piast rulers and their officials copied these models and, as a result, old dues owed to rulers became more regularly formulated as 'regalia'. Only in the thirteenth century were subjects' obligations towards rulers regulated by 'Polish ducal law' (*polskie prawo książęce*).[76]

Only after the end of the twelfth century were serious efforts made to create a more coherent system of collecting dues and using labour services for the benefit of a ruler. But the framework for the system was a set of traditional and widely known obligations. This is suggested by the fact that during the regulation process of the thirteenth and fourteenth centuries, when dukes offered liberties to the Church and new settlers, very similar duties were mentioned in all regions of the Piast realm. Most of them had Polish or Slavic names common across the whole country. It is possible that an endeavour to create a more homogeneous system of dues and rulers' rights was inspired by the administrative regulation known in the Empire. But it seems most probable that expectations expressed by rulers and enforced commonly by their officials were imposed over heterogeneous sets of local, traditional norms organizing the life of small societies (*vicinia, opole*). The problem is that all those norms and customs existed only in verbal tradition. The first time they appear in written sources was during the thirteenth and fourteenth centuries, a time when both western administrative patterns and Roman law influenced the written formulation of norms, so that it is almost impossible to distinguish between traditional, local or commonly used and newly introduced norms.[77]

[76] Gawlas, 'Fürstenherrschaft, Geldwirtschaft und Landesausbau'.

[77] Karol Modzelewski, 'Le système du ius ducale en Pologne et le concept de féodalisme', *Annales ESC* 37, 1 (1982), 164–85; on the creation of legal systems see Modzelewski, *L'Europe des barbares: germains et slaves face aux héritiers de Rome*

The traditional approach to law was challenged by ecclesiastical efforts to base the institutional structure of archbishoprics, bishoprics and monasteries on the permanent foundation of written law. During the visit of the papal legate Egidius of Tusculum, Duke Bolesław III the Wrymouth agreed to record in writing certain donations he and his ancestors had made to the Church (1105). The activity of his chancery is confirmed by recent finds of four lead bulls bearing the portraits of St Vojtěch (Adalbert) and the duke himself. Pope Innocent II's bull in 1136 guaranteeing the autonomy of the archbishopric of Gniezno probably (as the authenticity and dating of the extant copy remain controversial) also included a detailed list of the archbishopric's estates. This landmark document opened a new chapter in the functioning of law in Poland. From then on, dukes making donations to the Church would increasingly often issue documents in which, in addition to listing pertinent benefactions, they also confirmed all previous donations made by other benefactors. When Kazimierz the Just issued the first charter of immunity in 1180, this sealed the acceptance of writing as the important instrument of transmission of law.

Apart from ecclesiastical needs, the massive social and economic movement of colonization and establishing new, western legal norms for both villages and towns played a decisive role in the spread of written law in the thirteenth and fourteenth centuries. Although the first villages and towns of the new type were organized in the last quarter of the twelfth and first half of the thirteenth century, they received a foundation charter only extremely rarely. As before, their rights were guaranteed by a ruler's word and social memory. The latter was structured by rituals and visual signs which helped witnesses to memorize the deed. For example, different marks were cut in the trees and stones during official delimitations of estate borders (*ujazd*). The strength of social attachment to traditional rituals establishing law can be illustrated by a thirteenth-century charter which described estate borders; the written narration focused on describing a traditional *ujazd* of the estate. At the end of the twelfth and during the thirteenth centuries two forms of a law, oral and written, coexisted. Writing became a fully accepted

(Paris, 2006) and in Italian *L'Europa dei barbari: le culture tribali di fronte alla cultura romano-cristiana* (Turin, 2008).

and dominant means of codifying law in Polish society only in the fourteenth century.[78]

In the earliest sources (e.g. Thietmar of Merseburg's Chronicle) Piast rulers were portrayed not only as law-makers but also as judges. Even in the chronicle of Anonymous (seconds decade of the twelfth century) just dukes did not delegate their power of judging to their officials. Władysław Herman, who trusted his palatine Sieciech too much – according to the chronicler – and let him judge his peers, was condemned. The power of judging was still one of the duke's ultimate rights. Only at the end of the twelfth century, in the chronicle of Master Vincent, can one find passages about *praeses provintiae* appointed by the duke, and his officials of lower rank who sentenced subjects breaking ducal monopolies in Cracow land.[79] And, significantly, their meticulous activity was seen by the chronicler as a violation of subjects' freedom. Among the ducal court officials known from the second half of the twelfth century judges (*iudices*, sing. *iudex*) appeared scarcely. Apparently, dukes still tried to judge personally most cases restricted to ducal courts. That was made possible by the small scale of their duchies. When the duchy grew, palatines and voivodes rather than castellans were appointed to replace the duke in the courts.

Rulers held assemblies (*wiece* or *colloquia*) with their magnates, knights and sometimes with the most important representatives of the local Church. Although some historians argue that these assemblies were traditional, it seems possible that they became the scene of political and juridical life no earlier than after the middle of the twelfth century. Before that time, a ruler met only with his closest council to discuss his policy. Assemblies were not summoned regularly. The most important political and administrative questions were discussed there, but some minor cases were also judged and estate transactions of

78 Karol Maleczyński, Maria Bielińska and Antoni Gąsiorowski, *Dyplomatyka polska wieków średnich* (Warsaw, 1971); Karol Maleczyński, 'Rozwój dokumentu polskiego od XI do XV w', in Maleczyński, *Studia nad dokumentem polskim* (Wrocław, 1971), 242–76.

79 In Poland a 'terra' was a more stable administrative unit than a *provincia* or a duchy. In some cases a 'land' was identical to a high medieval duchy, but in other instances it was part of a larger unit. 'Cracow land' was part of Lesser Poland. It sometimes appeared as a separate duchy, and at other times as part of the Duchy of Cracow together with 'Sandomierz land'.

various kinds were confirmed. This was the place where a duke could appear in front of his subjects as judge. But it was also a sign of change in the means of communication. A ruler's authority had to be always displayed publicly. But after 1138, when the power of dukes weakened, they increasingly needed the co-operation of their magnates, sometimes even directly of knights, especially after the second half of the twelfth century, when nobles strongly influenced the processes of succession and policy-making.[80]

## *Hungary*

Royal legislative activity was an important aspect of royal power in Hungary from the reign of the first king, whose legislation was discussed in Chapter 3. Because of lack of evidence, it is often impossible to know the extent to which the population adhered to such legislation. Throughout the period, mixed assemblies of ecclesiastics and lay elites headed by the king issued legislation.[81] The influence of Carolingian conciliar decrees on these texts is especially marked. Laws of László I (1077–95) survive in three law-books in fifteenth–sixteenth-century manuscripts; no earlier manuscripts survive. According to some scholars, the first synod of Esztergom was also held during László's reign, but the majority opinion dates it to the reign of Kálmán (1095–1116). The collection called László's 'first law-book' is in fact the synod of Szabolcs from 1092, but the text that has come down to us may also contain ecclesiastical regulations issued at other times, because some topics, such as regulations on the tithe, appear in various canons scattered throughout the text. The second and third books are undated and, according to some scholars, the 'third book' contains not the legislation of László himself, but the laws of Salamon from 1064 or of Géza I (1074–7). This view is based on internal evidence, most notably a reference to the count palatine of the duke, suggesting that the duke had his own territory

[80] Piotr Boroń, *Słowiańskie wiece plemienne* (Katowice, 1999); Karol Modzelewski, 'Thing und Acht. Zu vergleichenden Studien der germanischen und slawischen Stammesverfassung' in *Leges-Gentes-Regna. Zur Rolle von germanischen Rechtsgewohnheiten und lateinischer Schriftstradition bei der Ausbildung der frühmittelalterlichen Rechtskultur*, ed. G. Dilcher and E.-M. Distler (Berlin, 2006), 79–89.

[81] On the following paragraphs, see Bak *et al.*, eds., *Laws*, 12–33, 55–68; Jánosi, *Törvényalkotás*.

(true for the period *c.* 1048–77, but more controversial during László's reign, when according to some historians the duchy did not exist); and legislation on those holding stray animals and fugitive slaves from the reign of Béla in the 1060s, which would make little or no sense under László (1077–95). The compilation of the texts and the numbering of the law-books are definitely much later than the reign of László; errors were perhaps also introduced into the text during copying. Contradictory regulations of the same issue within a law-book demonstrate that the legislation was issued piecemeal over the course of the reign and compiled into books subsequently.

The text of the 'synod of Esztergom' contains a collection of various synodal decrees, seventy-two canons from one synod held at Esztergom and the rest from others. The dating of the Esztergom synod itself is debated: only a very late manuscript refers to the synod taking place under Archbishop Lawrence of Esztergom (1105–16). Some scholars argue, based on the nature of the regulations of the synod, that these decrees predate the synod of Szabolcs (1092). The oldest manuscript containing the text (*Codex Prayanus*) dates from the late twelfth century. The law-book of King Kálmán was probably compiled before 1104, because the preface is dedicated to an ecclesiastic who died that year. The earliest manuscripts containing the law are from the fifteenth and sixteenth centuries. This is probably also a compilation of various pieces of royal legislation. Kálmán also issued statutes on the Jews. No other legislation from the twelfth century exists; whether because no new legislative activity took place or due to the subsequent loss of texts is an open question.

Despite the existence of an early body of written legislation, both government and legal processes were predominantly oral until the later twelfth century. The judicial system can be traced from the early laws and documentary evidence. The king was the highest judge. Law-days on the Feast of the Assumption of the Virgin Mary (15 August), later on St István's feastday (20 August), at Fehérvár provided royal judgements especially on issues relating to larger segments of society. The king also delegated judicial powers, in the eleventh century especially to the count palatine (*palatinus comes, nádor*). He could exercise judicial functions only by royal appointment; otherwise he only judged the *udvarnokok*. Then István II made the palatine a permanent judge; by the thirteenth century the palatine was the king's deputy in this capacity and his jurisdiction extended to the whole realm. He represented the king at the yearly law-day if necessary, and could judge all cases except those belonging to ecclesiastical courts. Nonetheless, he could not bring sentences of death and confiscation of goods against nobles without the approval of the king. He exercised his judicial function mainly as an itinerant judge, holding assemblies in various counties.[82]

At a lower level, each county *ispán* had judicial functions within his county. In addition, the king conferred judicial powers on royal judges who appear in the legislation of László I as those sent out in cases of theft, and in Kálmán's laws as judges in the countryside. By the early twelfth century, however, they could judge royal officials only together with the *ispán* of the county. By the early thirteenth century, they had become judicial officials of the *ispán*, and finally disappeared in the 1240s. Kálmán's early twelfth-century legislation (c. 2) mitigated the problem of travelling great distances to go to court: every bishopric was to hold a synod twice a year, where the *ispán*s and dignitaries assembled.[83]

Legal process was first based on oral presentation; only from the twelfth century was writing increasingly used. The *poroszló* (*pristaldus*, from southern Slavic *pristav*) was either permanently employed by a judge or appointed to take part in a specific legal case. They were laymen, who had to have lands so they could be held responsible for their actions. He was both an official and a witness whose testimony was legally valid concerning the decisions in legal cases in which he acted. *Poroszlók* were delegated by the judge to carry the summons seal, used to summon both ecclesiastics and laypeople before the judge. A few summons seals (*sigilla citationis*) survived. These are single-sided metal seals, which could be suspended from a strap around the neck and in this manner carried to those summoned before the court. The *poroszló* then accompanied the parties in a case to appear before clerics if they needed to take an oath or undergo an ordeal, and returned to the judge to relate the outcome. He also inducted new owners into their estates. The proceedings were not put into writing; the parties relied on the memory of the *poroszló*. This official disappeared with the rise of literacy by the thirteenth century.

[82] Bak *et al.*, eds., *Laws*, 34–7, c. 1, 8, 30; 'Nádor', in *KMTL*, and see n. 48.

[83] Bak *et al.*, eds., *Laws*, 26.

Proof was provided by witnesses, oaths and ordeals before the rise of written instruments. Ordeals took place in ecclesiastical institutions: from around 1100 King Kálmán restricted the institutions where ordeals could be administered to cathedral and important collegiate chapters, about fifteen to twenty locations in total. Ordeals were part of the process of proof; later, their outcome was recorded in writing. In Hungary, these were hot-iron ordeals. The person obliged to undergo the ordeal took a piece of red-hot iron in his hand and carried it for a given distance. His hand was then bandaged and sealed. After three days, the seal was broken: if the hand was healing, it meant innocence, if it was infected, culpability. A lay judge then brought in his verdict based on the ordeal. Ordeals were discontinued around 1230. Charters as proofs started to take priority instead.[84]

During the twelfth century charters started to be drawn up to record judgements; for example, decisions in cases of disputed estates were sometimes written down. Ecclesiastical institutions that had no direct interest in the case, but that were involved in some way (e.g. the judge gave his verdict there or they administered the proof) put the judgement in writing: the first such charter is known from 1121. When increasing numbers of both laymen and ecclesiastics wanted to have written proof of sales, donations and other private actions of juridical significance, they asked these ecclesiastical institutions for charters, from the end of the twelfth century, at first occasionally. Charters recording the verdict were sometimes sealed with the royal seal. In such cases the beneficiary took part in having the decision put into writing, and asked the royal chapel to append a seal. When during the reign of Béla III a separate chancery was created, royal charters replaced this type of charter. From the end of the twelfth century, non-royal sealed charters appeared as well. After that point, royal charters of judgements, non-royal sealed charters issued by the judge, and charters recording verdicts issued by chapters coexisted. From the first decades of the thirteenth century, Benedictine, Premonstratensian and Hospitaller convents also started to issue

[84] On Kálmán, see Bak *et al.*, eds., *Laws*, c. 22. Nora Berend, 'Oath-taking in Hungary: a window on medieval social interaction', in Górecki and Van Deusen, eds., *Central and Eastern Europe in the Middle Ages*, 42–9; László Solymosi and Kornél Szovák, eds., *Regestrum Varadinense (1208–1235): Ritvs explorandae veritatis, qvo Hvngarica Natio in dirimendis controuersijs ante annos trecentos & quadraginta vsa est, & eius testimonia plurima, in sacrario sumi temple Varadien. reperta. Colosuarij 1550* (Budapest, 2009).

charters for private transactions, and these so-called *loca credibilia* became significant social institutions.[85]

## TWO EMPIRES AND OTHER NEIGHBOURS

The central European polities existed in a sphere of interlocking and clashing interests between various neighbours and each other. The German Empire played a significant role in the birth of the new polities (see Chapter 3). Bohemian rulers' politics from the second half of the tenth century were closely related to the situation in the Eastern Frankish, then German Empire. Most Přemyslid dukes accepted a more or less formal dependence on a German king or emperor. They used their suzerain's protection as a weapon against their internal and external enemies. Among the latter, the Piasts and the Árpáds were both the most dangerous and most useful. The ultimate goal of every Přemyslid ruler from the middle of the eleventh century was to hold unquestioned power over Bohemia and Moravia and, if possible, to conquer Silesia (the borderland between Poland and Bohemia) or another province lost after the tenth-century collapse of the empire of Boleslav I the Cruel and Boleslav II the Pious. Internal and external targets were achieved when Bohemian dukes maintained a higher political and therefore military position than the Árpáds and the Piasts.

Piast political horizons were a little different. They also tried to regain control over territories lost after the reign of Bolesław I the Brave at the turn of the tenth and eleventh centuries: Silesia and Pomerania. Similarly to the Bohemian rulers they took part in the political life of the Empire. But they also tried constantly to broaden their political influence not only in the Empire, Bohemia and Hungary, but also in Sweden and Denmark, Kievan Rus', Prussian

85 Iván Bertényi, 'L'utilisation des sceaux dans la chancellerie "judicum curiae regiae" en Hongrie aux XIIIe–XIVe s.', *Archives et bibliothèques de Belgique* 58 (1987), 21–32; László Solymosi, *Írásbeliség és társadalom az Árpád-korban* (Budapest, 2006); Solymosi, 'Die Anfänge der weltlichen Gerichtsbarkeit und die Urkundenausfertigung in Ungarn', in *La diplomatica dei documenti giudiziari (dai placiti agli acta – secc. XII–XV) Atti del X Congresso internazionale della Commission Internationale de Diplomatique, Bologna, 12–15 settembre 2001*, ed. Giovanna Nicolaj (Vatican City, 2004), 445–62; Zsolt Hunyadi, 'The locus credibilis in Hungarian Hospitaller Commanderies', in *La commanderie: institution des ordres militaires dans l'Occident médiéval. Actes du premier colloque internationale du Conservatoire Larzac templier et hospitalier tenu à Sainte-Eulalie-de-Cernon (Aveyron), du 13 au 15 octobre 2000*, ed. Léon Pressouyre and Anthony T. Luttrell (Paris, 2002), 285–96.

and Lithuanian lands. The Piasts were always in pursuit of new alliances that could guarantee the stability of a balance of power in relations with the three above-mentioned main players, especially the Empire. From the second half of the eleventh century the papacy began to play a growing role among these distant allies of the Piasts, but became one of their major political partners only in the thirteenth century.

The political goals, alliances and enmities of Bohemia, Poland, Rus' and the two Empires, German and Byzantine (eventually the independent polities of the Balkans), steppe formations and the papacy created the background against which Hungarian rulers pursued their own interests. Political alliances and interests should not be imagined to have had long-term consistency similar to the rigidity of Cold War antagonisms. Indeed, foreign relations were sometimes extremely volatile; changing sides in alliances could happen rapidly. Thus for example a German king could be the Hungarian ruler's ally and then, in the space of a few months, back a pretender to the throne against the same king.

## *Bohemia*

The alliance or enmity of emperors played a significant role. Bohemian rulers received the royal title from emperors (see above). Succession struggles led to imperial intervention, although not all of them were decisive. For example, in 1126 King Lothar III backed Ota (Otto) the Black, expelled by Soběslav I, from his duchy of Moravia. Ota claimed his right to the throne in Prague as the eldest Přemyslid. Lothar preferred the ruler in Prague to be a military ally but in a weak position internally, and thus to be unable to hold on to his power without the help of imperial authority. Lothar III's army was defeated by Soběslav at the battle of Chlumec, Otto died in the battle, and Lothar III was captured and released only after approving Soběslav. Nonetheless, Soběslav did not fight for independence and accepted the dominant position of the German king. In 1127 Lothar III, seeking allies against the Staufs, assigned Bohemia to Soběslav I as an imperial fief, in fulfilment of the promise made after the battle of Chlumec. To protect himself from internal disorder, Soběslav strengthened his alliance with the emperor, supporting Lothar III in his struggle with Conrad Stauf. In 1142 Konrád of Znojmo rebelled against the duke of Prague, Vladislav II, winning battles and taking

Prague. Yet he abandoned his claim and retreated when King Conrad III clearly expressed his support for Duke Vladislav.[86] The latter had to repay Conrad by sending him supporting troops, and even took command personally when Conrad III led his armies into Italy. Numerous other examples exist of Bohemian dukes' support for the emperor.[87]

Military support for the imperial cause was usually rewarded, although only rarely by a grant of royal dignity. Soběslav took political advantage of the imperial rights over Bohemia to secure the German king's protection for his son, Vladislav, as the successor and future duke of Prague. Henry V gave gifts to Duke Vratislav II. In 1080 he sent a copy of the imperial lance to Bohemia, soon declared the 'lance of St Václav' and mounted with the so-called 'banner of St Vojtěch [-Adalbert]'. In 1081 Vratislav II received Austria as a fief on the condition that he expel the Babenbergs.[88] Vladislav I was rewarded in 1114 with the hereditary title of imperial 'cupbearer' (*summus pincerna*), which offered the dukes increased opportunities to engage in the internal affairs of the empire. Vladislav II in 1157–58 supported Frederick Barbarossa's campaigns in Poland and Italy and received a royal crown. He continued to send troops to imperial campaigns, and in 1169 Barbarossa granted Bohemian dukes the right to participate in the election of German kings.

Bohemian rulers may seem to have focused their political activity only on the Empire, trying to reach a status equal to members of higher imperial aristocracy. From the ninth century, Bohemia was indeed closest politically to the East Frankish realm, and then the Empire. Yet they did not give up completely an independent policy towards other neighbours, especially Poland and Hungary. The Přemyslids wanted to dominate in this part of Europe as much as their neighbours. But, ruling over a relatively small country, they had to rely on a powerful ally. Due to the existence of many power centres within the Empire, political relations with it were never restricted to the imperial court. Bavarian rulers appeared as privileged allies of Bohemian dukes. Břetislav II sustained good relations with the Empire while also strengthening the traditional alliance with Bavaria. In 1094 he married Liutgarda of the powerful von Bogen family. This may have been part of a strategy to seek allies within

[86] Vaníček, *Soběslav I.* [87] Žemlička, *Čechy v době knížecí*, 324–6.
[88] Cosmas II.35.

Germany, helping to promote Bohemian interests at a time when Emperor Henry IV had been challenged by his two sons. The alliance was soon reinforced through the arrangement of a marriage between Břetislav II's half-brother, Bořivoj, and the sister of Margrave Leopold of Austria.[89]

## *Poland*

From the middle of the eleventh century, depending on their political interests, Polish rulers sometimes relied on imperial help, while in other conflicts took the anti-imperial side. Around 1089 the Polish dukeWładysław Herman married Emperor Henry IV's sister, Judith Maria. No other Piast was so closely connected with the imperial family, although Piast dukes married women from the higher imperial aristocracy. Bolesław III the Wrymouth, the arch-enemy of King Henry V, married Salomea from the Swabian comital family from de Berg Castle. Bolesław III's oldest son married Agnes of the Babenberg family, daughter of Margrave Leopold III of Austria. One of Bolesław's daughters, Judith, married Otto, margrave of Brandenburg, while the other, Dobronega, wedded Margrave Dietrich of Lausitz. Over the course of the twelfth century, with the weakening position of the Piast dukes, the rank of their spouses' family in the aristocratic social order slightly diminished. Nevertheless, in 1188 Duke Henryk I the Bearded (Brodaty) of Silesia (1201–38) married Hedwig, daughter of Duke Berthold IV (VI) of Merania, sister of the queens of Hungary and France.[90] Despite family ties, during the twelfth century the Piast dukes never became so intricately involved in the political life of the Empire as did Bohemian rulers.

Nonetheless, several claimants appealed for imperial help during succession struggles. The ousted Władysław II the Exile, sought support from Conrad III, since his half-sister Agnes was Władysław's wife. Bolesław I the Tall, expelled by his son and younger brother, in 1172 asked Emperor Barbarossa for help. The latter accused all Piasts allied against Bolesław I, 'his vassal', of insulting imperial majesty.

[89] Barbara Krzemińska, 'Břetislav II: pokus o charakteristiku osbnosti panovnika', *Československy Časopis Historický* 35 (1987), 722–31; Max Piendl, '*Böhmen und die Grafen von Bogen*', *Bohemia* 3 (1962), 137–49.

[90] Zientara, *Heinrich der Bärtige*; Wiszewski, *Domus Bolezlai*, 375–379.

That sufficed to induce Bolesław IV to surrender as senior duke; his brother Mieszko III the Old went to Magdeburg at the head of an embassy, accepted that the expelled duke return to his duchy in Silesia, and promised compensation to the emperor (8,000 silver marks). The Piasts, unlike Přemyslids, acknowledged but never fully respected Barbarossa's authority as the highest judge in political quarrels among the Piasts or between them and their neighbours. It seems the emperor was uncertain about the extent to which he could subordinate the Piasts.

Under Frederick Barbarossa's successors, Henry VI and Frederick II, there was less pressure on the Piasts to behave as imperial vassals or even allies. Piast lands were not incorporated into the Empire, nor was their subordination necessary for the safety of its eastern borders of the Empire. Kings of the Romans propagated the idea that the Piast realm was an imperial fief, at least since Władysław II the Exile's oath of fidelity. Sometimes they succeeded in obtaining formal confirmation of their claims from the Piast dukes, and at other times they failed. Yet they invariably failed (with the exception of Bolesław I the Tall) to ensure that ducal oaths of fidelity were fulfilled.[91]

Piast marriage ties served to build alliances with a variety of powers. Bolesław III married Zbislava, the daughter of Grand Prince Svyatopolk of Kiev.[92] Bolesław III's diplomatic strategy was supported by his daughters' marriages. The oldest, Adelaida, married Margrave Albrecht II 'the Pious' of Austria. Three younger daughters were offered to Saxon lords: one in 1131/32 to Margrave Conrad, who ruled the Northern March; Judith to Otto, the son of Albrecht the Bear, creator of the Brandenburg March; and Dobronega to Detrich, margrave of Lower Lusatia. To secure his gains on the Baltic coast, Bolesław III arranged the wedding of his twelve-year-old

[91] Robert Holtzman, 'Über den Polenfeldzug Friedrich Barbarossas vom Jahre 1157 und die Begründung schlesischer Herzogthümer', *Zeitschrift des Vereins für Geschichte Schlesiens* 56 (1922), 42–55; Gerard Labuda, 'O stosunkach prawnopublicznych między Polską a Niemcami w połowie XII w. (Merseburg 1135, Kaina 1146, Krzyszkowo 1157)', *Czasopismo Prawno-Historyczne* 25 (1973), 25–58. For recent Polish literature citations, see Magdalena Biniaś-Szkopek, *Bolesław IV Kędzierzawy: książę Mazowsza i princeps* (Poznań, 2009), 239–53. See also Maciej Przybył, *Mieszko III Stary* (Poznań, 2002); Józef Dobosz, *Kazimierz II Sprawiedliwy* (Poznań, 2011); Knut Görich, *Friedrich Barbarossa. Biographie* (Munich, 2011).

[92] This marriage required special papal dispensation because they were both great-grandchildren of Mieszko II.

daughter Richeza/Riksa to King Magnus of Sweden in 1129/30. When Magnus died, she was given to Vladimir, prince of Novgorod, who died when his bride was still only twenty-three years old. Richeza's third wedding was to King Sverker I of Sweden. The youngest of Bolesław's daughters, Agnes, was sent to Kiev to marry Mstislav II. Around 1177 Mieszko III married his daughter Anastasia to the Pomeranian prince Boguslav I, and his second daughter Salomea to Boguslav's son, Racibor.

### *Hungary*

The German and Byzantine Empires contributed to the formation of the Hungarian realm, and played similar, but more prominent roles as potential marriage markets, allies or military enemies than the smaller neighbouring polities.[93] István's Bavarian marriage ensured good relations with his brother-in-law Henry II. After the latter's death, however, Conrad II attacked the kingdom in 1030, but was defeated. Many times German rulers backed one of the rivals who fought for the Hungarian throne. Peter allied himself with the Czech Břetislav against Henry III, but then escaped to Henry when his own subjects revolted. It was Henry's military victory against Samuel Aba in 1044 that allowed Peter's return; according to some historians the intervention led to Peter's vassalage to Henry. Henry captured the regalia, including the crown, and sent it to the Papal Curia as a sign of the divine approval of his victory. András I defeated Peter, who was backed by German troops (Henry attacked again in 1051 and 1052, but was unsuccessful), then fourteen years later he himself used German knights to fight against his brother Béla (who used Polish troops).

The regent Agnes in the name of the under-age Henry IV, whose sister was betrothed to Salamon, sent an army to put Salamon on the throne. After Salamon was ousted, Moson was occupied by Henry IV during his unsuccessful and short-lived campaign to regain Salamon's throne in 1074. (The town was reconquered by László I in 1079.) Henry V in 1108 backed Álmos against his brother Kálmán, but eventually gave up his campaign, as he could not triumph over the Hungarians, who were helped by Polish troops. Conrad III aided the

[93] For an overview, see Ferenc Makk, *Ungarische Außenpolitik (896–1196)* (Herne, 1999).

pretender Boris, who recruited warriors in Austria and Bavaria and launched an attack against Géza II in 1146. This led to Hungarian involvement in internal rivalry in Germany in retaliation: Géza II fought with the Welfs against the king in 1146. Such German aid for pretenders, however, was far from automatic, as it depended on the current preoccupations of the German ruler. For example, Géza II's brother István first tried to gain the support of Frederick Barbarossa, but, being unsuccessful, he went to the Byzantine court instead. Géza vacillated between appeasing Frederick, sending Muslim soldiers to help him in his siege of Milan in 1158, and pursuing his own divergent interests in alliance with the papacy. Eventually he sided with Pope Alexander III against Frederick's pope Victor IV.

Hungarian rulers took sides in internal German rivalries according to their own interests. When Emperor Henry III deposed Duke Conrad of Bavaria from his duchy in 1053, he revolted and took refuge in Hungary, whose ruler was a natural ally because Henry had been attacking the country; based in Hungary, Conrad kept ravaging the Bavarian frontier zones. Later, László I sided with the antiking Rudolf, and then gave refuge to German counts who rebelled against Henry IV.

Although earlier historiography often emphasized a German desire for the feudal subjugation of Hungary, a better understanding of medieval politics has led to a reinterpretation of recurrent German military intervention. Given the significance of bonds of friendship and alliance in the period, such interventions were connected to the creation and maintenance of zones of interest, ensuring that a friendly ruler occupied the throne. Moreover, much of the warfare in the twelfth century consisted of border clashes, with Hungarian armies ravaging Austrian areas and Austrian/Czech armies breaking into and devastating western parts of Hungary.[94]

Relations with the Byzantine Empire became important soon after the time of the Hungarians' appearance in written sources in the middle of the ninth century, and continued in the earliest period of Hungarian settlement, as discussed in previous chapters: Hungarians were in Byzantine military service against enemies of the Empire; they

[94] Gyula Kristó, *Háborúk és hadviselés az Árpádok korában*, 2nd edn (Szeged, 2003); László Veszprémy, *Az Árpád-és Anjou-kor csatái, hadjáratai* (Budapest, 2008), 99–110; Gábor Varga, *Ungarn und das Reich vom 10. bis zum 13. Jahrhundert. Das Herrscherhaus der Árpáden zwischen Anlehnung und Emanzipation* (Munich, 2003).

also raided Byzantine lands, and then some leaders became allies of Byzantium, accepting baptism in Constantinople. In the second half of the eleventh century, Byzantine governors in areas adjoining Hungary built up their own relations with the Hungarian dynasty. A niece of Nikephoros Botaneiates married Prince Géza. According to Michael Attaleiates, before becoming emperor in 1068, Romanos (IV) was drawing the Hungarians into an alliance to overthrow Constantine X. Hungarian hostility did not cease: under Salamon's reign, Hungarians attacked Belgrade and Niš and looted them.[95]

During the late eleventh and twelfth centuries, enmity and alliance between Hungary and Byzantium alternated. The issues bearing on Hungarian–Byzantine relations revolved around spheres of influence (especially over Serbia), the Byzantine desire to neutralize potential enemies, and contested territorial control in zones of common interest. From the late eleventh century on, such contest focused especially on Croatia and Dalmatia. Warfare often recurred, though many of these wars consisted of attacks against borderlands. Alliances, which were attempts to find resolution to conflicts, punctuated hostility.

Such alliances were often based on dynastic marriage. According to one view, István I's son Imre had a Byzantine wife, but the first reference to this is very late, and not necessarily reliable. Emperor Alexius I and Kálmán negotiated the marriage of László I's orphan daughter, Piroska (Eirene, d. 1134) and Alexius's son, John II Komnenos. They were married around 1105–6 and had eight children. Subsequently, she was revered in Byzantium as a saint for her piety. Géza I had a Byzantine wife, and Isaac II married a Hungarian princess. Hungarian rulers fought on the side of Byzantine emperors in several wars, for example, István I against the Bulgars, or Kálmán against the Normans. In the middle of the eleventh century, András I sent Hungarian troops to fight on the Byzantine side in Calabria.[96]

Along with the Byzantine crown sent to Hungary in the mid 1070s (discussed in Chapter 3), the so-called Monomachos crown may also be the material remains of a Hungaro-Byzantine alliance. This

[95] Gyula Moravcsik, 'Hungary and Byzantium in the Middle Ages', in *The Cambridge Medieval History*, vol. IV, pt 1 (Cambridge, 1966), 566–92; Moravcsik, *Byzantium and the Magyars* (Budapest, 1970); Ferenc Makk, *The Árpáds and the Comneni: Political Relations between Hungary and Byzantium in the Twelfth Century* (Budapest, 1989).

[96] Thérèse Olajos, 'Contingent hongrois au service de Byzance en Italie', in Csernus and Korompay, eds., *Les Hongrois et l'Europe*, 223–9.

Byzantine open crown, found in the late nineteenth century, bears a representation of Constantine IX Monomachos and the Empresses Zoe and Theodora, and therefore has been dated to 1042–50. Opinions about its provenance, however, range from the idea that it was a gift from the emperor to András I (perhaps at the latter's request to replace the royal crown taken by Henry III in 1044) to the hypothesis that it was plundered from Constantinople in 1204.[97]

Pretenders to the throne, or those who were unsuccessful in their bid for power, could find refuge in Byzantium (just as others did in Germany). Even if current political interests or the practical situation did not favour the active backing of a pretender, the Byzantine court was mostly accommodating to such high-ranking figures, in case they proved to be useful in future diplomacy or war. In other cases, pretenders could even solicit active military help to try to gain the throne. Thus, for example, Prince Álmos (Kálmán's brother, d. 1127), Boris (d. *c.* 1153–4, son of Kálmán's repudiated second wife) and Prince Géza (son of Géza II, d. 1210) lived in the Empire. This in itself sometimes led to armed conflict between the Hungarian and Byzantine rulers. Notably, Álmos's favourable reception in Byzantium was one of the reasons for the wars of 1127–9, with István II capturing and damaging various towns as far as Philippopolis (Plovdiv). Although Álmos died after the start of hostilities, warfare continued, with a Byzantine counter-attack.

Hostilities escalated in the middle of the twelfth century, with Géza II fighting in the Balkans and at the Lower Danube. Scholars are divided over whether the Hungarians were actively involved as early as 1149 on the side of Serbs in war against Byzantium. Hungarian involvement was certainly linked to attempts to strengthen Hungarian influence in the Balkans. It eventually led to Byzantine counter-attack. The older view, that Byzantium tried to subject the Hungarian king as a vassal, advanced as an explanation for the mid-twelfth-century hostilities, has been refuted. Mid-twelfth-century warfare is now interpreted as retaliatory, aiming to re-establish the status quo and preserve Byzantine influence over the Balkans. Peace treaties were broken several times, with the relaunching of Hungarian offensives in the 1150s, partly in the hope of backing Manuel's cousin

[97] Nicolas A. Oikonomidès, 'La couronne dite de Constantin Monomaque', *Travaux et Mémoires du Centre de Recherche d'Histoire et Civilisation de Byzance* 12 (1994), 241–62.

Andronicus in his bid for the throne. Faced with a rapprochement between Germany and Byzantium, Géza II established a marriage alliance with Bohemia and peaceful relations with Frederick Barbarossa.

Other pretenders, such as László II and István IV, had Byzantine backing. Princes István and László, brothers of Géza II, were already living in the Byzantine Empire when, at the news of Géza's death, Emperor Manuel decided to give them military help against the crowned king István III. After diplomacy failed to convince the elites to back István (IV), Manuel launched a military offensive. He finally succeeded in putting László II on the throne (1162), with István III first fleeing to Austria, then building a power base in western regions of Hungary. Archbishop Lukács and some of the elite never accepted László; Lukács excommunicated both him and then his brother and heir István IV, who gained the throne on László's death in 1163. István IV's only supporters seem to have been from the southern part of the kingdom, directly next to Byzantium, and he had to ask for Byzantine military help to keep his crown against internal discord. This did not prevent István III from returning, backed by foreign military help and by the majority of the local elite; he defeated and captured his uncle István IV, who was ultimately freed, and fled to lands under Byzantine control.

One of the most interesting and controversial periods of Byzantine–Hungarian alliance was the second half of the twelfth century. In 1163, Manuel I Komnenos (himself descended from a Hungarian mother, Piroska) and the Hungarian king István III concluded an agreement. Manuel acknowledged István's kingship and promised to cease supporting István IV's claims to the throne. István III in exchange promised to cede Croatian and Dalmatian areas and Srem[98] to the emperor, and sent his younger brother Béla, who from around 1161 had been duke of Croatia and Dalmatia (and according to some historians, also of Srem) to Manuel's court in Constantinople. There, he received the rank *despotés* and was betrothed to Manuel's daughter Maria. He took part in a war against Hungary, which recurred between István III and Manuel until 1167, because István did not keep to the original agreement. Hungarian troops invaded Dalmatia to prevent a Byzantine takeover. Manuel attacked Hungary's

[98] Srijem, Szerémség, Syrmia: an area between the Danube and the Sava Rivers, divided between modern Serbia and Croatia.

borderlands several times in order to gain the disputed territories; his attacks were often also linked to István IV's attempts to regain the throne. When the disputed lands were wrested away by or ceded to Byzantium, invariably Hungarian attacks were renewed to regain the territories, thus starting a new cycle.

According to Niketas Choniates (also copied in later historical tradition), Béla was appointed as heir to the Byzantine throne but, after the birth of Manuel's son, in 1170 the emperor separated Béla from his daughter, married him to Agnes (called Anna in Byzantium) of Châtillon from Antioch, and sent him back to rule Hungary, taking advantage of the sudden death of István III in 1172. Ioannes Kinnamos, on the other hand, cites Manuel's desire to attach the lands of the Hungarians as a motive for proposing a marriage alliance. Although noting Béla's high status at the court of Constantinople, he claims it was canonical impediment rather than political calculation that nullified the proposed marriage. He also attributes Béla's return to Hungary to Hungarian demands rather than to Manuel's desire to get rid of an inconvenient possible heir. In Kinnamos's account, the purpose Béla fulfilled at the court in Byzantium was the same as his role when he went back to rule Hungary: the personal tie was a means of ensuring the subordination of lands to Byzantium.[99]

Hungarian historians had argued that Manuel planned a personal union of Byzantium and Hungary in 1163, intending Béla to be one day both Byzantine emperor and king of Hungary. More recent consensus, however, rejects this idea: Manuel changed his ideas about Béla's position according to political needs, never intending him to create a personal union. Older scholarship also interpreted an initiative of Béla III himself as an attempt to create a personal union: in 1185 he asked for a relative of Manuel, Theodora, as wife. Instead, Isaac II and Margit (Margaret, then renamed Maria), Béla's daughter, were married eventually. Again, the current interpretation is much more convincing: Béla's marriage plans were not another way to achieve the personal union that had slipped out of his grasp earlier, but instead served to strengthen the Byzantine–Hungarian alliance against the Normans and to stabilize the respective rights of each realm to contested lands. After the end of the twelfth century, with the birth

[99] Harry J. Magoulias, tr., *O City of Byzantium, Annals of Niketas Choniatēs* (Detroit, 1984), 72–8, 96; Charles M. Brand, tr., *Deeds of John and Manuel Comnenus* (New York, 1976), 163–72, 174–5, 179–87, 193–7, 202–5, 214–15.

of new independent polities in the Balkans, Byzantium and Hungary ceased to have a common border, and relations became less intense, although they continued.[100]

Unlike most medieval polities in Europe, the kingdom of Hungary did not interact simply with other settled societies, but also with nomads. Situated at the meeting point of Christendom and nomad societies, Hungary's experience was similar to that of settled neighbours of nomads throughout history, such as Georgia, Rus' or China, albeit in the eleventh and twelfth centuries on a much smaller scale: nomad raids, the possibility of employing nomadic warriors, and the settlement of nomads within the kingdom. A variety of Turkic nomads – Pecheneg, Oghuz and then Cuman groups – were involved in these relations. Nomad raids for booty were part of nomadic societies' economies, and thus a constant threat. At times, the attacking nomads could also be in the employ of a sedentary political power: Byzantine emperors especially hired such troops to ward off their enemies. For example, Pechenegs raided the realm several times (such as in 1068) simply for booty, but were in Byzantine service against Hungarians in 1071. The Byzantine emperor Alexius I unleashed a Cuman attack against Hungary in 1091, perhaps to counter László's Croatian conquest. The Cumans raided the realm, but the king was finally victorious after he overtook the Cumans as they were withdrawing. The following year the Cumans attacked again, possibly at the instigation of Vasilko Rostislavich, one of the Rus' princes.

During the first two centuries of the Christian kingdom's existence, Hungary's kings both tried to guard against the raids and took advantage of the possibility offered by nomadic warrior neighbours. Obstacles in the border areas and border guards who alerted the king to invaders could not stop raids, but a quick counter-attack could minimize their impact. Having nomads for neighbours had its distinct advantages as well. For example, some Pechenegs entered to settle probably from the late tenth century on, and they were in the

[100] Márta F. Font, 'Emperor Manuel Comnenos and the Hungarian Kingdom', in *Byzantium, New Peoples, New Powers: The Byzantino-Slav Contact Zone, from the Ninth to the Fifteenth Century*, ed. Milijana V. Kajmakamova, M. Salamon and Malgorzata Smorag Rózycka (Cracow, 2007), 223–36; Paul Stephenson, 'Manuel I Comnenus, the Hungarian crown and the "feudal subjection" of Hungary, 1162–1167', *Byzantinoslavica* 57 (1996), 33–59.

employment of the king. András I used them against the Germans in 1051. István II even admitted the remnants of the primarily Pecheneg armies after their defeat by Byzantium (1122). István relied on Pechenegs due to the growing internal opposition to his wars. According to the medieval chronicle, their leader was constantly at the royal court, their elite were among the closest councillors of the king, and their warriors were among his most reliable supporters. Salamon, the exiled king, gained Pecheneg backing, and attacked the realm to regain his throne; after his defeat, he joined the Pechenegs in an unsuccessful anti-Byzantine war.[101]

Hungary lay not just on the route of nomad raids, but also on that of crusader armies heading east. The pilgrimage route through Hungary to Jerusalem was opened by King István in 1018 and, from the late spring of 1096, crusaders passed through the kingdom. The passage of the first crusader armies caused significant tensions and led to long-lasting mistrust on the part of Hungary's kings. During the first crusade, hostilities mounted as successive bands plundered and attacked the realm. The first group to traverse Hungary, under the leadership of Walter Sans-Avoir, passed through the kingdom before trying to plunder Zimony (Zemun, German Semlin, now part of Belgrade, Serbia), just inside the realm, before going on to Belgrade. Then Peter the Hermit's band killed many in Zimony in retaliation, seeing the armour of crusaders from previous bands hanging on the walls. Foucher (Volkmar)'s and Gottschalk's bands started plundering immediately after entering the kingdom, and were defeated and dispersed by King Kálmán. After that, Emich of Leiningen's troops were denied entry to the realm; they besieged the fort of Moson, which was to be their entry point into the kingdom, but were defeated by the king. When the main army under Godfrey of Bouillon finally arrived in September 1096, Godfrey and Kálmán concluded an agreement: while the crusaders crossed Hungary, Kálmán took Godfrey's brother Baldwin as hostage, and the king with his army escorted the crusaders through the realm from Sopron on the western border to Zimony on the eastern one.

Subsequent crusaders in 1101 passed through the kingdom without disturbances. Conrad III's passage in 1147 was also a tense occasion:

[101] András Pálóczi Horváth, *Pechenegs, Cumans, Iasians: Steppe Peoples in Medieval Hungary* (Budapest, 1989); N. Berend, *At the Gate of Christendom*, 6–41, 68–73.

according to the Hungarian chronicle, he lied in order to gain entry, and then proceeded to force churches and monasteries to hand over money, so that not a single church or monastery remained in Hungary that did not pay the king of the Romans out of fear. Although the French king Louis VII seemed to pass through the kingdom as a friend, he protected the pretender Boris in his entourage, and refused to hand him over to King Géza. In 1189 Emperor Frederick I made his way through Hungary on the third crusade.

The Hungarian kings' involvement in crusading dates from this time. King Béla III took the cross after crusader defeats in 1195/6, but fell ill and died in 1196, leaving the fulfillment of his vow to his younger son András II (Endre, Andrew; 1205–35). András took the cross shortly before his father's death, but was then preoccupied by trying to get a share of the realm from his older brother King Imre; the two fought a lengthy civil war. In 1200 a papal legate facilitated the peace agreement between the brothers and Imre also took the cross. Because of a war against the Bulgars, he put off the crusade, however, and died in 1204. András became king, and participated in the fifth crusade (see Chapter 7).[102]

Hungarian kings often responded to calls for military help from various neighbours, and occasionally resolved disputes among other rulers. Some examples illustrate this. László I helped the Polish duke Władysław I Herman against rebels in 1093. Kálmán intervened unsuccessfully in the principality of Galich (Galicia) in 1099 on the side of Svyatopolk, grand prince of Kiev, in the latter's war against the prince of Galich and other Rus' princes. István II in 1123 intervened on the side of Yaroslav of Volhynia against Vladimir II Monomakh. Such interventions recurred in internal rivalries in 1126 and the 1130s. Géza II led or sent troops to help his brother-in-law, Izyaslav Mstislavich, grand prince of Kiev, against other Rus' princes repeatedly between 1148 and 1152.[103] Kálmán joined a Byzantine–Venetian alliance, forcing Bohemond I of Antioch to agree to a peace with Byzantium in 1108. Béla III pressured both Isaac Angelos II, his

[102] Sándor Csernus, 'La Hongrie, les français et les premières croisades', in Csernus and Korompay, eds., *Les Hongrois et l'Europe*, 411–26; James Ross Sweeney, 'Hungary in the Crusades, 1169–1218', *International History Review* 3 (1981), 467–81; József Laszlovszky, Judit Majorossy and József Zsengellér, eds., *Magyarország és a keresztes háborúk* (Máriabesnyő and Gödöllő, 2006).

[103] For a detailed study of Hungarian–Rus' relations, see Márta Font, *Árpád-házi királyok és Rurikida fejedelmek* (Szeged, 2005).

son-in-law, and Frederick Barbarossa, whose son was betrothed to one of Béla's daughters, to make peace with each other in 1190. (Because of the prince's death the following year, the marriage did not take place.) Such interventions and alliances were often the consequence of ties created by dynastic marriages.

Some examples illustrate how marriage ties bound Hungary's ruling dynasty to immediate neighbours and lands further afield in every geographical direction. German lands continued to be important: Salamon married Judith (Jutta), sister of Henry IV. László married Adelhaid, the daughter of Rudolf of Swabia, antiking against Henry IV. István III married Agnes, the daughter of Duke Henry II (Jasomirgott) of Austria. The other empire, Byzantium, was also an active partner in marriage alliances: Géza I, István IV and Prince Géza (Géza II's son) married Byzantine princesses, while Piroska married John Komnenos, and Béla III's daughter Margit (Maria) married Isaac Angelos II. Rus' was also significant: for example, András I married a daughter of Yaroslav, grand prince of Kiev, and Géza II married Euphrosyne, sister of Izyaslav Mstislavich of Volhynia and eventually grand prince of Kiev. Rus' marriage alliances (members of Géza's family had Rus'ian wives; one of the daughters of László I married a Riurikid, perhaps Yaroslav Svyatopolkich; András I married a Rus'ian princess; Prince Álmos's wife and Kálmán's second wife were from Rus') and Rus' as a refuge for princes (e.g. András I was there prior to his ascent to the throne) later on led to Rus' becoming an area of Hungarian interventions (see below).

The new Norman power of southern Italy and Sicily played a role: Kálmán married the daughter of Roger I of Sicily (1097). István II married the daughter of the Norman Robert of Capua. Bohemian spouses were found for many Hungarian princesses: Adelhaid, daughter of András I, married the Czech ruler Vratislav I; Géza II's daughter Erzsébet married Vladislav II of Bohemia. Béla II's sister married the Czech ruler Soběslav. Prince Svatopluk, the son of the Czech ruler Vladislav II, was betrothed to István III's sister. A daughter of Béla III married Přemysl Otakar I, the king of Bohemia. Marriage ties with Poland were less frequent: Béla I married the daughter of Mieszko II; a daughter of Béla II married Mieszko III. Occasionally in the late twelfth century, great powers of the Latin principalities of the east and western Europe provided princesses for Hungarian rulers: Béla III married Agnes (Anna) of Châtillon (of Antioch), and after her death Margaret Capet, sister of Philip Augustus II of France in 1186. Imre married Constance of Aragon at the end of the twelfth century. Rising, rather than established, powers could also be important at times: probably as part of the anti-Byzantine alliance with the Serbs, István II arranged for his blind cousin Béla (II) to marry Helena, the daughter of Uroš I of Serbia. Some alliances were sealed by betrothals that ultimately never resulted in marriage due to the changing political circumstances. For example, Béla II's daughter was betrothed to the German king Conrad III's son, but the marriage never took place; in the end, she became a nun in Admont.[104]

## RELATIONS BETWEEN THE CENTRAL EUROPEAN POLITIES

The three central European polities also had complex relations with each other, ranging from marriage ties to warfare, especially in the eleventh century. The last Přemyslid ruler who tried to achieve a dominant political position in the region was Břetislav I. After his death, constant fights for succession reduced the Bohemian dukes' ability to influence their neighbours' policy. Although the Přemyslids continued to fight against them throughout the twelfth century, it was mostly as allies of the German kings/emperors. Bohemian warriors could invade the Polish or Hungarian realms without the necessity of long marches and preparations by the imperial army. Therefore, the Árpáds and the Piasts tried to eliminate the threat posed by dukes of Prague. They sought to neutralize them through alliance, although almost without exception that was possible only when Árpáds and Piasts were imperial allies. At those times, however, it became less important to neutralize the Přemyslids.

Sometimes 'alliance' became 'dependence'. When Władysław Herman became ruler of Poland (1079), changing his predecessor's policy, he strove for amicable relations with the imperial and Bohemian courts. Yet his ally, Duke Vratislav II, was crowned by the emperor in 1086 as 'king of Bohemia and Poland'. The title might seem to be honorary, but it emphasized the position of each ruler in the political system of the Empire. And when Władysław refused to honour it and pay Bohemian rulers a tribute from Silesia, Břetislav II supported Władysław's opponents, especially exiled magnates, who

[104] On Hungarian queens, see Attila Zsoldos, *Az Árpádok és asszonyaik: a királynéi intézmény az Árpádok korában* (Budapest, 2005).

were thus able to start a civil war, breaking Władysław's authority. Alternating alliance and hostility characterized Přemyslid relations to the Piasts and the Árpáds in the following decades.

Moravian dukes sometimes had their own alliances with Polish or Hungarian rulers to protect themselves against the Prague dukes' possible changing attitudes towards them. For example, this may have dictated the marriage alliance between Konrád II Ota of Znojmo's sister and Kazimierz the Just, duke of Wiślica *c.* 1166, who later became the most powerful of the Piasts. In the 1160s and 1170s Konrád was threatened by Vladislav II's attempts to strengthen his control over Moravia. Vladislav II actively supported Barbarossa's war against the Piasts in 1157. Thus the Piasts and Konrád II had a common enemy, resulting in their alliance. While in reality the Piasts were too weak to threaten Vladislav II, their alliance with Konrád might have been a decisive factor to convince Moravian nobles to support the duke of Znojmo.

Czech and Polish rulers were sometimes drawn into alliances through marriage and occasionally provided military help to one side in internal rivalries in Hungary, sometimes in the retinue of the German emperor.[105] For example, Vazul's sons, András, Béla and Levente, went possibly first to Bohemia when exiled; they then lived in Poland; and András and Levente finally went on to Rus', while waiting for the opportunity to return. Béla (I) married a Polish wife and had Polish help through his wife's family (Bolesław II was her nephew) to gain the throne. Béla's sons, Géza, László and Lampert, also escaped to Poland when Salamon ascended the throne. In 1063 Bolesław II promoted their cause. Álmos received Polish help before Bolesław III and Kálmán created an alliance. Boris also received Polish help. Bolesław III also intervened in support of Kálmán, who would later remain his ally. Similarly, Bohemian intervention in Hungarian succession struggles resulted from marriage ties. Around 1171, the brothers Friderich/Bedřich and Svatopluk, married to Hungarian princesses, responded to their mother-in-law's appeal for assistance, lending military support to their brother-in-law, István III, claiming the throne, against István IV.

[105] Gyula Kristó, 'Les relations des Hongrois et des Polonais aux Xe–XIIe siècles d'après les sources', *Quaestiones Medii Aevi Novae* 7 (2002), 127–143.

At times warfare occurred between Hungarian and Polish or Czech rulers. For example, a meeting gone wrong between the rulers István II and Vladislav I of Bohemia escalated into a battle in 1116.

## EXPANSION

### *Bohemia*

The period of territorial expension ended at the close of tenth century. Duke Bolesław II the Pious's realm comprised the Bohemian Valley, Moravia, Silesia, and Lesser Poland with Cracow and Sandomierz. During the last years of his reign or soon after his death, Piast dukes took control over the three latter regions. Over the next two centuries, rulers of Prague fought to keep Moravia under their control as closely as possible, and looked for possible new spaces of territorial expansion. After Duke Oldřich I regained power over Moravia and expelled warriors of Bolesław the Brave (1019/20, as Czech historians mainly argued) or Mieszko II Lambert (1029, as most of Polish medievalists suggest) Bohemian rule over Moravia remained stable. But its character changed. Břetislav I, Oldřich I's son, appointed governor of Moravia, treated the province as a conquered country. He erected a military administrative system (from 1041) and removed the old Moravian aristocracy from power, imposing men from Bohemia. Differences between Bohemia and Moravia remained due to the creation of three different duchies in Moravia and a fourth for the Bohemian Valley to solve succession problems. These differences did not diminish over time, despite attempts by several Prague dukes during the twelfth century to eradicate or diminish the independence of Moravian dukes. Instead, differences were reinforced by the tradition of separate courts and, from the second half of the twelfth century, separate Moravian branches of the Přemyslid dynasty.

Moravian rulers accentuated the territorial character of their power from the beginning of the twelfth century. But because of the dominant position of the Prague duke, many aspired to possess the throne of Prague, making them part of the Czech political system. Yet some of Moravian dukes, such as Konrád II Ota, tried to formalize their quasi-independent rulership with the help of the emperor. Therefore the Moravian margraviate was created as imperial fief at the end of the twelfth century. This did not break political and administrative bonds between Bohemia and Moravia, at least partly because the Moravian branches of the Přemyslid dynasty rapidly died out, replaced by sons and close relatives of the Prague dukes, making Moravia more or less a 'colony', even if a valuable one.[106]

Territorial expansion towards lands lost around 1000 or newly desired by rulers was less successful. Fights for Silesia (see Chapter 3) created a strong tradition of claiming the right to rule the province by the elite. But until the end of thirteenth century the real results of these struggles were unfavourable for the Bohemian rulers. The same is true concerning Lusatia. It was held as an imperial fief by Vratislav II between 1075 and 1081–6. The Bohemian king tried to strengthen his influence in Lusatia and extend it to neighbouring Meissen, prompting Emperor Henry IV to give Lusatia and the title of its margrave to Henry I the Older from the Wettin clan in 1081. In 1086 he also received Meissen Margraviate. Both provinces remained in the sphere of Přemyslid political influence, although they never achieved direct rule over both of them simultaneously during the twelfth century. The Czech duke Soběslav I succeeded in one aim at least: in 1136 the emperor Lothar III gave him Upper Lusatia as his fief. The personal nature of this gift was forgotten and Upper Lusatia province became tightly connected with Bohemian rulers until the second half of the thirteenth century. The whole Lusatian Margraviate was incorporated into the Czech Crown in 1367 by the Bohemian king and emperor Charles IV.

Henry IV gave Vratislav II the Eastern March (Austria) ruled by the Babenberg dynasty as his fief to secure his alliance when he deprived him of Lusatia. The Czech king's rule over Austria remained purely nominal. Yet it pointed the way to another possible direction for Czech expansion. After the Austrian line of the Babenbergs died out (1246), the Czech king Václav I with his son, the future king Přemysl Otakar II, gained possession of Austria (1251).[107]

106 Martin Wihoda, *Morava v dobe knížecí* (Prauge, 2010); Josef Žemlička, 'K ústrojí přmyslovského státu. Čchy a Morava jako zeme, království, markrabství', *Česky Časopis Historický* 108 (2010), 361–405.

107 Ivan Hlaváček, '*Böhmisch-österreichischen Nachbarschaft bis zu den Anfängen Přemysl II*' in *Böhmisch-österreichische Beziehungen im 13. Jahrhundert. Österreich (einschliesslich Steiermark, Kärnten und Krain) in Grossreichsprojekt Ottokars II. Přemysl, König von Böhmen*, ed. Marie Bláhová and Ivan Hlaváček (Prague, 1998), 11–23; Friedrich Prinz, 'Das Reich, Bayern, Böhmen und Österreich: Grundzüge einer historischen Nachbarschaft. Einige Vorüberlegungen', in *Prinz, Nation und Heimat. Beiträge zur böhmischen und sudetendeutschen Geschichte* (Munchi, 2003), 50–68; *Tschechen und Österreicher. Gemeinsame Geschichte, gemeinsame Zukunft* (Vienna, 2006), articles by Libor Jan and Marcin Pauk.

The deep political divisions and bloody internal fights in twelfth-century Bohemia limited the possibility for territorial expansion. But it is still the case that the main directions of thirteenth- and fourteenth-century expansion developed during the second half of the eleventh century and the twelfth century.

### *Poland*

Piast expansion during the twelfth century was connected not only to their geo-political situation, but also to the tradition of the 'golden age' of the reign of Bolesław I the Brave, who conquered Meissen, Lusatia, Bohemia, Moravia and part of Red Ruthenia (Grody Czerwieńskie), controlled Pomerania and subordinated – for a short time – Kievan Rus'. After the crisis of 1034–9, attempts of Polish rulers to achieve direct, personal domination over the lands of the Empire (Meissen, Lusatia or Bohemia) were unthinkable. But a new perspective for expansion over pagan – or Orthodox – lands opened, especially when crusading provided sufficient justification to wage war for pagans' salvation and the safety of the Church. In some territories, however, Piast aspirations to annex new areas were in conflict with desires of other Christian rulers, including the emperor.

Kazimierz the Restorer until his death in 1058 fought to regain power over his father's lands, but with only partial success. His son, Bolesław II the Bold, inherited rule over Greater and Lesser Poland, Silesia (for which he paid tribute to Bohemia), Mazowia and Pomerania. The chronology of the conquest and the character of dependence of Pomerania are debatable. Bolesław II certainly lost the province at the beginning of his rule, and had to fight Pomeranian raids during his entire reign. This implies that his father, Kazimierz, had subdued the inhabitants, but it is improbable that his domination was similar in character to that over the rest of his lands. Pomeranians were pagans, and no traces of their Christianization exist during the reigns of Kazimierz I and Bolesław II. No archaeological traces of defensive structures (strongholds) such as those built in other parts of the Piast realm have been found. This suggests a lack of administrative structure similar to that observed in Polonia in the middle of the eleventh century. Pomerania remained a newly subdued territory with a large margin of independence, rather than a regular province.

Duke Władysław Herman around 1090 brought Pomerania under his rule, possibly with the political or even military help of his new brother-in-law, the emperor Henry V. Historians argue that the duke tried to introduce in Pomerania a Polish administrative system with garrisons of ducal warriors in every major stronghold, under the command of officials nominated by the duke and coming from outside the province. But in the same or the following year, a Pomeranian uprising swept away Piast rule.

Bolesław III the Wrymouth as co-ruler attacked Pomeranians many times, causing his half-brother Zbigniew's discontent; the latter's dominion was Pomerania's immediate neighbour, and he tried to allay conflicts. When Zbigniew was expelled from Poland (1107), his brother began the war against Pomeranians on a large scale. His aim was to annex Pomerania as a regular province of Poland. Therefore he ended predatory raids and started to take strongholds one by one. At the same time he planned the Christianization of the province. According to the same historians, Bolesław's ambition was to regain access to the Baltic coast, and especially to the estuaries of the Oder and Vistula, which provided transport arteries through the whole of Poland and offered access to profitable Baltic trade routes. Yet this explanation is merely hypothetical; no sources suggest ducal interest in tradesmen or trade. His ambitions were to control more land and to take more taxes from these lands.

Bolesław III sometime after 1115 subordinated the west Slavic principality of Kopanica (today Köpenick, a suburb of Berlin). From 1116 to 1119 he managed to re-expand Polish territory into east Pomerania, which included the crucial Vistulan port of Gdańsk. From 1121/2, central and western Pomerania fell to Bolesław III, as did the trans-Oder Cispomerania and the island of Rügen.[108] A Christianizing mission was launched under the leadership of a certain Bernard in 1123, but his efforts failed.[109] A disenchanted Bernard entered the Benedictine monastery of Bamberg with permission from the local bishop Otto, who was later called to continue Bernard's mission. In 1124 Otto arrived in Poland and set off for the mission to Pomerania.[110] In the space of six months, backed by

108 This fact, overlooked in Polish sources, is confirmed by the agreement reached at Merseburg in 1135.

109 *Ebonis Vita s. Ottonis episcopi Babembergensis*, ed. Jan Wikarjak, preface and commentary Kazimierz Liman, Monumenta Poloniae Historica s.n., 7/2, II,I.

110 J. Petersohn, 'Apostolus Pomeranorum. Studien zur Geschichte und Bedeutung des Apostelepithetons Bischof Otto I von Bamberg', *Historisches Jahrbuch* 86/2 (1966), 257–94.

Bolesław III's military power, he performed mass baptisms and destroyed pagan temples, idols and cult objects. He understood well the features of the political system in Pomerania, where assemblies were closely connected to pagan temples. Therefore, the conversion of these societies did not simply rest on the destruction of pagan institutions, but also on securing a level of acceptance of the new religion from local assemblies. Even if these bodies typically acted under the threat of military action, they provided some political sanction to the changes imposed.[111] In that same year the papal legate, Cardinal Aegidius/Eid of Tusculum, established two new Polish bishoprics in Włocławek and Lubusz, which were to support missionary work in the newly converted northern provinces.

Taking advantage of Henry V's death in 1125, Bolesław III refused to pay tribute to the Empire for lands that he had taken west of the Oder. Cispomerania and Rügen, conquered by Poland, also attracted claims from Germany and Denmark. The political interests of the Empire and the Piasts were in conflict not only in the north, but also in Hungary and Bohemia. The emperor called a summit at Merseburg in 1135, where personal negotiations between Lothar III and Bolesław III led to a compromise. The Polish duke kept the territories in Cispomerania but accepted that they were fiefs of the Empire and agreed to pay tribute for the previous twelve years.

After Bolesław III's death (1138) his descendants gradually lost influence over Pomerania. Western regions of the province were under growing pressure from Saxons. Denmark also refused to give up its traditional interests in the area. Eastern Pomerania was under the direct administration of the Piast senior duke. But even there ducal governors of Eastern Pomerania started to become increasingly independent. Polish rule in the north was disintegrating: Mieszko III's brother-in-law, Boguslav I, duke of Western Pomerania, subordinated his domain to Germany between 1180 and 1181. This failed to prevent Canute IV from conquering his principality, however, and in 1185 the Pomeranian duke was forced to swear allegiance to the Danish king. The duke of Greater Poland, Władysław III Spindleshanks (Laskonogi, 1202–29), tried at the beginning of the thirteenth century to regain influence over Pomerania, and in 1205 his warriors fought together with Western Pomeranian duke Boguslav II against Danish troops. But his efforts did not produce lasting results. Around the same time the

[111] Rosik and Urbanczyk, 'Poland', 306.

governors of Gdańsk rejected Polish sovereignty and declared themselves to be hereditary dukes. Finally in 1231 the pope declared the duchy of Gdańsk and its ruler Swentopelk to be fully independent. Nevertheless, in the last quarter of the thirteenth century, due to matrimonial and political connections, Eastern Pomerania was connected to Greater Poland.[112]

Apart from the conquest of Pomerania, there was limited and only local Polish interest in crusading. Two of the junior dukes of Poland answered the call to the second crusade: in 1147 Bolesław IV attacked the Prussians while Mieszko III took his forces to Polabia, where he fought together with Henry the Lion of Saxony, Margrave Albrecht the Bear of the Northern Mark and Conrad Wettin, margrave of Meissen. Despite the co-ordinated attack, the war achieved nothing, ending with the siege of already Christian Szczecin/Stettin.

Attempts to conquer Prussia were longer lasting, although their impact was limited. In 1166 Bolesław IV and his younger brother Henryk of Sandomierz launched an unsuccessful attack against the Prussians in which Henryk lost his life. The aim of the attacks is debatable: either conquest or subjugation. The latter seems more probable, as the chronicler Master Vincent wrote that Bolesław IV the Curly forced Prussians to pay tribute, but did not Christianize them.

Piast attempts to influence the political situation in Ruthenia from the second half of the eleventh century seldom took the shape of territorial expansion. Only Bolesław II the Bold was successful in expanding his eastern boundaries. While ostensibly coming to the aid of his uncle-in-law, Izyaslav, who had been deposed from the throne as the grand prince of Rus', Bolesław seized Kiev in 1069 and remained there for almost a year. He attached Red Ruthenia to his realm, yet this was not a stable conquest. In 1073 Izyaslav was deposed again from the Kievan throne, but Bolesław refused to help. Izyaslav sent his son Yaropolk to Rome with an offer to subordinate the Rus' Orthodox Church to the papacy. Pope Gregory VII ordered the pro-papal Bolesław II to intervene on Izyaslav's behalf, and in 1077 he helped the deposed grand prince to recover his throne. Family and political relations in the twelfth century led to many interventions by Piast dukes in Ruthenia. Yet these did not amount to expansion. The

[112] Piskorski, ed., *Pommern im Wandel der Zeiten* (Szczecin, 1999); Rudolf Benl, 'Pommern bis zur Teilung 1368/1372', in *Deutsche Geschichte im Osten Europas. Pommern*, ed. Werner Buchholz (Berlin, 2002), 21–126.

first duke who tried to subject those Ruthenian dukes who were to his power base geographically closest was Kazimierz II the Just. During the 1080s he intervened together with duke of Mazowsze, Leszek (son of Bolesław IV the Curly), many times in Brzešć Ruthenia. As a result, the dying duke of Drohiczyn, Wasylko, chose Leszek as his heir and successor on Drohiczyn's throne. After Leszek's death (1186), the Drohiczyn duchy passed to Kazimierz. Kazimierz focused his interests on strengthening his political influence in Brzešć-Włodzimierz Ruthenia. In 1187 Kazimierz and King Béla III of Hungary began to compete for political control over the principality of Galich. After Béla imposed his son (see below), Kazimierz ceased to intervene, until Emperor Frederick I Barbarossa ordered him to expel András when he sent his warriors. In 1190 a Polish expedition successfully reinstalled Duke Vladimir, who had been deposed by the Hungarians. After Kazimierz's death, his Ruthenian policy forced successive Cracow and Mazovia dukes to participate in the political life of Rus' principalities. Piast political influence there was traditional, but by no means decisive for Rurikid internal or external policies.[113]

## *Hungary*

Hungary's rulers from the late eleventh century on attempted, with more or less success, the expansion of their realm. The first areas of interest were the territories between Hungary and the Adriatic: Croatia and Slavonia. The area which eventually became Croatia had been under Frankish rule, with Slav rulers emerging in hillforts from the early ninth century. A number of dukes vied with each other; some, like Branimir, gained papal acknowledgement of their independent rule. The population seems to have been converted by around the middle of the ninth century through Carolingian influence.[114] Debates surround

[113] Grudziński, *Boleslaus the Bold*, 15–74; Dobosz, *Kazimierz II Sprawiedliwy*; Christian Lübke, 'Das Reich von Kiev als Faktor der Beziehungen zwischen Deutschland und Polen (10.–11. Jahrhundert)', in *Mittelalter – eines oder viele? / Średniowiecze – jedno czy wiele?*, ed. Sławomir Moździoch, Wojciech Mrozowicz and Stanisław Rosik (Wrocław, 2010), 127–39.

[114] For a detailed history of Slavonia and Croatia, see John V. A. Fine, *The Early Medieval Balkans: A Critical Survey from the Sixth to the Late Twelfth Century* (Ann Arbor, 1991), ch. 8; Curta, *Southeastern Europe*, 191–201, 256–67; Stanko Guldescu, *History of Medieval Croatia* (The Hague, 1964); John V. A. Fine, *When Ethnicity Did Not Matter in the Balkans: A Study of Identity in Pre-Nationalist Croatia, Dalmatia and Slovenia in the Medieval and early Modern Periods* (Ann Arbor, 2006).

the status of Slavonia (the part of modern Croatia that lies between the River Drava and the Kapela Mountains)[115] from the middle of the tenth century: whether it was subordinated in some form to the nascent realm of Hungary, was conquered by Tomislav of Croatia, or was independent. The latter claim is based on a late twelfth-century text. The special tax its inhabitants later owed to the Hungarian king (*marturina*, marten fur, eventually transformed into a monetary tax in the early twelfth century) gave rise to the hypothesis that the Slavs had come under the overlordship of Hungary's rulers early on, as this archaic form of taxation is similar to tribute extracted by nomadic rulers from Slavic neighbours. The contradictory and later written sources cannot provide a firm basis for historical arguments; archaeological evidence suggests that a new population appeared in the area, but is inconclusive in explaining who they were and where they came from.

In the early tenth century, Tomislav was styled 'king' by the pope, and seems to have extended some type of control (perhaps the collection of tribute) over at least parts of Dalmatia. The royal title was used by the tenth-century rulers as well, although not exclusively. Peter Krešimir IV (1060–74) received a royal title from the pope, and after him, Zvonimir gained a papal crown in 1075 from Gregory VII. Zvonimir had married László I's sister, and a strong alliance bound the two kings until Zvonimir's death in 1089 or 1090. The widowed queen, faced by internal opposition, requested the intervention of her brother King László of Hungary. In 1091, László invaded Croatia and, between that date and the early twelfth century, Hungarian rule was extended to the area. Sometime between 1091 and 1094, Slavonia was organized into one diocese under the newly founded bishopric of Zagreb, suffragan of Kalocsa, and attached to the kingdom of Hungary. László's nephew Álmos was appointed ruler of Croatia, but historians offer different interpretations of the exact chronology and the character of Hungarian rule during this decade.

Kálmán attached the rest of Croatia to the realm. According to one version of events, he defeated a local rival in 1097. According to another interpretation, the alleged rival is a later folk-etymological invention based on a toponym. In 1102 Kálmán was crowned king of Croatia. The *pacta conventa* that he supposedly made with Croatian

[115] Until the thirteenth century, 'Sclavonia' referred to the whole of Croatia in some texts, and to Slavonia in others.

nobles, recognizing their privileges, is a later forgery.[116] Only briefly did Byzantine and Venetian claims to suzerainty interrupt Hungarian rule in the late twelfth century. Apart from that, from Kálmán's reign, Hungarian kings also ruled as kings of Croatia until the twentieth century. Yet Croatia retained its status as a separate kingdom and independent administrative unit: the kings of Hungary added the title 'rex Croatiae' to their titulature. An appointed *ban* (*banus*) governed in the name of the king. Throughout the period the *ban* was chosen from members of the Hungarian nobility. He mostly served as military leader. Croatian nobles retained their privileges, independence in internal matters, and owed military service to the king only within Croatia and not in Hungary.

Kálmán also extended Hungarian rule to Dalmatia (the coastal area and islands of the Adriatic Sea). He invaded in 1105 and besieged Zadar (Zara). Over the next two years, the other Dalmatian cities also accepted his rule. Hungarian rule here meant taxation (two-thirds of the customs duties were to go to the king); in other respects, the king confirmed the towns' autonomy and privileges in 1108. Dalmatia was even less incorporated into Hungary than Croatia. 'Rex Dalmatiae' was duly added to the royal title, but the territory did not become a permanent acquisition, largely due to prior claims. Dalmatian towns both on the coast and on the islands had been dependants of the Byzantine Empire, with a military governor in Zadar since the establishment of the *theme* of Dalmatia in (or just before) 870. Around 1000, Venice became involved in maintaining nominal Byzantine control over Dalmatia and, by the late eleventh century, many towns had become *de facto* independent from Byzantium. In the 1080s, Emperor Alexius I turned to the Venetian doge for help against the Normans and appointed him duke of Dalmatia and Croatia and imperial *protosebastos*.

Venice never gave up its claims to Dalmatia (nominally as the representative of Byzantium), and attacked it immediately after Kálmán's death. Dalmatian cities acknowledged Venetian rule once

[116] For the opposing view, see Stjepan Antoljak, *Pacta ili Concordia od 1102 godine* (Zagreb, 1980); but for a recent bibliography of the voluminous Croatian literature and debates, see Gábor Szeberényi, 'A Pacta Conventa és a középkori horvát nemesi társadalom: Historiográfiai áttekintés', in *Középkortörténeti tanulmányok 5. Az V. Medievisztikai PhD-konferencia (Szeged, 2007. június 7–8.) előadásai*, ed. Éva Révész and Miklós Halmágyi (Szeged, 2007), 165–79.

again, and thereafter for the rest of the century Hungarian rulers and Venetians, and in the second half of the twelfth century also Byzantines, who reasserted direct control, continued to compete for lordship over the territory. Dalmatian lands changed hands repeatedly, sometimes as often as every year. Manuel Komnenos secured Byzantine rights to these lands through his alliance with Béla III, but after he died the Hungarian king once more recovered the Dalmatian towns (1180–81). Yet this was by no means the end of the territorial disputes: the most infamous episode of the continued conflict was the siege and capture of Zadar by the fourth crusade for the Venetians in 1202.[117]

The territorial ambitions of Hungary's kings did not stop at the closest neighbouring lands; they tried to continue to extend their power over more distant areas of the Balkans. Some modern historians hypothesized that László I (1077–95) or Béla II (1131–41) had conquered a part of Bosnia (or Bosna). No evidence of this exists, however; even the Hungarian expedition to Bosnia in 1137 did not result in any conquests. Béla II or one of his successors added 'king of Rama' to his royal title; as the earlier charters only survive in later copies that may be interpolated, there is no certainty about the exact date. The reality behind this claim of suzerainty is also debated. Historians have speculated that an agreement linked to Béla II's marriage to the daughter of Uroš I of Raška created a basis for this claim, while others suggest it was devoid of any firm base and meant little more than an additional item in the royal title. Bosnia was governed by a *ban*, and Bosnian troops under the *ban* are known to have helped the Hungarian side against Byzantium in the middle of the twelfth century. Hungarian suzerainty over Bosnia, if it had existed, was lost to Byzantium in 1165. After 1180, the *ban* was to all practical purposes independent, until from the 1230s Hungarian kings once again claimed suzerainty.[118]

[117] Fine, *Early Medieval Balkans*, ch. 8; Stephenson, *Byzantium's Balkan Frontier*, ch. 5–8; Curta, *Southeastern Europe*, 338–50; György Györffy, 'Le relazioni bizantino-ungheresi e la Dalmazia all'inizio del secolo XII', in *Über das letzte Jahrzehnt der ungarischen Byzantinistik. Akten der am 3–4. November 1980 gehaltenen Szegeder Konferenz*, ed. Samuel Szádeczky-Kardoss, Acta Universitatis Szegediensis de Attila József Nominatae Opuscula Byzantina 7, 1 (Szeged, 1981), 65–75.

[118] Stephenson, *Byzantium's Balkan Frontier*, 226–7, 233; Fine, *Early Medieval Balkans*, ch.7; Tibor D. Živković, 'Рама у титулатури угарских краљева (with English summary)', *Zbornik radova Vizantoloskog Instituta* 41 (2004), 153–64.

Towns and areas that lie in present-day Serbia were also targets of Hungarian expansion. The area of Srem and its centre, the town of Sirmium (the modern Sremska Mitrovica), was already under attack from the Hungarians at the time of the Hungarian conquest. Parts of this territory were incorporated in a march by István I. In 1071, Sirmium and the whole area north of it (Frangochorion) was attached to Hungary, and remained under Hungarian rule with the exception of the years between 1165 and 1181, when Byzantium reclaimed it – although even then Byzantine authority was at first exercised through allied Hungarian princes, István (IV) and Béla (III) – and warfare over the area flared up a number of times. Finally the area was reattached to the kingdom of Hungary by Béla III. This area between the Sava and Drava Rivers became the county of Szerém within the realm, famous for its wines.

Lands further south along the Danube and Velika Morava Rivers under Byzantine control were in the line of Hungarian–Byzantine conflicts. Hungarian kings often fostered alliances with Serb *župans* of Raška – adjacent to these lands – against Byzantium. In the first half of the twelfth century, Hungarian armies devastated several towns including Braničevo in expeditions against Byzantine-held lands. A Hungarian–Serb alliance was created through the marriage of Béla (II) of Hungary and Helena, the daughter of the Serb *župan* Uroš I. Their son, Géza II, fought against Byzantium in a Serb alliance. A series of Hungarian attacks and Byzantine counter-attacks were punctuated by peace agreements. In 1154 Géza attacked once again, relying on his alliance with Adronicos, Emperor Manuel's cousin. Andronicos was duke of Niš and Braničevo, and promised to cede the region to Géza in exchange for help in gaining the crown. Andronicos, however, was imprisoned, and Géza, who took Braničevo, had to give it up and renew the peace. Serb lands became increasingly independent from Byzantium. After Manuel Komnenos's death in 1180, the Serb grand *župan* Stefan Nemanja entered into an alliance with King Béla III of Hungary. The latter led successful military campaigns against Niš, Braničevo, Belgrade and Sardica in 1182, while Nemanja extended the areas under Raškan control. In 1185, Béla gave up these latest conquests south of the Danube–Sava line, as the dowry of his daughter Margit, who married the Byzantine emperor Isaac II Angelus.[119]

[119] Fine, *Early Medieval Balkans*, 234–47; Curta, *Southeastern Europe*, 328–38.

Until the late twelfth century, Hungarian interventions in Galich (Galicia) were in support of local candidates, without any expansionary aim. Béla III, himself the son of a Rus'ian mother, went further than his predecessors and tried to annex Galich, when in 1188 Prince Vladimir Yaroslavich, expelled by his magnates, sought help in Hungary. Béla III imprisoned him, invaded Galich and put his son András (Endre, Andrew) on the throne. András's subjects rebelled and Vladimir escaped from Hungary and regained the throne with Polish help in 1190. After the death of his successor, Roman Mstislavich, the latter's widow Anna turned to András, who in the meantime became king of Hungary as András II, and to Leszek the White (Biały), prince of Cracow (1194–1227), on behalf of her children in 1205. This prompted a new phase of Hungarian interest in Galich; Hungarian–Polish military interventions recurred for more than a decade, and briefly these rulers' minor children, married to each other, were installed on the throne of Galich. Eventually, the prince of Novgorod claimed Galich.[120]

[120] Font, *Árpád-házi királyok*; Márta F. Font, 'Politische Beziehungen zwischen Ungarn und der Kiever Rus' im 12. Jahrhundert', *Ungarn Jahrbuch* 18 (1990), 1–18, epa.oszk.hu/01500/01536/00018/pdf/UJ_1990_001-018.pdf.

# 5

# SOCIETY AND THE ECONOMY, ELEVENTH–TWELFTH CENTURIES

The economy of Bohemia, Hungary and Poland remained mainly agricultural in the period, although towns started to play a role everywhere in the twelfth century. Society in all the polities became more complex and hierarchical over the period.

## POPULATION SIZE

The size of the population can only be guessed at hypothetically: rare contemporary population numbers for certain groups (which are not statistics in the modern sense), archaeological or other indicators for sizes of villages and churches, analogies with western Europe (where the calculation of medieval populations cannot be precise either) and the use of theoretical frameworks for the size of families or likely population growth combine to provide very provisional and debatable estimates.

It is extremely difficult to estimate the population of the Piast realm in the eleventh and twelfth centuries in absolute numbers. Using regression analysis applied to later data on the collection of Peter's pence, it has been estimated that around the year 1000 Poland's population was about 1.25 million, but this figure is rough and appears too high. Estimates of population density in particular areas based on archaeological data seem more trustworthy, and can be added up for the entire country. Keeping in mind their hypothetical character and modifications introduced to make them consistent with historical studies, scholars have pointed to the systematic growth of population density during the period in question. In the seventh century, population density in the area of the future Piast state has been estimated at 2 persons per km$^2$ to reach 5 persons by the early eleventh century. Only in the thirteenth century did population density grow to 10 persons per km$^2$ across the country, thanks to immigration from western Europe, the development of a new system of urban and rural settlements and – above all – the introduction of new, more productive farming methods which could support a larger population. As the total area of the Piast state in the eleventh and twelfth centuries is estimated at 250,000 km$^2$, it follows that it was inhabited by some 500,000 people in the seventh century; in the eleventh century the population did not exceed 1.25 million, and it reached 2.5 million by the thirteenth or – more likely – fourteenth century.

Bohemia's population has been estimated *c.* 1050 as 450,000, and Moravia's as 230,000, which doubled by 1200; thus the Přemyslid realm may have been inhabited in the late twelfth and early thirteenth century by *c* 1.36 million. Population density varied even in relatively densely settled areas. In the Přemyslid realm for the middle of the eleventh century an average population density is estimated as 8.7 persons per km$^2$, and 20.4 persons per km$^2$ for settlements situated on fertile soil or serving as administrative centres. Calculations for Hungary suggest a maximum population of 1 million at the time of the conquest at the end of the ninth century (including both the conquerors and the local inhabitants), and by 1200 they range between 1.1 million and 2.2 million. Population concentration was uneven everywhere, the densest in plains and the sparsest in mountainous areas.[1]

[1] 'Obyvatelstvo českých zemí ve středověku' (chapter), in Milan Stloukal, Eduard Maur, Ludmila Fialová, Pavla Horská *et al.*, *Dějiny obyvatelstva českých zemí* (Prague, 1996), 2nd edn 1998, 35–73 (textbook with bibliography); Josef Žemlička, *Čechy v době knížecí (1034–1198)* (Prague, 1997), 18; Tadeusz Ladenberger, *Zaludnienie Polski na początku panowania Kazimierza Wielkiego* (Lviv, 1930); Tadeusz Ładogórski [Ladenberger], *Studia nad zaludnieniem Polski XIV w.* (Wrocław, 1958); Henryk Łowmiański, *Początki Polski*, vol. III (Warsaw, 1967), 311–14; Cezary Kuklo, *Demografia Rzeczpospolitej przedrozbiorowej* (Warsaw, 2009), 36–50, 210–20; Kristó, 'Die Bevölkerungszahl Ungarns in der Arpadenzeit'; Font, *Im Spannungsfeld der christlichen Großmächte*, 215–16.

## POPULATION GROUPS

Many immigrant groups played a role in central Europe. Of these, two especially have been the focus of attention: Germans and Jews. German immigration in central Europe, traditionally seen as part of the *Drang nach Osten*, has been the centre of contention. Long hailed by many German historians as a civilizational drive to the east of Germany and criticized by historians from central European countries as a negative force, even a kind of proto-Nazi expansion, a more balanced analysis shows that local rulers and agents were active in recruiting German settlers. They were motivated by the benefit they could derive from such immigration, including gaining a larger workforce to cultivate land: empty lands did not bring income, and in all three countries attractive conditions were offered to immigrant settlers. We cannot speak of German colonization in the sense of German subjugation of unwilling local populations. German merchants in central European towns and peasant settlers were already present in the period we cover. A German role both in mining and as urban elites became important only in the later medieval period, after the thirteenth century.

The legal status of Jews in Hungary and Poland was on the whole more favourable than in western Europe. Both realms recognized the rights of Jews as *hospites* (immigrants who had privileges), unless their status was specifically regulated in other ways. Restrictions on the interaction between Jews and Christians and on the possible sphere of Jewish activities, spreading in western Europe at the time, remained more limited in Hungary and were not introduced in Poland.

### *Hungary*

The population of Hungary was mixed from the start.[2] The 'Hungarians' themselves were not ethnically homogeneous; in addition, they also assimilated the local peoples (Slavs and probably descendants of the area's earlier populations) inhabiting the area at the time of the conquest, as well as subsequent immigrants. In the early eleventh century Slavs may have formed a majority of the population. An unresolved question concerns the origin of the

[2] Erik Fügedi, 'Das mittelalterliche Königreich Ungarn als Gastland', in Fügedi, *Kings, Bishops*, no. VIII; Gyula Kristó, 'Magyarország népei Szent István korában', *Századok* 134 (2000), 3–44, see 41–2; Kristó, *Nichtungarische Völker*, 21–35.

Székely (Seklers). Scholars disagree whether they were Turkic immigrants or part of the Hungarian confederation at the time of the conquest and, if the latter, whether descendants of the Kabars or not; whether they were of Turkic or Finno-Ugric stock is also debated.[3] In addition, Hungary, at the crossroads of Latin and Byzantine Christianity and the world of the steppe nomads, was home to immigrants from the east and the west throughout the period.

Slavs played an important role, as attested by the significant borrowings in early administrative and Christian vocabulary from Slavic languages. The Slavic population of the kingdom did not simply consist of those already living in the area in the late ninth century. Slav immigrants from Bohemia and Moravia, Poland and Rus' also settled after the Hungarian conquest. István I's son, Imre, held the title *Dux Ruizorum*, and historians have interpreted this as an indication that István settled Rus' warriors in the borderlands in the early eleventh century. The early twelfth-century laws of King Kálmán mention that *hospites* such as Slavs who worked on the fields of others had to pay for their freedom only and did not owe other monetary payments. Thirteenth-century sources mention Rutheni (Rus'), Czechs and Poles as *hospites*, that is, immigrant settlers, who were given various, usually uninhabited, lands; several times they are explicitly mentioned as peasants. The majority of the Slav *hospites* obtained rights as peasant settlers, while some others became *várjobbágyok* (castle warriors) and eventually nobles. There were also groups of Slavs living from hunting and fishing, paying their tax in marten skins until the mid thirteenth century. From that time on, many Slav peasants immigrated without receiving *hospes* status, although they enjoyed some limited rights.[4]

Settlers from the west included knights and members of the elite who arrived, sometimes in the entourage of queens, and received high status at the royal court. Larger groups of immigrant settlers began to arrive from the early twelfth century: Romance-speakers, called

[3] Zoltán Kordé, 'Kabars, Sicules et Petchenègues: les Hongrois et les auxiliaires militaires', in Csernus and Korompay, eds., *Les Hongrois et l'Europe*, 231–9; Nathalie Kálnoky, *Les constitutions et privilèges de la noble nation Sicule* (Budapest, Paris and Szeged, 2004); Kristó, *A székelyek eredetéről* (Szeged, 1996); Kristó, 'Quelle est l'origine des Sicules?', *Cahiers d'études hongroises* 10 (2002), 115–28.

[4] Kristó, *Nichtungarische Völker*, 84–128; for Kálmán's law, see Bak *et al.*, eds., *Laws*, 32, c. 80.

*Latini*, who were north Italians (Lombards and Venetians) and Walloons (French-speakers).[5] From the use of the Latin and Hungarian terminology (*Latini* and *Olasz* respectively), neither of which distinguished between these groups, it is impossible to tell whether Italians or Walloons settled in any given location, but some toponyms, derived from Old French, point to Walloon settlement. Some of the *Latini* were peasants, and had an important role in the development of viticulture. Many were townsmen, and played a key role as merchants and sometimes as artisans. Their communities settled in royal towns in their own quarter (*vicus Latinorum*), with their own privileges before the Mongol invasion (1241–2); they did not, however, settle in those towns that developed after the invasion.

German settlers started to arrive in Hungary as early as the eleventh century, but more substantial German immigration took off from the middle of the twelfth century. Initially designated as *Theutonici*, during the early thirteenth century the main denomination for German-speakers became *Saxones* (a term appearing from 1206). This reflected their legal status rather than their ethnic origin: most were not Saxons, but arrived from various regions of the German lands. Diverse origins are attested by the variety of their pottery, art and liturgy. According to a later reference, it was King Géza II who invited German-speakers in and settled them in southern Transylvania from 1149. This was a large area (German Altland) containing many separate German villages, interspersed with villages of non-German inhabitants. Subsequently German settlement in southern Transylvania expanded (the entire settlement area was called Königsboden). In the twelfth and thirteenth centuries German settlements also developed in northern Transylvania. Many of the German settlers in Transylvania were free peasants who brought land under cultivation and kept animals. German townspeople started to play a significant part in Hungary beginning only in the thirteenth century, especially from the middle of the century on.[6]

[5] Kristó, *Nichtungarische Völker*, 182–95; Mihály Auner, 'Latinus', *Századok* 50 (1916), 28–41.

[6] On Géza II's role, see Zsigmond Jakó, ed., *Erdélyi okmánytár*, vol. I, *1023–1300* (Budapest, 1997), 22, 132; Kristó, *Nichtungarische Völker*, 131–40; Harald Zimmermann, *Siebenbürgen und seine Hospites Theutonici. Vorträge und Forschungen zur südostdeutschen Geschichte. Festgabe zum 70. Geburtstag*, ed. Konrad Gündisch (Cologne, 1996); Horst Klusch, *Zur Ansiedlung der Siebenbürger Sachsen* (Bucharest and Klausenburg, 2001).

Minority groups adhering to different religions were also present in the kingdom. Although Jews already lived in Roman Pannonia, no evidence exists of a continuity of Jewish life to the Middle Ages. Speculations about the immigration of Jewish Khazars at the time of the Hungarian conquest of the Carpathian basin in the late ninth century cannot be substantiated. Jews, however, appeared in Hungarian territories by the second half of the tenth century. Around 955, Ḥasdai ibn Shaprut mentioned sending his letter from Cordoba to the Khazars via the Jewish communities of the lands that later became the kingdom of Hungary, and Ibrāhīm ibn Ya'qūb around 965 wrote about Jews from there trading in Prague. Jewish communities appeared initially in western Hungary, and their immigration was probably mostly linked to trade in the first instance: they are attested along a trade route between Regensburg and Kiev from the eleventh century on. Long-distance trade between western Europe and eastern lands early on included Jewish merchants among others; Jews also started to trade commodities in the local markets. Sources refer to commerce between Jewish communities in Hungary and Jews from Mainz and other German and Austrian towns during the period. Various types of evidence testify to the western origin of Jews, especially migration from German lands: links to rabbis and the similarity of customs noted in *responsa* (*sheelot u-teshuvot*), naming patterns and the technique and lettering of tombstones.[7]

Both László I and Kálmán prohibited Jews from holding Christian slaves. László also prohibited marriage between Jews and Christian women. Kálmán restricted Jewish settlement to episcopal centres, and allowed only the use of pagan slaves to work lands owned by Jews, in line with earlier imperial legislation. Commercial transactions between Jews and Christians were to be put in writing in sealed charters, and loans were minutely regulated. Other ecclesiastical prohibitions were not issued locally. Moreover, the practical effect of the legislation seems to have been minimal: for example, Jews settled in non-episcopal centres, and sealed charters did not become a feature of

[7] For the Hebrew text and a Hungarian translation of all Hebrew sources concerning medieval Hungary, see Shlomo J. Spitzer and Géza Komoróczy, ed. and tr., *Héber kútforrások Magyarország és a magyarországi zsidóság történetéhez a kezdetektől 1686-ig* (Budapest, 2003), which includes a list of all previous editions. See also Alexander Scheiber, *Jewish Inscriptions in Hungary from the Third Century to 1686* (Budapest, 1983). For an overview, see N. Berend, *At the Gate of Christendom.*

Jewish–Christian trade. Jews in both Hungary and Poland became involved in minting, and in the thirteenth century in tax-farming. Around the middle of the eleventh century two (probably German) Jews litigated in Mainz about a failed attempt to mint coins at the royal mint in Hungary. Jewish lessees of the treasury in thirteenth-century Hungary were involved in minting, signalled by Hebrew letters serving as identifying marks on the coins.[8]

Muslims constituted a small minority in the kingdom of Hungary, and scholars have speculated both about their place of origin (the Khazar Empire, Volga Bulgaria, the Balkans and Khwarezm) and about the period of their immigration, from the ninth through the eleventh centuries. They most likely arrived from different areas and in several waves. Muslims served the kings as officials of the treasury and oversaw the sale of salt in southern Hungary. Legislation in the late eleventh and early twelfth centuries aimed at the conversion of Muslims to Christianity, and legal prohibitions in the service of conversion attest to a good knowledge of Muslim practices such as ritual ablutions and abstention from pork. In the middle of the twelfth century, a Muslim author, Abū Ḥāmid al-Ġarnāṭi spent several years in the kingdom, and wrote about converts who practised Islam in secret as well as Muslims who openly adhered to their religion and served in the royal army. By the time he was writing, the Hungarian king was encouraging Muslim immigration, wishing to draw on their military service. By the end of the thirteenth century, Muslims disappeared from Hungary: mostly they probably integrated through conversion, but almost no evidence of the process survives.[9]

No less attractive to the kings of Hungary were immigrant groups from the steppes east of the kingdom. Some of the Turkic nomads who periodically raided the kingdom eventually settled there, usually fleeing west following a defeat. The Pechenegs were the most important such population until the thirteenth century; and they may have started settling in the Carpathian basin already in the tenth century, but Hungarian sources mentioning them only exist from the eleventh; further groups arrived in the eleventh and twelfth centuries. The texts are more informative on their legal status from the end of the twelfth century. Many villages of Pechenegs were donated by the king from the eleventh century on to monastic institutions, which from then on had jurisdiction over these villages. Another group of Pechenegs at

[8] On minting, see N. Berend, *At the Gate of Christendom*, 120–9. [9] *Ibid., passim.*

Árpás came under the jurisdiction of the count palatine. Pechenegs and other nomads who settled before the thirteenth century converted and assimilated.[10]

The military significance of many immigrants was crucial for the kings, who repeatedly needed more reliable support than that provided by nobles. Western immigrants often had a military role. Beginning with the marriage of István I to the Bavarian princess Gisela, German-speaking warriors from different German lands started to arrive in the kingdom. As heavy armoured cavalry, they helped the king defeat powerful local leaders with territories of their own and incorporate their lands into his kingdom. Many of these immigrant warriors received large estates and became part of the nobility. Crusaders of the first and second crusades crossed Hungary on their way to the Holy Land and, as charters attest, subsequently in the early twelfth century some knights settled in Transylvania. Peasant settlers also provided military service through several villages together equipping a soldier. This was part of the obligation of the German ('Saxon') population of southern Transylvania, for example. Nomads provided a radically different type of military service, as light cavalry. They fought in the royal army with bows and arrows, using nomadic tactics, which involved feigned retreat and then suddenly firing arrows at the enemy. They were also part of the bodyguard for several rulers. In the early period after the Hungarian settlement, many groups including Pechenegs guarded the frontier regions of the kingdom, as well as serving in the army as vanguard or rearguard. Muslims also participated in the army in royal service as light cavalry.[11]

The military, economic and political usefulness of immigrants was therefore substantial for the kings of Hungary, who initially guarded the monopoly of settling them on their own lands. The taxes and service of immigrants were an important source of revenue and power for the kings. It is not surprising, therefore, that many immigrants were granted privileges by the king; these were in written form, especially from the thirteenth century.

[10] Pálóczi Horváth, *Pechenegs*; Kristó, *Nichtungarische Völker*, 70–83.

[11] Göckenjan, *Hilfsvölker und Grenzwächter*; N. Berend, *At the Gate of Christendom*, 140–7; Gyula Kristó, *Háborúk és hadviselés az Árpádok korában*, 2nd edn (Szeged, 2003), 232–83; Szabó, *A honfoglalóktól a huszárokig*.

## Bohemia and Poland

Bohemia and Poland were far less ethnically diverse than Hungary in the eleventh and twelfth centuries. Both states were inhabited mostly by different groups of Slavic origin. The subjects of the Přemyslid duchy no later than in the tenth century were called *Boemi* or *Bohemi*, and they were seen from the outside as a stable, undivided group. Historians argued that in reality at least until the middle of the tenth century tribal divisions among inhabitants of the Bohemian basins could be observed. The Piasts ruled over a more heterogeneous society which originated from different pre-state social formations scattered over the area. Only around the year 1000 was their realm first called *Polonia*, and the people *Poloni*. Albeit socially or politically different, these people since the eleventh century were similar as far as civilization and culture are concerned. Based on information from archaeological excavations and several mentions in written sources, one can find several ethnically different groups on the territory of Bohemia and Poland, but they are of only marginal importance. This situation changed in the thirteenth century. From that time, multiethnicity became a trademark of and a factor supporting the development of the whole of central Europe, including Bohemia and Poland.[12]

In the Piast realm, Norman settlements can be identified among the dominant Slav population, mostly in the period from the end of the tenth to the middle of the eleventh century, but their size and significance remain debatable. The majority of scholars connect their existence to the organization of ducal armed forces and the presence in them of Norman mercenaries. Some, however, argue for the possibility of broader cultural influences linked to the settlement of entire families and trade contacts. Even more controversial is a hypothesis concerning Hungarian warriors serving Piast dukes in the eleventh century. The arguments for their presence are unconvincing:

[12] Christian Lübke, 'Multiethnizität und Stadt als Faktoren gesellschaftlicher und staatlicher Entwicklung im östlichen Europa', in *Burg – Burgstadt – Stadt. Zur Genese mittelalterlicher nichtagrarischer Zentren in Ostmitteleuropa*, ed. Hans Brachmann (Berlin, 1995), 36–50; Lübke, 'Ethnic diversity in East Central Europe and the beginnings of the economic change in the High Middle Ages', in *Movimientos migratorios, asentamientos y expansion (siglos VIII–XI): en el centenario del profesor José María Lacarra: XXXIV Semana de Estudios Medievales, Estella, 16 a 20 de julio de 2007* (Pamplona, 2008), 289–304.

a limited number of burials with parts of equipment linked to Hungarian culture. Only the topographical names 'Węgry, Węgrzyce' (i.e. Hungarian people) suggested organized Hungarian settlement. But these settlements were traditionally understood to have been inhabited by prisoners of war, and only recently did the hypothesis emerge that these villages should be seen as centres of warriors' settlements. No sources indicate the presence of Norman or Hungarian warriors – at least in the service of local dukes – in Bohemia. But both in Bohemia and Poland warriors who originated from the Empire were present. They were sent to these countries by emperors or kings of Germany in support of their allies, but, especially in the second half of the twelfth century, they also arrived looking for career opportunities. Although they were not numerous, their number grew over the next century.[13]

In Bohemia, the commercial activity of Sephardic Jews is attested already in the tenth century in the context of their involvement in the slave trade. Evidence of Jewish settlement has been found in Prague but it seems to have disappeared by the late tenth or early eleventh century. In the late eleventh century, a multi-ethnic community was active in Prague, which comprised German, Romance and Jewish elements. Its German members were granted a written privilege by Vratislav II which released them as 'guests' from many dues payable to the duke and took them under his protection. It is possible that similar legal privileges – albeit not put into writing – were enjoyed by other ethnic groups. Jews, although they had legal autonomy in internal matters, were under ducal authority in economic issues and in cases of litigation with ducal subjects. The ruler was represented by an official of the ducal treasury, the bailiff (*camerarius*). He was also entitled to judge disputes between Jews and Christians, and collect dues for the duke.

The Jews continued to thrive, thanks to the dukes' protection and their own financial, commercial and trade activities, until the late eleventh century. In the heated crusading atmosphere, the first pogrom of the Jews in Prague took place in 1096. Under the protection of the bishop of Prague, the Jewish community recuperated, but only for a short time. In 1098, Duke Břetislav II accused the Jews of conspiring

[13] Halina Modrzewska, *Osadnictwo obcoetniczne i innoplemienne w Polsce wcześniejszego średniowiecza* (Warsaw, 1984); Tomasz Jurek, 'Fremde Ritter im mittelalterlichen Polen', *Questiones Medii Aevi Novae* 3 (1998), 20–5.

to flee with their assets to Poland and Hungary, and confiscated all their property, arguing that they had acquired their fortunes in Bohemia and thus had no right to transfer them abroad. The Jews returned after a short time. Their uncertain legal and social position, due to dependence upon the will of each duke, lasted until the first written privileges for them were issued in 1255, during the reign of King Přemysl Otakar II of Bohemia (1261–78). The most important Jewish community in the realm was always situated in Prague. It flourished not only economically, but also as a centre of intellectual life, especially Talmudic culture. Most newcomers, who usually migrated from the Empire, gravitated towards Prague and its prosperous market. During the thirteenth century, the number of independent Jewish communities in the Přemyslid realm increased slightly. They emerged in Znojmo and probably in Brno and Cheb (Eger). It was no accident that almost all of them were organized near the ducal or, in the case of Moravian communities, ruler's court. Although sometimes a ruler's anger – used for political ends – could be dangerous for them, most of the time it was his authority that sheltered them against the hostility of Christian debtors.[14]

Jews first settled in Poland at the beginning of the eleventh century. They were mentioned as living in Cracow and – probably – Przemyśl, near Kievan Rus'. They are attested in the early eleventh century as merchants and in financial roles. In Greater Poland Jewish communities appeared from the second half of the twelfth century in Kalisz and probably Gniezno and Poznań. In Mazovia a small community of slave merchants was present in Płock in the eleventh century, which probably continued during the twelfth century: a 'Jews' well' was mentioned in a charter from 1237. In the late twelfth century (*c.* 1186–94) 'ducal Jews' were involved in minting coins with Hebrew inscriptions for the duke of Greater Poland Mieszko III the Old (1173–1202).[15] This may be a sign of the growing importance of Jews dealing

[14] *CDB*, vol. V, fasc. 1, eds. J. Šebanek and S. Dušková (Prague, 1974), no. 41, p. 85; Peter Hilsch, 'Die Juden in Böhmen und Mähren im Mittelalter und die ersten Privilegien (bis zum Ende des 13. Jahrhunderts)', in *Die Juden in den Böhmischen Ländern. Vorträge der Tagung des Collegium Carolinum in Bad Wiessee vom 27. bis 29. November 1981*, ed. Ferdinand Seibt (Munich, 1983), 13–26; Vladimír Sadek, 'Medieval Jewish scholars in Prague', *Review of the Society for the History of Czechoslovak Jews* 5 (1992–3), 135–49; Daniel Polakovič, 'Medieval Hebrew inscriptions in Cheb (Eger)', *Judaica Bohemiae* 42 (2006), 5–52.

[15] Marian Gumowski, *Hebräische Münzen im mittelalterlichen Polen* (Graz, 1975).

as creditors with financial matters of the Polish realm, or just at the Piast court. These coins were minted in Kalisz, where a significant Jewish colony was present and which temporarily became Mieszko the Old's capital. Coins with Hebrew inscriptions have also been found during archaeological excavations in Poznań and Gniezno, the most important cities of Greater Poland. That suggests that at the end of the twelfth century Jewish communities were active there in financial operations. It is very probable that at the end of the twelfth century ducal coins with Hebrew inscriptions were also minted in Gniezno and, up to the beginning of the thirteenth century, in Cracow. From the second half of the twelfth century Jews were also present in Silesia, actively participating in a credit market. Silesian Jews owned whole villages which passed into their possession probably as pledges. The first such case occurred before 1153, and the practice continued during the first half of the thirteenth century. The first groups of Jews settled in the province apparently in Wrocław. Then, up to the end of the thirteenth century, new communities appeared in Bolesławiec, Bytom and Głogów, and probably in Legnica, Lwówek, and Świdnica. Historians pointed out that Silesia was the first Piast province where, in the second half of the twelfth and first half of the thirteenth centuries, Jews migrating from the central parts of the Empire settled. In other provinces of Poland Jewish settlement density was lower.[16]

[16] *Schlesisches Urkundenbuch*, ed. Heinrich Appelt, vol. I (Vienna, 1971), no. 58: 'villam Tinech emit comes Petrus a Iudeis' (*c.* 1200), no. 83: 'pars ville falcinariorum in Vratizlav, quam Ioseph Iudeus habuit' (*c.* 1202), no. 95: 'tota villa falconariorum, quam Iozof et Kazchel Iudei habuerunt' (1204); *Zbiór dokumentów i listów miasta Płocka*, ed. Stella Maria Szacherska, vol. I: *1065–1495* (Warsaw, 1975), no. 23. Aleksander Gieysztor, 'Les Juifs et leur activité économique en Europe Orientale', in *Gli ebrei nell'alto medioevo: settimane di studio del centro italiano di studi sull'alto medioevo*: 261 (Spoleto, 1980), 498–528; Mateusz Goliński, 'Jews in medieval Legnica: their location in the municipal area', in *Jews in Silesia*, ed. Marcin Wodziński and Janusz Spyra (Cracow, 2001), 17–32; Hanna Zaremska, 'Organizacja wczesnośredniowiecznych gmin żydowskich w Europie Środkowej: Ostrzyhom i Kraków', in *Ludzie. Kościół. Wierzenia. Studia z dziejów kultury i społeczeństwa Europy Środkowej (średniowiecze – wczesna epoka nowożytna)*, ed. Wojciech Iwańczak and Stefan K. Kuczyński (Warsaw, 2001), 303–12; Zaremska, 'Statut Bolesława Pobożnego dla Żydów: uwagi w sprawie genezy', *Roczniki Dziejów Społecznych i Gospodarczych* 64 (2004), 107–34; Zaremska, *Żydzi w średniowiecznej Europie Środkowej* (Poznań, 2005); Zaremska, *Żydzi w średniowiecznej Polsce. Gmina krakowska* (Warsaw, 2011).

As in Bohemia, their legal autonomy was guaranteed by ducal authority. At the beginning of the thirteenth century the 'elders' of the Jewish community of Cracow were mentioned as judges in cases between local and visiting merchants. Much later – first mentioned in 1264 – a special ducal official, the 'Jews' judge' (*iudex Judeorum*) is mentioned in charters as an arbiter in such procedures. In the fourteenth century these officials were appointed by a ducal voivode and were all Christians and the ruler's representatives, although they judged Jewish matters according to the latter's own rights. It is highly probable that earlier, in the eleventh and twelfth centuries, another ducal official appeared as an intermediary between Jews and Christians, and especially between Jewish communities and ducal power. In the thirteenth century the voivode of the province was mentioned in such a position. But historians have suggested that he took over the responsibilities of the ducal bailiff. If this is correct, then during the eleventh and twelfth centuries the organization and shape of ducal protection over Jews were similar in Poland and Bohemia. But we know little about their economic or social situation in the period before thirteenth century. The fact that in 1098 Poland was named as the destination for the Bohemian Jews allegededly attempting to escape suggests that the Jewish community in Poland was safe and affluent. Historians argue that Jews' dependence on ducal authority was advantageous for both sides. For dukes, their right to control Jews was a source of such significant income that they did not give up this right even after chartered towns replaced strongholds, older centres of exchange and financial operations. Whereas in the Empire Jews living in towns were subject to the law of the town, in Poland they had their legal autonomy from it and, at the same time, were fully dependent upon the duke's will. As in Bohemia, their rights were written down not earlier than the second half of the thirteenth century. This was first done by the duke of Greater Poland, Bolesław the Pious in 1264, then by Silesian dukes; all charters were more or less closely modelled on general privileges issued after 1250 by rulers of Austria, Hungary and Bohemia.[17]

[17] *KDWp* I, no. 605; Zofia Kowalska, 'Die grosspolnischen und schlesischen Judenschutzbriefe des 13. Jahrhunderts im Verhältnis zu den Privilegien Kaiser Friedrichs II (1238) und Herzog Friedrichs II von Österreich (1244). Filiation der Dokumente und inhaltliche Analyse', *Zeitschrift für Ostmitteleuropa Forschung* 47 (1998), 1–20.

From the second half of the twelfth century groups of village settlers from western parts of Europe, mostly from German lands but also Walloons, arrived in Poland (Silesia) and at the end of the twelfth and early thirteenth centuries in Bohemia. Their compatriots, mostly merchants, had lived in several strongholds in both countries in small groups recognized by local law as *hospites* ('guests') since the eleventh century. From the second half of the twelfth century another group of highly qualified foreigners arrived from German and Italian areas to both countries – miners. They were seldom mentioned as workers in mines, although it is highly possible that they popularized more efficient and up-to-date ways of mining than hitherto known locally. More frequently, but during the thirteenth rather than the twelfth century, they were required to organize the whole process and set up a mine. But in the period under consideration their numbers were very small. Immigration eventually leading to change in the ethnic character of the population took place in the thirteenth and fourteenth centuries.[18]

## SOCIAL STRUCTURE AND ORGANIZATION

In all three realms, social organization changed over time, with the emergence of an increasing number of diverse status groups. This also meant a growing hierarchization of society. The significance of warriors was crucial in each area, but a stratified nobility developed only gradually. Scholarly debates focused on the ruler's role in social organization. Society in all three realms included slaves, free peasants and guests (*hospites* – settlers with privileges). Numerous debates focused also on the existence and role of service villages: whether they were organized by the ruler (and thus what implication they held for the ruler's power), whether they were local or imported in origin, when they came into existence and what their exact characteristics were.

[18] Benedykt Zientara, 'Walloons in Silesia in the twelfth and thirteenth centuries', *Quaestiones Medii Aevi* 2 (1981), 127–50; Danuta Molenda, 'Mining towns in Central-Eastern Europe in feudal times: problem outline', *Acta Poloniae Historica* 34 (1976), 165–88; Molenda, 'Die Beteiligung fremder Fachleute im Erzbergbau im mittelalterlichen Polen', *Questiones Medii Aevi Novae* 3 (1998), 179–83, 194.

## Bohemia

According to Ibrāhīm ibn Ya'qūb, a Hispano-Arab Jewish merchant and traveller, members of the Polish (and probably Czech) warrior elite completely relied on the ruler for their sustenance and received from him everything needed to perform their functions in society. They also enjoyed his protection, which extended to their families. With these remarks put in the context of Třeštík and Krzemieńska's general model (see Chapter 4), it has been argued that the ruler supported the members of his *druzhina* by letting them share in ducal revenues. Bestowing offices upon them, the ruler would grant them a share in the revenues related to the relevant office. The ruler was the sole landowner and this ducal monopoly would be broken only in the thirteenth century.[19] Recently Czech scholars criticizing this thesis have pointed to twelfth-century sources confirming the ownership of land by nobles in Bohemia. During this period, noble estates were modest, comprising from several to a dozen or so small villages, and expanded into large landholdings during the second half of the twelfth and first half of the thirteenth centuries. Of the ordinary warriors (*milites*), some had the status of mere peasants only occasionally called to arms (*milites secundi ordini*).[20]

Debate on the social structure of the rural populations in the Přemyslid state in the tenth through the twelfth centuries has continued for decades. Since the 1970s, the dominant theory has held that under the influence of the state's rule the originally free people split into groups of ducal subjects of diverse legal status. Those holding the whole land controlled it in such a way as to respect the particular rights of each group. Among the rural population, the top position in the social hierarchy was occupied by free settlers and *hospites* who enjoyed personal freedom and could not be transferred by the ruler to any third party against their will. There also existed a separate group of free warriors who were not knights (the *milites secundi ordinis* mentioned above).

A step below in the social hierarchy were the so-called inheritors, in sources referred to as *rustici* or *rustici ducis* (the term *heredes* appears in

[19] Barbara Krzemieńska and Dušan Třeštík, 'Hospodářské základy raně středověkého státu ve střední Evropě (Čechy, Polsko, Uhry v 10. a 11. století)', in *Hospodářské dějiny / Economic history. Praha, Ústav československých a světových dějin Československé akademie věd* 1 (1978), 149–230.

[20] Jan, *Václav II*, 172–93.

the twelfth century). They were freemen who had hereditary rights to their land, fell under the exclusive jurisdiction of ducal courts and paid the dues called *tributum pacis*, which indicated and confirmed their status as freemen. Still, they were the duke's subjects and he had the right to pass them on, together with their land, to a third party. Below them were the unfree settlers cultivating the land assigned to them by the duke, and at the bottom of the social ladder were the slaves working at his court or estates. The *ministeriales* supposedly occupied an in-between position: they were unfree settlers cultivating the land belonging to the duke. They paid dues in kind (specified craft goods, services or foodstuffs, such as honey) and could keep the remainder of the crops. Their settlements (service villages) were concentrated around the ducal strongholds, ensuring necessary provisions.[21]

Debate has centred on the precise meaning of the social categories that the sources designate as 'free settlers', *hospites*, *heredes*, *ministeriales* and others. It is generally accepted that there existed a variety of legal relations between the freemen and the overlord, as well as different forms of landholding rights. Likewise, the important role of the unfree population in the ducal and noble villages seems indisputable, and studies have focused on the origins of their significant role in the social structure of villages on the one hand, and on the precise character and evolution of their unfree status on the other. Recent studies paint a more dynamic picture of social changes during the period of the tenth through the twelfth centuries.

More traditionally oriented historians argue that in the tenth century there existed two social groups: the ruler and his *druzhina* on the one hand and the free peasants on the other. Over time, the growing burden of various dues levied by the state apparatus resulted in limits on the peasants' freedom. The state administration's control over the free settlers on the ducal estates (*rustici duces*, later *heredes*) continued to grow. Dues paid by them constituted the basic part of ducal revenues. Still, they retained personal freedom. When demographic growth in the eleventh century made it impossible to sustain the growing number of freemen living on lands received from the duke, many resettled on ducal, noble or ecclesiastical estates as *hospites*. They retained their personal freedom, but their economic dependence from the landowner increased. Over time, the pressure exerted by

[21] Jan Klápště, 'Studies of structural change in medieval settlement in Bohemia', *Antiquity* 65, 247 (1991), 396–405.

the ducal administration resulted in the shift of some freemen to the group of service craftsmen and *ministeriales*. They held lands granted by the duke on which no dues were levied. In exchange, they paid dues in the form of specified craft goods or services to the ducal court. These obligations were hereditary. Over time, their status became identical to that of the unfree service population. The latter would be settled by the duke on his lands and initially obliged to pay higher dues. At the bottom of the social hierarchy were the slaves serving directly at the ducal court. The distinction between the free and unfree peasants disappeared finally only in the second half of the twelfth century. At this time, the term *heredes* became widely used to indicate the land-cultivating rural population of ducal or noble subjects.[22]

This mostly conventionally sketched and widely accepted picture has been challenged by new approaches. Historians recently pointed out two aspects of the socio-economic organization of the Bohemian village in the period between the tenth and twelfth centuries. First, they emphasized the efficiency of the system imposed by ducal authority: despite recurring political turmoil, ducal revenues remained stable enough for the rulers to be very active on the domestic and international political scene. Second, they argued that unfree status was much more common than hitherto suggested. Until the twelfth century, only the free settlers, cultivating their own land to which they had hereditary rights, and the *hospites*, cultivating the lands granted to them, enjoyed personal freedom. All other categories of population in villages and ducal estates other than members of the elite were unfree. Dues and services they owed to the duke, local lord or landowner could assume diverse forms, but there was a common factor that determined their status: they could all be transferred to a third party without their consent.

At the same time, researchers argued against viewing the unfree as functioning in isolation from the remainder of the rural population. The economic organization of the ducal domain was based on the system of manorial estates (*curia*) rather than service villages. Of various sizes, they were spread across the realm and their administrators collected various dues in kind and goods, including those produced by unfree craftsmen, and either transported them or stored them on site to provide sustenance for the itinerant court and ducal

[22] Žemlička, *Čechy v době knížací*, 153–8.

entourage. This system, characteristic of the Přemyslid domain, emerged in the tenth century, and continued almost unchanged throughout the twelfth.[23]

In the thirteenth century, the organization of Bohemian village society changed drastically as a result of the appearance of new settlements chartered according to Teutonic law, with their settlers having their rights and obligations precisely defined. Usually, they were also granted hereditary ownership of the land and were free to leave the village if they so wished. In Bohemia, chartered settlements (villages and towns) developed later than in neighbouring Poland, which may suggest that the performance of the Přemyslid system of manorial estates was more efficient.[24]

## *Poland*

For decades scholars had maintained that the process of the gradual transfer of landholdings to the warriors, particularly those forming the ruler's inner circle, had started in the middle of the eleventh century. Thus, the monopoly of the ruler as the sole landholder would have come to an end earlier than in Bohemia. Already in the second half of the eleventh century, landholdings started to provide a livelihood for the warriors but at the same time the ownership of land on the one hand reduced their dependency upon the ruler, and on the other resulted in the diversification of economic status within the group. In the end, an elite of influential high nobility emerged as distinct from ordinary warriors. This model has now been modified considerably. The first landholdings granted to the duke's warriors were small and could not provide the holder and his family with a permanent base from which to maintain an elevated status and activity among the realm's elite. Through the whole period considered here, irrespective

[23] Tomáš Petráček, *Fenomén darovaných lidí v českých zemí ch 11.–12. století: k poznání hospodářských a sociálních dějin českých zemí v době knížecí* (Prague, 2003); Petráček, 'Rustici, hospites, duces: k problému svobodných rolníků v Přemyslovských zemí ch 11. a 12. století', *Časopis Národního Muzea, řada historická* 171, 3–4 (2002), 137–64.

[24] Rudolf Procházka, 'Pocátky jihomoravských mest a etnické zmeny', *Archeologia Historica* 28 (2003), 267–95; Michael Brauer, Pavlína Rychterová and Martin Wihoda, 'Kolonisation und Akkulturation im Mittelalter: vergleichende europäische und regionale Perspektiven. Einleitung', in *Die mittelalterliche Kolonisation: vergleichende Untersuchungen; studentische Arbeiten aus dem internationalen Seminar, veranstaltet in Prag vom 7. bis 11. März 2005*, ed. Michael Brauer (Prague, 2009), 7–20.

of his status in the duke's circle, the warrior's principal source of income remained his service to the ruler. Only in the late twelfth and, especially, in the thirteenth century did the elite's sustenance become independent of holding court offices, through the process of accumulating landholdings; thus the warriors' livelihood no longer relied on the ruler's gifts and war booty.[25]

The elite itself was differentiated. Ordinary warriors (*nobiles, milites gregarii*) were clearly separated from the close associates and counsellors of the duke. But in twelfth century this narrow circle was also divided into two layers. The highest position in the elite was that of the *palatinus*, the closest to the duke. He led the army in place of the duke, and appointed officials of almost all ranks. In return, he could share ducal rights, and not only as a founder of church institutions (sometimes of substantial significance, such as the Benedictine cloister of St Vincent in Wrocław or the collegiate church of St Andrew near Cracow). The most powerful and closest collaborators of the duke were called *principes* by the Anonymous chronicler in the first quarter of the twelfth century. They ruled whole provinces (*regiones, provinciae*) of the Piast realm as ducal representatives and were commonly acknowledged as guardians of both local traditions and laws stated by the duke. One rung below on the social scale were *comites*. They mostly oversaw strongholds and represented ducal authority in the province.[26]

It is likely that already from the late eleventh century one had to be knighted to become a fully fledged member of the *druzhina*. According to Gallus Anonymous, the knighting ceremony had a dual character: religious and lay. That of young Bolesław the Wrymouth was staged on the Feast of the Dormition and celebrated with a splendid banquet. The chronicler seems to suggest that all young warriors of the *druzhina* would be eventually knighted but the moment would be chosen solely by the duke. We do not know to what extent the customs relating to the knighting ceremony resembled those practised by knights in western Europe. Armaments and accoutrements correspond to contemporaneous European

[25] Karol Modzelewski, 'L'organizzazione delle Stato polacco nei secoli X–XIII. la società e le strutture del potere', in *Gli slavi occidentali e meridionali nell'alto medioevo*, Settimane del Centro italiano di studi sull'alto medioevo, 30 (Spoleto, 1983), vol. II, 557–96.

[26] Modzelewski, 'Comites, principes, nobiles'.

standards but there is no evidence of the participation of Polish knights in the emerging chivalrous culture. Their very modest involvement in crusading and rare endowments of monastic foundations prior to the thirteenth century also suggest the absence of interest in cultural models popular in the west.

No sooner than the beginning of the thirteenth century can one trace in the sources elements of institutions such as beneficia tied to an oath of *fidelity*. The chronicle written by Anonymous testified to the high ranking of *fides* as a knight's moral virtue. But this was not linked to local rituals of taking a beneficium from the hands of a ducal senior, or an oath of fidelity. In eleventh-century Poland, a specific chivalrous ethic evolved, which focused on loyalty to the ruler. In the second half of the eleventh century and in the twelfth at the latest, new ideas began to emerge and inform the knightly ethos: loyalty towards Poland as the *patria* and giving the *patria*'s interests priority above one's individual concerns; respect for and support of the Church; and integrating lay customs with those propagated by the clergy. Yet the political and social organization of the Polish elite's life was far from reflecting classical models of feudal society.[27]

From the second half of the twelfth century, special conditions on which landholdings were granted constituted the specific *ius militare* and comprised: hereditary ownership rights over land; landholdings free of taxes and dues payable to the ruler; reduction of tithes (privileges regarding the manner of their calculation). Simultaneously, warriors recruited from peasants and castle warriors were reduced to doing agricultural work on the estates of lay lords.

The social position of the rural population was diverse in the late tenth century. Free villagers constituted the largest group. They lived in small settlements comprising usually five to seven and occasionally up to several dozen farms. To each farm belonged a number of small fields dispersed within a diameter of several kilometres which together made up the family's landholdings, referred to as *sors* in Latin or *źreb* in

[27] Sławomir Gawlas, 'Die Probleme des Lehnswesens und Feudalismus aus polnischer Sicht', in *Das europäische Mittelalter im Spannungsfeld des Vergleichs. Zwanzig internationale Beiträge zu Praxis, Problemen und Perspektiven der historischen Komparatistik*, ed. Michael Borgolte and Ralf Lusiardi (Berlin, 2001), 97–123; Lech Leciejewicz, 'Die sozialen Eliten im frühpiastischen Polen', in *Die frühmittelalterliche Elite bei den Völkern des östlichen Mitteleuropas (mit einem speziellen Blick auf die großmährische Problematik); Materialien der internationalen Fachkonferenz, Mikulcice, 25.–26.5.2004*, ed. Pavel Kouril (Brno, 2005), 353–8.

Polish. The origin of the Latin term, which apparently refers to the drawing of the lots as a way to distribute the allocated land, is not clear. We do not know at which stage and how often, if it was repeatable, such a procedure took place. Pastures were communal. Groupings of several (up to a dozen or so) villages made up neighbourhood communities referred to as *vicinia* in Latin and *opola* in Polish.

The *vicinia* performed auxiliary administrative functions but we know nothing about their juridical powers. Formally, only the duke and his representatives could discharge judicial functions. However, in the tenth and eleventh centuries they would not be available in a particular *vicinium* or village to perform them on any regular basis. In this situation, it seems plausible that, despite the formal monopoly of the ducal judiciary, local common law harking back to the tribal past continued to be applied to regulate the villagers' life. A major change would only follow the establishment in the twelfth century of a regular, albeit not very dense, network of castellanies and corresponding court districts which did not eliminate the *vicinia* altogether but likely limited their functions. The demise of the *vicinia* system would come only in the second half of the thirteenth and in the fourteenth centuries, with the foundation of villages chartered according to Teutonic law. The new patterns of rural life, the emergence of towns following the west European model and a new system of territorial administration of justice would turn the *vicinia* into a relic deprived of real relevance.[28]

Evidence of the diversified status of free villagers dates to as early as the eleventh and the first half of the twelfth century. The so-called *heredes* (freeholders of village land) formed the elite. Other than dues payable to the ruler, they did not owe anything to any other lord. Part of the population of the ducal villages were slaves (*servi*). Some of the latter, and also some of the former, category would become serfs bound to the land (*ascriptici*). They retained their freeman status but could not leave their place of residence for good without the permission of their lord – the duke, the Church or (rarely) a lay lord – and additional dues could be levied upon them.

The majority of villages were controlled by the ruler through his representatives residing in strongholds and later castellanies. From the second half of the eleventh century, some would be donated by the

[28] Karol Modzelewski, 'L'organisation de l'opole (vicinia) dans la Pologne des Piasts', *Acta Poloniae Historica* 57 (1988), 43–76.

ruler to the Church or lay lords. Some historians argue that already by the late tenth and in the eleventh century, but according to others not earlier than in thirteenth century, new types of economic and settlement centres appeared in the rural landscape: ducal manorial estates (*curia*) and service villages located in the vicinity of strongholds. Ducal manorial estates were cultivated partly by unfree peasants organized in 'tenths' (*decimi*) and partly by free ploughmen. But the system of ducal landholding in the form of centralized manorial estates became prevalent, or more popular, only in the twelfth and thirteenth centuries.

At first most of the peasants were called *rustici ducis*, freemen with hereditary obligations to the duke. The nature of this obligation is unclear. Most historians assumed that dues and labour owed by peasants to a ruler were determined by special 'ducal law' (*ius ducalis*), which originated from the traditional duties of the subjects. During this period a new category is attested in the population: the *rataje* (*aratores*). They worked mostly on ducal farms, and were freemen who held no land and thus served as hired hands or settled there as leaseholders of small farms. Few ducal villages were inhabited exclusively by the unfree, and they were usually founded to settle an ethnically different group of prisoners of war. More often, the unfree would be settled individually or in small groups among the freemen on the ducal estates as specialists (craftsmen, hunters or gatherers of forest products). Service villages had a different character. They were inhabited by free peasants obliged to provide specified services or dues in kind (craft goods, crops or agricultural products) to sustain the local stronghold, its personnel and residents.[29]

During the second half of the twelfth century, parallel with the growing number of ducal donations of land to the elite warriors and nobles, the social status of peasants changed. Landowners strove for control over the free villagers and so tried to remove all the freedoms they could, leaving only the freedom to move out of the village, and also strove to replace ducal jurisdiction over the village's inhabitants with their own. As a result of this process, the category of free peasants

[29] Karol Modzelewski, 'La division autarchique du travail à l'échelle d'un État: l'organisation "ministériale" en Pologne médiévale', *Annales ESC* 19 (1964), 1125–38; Modzelewski, 'The system of the ius ducale and the idea of feudalism (comments on the earliest class society in medieval Poland)', *Questiones Medii Aevi* 1 (1977), 71–99; Modzelewski, 'Le système des villages de "ministeriales" dans l'organisation économique de l'État polonais aux Xe–XIIIe siècles', *Fasciculi Historici* 9 (1977), 21–8; Modzelewski, 'Ius ducale et féodalisme'.

(*heredes*, formerly *rustici ducis*) in the thirteenth century slowly disappears from the sources, replaced by peasants bound to the land (*ascriptici*). Simultaneously, in the thirteenth century, the unfree population likewise disappeared, with some joining the *ascriptici* and others becoming serfs (*ministeriales* or *aratores*). *Ascriptici* inherited both the land they cultivated and the obligation to pay dues for its suzerain. But they could not leave the village voluntarily, losing the 'right to depart' (*ius recedendi*), nor sell or change the land they possessed. Some of them were described as unfree men, former ducal slaves, deliberately separated from the *ministeriales* of an owner. For example, the duke gave to the bishopric of Płock at the beginning of the thirteenth century 'ascriptici decimi episcopales' next to 'ministeriales, sicut coci, lagenarii, pistores, aucupes, conarii siue cuiuscumque oficii'.[30]

Over the course of the twelfth century, in the villages organized according to local law, the diversity of the peasants' personal legal status did not vanish, although their direct dependence on the duke and his officials started to be replaced by bonds to a specific landowner. The latter tended towards strengthening – in comparison with ducal administration – control over peasants on his land. Free and unfree men were both treated as part of the owners' property. That created new forms of dependence and new social groups. Some historians argue that not only these new groups of peasants, but also the entire system of Piast *ius ducale* and service villages, relatively homogeneous for the whole realm, were created not earlier than the twelfth century. In addition, these historians suggest that this system was not rooted in local traditions, which were diverse and unknown to us. It was shaped under the influence of west European reforms of estates management, which in the Empire led to the emergence of the so-called *Grundherrschaft*.[31]

[30] *Villae capituli Plocensis*, ed. Wojciech Kętrzyński, MPH 5 (Lwów, 1888), 433–8.

[31] Stanisław Trawkowski, 'Heredes im frühpiastischen Polen', in *Europa Slavica – Europa Orientalis. Festschrift für Herbert Ludat zum 70. Geburtstag*, eds. Klaus-Detlev Grothusen and Klaus Zernack (Berlin, 1980), 262–85; Karol Modzelewski, 'Servi, heredes, ascripticii: la conditio paysanne aux yeux du groupe dirigeant en Pologne médievale', *Questiones Medii Aevi* 4 (1990), 45–69; Sławomir Gawlas, *O kształt zjednoczonego królestwa: niemieckie władztwo terytorialne a geneza społecznoustrojowej odrebności Polski* (Warsaw, 1996); Gawlas, 'Fürstenherrschaft, Geldwirtschaft und Landesausbau'.

The foundation of villages chartered according to Teutonic law would result in a major change in the rural social structure from the late twelfth century. These foundations were preceded in the second half of the twelfth century by the appearance of the communities of the *hospites*. These newly arrived settlers were exempted from most services to the duke or local lord. In exchange, they were obliged to settle in a certain area and turn the local forest or wasteland (marshes, for example) into farmland. Their legal status would be regulated by a contract concluded with the landholder. Such individual contracts were quite inconvenient to the landowner forced to negotiate conditions with the particular community, and thus acknowledge its autonomous legal status as a carrier of rights. This in turn weakened the lord's position as the giver of law. As a result, this model would soon be abandoned in favour of giving charters to new villages, or modifying the status of existing ones in accordance with legal models imported from the West, with the ruler acting as the sole giver of law. This new model of organization would become widespread only in the thirteenth and fourteenth centuries.[32]

## *Hungary*

Social transformations radically changed the nature of society between the beginning and the end of the period covered in this book. Early on, there was little differentiation beyond the elite, freemen and the unfree. By the end of the thirteenth century, however, complex legal statuses had developed, with the king at the top; the high nobility who participated in political power; a lower nobility, who had started to acquire local power through the institution of county assemblies; a hierarchically differentiated stratum of other freemen, from those who were fairly high-ranking locally to poor peasants; and slaves.[33] Social change did not simply mean stratification. Linked to

[32] Stanisław Trawkowski, 'Die Rolle der deutschen Dorfkolonisation und des deutschen Rechtes in Polen im 13. Jahrhundert', in *Die deutsche Ostsiedlung des Mittelalters als Problem der Europäischen Geschichte*, ed. Walter Schlesinger (Sigmaringen, 1975), 349–68.

[33] Antal Bartha, *Hungarian Society*; László Solymosi, 'Liberty and servitude in the Age of Saint Stephen', in *Saint Stephen and His Country*, 69–79; Ilona Bolla, *A jogilag egységes jobbágyosztály kialakulása Magyarországon* (Budapest, 1983, repr. 2005); Erik Fügedi, *The Elefánthy: The Hungarian Nobleman and His Kindred* (Budapest, 1998), ch. 1.

Christianization, fundamental aspects of life, such as marriage, also changed. Traditional methods of acquiring wives, such as abduction and rape, were to be punished. The early twelfth-century synod of Esztergom required that marriages take place in the presence of a priest before witnesses and with the consent of both partners. While some of the early laws accepted the right of a husband to kill an adulterous wife and remarry, eventually penance was prescribed for the woman and the spouses had to choose between either reconciliation or spending the rest of their lives unmarried: the traditional rights of the husband were replaced by ecclesiastical norms.[34]

The original social structure of the conquest-period Hungarians was radically transformed in the first centuries of settlement, Christianization and the extension of the ruler's authority. Independent local leaders lost their power in line with the reorganization of power structures; new social categories also appeared. Only two distinct categories, freemen and slaves, are mentioned in the early laws in the first half of the eleventh century; the laws reinforce this fundamental distinction through divergent penalties. István's laws punish the murder of a freeman by the payment of 110 gold *pensae*, while killing someone's slave only entailed payment of the slave's price. For theft, while a freeman could pay compensation, or was sold as a slave, slaves were punished by mutilation and, ultimately, death: after a first offence the nose was cut off; for the second, the ears, unless the slave was able to pay compensation (five oxen in each case). For a third offence, the death sentence could not be commuted. By the later eleventh century, however, for theft over a certain value (the equivalent of 10 deniers for freemen, 6 for slaves), freemen lost their lives, slaves their eyes.[35]

Although the distinction between freemen and slaves persisted, over the course of the eleventh and twelfth centuries, many other social categories and a more complex social hierarchy emerged. From the middle of the eleventh century (when the so-called third lawbook of László I was probably compiled), and during the reign of László I, extensive and strict legislation aimed at the eradication of theft: 60 per cent of the laws concern punishment for theft of animals, goods and servants. This has been linked by modern scholars to social transformations, either to the impoverishment of middling freemen as the clan structures fell apart, or to resistance to the establishment of

[34] N. Berend *et al.*, 'The kingdom of Hungary', 333–4.

[35] Bak *et al.*, eds., *Laws*, 4, 9–10, 20.

private property. Given that strict punishments were also meted out to members of the lower class for theft in Victorian England, for example, such legislation is perhaps better understood as intended to create and uphold distinctions and boundaries between status groups.[36]

The elite consisted of the most powerful families in the entourage of the king (members of the royal council); scholars argue that this elite developed from the heads of clans who were powerful at the time of the conquest, and eventually immigrant west European knights. Noble lineages (kindreds), however, are only firmly traceable through the written sources in exceptional cases from the eleventh and, in most cases, from later centuries. This aristocracy was designated in the sources by different terms: *maiores* (from the earliest sources to the 1160s); *optimates* (1070s–1160s); *proceres* (1090s–1140s); during the reign of István III (1162–72) *magnates*, which was then rarely used until the late Middle Ages; and, from the thirteenth century, *barones*. Another group had emerged by the beginning of the thirteenth century, the *servientes regis*, who by the end of the century formed part of the nobility ('lesser nobility'; see Chapter 7). The term *nobilis* appeared in the eleventh century to distinguish those freemen who possessed their own lands and gave only military service from the less well-to-do freemen living on the land of others, providing various services. From the thirteenth century it became the designation of the *servientes regis*. Warrior status (*miles*) in the eleventh century did not entail a uniform social or economic status, and included immigrant western knights as well as local commoners. By the twelfth century some freemen could no longer assume this role and instead were obliged to pay taxes.[37]

Dependent populations were organized in somewhat divergent ways on royal, ecclesiastical and lay noble estates, although unfree populations provided services on all. The royal estate (*curia, curtis*) organization was based on the unfree *udvarnok*s (from Slavic 'court', *dvor*), who provided produce and labour services for the royal court.

[36] *Ibid.*, 12–23.

[37] Attila Zsoldos, *A szent király szabadjai* (Budapest, 1999); Fügedi, *Ispánok, bárók, kiskirályok*; Fügedi, 'The aristocracy in medieval Hungary (theses)', in Fügedi, *Kings, Bishops*, 1–14; Fügedi, 'Some characteristics of the medieval Hungarian noble family', *Journal of Family History* 7 (1982), 27–39; Zsolt Hunyadi, 'Maiores, optimates, nobiles: semantic questions in the early history of the Hungarian nobility', *Annual of Medieval Studies at the CEU* (1996/1997), 204–11; Martyn Rady, *Nobility, Land and Service in Medieval Hungary* (Basingstoke, 2000).

The population of the castle districts was organized into castle servants and castle warriors. Castle servants (*civiles*, *cives*, *castrenses*) provided agricultural products and craft goods for the royal court. Some also had other duties, serving for example as prison guards, and most provided occasional military service. Castle warriors under the *ispán* were soldiers on a permanent basis, ensured defence, and went on military campaigns with the king outside the realm. They also had juridical and administrative tasks. In return, they received a share of the taxes of the castle servants, and use (but not ownership) of castle lands. The status of castle warrior (*iobagio castri*) entailed privileges, but only within the framework of the castle organization, as dependants of the king; they were not freemen. This group, however, was not unified; it included people who joined the castle organization with their own lands which they retained in their possession. By the thirteenth century, the highest echelon (*liberi* or *iobagiones S. Regis*) claimed their status originated from service to St István. With the fragmentation of royal castle lands, over the course of the thirteenth and fourteenth centuries most castle warriors became the dependent peasants of noble beneficiaries of land donations. The elite, however, became part of the nobility, either spontaneously or through royal donation of noble status. In the thirteenth century a more unified peasantry also developed (entailing the change of meaning of *iobagio*), as discussed in Chapter 7.[38]

Dependent populations included slaves, working at the will and on the lands of their lord. Slaves could be freed and gain *libertinus* status, but the meaning of this changed over time. Initially, *libertini* gained full freedom, yet by the late eleventh century there is evidence of conditional freedom: slaves freed in order to serve the Church. In the twelfth century, the term designated the unfree who were given lands to cultivate by their lords but, unless they paid for their freedom, they remained the property of their lord and could be sold. Slaves could gain full freedom through manumission, which could be granted for

[38] Beatrix F. Romhányi, 'Kolostori gazdálkodás a középkori Magyarországon', in András Kubinyi, József Laszlovszky and Péter Szabó, eds., *Gazdaság és gazdálkodás a középkori Magyarországon: gazdaságtörténet, anyagi kultúra, régészet* (Budapest, 2008), 401–12, with a detailed bibliography; Zsoldos, *A szent király szabadjai*; Székely and Bartha, eds., *Magyarország története*, II, 966–1001; István Tringli, 'The liberty of the holy kings: Saint Stephen and the holy kings in the Hungarian legal heritage', in *Saint Stephen*, ed. Zsoldos, 127–82.

the benefit of the soul of a testator or could be bought. Slavery was inherited, but could also be imposed on freemen for various offences, for example, for repeated theft. Marriage to a slave also resulted in loss of free status. Slavery remained significant throughout these two centuries. On royal and ecclesiastical estates, and increasingly on the estates of lay lords, there were also groups who were given land and a house for service, who cultivated their lands and provided different types of agricultural work. Whether they were slaves or not has been debated.[39]

Charters refer to various categories of subject populations on estates: for example, vinter, tiller, swine-herd, hunter, stone cutter, furrier, baker, bell-ringer, cook, butcher, miller, carpenter, potter and smith. There were also people designated as serving with a horse. According to some scholars, they may have been the descendants of pastoralists who lost their freedom and their access to communal lands as a result of social reorganization. Although the sources specifically designate some of the subject population as agricultural producers (e.g. *arator*), they were not the only ones to do agricultural work. Members of other categories, such as bee-keepers or fishermen, also gave bread or flour as tax in kind to their lords from their own produce; the same was true of giving animals in tax by those not specifically labelled as participating in animal husbandry. According to one view, subject artisans in the same occupation were resettled by their lords as much as possible into one settlement, working on the tools provided by the lord, in the lord's workshop (for the twelfth century, data come only from ecclesiastical estates; for the thirteenth century, also from royal ones).

Strongholds were not just the centres of royal power, but also the bases for organizing the sustenance of the ruler and his entourage. Around them, toponyms have been interpreted as names of service settlements, which provided for the royal court. Periodically renewed debate surrounds the existence of these communities. In all three countries one finds toponyms in charters that designate an

[39] Cameron Sutt, 'Slavery in Árpád-era Hungary in a comparative context', unpublished Ph.D dissertation, University of Cambridge, 2008; János M. Bak, 'Servitude in the medieval kingdom of Hungary (a sketchy outline)', in *Forms of Servitude in Northern and Central Europe: Decline, Resistance, Expansion*, ed. Paul Freedman and Monique Bourin (Turnhout, 2005), 387–400; synod of Szabolcs (Ladislas I, bk I) c. 30, and Stephen, bk II, c. 7; bk I, c. 31; bk I, c. 29, both in Bak *et al.*, eds., *Laws*, 7, 10, 59.

occupation, from various aspects of agricultural work to a range of crafts, for example, smith, carpenter, cook or fisherman. Scholars have interpreted these as designating communities that communally owed the royal court the service reflected in the name of the village. Some scholars maintain that these villages consisted solely of craftsmen designated by the name of the village, while others suggest that the inhabitants must have had a more diverse range of occupations than signalled by the name of the settlement; the latter simply indicated the specific service the inhabitants had to provide the court. Based on whether the toponyms derive from Slavic on the one hand or Finno-Ugric and Turkic on the other, scholars have argued for the ethnic origin of the population inhabiting such settlements, a risky undertaking since there is no proof that the inhabitants themselves gave the settlements their name. Hypotheses of ninth-century Moravian and Carolingian and tenth-century Hungarian origins for such settlements have been refuted. The assumption that rulers could create such settlements at will and that the inhabitants were moved there and were of unfree status cannot be substantiated. Comparison between the three cases also shows divergence: in Bohemia and Poland such names appear later (in the thirteenth century) and reflect a more variegated range of services; such a system may have been instituted there later.[40]

## THE RULER'S REVENUES

The best-documented aspect of the early medieval economy relates to generating revenues for the ruler, although many of its elements and its extent have been debated. According to the Třeštík–Krzemieńska model, the area supervised by the stronghold's commander generated dues, which were subsequently consumed on site by the ruler's

[40] Gusztáv Heckenast, *Fejedelmi (királyi) szolgálónépek a korai Árpád-korban*, Értekezések a történeti tudományok köréből 53 (Budapest, 1970); György Györffy, 'Az Árpád-kori szolgálónépek kérdéséhez', *Történelmi szemle* 15 (1972), 261–342; Font, *Im Spannungsfeld der chridtlichen Großmächte*, 240–9; Florin Curta, 'The archaeology of early medieval service settlements in Eastern Europe', in Górecki and Van Deusen, eds., *Central and Eastern Europe*, 30–41; Christian Lübke, *Arbeit und Wirtschaft im östlichen Mitteleuropa. Die Spezialisierung menschlicher Tätigkeit im Spiegel der hochmittelalterlichen Toponymie in den Herrschaftsgebieten von Piasten, Premysliden und Arpaden* (Stuttgart, 1991).

representatives or his itinerant court or sent to the treasury. Dues were paid in kind, in produce or in labour services, by subject populations living in settlements located in the vicinity of the stronghold. They were obliged to provide specified produce or render precisely defined services to the officials of the stronghold or to the ruler. These service villages ensured the state administration a fixed level of income in exchange for protection guaranteed by the warriors manning the stronghold. Over time, residents of service villages and other villages would become the peasantry, while warriors residing in strongholds and members of the ruler's bodyguard would evolve into the knightly estate. As the centres of administration, exchange and handicrafts, strongholds would become proto-towns, and their dwellers, along with those of chartered towns, would over time form the estate of burghers. More recent studies question many aspects of that model.

## *Bohemia*

The basic form of taxation levied upon all freemen was the so-called *tributum pacis*, paid to the duke. But that was only a part of the ruler's income. The character of these revenues is now an open question, strongly disputed among Czech historians. Traditionally it was postulated that the duke was the owner of all cultivated land in Bohemia and Moravia, receiving income from all immovable properties in the state. He gave some of income to magnates and warriors, dignitaries, allies and those of lesser social status who provided aid. In exchange, he was entitled to profit from their work of various characters. Dues were paid by providing products of craft (goldsmithing, blacksmithing and so on), but also by common, general service (such as fortress maintenance or building repairs).

A younger generation of Czech medievalists argues that the ruler's share of the land was much smaller. At least from the beginning of the twelfth century private estates were common in Bohemia. It was not just powerful families with fortified strongholds who held land, but even warriors lower down the social hierarchy had landed properties of one or two villages. At the same time, dukes not only gave estates to ecclesiastical institutions and lay supporters, but also bought land from private landholders. This system of mixed landed property was stable before the thirteenth century and may have already existed in the eleventh century. Accepting the latter view entails revising the estimate of the ruler's income, which must have been much smaller than hitherto suggested. Yet its extent remains pure guesswork.[41]

Regardless of whether a historian agrees with a more traditional or more modern approach to the question of landed property, the major outline of the rulers' estate administration is presented in the same way. The *curia ducis* was mentioned as the local centre of economic administration. Different types of such centres existed according to the economic features of the places where they were situated. So-called hunting manors, used by dukes as residences during hunts, which existed in the middle of forests (for example, Starý Knín, Kamýk, Chvojno), were less important. It seems probable that these manors operated as centres of the entire forest economy (hunting, fur, tar, potash and wood trade etc.). Of more importance were manors designed for agricultural management and the collection of dues from peasant tenants. They were situated on farmland, near major rivers (Týnec at the Elbe river, Radonice and Budyně at the Ohra River). Historians suggested that manors situated near administrative centres were treated as centres of craft production for dukes and their court. It is certain that in some manors specialized units of slaves – male and female (*gynecea*) – produced goods needed by their owners (dukes, then bishops, cloisters etc.). Some of these manors evolved into major economic centres of regional importance, being places of dues collecting, cattle-breeding and craft production. But even for these, the scale and range of production are unclear and are sometimes a matter of guesswork rather than estimates. Traditionally it is believed that the major part of the revenues was transferred to local administrative centres (strongholds, *hrady*). Here it was divided between the duke and local officials as their salary. It is believed that this early

[41] Josef Žemlička and Dušan Třeštík, 'O modelach vývoje přemysloského státu', *Český Časopis Historický* 105, 1 (2007), 122–64; Libor Jan, 'Skryty půvab "středoevropského modelu"', *Český Časopis Historický* 105, 4 (2007), 873–902; Jiři Macháček, 'Středoevropský model a jeho archeologické testování', *Český Časopis Historický* 106, 3 (2008), 598–625; for a response, see Josef Žemlička, 'O "svobodné soukromosti" pozemkového vlastnictví (k rozsahu a kvalitě velmožské držby w přemyslovských Čechach', *Český Časopis Historický* 107, 1 (2009), 269–306; Libor Jan, 'Nekolik postrehu k vývoji panovnické komory, soudu a správy zeme', in *Pocta Janu Janákovi: predsedovi Matice moravské, profesoru Masarykovy univerzity venují k sedmdesátinám jeho prátelé a záci*, ed. Bronislav Chocholác (Brno, 2002), 75–83.

system of rulers' revenues was characteristic of a type of autarchic economy.[42]

But money and luxury objects were needed by dukes even if the autarchy hypothesis is correct. This was necessary both for rulers' status symbols within Bohemia and for political relations with the Empire. Rulers acquired money from market taxes (*theloneum forense, theloneum fori*), perhaps instead of receiving dues. Also penalties were paid in currency by perpetrators sentenced by a duke and his officials, forming a third general source of a ducal income. The penalty was determined in money but – as in Poland – we cannot be sure if it was always paid in money or in its equivalent in goods. Ducal monopolies were also an important source of revenues. For example, only a ruler could take profits from mining. But up to the second half of the thirteenth century, the latter was of small importance for Czech rulers.

The fourth type of income was sometimes very important, sometimes only symbolic, but almost impossible to quantify: spoils of war. Even when we know that booty was substantial and valuable, we cannot estimate its value. For example, Duke Břetislav I brought enormous spoils from his raid into Poland in 1038. Cosmas in his chronicle wrote that apart from the relics of St Vojtěch-Adalbert he led into Prague numerous carriages full of golden and silver liturgical objects lined with precious stones taken from Piast churches. The value of the booty was significant enough to prompt the emperor to ask for his share of it, as Bohemia's suzerain. The duke, after an armed conflict, paid the lion's share to the emperor, yet he still had enough resources to build and endow a new, monumental church. But one has to remember that the war of 1038 was exceptional for the Czech rulers in the eleventh and twelfth centuries. Other conflicts brought them some income but it was never so splendid.[43]

[42] Barbara Krzemieńska and Dušan Třeštík, 'Zur Problematik der Dienstleute im frühmittelalterlichen Böhmen', in *Siedlung und Verfassung Böhmens in der Frühzeit*, eds. František Graus and Hermann Ludat (Wiesbaden, 1967), 70–98; Krzemieńska and Třeštík, 'Hospodářské základy raně středověkého státu ve střední Evropě' Jindřich Tomas, 'Řemeslníci 11.–13. století v českých zemích v písemných pramenach', *Acta Historica* 8 (1983), 73–84.

[43] Cosmas II. 5, p. 90.

## Poland

The central administration's revenue sources were diversified, but the picture remains somewhat obscure. The extra revenue gained as booty during military campaigns was essential for maintaining the ruler's prestige: precious ornaments, gold and silver coins and bullion, which the ruler would subsequently distribute among the members of the elite. The chronicler Gallus Anonymous depicted Bolesław II the Bold ostentatiously showing off his riches following the victorious raid on Kiev. The king sat on the throne and publicly presented the spoils. One poor churchman was so impressed with the display that the bemused king allegedly let him take as much gold as he was able to carry.[44] The anecdote does not necessarily correspond to the reality of the second half of the eleventh century, but certainly reflects the expectations of the Polish elite concerning the ruler's behaviour in the first half of the twelfth. The ruler was expected to be rich and to share his riches with the members of his retinue. The same chronicle describes the legendary splendour of the court of Bolesław I the Brave: gold jewellery, costly gowns and general resplendence are symbolic attributes of the imagined Piast 'golden age'. Yet, notably, even in this imaginary world only members of the ruler's inner circle partook of the riches, and this picture accurately reflects the reality of the early twelfth century.[45]

It is certain, however, that from the beginning, commoners bore the lion's share of the burden of providing for the ruler and his court. Some historians suggested that the whole system of dues was inherited from tribal times and emerged as a coherent structure parallel with the beginnings of the realm. Others rejected such a supposition and emphasized that it is impossible to find traces of a complete 'system' of royal revenues during the period from the tenth to the twelfth centuries; instead, more or less pragmatic and evolving practices existed. These practices changed only during the thirteenth century, a period of modernization; they were moulded into a system-like shape modelled on the Empire's *Landesherrschaft*. No precise records exist, and we only know the names of dues paid in the twelfth century

[44] *Galli Anonymi Cronicae* I.26, pp. 50–2.

[45] *Galli Anonymi Cronicae* I.6, p. 19; Gerd Althoff, 'Symbolische Kommunikation zwischen Piasten und Ottonen', in *Polen und Deutschland vor 1000 Jahren. Die Berliner Tagung über den 'Akt von Gnesen'*, ed. Michael Borgolte (Berlin, 2002), 303–7.

in various localities and territories to benefit the central administration. It remains unclear, however, whether the similarity of names also implied the equivalence of the designated dues. At the latest in the twelfth century the customary names of two basic types of dues paid to the duke were established: the *poradlne* on crops (or – more likely – the cultivated farmlands) and the *narzaz*, on livestock. In addition to these dues in kind, rural residents also rendered services to the ruler, for example, the *stan*, the obligation to host the duke and his itinerant court during their journey through the relevant *vicinia* (*opole*); the *przewóz*, providing the ruler or his representatives with carts to drive through the district; the *stróża*, upkeep of the local stronghold's fortifications; and many others.[46]

Other revenues were drawn from the judiciary and from various forms of economic activity exclusively reserved for the royal treasury (*regale*). The ruler (through his representatives) was entitled to receive a certain portion of the fines adjudged in cases reserved for ducal jurisdiction. But it is difficult to say how often and what kind of cases involving the life of rural communities were referred to the decision of ducal judges in the eleventh century. In this context, one must note the violent and effective popular resistance against Duke Mieszko the Old's efforts to impose ducal jurisdiction and monopolies in the late twelfth century.

Among the Piasts' *regale*, the exclusive right to mint coins – or more precisely the right to replace circulating coins with new ones – became an important source of revenue in the twelfth century. The duke's monopoly on minting money was combined with the subjects' obligation to pay dues and fines in coins which the ruler regarded as current. Twice a year, he would change the coinage and introduce a new coin with a smaller bullion content, but the obligatory exchange rate was 1:1. This affected both the elite and commoners and occasionally inspired active protest against rulers who used this source of supplementary revenue too aggressively.[47] Nonetheless, up to the end of the period in question rulers' coins were used to demonstrate the

[46] For the traditional picture, see Henryk Łowmiański, 'The problem of the origins of the Polish state in recent historical research', *Questiones Medii Aevi* 1 (1977), 33–70 (esp. 57–8); Modzelewski, 'The system of the ius ducale'. For a more recent approach, see Gawlas, 'Fürstenherrschaft, Geldwirtschaft und Landesausbau'.

[47] Stanisław Suchodolski, 'Hatte die Münzprägung im Mittelalter einen Einfluß auf die politischen Ereignisse in Polen gehabt?', *Numismatische Zeitschrift* 103 (1995), 57–66.

ruler's right to control the economic conditions of life and the symbolic language of power.[48]

Hunting was also among rulers' monopolies. Historians traditionally believed that the ruler possessed the sole right to hunt either specific species of animals (bears, dears, boars and beavers) or in a specific manner (with falcons, dogs etc.). But recent research suggested that Piast rulers had the right, like their western counterparts, to hunt anywhere within the whole realm, and also had the exclusive right to hunt on special, restricted grounds manned and supervised by dedicated groups of servants. These grounds were called *gaje* ('groves'), *knieje* ('wilderness, forests') and *łowiska* ('hunting grounds'). Peasants who oversaw them and helped rulers during the hunt were settled in separate villages near these forests, named after their specialization: Bobrowniki (village of beaver-keepers), Psary (dog-keepers' village), Sokolniki (falconers' village), Strzelce (huntsmen's or shooters' village). Hunting restrictions were treated partly as another sign of the rulers' status, but were also used to gain support. Therefore a ruler might give his allies a right to hunt on his grounds, or sell a whole property together with the right to hunt. The ruler's hunting privilege, however, did not deprive other men of the right to hunt on their own, even if not on the ruler's special grounds.

In the late twelfth century, the rulers' efforts to enforce the hunting *regale* met with resistance from people living near rulers' forests. In duchies smaller than the ones created in 1138, rulers had to guard their privileges more closely in order to generate sufficient income and to secure for themselves political support by donating privileges to magnates and knights. Therefore by the end of the period, together with the efforts to tighten the fiscal system, the rulers also strove (we do not know how effectively) for more control over their subjects' hunting activities. They hunted on grounds supposedly reserved for the ruler, which stimulated the fur and skin trade and also supplied the craftsmen residing in strongholds, service villages and other villages. The very fact that rulers undertook to limit hunts organized without their permission may testify to such practices being commonplace. The resistance against such limitations and consequently the fines

48 Borys Paszkiewicz, 'ALENA DVCTRIX – brakteat księżnej Heleny', *Wiadomości Numizmatyczne* 44, 1 (2000), 55–62; Borys Paszkiewicz, 'Beginning of the Polish provincial coinage: some remarks', *Peníze v promenách casu. 4 / Money in Metamorphosis of Time / Geld im Wandel der Zeit* (Ostrava, 2007), 21–40.

imposed for breaking the ban suggest that hunting played a significant role in the economic activity of villagers.[49]

Similarly to rulers elsewhere in Europe, the Piasts also had a monopoly on mining, but used it to a limited degree. Only by the end of the twelfth century did the first larger mining settlement appear (Złotoryja/Goldberg in Silesia), its residents washing out natural gold deposits rather than digging underground mines. More important for both fiscal and economic reasons, although on a modest scale even during the thirteenth century, was lead-mining in Silesia and Lesser Poland. The quantity of ore-mining increased significantly only in the fourteenth and fifteenth centuries. The beginnings of salt-mining in Poland remain obscure. Tradition links them to the duke of Cracow, Bolesław V the Bashful (1243–79), and his wife Kinga which implies that, like gold-mining, the development of this branch of the economy started in the thirteenth century.[50]

The mining *regale* often included the ruler's exclusive right to sell goods produced in connection with their monopoly; this concerned salt in the first instance. With salt being an essential commodity, the control of its trade could bring hefty profits for the royal treasury. The connection between the relevant monopoly and the levying of customs duties and tolls seems less obvious. Hypothetically, it was connected to the land *regale*, that is, the ruler's exclusive ownership rights to all land which was not held by private owners. But it appears more likely that, at least in the beginning, customs duties and tolls were paid by travellers because ducal protection extended over them in the course of their journey. Customs houses were mentioned for the first time in the first half of the twelfth century and located in several bigger ducal strongholds: Gdańsk, Gniezno, Kalisz, Łęczyca, Małogoszcz, Sieradz and Wyszogród. More detailed information and data on customs duties come only from thirteenth-century charters. The growing number of customs houses after 1138 was

[49] Agnieszka Samsonowicz, 'The right to hunt in medieval Poland', *Fasciculi Archeologiae Historicae* 21 (2008), 65–70; Samsonowicz, *Łowiectwo w państwie Piastów i Jagiellonów* (Wrocław, 1990).

[50] Jerzy Wyrozumski, *Państwowa gospodarka solna w Polsce do schyłku XIV wieku* (Cracow, 1968); Danuta Molenda, 'Der polnische Bleibergbau und seine Bedeutung für den europäischen Bleimarkt vom 12. bis 17. Jahrhundert', in *Montanwirtschaft Mitteleuropas vom 12. bis 17. Jahrhundert. Forschungsprobleme: Stand, Wege und Aufgabe der Forschung*, ed. Werner Kroker and Ekkehard Westermann (Bochum, 1984), 187–98.

connected to Poland's partition (1138–*c.* 1300) into a dozen or so duchies. It is believed that the locations of customs houses were determined both by new political aims and by the economic needs of dukes, and thus that they do not necessarily correspond to the sites of collection of customs duties and tolls during the preceding period.[51]

## *Hungary*

Royal revenues came from three main sources: the king's own estates, taxes and royal monopolies (such as tolls, salt-mining, minting).

Historians maintain that the king was the greatest landholder in the realm until the thirteenth century. Although he donated lands both to ecclesiastical institutions and to the laity for faithful service or in order to secure fidelity, he also had the right to all empty lands, which until the thirteenth century were considerable. Additionally, the lands of families without heirs reverted to the possession of the king. In the eleventh and twelfth centuries, an estimated 10% of the realm consisted of ecclesiastical estates along with about 15% of lay estates, signalling the preponderance of royal lands. This, however, was more notional than real, since the remaining 75% included all uninhabited areas, which brought in no revenues. Substantial change, which eventually shifted the balance of power to the nobility, started during Béla III's reign. He donated Modrus county to *comes* Bertalan in 1193, the first royal donation of a whole county. The county no longer owed revenues to the king, nor did royal officials do business there. In return, Bertalan was to send armoured warriors to the royal army.[52]

Throughout the period, a significant but incalculable part of royal revenues came from the taxes in kind and labour services of the population of royal estates and strongholds. The foodstuffs and animals provided as revenues in kind were consumed by the itinerant royal court during its yearly stay on each estate. In the eleventh and twelfth centuries royal revenues predominantly came from the land. Direct taxation is supposed to have been introduced by István, based on a Byzantine model, the *kapnikon* (the basis of this inference is that

[51] Janina Nowakowa, *Rozmieszczenie komór celnych na Śląsku do XIV wieku* (Wrocław, 1952).

[52] Székely and Bartha, eds., *Magyarország története*, vol. II, 1247–8.

the silver content of the tax in Hungary was the same as that in Byzantium). This tax of 8 deniers (*liberi denarii*), imposed on all freemen, whether introduced by István or not, was reformed by Kálmán, who linked the sum to the type of military service provided. Kálmán's laws describe how each *ispán* had to transport the deniers paid by freemen of his county to Esztergom once a year; there he could take his third from that, leaving the rest for the king. Kings also secured revenues from the regulation of trade. From the late twelfth century monetary revenues increased (from minting, customs duties, the thirtieth tax and salt sales) in coins or unminted silver. Royal revenues also included payments related to judicial activity.[53]

A source from the end of the period throws more light on the question of royal income. A list of revenues compiled for Béla III suggests that half of the royal revenues came from the king's own estates and taxes from the counties. Exactly when and why the list was compiled has been debated: according to one view, it was meant to impress Béla's future father-in-law before his second marriage; according to another, it was in preparation for the Aragonese marriage of his son Imre. The sums provided have been criticized as exaggerated and unreliable, but the structure of royal revenues described in the list is generally seen as reliable. Monetary revenues derived from the exchange of money, the sale of salt, customs duties on fairs, trade and shipping, immigrant *hospites* in Transylvania, two-thirds of the monetary revenues of each county *ispán*, payments from the duke of Slavonia and gifts from *ispáns*. Revenues in kind from the population ensured that the king and court had food, and the royal family was provided with textiles, horses and other valuables.[54]

Minting started during the reign of István I (as discussed in Chapter 3), but money did not play a crucial role in the economy of the first two centuries of the Christian kingdom. Silver coins as well as unminted silver started to be used more widely during the twelfth century. Minting was a royal monopoly (extended to the eleventh-century princes at the head of the duchy) and was carried out at

[53] Kálmán, c. 35, 45, 79 in Bak *et al.*, eds., *Laws*, 28, 29, 32; Kubinyi *et al.*, eds., *Gazdaság*, section 7 on trade; Zoltán Kordé, 'Adó', in *KMTL*, 29–30.

[54] Gábor Barta and János Barta, 'Royal finance in medieval Hungary: the revenues of King Béla III', in W. M. Ormrod, Margaret M. Bonney and Richard J. Bonney, eds., *Crises, Revolutions and Self-Sustained Growth: Essays in European Fiscal History, c. 1130–1830* (Stamford, 1999), 24–40.

Esztergom. Hungarian silver coins were light and small, even as light as Géza II's 0.13 gram silver coins. During the eleventh and twelfth centuries, designs were simpler, using punches to impress the die; from the thirteenth century, dies were engraved and designs developed, including more figures, buildings and so on. Copper coins were issued during the reign of Béla III; scholars have advanced numerous hypotheses to account for this. Beginning in the middle of the thirteenth century, the *bans* of Slavonia minted coins as well.

King Salamon introduced the system of minting new coins every two years; the old ones had to be exchanged at a fixed rate, bringing revenues for the king as the older coins were no longer accepted. During László I's reign, the *lucrum camerae*, revenues from minting and the exchange of old for new money, was one of the most significant sources of monetary revenue. László also had heavier deniers minted, of which 40 equalled 1 Byzantine golden coin that circulated in the realm. From the reign of Béla II (1131–41) new coins started to be issued every year. Initially the silver content of the coins was also decreased at each minting, increasing royal revenues, but such debasement was discontinued under Géza II (1141–62). Because of the unreliability of minted coins, real value was represented by silver bars according to weight and silver content. From the end of the twelfth century, deniers of Friesach (minted under the archbishop of Salzburg) circulated in Hungary, and form the most important group in coin-finds until the middle of the thirteenth century.[55]

## AGRICULTURE AND ESTATE ORGANIZATION

Agriculture remained the key component of the early medieval economy; the extent to which each polity was autarchic has been

[55] László Réthy, *Corpus Nummorum Hungariae I.* (Budapest, 1899, repr. 1982); Lajos Huszár, *Münzkatalog Ungarn von 1000 bis heute* (Budapest, 1979) (Géza II's 0.13 g coin: Réthy, *Corpus Nummorum Hungariae*, 92; Huszár *Münzkatalog*, 106); Nora Berend, 'Imitation coins and frontier societies: the case of medieval Hungary', *Archivum Eurasiae Medii Aevi* 10 (1998–9), 5–14; István Gedai, 'Friesach Denars and their historical background in the Hungarian Kingdom', in Gedai, *Die Friesacher Münze im Alpen-Adria-Raum* (Graz, 1996), 191–207; Kovács, *A kora Árpád-kori magyar pénzverésről*; László Kovács, 'Die zwischen 1000 und 1141 verborgene Hortfunde des Karpatenbeckens', *Acta Archaeologica Academiae Scientiarum Hungaricae* 59 (2008), 429–55; Bálint Hóman, *Magyar pénztörténet* (Budapest, 1916, repr. 1991); Csaba Tóth, 'Pénzverés és pénzügyigazgatás 1000–1387', in Kubinyi *et al*, eds., *Gazdaság*, 163–84.

debated. Estate and village organization was diverse, but the ruler's lands played a crucial role in all three areas in this period. Land use was based on traditional patterns, with the two- or three-field system introduced in the latter part of the period. Agricultural technology developed everywhere in the late twelfth and thirteenth centuries, including through borrowing from western, especially German, lands.

### *Bohemia*

The acreage of the arable land is estimated as around 15 per cent of the whole Přemyslid realm at the beginning of the twelfth century. From the beginnings of the polity (in the tenth century) the acreage of fields was expanding at a stable rate. But the character of the process was different in the tenth and eleventh centuries from that in the twelfth. At first, it was strictly connected to the administrative structure of the realm. In the middle of the tenth century, Bohemia was covered with a relatively regular network of small settlements among the dominating deciduous forest. But when the Přemyslids strengthened their power, they concentrated their administrative and economic tasks in manors of different importance. In the immediate vicinity of the manors, the field acreage started to grow rapidly; the scale of the process was connected to the importance of the administrative centre. As an example, the landscape around Prague in the twelfth century consisted more of fields and meadows than forests. At the same time, in the case of regional administrative centres, the ratio of forest to cultivated land was more or less equal. The increase in cultivated land was at least partially a result of conscious settlement activities carried out by dukes. They not only translocated their 'own' people organized in so-called tens and living on the land. They also settled their slaves, mostly prisoners of numerous wars. These actions were sometimes planned on a large scale. During the war of Břetislav I against Poland in 1038, he was supposed to resettle in Bohemia the whole population of one of the most important Piast strongholds, Giecz, because they were famous as good craftsmen. Yet even after such activity, forests still covered around 85 per cent of the Přemyslid duchy.

Traditionally, historians have suggested that the situation rapidly changed only due to the thirteenth-century 'German colonization'. But nowadays Czech medievalists accentuate instead the importance of the so-called internal colonization of the twelfth century. They connected it with a continent-wide process of increasing population in the eleventh and especially twelfth centuries. As a result, first, reserves of uncultivated lands around old settlements were turned into fields and meadows. But around the middle of the twelfth century this turned out to be insufficient. Hundreds of new small villages or settlements appeared in the woods, connected to technological changes: the yoke was replaced by the horse-collar, and horseshoes appeared at the same time. These made it possible to plough heavy soil and generally to plough more effectively. We should also add new types of carriages and, last but not least, the appearance of mills and windmills. But we should not exaggerate their importance: mills were mentioned very rarely, and they appeared in larger numbers only in the thirteenth century. Nevertheless, colonization was a fact. Unlike in the eleventh century it was not connected to forced migrations ordered by the duke. Dukes, but on a larger scale the Church and magnates, profited from a voluntary migration movement. Younger sons of free ducal peasants together with knights of lesser social status migrated from their villages and settled down as *hospites* in new places. They were freed for several years from any dues and payments. The numeric significance of this process for the whole Bohemian economy cannot be calculated. But for contemporaries its importance was clear: ecclesiastical officials distinguished the tithes collected from old and new villages (or fields) as 'decimae prediales veteres' and 'decimae praediales novales'.[56]

Apart from this 'internal colonization' movement – which, as described below, is not unanimously accepted – the features of Bohemian agriculture were more or less similar to those characteristic of the Piast realm. The average yield has been estimated at 3 grains per 1 sown grain on the best type of soil and 2.5 for less fertile types of soil. The spatial organization of an average manor, known to us from the so-called Únětice charter from around 1125–40, was simple. Arable fields (*ager* or *terra ad aratrum*) were located in the direct vicinity of a house (in a village or settlement). At a certain distance from the house was a transitional zone (*campus*), a space between a forest and a field,

[56] Tomáš Vélimský, 'K problematice rané kolonizace 12. stoleti v Českém středohoří a vzniku feudální pozemkové držby', *Medievalia Historia Bohemica* 4 (1995), 81–101; Jan Klápště, 'Změna – středověká transformace a její předpoklady', in *Medievalia archeologica bohemica* (*Památky Archologické*, Supplementum 2) (Prague, 1994), 18–27; Žemlička, *Čechy v době knížecí*, 272–82.

but which cannot be called a meadow. The meadow proper (*pratum*) was mentioned as an entirely different type of agricultural space.[57] The *campus* was overgrown with bushes, then trees and – to some degree only – grass. It had been cultivated many years previously, but as a *campus* it rested and was used as pasture, albeit of mediocre quality. It was also an energy reserve for peasants: young trees and bushes were easier for a man with an axe to fell for domestic usage than large, old trees of proper wood. Last but not least, it was reserved for future agricultural activity: after a while, it was again turned into an arable field.[58]

The above analysis of the meaning of the term *campus* in the Únětice charter, proposed by Zdeněk Smetánka, is important for a wider view of the medieval Bohemian economy. He proved beyond any doubt that assumptions made on the basis of this charter that the three-field system was known in Bohemia in the first half of the twelfth century were false. Accepting this, one has to ask: if the only agricultural system that existed around the middle of the twelfth century was a traditional one, could the hypothesis of a massive 'inner colonization' movement, sketched above, carry weight? The estimated amount of crops obtainable from arable land and meat derived from livestock and fishing, perhaps together with seeds and fruits gathered on the *campus* and in forests, were barely enough to provide for four to five members of a family. On the one hand, with such a limited amount of reserves, could population growth reach the scale needed to allow a massive migration and settlement movement? On the other hand, the poor level of productivity may have encouraged young men starving at home to migrate from their villages, and broaden extensive production by the colonization of uncultivated areas. Currently these are still open questions in face of contradictory results from source analysis.

Typically villages were situated along one watercourse or more, although classic 'dispersed' or 'nucleated/compact' village types were also present. If a village was large enough, its centre was a manorial hall, or halls if a village had more than one owner. In local administrative or exchange centres, a church was erected near the house of the owner. Village arable fields and meadows stretched for 1–1.5

[57] *CDB* I, no. 124, p. 130.

[58] Zdeněk Smetánka, *Legenda o Ostojovi: archeologie obyčejného života*, 2nd edn (Prague, 2010), 25–6, 66–78, 92–102.

kilometres, but together with wooded areas, forests and *campi* its territory could stretch much further.[59]

## *Poland*

From the Neolithic era, arable land was divided into zones according to their proximity to human dwellings. Adjoining the houses, the garden zone was intensively and usually manually cultivated but its significance had gradually diminished and in the period discussed it mainly provided the villagers with vegetables, mostly leguminous crops. Once extremely important, the zone of fields and pastures located in the direct vicinity of large cattle pens played only a marginal role in the Middle Ages. Fields fertilized with manure were manually cultivated and used for intensive cereal-growing. But most important during the eleventh and twelfth centuries was the zone of fields cultivated using draught animals. These fields were usually planted with rye, millet, wheat (usually of the common (bread) variety), barley (two varieties) and oats. The average yield in the eleventh and twelfth centuries has been estimated at 2–3 grains per 1 sown grain. A radical increase in crop yield following the introduction of more intensive agriculture, with 1 sown grain yielding 3–3.5 grains, would come only in the thirteenth or fourteenth centuries.[60]

Low crop yields resulted from the organization of agriculture. For a long time, the fallow land system dominated: a piece of land would be cultivated for several years in a row and then be allowed to lie fallow for several years. Reforestation could be prevented by livestock grazing but this was not a rule since pastures were generally located closer to the village. The fallow land system evolved into the more sophisticated two-field system. Then arable land was divided into two (groups of) fields: one was planted with cereals, while the other was allowed to lie fallow until the next planting season to recover its fertility before being planted by cereals again. Quick crop rotation

[59] Jan Klápště and Zdeněk Smetánka, 'The archeology of medieval villages in Bohemia and Moravia (Czech Republic)', *Ruralia* 1 (1996) (*Památky Archologické*, Supplementum 5), 331–8; Klápště and Smetánka, 'The settlement pattern within the medieval landscape near Kostelec nad Černými lesy (Central Bohemia)', Ruralia 2 (1999) (*Památky Archologické*, Supplementum 11), 226–36.

[60] Andrzej Wyczański, 'Gospodarka wiejska w Polsce XIV wieku w ujęciu liczbowym (próba oceny)', *Roczniki Dziejów Społecznych i Gospodarczych* 62 (2002), 169–72.

required additional fertilization of the soil by allowing the livestock to graze and enrich it with their manure and by the further spreading of manure. The two-field system was more labour-intensive but yielded more balanced crops than the fallow land system, which progressively diminished the soil's fertility. In the climate of central Europe, a four-year cycle of crop rotation might have been employed as a variant of the two-field system, though solid evidence is lacking so its employment remains hypothetical. It would have involved: (1) planting the field with a spring crop; (2) allowing the land to lie fallow; (3) planting the field with a winter crop; (4) allowing the land to lie fallow. This would give the advantage of a longer interval between sowing the same type of crops (three years instead of one year) to restore the fertility of the soil. The well-documented agricultural breakthrough caused by the introduction of the three-field system would come only in the later thirteenth and fourteenth centuries.[61]

Land cultivation methods also influenced the crops. Ploughing with draught animals, usually oxen, was common in the eleventh and twelfth centuries, but during this period a major change occurred in the ploughing equipment. The wooden lister (sulky plough) only had iron fittings occasionally and this no earlier than the tenth century; even with such fittings it could only work light soil, which had a relatively low crop yield. The revolutionary modifications to the lister included the replacement of its frame with a runner and fitting it with an iron-clad mould-board to slice through the soil more easily and an iron coulter making a deeper vertical cut. The ploughed field would be then worked with a harrow and sometimes also ploughed again with a simpler chisel lister immediately before sowing in order to break up larger clods of earth. This method made possible the cultivation of heavy soils, and also meant a more productive use of the time the land was allowed to lie fallow, as the overgrowing plants could be ploughed over to enrich the soil. Later, in the thirteenth century, the lister would be replaced with a plough which (especially the wheeled plough) performed the task twice as efficiently.

The expansion of arable land in the eleventh and twelfth centuries was gradual, as the deforestation process continued. It has been estimated on the basis of archaeological evidence that in Greater Poland 20% of the province's area was deforested in the tenth century,

[61] For an overview, see *Historia kultury materialnej Polski*, vol. I, *Od VII do XII wieku*, ed. Zofia Podwińska and Maria Dembińska (Wrocław, 1978), 72–116.

and the proportion rose steadily to 30% in the twelfth, rapidly to reach 40% in the thirteenth century as a result of demographic growth and developments in agricultural organization and farming methods. Thus, the eleventh and twelfth centuries may be regarded as a period of continuous change occurring within the traditional model of land cultivation.[62]

A similar process of limited change concerned animal husbandry. As compared to the preceding centuries, the importance of cattle-breeding gradually decreased, while raising pigs become more popular, perhaps because it was less labour-intensive and thus more economical at a time when cereal cultivation required a greater labour input than before. But this proved a temporary trend. Following the introduction of the two-field and particularly of the three-field system, cattle-raising regained its importance but – as with growing crops – the major change would come only in the later thirteenth and in the fourteenth centuries. More intensive farming provided more fodder for the cattle. The emergence of towns as the centres of trade and of craft rather than agricultural production likely generated greater demand in the home market for both meat and draught animals (transport of goods and raw materials). Overall, in agriculture the period of the eleventh and twelfth centuries is marked by the continuation of changes which had started earlier, but real breakthroughs would come only in the following centuries.[63]

From the beginnings, the Piast realm was geographically diversified. Therefore, no common type of village location or village spatial organization existed. For example, in Pomerania the most popular location of villages was on a small hill or other kind of elevation, while in Greater Poland most villages were founded in valleys. This regional difference was interpreted as strictly connected to differences in the natural environment, and not to cultural traditions. Open settlements everywhere more or less corresponded to classical types of medieval villages: concentrated (regular) or dispersed. The first type was organized around a central open area, either round or oval, or alongside a

[62] On village life, see Andrzej Buko, *The Archeology of Early Medieval Poland: Discoveries – Hypotheses – Interpretations* (Leiden and Boston, 2008), 333–50 (with bibliographical remarks).

[63] Alicja Lasota-Moskalewska, 'Polish medieval farming in the light [of] archeozoology', *Questiones Medii Aevi Novae* 9 (2004), 205–16 (on the ninth–eleventh centuries).

path or road, by which houses stood facing each other in one or two lines. Typical farm units consisted of a dwelling house and outbuildings of different, sometimes now unknown, functions (farm houses, crafts workshops, granaries, etc.). Most villages occupied no more than 0.5 ha of residential land (between 40 to 65% of all known villages, in different proportions in different provinces). The percentage of villages of 1–5 ha is estimated at 30–40%. Any population numbers are highly hypothetical, which is also the case for figures cited below. Average-size villages with five to seven farm units were inhabited by twenty to forty-five people, and bigger ones contained eight to twelve dwelling houses with thirty-five to seventy people. Villages of one to three homesteads could be inhabited by five to eighteen peasants. The number of inhabitants in a few large, archaeologically excavated villages was calculated as 100 and more people. Until the end of the twelfth century, most houses in these villages were built as sunken houses. But during the period under investigation, the number of timber-framed houses steadily increased and consequently the percentage of pit-houses in the general number of dwelling houses decreased.[64]

Over the course of the eleventh and twelfth centuries significant changes occurred in the functioning of settlements on all levels of the system. As mentioned before, a simple scheme dominated in the early eleventh century: small rural settlements delivered dues to the local stronghold manned by ducal warriors. Most rural settlements were obliged to pay taxes in the form of a set portion of their crops. The remainder constituted a very diverse group of service villages. Located around the stronghold, they were obliged to provide precisely defined products and labour services to the duke and his warriors, for example, armaments or assistance during hunt. As noted, toponyms, some still in use, were likely names of service settlements reflecting the kind of service or products communally owned to the ducal court. For example, Szczytniki once provided *szczyt*s (shields) and Kowale was a village of *kowal*s (blacksmiths).

The scale of goods exchange in society remains difficult to determine. The activity of market centres is attested only in the second half of the twelfth century. Their emergence was related to broader socio-fiscal changes and cannot be interpreted as an argument for the

[64] Sławomir Moździoch, 'Das mittelalterliche Dorf in Polen im Lichte der archäologischen Forschung', *Ruralia* 1 (1996) (*Památky Archologické*, Supplementum 5), 282–93.

existence of a system of markets as early as the eleventh century. Market settlements served as the centres of exchange, mainly for the population of local villages, and possibly also of handicrafts, but the scale of the latter remains undeterminable. Their establishment was closely related to castellanies as the centres of ducal political and/or economic administration.

Rulers tried to improve the organization of exchange by having the *hospites* settled in the vicinity of strongholds. By granting them special rights (see above), they wanted these small migrant communities to strengthen economic centres. The experiment proved only partially successful. The *hospites'* settlements achieved a degree of economic success but, constrained by ducal authority, they did not grow as quickly as their founders had expected. As a result, from the 1160s models based on those of the Empire were adopted. Resorting to internal colonization, settlers were brought to Poland to found new rural settlements or reform extant ones in accordance with Teutonic law. In rural settlements, dispersed development was replaced by continuous development, often lining the road running through the village. Replacing market settlements and administration centres in strongholds with towns chartered in accordance with Teutonic law constituted an even bigger revolution. This process was part of a much broader transformation of society; although initiated in Silesia already in the late twelfth century, it became more widespread only in the thirteenth and fourteenth centuries and allowed the appearance of a state society (*Standesgesellschaft*) in Poland, which replaced traditional forms of social organization (see Chapter 7).[65]

## *Hungary*

Throughout the period agriculture retained its primacy in the economy. Most of the Carpathian basin was suitable for cultivation,[66]

[65] Sławomir Gawlas, 'Polen – eine Ständegesellschaft an der Peripherie des lateinischen Europa', in *Europa im späten Mittelalter. Politik – Gesellschaft – Kultur*, ed. R. C. Schwinges, Ch. Hesse and P. Moraw (Munich, 2006), Historische Zeitschrift – Beihefte n.s. 40, 237–61; Gawlas, 'Die zentrale Funktion der Städte in Ostmitteleuropa in der Zeit des Landesausbaus', in *Städtelandschaften im Ostseeraum im Mittelalter und in der frühen Neuzeit*, ed. Roman Czaja and Carsten Jahnke (Toruń, 2009), 9–28.

[66] József Laszlovszky, 'Földművelés a késő középkori Magyarországon', in Kubinyi *et al.*, eds., *Gazdaság*, 49–82.

which in this period focused on cereals. Large areas were used to grow grains – wheat on central lands, and on more peripheral lands rye, barley, oats and millet – as both autumn and spring sown crops. These cereals were both mentioned in written sources (for example, bread, beer and so on as revenues in kind, and obligations to grow cereals) and found during archaeological excavations. The paucity of sources precludes the calculation of yields. Cereals were ground in mills. Hand-mills and grindstones existed throughout the period, while water mills appeared at the end of the eleventh century, their number and importance growing from the middle of the twelfth century. By the early thirteenth century, cereal cultivation was widespread in all the lands of the plains. Moreover, forests started to be cleared, especially during the thirteenth century, to bring more land under cultivation. Along the rivers, especially the Danube, Tisza and their confluents, 4–15-km-wide areas were regularly flooded, and were therefore not available for cultivation. These areas as well as the swamps near Lake Balaton and elsewhere were, however, used for fishing, and during the dry season in summer, for grazing animals and collecting fodder.[67] In contrast, large parts of the Plains area that in later centuries became sandy or barren were densely settled by agricultural villages in the Árpád age, according to archaeological evidence.

Royal, ecclesiastical and noble landowners all had scattered possessions. The same landowner held lands (including villages or parts of villages) in many different locations, which could be separated by significant distances. At the same time, several landowners could hold land in the same village.[68] The best sources about economic organization and production on estates in the period are the lists compiled for ecclesiastical possessions. Throughout the eleventh and twelfth centuries, kings and then, increasingly, nobles continued to found and endow new ecclesiastical institutions and give donations to existing ones. Smaller institutions owned only one or two villages, but larger ones twenty to one hundred villages. One of the best-documented ecclesiastical institutions of the period is the monastery of

[67] Tibor Bellon, *Ártéri gazdálkodás az Alföldön az ármentesítések előtt* (Nyíregyháza, 1996); Miklós Takács, 'The importance of water in the life of the rural settlements of mediaeval Hungary', in *Ruralia 5: Water Management in Medieval Rural Economy*, ed. Jan Klápšte, Jean-Michel Poisson André Bazzana (Turnhout, 2005), 222–32.

[68] For maps, see Székely and Bartha, eds., *Magyarország története*, vol. II, 1048–51.

Pannonhalma, founded perhaps by Géza and enriched by a donation from István I in 1002. The monastery owned ten villages in the early eleventh century; at the end of the eleventh century almost thirty; and in the 1230s close to one hundred. The elite of ecclesiastical estates (called *iobagio*, then from the thirteenth century *iobagio nobilis*, finally *praedialis*) provided service by collecting the tithe, administering the estate – using their own horses to move around – and providing military service. They had land from the Church to provide their livelihood. In their origin, some were servile and others free, but the latter renounced their freedom when they accepted ecclesiastical lordship.

It is very difficult to gather data about lay noble estates, because royal donations of land to the laity were initially oral. The first charter of donation whose beneficiary was a nobleman survives only from the later half of the twelfth century. Lay donations to the Church and testaments provide some evidence concerning lay landholding. Noble estates consisted of different types of lands: inherited land and acquired land (either received through donation or purchased). Land that had been inherited within the family at least once passed into the first category. Ownership rights to the first type of landholding were invested in the lineage; therefore the consent of all kin who had a right to inherit was needed for the sale of such land. The inheritance system was based on the extended rather than the nuclear family. Lands were inherited by more distant relatives if nearer relations were lacking, although King Kálmán's legislation in the early twelfth century attempted to differentiate between lands received from István I, which could be inherited in this way, and lands received later, which were to revert to the king if no member of the immediate family was alive. The common right of ownership could be terminated through a division of land among the kin through common consent or judicial process. 'Acquired land' was personal property rather than that of the lineage, but lands held from royal donation could be alienated only with royal consent.[69] The buying and selling of land appear increasingly in the sources from the twelfth century. It seems that members of the lay elite normally held possessions of about ten to

[69] Rady, *Nobility*; Martyn C. Rady, 'The "title of new donation" in medieval Hungarian law', *Slavonic and East European Review* 79 (2001), 638–52; Kálmán, c. 20 in Bak *et al.*, eds., *Laws*, 27.

fifteen *praedia* (villages, estates or parts of lands), with the most significant properties amounting to perhaps up to thirty *praedia*.

The *praedium* was the organizational form of lay estates. Land was held by the lord and worked by the subject population. *Praedia* did not have a set size; for example, sources indicate that at the lower end of the spectrum, a *praedium* had only three servant families, while the large *praedia* equalled the size of a large village, with twelve families and an additional twenty-seven people. The entire *praedium* was the property of the landowner, but already in the eleventh century two types of work were carried out on it, which eventually led to a transformation of the relations between landowners and workers. Part of the estate was cultivated directly by the subject populations, who owed work service. A different model of exploitation was introduced on other parts, however: subject populations were assigned the use of a house, and increasingly of land which they farmed independently; in exchange, they owed taxes in kind to the lord.

Although some historians refrain from using the term 'slave', even they describe the 'servants' who owed unlimited labour service to their lords as 'similar to the slaves of antiquity'.[70] The distinction between the various categories of unfree population – a variety of terms appear in the sources – is debated, and so is the process of the disappearance of slavery. Manumission and a changing economic system (a shift away from the direct cultivation of the landlord's estates using labour service) probably played a key role. The unfree owed (sometimes fixed) labour services and dues in kind. Increasingly, and at the latest in the thirteenth century, they acquired the use of plots of land (owned by the lord, but used by the subject population) and became eventually small producers who owed dues in kind to their lords. Transfer to ecclesiastical ownership also contributed to this process. One example illustrates this transformation of status. In 1165, the *praedium* of Kisszelepcsény with six *servus* families, lands and *arator* slaves was donated to the monastery of Garamszentbenedek (today Hronský Beňadik, Slovakia). In 1247 when Kisszelepcsény appears in the sources, it is called a village, signalling the change in its status, and its inhabitants are serfs. Their duties were recorded in detail (in contrast to the earlier situation when the landlord could

70 Székely and Bartha, eds., *Magyarország története*, vol. II, 1054.

determine the services owed), including dues in kind and money, and service as messengers on their own horses.[71]

There are no precise data on the system of land use. From indirect references and archaeological excavations it is thought that as late as the twelfth century land first used by animals as pasture, and therefore well prepared by their manure, was subsequently continuously cultivated as long as it was productive; when the soil was exhausted, the area was abandoned. Cultivation then moved on to a new area, whereas the previously cultivated land once more came to be used for animal pasture. Such a system was based on the fertility of the land rather than any pre-planned organization and was made possible by the existence of extensive areas suitable for cultivation. Excavations of villages showed that houses had large areas of land around them, surrounded by ditches. It is thought that these areas were used to grow crops; then, after the harvest, the animals were kept in the same area. When the land became infertile or the houses uninhabitable (the buildings were not durable), the occupants moved to another location in the settlement. Eventually, the whole settlement had to move. Historians used to interpret such moving settlements as signs of the survival of nomadism (or semi-nomadism), which probably preceded the development of a settled economy (see Chapter 2). The fact that villages were not attached to a permanent location – late-eleventh century legislation that warned villagers against moving their settlement away from churches, as well as occasional evidence of villages changing their location even in the thirteenth century – were seen as proof of the slow development of permanent settlement. Now, however, moving settlements are seen as an inevitable outcome of the system of land use: villages had to move as lands around them became infertile exactly because life was based on cultivation and settled agriculture, rather than on nomadism.[72]

[71] On estate organization, see *ibid.*, vol. II, 1035–59; Rady, *Nobility*; István Szabó, 'The praedium: studies on the economic history and the history of settlement in early Hungary', *Agrártörténeti Szemle* 5 (1963 Supplementum), 1–24.

[72] Laszlovszky, 'Földművelés'; László Makkai, 'A feudális mezőgazdaság', in Péter Gunszt and László Lökös, eds., *A mezőgazdaság története* (Budapest, 1982), 35–61; László Földes, 'Telek és költözködő falvak a honfoglaláskori és Árpád-kori magyarság gazdálkodásában', in Ferenc Tőkei, ed., *Nomád társadalmak és nomád államalakulatok* (Budapest, 1983), 327–49; István Szabó, *A falurendszer kialakulása Magyarországon (X–XV. század)* (Budapest, 1966).

Village landholding patterns are frequently mentioned in charters. Both arable lands and forests are often described as held in common by the villagers. It has been suggested that lands were assigned to individual families by drawing lots and that they were periodically redistributed. Landowners including ecclesiastical institutions could hold land in common with the villagers and participate in these distributions of parts. Subject populations, even slaves, often had fixed rights of land use. Two- and three-field systems were introduced only in the later Middle Ages. Boundaries between village communities were signalled by natural and artificial border-markers, described in charters, but not all land within these was cultivated. The crucial equipment for agriculture was the plough pulled by oxen. Charters of donation and wills mention different numbers of oxen as necessary for pulling a plough: eight, four or two. This evidence as well as archaeological finds indicate that two types of ploughs were used: the heavy ploughs, made with an iron ploughshare, effective even in cultivating heavy soil, and wooden ploughs for light soil. Coulters, and from the thirteenth century increasingly assymetrical ploughs, were also introduced. Several families subject to the same lord used the same plough. Iron agricultural tools were so valuable that they are found among the treasures hidden at the time of the Mongol invasion.[73]

It is thought that external influences played a role in changes in agricultural technology and the introduction of more intensive agriculture. Benedictine monasteries introduced intensive garden-cultivation and a specialized production. Viticulture and fruit trees spread as a result.[74] From the eleventh century on, sources show the importance of viticulture and the making of wine. The numbers of recorded vintners increased over the course of the twelfth century. Some areas, notably the regions around Buda, Sopron and Pozsony (Bratislava, Slovakia) exported wine in long-distance trade. Narrative

[73] Márta Belényesy, 'La culture permanente et l'évolution du système biennal et triennal en Hongrie médiévale', *Ergon* 2 (1960), 311–26; József Laszlovszky, 'Field systems in medieval Hungary', in *The Man of Many Devices*, 432–44; Ágnes Ritoók and Éva Garam, *A tatárjárás (1241–1242) Katalógus* (Budapest, 2007), 104–6.

[74] Laszlovszky, 'Földművelés'; Ferenc Gyulai, *Archaeobotany in Hungary: Seed, Fruit, Food and Beverage Remains in the Carpathian Basin from the Neolithic to the Late Middle Ages* (Budapest, 2010); Gyulai, 'A Kárpát-medencei szőlő és borkultúra régészeti-növénytani emlékei', in Zoltán Benyák and Ferenc Benyák, eds., *Borok és korok* (Budapest, 2002), 101–15.

sources and the analysis of archaeological remains also show the variety of fruits and vegetables: notably apples, sour cherries, cherries, walnuts, hazelnuts, peaches, watermelons, peas, onions, beans, lentils and buckwheat. The Cistercians introduced new estate-organization techniques.

From the second half of the twelfth and especially from the thirteenth century, German- and Romance-speaking peasant immigrants (*hospites*) settled under the direction of *locatores*, introducing new settlement types as well as contributing to the extension of agricultural lands and more intensive cultivation. Assarting started in the twelfth century, and other ways of improving cultivation in the thirteenth. Assarting was linked to the plantation of new villages and invition to new settlers, mostly immigrants. From this period on, there is evidence of clearing forests in order to gain new arable lands and extend cultivation. Immigrants probably introduced the assymetrical heavy plough (which appeared in this period in Hungary), mentioned above, that could turn the soil even on newly cultivated land.[75] As a result, plots became longer, in order to necessitate fewer turns with the plough. Specialization in agricultural production, urbanization and growth in the trade of produce were intertwined from the late twelfth and thirteenth centuries.

Animals were kept in a variety of different ways: as a complement to agricultural cultivation in villages; as part of extensive agriculture, on pasture under shepherds; and seasonally migrating to different pastures. The significance of livestock in the period is shown by the fact that cattle became the basis for designating the trade value of objects. In mountainous areas, cultivation was impossible and animals were kept instead but, overall, both growing crops and raising livestock were important in the eleventh and twelfth centuries. Archaeozoological studies indicate the relative numbers of animals kept: cattle, sheep and goats, horses and pigs were the most important. The greatest single element in some villages are cattle bones, which constitute up to 60% of the total, while in others sheep and goat bones reach 57–8% of the total. The number of horses was also higher than in the late medieval period. Horses, sheep and goats were

[75] Róbert Müller, 'A középkor agrotechnikája', in Lívia Bende and Gábor Lőrinczy, eds., *A középkori magyar agrárium* (Ópusztaszer, 2000), 27–44; Müller, *A mezőgazdasági vaseszközök fejlődése a késővaskortól a törökkor végéig* (Zalaegerszeg, 1982); Iván Balassa, *Az eke és szántás története Magyarországon* (Budapest, 1973).

the typical animals of nomadic open-air animal-raising, and some historians have interpreted the presence of a high number of livestock as a sign of continued nomadism. Yet it has been shown that such livestock were also kept within the framework of settled life, on estates. According to one study of the 118 known *praedia* in the written sources between 1067 and 1250, four engaged exclusively in animal husbandry, and flocks were mentioned in relation to a total of 33.[76]

Animals were recorded in estate lists and testaments; they were important not only in order to work the land (oxen) but also to provide food and materials for clothing. Sheep, goats, cows, pigs and horses were commonly listed as belonging to estates. While initially animal herds belonged to lords, soon subject populations on estates themselves kept animals. There are signs of the emergence of animal husbandry using stables as well: the synod of Esztergom (canon 65, *c.* 1100) and *c.* 1151 a charter both mention sheep pens, and another twelfth-century charter refers to stables. Geese and poultry are often mentioned as tax in kind, and they amount to 1–8% of animal bone remains in villages of the period. Bee-keeping was widespread – bees often appear among the goods of estates – and honey was used to make beer.

Fishing and hunting are attested; many communities had to pay tax in kind in fish or game. Hunting was a pastime of lords as well as the obligation of subject populations. Marten, beaver, aurochs, boar, deer, hare and various wild birds are either mentioned in the sources or were identified by archaeozoological studies. Although written sources often praise the land's richness in wild animals, according to the excavated material, such animals formed an insignificant part of the diet; the main source of meat was animal husbandry. Fishing, however, was a significant source of food. Rivers and lakes were not the only important sources of fish; fish ponds also often appear in the sources. The analysis of human remains suggests that people regularly had sufficient food at their disposal, and did not suffer from famine or food shortages apart from exceptional circumstances.

[76] Kubinyi *et al.*, eds., *Gazdaság*, section 2 on animals (including fishing and hunting); László Bartosiewicz, 'Animal husbandry and medieval settlement in Hungary: a review', *Beiträge zur Mittelalterarchäologie in Österreich* 15 (1999), 139–55; Székely and Bartha, eds., *Magyarország története*, vol. II, 1029–30.

## CRAFTS, TRADE AND URBANIZATION

A monetary economy appeared significantly earlier in Bohemia than in the other two realms. Yet everywhere, by the end of the period, urbanization and monetarization had started to change the economic system. The role of foreigners, particularly Germans in Bohemia and Poland, in the formation of towns has been debated by generations of scholars (see Chapter 7).

### *Bohemia*

That Prague was one of the biggest marketplaces of eastern and central Europe during the period of the tenth and eleventh centuries is well known. It was an important centre of the slave trade. In addition, part of the tribute paid to dukes was exchanged by ducal officers for luxury goods during monthly markets. The latter were visited by merchants from Rus', Hungary and western Europe to buy slaves, furs, potash, tar and sometimes grain. But in what traditionally has been seen as the autarchic economy of the Přemyslid realm, trade was of mediocre importance for most of the population. It is significant that the position of Prague changed radically and quickly from the middle of the eleventh to the middle of the twelfth century. Its marketplace became local, or at the most significant within the realm. In the whole realm, local exchange took place at special market settlements, called *loca forensia* or *fora*. Their inhabitants, however, worked as ordinary peasants. They participated in seasonal market exchange only from time to time. These *loca* were not in any way centres of craft production, but only of exchange between inhabitants of widely dispersed, locally situated villages. As in Poland, in the twelfth century, when monetary circulation started to be more lively, *fora* played an important role for peasants selling the necessary quantity of goods at the local market to be able to gather coins for paying dues in standard silver coins (*denari*).

More frequently, strongholds were supposed to be 'proto- or early towns' on the basis of the same theoretical and conceptual framework as in case of Poland. Local administrative centres were situated there, together with a cluster of warriors, officials and sometimes ecclesiastics. There were granaries and other types of storage houses for goods brought by peasants as dues. Ducal mansions were located in larger strongholds. A ruler, together with his entourage, could rest there during their usual itinerant movement around the land, but above all he held court and issued political, religious and economic privileges during meetings with knights and local landowners. Ecclesiastical communities were also founded: not only parochial churches, but also Benedictine and Premonstratensian cloisters, and collegiate churches (Litoměřice, Mělaník, Stará Boleslav).

It is supposed that in order to provide for the needs of all the non-productive groups both in and around the stronghold, a number of craftsmen were settled and worked in the *suburbia*. Magnates' halls and their churches were also built in this suburban zone. The multiplicity of settlers of different social status enriched these suburban communities, providing new possibilities for exchange and co-operation. Strong internal cohesion led to some of these settlements bearing their own name, although they were part of a stronghold's suburban structure.[77]

The more functions a stronghold had – political, administrative, military, religious – and the higher its position was in the administrative structure, the greater the chance that it evolved from a simple power centre to a so-called proto-town. For example, in the twelfth century in Litoměřice several families of specialized craftsmen lived in the suburban zone: apart from smiths, shoemakers and furriers, also wine-makers and others. At the end of the century, a small group of Saxon merchants was mentioned there as well. In Prague, where social relations were the most complex, a special socio-topography even appeared. The most prestigious suburban areas were called *suburbium Pragense* (now Malá Strana) and *vicus Wissegradensis*. According to Cosmas, there was where the richest people lived. Many of them were of foreign origin: Saxons, other Germans, Jews and last but not least Romance-speaking merchants. But even though the suburbs were as large as the area around the Prague stronghold was, the only bearer of the name was the stronghold. Its surroundings were only of secondary importance; when the stronghold's importance weakened,

[77] Krzemieńska and Třeštík, 'Zur Problematik der Dienstleute im frühmittelalterlichen Böhmen'; František Kavka, 'Die Städte Böhmens und Mährens zur Zeit des Přmysliden Staates', in *Die Städte Mitteleuropas im 12. und 13. Jahrhundert*, ed. Wilhelm Rausch (Linz, 1963), 137–53; Jiří Kejř, 'Zwei Studien über die Anfänge der Städteverfassung in den böhmischen Ländern', *Historica* 16 (1969), 81–142. On craftsmenm, see Jindřich Tomas, 'Řemeslnící 11.–13. stoleti v českých zemích v písemných pramenach', *Archeologia historica* 8 (1983), 73–84.

all suburban activity faded away. Craft production and goods exchange were important as long as the administrative or political centre existed. Yet this should not lead us to belittle the role played by local marketplaces, both *fora* and those affiliated to strongholds, for the inhabitants of the Přemyslid realm. They proliferated in a quite regular pattern across the entire country, and their number at the end of twelfth century is estimated at between 90 and 120.[78]

Yet, like all other elements of the traditional model of social change in early and high medieval Bohemia, the theory of early towns is also contested. The interpretation of archaeological data as proof of well-organized and developed craft settlements has now been revealed to have been over-ambitious. A single, finished product found in a hut in the suburbia was treated as a trace of craft workshop activity, or even of a settlement of a whole cluster of craftsmen. The underlying reason was the desire to prove the existence of Slavic towns before German migration of the thirteenth century.[79] What remains a fact is that ducal strongholds, more or less regularly situated across the realm, together with *loca forensia* and ducal manors, created a network of local exchange activity. Craft production was situated in villages rather than in strongholds. Activity in suburbs was closely correlated to the dominant function of the stronghold. Exchange, distribution and trade did not make a settlement important. Power was the key to development. The situation may have changed when 'inner colonization' started, but radical changes took place only when the

[78] Ladislav Hrdlička, 'The archeological study of the historical centre of Prague: 1969–1993', in *25 Years of Archeological Research in Bohemia* (Prague, 1994) (*Památky Archologické*, Supplementum, vol. 1), 174–84; Tadeusz Lalik, 'Targ', in *Słownik Starożytności Słowiańskich* (Wrocław, 1977), 30; Miroslav Richter, 'Zur ältesten Geschichte der Stadt Prag', in *Frühgeschichte der europäischen Stadt. Voraussetzungen und Grundlagen*, ed. Hans Jürgen Brachmann and Joachim Herrmann (Berlin, 1991), 174–9; Josef Žemlička, 'Leitmeritz (Litoměřice) als Beispiel eines frühmittelalterlichen Burgerzentrums Böhmens', in *Burg – Burgstadt – Stadt*, 256–64.

[79] The existence of 'proto-towns' was already being debated in the 1970s: see Andrzej Wędzki, *Początki reform miejskiej w Środkowej Europie do połowy XIII w. (Słowiańszczyzna Zachodnia)* (Warsaw, 1974), on the existence of Slavonic 'early towns', which was criticized by Benedykt Zientara, 'Przełom w rozwoju miast środkowoeuropejskich w pierwszej połowie XIII wieku', *Przegląd Historyczny* 67 (1976), 219–43.

great thirteenth-century colonization started and chartered towns appeared.[80]

## *Poland*

Mieszko I's intensified contacts with surrounding Christian states also resulted in foreign trade, testified by the inflow, already in 970–85, of German, Italian, French, Bohemian, English and Danish coins. Earlier monetary deposits had consisted almost exclusively of Samanid coins.[81] At the same time, former contacts with the Middle Danube region and with Scandinavia were sustained, as seen through the inflow of status-markers from both directions.[82]

Northern contacts were facilitated by the strong presence of Scandinavian merchants, warriors and settlers along the Baltic coast, where they established rich emporia inhabited by multi-ethnic communities. Of these settlements, Truso, by the Vistula estuary, was already in decline, although Wolin, on the Odera estuary, was in full bloom. An opulent cemetery in Świelubie-Bardy near Kolobrzeg suggests the presence of a third emporium on the central coast of Pomerania, but the precise site has not been discovered.

Little research has been done regarding the volume of trade. The slave trade was important in both Bohemia and Poland as late as the tenth century. It has been suggested that the Piasts could have financed their investments in infrastructure and the military sphere by the substantial 'export' of slaves, whom Scandinavian merchants shipped to Muslim markets in eastern Europe.[83] The significance of the slave trade decreased in the eleventh century, and it completely disappeared in the twelfth. During this period, trade in Poland (and Bohemia) focused on importing luxury goods: men's and women's jewellery, luxurious fabrics (silk from the East), game sets, items of

80 Petr Meduna, 'K rekonstrukcíivnitřni struktury hradské organizace Přemyslovců v severozápadnich Čechách', in *Lokalne ośrodki władzy państwowej w XI-XII w. w Europie Środkowo-Wschodniej*, ed. Sławomir Moździoch (Wrocław, 1993), 91–108; Rudolf Prochazka, 'K vývoji a funkčnímu rozvrstvení hradů 11–12. stoleti na Moravě', in *Lokalne ośrodki*, 109–42.

81 Cf. Michael Müller-Wille, 'Fernhandel und Handelsplätze', in *Europas Mitte um 1000*, ed. A. Wieczorek and H.-M. Hinz (Stuttgart, 2000), Abb. 84 and 85.

82 Michał Kara, 'Archeologia o początkach państwa Piastów (wybrane zagadnienia)', in *Kolory i struktury średniowiecza*, ed Wojciech Fatkowski (Warsaw, 2004), 241–276 (here 269–71).

83 E.g. H. Samsonowicz, *Dzień chrztu i co dalej. . .* (Warsaw, 2008).

precious metal (tableware, ecclesiastical objects) and perhaps also books; and exporting mostly furs and skins (once the slave trade had ceased). The magnitude of changes in trade before the thirteenth century remains difficult to ascertain.[84]

In the eleventh century, craftsmen produced goods for the duke and his administration as well as for their respective local communities. Closely connected to the ruler were the teams of stonemasons erecting his *palatia* and churches in the principal strongholds. Still, few such monumental structures were built and their similarities to particular architectural models in the Empire and, less often, in Italy suggest that the workers, or at least the site managers, were foreigners. We do not know to what degree they relied on local stonemasons. The toponyms suggesting some settlements' specialization in goldsmithing (e.g. Złotniki) do not necessarily reflect any significant activity of local specialists, as the gold objects that have survived have been identified as imports from western Europe. Local craftsmen would likely make small silver objects and reclaim metals, particularly silver, needed for minting coins. Precious metals were in short supply in Poland, and sources attest the practice of removing gold and silver threads from worn clothes, but we do not know whether they would be reused to decorate new clothes or melted down.

The warriors' needs were hypothetically catered to by the craftsmen settled in service villages who made everything from armaments to clothes. Goods produced in service villages were likely delivered to the users through the system of dues in kind paid to the duke's representatives. Thus, the needs of the biggest consumer on the home market – that is, the ducal administration – were satisfied without developing any system for exchanging goods and services. It is possible that at least some in service villages, particularly the smiths, produced goods for neighbouring agricultural villages. On the other hand, slave craftsmen also worked for the duke and his officials. The duke's founding of special houses of female slave weavers is attested in eleventh-century Bohemia. In Poland, a large number of weaving implements excavated in strongholds testifies to their female residents' involvement in textile production, but there is no way of establishing whether they were slaves, free servants or members of the warriors' families. Craftsmen working for rural

[84] Sławomir Moździoch, *Organizacja gospodarcza państwa wczesnopiastowskiego na Śląsku: studium archeologiczne* (Wrocław, Warsaw and Cracow, 1990).

communities formed a separate category. It must be remembered, though, that in the eleventh and twelfth centuries the villagers whose basic occupation was farming would also make their own clothes (of textiles, leather and fur) and pottery. Specialization primarily concerned metalwork and the production of stone implements, such as quern-stones, distaffs and spindle-whorls. It is also possible that the agricultural villages were supplied with craft goods of this kind by the service villages.[85]

In the twelfth century, thanks to the expanded circulation of ducal coinage, the residents of castellanies were also able increasingly to rely on trade exchange through the system of fairs. The centres of ducal estates stored foodstuffs delivered by the farming villages as dues in kind: their demand for craft goods was limited to those needed for their own sustenance. The personnel of former strongholds, who used to rely on the dues of peasants and probably on service villages for their supplies, had now to procure them using funds allocated by the ruler. This stimulated trade and encouraged the craftsmen residing in the farming villages to specialize and offer their wares for sale at fairs. The traditional system of producing craft goods mainly for the village's owner continued to some degree in the large ecclesiastical estates established in the late eleventh and the twelfth centuries. An additional stimulus conducive to specialization was the arrival of the *hospites* invited from western Europe by the rulers in the twelfth century. Their experience with a greater degree of specialization provided a stimulus for the development of the exchange of goods and services within the system of fairs. As middlemen involved in long-distance trade, they also opened new trade routes, particularly in the fur trade.[86]

From the beginning of the twentieth century, Polish historians and later archaeologists have worked with a theory of the evolutionary character of the urbanization process in Polish lands. According to this theory, towns or their direct predecessors appeared soon after the arrival of the Slavs (or the disappearance of Germans, depending on

[85] *Historia kultury materialnej Polski*, vol. I, *Od VII do XII wieku*, 117–200; Sławomir Moździoch, 'Problem produkcji rzemieślniczej w śląskich grodach kasztelańskich z XI–XII wieku', in *Zkoumání wyrobních objektu a technologií archeologickymi metodami*, vol. V (Brno, 1989), 18–31.

[86] On local markets (*fora*), see Tadeusz Lalik, 'Märkte des 12. Jahrhunderts in Polen', *Kwartalnik Historii Kultury Materialnej* 10, 3 (1962), 364–7.

the accepted beliefs concerning the ethnogenesis of Poles) to these lands, around the eighth century. As a proof of this theory, the entire Lausitz Culture and especially the stronghold of Biskupin have been pinpointed (see Chapter 2). The next step supposedly was tribal strongholds of the ninth and the first half of the tenth century. Quite densely populated Piast strongholds – with their service villages and boroughs, a multi-segmented structure, a differentiated community of administrators, warriors, priests, trade- and craftsmen – were accepted as the final stage of the 'early town' development process. Chartered towns were understood as a natural consequence of the long, historical process of urbanization common to all societies in central Europe.

But since the last two decades of the twentieth century, the evolutionary vision of urbanization has been strongly criticized. Deep, functional differences are stressed between different kind of strongholds and chartered towns. The twelfth-century centres of ducal administration are sometimes still referred to as 'proto-towns'. They comprised the stronghold surrounded by the boroughs of artisans where trade took place between merchants and the members of the elite residing in the castle, but the inhabitants of neighbouring villages could also participate in commercial exchange. It is often suggested that the former Piast stronghold, as the centre of consumption stimulating the production of specified goods, evolved into the centre of production and exchange. But that is merely a hypothesis. It seems more convincing that the residents' economic activity was never the primary reason for the strongholds' existence. It is supposed that, in the tribal period, ritual functions of strongholds were much more important than economic ones. For the Piast period, the political and administrative functions of well-fortified settlements were crucial for the creation and maintenance of a web of strongholds. The economic activity of the strongholds' inhabitants could be seen only as consequences and tools enabling the realization of the fundamental objectives of their existence. Proper towns, where the economy played a dominant role in the spatial, social and political organization of life, appeared in Poland only in the late twelfth century with the foundation of the first chartered towns, and became commonplace in the thirteenth and fourteenth centuries, as such towns spread throughout the land.[87]

[87] Sławomir Moździoch, 'Problemy badań nad początkwami miast i wsią wczesnośredniowieczną w Polsce', *Slavia Antiqua* 37 (1997), 39–63; Przemysław Urbańczyk,

### *Hungary*

Initially there were no artisans solely dedicated to craftsmanship, to the exclusion of agricultural labour. Rather, artisans were among the subject populations of lords and, according to the evidence of some charters, also held lands which they farmed, but owed their dues especially in artefacts to their lord. For example, the potters of the church of Dömös owed 500 bowls two or three times a year. Sometimes artisans were not even distinguished from other unfree inhabitants of the estate by specific terminology in the lists, which simply mentioned their dues in artefacts rather than in agricultural produce. Because of the lord's needs for such products and the necessity for artisans to have time for such work, their other servile dues were fixed. This provided a relatively privileged position for artisans within the subject population, although from the thirteenth century artisans' complaints show that some had to do significant amounts of other work.

Artefacts produced in Hungary included goldsmith work. The artistic heritage of the conquest-age Hungarians, known almost exclusively from metal decorations on clothing and horse accoutrements, was not continued in the eleventh century. Rather, the adoption of Byzantine and western styles is manifest in silver, gold and other objects. Certainly documented from the last quarter of the twelfth century, but according to some scholars already functioning from the first half of the eleventh, a royal goldsmiths' workshop provided jewels and objects for the royal court. Finds of earrings, hair-rings, dress ornaments, rings and necklaces made of copper and silver attest the existence of local production for a wider population as well. Iron production, which existed in western Hungary in the twelfth century, probably ceased in the thirteenth, due to the import of Styrian iron. Smiths played an important part in producing horse

'Wczesna urbanizacja ziem polskich', in *Civitas et villa*: 37–45; on 'early towns', see Moździoch, 'Vorformen der Stadtentwicklung im südlichen Polen in 11.–12. Jh', in *Actes du XIIe Congres International des Sciences Préhistoriques et Protohistoriques* (Bratislava, 1993), 185–91, and Moździoch, 'The origins of the medieval Polish towns', *Archaeologia Polona* 32 (1994), 129–53; on the transition between 'early towns' and 'chartered towns', see Moździoch, 'Die frühstädtischen Siedlungskomplexe und Lokationsstädte in Schlesien im 12.–13. Jh. (Änderungen der Raumstruktur im Lichte der archäologischen Quellen)', in *Hausbau und Raumstruktur früher Städte in Ostmitteleuropa*, ed. Hansjürgen Brachmann (Prague, 1996) (*Památky Archeologické*, Supplementum 6), 87–100, and Jerzy Piekalski, *Von Köln nach Krakau. Der topographische Wandel früher Städte* (Berlin, 2001).

accoutrements, agricultural implements and armaments, which included maces (used in Hungary as a result of eleventh- and twelfth-century nomad immigration), short swords, and bows and arrows. Textile-work was based on flax and hemp, produced by peasants using spindles and treadle weaving looms. Pottery products until the late twelfth century were simple and for everyday use; glazed ware appeared in the thirteenth century; and glass jars and beads were also made.[88]

Trade was not significant in the early period of Hungary's economy; involvement in international trade started to increase from the twelfth century onwards. The most important east–west trade route in the tenth and eleventh centuries linked Kiev, Cracow, Prague, Regensburg and Mainz. Trade routes from the Carpathian basin joined this main route. Hungarian exports included slaves, salt, horses and probably other animals, agricultural products, metal and some artisanal products. Imports into Hungary included armaments, artisanal products and luxury items. Surviving items include ecclesiastical vessels and German metal objects. One branch of the Levantine trade route, going north from Constantinople, crossed Hungary, and Hungarian merchants travelled all the way to Constantinople. Laws stipulated that foreign merchants travelling through Hungary were to go to Esztergom and wait for a royal permit to exit the realm. The royal court and the archbishop of Esztergom were probably the most important buyers of imported luxury products. German, Rus'ian, and Venetian merchants are known to have frequented Hungary.[89]

Initially, the king controlled markets, held at royal seats and the seats of *ispán*s. All tolls from markets went to the king. From around

[88] László Szende, 'Középkori kézművesség', in Kubinyi *et al.*, eds., *Gazdaság*, 199–228; Éva Kovács, *Romanische Goldschmiedekunst in Ungarn* (Budapest, 1974); Gusztáv Heckenast, 'Eisenverhüttung in Ungarn im 9.–14. Jahrhundert', in *La formation et le développement des metiers au moyen âge (5e–14e siècles)*, ed. László Gerevich (Budapest, 1977), 85–94; Miklós Takács, 'Handwerkliche Produktion in den dörflichen Siedlungen im árpádenzeitlichen Ungarn (10.–13. Jahrhundert)', in *Arts and Crafts in Medieval Rural Environment*, ed. Jan Klápště and Petr Sommer *Ruralia* 6 (Turnhout, 2007), 53–70; Imre Takács, 'Opus duplex in der Goldschmiedekunst des 13. Jahrhunderts und die höfische Kultur', *Ars Decorativa* 26 (2008), 7–37.

[89] Károly Mesterházy, 'Der byzantinisch-balkanische Handel nach Ungarn im 10.–11. Jahrhundert im Spiegel der Gräberfunden', in *Byzance et ses voisins: mélanges à la mémoire de Gyula Moravcsik à l'occasion du centième anniversaire de sa naissance*, ed. Terézia Olajos (Szeged, 1994), 117–28; Kubinyi *et al.*, eds., *Gazdaság*, section 7.

the middle of the twelfth century on, kings both donated the right to collect tolls from certain markets and granted the right to hold markets to ecclesiastical institutions and lay lords. In this way, the *forum liberum* developed, where royal tolls were not collected.

Military roads formed the basis of trade and communication overland; one of them, leading to Fehérvár, is recorded in the first vernacular phrase included in a charter from 1055. Such roads connected the seats of *ispán*s. From the twelfth century on, records show that rivers were used to transport merchandise. Tolls were erected on the roads and next to river crossings. Kings began to donate the right to revenues from these to lords beginning in the middle of the twelfth century. By the end of the century, communities increasingly sought to receive royal exemptions from tolls, and early thirteenth-century examples of such exemptions abound, concerning Cistercians, Templars, *hospes* communities and individuals. Most of these exemptions were partial, that is, for a certain territory or from certain named tolls.[90]

Early urbanization was linked to centres of the ruler's power. Two cores, the residence of the ruler and suburbs of merchants and artisans, characterized the earliest towns. Unlike Prague and Cracow, which were important trade centres, no such town appeared in Hungary in the eleventh and twelfth centuries. Two towns served as the principal seats of the ruler, Esztergom and Fehérvár, which early on had suburbs of artisans and, from the middle of the twelfth century, a quarter inhabited by *Latini*. In addition, episcopal centres also developed into centres of trade, in many cases with *Latini* settlers. The *hospes* status of foreign merchants evolved into privileges of autonomy for the communities of western settlers. *Latini* especially contributed to urbanization in the kingdom: their privileges became the basis of town law.[91]

The end of the eleventh and beginning of the twelfth century represented a turning point, when private landed estates consolidated, although not in the territory of the entire realm: large uninhabited

[90] Boglárka Weisz, 'Vásártartás az Árpád-korban', *Századok* 141 (2007), 879–942; Weisz, 'A vásár és a vám Árpád-kori törvényeinkben', in *Tanulmányok a középkorról: a II. Medievisztikai PhD-konferencia, Szeged, 2001. április 3., előadásai*, ed. Boglárka Weisz, László Balogh and József Szarka (Szeged, 2001), 169–92.

[91] Erik Fügedi, 'Die Entstehung des Städtewesens in Ungarn', in Fügedi, *Kings, Bishops*, 101–18; Gerevich, ed., *Towns in Medieval Hungary*.

areas, as well as free land and freemen not subject to any lord, continued to exist. Most of the period was characterized by an autarchic economy with minimal internal trade. The towns of this period were above all royal and ecclesiastical centres of power. Another major transformation started during the reign of Béla III, and culminated in the middle of the thirteenth century, consisting of the growth of trade and monetization, and urbanization, as well as the growth of the nobility's political power.

# 6

# ECCLESIASTICAL HISTORY, ELEVENTH–THIRTEENTH CENTURIES

While Byzantine influence played a role, especially in Bohemia and Hungary, it was the Latin Church which mainly came to define ecclesiastical life. Ecclesiastical institutions developed, albeit at varying rates, in all three polities. By the thirteenth century, adoption and adaptation from western Europe were complemented by local ecclesiastical initiatives.

## CATHOLIC (LATIN) AND ORTHODOX (GREEK) CHRISTIANITY

While the newly Christianized lands became part of Latin Christendom, Byzantine influences were not negligible in Bohemia and Hungary and reached Poland in the early period, although such influences were fading at the latest by the thirteenth century.

Still open for debate is the extent to which the Great Moravian Slavonic legacy persisted within the Bohemian Church, for evidence is scarce. The first Bohemian church, founded in Levý Hradec, was dedicated to St Clement.[1] Later, other churches in ducal strongholds shared this dedication. This indicates that Clement's cult remained significant during the tenth and eleventh centuries; it is even claimed that his relics were once brought from the Black Sea area by St Constantine/Cyril and St Methodius. We also find evidence for the

[1] *Legenda Christiani*, chap. 2.

use of Slavonic script,[2] although no proof for the use of double liturgy. There are no sources to indicate how far the Slavonic liturgy was used after it was forbidden in 885 by Pope Stephen V.[3] The ban was repeated in 968.[4] However, it is telling that in 1080 King Vratislav II sent a plea to the Roman Curia asking that the use of Slavonic liturgy be permitted; the request was declined.[5] This appeal could have been made in an attempt to save a still-functioning 'Slavonic' Benedictine monastery founded in 1032 at Sázava near Prague.[6]

The influence of the Orthodox Church was felt along the eastern periphery of Piast Poland, in particular the south-eastern frontier (the eastern edge of Lesser Poland), which was conquered by Grand Duke Vladimir the Great in 981. Because of a lack of written sources, studying the penetration of eastern religious ideas must be based mainly on archaeological data. The zone of influence for eastern Christianity is generally indicated by finds of small pendant crosses with rounded extremities; some are of the type called *encolpia*, made of two folding halves, which were used by the adherents of the Orthodox Church. Their spread along the eastern frontier zone from the eleventh to the thirteenth centuries may be used to map the area of the indirect influence of Orthodox Christian culture. The crosses were mostly imported from the east but some of them were made in south-eastern Poland.[7] The same may be said about small crosses made by the pseudo-filigree technique, which include circular pendants with in-built crosses, crosses decorated with enamel and

[2] J. M. Clifton-Everest, 'Slavisches Schrifttum im 10. und 11. Jahrhundert in Böhmen', *Bohemia* 37 (1996), 257–70; Z. Hauptová, 'Církevněslovanské písemnictví v přemyslovských Čechách', in *Jazyk a literatura v historické perspektivě'* (Ústí nad Labem, 1998), 5–42.

[3] Letter of Pope Stephen V to Svatopluk in 885, in *CDB* I, no. 26, p. 23: 'Stephanus episcopus, servus servorum dei, Zuentopoco regi Sclavorum'.

[4] Cosmas I.22.

[5] *CDB* I, 88, no. 81; for discussion, see V. Novotný, 'Vratislav II. a slovanská liturgie', *Časopis pro moderní filologii* 2 (1912), 289–390.

[6] J. Kadlec, *Svatý Prokop* (Rome, 1968); K. Reichertová, E. Bláhová, V. Dvořáčková and V. Huňáček, eds., *Sázava* (Prague, 1988); P. Sommer, *Svatý Prokop: z počatků českého státu a církve* (Prague, 2007).

[7] Marcin Wołoszyn, 'Bizantyńskie i ruskie zabytki o charakterze sakralnym z Polski – wybrane przykłady', in *Człowiek, sacrum, środowisko miejsca kultu we wczesnym średniowieczu*, ed. S. Moździoch (Wrocław, 2000), 243.

small rectangular icons made of soft stones. Finds of these items are concentrated along the eastern border of medieval Poland.[8]

The Orthodox Church tolerated burial under mounds until the beginning of the thirteenth century; thus its area of dominance may be identified archaeologically from the eleventh century onwards. Mapping the extent of Christian mound burials reveals a zone along the Bug River, which was under more or less direct control by Rus' until the second half of the fourteenth century. This area had no parish church network. In the south-eastern periphery of the Piast domain, the influence of the Orthodox Church was supported by Rus' dukes. At the beginning of the twelfth century, Volodar Rostislavich, duke of Přemysl (1092 or 1097–1124), founded an Orthodox church on Castle Hill in that town, where there had earlier stood a *palatium* with chapel annex built by Bolesław the Brave. The high stone tower containing a chapel on its upper floor, still standing in Stołpie, near Chełm, is dated to the late twelfth century. According to one hypothesis, it is reminiscent of monasteries from the Balkans built at similar high points.[9]

In Hungary, Byzantine ecclesiastical influences were most notably manifest in the 'bishopric of Tourkia', whose bishops existed throughout the eleventh century, although we do not know the extent of their real authority (see Chapter 3), in Greek monasticism, possibly in the adoption of saints and religious practices, and in the presence of Greek texts, all discussed below. The Byzantine orientation of some early chieftains (Chapter 3) was not the only channel for influences; political ties to Rus' and Byzantium, the conversion of András I in Kiev and marriage to a Rus' princess and Béla III's ties to Byzantium provided continued means for ecclesiastical influence as well. A significant example of this is the so-called double cross (the two-barred variant of the cross, used in the Orthodox Church), which was used in royal heraldry, and became part of the Hungarian coat of arms. Although Hungarian interest in this form of representation may go back to the relic of the true cross István I received from the Byzantine emperor Basileos II, its documented use on the coat of arms, represented on coins, started around 1190, during the reign of Béla III, whose strong ties to Byzantium were discussed in Chapter 4. We only have glimpses of possible intellectual connections: for example, around 1190, Jób, the archbishop of Esztergom, corresponded in

[8] Map, fig. 7, Wołoszyn, 'Bizantyńskie'.

[9] Andrzej Buko, *Stołpie: tajemnica kamiennej wieży* (Warsaw, 2009).

Greek with Isaac Angelos II about doctrine. The extent of Byzantine ecclesiastical influence, however, is debated. Only one Greek charter survives, but is that due to the fact that the Greek language never became significant in Hungarian ecclesiastical life, or due to the proportionally greater later destruction of documents, once Hungary no longer belonged to the Orthodox ecclesiastical sphere and there was no reason to retain such texts? Were continued Byzantine references to an (Orthodox) archbishopric of Tourkia until the late twelfth century expressions of reality, or of a Byzantine legal claim upheld despite being unconnected to a continued existence of the archbishopric itself?[10]

## CONTINUED CHRISTIANIZATION

The implantation of an ecclesiastical organization was not the only challenge in the eleventh century. Continued missionary work among large numbers of people, some living in places that were difficult to access or in distant regions, and Christian legislation were to ensure the Christianization of the local populations. Traditions rooted in the pre-Christian past may have been more meaningful than new Christian solidarities for some communities.

[10] For the various aspects of Byzantine influence, see Moravcsik, *Byzantium and the Magyars*; Gyula Moravcsik, 'The role of the Byzantine Church in medieval Hungary', *American Slavic and East European Review* 6, 3/4 (1947), 134–51; Moravcsik, 'Byzance et le christianisme hongrois du moyen âge', *Corso di Cultura sull'Arte Ravennate e Bizantina* 16 (1969), 313–41; Alexander Szentirmai, 'Der Einfluss des byzantinischen Kirchenrechts auf die Gesetzgebung Ungarns im XI.–XII. Jahrhundert', *Jahrbuch der österreichischen byzantinischen Gesellschaft* 10 (1961), 73–84; Moravcsik, *Die byzantinische Kultur und das mittelalterliche Ungarn* (Berlin, 1956); Zsuzsa Lovag, 'Byzantinische Beziehungen in Ungarn nach der Staatsgründung. Archäologische Forschungen zwischen 1970 und 1984', *Mitteilungen des Archäologischen Instituts der Ungarischen Akademie der Wissenschaften* 14 (1985), 225–33; Nicolas A. Oikonomidès, 'À propos des relations ecclésiastiques entre Byzance et la Hongrie au XIe siècle: le métropolite de Turquie', in Oikonomidès, *Documents et études sur les institutions de Byzance (VIIe–XVe s.)* (London, 1976), no. XX, 527–33; Baán, 'The metropolitanate of Tourkia'; Jean Pierre Ripoche, 'Byzance et son art en Hongrie médiévale', *Byzantinische Forschungen* 6 (1979), 167–84; Gergely Kiss, 'Les influences de l'Église orthodoxe en Hongrie aux Xe–XIIIe siècles', *Specimina Nova Pars Prima Sectio Mediaevalis* 4 (2007), 51–71; István Kapitánffy, *Hungarobyzantina: Bizánc és a görögség középkori magyarországi forrásokban* (Budapest, 2003). On Hungarian–Rus' contact, see Font, *Árpád-házi királyok* (for András, see 130).

## *Bohemia*

This was not so problematic in Bohemia, which was relatively small and had been subject to increasing Christian influence from the early ninth century, both from the Bavarian west and the Moravian east. From as early as the later eighth century, the burning of dead bodies was gradually replaced by rites of inhumation. This process should not be ascribed only to the spread of Christianity, but also as part of a more general turn to burial rites, observed across large areas of central Europe.[11] This explains why some skeletons were still buried under mounds in the tenth century.[12] Moreover, elements of earlier burial customs were still observed, even at the sacral and administrative centres of the Přemyslids. In the stronghold of Stará Boleslav, where one of the oldest churches in Bohemia was built at the beginning of the tenth century, until the middle of the eleventh century graves of its inhabitants were placed outside the fortified, permanently inhabited area, and provided with humble personal jewellery characteristic of the pre-Christian period, without any elements suggesting the conversion of those buried. No earlier than the end of the eleventh century, a larger number of inhumations *ad ecclesiam* appeared, and they became predominant in the next century.[13] Evidence for heathen practices was identified in the cemetery of the ducal warriors at the Gardens of Lumbe, located within the northern bailey of Prague Castle.[14] This phenomenon is also well attested by grave gifts of animal bones and eggshells, as well as trunk (dugout) coffins, which were excavated in the graves of members of the ruling dynasty who were buried during the tenth and eleventh centuries at Prague's Castle Hill.[15]

[11] Ivo Štefan, 'Zmìna pohøebniho ritu v raném stødovìku jako archeologický a kulturnì-antropologický problem', *Archeologicke Rozhledy* 59 (2007), 805–36.

[12] M. Lutovský, 'Frühmittelalterliche Hügelgräber in Südböhmen', in *Archäologische Arbeitsgemeinschaft Ostbayern/West- und Südböhmen* 8 (Treffen and Rahden/Westf., 1999), 173–82.

[13] Ivana Boháčová, 'Christianizace české společnosti a vznik významných sakrálních center (příklad Staré Boleslavi)', in *Kościół w monarchiach Przemyślidów i Piastów*, ed. Józef Dobosz (Poznań, 2009), 90, 95–6.

[14] Z. Smetánka, L. Hrdlička and M. Bajerová, 'Výzkum slovanského pohřebiště za Jízdárnou na Pražském hradě', *Archeologické rozhledy* 25 (1973), 265–70; also Zdeněk Smetánka, Ladislav Hrdlička and Miroslava Blajerová, 'Výzkum slovanského pohřebiště za Jízdárnou Pražského hradu v roce 1973', *Archeologické rozhledy* 26 (1974), 386–405, 433–8.

[15] I. Borkovský, *Svatojiřská basilika a klášter na Pražském hradě* (Prague, 1975), 22–4.

In the countryside, so-called row-cemeteries were replaced in the late eleventh century by graveyards located on consecrated ground surrounding churches or chapels characterized by the orientation of heads to the west and no grave goods. However, even in places that were under the direct surveillance of a priest, some elements of pagan practice survived, often in the form of an '*obol* for the dead' (a coin placed in the grave) or in practices apparently aimed at combating vampires (such as displacing the head of a dead person).[16]

Archaeologists claim to have found material evidence for funerary feasts at Christian cemeteries.[17] The Přemyslid dukes repeatedly prohibited non-Christian practices such as burying dead bodies outside consecrated cemeteries or holding wild night-time wakes for the dead. From a Bohemian perspective, the translation of Vojtěch-Adalbert's relics to Prague (1038/9) may have been seen as an attempt to reconcile Bohemia with its martyred fellow countryman who twice escaped from the diocese on account of a lack of Christian morality, tolerated at the time by Duke Boleslav II.[18] Therefore, according to Cosmas, Břetislav I wished to impose the observance of key Christian regulations: polygamous or non-canonical marriages and divorces were forbidden; adultery and abortion would be punished by enslavement and the selling of the accused persons at the Hungarian market; accusations of murder and marital abuses would be decided by ordeal; beer-selling taverns were to be shut down; work and market trading were to be forbidden on Sundays and holy days; drunkards would be imprisoned until they paid the duke 300 coins; and the burying of dead bodies outside 'the cemeteries of the faithful' was prohibited.[19] Although this decree is not confirmed by any other source, Cosmas of Prague, quoting edicts apparently issued by Břetislav I (1039) and Břetislav II (1092), still considered Bohemians to be 'half-Christians' in the early twelfth century.[20]

The chronicler could describe in this way not only peasants with their continued observance of traditional forms of cults of natural powers, but also Christian clergy resistant to the recommendations

[16] Z. Krumphanzlová, 'Der Ritus der slawischen Skelettfriedhöfe der mittleren und jüngeren Burgwallzeit in Böhmen', *Památky archeologické* 57 (1966), 277–327.

[17] P. Sommer, 'Heidnische und christliche Normen im Konflikt. Die Vorstellungswelt der böhmischen Gesellschaft im frühen Mittelalter', in *Prozesse der Normbildung und Normveränderung im mittelalterlichen Europa*, ed. D. Ruhe and K.-H. Spieß (Stuttgart, 2000), 162–3, 172–3.

[18] Vita I, 12; Vita II, 11. [19] Cosmas II.4. [20] Cosmas II.4 and III.1.

of papal envoys (see below) and secular elites promoting a social ethos deeply rooted in pre-Christian realities. Especially the latter problem was the subject of intensive attention by Czech clergy. The tenth-century historiography (*Legenda Christiani*) tended clearly towards proposing Christian models of elite behaviour, including especially members of the Přemyslid dynasty.[21] A Czech medievalist has suggested that, despite their obvious Christian character in the literary sources, St Václav and Ludmila had so many features of mighty, divine and pagan persons that they might easily be treated not as historical rulers but as mythical, pagan deities.[22] Although this theory was heavily criticized, the main problem was acknowledged: the ideological image of Přemyslid power, their ducal charisma, in the tenth and eleventh centuries bore a resemblance to what we know about pagan rulers' ideology in different regions of early medieval Europe, including Sweden and Ireland. Cosmas's chronicle may be seen as an attempt at Christianization of the complex of stories organizing a ruler's image among Czech elites at the beginning of the twelfth century. Historians pointed out elements of this pre-Christian concept of power: a strong connection between a ruler and the fertility of nature under his rule; the important role of a woman – both as the founder of the ruling dynasty and as a prophet (Libuše: see above), a distant echo of a goddess corroborating a ruler's power; a horse as a tool of divination during an enthronement ritual; the bipolar system of central places – Vyšehrad as a sacral centre connected with pagan rituals of enthronement and Prague as an administrative centre. These elements were transformed by Cosmas in his chronicle in order to 'Christianize' the past of the ruling dynasty. Writing down stories about the Přemyslids' beginnings as properly Christian in shape and meaning was an important element of the process of creation of the new power's ideology in the twelfth century. It comprised also a new, Christian ideology of Czech rulers built on the idea of a royal dignity and charisma derived from western culture.[23] Czech knights

[21] *Legenda Christiani*, chap. 2, on 'Peoples and dynasties'.

[22] Zaviš Kalandra, *České pohanství* (Prague, 1947).

[23] Vratislav Vaníček, 'Sakralita české panovnické hodnosti, dynastie Přemyslovců a Vyšehradu v proměnách Christianizace a středověké modernizace', in *Královský Vyšehrad*, vol. III, *Sborník příspěvků ze semináře 26.9.2006 Vyšehrad a Přemyslovci pořádaného Královskou Kolegiátní Kapitulou sv. Petra a Pavla na Vyšehradě a Archeologickým ústavem AV ČR* (Prague, 2007), 20–37.

treated suspiciously rulers' attempts to change traditional ideas about power. The new prevailed but no earlier than in the middle of the twelfth century.[24]

Archaeological finds suggested that, although elites of Bohemia became Christian in the sense of the word accepted by the Roman Church between the second half of the ninth and the twelfth century, the Christianization of the countryside took much longer and even lasted into the modern era.[25] Nevertheless, some research has suggested, that the disappearance of the traditional practice of providing the dead with special gifts, the so-called *milodary*, observed during the twelfth century, can be treated as an indicator of progress in the Christianization of the Přemyslids' subjects of lower social rank. Apparently there was no Church legislation against this custom; its disappearance was a result of acculturation, which influenced a general change in burial practices.[26] The decisive role of the twelfth century for the Christianization of the countryside is also visible in ducal legislation. Although it is supposed that Břetislav I passed laws in 1039 against and penalties for practising magic, it is certain that Duke Břetislav II repeated them in 1092. There is evidence for such laws and enforcement of penalties against all who dared to deal with any kind of magic (among them, prophets and magicians had to be expelled from the country, and traditional forms of communications with the dead were prohibited), who practised pagan cults in forests or who buried the dead outside Christian cemeteries, especially in fields or woods.[27] After the twelfth century, although some of these practices survived, their popularity shrank visibly and there was no need for further administrative, ducal legislation against them. From the twelfth century Christianization carried on, but mostly as a process of continuing acculturation, and with the clergy rather than ducal officials being responsible for it.

[24] David Kalhous, *České země za prvních Přemyslovců v 10.–12. století* (Prague, 2011), 104–23.

[25] Josef Unger, 'Odraz christianizace Moravy v archeologických pramenech', in *Christianizace českých zemí ve středoevropské perspective*, ed. Jiří Hanuš, Matice moravská. Země a kultura ve střední Evropě, 19 (Brno, 2011), 19–71.

[26] Pavlína Mašková, 'K obrazu středověkého pohřebiště – cirkevní normy a výpověď' archeologických pramenů', in *Kościół w monarchiach*, 78.

[27] Cosmas III.1, p. 161.

## *Poland*

No cemeteries or even single burials in Poland indicate an acceptance of Christian eschatology before the late tenth century. After that, Christianization proceeded gradually and pre-Christian traditions persisted even in central areas. The connection of characteristic landscape formations to pagan hierophanies – elements of the environment believed to represent the sacred – posed a serious challenge to the Church because they were such important parts of collective identity at the local level. Therefore, some of these ideas were Christianized in order to maintain some control over their symbolic power. In most cases, condemnation and the placing of a cross proved sufficient. In some instances monasteries were built on the traditionally venerated mountains of Łysiec (in central Poland) and Ślęża (in Silesia) during the twelfth century.

Archaeological evidence for individual burial practices, as well as collective decisions taken over the localization and organization of cemeteries provide evidence for the process of Christianization. Helena Zoll-Adamikowa outlined how the penetration of Christianity into Poland varied enormously: some areas were nominally Christianized without the conversion of inhabitants; some were individually converted by single people; some areas underwent a 'temporary' Christianization that was halted due to the negligence of the clergy or mass resistance; and only certain regions experienced a formal, durable Christianization that led to the common acceptance of all the rules of the faith. According to this model, one should also distinguish between two different types of relevant ecclesiastical activity. An 'early' missionary stage was followed by a second effort, when the Church was supported by more effective administrative and coercive measures. No single chronology is suitable for the whole realm, and every area must be studied separately. Due to the scarcity of relevant written evidence, much of our knowledge is provided by archaeology.[28]

The practice of cremation, typical for early medieval Slavs, may serve as a useful indicator of how pagan death rituals survived in some areas of Poland, while the growing acceptance of Christian

[28] H. Zoll-Adamikowa, 'Zum Beginn der Körperbestattung bei den Westslawen', in *Rom und Byzanz im Norden*, vol. II, 227–38; 'Postępy chrystianizacji Słowian przed rokiem 1000', in *Święty Wojciech i jego czasy*, ed. A. Żaki (Cracow, 2000), 104.

eschatology is proven elsewhere by the disappearance of cremation graves and grave-mounds; the east–west orientation of bodies; a reduction in grave goods; the location of cemeteries near churches; and a series of changes to the arrangement of arms – having once been laid straight at the sides, they became crossed over the pelvis and, finally, crossed over the chest.[29]

Both 'nominal' and 'temporary' Christianization, as well as missionary activity, could be indicated by the parallel appearance of inhumation alongside cremation, flat graves alongside grave-mounds, and the east–west orientation of skeletons. Formal Christianization resulted in the introduction of so-called village or row-cemeteries, which involved only skeleton burials but could still retain pagan elements such as grave-mounds, an orientation other than east–west and numerous grave goods. Elevated sites were typically preferred for these cemeteries, although not at the same locations where earlier pagan necropolises had been situated.[30] Only after a period of between 150 and 200 years after Mieszko's baptism do the concentration of all burials around churches and lack of grave goods demonstrate that the Church had gained full control over the burial rites of the local populations. The process was faster around the ecclesiastical-political centres and slower in marginal areas. In general, the 'real Christianization' of Poland began some time before the middle of the twelfth century with the development of a network of parish churches and monasteries.[31]

The Christianization of less accessible areas and peripheries was much slower. In these regions, a syncretism of Christian and pagan elements seems to have survived: various orientations of the skeletons; partially burned skeletons; cemeteries with evidence for both cremation and inhumation burials; special objects placed into the graves, such as amulets made of animal teeth, coins and half-moon pendants; and mutilation of dead bodies. From the eleventh to the twelfth centuries, pagan amulets were still popularly in use while cemeteries in north-eastern

[29] An exception must be made for a narrow zone in the east which came under the influence of the Orthodox Church and which tolerated barrow graves until the twelfth century.

[30] H. Zoll-Adamikowa, 'Usytuowanie cmentarzy Słowian w środowisku (doba pogańska i pierwsze wieki po przyjeciu chrześcijaństwa)', in, *Człowiek, sacrum, środowisko: miejsca kultu we wczesnym średniowieczu*, ed. S. Moździoch (Wrocław, 2000), 217.

[31] Zoll-Adamikowa, 'Zum Beginn', 233.

Poland contained necklaces made of several crosses.[32] In eastern Poland, the openly pagan cremation ritual survived locally until the thirteenth century.[33]

According to Thietmar's chronicle, Bolesław the Brave acted cruelly against sinners: those who did not observe compulsory fasts had their teeth knocked out while men found guilty of adultery had their testicles nailed to a bridge.[34] Even if there is a basis in historical fact, such measures directed in the main towards members of the higher classes could not effect change among the masses.

Therefore, the Polish duke sent several envoys to Rome asking for missionaries to teach the population.[35] In 1001, Otto III sent two Benedictine monks – John and Benedict – from the monastery in Pereum, near Ravenna.[36] With Boleslav's help they built a hermit's monastery in *Meserici* (Międzyrzecz?) in 1002 (?), where they were joined by three local devotees, Isaac, Matthew and Christinus.[37] In 1002 the missionary archbishop Bruno of Querfurt was ordained in Rome and sent to Poland in order to lead the work, although because of obstacles raised by the German king, Henry II, Bruno reached his destination only in 1007/8.[38] In the meantime, his five fellow Benedictine brothers in Poland were killed in an attempted robbery in 1003. Bishop Unger of Poznań pronounced them martyrs and buried them in Gniezno. After Archbishop Bruno arrived in Poland, he wrote a highly emotional commemorative text known as the *Vita quinque fratrum*. Bruno appreciated Bolesław's engagement in missionary work, leading him to reproach Henry II for employing 'diabolical pagans' (the Polabian Liutizi) in his conflict with the Polish Christian ruler.[39] New pagan areas came under Polish rule

[32] D. Krasnodębski, 'Średniowieczni mieszkańcy pogranicza', in *Gazociąg pełen skarbów archeologicznych*, ed. M. Chłodniki and L. Krzyżaniak (Poznań, 1998), 96, figs. 134 and 135.

[33] J. Kalaga, *Ciałopalny obrządek pogrzebowy w międzyrzeczu Liwca, Bugu i Krzny* (Warsaw, 2006), 186.

[34] Thietmar of Merseburg VIII.2.

[35] *Vita quinque fratrum eremitarum [seu] Vita uel passio Benedicti et Iohannis sociorumque suorum auctore Brunone Quesrfurtensi*, ed. Jadwiga Karwasińska, MPH s.n., 4/3 (Warsaw, 1973), chap. 12–13, 21.

[36] *Vita quinque fratrum*, chap. 2; *Petri Damiani Vita Beati Romualdi*, ed. Giovanni Tabacco (Rome, 1957) (henceforth Peter Damian), chap. 28.

[37] *Vita quinque fratrum*, chap. 13.

[38] Thietmar of Merseburg VI.94–5.

[39] Bruno of Querfurt, 85–106.

through conquest in the north in the first half of the twelfth century. Supported by Duke Bolesław III the Wrymouth, Bishop Otto of Bamberg sucessfully Christianized Pomerania between 1124 and 1128 (see Chapters 3–4).

## *Hungary*

Extensive legislation produced during the second half of the eleventh and early twelfth centuries aimed at ensuring the Christianization of Hungary's population, adding to and modifying István's laws (see Chapter 3). Basic demands were formulated and outward conformity to prescribed Christian behaviour was required. The legislation emphasized punishments for the infringement of prescriptions. The eradication of 'pagan' religious rituals preoccupied legislators until the twelfth century. According to the synod of Szabolcs (1092), those who made sacrifices next to wells or made offerings to trees, springs or stones according to pagan custom had to pay an ox as a penalty.[40] The synod of Esztergom (according to the majority of scholars, early twelfth century, but according to others, predating the synod of Szabolcs) punished the observation of pagan rites according to social status. High-ranking people (*maiores*) were to do penance for forty days; commoners (*minores*) for seven days but were also to be flogged.[41] Those in contact with the supernatural outside the bounds of the Christian Church – *strigae* (form-changing witches or vampires), *malefici* (practitioners of black magic) – were explicitly targeted, although their punishment changed over time.[42]

The new Christians had to contribute to the construction of churches, pay the tithe, observe feastdays and fasts, make a deathbed confession and attend church on Sundays.[43] Those guarding the fire were allowed to stay at home, and the synod of Szabolcs also allowed villages that were too far away from the church to send just one representative per village. Yet this was not intended to provide an escape from obligations of attendance: villagers who abandoned their church were to be compelled to return. Another synod imposed a fine

40 Bak *et al.*, eds., *Laws*, 58, c. 22; Géza Érszegi, 'The emergence of the Hungarian state, the adoption and consolidation of Christianity (970–1095)', in *A Thousand Years of Christianity in Hungary*, ed. István Zombori *et al.* (Budapest, 2001), 25–36.

41 Bak *et al.*, eds., *Laws*, 62, c. 7.

42 *Ibid.*, 8, c. 33–4; 60, c. 34; 30, c. 57 and c. 60; 65, c. 49.

43 *Ibid.*, 3, c. 8–13; 10, c. 1; 11, c. 20; 57, c. 11–12; 58, c. 15–16; 59, c. 25, c. 30; 60, c. 37–38; 61, c. 40; 62, c. 8; 67, c. 87.

on villages that tried to move to a different location.[44] The synod of Esztergom prescribed punishments for relatives and village elders of the dying for the omission of deathbed confession.[45] Beginning with the late eleventh-century synod of Szabolcs and the early twelfth-century laws of Kálmán, there was an insistence on the burial of Christians in churchyards.[46] Christian burial was denied to those who died excommunicated. The dogs and horses of those out hunting on Sundays, and the horses of those visiting markets (which in any case were prohibited on Sundays), were to be confiscated. If the offenders out hunting were priests, they were to be suspended.[47] The synod of Szabolcs decreed that non-observance of Sundays, feastdays or fasts was punishable by fasting at the pillory.[48] Another canon incorporated into the textual tradition of the synod of Esztergom prescribed penance for freemen and flogging for the unfree for not celebrating compulsory feastdays.[49] The synod of Esztergom was the first to introduce more detailed regulations concerning the teaching of the content of the new religion: it defined the material to be explained to the people on Sundays (the Gospel, Epistle and Creed, but in lesser churches only the Creed and the Lord's Prayer); and prescribed confession and communion at Easter, Pentecost and Christmas.[50]

The prologue of the law of King Kálmán contradicts the synodal legislation of the period. It includes a lengthy argument concerning the complete Christianization of the population.[51] Alberich, who may have been a monk, compiled the text of the legislation passed at the council of Tarcal, in the early years of King Kálmán's reign, at the end of the eleventh or beginning of the twelfth century, at the request of the archbishop of Esztergom, Seraphin (*c.* 1095–1104). He compares István I's legislation in the context of conditions in the past with his own times and Kálmán's legislation as a reflection of contemporary conditions. During István's reign, coercion was central, because Christianity was fragile. People had to be forced to obey Christian precepts and they resisted. By the time of King Kálmán, however, piety and even a willingness to die for the faith characterized Hungary's population.

Ecclesiastical legislation insisted on Christian burial, and therefore cemeteries developed around churches. This process has been

[44] *Ibid.*, 57, c. 11; 58, c. 19; 67, c. 85. [45] *Ibid.*, 62, c. 10.
[46] *Ibid.*, 31, c. 73; 59, c. 25. [47] *Ibid.*, 57, c. 12; 58, c. 15–16. [48] *Ibid.*, 59, c. 25.
[49] *Ibid.*, 67, c. 87. [50] *Ibid.*, 62, c. 2–3. [51] *Ibid.*, 24–6.

analysed on the basis of archaeological excavations. Pagan cemeteries continued to exist, proven by finds of coins of László I and Kálmán in them. Christian cemeteries around churches started to be established during the eleventh century and at the latest by the twelfth, and some were used until the modern period. A number of them were set up on top of pre-Christian burials. But while in towns burials by the twelfth century centred around churches, graveyards not associated to churches continued until the early thirteenth century in some villages. The process of transition from pagan to Christian graveyard is debated, revolving around the classification of tenth- and eleventh-century row-cemeteries: whether they were pagan, Christian or started as pagan and were then turned into Christian cemeteries. Grave finds in Christian cemeteries mostly comprise jewellery (rings, hair-rings, etc.) and other ornamental pieces. Some graves contained coins – these had disappeared from some cemeteries already in the eleventh century, while they were included in others even in the thirteenth – understood as the obol for the dead, placed in the mouth or hands or on the body. Certain grave goods such as sharp iron objects (e.g. knives) and eggs have been interpreted as signs of traditional beliefs. Bodies were mostly buried on their back, with the hands parallel to the body or across the lap, but other forms, such as with arms crossed and hands resting on the shoulders, also occurred. Coffins were in use, but not in all graves; dead bodies could also be wrapped in cloth instead, and brick graves occurred frequently in some cemeteries.[52]

## ECCLESIASTICAL INSTITUTIONAL STRUCTURES

In all three realms, the first Christianizing rulers introduced ecclesiastical institutions and structures into their territories. Bishoprics were the first to be founded, accompanied by the building of churches. Strong royal involvement in the foundation of ecclesiastical institutions, and their use in the administration of the realm, was

[52] *Ibid.*, p. 31, c. 73; p. 59, c. 25; Ágnes Ritoók and Erika Simonyi, eds., '*. . . a halál árnyékának völgyében járok': a középkori templomok körüli temetők kutatása* (Budapest, 2005) (with English summaries); Mariann Bálint, József Laszlovszky, Beatrix Romhányi and Miklós Takács, 'Medieval villages and their fields', in Visy, ed., *Hungarian Archaeology*, 383–8 (here 386); N. Berend *et al.*, 'The kingdom of Hungary', 338–9.

characteristic of central Europe for the greater part of the first Christian centuries.

## Dioceses

Whereas Hungary and Poland each received their own independent archbishopric (Esztergom and Gniezno) in 1000–1, the founding of an independent archbishopric in Bohemia took place only in 1344, despite recurrent efforts to create one from the eleventh century. Until then, the bishopric of Prague was a suffragan of the archbishopric of Mainz. Although an independent archbishopric was clearly desirable for rulers, its lack did not prevent them from exercising power.

### *Bohemia*

Following its establishment in 967, the Prague diocese formed a part of the archbishopric of Mainz. Although documentary sources are lacking, the former Moravian (arch)bishopric seems to have ceased to operate in the early tenth century; certainly no evidence suggests its reappearance before the second half of the eleventh century. The often-cited letter of Pope John XIII to Boleslav I, which mentions a Moravian bishop in 967, appears only in an unreliable twelfth-century passage from Cosmas of Prague, who praised the activity of the duke's daughter, Mlada-Maria.[53]

Bohemia entered the eleventh century with a well-developed ecclesiastical organization, but one that remained subordinate to the German Church. In 997 Boleslav II appointed as bishop a German monk Thiadag/Dydak, who had previously served the court as a doctor. Despite Thietmar's critical stance,[54] Thiadag remained in his diocese for the next twenty years, serving six occupants on the Prague throne. Břetislav I's sack of Gniezno, his transfer of its relics to Prague and his attempt to punish sinners through legislation (1038/9) may also be interpreted as part of his failed strategy to acquire his own ecclesiastical province, requiring reconciliation with St Vojtěch-Adalbert.[55] Vratislav II restored the Moravian diocese with its centre in Olomouc in 1063, which led to a prolonged conflict with the bishop of Prague (see below).

[53] Cosmas I.22. [54] Thietmar of Merseburg VII.56–8.
[55] Krzemieńska, *Břetislav I*, 188–229.

*Poland*

The territorial organization of the Polish Church province coincided with the establishment of the archdiocese in 1000. Poppo of Cracow, Jan of Wrocław and Reinbern of Kołobrzeg were placed under Archbishop Radim-Gaudentius.[56] Bishop Unger of Poznań maintained an independent position. Arrested in 1004 by Henry II on his way to Rome, Unger was likely forced to submit to the archbishop of Magdeburg; this would have lasted until his death in 1012–13, at which point the Poznań bishopric was subordinated to Gniezno. The three peripheral bishoprics in Cracow, Wrocław and Kołobrzeg may not have had precise boundaries until the late eleventh century. Nevertheless, they probably covered the so-called *pertinentia* of the Piast state: Lesser Poland in the south-east, Silesia in the south and Pomerania in the north.[57] We do not know whether the early bishops came from abroad or were ordained from among the active clergy.

The position of the first archbishop in the Piast realm is unclear. A hundred years later, Gallus Anonymous mentioned Archbishop Radim-Gaudentius laying an anathema on Poland. This, however, has no confirmation in contemporary sources. More importantly, these sources are also silent concerning the archbishopric's metropolitan status. Even Bruno of Querfurt, who knew Radim-Gaudentius personally and wrote several important texts in Poland in 1008–9, does not mention the archbishopric or the archbishop at all. At the same time, he referred to the elderly Bishop Unger as *episcopus terrae*.[58] Polish sources substituted for Radim in the tradition of the Polish Church his brother, St Vojtěch-Adalbert, who was seen to be the founder of the Gniezno archbishopric. Thus, without the direct testimony of Thietmar of Merseburg, the establishment of Radim as the first archbishop of Gniezno could easily have passed unnoticed by historians. According to some historians, this collective amnesia on the part of the Polish Church implies an attempt to disguise uncertainty within the early history of the ecclesiastical province. Others explain this absence of knowledge in the context of disappearance of the Polish Church organization and almost all its institutions after the rebellion and Bretislav I's raid in 1038–9. If the bishoprics and

[56] Thietmar of Merseburg IV.45.

[57] Gerard Labuda, *Studia nad początkami państwa polskiego*, vol. II (Poznań, 1988), 474–510.

[58] *Vita quinque fratrum*, 30.

archbishoprics served as points and archives of a collective memory, their content vanished when the organization collapsed. The only place where detailed information about the deep past remained was Cracow, the bishopric which remained untouched by the events of 1038/9.

The three bishoprics probably concentrated on missionary activity. Most challenging of all was the situation in Pomerania, where Polish sovereignty was more of an aspiration than a reality. Bishop Reinbern began his work in Kołobrzeg with the destruction of some *fana idolorum* and the Christianization of the sea by throwing in stones sprinkled with holy oil.[59] The diocese must have quickly collapsed, because as early as 1003 Reinbern travelled with Boleslav the Brave to Prague,[60] and later to Kiev, where he died.[61] There are no further accounts concerning that Pomeranian bishopric.

After the crisis of the Polish Church (see Chapter 3), the rebuilding of ecclesiastical infrastructure was a prolonged process, not aided by the unstable political situation under Kazimierz the Restorer. The cathedral in Gniezno was only reconsecrated by his son, Bolesław II the Bold, in 1064. In 1075, Pope Gregory VII complained to the duke that there were not enough bishoprics in Poland and expressed his displeasure that the archbishopric was still not functioning.[62] Probably in the following year it was the archbishop of Gniezno who crowned Bolesław, yet the cathedral was again reconsecrated in 1097.[63] Other dioceses also recovered only gradually. The bishopric at Cracow was active again in 1046, or perhaps earlier, since Aaron, Benedictine

59 Thietmar of Merseburg VIII.72–3. 60 Thietmar of Merseburg VIII.10.

61 Thietmar of Merseburg VIII.72–3; see also comment by Stanisław Rosik, *Reinbern – Salsae Cholbergiensis aecclesiae episcopus*, in *Salsa Cholbergiensis. Kołobrzeg w średniowieczu*, ed. Lech Leciejewicz and Marian Rębkowski (Kołobrzeg, 2000), 85–93.

62 *List Grzegorza VII Papieża do Boesława Śmiałego roku 1075*, in *KDWp* I, no.4; MPH I, pp. 367–8.

63 *Rocznik kapituły krakowskiej*, ed. Zofia Kozłowska-Budkowa, in *Najdawniejsze roczniki krakowskie i kalendarz*, ed. Zofia Kozłowska-Budkowa, MPH s.n., 5 (Warsaw, 1978), 19–105 (here 48); *Vita sancti Stanislai cracoviensis episcopi (Vita maior)*, ed. Wojciech Kętrzyński, MPH, 4 (Lwów, 1884), 319–438 (here 383); Marek Derwich, 'Les fondations de monastères bénédictins en Pologne jusqu'au début du XVIe siècle', in *Moines et monastères dans les sociétés de rite grec et latin*, ed. Jean-Loup Lemaitre, Michel Dmitriev and Pierre Gonneau, École Pratique des Hautes Études, IVe Section, Sciences historiques et philologiques V, Hautes Études Médiévales et Modernes, 76 (Geneva, 1996), 49–69 (here 53).

abbot of the monastery of Tyniec, is mentioned in the Polish annals as the sole operational bishop in the whole of Poland for that year.[64] The episcopal see of Wrocław was destroyed by a pagan uprising during the 1030s, and bishops may have moved to other strongholds (local, Silesian medieval tradition indicates Smogorzewo or Ryczyn). A bishop came back to Wrocław only around 1050. The bishopric of Poznań ceased to function and appears to have been restored only by 1075/6. A new bishopric at Płock was established in 1075 by King Bolesław II for the province of Masovia.

At the very beginning of the following century, Władysław Herman reformed the organization of episcopal clergy. In episcopal sees he established groups of canons with their separate prebends and granted them the power to elect a candidate for the bishopric (who had to be accepted by the ruler). He and his wife Judith of Bavaria furnished bishoprics and the Benedictine abbey in Tyniec with several landed properties, men (and slaves) and revenues. In several cases the Church was granted jurisdiction over the peasants who lived in these lands.

Bolesław III reconquered pagan Pomerania during the second decade of the twelfth century. Its effective integration depended on a rapid process of conversion, but the Polish Church seemed ill prepared for missionary work on such a scale. In response, and with the aim of reinforcing the institution of the Church, the duke established a series of new northern bishoprics around 1124. Two of these, at Włocławek and Kruszwica, were founded in Kuyavia and merged in 1156, while the other was situated in Lubusz, on the river Oder. The latter was consecrated by a papal legate, Idzi (Eid) of Tusculum. Bolesław III also relied on foreign missionaries. After a failed attempt by the Spanish bishop Bernard in 1122, the Saxon bishop Otto of Bamberg was sent to Pomerania (see Chapter 3). The Polish ruler wished to set up a new bishopric at Wolin as a suffragan of Gniezno, but a diocese in Wolin was only granted in 1140, fifteen years after the region was officially Christianized, and was directly subordinate to the Holy See. It later moved to Kamień Pomorski on the opposite side of the Dziwna River.

64 E.g. *Rocznik Traski*, a. 1046; cf. Józef Dobosz, *Monarchia i możni wobec Kościoła w Polsce do początku XIII w.* (Poznań, 2002).

*Hungary*

The exact beginning of the introduction of episcopal organization in Hungary is debated. According to some historians, Géza founded the first bishopric, that of Veszprém. According to the majority opinion, however, although Géza may have had a missionary bishop permanently at his court (this hypothesis, not widely accepted, is based on a sole reference, by Thietmar of Merseburg, to Géza being upbraided by 'his priest'), the foundation of Veszprém, the first permanent bishopric, was the work of his son István, the first Christian king. Traditionally, historians credited István with the establishment of ten bishoprics, and argued that he fulfilled a conscious programme based on canon law, in order to create the ecclesiastical structure of an independent kingdom. It has now been shown that István founded bishoprics gradually, rather than according to a pseudo-Isidorian plan; and he did not establish all ten of the earliest ones. The early ecclesiastical structure was strongest in the lands west of the Danube, under the firm control of the dynasty, and extended only slowly, in parallel to territorial consolidation. Moreover, there was fluidity and change in the seats and extent of bishoprics, and in the alignment between archbishoprics and their suffragan dioceses. By the first years of the eleventh century, the bishoprics of Veszprém and Győr (some time before 1009) and the archbishopric of Esztergom (1001) were organized in the territories under the rule of the Árpáds. As István subjugated new areas, he also founded more bishoprics: Transylvania in perhaps 1003; in 1009 Pécs; according to some historians Eger and Kalocsa (others date the foundation of these two earlier in the eleventh century); and perhaps in 1030 Csanád (Cenad, Romania).[65]

[65] For a summary and a criticism of the view that Géza founded Veszprém, see Gyula Kristó, 'Géza fejedelem megítélése,' in Veszprémy, ed., *Szent István*, 369–80 (see 373, 378); László Koszta, 'Egyház- és államszervezés', in Gyula Kristó, *Államalapítás, társadalom, művelődés* (Budapest, 2001), 65–74; Koszta, 'L'organisation de l'Église chrétienne en Hongrie', in Csernus and Korompay, eds., *Les Hongrois et l'Europe*, 293–311; Koszta, 'State power and ecclesiastical system in eleventh-century Hungary (an outline to the dynamics of the development of Hungarian Christian Church)', in *Capitulum VI*, ed. István Petrovics, Sándor László Tóth and Eleanor A. Congdon (Szeged, 2010), 67–78; Gábor Thorockay, 'Szent István egyházmegyéi – Szent István püspökei', in Veszprémy, ed., *Szent István*, 482–94 (the English version is in Gábor Thorockay, 'The dioceses and bishops of Saint Stephen', in Zsoldos, ed., *Saint Stephen and His Country*,

The status of Kalocsa (from the thirteenth century Bács-Kalocsa) has been the subject of much debate, and the following interpretations all have advocates in recent scholarship. Some argue that Kalocsa was founded as an archbishopric without an ecclesiastical province, others that it was established as a bishopric and promoted later to archiepiscopal status. According to one view, it was a Byzantine archbishopric, according to another, a Latin titular archbishopric, without an ecclesiastical province initially, created in order to honour a prelate, Asericus (Astrik), who played a crucial role in early ecclesiastical organization.[66] It was certainly already an archbishopric in the middle of the eleventh century. Hartvic's story, the only narrative about the creation of the archbishopric of Kalocsa, cannot be taken as a factual description. According to him, Sebastian, archbishop of Esztergom, became blind and thus had to be replaced as prelate (by Asericus, the bishop of Kalocsa, who was elevated to the position of archbishop of Esztergom), but was subsequently healed and so restored to his see. Presumably not to offend Asericus, who had to return to his see of Kalocsa, he received a pallium from the pope, thus elevating Kalocsa to an archbishopric.[67]

With the territorial expansion and consolidation of royal power, István's successors founded more bishoprics and reorganized the existing ones: Vác (some historians argue for its foundation by István I, but more likely sometime between 1038 and 1075), around the middle of the eleventh century Bihar (modern Biharea, Romania, the seat of which was moved to Várad, modern Oradea, Romania, by László I after 1091), Zagreb (1080s) and *c.* 1100 Nitra (Hungarian Nyitra, today

49–68); Kristó, *Szent István*, 88–93; Gergely Kiss, 'A középkori magyar egyházszervezet kialakulása (10. század vége–12. század eleje)', *Magyar Egyháztörténeti Vázlatok/Essays in Church History in Hungary* (2009/1–4), 105–16; Tamás Fedeles, Gábor Sarbak and József Sümegi, eds., *A pécsi egyházmegye története I: a középkor évszázadai (1009–1543)* (Pécs, 2009); Tamás Fedeles and László Koszta, *Pécs (Fünfkirchen). Das Bistum und die Bischofsstadt im Mittelalter* (Vienna, 2011).

66 Kristó, *Szent István*, 91–2; István Baán, 'The foundation of the archbishopric of Kalocsa: the Byzantine origin of the second archdiocese in Hungary', in *Early Christianity in Central and East Europe*, ed. Przemysław Urbańczyk (Warsaw, 1997), 67–73; László Koszta, 'Esztergom és Kalocsa kapcsolata a 11–12. században (az egységes magyar egyháztartomány megosztása)', in *'Lux Pannoniae' Esztergom: az ezeréves kulturális metropolis* (Esztergom, 2001), 57–63; József Török, *A tizenegyedik század magyar egyháztörténete* (Budapest, 2002), 37, 131–8. See also the works listed in n. 10.

67 Bartoniek, ed., *Legenda S. Stephani regis ab Hartvico episcopo conscripta*, 416–17; Eng. tr., N. Berend, 'Hartvic', 385.

Slovakia). The foundation of several of these is not well attested and their exact dating is debated. Although by the end of the period all the bishoprics were subordinated as suffragans to one of the two archbishoprics, this was not the case from the beginning: Nitra, for example, functioned for almost a century as an independent bishopric before becoming a suffragan of Esztergom. The bishops of Transylvania, Csanád, Várad and Zagreb eventually became suffragans of Kalocsa. Croatian bishops were initially suffragans of Split, then from 1154 of Zadar. A late-twelfth-century list includes the purported revenues of the dioceses: those of Esztergom (6,000 marks), Eger (3,000) and Kalocsa (2,500) were the highest, those of Nitra, Zadar and Split (less than 500 marks) the lowest. It has been suggested that these sums vastly under-represent real revenues, perhaps to give misleading information to the papacy. Missionary bishoprics continued to be created parallel to the kingdom's (attempted or real) expansion: Bosnia from the late twelfth century, Srem from 1229, Nándorfehérvár (Beograd (Belgrade), Serbia) in the late thirteenth century, all suffragans of Kalocsa, and the short-lived Cuman bishopric (Chapter 7).[68]

## *Archdeaconries, canons and parishes*

In Bohemia 'archpresbytrii', also called 'archidiaconi', first appeared in the so-called Gniezno statutes, cited by Cosmas of Prague as decrees from 1038 by Duke Břetislav I for the Bohemian Church. According to this law 'archipresbyterii' had to co-operate with the ducal administration in law enforcement. Most historians argued that 'archipresbyterii' were seated by rulers at churches founded by dukes in main, castellan strongholds. They were above all ducal rather than episcopal officials, taking part in the administration at the request of rulers.

[68] In addition to the works in n. 65, see László Koszta, 'La fondation de l'éveché de Vác', *Specimina Nova Pars Prima: Sectio Mediaevalis* 1 (2001), 87–105; Koszta, 'A nyitrai püspökség létrejötte (Nyitra egyháztörténete a 9–13. században)', *Századok* 143 (2009), 257–318; Géza Érszegi, 'The emergence of the Hungarian state, the adoption and consolidation of Christianity (970–1095)', 25–36; József Török, 'The development of the Hungarian dioceses in the last millennium', in *A Thousand Years of Christianity*, 176–82.

Recently this hypothesis has been questioned: the 'castellan stronghold system' was not correlated with early Church foundations. Presbyterii as heads of local churches appeared not only at ducal, but also at episcopal or magnates' foundations. Consequently, they cooperated with ducal administration not as officials but as educated men, who were able to use writing in legal procedures. In the first half of the twelfth century 'archipresbiterus' and 'archidiaconus' ceased to be merely honorary titles. Reforms administered by Bishop Daniel in Prague and Bishop Zdík in Olomouc (1126–50) stabilized the system of inner church administration which was born decades earlier. Archdeacons were now heads of local administrative units, representatives of the bishop who overlooked the parishes and private churches. At some point between 1135 and 1140, six archdeacons from churches across the main Moravian stronghold joined the twelve members of the newly established cathedral chapter.[69]

From the 1170s, the diocese of Prague was divided into ten archpresbyterates, and from 1130s the dioecese of Olomouc into six archpresbyterates. A decanates network was evolving until the middle of the fourteenth century, but the general outline of the system was in place by the last quarter of the thirteenth century (more than fifty decanates in the Prague diocese and more than thirty in the Olomouc diocese). Also, the parish system was constructed in these times, with more than 2,000 parishes in the Prague diocese (the number of parishes in Olomouc bishopric is not known precisely). All these posts were diverse not only in their geographic but also economic conditions. The income of an archpresbyter of Kouřim was more than five times that of the same official in Litoměřice or Plzeň. Such economic differences were also typical of all other Church offices.

The beginnings of Polish archdeaconries are obscure and dated differently for different regions. An archdeacon as the representative of an (arch)bishop for all the clergy of a diocese appeared relatively early, at the beginning of the twelfth century (the archdeacon of Gniezno in the Chronicle of Gallus Anonymous) and throughout the twelfth and thirteenth centuries (that of Cracow in 1166;

[69] *CDB* I, 116–23, no. 115; 124–5, no. 116; M. Zemek, 'Das Olmützer Domkapitel. Seine Entstehung und Entwicklung bis 1600', *Archiv für Kirchengeschichte von Böhmen-Mähren-Schlesien* 9 (1988), 66–86; second part published in vol. 10 (1989), 58–88; Libor Jan, 'K otázce hradských kostelů, velkofar a arcikněží v přemyslovském panství (10.–12. stol.)', in *Kościół w monarchiach*, 193–203.

Włocławek in 1198; Wrocław in 1200; Płock in 1207; Poznań in 1210; Lubusz in 1276). But archdeacons as heads of smaller territorial units of episcopal organization appeared later. In cases of provinces where population density was relatively high and consequently Christianization was faster, as in Greater and Lesser Poland, territorial archdeaconries appeared in the second half of the twelfth century; in Kraków land the first archdeaconries were mentioned in 1171, and the archdeaconry of Lublin was specified in 1198. But in other bishoprics a system of archdeaconries and deaconries developed later, at the beginning or even in the second half of the thirteenth century or at the beginning of fourteenth century. The territorial reorganization of archdeaconries, which adjusted their boundaries to the administrative needs of the Church, was still happening during the fourteenth and fifteenth centuries. The precise moment of the appearance of deaconries is disputable. Most historians previously suggested that in Piast lands archdeaconries were created earlier than deaconries. But nowadays researchers claim that both types of Church administrative units may have been created at the same time, at least in aforementioned provinces. According to some researchers, the territorial coverage of archdeaconries may have been related to boundaries of old tribal territories or early state administrative units, but neither hypothesis can be proven.[70]

In Hungary, archdeaconries probably formed in the eleventh century. Archdeacons appear in the synod of Esztergom (probably at the beginning of the twelfth century) in a judiciary capacity over priests; synodal legislation also demanded that they possess a compendium of canon law.[71] Archdeaconries are thought to have initially coincided with royal counties, and the churches in *ispáns*' strongholds are understood as archdeaconal centres. Such churches were excavated in Borsod, Szabolcs and Visegrád; the lack of burials around the excavated church of Borsod county, and the existence of another nearby church with a cemetery led to this interpretation. Archdeacons are

[70] Bernhard Panzram, *Die schlesischen Archidiakonate und Archipresbyteriate bis zur Mitte des 14. Jahrhunderts* (Breslau, 1937); Tadeusz Silnicki, *Organizacja archidiakonatu w Polsce* (Lwów, 1927); Józef Szymański, 'Uwagi o organizacji archidiakonatu polskiego', *Rocznik Teologiczny Krakowski* 6, 3 (1953), 33–55; Bolesław Kumor, 'Archidiakonat: w Kościele polskim', in *Encyklopedia katolicka*, vol. I (Lublin, 1989), cols. 871–2; Jacek Chachaj, 'Pierwotna średniowieczna sieć dekanalna w diecezji krakowskiej', *Archiwa, Biblioteki i Muzea Kościelne* 71 (1999), 379–87.

[71] Bak *et al.*, eds., *Laws*, 64–5, c. 47; 66, c. 65.

thought to have had the tasks of conversion, ecclesiastical organization and supervision, rather than the care of souls. Archdeacons eventually fulfilled judicial and administrative functions at bishops' sees.[72]

In Hungary, royal chapels that were established beginning in the early eleventh century gradually developed into collegiate churches. Cathedral chapters appeared beginning in the late eleventh century. The synod of Esztergom (probably early twelfth century) legislated on the life of the canons: it emphasized the need for episcopal regulation and the requirement that they live according to the rule of regular canons.[73] The first cathedral chapters in Poland were organized by the late eleventh and early twelfth centuries. During reforms initiated by Duke Władysław Herman, twenty-four prebends for canons were created in Cracow in 1080s (see above). Slightly later, the same duke created chapter of canons in Gniezno, Płock and perhaps Wrocław. At the end of twelfth century of chapters canons functioned at all cathedral churches in Piast lands. In parallel, apart from chapters in archbishoprics and bishoprics, smaller units of canons were founded at the turn of eleventh and twelfth centuries at local churches in Zawichost, Sandomierz and Cracow (St Andrew's collegiate church).[74] In Bohemia, Spytihněv II founded a collegiate chapter in Litoměřice. The Prague cathedral chapter was reorganized in 1068 by Provost Marek, who limited the number of its members to twenty-five and demanded that they wear priestly attire. The finances of the congregation were also secured.[75] At Vyšehrad, where dynastic legends placed the home of the first Přemysl and his wife, Libuše, a collegiate chapter was founded around 1070. Its provost also served as

[72] Mária Wolf, 'Ecclesia baptismalis, ecclesia parochialis – a borsodi ispánsági vár templomai/The churches of the ispán's castle at Borsod', in Ritoók and Simonyi, eds., '. . . *A halál árnyékának völgyében járok*', 131–9.

[73] László Koszta, 'Die Domkapitel und ihre Domherren bis Anfang des 12. Jahrhunderts in Ungarn', in *The Man of Many Devices*, 478–91; László Koszta, 'Conclusions drawn from the prosopographic analysis of the canons belonging to the cathedral chapters of medieval Hungary (1200–1350)', in *Carreiras eclesiásticas no Ocidente Cristão: séc. XII–XIV / Ecclesiastical Careers in Western Christianity: 12th–14th c.* (Lisbon, 2007), 15–30; Gergely Kiss, 'Contribution à l'évolution des chapitres dans la Hongrie médiévale,' *Specimina Nova Pars Prima: Sectio Mediaevalis* 1 (2001), 107–19; Bak *et al.*, eds., *Laws*, 63, c. 26; 66, c. 58.

[74] Józef Szymański, *Kanonikat świecki w Małopolsce od końca XI do połowy XIII w.* (Lublin, 1995).

[75] Cosmas II.26; Z. Hledíková, 'Pražská metropolitní kapitula, její samospráva a postavení do doby husitské', *Sborník historický* 19 (1972), 5–48.

ducal chancellor. Members of the chapter were directly subject to the pope, who was to receive from them 12 talents of silver.[76]

Parishes were the last element among ecclesiastical structures to take shape. As everywhere in Europe, they developed gradually over several centuries. In Hungary, those in charge of the care of souls oversaw a very large area for centuries, rather than something akin to the 'parish' of late medieval western cities. Thus even in István's prescriptive legislation ten villages belonged to one church and the population attended mass there; initially even this programme may not have been fulfilled. Subsequent legislation called for every church to have a parish around it. Throughout most of the period, not every village had a church and priest. We can only glimpse the practical difficulties this caused through legislation itself: as noted, villages too far away were allowed to send one representative to mass. The *ecclesia parochiana* of late eleventh-century legislation, and the synod of Esztergom's *parochianus presbyter* are understood by some scholars as references to parishes, but by others as references to archdeaconal churches. According to this view, the *ecclesia parochiana* was the church inside the fortified area of county centres, while the *ecclesia baptismalis*, also in the *ispán*'s seat, but outside the castle, was the one charged with the care of souls, around which a cemetery developed, as discovered by archaeologists in Borsod county.[77]

Preaching, dispensing the sacraments and burial were also performed by monks, and initially no distinction was made in the respective spiritual functions of monks and parish priests, as shown by both textual and archaeological evidence. Thus, cemeteries around early monasteries contained the bodies of women and children, interpreted as laypeople buried in monastic cemeteries. The earliest known prohibition of monastic involvement in preaching, baptism

[76] *CDB* I, 365–7, no. 384, 371–91, no. 387; A. Pleszczyński, *Vyšehrad: Rezidence českých panovníků. Studie o rezidenci panovníka raného středověku na příkladu českého Vyšehradu* (Prague, 2002).

[77] Bak *et al.*, eds., *Laws*, 58, c. 19; 63, c. 16; Wolf, 'Ecclesia baptismalis'. On parish formation, see Jerzy Kłoczowski, 'Les paroisses en Bohême, en Hongrie et en Pologne (XI–XIII siècles)', in *Le istituzioni ecclesiastiche della 'Societas Christiana' dei secoli XI–XII: diocesi, pievi e parocchie. Atti della sesta settimana internazionale di studio Milano, 1–7 settembre 1974*, Miscellanea del Centro di Studi Medioevali 8 (Milan, 1977), 187–98; Marie-Madelaine de Cevins, 'Les paroisses hongroises au Moyen Age', in Csernus and Korompay, eds., *Les Hongrois et l'Europe*, 341–57; N. Berend *et al.*, 'The kingdom of Hungary', 355–6.

and the giving of absolution can be found in the text of the synod of Esztergom (probably early twelfth century), but such prohibitions recurred in the thirteenth and fourteenth centuries: against monks holding masses, taking confessions, performing burials and other activities now relegated to parish priests. The key period in the evolution of the parish system was probably from the end of the twelfth to the middle of the thirteenth century, although little is known about the details of this process, and parish organization was completed in the fourteenth and fifteenth centuries. Parish churches came into existence in a variety of ways. The transformation of private churches into churches with rights of patronage also meant that these became the centres of parishes. In addition, especially during the later thirteenth century, many small churches were built. The fourteenth-century papal tithe lists are the best sources for parish organization.[78]

The most broadly accepted hypothesis concerning the beginnings of parochial organization in Bohemia is connected to the idea of 'stronghold organization' as a framework for the ducal administration system in the tenth–twelfth centuries. According to the theory, churches founded in castellan strongholds were not only places of cult for Christian elites, but also missionary centres and seats of 'large parishes' whose priests bore the title of archdeacon. Huge in size, 'large parishes' had their centres in seats of ducal representatives and their functions were related to them. But the functions of these 'large parish' priests in relation to inhabitants of villages within stronghold administrative units is an open question (whether it was obligatory or voluntary to receive sacraments and attend masses, the choice of burial place, etc.), as is the moment of their foundation. It seems that clergymen appointed to strongholds' churches focused mainly – or even exclusively – on the spiritual care of the forts' inhabitants. Archaeologists have pointed out that in nearby villages local cemeteries, sometimes going back to the ninth century, were still used without any trace of Christian supervision. They were abandoned no earlier than the turn of eleventh and twelfth centuries.

At the same time, the number of village churches also rapidly grew. The main place of burial for local inhabitants became the interior of churches and new cemeteries located in their vicinity. Recently,

[78] In addition to the works in the previous note, see Bak *et al.*, eds., *Laws*, 64, c. 34; Elemér Mályusz, 'Die Eigenkirche in Ungarn', *Studien zur älteren Geschichte Osteuropas (Festschrift für Heinrich Felix Schmid)* (Graz, 1956), 76–95.

several historians have argued that the theory of 'large parishes' is entirely misleading and that they were created no earlier than the second half of the eleventh century. At the turn of the eleventh and twelfth centuries the title of their priests changed from archpriests to archdeacons, and only then was the whole system of ecclesiastical administration formalized. Local parishes in Bohemia began to function more regularly at that time, but the process of creation of a system of parishes extended until the middle of the thirteenth century, when the inner colonization process established new standards of spiritual care over villagers.[79]

Historians who identify 'parochial church' with *ecclesia baptismalis*, date the beginnings of parishes in Poland to the first half of the eleventh century. Recently, some archaeologists have backed this theory by suggesting that ducal foundations built as elements of *ostentatio ducis* in main strongholds were the centres of the Christianization process of elites up to 1038/9. But after the crisis of the Piast realm, a building for a clergyman taking care of local flock appeared at the edge of or near the stronghold, alongside a church for the elite, located in the stronghold's centre. Adjacent to it was a cemetery with burials of a humble character, which are unlike the richly furnished sites known from churches located in strongholds. In addition, architectural features of buildings, built of wood, suggested that they served as centres of spiritual care over local inhabitants (Poznań, Giecz, Ląd, Kalisz). According to researchers these churches were centres of 'large parishes' similar to those supposedly known from Hungary and Bohemia.

Apart from these 'large parishes', there were other forms of 'proto-parochial' units that might also have existed before the thirteenth century. Clergymen with the title *prepositus*, appointed by bishops, administered to inhabitants of vast territories in the eleventh century, and these units mainly evolved into archdeaconries (bishopric of Kamień Pomorski), although sometimes they became parishes in the thirteenth century (Santok, at first the seat of an archdeaconry, but

[79] Zdenek Fiala, 'Die Organisation der Kirche in Přemyslidenstaat des 10.–13. Jahrhundert', in *Siedlung und Verfassung Böhmens in der Frühzeit*, ed. František Graus and Herbert Ludat (Wiesbaden, 1967), 133–43; Libor Jan, 'Die Anfänge der Pfarrorganisation in Böhmen und Mähren', in *Pfarreien im Mittelalter. Deutschland, Polen, Tschechien und Ungarn im Vergleich*, ed. Nathalie Kruppa and Leszek Zygner (Veröffentlichungen des Max-Planck-Instituts für Geschichte, 238) (Göttingen, 2008), 183–99.

from 1298 a parish with the church in castellan stronghold). Also churches in villages with Benedictine or Cistercian monasteries, which were used as centres of Christianization in the eleventh and twelfth centuries (Mogiła, Lubiń, Łekno), in some instances became in the thirteenth century centres of newly organized parishes. These early forms of Church administrative system in Poland are mostly hypothetical. Better evidence exists for the spiritual care provided by clergymen appointed as heads of local churches founded by dukes or magnates and endowed in the twelfth century with income from the surrounding villages. In some cases, villages surrounding these Churches made up regular parishes in the thirteenth century with the aforementioned church as its centre. A stable system of smaller, basic units of parishes with more strictly defined borders, confirmed by written sources, appeared no earlier than the second half of the twelfth and – mainly – during the thirteenth century.[80]

## *Churches*

Building churches was crucially important for the introduction and maintenance of Christianity.

### *Bohemia*

In Bohemia, the popularity of round churches may have resulted from traditions inherited from Great Moravia. In Prague, the rotunda of St Vitus, built as a royal chapel between 920 and 940, became the bishop's seat. Its original, single apse positioned to the east was later supplemented by apses built into the north and south walls to accommodate the shrines of St Václav and St Vojtěch-Adalbert.[81] The church also served as the mausoleum for members of the Přemyslid dynasty. Then the rotunda of St Vitus was dismantled and a large cruciform Romanesque basilica with east and west choirs was built on

[80] Leszek Zygner, 'Die Pfarrei im mittelalterlichen Polen. Ein Forschungsüberblick', in *Pfarreien im Mittelalter*, 67–82; Piotr Plisiecki, '*The parochial network and the tithes system in the medieval dioecese Cracow*', in *Pfarreien im Mittelalter*, 223–34; Zofia Kurnatowska, 'Początki organizacji parafialnej w Polsce', in *Kościół w monarchiach*, 37–48; Eugeniusz Wiśniowski, *Parafie w średniowiecznej Polsce: struktura i funkcje społeczne* (Lublin, 2004).

[81] Jan Frolík *et al.*, *Nejstarši sakrálni architektura Pražského hradu* (Prague, 2000); K. Benešovska *et al.*, *Ten Centuries of Architecture*, vol. I, *Architecture of the Romanesque* (Prague, 2001).

the same site between *c.*1060 and 1090.[82] At Vyšehrad another twin-choir basilica was built.[83] St Mary's church in Prague was built in stone in the tenth century, where Duke Spytihněv I (d. 915) was buried together with his wife. Originally the tomb may have been intended to house the body of Duke Bořivoj I (d. 888/9).[84]

Czech archaeologists have dated stone or wooden churches built in main Přemyslid strongholds (Levý Hradec, Starý Plzenec, Stará Boleslav) and by powerful magnates (ducal) families (Libice) to the tenth century, even possibly to its first half. Besides Prague and Olomouc (where the Romanesque cathedral church of St Václav was consecrated in 1131), which were bishopric sees, stone churches were built during the eleventh century in other main strongholds, especially in the seats of local dukes (Brno, Znojmo – although historians debate whether the rotunda of St Catherine was built in the eleventh or the first half of the twelfth century). Benedictine abbeys, such as Břevnov, Ostrov, Sázava, Rajhrad and others, were at first constructed of wood but after several decades, mostly in the eleventh century, their churches were rebuilt in stone, followed later by the other buildings. Monasteries founded in the twelfth century sometimes had stone chapels and churches from the very beginning. Village churches appeared as chapels in larger numbers at the beginning of the twelfth century, but they were mostly wooden structures. No earlier than the middle of the twelfth and in the thirteenth century they were rebuilt in brick or stone, or dismantled and replaced by new, massive buildings with parochial functions.

### *Poland*

There is no unambiguous material evidence for the building of churches in poland during the tenth century. Very few traces of early wooden ecclesiastical architecture have been discovered there, although this may be because masonry is more likely to be found by archaeologists, and because of the difficulties of identifying early wooden structures. In Cracow, apart from the early phases of St

[82] Anezka Merhautová, ed., *Katedrála sv. Víta v Praze* (Prague, 1994).

[83] B. Nechvátal, 'Vyšehrad a archeologie', in *Královský Vyšehrad: sborník příspěvků k 900. výročí úmrtí prvního českého krále Vratislava II. (1061–1092)*, ed. B. Nechvátal (Prague, 1992), 112–39.

[84] Jan Frolik, 'Hroby Přemyslovskych knižat na Pražskem Hrade', In *Pohrbivani na Pražském hradě a jeho předpolích*, ed, Katerina Tomkova, vol. I.1 (Prague, 2005) (Castrum Pragense, vol. 1), 25–46 (here 29).

Vojtěch-Adalbert's church,[85] there is evidence for a possible tenth-century wooden church under the pre-Romanesque cathedral at the royal complex on Wawel Hill.[86] There is more evidence of functioning wooden churches in the eleventh century (Tyniec near Cracow,[87] Ostrów Lednicki[88] and perhaps Kalisz-Zawodzie, where the wooden church was used also in the first half of the twelfth century).[89] Bolesław the Brave and his son Mieszko II between 992 and 1034 created a network of stone churches in main ducal residences, where they were exemplary symbols of the new Christian era promoted by the monarchy (Giecz, Gniezno, Poznań and Ostrów Lednicki). Princess Mathilde of Lotharingia congratulated King Mieszko II in 1028 on building 'more churches than anybody else'[90] before in Poland (although whether this is true or not is unknown).

There are around eighty remnants of stone buildings in Poland that may be safely dated to between the tenth and twelfth centuries.[91] It took more than 150 years for stone churches to appear in the peripheries. Two clear trends can be identified in the oldest stone architecture from Poland. The overwhelming tendency was to build round churches or, rather, chapels with one or more apses. They could be erected relatively quickly and cheaply.[92] There is an on-going debate concerning the origin of early architectural influences. An initial hypothesis identified the main inspirations as being from the Carolingian–Ottonian zone and from neighbouring Bohemia. Later, Byzantine and/or south Slavic elements were identified; Italian

85 Zygmunt Świechowski, *Katalog architektury romańskiej w Polsce* (Warsaw, 2009), 240.

86 Zbigniew Pianowski, 'Początki zespołu architektury sakralnej na Wawelu: stan badań i interpretacji do roku 2000', in *Dzieje Podkrapacia*, vol. V, *Początki chrześcijaństwa w Małopolsce*, ed. J. Gancarski (Krosno, 2000), 67.

87 W. Kalinowski, 'Przedmioty liturgiczne znalezione w grobach pierwszych opatów tynieckich', *Folia Historiae Artium* 6–7 (1971), 175–207.

88 Kurnatowska, 'Ostrów Lednicki in the early Middle Ages', 173–80.

89 Tadeusz Baranowski, 'The stronghold in Kalisz', in *Polish Lands*, 295–7.

90 *Epistola Mathildis Suevae*, ed. Brygida Kürbis, in *Kodeks Matyldy: Księga obrzędów z Kartami dedykacyjnymi*, ed. Brygida Kürbis, Monumenta Sacra Polonorum, 1 (Cracow, 2000), 139.

91 Zygmunt Świechowski, *Katalog architektury romańskiej w Polsce* (Warsaw, 2009). For data on accelerator dating of mortar samples, see www.archaeology.pl.

92 Teresa Rodzińska-Chorąży, 'Architektura kamienna jako źródło do najwcześniejszych dziejów Polski', in J. M. Małecki, ed., *Chrystianizacja Polski południowej* (Cracow, 1994), 148.

connections have also been suggested.[93] Recent views accept that there was a combination of various influences.[94]

We do not know where the first royal church was built. Three royal chapels built by Bolesław the Brave were discovered in Ostrów Lednicki and Giecz, both in Greater Poland, as well as in Przemyśl, south-eastern Poland. All were small, round annexes attached directly to royal residential buildings (*palatia*). A very recent (and as yet unpublished) discovery of a tiny stone chapel adjacent to the alleged *palatium* of Mieszko I in Poznań may be the oldest example of such a combination. Several churches were built in relatively remote areas of the country. In the stronghold in Kałdus, near Chełmno in north-east Poland, the foundations of a large basilica were unearthed from the first half of the eleventh century. The church may be compared only to the cathedrals erected at Gniezno and Poznań.[95] We might connect the investment to the early Piasts' missionary ambitions, aimed not only at their own territory, but also at foreign countries (for example, Bruno of Querfurt's attempt to convert the Yatvingians in 1009).[96]

In the archiepiscopal see at Gniezno, a simple, probably temporary, rotunda building was erected shortly before the large Romanesque cathedral was built in the early eleventh century. This earlier structure is understood to have been a shrine in which the body of St Vojtěch-Adalbert was kept until the visit of Otto III in 1000.[97] In Poznań, an impressive cathedral was built in the late tenth or early eleventh century. In Cracow, there is no material evidence to suggest the existence of any solid stone tenth-century construction on Wawel Hill. The impressive St Wacław's cathedral was, however, built there

[93] E.g. J. Hawrot, 'Kraków wczesnośredniowieczny', *Kwartalnik Architektury i Urbanistyki* 4 (1959), 125–69; K. Żurowska, 'Studia nad architekturą wczesnopiastowską', *Zeszyty Naukowe Uniwersytetu Jagiellońskiego: Prace z Historii Sztuki* 17 (1983), 164.

[94] Z. Świechowski, *Architektura romańska w Polsce* (Warsaw, 2000), 33.

[95] W. Chudziak, 'Problem chrystianizacji ziemi chełmińskiej w świetle źródeł archeologicznych', in *Człowiek, sacrum, środowisko*, 130.

[96] Miłosz Sosnowski, *Anonimowa Passio s. Adalperti martiris (BHL 40) oraz Wiperta Historia de predicatione episcopi Brunonis (BHL 1471b) – komentarz, edycja, przekład, Rocznik Biblioteki Narodowej* 43 (2012), 5–74 (here 70, 72); also Peter Damian, chap. 27; Thietmar of Merseburg VI.94–5.

[97] T. Janiak, 'Gniezno – stołeczny ośrodek monarchii wczesnosredniowiecznej', in *Civitates principales: wybrane ośrodki władzy w Polsce wczesnośredniowiecznej*', ed. T. Janiak (Gniezno, 1998), 17–21; Z. Kurnatowska, 'The stronghold in Gniezno in the light of more recent studies', in *Polish Lands*, 191–4.

in the eleventh century. At the same time, more than ten churches and other stone buildings of various shapes, sizes and functions were established on Wawel.[98]

In the second half of the twelfth century, old churches were refurbished and new ones were built. In Płock a new cathedral was consecrated in 1144 by Bishop Alexander of Mallone from Liège. From the late twelfth century onwards, the Church gained effective control over the already largely Christianized masses, now served by a network of parish churches. Numerous village churches were built in Poland during the aftermath of the Fourth Lateran Council in 1215, which stressed the function of parishes as the basic units of the territorial Church. Thus, the ecclesiastical network expanded into the countryside. Approximately 150 remnants of stone Romanesque buildings in Poland still survive, and most were erected as parish churches in the thirteenth century.[99]

### *Hungary*

As early as the reign of István I, the laws stipulated that every ten villages had to build a church; the provision of churches with vestments, liturgical objects and books was to be shared between king and bishops.[100] To what extent such regulation was carried out in practice is unknown, because little information exists on the early small churches serving the population. The earliest churches were wooden or wattle-and-daub constructions. In Hungary, either nothing remains of them, or only traces, such as sometimes remains of timber frames. In the twelfth century, stone as well as brick churches appeared and perhaps about one-tenth of villages did indeed possess a church. In the late thirteenth century more intensive church-building started, as shown by the fact that the first architectural layer of most medieval village churches comes from that period. It seems that these were austere and usually small, for about twenty to twenty-five people. They did not usually have towers.[101] Private churches founded by the nobility proliferated; such churches were inherited or

98 A. Żaki, 'Kraków wislański, czeski i wczesnopiastowski', in Małecki, ed., *Chrystianizacja Polski południowej*, 64.

99 For an overview, see Świechowski, *Katalog architektury romańskiej w Polsce*.

100 Bak *et al.*, eds., *Laws*, 9, c. 1.

101 Ernő Marosi, *Magyar falusi templomok: építészeti hagyományok,* 2nd rev. edn (Budapest, 1975); Bálint *et al.*, 'Medieval village', 385–6.

sold as part of the property of the lay owner, who also had the right to appoint the priest. The papal legate Philip at the synod of Buda (1279) issued legislation against private churches and decreed their transformation into churches with the right of patronage to comply with canon law.

Royal churches and cathedrals were an important part of the early building programmes, although none of them has survived in its original form. Almost all eleventh-century churches and cathedrals were rebuilt. Although hypothetically the destruction caused by the pagan uprising may have been responsible, no archaeological evidence indicates the rebuilding of burnt or violently destroyed buildings. Rather, it seems that the wood and wattle-and-daub building technique of the early period necessitated rebuilding, as did the desire to replace old-fashioned buildings with ones in the new Romanesque style. The new 'Benedictine plan' was used for the rebuilding of the cathedrals of Eger, Győr and Gyulafehérvár (Alba Julia, Romania). Art historians date these to the late eleventh and early twelfth centuries.

The cathedrals of Veszprém, Győr, Pécs and Nitra retain some of their early features. Archaeological excavations uncovered extensive remains in the case of the cathedrals of Eger and Kalocsa. Carved stone decorations remain from the middle of the eleventh century (Veszprém) and the twelfth (Győr, Pécs). Only descriptions and fragments remained of the cathedral of Esztergom. The three-aisled royal basilica at (Székes)Fehérvár was the king's chapel, but it was one of the largest buildings in the kingdom. It housed the tombs of István and his son Imre, as well as those of several later kings, and the regalia; it was also the coronation church of the kings. Italian, Swabian and, according to some art historians, Byzantine influence is manifest in decorations and groundplans of ecclesiastical buildings. While the palmette decorations and centralized building plans are Byzantine in origin, art historians have argued that the Hungarian examples are closer to Italian than to Balkan parallels. Thus the transmission of 'Byzantine' style to Hungary – seen in royal and noble private churches and monasteries of the eleventh century – is debated; the stone carvings from Szekszárd may have been influenced by San Marco, Venice. Lombard and other Italian influences are seen in the few remaining frescoes.[102]

102 Altmann *et al.*, *Medium regni*; N. Berend *et al.*, 'The kingdom of Hungary', 336–7, 352–4; Béla Zsolt Szakács, 'Western complexes of Hungarian churches of the

From the twelfth century – according to the generally held view, through Lombard influence – Romanesque-style stone carvings, including carved animals and monsters, started to spread. South German monastic building styles also influenced Benedictine monasteries of the twelfth century. The cathedral of Esztergom was rebuilt; the most up-to-date Parisian early Gothic encrusted marble decorations were used for its western entrance, the Porta Speciosa (destroyed in the eighteenth century) in the 1190s. In the thirteenth century, a variety of late Romanesque and Gothic styles were used to rebuild existing ecclesiastical structures, such as the cathedral of Kalocsa and abbey church of Pannonhalma, and to build new ones, for example a cloister for the Benedictine abbey of Somogyvár, and buildings for aristocratic monasteries, such as the Premonstratensian priory of Bény (Hont-Pázmány kindred). A few remaining objects attest the liturgical equipment of churches: vessels, altarcloths and crosses include imports from both the west and Byzantium, and artistic influences on crosses and metal vessels demonstrate ties to south German and Lower Saxon areas, and to Flanders. Thirteenth-century frescoes show Byzantine and Italian influence.[103]

Relics had to be acquired for the altars of the new churches. The first data on such acquisitions come from the reign of István I, who was keen to acquire relics from various sources. Reportedly, he received relics from Emperor Otto III, and perhaps from Cluny, and he took them from Ochrid when he was on a military campaign there. His successors continued to collect relics: King Peter received the relics of a martyred pilgrim from Trier, and László I in 1091 asked for part of the relics of St Benedict from the abbot of Monte Cassino.

early eleventh century', *Hortus Artium Mediaevalium* 3 (1997), 149–63; Ernő Marosi, 'Die Rolle der byzantinischen Beziehungen für die Kunst Ungarns im 11. Jh.', in *Byzantinischer Kunstexport. Seine gesellschaftliche und künstlerische Bedeutung für die Länder Mittel- und Osteuropas*, ed. Heinrich Leopold Nickel (Halle an der Saale, 1978), 39–49; Béla Zsolt Szakács, 'The Italian connection: theories on the origins of Hungarian Romanesque art', in *Medioevo: Arte e Storia*, ed. Arturo Carlo Quintavalle (Milan, 2008), 648–55; Endre Tóth and Gergely Buzás, *Magyar építészet I: a rómaiaktól a román korig* (Budapest, 2001); Ernő Marosi and Tünde Wehli, *Az Árpád-kor művészeti emlékei* (Budapest, 1997), with many photos; Melinda Tóth, *Árpád-kori falfestészet* (Budapest, 1974). On the cathedral as well as other early ecclesiastical architecture of the diocese of Pécs, see Gergely Buzás, 'Az egyházmegye építészeti emlékei', in Fedeles *et al.*, eds., *A pécsi egyházmegye története I*, 611–713.

103 In addition to works listed in the previous two notes, see Ernő Marosi, *Die Anfänge der Gotik in Ungarn. Esztergom in der Kunst des 12.–13. Jahrhunderts* (Budapest, 1984).

Kálmán decreed that the relics of saints were to be carried by 'good and religious' ecclesiastics during processions. Royal collection of relics continued throughout the period: András II reportedly returned to Hungary from his none-too-successful crusade in 1218 laden with relics, including bodily remains of several saints and one of the vessels used by Christ at Cana. Relics from local saints (see below) were added to these collections: contemporary sources refer to István's right hand and a chain worn by St Zoerard.[104]

## MONASTICISM AND REGULAR CLERGY

Monasteries were founded by members of the royal dynasty and eventually of the nobility. In Bohemia and Hungary, monasticism was introduced at the time of the first rulers' conversion to Christianity, while in Poland the implantation of monasticism followed about thirty years after the introduction of Christianity. New orders (such as the Cistercians or military orders) were introduced from the twelfth century, and some locally founded orders appeared as well. In the thirteenth century, the newly founded mendicant orders arrived within a very short time in the three polities.

### *Bohemia*

The ducal stronghold in Prague boasted an important royal foundation, the convent of St George, most likely founded by Vratislav I, who was also buried there. When the first bishop, Dětmar, adopted St Vitus's as his main church, a Benedictine nunnery was added to St George's and the two buildings were connected by a covered passageway – a *via longa*.[105] The nunnery was governed by the ruling Přemyslid dynasty, through female members of the family as abbesses. Around 1000, a new Benedictine monastery was founded in Ostrov, central Bohemia. In the early eleventh century, the monastery at Břevnov (now in Prague), which was established in 993 by St Vojtěch-Adalbert, underwent a programme of restoration before being settled by Benedictines from Niederaltaich in Bavaria. Vratislav II enlarged the monastery at Břevnov and ensured that the whole complex, together with the convent's basilica, was completed

[104] N. Berend *et al.*, 'The kingdom of Hungary', 337–8.

[105] A. Merhautová-Livorová, *Bazilika sv. Jiří na pražském hradě* (Prague, 1972).

around 1089.[106] Three years earlier monks from Břevnov had been introduced by Duke Vratislav I to the monastery in Opatovice, where earlier a hermitage functioned. Through an unusual initiative, Duke Oldřich in 1032 allowed the foundation of a Benedictine monastery in Sázava, where a Bohemian hermit named Prokop (d. 1053, canonized in 1203) officially (re)introduced the Slavonic liturgy. The Přemyslid sympathy towards the Benedictine movement did not end with the eleventh century, although it weakened over time. In 1115 Duke Vladislav I founded another Benedictine abbey in Kladruby (south-western Bohemia). Prague rulers were perhaps responsible before 1140 for the origin of the Benedictine abbey in Postoloprty. But during the twelfth century magnates also created new Benedictine monasteries, as did Vrbata, who founded the abbey in Podlažice *c.* 1150. The beginnings of the Benedictine abbey in Vilémov are dated to *c.* 1119. It is possible that a noble took a decisive role in its foundation.

At the end of the eleventh century, a new wave of monastic foundations was connected to new religious orders and to the growing position of nobles, who by such foundations emulated ducal gestures of power. In 1142, the Norbertines opened their monastery in Strachov, founded by the bishop Jindřich Zdík. Three years later, a Norbertine nunnery was founded in Doksany. Between 1184 and 1187 the nobleman Jiří of Milevsko founded a Norbertine house in his family village, Milevsko. In 1193 Hroznata, one of the mightiest Bohemian nobles, founded a monastery in Teplá, filial to Strachov. The same magnate, returning from crusade, set up a Norbertine nunnery in Chotěšov between 1202 and 1210. Supported by magnates, the Premonstratensians were even able to take over some Benedictine monasteries founded earlier by dukes. In 1139 Duke Soběslav I founded a Benedictine monastery in Želiv, filial to Sázava. Ten years later Benedictine monks were expelled and replaced by Norbertines with the help of the bishop Jindřich Zdík.

Taking part in the second crusade had attracted the Bohemian duke Vladislav II to the Cistercians and the knightly orders. He founded one of the Knights of St John houses at Mala Strana in Prague. The order soon expanded and was given estates by dukes in Kadaň (1183), Kladsko (before 1186), Manětín (1169) and Stříbro. New monasteries

[106] P. Sommer, 'Early mediaeval monasteries in Bohemia', in *Twenty-Five Years of Archaeological Research in Bohemia*, 206–11.

were built in Kadaň and Manětín. Members of the Order of the Holy Sepulchre also obtained a property in Zderaz, near Prague. Duke Vladislav II tried to expand the number of Cistercians too. The first Cistercian abbey in Bohemia was founded in the village Sedlci by the noble Miroslav, suposedly a relative of Bishop Jindřich Zdík, in 1143. A year later, the duke together with his wife founded a second abbey in Plasy, near Plzeň, and these were soon followed by monasteries at Pomuk, near the castle Zelena Hora (1144). Not all foundations occurred without trouble. At the end of the twelfth century a noble called Milhošt' invited monks from the abbey Waldsassen to set up a monastery in his village Mašt'ov. But after a short period he expelled the monks, probably for economic reasons. They found shelter under the protection of another noble, a royal high official called Slávek, who prepared for them a mansion in Osek, where they started a new monastery *c.* 1198. Another new trend in the monastic life in Bohemia during the twelfth century was growing number of nunneries, mostly Norbertine and created by lay magnates. Apart from the above-mentioned ones, Norbertine nunneries were built in Louňovice pod Blaníkem (1149) and Dolní Kounice (1181, known as *claustrum Rosa coeli*). Queen Judith of Thuringia built a Benedictine abbey in Teplice between 1152 and 1167 and settled nuns from St George's cloister in Prague there.

Monastic foundations were less numerous in Moravia. The first monastery, a dependent priory of Břevnov, was founded by Duke Břetislav I *c.* 1045 in Rajhrad. The first independent abbey was founded in 1078: Duke Ota I of Olomouc established a Benedictine monastery in Hradisko (Hradiště) near Olomouc. The Benedictine monastic community was expelled and replaced by a Norbertine convent in the 1140s. At the same time, a Benedictine priory was created by monks in Komárov. But the twelfth century was the time of Norbertines in the Přemyslid realm, and in 1190 Konrád II Ota founded a new monastery together with his mother in Loucka, near Znojmo. This foundation was a political demonstration. In 1101 Dukes Litold of Znojmo and Ondřej of Brno together founded a Benedictine abbey in Třebíč, near the border of their respective realms, as the sign of their ever-lasting alliance. At the beginning of the thirteenth century a Cistercian abbey was founded by the Moravian margrave Vladislav Jindřich in the village Veligrad, the foundation of which was successfully completed in the 1140s. Although magnates in Moravia were not so active in foundations as their Czech counterparts, in 1211 Markvart of Hrádek founded a Norbertine nunnery in Nová Řiše.[107]

During the thirteenth century two major tendencies appeared in the monastic foundation activity of Bohemian kings and magnates. First, the royal dynasty focused on supporting the mendicant orders. In 1232, Václav I the One-Eyed's (Jednooký, 1230–53) youngest sister, Anežka, built a hospital in Prague, and after two years a convent of the Poor Ladies living under the rule of St Francis was also founded there. Around that time (after 1228) the first Franciscan convent in Prague, at the church of St Jacob, was built on the initiative of King Václav I. Soon in several major towns of Bohemia and Moravia mendicant houses appeared, supported by rulers and their officials (during the 1230s: Olomouc, Brno, Znojmo, Kadaň, Litoměřice, Opava, Hradec Králové). Less numerous were Dominican order's houses founded by the royal dynasty and nobles (Prague, Znojmo, Olomouc, Plzeň) as well as by female members of the court's nobility (Turnov, Jablonné v Podještedi). Second, until the 1270s magnates increased the number of their foundations, which played the role of both economic centres of newly gained estates and symbols of prestige, sometimes becoming also the necropolis for several generations of the founders' families (Cistercian abbeys of Vyšši Brod and Žd'ar). Among monasteries founded by nobles, those of the Cistercian order dominated, together with Knights of St John and the Teutonic Order (small dependencies) but also numerous small nunneries. From the 1270s the number of new nobility foundations decreased rapidly, according to some historians, as a result of internal fights for power in Bohemia. Perhaps the strengthening of royal power also negatively influenced the creation of new symbols of prestige and independence of the nobility.[108]

Throughout the thirteenth century thanks to royal liberties bishops, monasteries and chapters built their own landed estates with full rights for inhabitants and independence from royal administration. Ecclesiastics, earlier closely subjected to royal power, evolved into a separate and quasi-independent social group. Yet this independence was relative, as a result of two aspects of their relations with nobles: economic relations between ecclesiastics and their families, and

[107] Dušan Foltýn, *Encyklopedie moravských a slezských klášterů* (Prague, 2005).

[108] M. R. Pauk, *Działalność fundacyjna możnowładztwa czeskiego i jej uwarunkowania społeczne (XI–XIII wiek)* (Cracow, 2000).

quasi-cliental bonds linking chaplains with noble families who were patrons of Church institutions. Well-endowed posts and dignities would be in the hands of one family or clan for at least two, sometimes several, generations. Patrons of rural churches or founders of altars in bigger institutions had the right to nominate a candidate for these benefices. Apart from members of their families, these candidates were often their former subjects. Their dependence on benefactors derived both from holding the post under their patronage and from a subject's service due to former lords.

During the entire period the upper nobility dominated in recruitments for higher dignities, especially for chapters in Prague and Vyšehrad. Canons of other chapters and rectors of wealthy parochial churches were recruited from the middle nobility. Townsmen only began to appear as holders of low-ranking posts. The *pauperes clerici*, who served as altarists and curates in place of actual rectors who accumulated benefitia, originated from the lowest-ranking nobility and peasants, subjects of wealthy patrons.

## *Poland*

The restoration of the Polish Church after the 1030s included the arrival of new clergy. From the middle of the eleventh century there was an influx of Benedictine monks settling in Poland, encouraged and financed by Kazimierz. The oldest Benedictine monastery whose location we know was founded around 1044 in Tyniec, near Cracow, where Aaron, soon to be bishop of Cracow, was then abbot. Around the year 1050, the next one was founded in Mogilno, soon contributing to the establishment of a new bishopric in Płock (1075/6). A third abbey was founded around 1075 by King Bolesław II the Bold in Lubiń, near Kościan. At the beginning of the twelfth century, Bolesław III the Wrymouth contributed to the foundation by magnates of a new Benedictine abbey atop Mount Łysiec, which gained a new name, Święty Krzyż (Holy Cross). The next wave of monastic foundations came with the expansion of the Cistercians, who arrived in Poland during the middle of the twelfth century. Their first monastery was founded in Greater Poland to house those who arrived from Altenberg, near Cologne. A noble by the name of Zbylut donated an estate in Łekno to the community in 1153.

Noble families attracted foreign monks by the foundation of new monasteries. Thus in 1122 the Sieciech family founded a Benedictine abbey in Sieciechów, while in 1139 Piotr Włostowic founded a Benedictine abbey in Wrocław. In 1140 nobles from the Gryf family invited the first group of Cistercians from Morimond and presented them with a monastery in Brzeźnica (then Jędrzejów). The same order set up a number of other monasteries founded by Piast dukes: Lubiąż (1163), Ląd (1175), Sulejów (1177), Koprzywnica (1185); by Pomeranian rulers: Oliwa (1186); by Church officials: Wąchock (1179); and by lay nobles: Kołbacz (1173). Besides monks, regular canons of different orders were generously supported by both rulers and nobles. The origin of houses founded in the first half of the twelfth century are obscure. During the reign of Bolesław III, two monasteries of regular canons of the Lateran started: in Trzemeszno and top of Ślęża Mountain (near Wrocław), then transferred to Wrocław. The first was supported by Duke Bolesław III; the second was founded by the noble, ducal palatine Piotr Włostowic. A third monastery of the order was founded in Czerwińsk by Alexsander of Malonne, bishop of Płock (1148–55). A growing role for nobles in supporting new foundations is clearly visible in the history of Norbertine order in Poland. As in Bohemia, nobles were keen to support canons of Norbertine order, but at least one, the Silesian branch of the Piast dynasty, shared that interest. First, a small house was built for Norbertine canons in the village Kościelna Wieś near Kalisz (Greater Poland) *c.* 1150 in unknown circumstances, probably at the initiative of a nobel or nobles. Apparently, lay nobles initiated the foundation of the first Norbertine monastery in Lesser Poland, in the village Brzesko (*c.* 1149, then transferred to Hebdów). It was settled probably by canons from Strahov. When the noble Jaksa of the Gryf family initiated the foundation of a Norbertine nunnery in Zwierzyniec near Cracow (*c.* 1162) he also established a convent from the Bohemian cloister Doksany. The same magnate participated in the foundation of another Norbertine nunnery in Krzyżanowice (before 1176), and was responsible for calling in members of the Order of the Holy Sepulchre. When Jaksa returned from the crusade (after 1160) he founded a cloister for the order in Miechów, which was soon generously endowed by dukes. In 1165–6, ten years after he had undertaken a pilgrimage to the Holy Land, Duke Henryk of Sandomierz founded a monastery and hospital in Zagość for the Knights Hospitaller. In 1170 the same order received a hospital in Poznań from Duke Mieszko III the Old.

If the Norbertines dominated among twelfth-century foundations, this was the result of actions undertaken by their promoters; nobles provided support for the canons. The nobleman Dzierżko not only participated in the foundation of the double monastery in Busko, but also in his last will ordered his wife to enter the cloister after his death (*c.* 1190). His brother, Wit, bishop of Płock, founded the cloister in Witów (*c.* 1179). He was also involved, together with the castellan of Płock, in the creation of the new cloister in the capital of his bishopric (*c.* 1190). Before 1193 a Norbertine nunnery was created in Strzelno, Kuyavia, probably also as a foundation of relatives of Piotr Włostowic. Among the Piasts, only rulers from the Silesian branch supported the order, for political reasons according to some historians (as revenge on the Benedictines, who conspired against Duke Władysław II the Exile – founder of the Silesian branch of the dynasty). With the help of dukes of Wrocław, Norbertines took over the Benedictine abbey in Ołbin, near Wrocław. Norbertine canons entered there before 1193.[109]

The foundation activity of the Piast dynasty was reduced during the eleventh and twelfth centuries. The strengthening independence and social position of nobles resulted in their seeking adequate means of expression of their new prestige. The foundation of family monasteries of regular canons, less expensive than the more prestigious monastic abbeys, and more in fashion, became an ideal solution for many wealthy and powerful magnates.

In the thirteenth century, the Cistercians received a series of new monasteries: Trzebnica, the first nunnery (1202), Kamieniec Ząbkowicki (1222), Mogiła (1223), Henryków (1225–7), Obra (1231), Bledzewo (1232), Szczyrzyc (1239), Paradyż (1234), Koronowo (1254), Rudy (1255), Pelplin (1276), Przemęt (1278) and Bierzwnik and Krzeszów (both 1292). The Premonstratensians were based in Żukowo, near Gdańsk (1212–14), and established nunneries at Ibramowice (1218–29) and Cracow (1250). In 1220 Bishop Iwo Odrowąż settled a group of 'Regular Canons of the Holy Ghost of Saxia' in Prądnik, where a hospital was later built. In 1226 the Knights Templar were invited to Silesia by Prince Henryk the Bearded.

109 Marek Derwich, 'Die Prämonstratensenorden im mittelalterlichen Polen. Seine Rolle in Kirche und Gesellschaft', in *Studien zum Prämonstratensenorden*, ed. Irene Crusius and Helmut Flachenecker (Göttingen, 2003), 311–47; Dobosz, *Monarchia i możni*; Zbigniew Piłat, 'Fundator i fundacja klasztoru Bożogrobców w Miechowie', in *Bożogrobcy w Pilsce* (Miechów and Warsaw, 1999), 11–43; Jerzy Rajman, The origins of the Polish Premonstratensian Circary, *Analecta Praemonstratensia* 66 (1990), 203–19.

The mendicant orders settled in a number of towns and had built around seventy convents by the end of the thirteenth century: the first Dominicans arrived at Cracow following St Jacek Odrowąż and Blessed Czesław; the Franciscans came to Poland in 1237. At some point before 1241, the Franciscan Sisters of St Clare established a nunnery in Zawichost. Their second foundation, in 1267, was located at Skała, near Cracow, while a third was at Stary Sącz in 1280.

New forms of religious behaviour were recorded in Poland from 1261, when for the first time the presence of flagellants was noted in Silesia. The gravitation of the masses towards more extreme displays of religiosity found support within the Church, although the religious orthodoxy of elites was guarded much more carefully. An extreme example of this can be found from 1284, when Bishop Tomasz II of Wrocław declared Prince Henryk IV the Righteous (Probus, 1266–90) anathema for participating in too many tournaments.

### *Hungary*

Monasteries were initially founded by rulers. Of these early structures, none survives in their entirety; and few traces remain of the earliest buildings. Most of the early houses were Benedictine, but some were Greek Orthodox monasteries. Pannonhalma was the most significant Benedictine house. Its interpolated charter of privileges mentions the founder as Géza, with the foundation completed by István (see Chapter 3). The existing monastery at Pannonhalma still preserves some of its original architecture: fragments of a western apse and a crypt, and possibly a transept and tower(s). István founded several other Benedictine monasteries, at Pécsvárad, Zalavár, Bakonybél, Somlóvásárhely and Zobor. Of these, a sixteenth-century drawing remains of the St Hadrianus monastery at Zalavár (Mosaburg). A two-story chapel of the monastery of Pécsvárad preserved its early structure on the ground floor, which may go back to István's reign, although the dating is uncertain.[110]

[110] Gyula Kristó, 'Tatárjárás előtti bencés monostorainkról', *Századok* 138, 2 (2004), 403–11; Imre Takács, ed., *Mons Sacer, 996–1996: Pannonhalma 1000 éve* (Pannonhalma, 1996); Imre Takács, ed., *Paradisum plantavit. Bencés monostorok a középkori Magyarországon / Benedictine Monasteries in Medieval Hungary. Kiállítás a Pannonhalmi Bencés Főapátságban 2001. március 21-től november 11-ig / Exhibition at the Benedictine Archabbey of Pannonhalma 21 March–11 November 2001* (Pannonhalma, 2001); Gergely Kiss, 'The exemption of the royal Benedictine monasteries in

István also founded Greek monasteries. The convent of nuns in Veszprémvölgy probably followed the Greek rite. Its foundation charter, originally in Greek, issued by 'Stephanos kralés', survives in a bilingual (Greek and Latin) royal transcript from 1109. According to one opinion, the convent was founded by Géza, who according to Adémar de Chabannes also received the name Stephanus in baptism. There is no independent corroboration of this, and Adémar's text is certainly erroneous in many details. Géza's son István (Stephen), who certainly received that baptismal name, as well as a royal title, is a more likely candidate as the founder. The dating of the monastery's remains is controversial. Reportedly Ajtony, one of the potentates subjugated by István, and a convert to Orthodox Christianity, also founded a Greek monastery at Csanád; this was supposedly moved to Oroszlámos (today Banatsko Aranđelovo, Serbia) by the military leader who defeated him. According to tradition, communities of Greek monks at Szávaszentdemeter (Sremska Mitrovica, Serbia) and Pentele were established by or received donations from István, although a lack of contemporary evidence precludes firm conclusions. In the eleventh century, Greek monasteries were also founded by King András I, who had married a Kievan princess, and members of the elite. Bizere, in Arad county (today Romania), has been recently excavated. Greek monasteries continued to exist into the thirteenth century, when they were abandoned and turned over to other monastic orders.[111]

Hungary in the 11th–13th centuries', *Specimina Nova Pars: Prima Sectio Mediaevalis* 2 (2003), 25–63; József Laszlovszky and Beatrix Romhányi, 'Cathedrals, monasteries and churches: the archaeology of ecclesiastic monuments', in Visy, ed., *Hungarian Archaeology*, 372–7. A register of all monasteries can be found in Beatrix F. Romhányi, *Kolostorok és társaskáptalanok a középkori Magyarországon* (Budapest, 2000).

111 Györffy, *Diplomata Hungariae*, 81–5, no. 13; Miklós Komjáthy, 'Quelques problèmes relatifs à la charte de fondation du couvent des religieuses de Veszprémvölgy', in *Mélanges offerts à Szabolcs de Vajay à l'occasion de son cinquantième anniversaire par ses amis, ses collègues et les membres de l'Académie*, ed. Adhémar de Panat and Chevalier Xavier de Ghellinek Vaernewyck (Braga, 1971), 369–80; Géza Érszegi, 'A veszprémvölgyi alapítólevél', in *Válaszúton. Pogányság – Kereszténység. Kelet – Nyugat. Konferencia a X–XI. század kérdéseiről*, ed. László Kredics (Veszprém, 2000), 159–75; *Ademari Cabannensis Chronicon*, ed. Pascale Bourgain, Corpus Christianorum Continuatio Mediaeualis 129 (Turnhout, 1999), III.31 (at 152); András Fülöp and András Koppány, 'A veszprémvölgyi apácakolostor régészeti kutatása (1998–2002)', *Műemlékvédelmi Szemle* 12, 1 (2002 [2004]), 5–40; *Legenda S. Gerhardi episcopi*, 492; Gyula Moravcsik, 'Görögnyelvű monostorok Szent István korában', in Jusztinián Serédi, ed., *Emlékkönyv Szent István király halálának kilencszázadik*

Later eleventh-century monastic architecture is slightly better documented than the earliest structures. The crypt of the Benedictine abbey of Tihany, founded in 1055 by King András I, is still preserved. The ground plans of Szekszárd (founded in 1061 by King Béla I), Feldebrő (founded before 1044 by a member of the Aba family, possibly King Samuel Aba), and Zselicszentjakab (founded in 1061 by *comes* Otto) have been reconstructed. Many of these churches had a centralized ground plan but, in the last quarter of the eleventh century, the so-called Benedictine plan became fashionable. The first dated examples of this new style are the royal monasteries of Garamszentbenedek (Hronský Beňadik, 1075) and Somogyvár (1091). Nobles founded monasteries already in the eleventh century, and continued to do so in increasing numbers during the twelfth. These monasteries served as burial places for noble lineages, as the royal ones did for early rulers. From the thirteenth century, several representations of aristocratic founders survive as frescoes or carvings on the tympanon: the couple are always shown in a prostrate position, beseeching Christ for their eternal reward.[112]

The royal foundation of monasteries continued throughout the period, and reflected the rise of new orders: although Benedictine monasteries and nunneries continued to be established in the twelfth century, kings also started to found Cistercian and Premonstratensian ones. The first Cistercian monastery in Hungary, Cikádor, was founded by monks from Heiligenkreuz, Austria, at King Géza II's request in 1142. After a short hiatus, the Cistercian order started to

*évfordulóján* (Budapest, 1938), 387–422; Ileana Burnichioiu and Adrian A. Rusu, *Mozaicurile medievale de la Bizere the Medieval Mosaics from Bizere die mittelalterlichen Mosaiken von Bizere* (Cluj-Napoca, 2006); Ileana Burnichioiu and Adrian A. Rusu, *Manastirea Bizere* (Cluj-Napoca, 2009).

112 Takács, ed., *Paradisum plantavit*, 229–66, 335–45, 350–8, 461–547 (in the period 1142–1241 between forty and eighty Benedictine monasteries were founded by families); Béla Zsolt Szakács, 'Állandó alaprajzok – változó vélemények? Megjegyzések a "bencés templomtípus" magyarországi pályafutásához', in *Maradandóság és változás*, ed. Szilvia Bodnár (Budapest, 2004), 25–37; Béla Zsolt Szakács, 'The research on Romanesque architecture in Hungary: a critical overview of the last twenty years', *Arte Medievale* n.s. 4, 2 (2005), 31–44; Erik Fügedi, 'Sepelierunt corpus eius in proprio monasterio: a nemzetségi monostor', *Századok* 125, 1–2 (1991), 35–67; Fügedi, 'Quelques questions concernant les monastères des grandes familles en Hongrie (XIe–XIVe siècle)', in *L'Eglise et le peuple chrétien dans les pays de l'Europe du Centre-Est et du Nord (XIVe–XVe siècles). Actes du colloque organisé par l'Ecole française de Rome, 27–29 janvier 1986*, Collection de l'Ecole Française de Rome 128 (Rome, 1990), 201–9; Marosi and Wehli, *Az Árpád-kor művészeti*, 44.

spread in Hungary during the reign of Béla III. He asked for monks from France, and founded several new Cistercian houses: Egres, by monks from Pontigny (1179), Zirc by monks from Clairvaux (1182), Szentgotthárd by monks from Trois Fontaines and Pilis by those from Acey (1184), while monks from Pilis itself took Pásztó over for the order (1191). In 1183, the king gave the same privileges to Cistercian monasteries in Hungary as they possessed in France. In the thirteenth century, King Béla IV (1235–70), bishops and nobles founded more Cistercian houses; that of Bélapátfalva remains, in early Gothic style. Only the groundplans of others are known.[113]

Sometime between 1157 and 1186, the Knights Hospitaller (Order of the Hospital of St John of Jerusalem) were introduced into Hungary, perhaps due to their charitable rather than military role. The first preceptory was just outside (Székes)Fehérvár, the royal centre. The support of King András II in the early thirteenth century led to the growth of the order, who by now played a military role in the realm. More houses were founded, and the order started to play a role in the authentication of documents (see below).[114] Another order, which scholars used to confuse with the Knights Hospitaller, was founded in the middle of the twelfth century by Géza II: the Order of Hospitaller Canons Regular of St Stephen (Stephanites).[115]

The two newly founded mendicant orders, the Dominicans and the Franciscans, settled very quickly in Hungary. Paulus Hungarus, who taught at the University of Bologna, was sent to Hungary to found the Dominican province there in 1221; by 1304 a *studium generale* (Dominican school) existed in Buda. The Franciscan province was founded in 1232. The main task of the new orders was preaching to the laity; three Dominican collections for preaching survive from

[113] There were seven Cistercian monasteries in the twelfth century: Ferenc Levente Hervay, *Repertorium historicum Ordinis Cisterciensis in Hungaria* (Rome, 1984); László Koszta, 'Die Gründung von Zisterzienserklöstern in Ungarn 1142–1270', *Ungarn Jahrbuch* 23 (1997), 65–80.

[114] Zsolt Hunyadi, *The Hospitallers in the Medieval Kingdom of Hungary c. 1150–1387* (Budapest, 2010); Hunyadi, 'Milites Christi in the medieval Kingdom of Hungary: a historiographical overview', *Chronica: Annual of the Institute of History, University of Szeged* 3 (2003), 50–7.

[115] Károly-György Boroviczény, 'Cruciferi Sancti Regis Stephani: tanulmány a stefaniták, egy középkori magyar ispotályos rend történetéről', *Orvostörténeti Közlemények: Communicationes de Historiae Artis Medicinae* 133–40 (1991–2), 7–48; Hunyadi, 'Military-religious orders in the medieval kingdom of Hungary: a historiographical overview'.

the thirteenth century, and two Franciscan ones containing sermons survive from late thirteenth-century Hungary. Both orders' books transmitted the most up-to-date French and Italian sermon material. Paulus Hungarus also annotated a canon-law collection (Compilatio I–III). The Franciscans had forty-one houses by 1300, and the Dominicans thirty-five by 1303. Both orders played a significant role at the rulers' courts. The Dominicans were favoured until 1260, when Princess Margit (Margaret), who had been offered to God as an oblate, took binding vows as a Dominican nun, refusing to marry. Her father, Béla IV, then started to patronize the Franciscans instead. The Dominicans were also important in conducting missions towards the neighbouring lands in the east, to the Cumans.[116]

The new religious spirit particularly affected royal women in the region. Apart from Margit, who espoused the Dominican way of life, several others became prominent proponents of the Franciscans. Erzsébet (Elizabeth; d. 1231), daughter of András II of Hungary and wife of Louis of Thuringia, founded a Franciscan hospital for lepers after becoming a widow, and lived a life of austerity and severe penance as a laywoman. Many other royal women were influenced by mendicant spirituality.[117] The new spirituality of the thirteenth century was not exclusively mendicant, however: an order of Pauline hermits was founded in Hungary in 1262, based on existing eremitical communities, the Ordo Fratrum S. Pauli Primi Eremitae, whose rule was granted in 1308.[118]

[116] Erik Fügedi, 'La formation des villes et les ordres mendiants en Hongrie', in Fügedi, *Kings, Bishops*, no. XII; Gergely Gallai, 'Some observations on Paulus Hungarus and his notabilia', in *Proceedings of the Eleventh International Congress of Medieval Canon Law: Catania, 30 July–6 August 2000*, ed. Manlio Bellomo (Vatican City, 2006), 235–44; Nora Berend, 'The Mendicant orders and the conversion of pagans in Hungary', in *Atti del XXVIII Convegno internazionale di studi Francescani Alle frontiere della cristianità: i frati mendicanti e l'evangelizzazione tra '200 e '300* (Spoleto, 2001), 255–79.

[117] Klaniczay, *Holy Rulers*, ch. 5; Gábor Klaniczay, 'Proving sanctity in the canonization processes: Saint Elizabeth and Saint Margaret of Hungary', in *Procès de canonisation au moyen âge: aspects juridiques et religieux*, ed. Gábor Klaniczay (Rome, 2004), 117–48; Dieter Blume and Matthias Werner, eds., *Elisabeth von Thüringen – eine europäische Heilige (3. Thüringer Landesausstellung 'Elisabeth von Thüringen – eine Europäische Heilige', Wartburg – Eisenach, 7. Juli bis 19. November 2007)*, 2 vols. (Petersberg, 2007).

[118] Ferenc Levente Hervay, ed., *Vitae fratrum eremitarum ordinis Sancti Pauli primi eremitae (Gregorius Gyöngyösi)* (Budapest, 1988); Gábor Sarbak, ed., *Der Paulinerorden. Geschichte, Geist, Kultur* (Budapest, 2010).

## LITURGY AND SAINTS

Liturgy was imported as well as rapidly produced locally. Saints' cults were introduced at the time of Christianization. The first to be established were universal cults (such as the cult of the apostles and the Virgin Mary), and the cults of saints popular in the areas from which Christian influences reached central Europe. Soon each polity also developed its own cults for local saints, which in Bohemia and Hungary included royal saints as well as ecclesiastics, and in Poland only ecclesiastics. The popularity of individual saints can be traced from evidence such as, for example, church dedications, texts and the appearance of saints on various objects, for example on coins and seals.

### *Bohemia*

The liturgical customs observed at the beginning in the Bohemian Church developed under influences of both Western (via the Empire) and Eastern (inherited from Great Moravian Christendom) Christianity.[119] The majority of liturgical books arrived at first from the Empire and specifically from Bavaria. The most ancient were *Gregoriánsko-gelasiánsky sakramentář* (written in the eight/ninth century) and *Franko-saský evangeliář* (*c.* 870). The first writing with elements of Czech orthography and grammar were the so-called *Kievian Letters*, preserved in an eleventh-century manuscript but originally probably composed in the tenth century. Several letters contained a Slavonic translation of the *Libellum missae* of Italian monastic origin, thought by researchers to have been a missionary aid. Their content also shows the influence of Byzantine liturgy, once again stressing the importance of both liturgical traditions for Bohemia. Into a book of Roman ritual, written in the first half of the eleventh century in Latin, several pages called *Pražské hlaholské zlomky* were inserted, written in the vernacular and in the Slavonic alphabet, and containing prayers supplementing Roman liturgy.[120] These few surviving sources are vivid testimony of the presence of Slavonic-rite elements in Bohemian Church liturgy (the language and grammar are probably from Great Moravian times but the orthography shows features

[119] Josef Vašica, *Literární památky epochy velkomoravské 863–885*, 2nd edn (Prague, 1996).

[120] David Kalhous, 'Slovanské písemnictví a liturgie 10. a 11. věku', *Český Časopis Historický* 108, 1 (2010), 1–33.

specific to Czech), although the Latin liturgy was by no means dominant.[121] And at the end of eleventh century these Slavonic elements in liturgy were treated by monastic writers only as ancient souvenirs.[122]

The Chronicle of Cosmas of Prague testified to the openness of the Bohemian Church to different liturgical influences. During Břetislav II's burial ceremony (1100) one of the clergymen exclaimed, uniting Latin, Greek and Jewish tradition: 'Anima Bracizlai Sabaoth Adonay, vivat expers thanaton, Bracizlaos yskiros.'[123] It is beyond doubt that a specific, Bohemian ritual connected with its specific liturgy existed during the early stage of Bohemian Church history, but we do not know the details.[124] Some elements of liturgical reforms were present in the activity of presbyter Marek who reformed the life of the cathedral chapter of Prague in 1068. Jindřich Zdík, the bishop of Olomouc from 1126 to 1150, reformed and unified liturgical customs in his diocese and issued rituals for his flock. *Legenda Christiani*

121 František Graus, 'Slovanksá liturgie a pisemnictvi v přemyslovských Čechá ch 10. století', *Československý Časopis Historický* 14 (1966), 473–95, reasonably opposed theories that the presence of Slavonic liturgical texts in the Přemyslid realm proved the existence of a complex Slavonic liturgy there. Although it is not possible to exclude such a possibility, much more probable is the existence of different versions of local liturgies in separate Church centres of the realm.

122 Franz Wenzel Mareš, 'Die slavische Liturgie in Böhmen zur Zeit der Gründung der Prager Bistums', in *Millennium dioeceseos Pragensis 973–1973. Beiträge zur Kirchengeschichte Mitteleuropas im 9.–11. Jahrhundert*, Annales instituti Slavici, 8 (Vienna, Cologne and Graz, 1974), 95–110; Emilie Bláhová, 'Literarische Beziehungen zwischen dem Sázava-Kloster und der Kiever Rus'', in *Der heilige Prokop, Böhmen und Mitteleuropa*, 237–53; Petr Kopal, 'Sázavský klášter jako středisko tzv. staroslověnské liturgie', in *Historia Monastica*, vol. I, *Sborník z kolokvií a konferencí pořádaných v letech 2002–2003 v cyklu 'Život ve středověkém klášteře'* (Prague, 2005), 141–4; Dušan Třeštík, 'Slawische Liturgie und Schrifttum im Böhmen des 10. Jahrhunderts. Vorstellungen und Wirklichkeit', in *Der heilige Prokop, Böhmen und Mitteleuropa*, 205–36. For more about the role of the Benedictine monastery of Sázava in preserving Slavic liturgy, see Květa Reichertová, Emilie Bláhová, Vlasta Dvořáčková and Václav Huňáček, *Sázava: památník staroslověnské kultury v Čechách* (Prague, 1988). See Martin Wihoda, 'Slovanská Sázava v paměti klášterního písemnictví', *Sázavsko* 11 (2004), 17–25, on traces of the pragmatic use of memory of the Slavic roots of the abbey in the cloister's historiography.

123 Cosmas III.13, p. 174.

124 On Slavonic prayers in Czech liturgy, see Miroslav Vepřek, 'Církevněslovanské modlitby českého původu: prieres en slavon d'origine tcheque', *Slavia* 77, 1–3 (2008), 221–30.

transmitted a description of liturgical burial practices that resembled those observed in Bavarian society. The Chronicle of Cosmas of Prague reports two types of lay participation in the liturgy: magnates during the bishop's enthronement in 975 sang the hymn 'Te Deum' in German and the common men shouted 'Krlessu'; the Czech elected Duke Spytihněv II (1055) and then sang 'kyrieleyson, cantilenam dulcem'.[125] Both incidents are more likely to have occurred in the first half of the twelfth century, the moment of composing the Chronicle, than the tenth or the eleventh century. But nevertheless they show the participation of laymen in the liturgical life of the Bohemian Church, although it was limited and rather stereotypical. Another example of lay activity in liturgical life is the common use of the so-called *calix ansatus*. These liturgical chalices were apparently used in Bohemia when laymen accepted communion in both forms and they ceased to be used after the Fourth Lateran Council.[126]

In the *Oppatowitz Homiliarium*, which was written in the middle of the twelfth century and contains the most ancient draft of the Czech liturgy, among the most popular Christian feasts connected with the life of Christ, his mother and the postles, two Czech saints were mentioned: Václav and Vojtěch-Adalbert. St Václav, the Bohemian duke murdered by his younger brother Boleslav I in 935, was the holy patron of the realm, the dynasty and the people. In the tenth to fourteenth centuries more than ten hagiographies and legends were written in Latin and Old Slavonic in various centres, from Monte Cassino to Kiev. In the eleventh century his portraits were struck on Bohemian coins and later also on royal seals. After the victorious battle of Chlumec over the German army in 1126, St Václav also was granted the title of the eternal military leader. Thus, he was no longer pictured as a monk but as a knight.[127] Such a transformation proved

[125] Cosmas, I.23, pp. 45–6, II.14, p. 103; Franz Zagiba, '"Krleš" und "Christe keinado" bei der Begrüssung Thietmars als ersten Bischof von Prag im Jahr 1076', in *Millennium dioeceseos Pragensis*, 119–26.

[126] Sommer, *Začátky křesťanství*, 23, 59; Sommer, 'Procession in early medieval Bohemia', in *Wallfahrten in der europäischen Kultur / Pilgrimage in European Culture*, ed. D. Doležal and H. Kühne (Frankfurt, 2006), 167–76; Sommer, *Svatý Prokop*, 37–54.

[127] Ferdinand Seibt, 'Der heilige Herzog Wenzel', in *Lebensbilder zur Geschichte der böhmischen Länder*, vol. IV (Munich and Vienna, 1981), 9–21; Anežka Merhautová, 'Vznik a význam svatováclavské přilby', in *Přemyslovský stat kolem roku 1000*, 85–92; Petr Charvát, *Václav, kníže Čechů* (Prague, 2011).

the vitality of the cult, whose object changed from classical, Ottonian saint king-Christianizer into saint warrior-patron of knights, much more popular in central Europe from the twelfth century. Slightly less popular was the cult of his mother, St Ludmila. The only Bohemian female saint of the period was strangled in Tetin in 921 on the order of her daughter-in-law Drahomira. Originally buried by the town wall, her relics were exhumed in 925 by Václav and reburied in Prague in St George's church. With time she became one of Bohemia's holy patrons. In *Legenda Christiani* she was pictured mainly as the wife of Břetislav I and the mother of Václav and Boleslav. According to the ideal of pious queens of the Ottonian dynasty, she was portrayed as a humble but wise woman, and above all as co-founder of Bohemian Christianity. Later she started to be remembered as the mother of the Přemyslid dynasty as well as of the Czech Christian nation.[128]

Vojtěch-Adalbert was born in 956/7 as a member of the mighty Slavnikids family. He started his clerical career early and in 982 was elected bishop of Prague. His strict observance of Christian ethics and Church law was coupled to admonishing and preaching his flock. He gradually lost the sympathy of, and the possibility of controlling, Czechs. Finally he left Prague in 989, went to Rome and became a Benedictine monk at the Aventine abbey. Urged by Pope John XV, he went back to Prague in 993 but left it again before his family was killed by Duke Boleslav II in 995. In 997 he tried to convert Prussia with the help of the Piast duke Bolesław I and was killed by pagans. His body was buried in Gniezno, one of Bolesław I's capitals. In 1039 the Czech duke Břetislav I brought to Prague relics of St Vojtěch-Adalbert and the Five Martyr Brothers (see Chapter 3).[129]

[128] *Legenda Christiani*, chap. 2, 'Peoples and dynasties', and Nad'a Profantová, *Kněžna Ludmila: vládkyně a světice, zakladatelka dynastie* (Prague, 1996); H. Jilek, 'Die Wenzels- und Ludmila-Legenden des 10. und 11. Jahrhunderts (Neuere Froschungsergbnisse)', *Zeitschrift für Ostforschung* 24 (1975), 79–148; Maria Y. Paramonova, 'Heiligkeit und Verwandschaft. Die dynastische Motive in den lateinischen Wenzelslegenden und den Legenden der Boris und Gleb', in *Fonctions sociales et politiques du culte des saints dans les sociétés de rite grec et latin au Moyen Age et á l'epoque modern: approche comparative*, ed. Marek Derwich and Michail Dmitriev (Wrocław, 1999), 433–55; Zdeňka Hledíková, 'Úcta sv. Ludmily mezi 12. a 14. stoletím a její formování v klášteře sv. Jiří na Pražském hradě', in *Nomine Liudmilam: Sborník prací k poctě svaté Ludmily / Nomine Liudmilam: Collection of Works in Honour of St. Ludmila*, ed. Renata Špačkova and Petr Meduna (Mělník, 2006), 41–53.

[129] Cosmas II and V.

The tomb of St Vojtěch-Adalbert in St Vitus's rotunda became the site of veneration which was later transferred to the Romanesque cathedral of Prague. In the early twelfth century he had became patron of the diocese of Prague and was popularly thought of as its founder.[130]

Prokop (*c.* 970–1053) was the third of the 'national' saints of Bohemia before 1200. He was the founder and first abbot of the monastery at Sázava as well as a determined spokesman for the use of post-Moravian Slavonic liturgy in central Europe. At first his cult was restricted to Sázava monks and laymen from their immediate social enviroment. That gradually changed when, thanks to Přemysl Otakar II, the abbot was canonized by Pope Innocent III in 1203. But even after that his cult was far from having a wide social range. No earlier than in the fourteenth century, and mainly thanks to the king and emperor Charles IV, his sanctity was well known, and he became the third holy patron of Bohemia, alongside the 'eternal king' St Václav and St Vojtěch-Adalbert.[131]

## *Poland*

Our knowledge about the early history of liturgy in Poland is worse than vague. Because several Polish liturgical terms were derived from Czech, historians argued that foundations of the liturgical life in

[130] See generally, Jaroslav Kadlec, 'Svatovojtěšská úcta v českých zemích', in *Svatý Vojtěch: sborník k mileniu*, ed. Jaroslav V. Polc (Prague, 1997), 42–75, and Franz Machilek, 'Die Adalbertsverehrung in Böhmen im Mittelalter', in *Adalbert von Prag. Brückenbauer zwischen dem Osten und Westen Europas*, ed. Hans Hermann Henrix (Baden-Baden, 1997), 163–83. On more specific problems, see Zdeněk Boháč, 'Svatovojtěšská patrocinia v českých zemích', in *Svatý Vojtěch: sborník k mileniu*, 76–87; Anežka Merhautová, 'Počátky úcty ke sv. Vojtěchu ve výtvarném umění', *Sborník Společnosti přátel starožitností* 3 (1992), 23–6; for the broader central European context at the turn of the tenth and eleventh centuries, see Dušan Třeštík, 'Sv. Vojtěch a formování střední Evropy', in *Svatý Vojtěch, Čechové a Evropa: sborník příspěvků z mezinárodního sympozia uspořádaného Českou křesťanskou akademií a Historickým ústavem Akademie věd ČR 19.–20. listopadu 1997 v Praze*, ed. Dušan Třeštík and Josef Žemlička (Prague, 1998), 81–108.

[131] Wojciech Iwańczak, 'Kult św. Prokopa w średniowiecznych Czechach', in *Środkowoeuropejskie dziedzictwo cyrylo-metodiańskie*, ed. Antoni Barciak (Katowice, 1999), 165–78; Jaroslav Kadlec, 'Der heilige Prokop', in *Tausend Jahre Benediktiner in den Klöstern Břevnov, Braunau und Rohr im Auftrag der Abteien Břevnov und Braunau in Rohr* (St Ottilien, 1993), 309–24; Sommer, *Svatý Prokop*, 173–210; Sommer, 'Der heilige Prokop und sein Kult im Mittelalter', in *Die Heiligen und ihr Kult im Mittelalter* (Prague, 2010), 275–97.

Poland were shaped by relations with the Bohemian Church. But when we consider the manuscripts imported and the clergymen who arrived to Poland from abroad, the influences of Bohemian Church are disputable for the eleventh–twelfth centuries. Liturgical manuscripts were written and probably imported from Bavaria (*Missale Gnesnensis*, written *c.* 1000, and the *Codex Aureus Gnesnensis* and *Codex Aureus Pultaviensis*, both written in the second half of the eleventh century) and the Rhineland (*Psalterium Egberti*, in Poland since *c.* 1020, and *Sacramentarium Tinecense*, brought to the Piast state *c.* 1050).[132] Also the first bishop of Cracow and *de facto* head of the Polish Church after the pagan reaction in the 1030s was Aaron, the Benedictine abbot of Tyniec, who originated from the Rhineland. During the twelfth century apart from Bavaria, Saxony, and the Rhineland, northern France and especially the region of Meuse became a main region of influence. From here came Alexander and Walter of Malonne, brothers and leading figures in a reform movement in the Polish Church of the twelfth century. Alexander as bishop of Płock (1129–56) and Walter as bishop of Wrocław (1149–69) tried to establish customs in accordance with the papal magisterium for clergymen and the liturgy. Alexander supposedly even brought a pontifical called *Pontificale Plocensis* with description of ecclesiastical ceremonials according to Roman rite.[133] Several years before the brothers of Malonne began these reforms, the papal legate to Poland, Cardinal Gilles of Tusculum, deposed several bishops as unworthy and ordered the adjustment of Polish ecclesiastical life to the Roman standard (*c.* 1125). If one of the fields of this reform was liturgical customs, this suggests that before these changes some kind of special Polish liturgy was observed in the Church, but its characteristics are completely unknown.

The beginnings of saints' cults in Poland are as vague as those of the liturgy. They were strictly connected with the ducal court but no member of the dynasty became a saint. Even Dobrava, Mieszko I's wife, memorialized in historical sources as Christianizing her

[132] Edward Potkowski, *Książka rękopiśmienna w kulturze Polski średniowiecznej* (Warsaw, 1984); for a short introduction, see Anna Adamska, 'The Introduction of Writing in Central Europe (Poland, Hungary and Bohemia)', in *The New Approaches to Medieval Communication*, ed. Marco Mostert (Turnhout, 1999), 175–6.

[133] Antoni Podleś, *Pontyfikał płocki z XII wieku. Bayerische Staatsbibliothek München Clm 28938. Biblkioteka Seminarium Duchownego Płosk, Mspł 29. Studium liturgiczno-źródłoznawcze. Edycja tekstu* (Płock, 1986) (edition and commentary in Polish).

husband's realm, was not described as a saint and had no cult. Several historians suggest that her son, Bolesław I the Brave, might have been treated as a dynastic saint in the eleventh century, but this hypothesis has no basis in evidence. It is possible that the absence of rulers who initiated the Christianization of Poland becoming saints is a result of the destruction of the Polish Church in 1038/9. Without ecclesiastical 'places of memory' founded during Christianization, the memorialization of those who began the process was lost, or at least any potential cult lost its fundamental basis. It is characteristic that the founder of Gniezno archbishopric from the twelfth century was believed to have been St Vojtěch-Adalbert, not his patron, Duke Bolesław I the Brave. Moreover, Bolesław I the Brave did not attempt to memorialize his father's merits nor did Mieszko II, son of Bolesław. Bolesław consciously created the cult of St Vojtěch-Adalbert as his and his realm's patron for political reasons (Vojtěch-Adalbert was closely related to the court of Emperor Otto III). He imitated his father, only more successfully. Mieszko I venerated St Godehard of Augsburg; that cult was strongly supported by the empress-widow Adelaide as an imperial cult. In this way, political cults fully supported by dukes could outshine locally important dynastic cults.[134]

Due to the efforts of Bolesław I the Brave, the most important Polish saint until the thirteenth century became St Vojtěch-Adalbert, bishop of Prague. Bolesław's and Emperor Otto III's influence led to Vojtěch-Adalbert's speedy canonization, and the founding of the archbishopric of Gniezno where Radim-Gaudenties, brother of the saint, was appointed as the first 'archbishop of St Vojtěch[-Adalbert]' in 999–1000. After the Bohemian duke Břetislav I took the saint's relics from Gniezno in 1039, his cult in Poland faded but it flourished once again at the beginning of the twelfth century with the help of Duke Bolesław III the Wrymouth. During his reign in 1127 the head of St Vojtěch-Adalbert was miraculously found in Gniezno (it was his second head, the first one being still in Prague). The saint was elevated as the main patron of the realm. On ducal coins and lead seals the saint was presented as protecting the duke.[135] Duke Bolesław I the Brave might

[134] Tomasz Janiak, 'Czy Bolesław Chrobry był czczony jako święty? Z badań nad przestrzenią liturgiczną przedromańskiej katedry w Poznaniu (do połowy XI w.)', *Slavia Antiqua* 44 (2003), 67–95.

[135] Alexander Gieysztor, 'Sanctus et gloriosissimus martyr Christi Adalbertus: un état et une église missionaires aux alentours de l'an Mille', in *La conversione al Cristianesimo nell'Europa dell'alto medioevo*, Settimane di Studi del Centro Italiano

also have planned to establish a cult of Bruno of Querfurt, whose martyred body he bought, just as he had done for Vojtěch-Adalbert in 997. His plans, failed however, because of radically different political circumstances. The new German king, Henry II, did not share the predication of his predecessor Otto III for Poland and went to war with Bolesław. In this context his fellow Saxon, Bruno, had little chance of becoming a new Polish saint.[136] More persistent was the cult of Five Martyred Brothers, hermits who lived in a cloister somewhere in Greater Poland (Meseritz). After their relics were transported to Bohemia in 1038/9, their cult survived in a weak form.[137]

Other saints whose cult was supported by the Piasts included St Peter throughout the eleventh century, St George and above all St Giles. The latter was believed to be the special protector of Bolesław III the Wrymouth. According to the Chronicle of Anonymous, his father, Władysław Herman, sent envoys to the abbey of St Giles with precious gifts and requests for prayers so that his wife, Judith of Bohemia, might conceive a son, the future Bolesław III. During his and his father's lifetimes several churches were founded under the name of St Giles. But that was a private cult that ended with the death of Bolesław III. More disputable is the character of the cult of Stanisław, a bishop of Cracow sentenced to death for treason by King Bolesław II the Bold in 1079. Some historians believe that as early as during Władysław Herman's reign the cult of Bishop Stanisław developed in Cracow. But the bishop's cult is confirmed no earlier than the thirteenth century, a period of struggle for the

di Studi sull'Alto Medioevo 14 (Spoleto, 1967), 611–47; 'Discussione sulla lezione Gieysztor', in *La conversione al Cristianesimo*, 683–4; Jerzy Strzelczyk, 'Die Rolle Böhmens und St Adalberts für die Westorientierung Polens', in *Adalbert von Prag* 141–62; Johannes Fried, 'Gnesen, Aachen, Rom. Otto III. und der Kult des hl. Adalberts. Beobachtungen zum älteren Adalbertsleben', in *Polen und Deutschland vor 1000 Jahren*, 235–79; Sławomir Gawlas, 'Der hl. Adalbert als Landespatron und die frühe Nationenbildung bei den Polen', in *Polen und Deutschland vor 1000 Jahren*, 193–233; Monika Siama, *La mythologie chrétienne en Pologne du haut moyen âge: le cas de saint Adalbert* (Grenoble, 2009); Lucas Wolfinger, 'Politische Handeln mit dem hl. Adalbert von Prag. Mittelalterliche Vorstellungen von einer civitas sancta', *Mitteilungen des Instituts für Österreichische Geschichtsforschung* 114 (2006), 219–50.

[136] *Bruno z Kwerfurtu: osoba-dzieło-epoka*, ed. Marian Dygo and Wojciech Fałkowski (Pułtusk, 2010).

[137] Brygida Kürbis, 'Brun z Kwerfurtu i początki kultu Pięciu Braci', in *Polska na przełomie I i II tysiąclecia. Materiały Sesji Stowarzyszenia Historyków Sztuki, Poznań, listopad 2000*, ed. Szczęsny Skibiński (Poznań, 2001), 115–27.

Polish Church's independence from ducal and magnate patronage. Stanisław's canonization in 1254 marked a symbolic victory for those who had worked to establish the independence of the Polish Church: he clearly represented the struggle against lay power. But his cult in the eleventh and first half of the twelfth century, during the times of strong ducal authority, is rather obscure. Strikingly, during the period in question, apart from the Virgin Mary, there were no cults of women in the Polish Church. The first widely popular local woman saint was St Hedwig, the wife of the Silesian duke Henryk the Bearded, canonized in 1267.[138]

## *Hungary*

Like other aspects of the ecclesiastical organization, early Hungarian liturgy was imported. The most important influences came from neighbouring ecclesiastical centres, such as Aquileia, Magdeburg, Mainz, Passau and Salzburg. Liturgical manuscripts primarily show the influence of southern German areas, the Rhineland, northern Italy and Lotharingia. Such influences were due both to missionaries who arrived in the kingdom bringing their local liturgical practices and texts, and to the imported ecclesiastical manuscripts. These were often acquired on the order of the king, who donated them to churches. The earliest known liturgical manuscript is a fragment of a sacramentary from the first half of the eleventh century. This follows southern German traditions, as do other early manuscripts donated to the newly founded bishopric of Zagreb at the end of the eleventh century. The Szelepchényi or Nitra Evangelistary follows a system known only from ninth- and tenth-century Lotharingian manuscripts. Occasionally, manuscripts from areas more distant from Hungary were imported, such as a northern French manuscript originally produced for the monastery of St Vaast. Byzantine influence has been debated: while some scholars detect it in certain liturgical formulas, the dates of some saints' feastdays, and the late eleventh-century prescriptions of fasting, others argue that these mirrored outdated western customs. Migrant clerics could contribute to the spread of specific liturgical influences: Arnold of Regensburg travelled

[138] Aleksander Gieysztor, 'Politische Heilige im hochmittelalterlichen Polen und Böhmen', in *Politik und Heiligenverehrung im Hochmittelalter*, ed. Jürgen Petersohn (Sigmaringen, 1994), 325–41.

to Esztergom in 1028 where he taught the office of St Emmeram to the canons of the cathedral.[139]

Liturgies were composed in Hungary already in the late eleventh century; for example, the Sacramentary of St Margaret includes a liturgy for the local saint István. The *Codex Albensis*, the earliest antiphonale with musical notations (*c.* 1120, probably from Transylvania), shows that common elements existed in the liturgical usage of the dioceses of Esztergom, Kalocsa and Transylvania. Thus a basic common liturgical structure developed in the Hungarian kingdom, distinct from the practice of neighbouring bishoprics, going back at least to the early twelfth century. New elements continued to be incorporated into the liturgy, for example, a newly invented type of Hungarian musical notation at the end of the twelfth century. Some ecclesiastical institutions had significant collections of liturgical manuscripts: a charter from the end of the eleventh century lists around forty of them in the possession of the Benedictine monastery of Pannonhalma.[140]

Both eastern and western saints appeared in Hungary, although the distinctions were often not clear cut, and therefore there is disagreement over the possible eastern influences on saints' cults in Hungary. According to some scholars, the cults of Nicholas, George, Cosmas and Damian clearly signal such influences, either due to Byzantine missions, or to an existing Orthodox population in the realm. However, some 'eastern' saints were also venerated in the German Empire (as St George's chapel in Regensburg testifies, for example) and, according to other historians, the influence of the Ottonian Empire may have been more important in introducing these cults to Hungary. Thus it is possible that Hungarian cults of

[139] N. Berend *et al.*, 'The kingdom of Hungary', 335–6.

[140] József Török, 'The history of liturgy in Hungary', in *A Thousand Years of Christianity in Hungary*, 155–9; József Török, 'Storia della liturgia medievale dell'Ungheria', *Folia theologica* 8 (1997), 143–56; N. Berend *et al.*, 'The kingdom of Hungary', 356–7; Zoltán Falvy and László Mezey, eds., *Codex Albensis. Ein Antiphonar aus dem 12. Jahrhundert* (Budapest and Graz, 1963); László Dobszay and Gábor Prószéky, eds., *Corpus Antiphonalium Officii, Ecclesiarum Centralis Europae: A Preliminary Report*, tr. Erzsébet Mészáros (Budapest, 1988); Benjamin Rajeczky, ed., *Magyarország zenetörténete I Középkor* (Budapest, 1988); Györffy, *Diplomata Hungariae*, pp. 295–301, no. 100; Polycarpus Radó, *Libri liturgici manuscripti bibliothecarum Hungariae et limitropharum regionum* (Budapest, 1973); László Dobszay, 'The system of Hungarian plainsong sources', *Studia Musicologia Academiae Scientiarum Hungaricae* 27 (1985), 37–65; Janka Szendrei, *A 'mos patriae' kialakulása 1341 előtti hangjegyes forrásaink tükrében* (Budapest, 2005).

some of these saints owed their origin to German, rather than Byzantine, influence.[141]

Church dedications include the Virgin Mary and Sts George, Martin, Nicholas, Michael and Peter. There are also dedications to St Adalbert (Vojtěch, the martyred bishop of Prague). The origin of his cult in Hungary is debated: it may have been linked to its promotion by Emperor Otto III, or to the role Adalbert's disciples played in Hungary or, according to some historians, to Adalbert's important role in the Christianization of Hungary. Other saints to whom churches were dedicated included Adrian (a fourth-century martyr from Nikomedia), Benedict (of Nursia), Demetrius (a fourth-century local martyr whose cult was important in the Carpathian basin), Giles (a supposed seventh-century hermit, whose cult was imported because of the links to the monastery of Saint-Gilles in France), and the first-century pope Clement I. The cult of St Gotthard, abbot of Niederaltaich and bishop of Hildesheim (d. 1038, canonized 1131), is attested in Hungary already in the twelfth century; his relics were preserved in Nitra and Pozsony (Bratislava). The chasuble that István and Gisela donated to the church of the Holy Virgin at (Székes) Fehérvár, and which was subsequently transformed into a coronation mantle, was decorated with a number of saints; these show both German and Byzantine influence: Sts Cosmas, Damian, Pantaleon, George, Vincent, Stephen proto-martyr (the bishopric of Passau was dedicated to him, and István – Stephen – was named after him), Clement, Sixtus, Cornelius and Lawrence. Narrative sources mention the Virgin Mary and St Martin as important patron saints for István, who prayed to them before battles. A late-eleventh-century synod prescribed the list of saints whose feasts were to be celebrated, which included the local saints, the apostles and feasts of the Virgin and of the Cross; that these cults became widespread can be seen in the choice of subsequent church titles.[142]

141 Károly Mesterházy, 'Adatok a Bizánci kereszténység elterjedéséhez az Árpádkori Magyarországon', *Debreceni Múzeum Évkönyve* (1968–70), 145–77; István Kapitánffy, *Hungarobyzantina: Bizánc és a görögség a középkori magyarországi forrásokban* (Budapest, 2003), 40–1; see also n. 10 in this chapter. For a detailed study of Demetrius, showing Byzantine connections, see Péter Tóth, ed., *Szent Demeter: Magyarország elfeledett védőszentje* (Budapest, 2007).

142 András Mező, *A templomcím a magyar helységnevekben (11.–15. század)* (Budapest, 1996); András Mező, *Patrocíniumok a középkori Magyarországon* (Budapest, 2003);

The first local saints in Hungary were canonized in 1083 by local synods: István I, his son Imre (Emeric) who died young, before his father, the Venetian monk Gerard (Gellért), who became bishop of Csanád in Hungary and who was martyred by pagan rebels after István's death in 1046; and two immigrant hermits, Benedict and Zoerard-Andrew (the forms Szórád, Svorad, Świerad are also used). The political circumstances of these canonizations have been analysed in detail. It was most probably the ruling king, László I, who initiated these canonizations. King András I (1046–60) had his son Salamon crowned king (1057), to which András's brother Béla objected. Civil wars followed, involving the intervention of Emperor Henry IV on the side of Salamon, who finally occupied the throne (1063–74), but was then attacked by Béla's sons Géza and László. The latter two were victorious, and Salamon was imprisoned. Géza I and then László I ruled Hungary but, in spite of their military victory and ability to rule, they suffered from a 'legitimacy deficit'. László had been ruling without having been crowned, and initiated the canonizations as a means of legitimation. In preparation for the canonizations, he freed Salamon from prison, who then escaped abroad.[143]

Thus the cult of King István I was initially organized for political reasons, and this laid the basis for his continued importance as a reference point. From being represented as the fount of various rights in medieval legislation, to his modern cult as the founder of the state, István has been central in ideas about the medieval kingdom and modern nationalism. István's hagiography also reflected political trends. Three *Lives* were written between his canonization and the early twelfth century, and all contained elements of political polemics. The first two depict István in very different ways. According to the *Legenda Maior*, he was a holy man, living an ascetic life dedicated to prayer and charity. In contrast, the *Legenda Minor* emphasized the cruel punishments István meted out, although in order to uphold justice. According to some scholars, this is a more authentic portrait of the first king; according to others, it served to legitimize King Kálmán's own deeds. The last *vita*, by Hartvic, commissioned by

Kovács and Bardoly, eds., *Coronation Mantle of the Hungarian Kings*; N. Berend *et al.*, 'The kingdom of Hungary', 337; Bak *et al.*, eds., *Laws*, 60, c. 38.

143 Klaniczay, *Holy Rulers*, ch. 3; László Veszprémy, 'Royal saints in Hungarian chronicles, legends and liturgy', in *The Making of Christian Myths in the Periphery of Latin Christendom (c. 1000–1300)*, ed. Lars Boje Mortensen (Copenhagen, 2006), 217–45.

King Kálmán, defended the Hungarian king's rights against both pope and emperor. Against papal claims, Hartvic asserted that the Hungarian ruler received the right from the pope to rule according to both laws as well as the right to be the head of the church as an apostolic king; and that he had offered the realm to the Virgin Mary. To counteract any imperial claims over Hungary, he invented the story of the sending of a papal crown to István, and used an earlier story about the Virgin Mary's miraculous intervention to protect Hungary against German invasion.[144]

The *Lives* of the other saints were written by different ecclesiastics: that of the two ascetic hermits not long after 1064, by Mór, former abbot of Pannonhalma, bishop of Pécs. Their cult was strong in the region of Nitra and in southern and south-western Poland. Gerard's cult was especially marked in Csanád, of which he was bishop, and Pest, where he was martyred. Of the two legends that were written, one, the *Legenda Maior*, dates from the second half of the fourteenth century in its present form and includes many elements that are incompatible with the early Middle Ages. Some scholars, however, argue that its basis was an earlier, no longer extant *vita*, written in the first half of the twelfth century, and that it contains authentic eleventh-century data, such as the stories about the bishopric of Csanád in the 1030s and the battle against Ajtony. The *Legenda Minor* is a text for the saint's feastday. It emphasizes Gerard's virtues, goodness and humility. It is dated variously to the end of the eleventh, first half of the twelfth or the early thirteenth century. The *Life* of Imre was probably written in the middle of the twelfth century, depicting him as a virgin. László I himself was canonized in 1192, and his *vita* was composed in the early thirteenth century.[145]

[144] Veszprémy, ed., *Szent István*; Bartoniek, ed., *Legenda S. Stephani regis ab Hartvico episcopo conscripta*; N. Berend, 'Hartvic'; József Gerics, 'Über Vorbilder und Quellen der Vita Hartviciana Sancti Stephani regis Hungariae', *Acta antiqua Academiae Scientiarum Hungaricae* 29 (1981), 425–44; József Gerics, *Egyház, állam és gondolkodás Magyarországon a középkorban* (Budapest, 1995); Gábor Thorockay, 'A Hartvik-legenda a XIX.–XX. századi történetírásban', in Thoroczkay, *Írások az Árpád-korról: történeti és historiográfiai tanulmányok* (Budapest, 2009), 171–214.

[145] Klaniczay, *Holy Rulers*, ch. 4; Gábor Klaniczay and Edit Madas, 'La Hongrie', in *Hagiographies: histoire internationale de la littérature hagiographique latine et vernaculaire en Occident des origines à 1550*, ed. Guy Philippart, vol. II (Turnhout, 1996), 103–60; Pál Cséfalvay, ed., *Magyar szentek tisztelete és ereklyéi: kiállítás a Keresztény Múzeumban, 2000. június 17–október 1.* (Esztergom, 2000).

## RULERS AND CLERICS

In all three realms, ecclesiastics, especially prelates, played a key role in royal government as royal counsellors, chancellors and diplomats; rulers therefore wanted to ensure that they were reliable. Rulers thus continued to exert an important influence over selections for episcopal sees and ecclesiastical legislation. There were differences between the three dynasties, however, in their preferences for foreign or local prelates.

### *Bohemia*

Because of their significance for royal government, the Bohemian clergy were financed by the dukes and were more dependent on their secular lords than on the authority of the bishops.[146] Even tithes, originally paid in grain,[147] were at first collected by ducal officials and given to the Church. The clergy was subject to the ruler's judicial, administrative and financial control; the rulers announced their expectations of Christian conduct and punished any transgressors.[148] The bishops of Prague, financially and politically dependent on the monarchs, were treated as royal officials and were expected to support the policies of the Přemyslids: at the end of the twelfth century, they were still regarded as 'chaplains' to the dukes.[149] At times, however, it was possible for the ruler to rely on another ecclesiastic instead of the bishop: Spytihněv II's main adviser was Meginhard, the German abbot of the monastery of Břevnov, rather than Bishop Sever. The will of dukes/kings who held the right of investiture was decisive in any nominations to sees. Even in Prague, where there had been a strong tradition of electing bishops, the dukes always had the final say.

The Bohemian dukes, mindful of the difficult coexistence between Boleslav II and the Bohemian bishop Vojtěch-Adalbert, preferred to 'import' their bishops, usually from Germany. This strategy allowed the dukes to avoid any problems that might result from the close involvement of Church leaders in local political communities, often themselves opposing the ruler. Even placing one's cousin or brother on the bishop's throne at Prague resulted in a serious conflict of interest, as happened

[146] J. Žemlička, '"Decimae trium provinciarum" pro klášter v Břevnově (k hmotnému zajištění nejstarších klášterních fundací v Čechách)', in *Ludzie, Kościół, Wierzenia*, 125–33.

[147] Cosmas I.40. [148] Cosmas II.4 and III.1. [149] *Letopis Jarlocha*, 480.

under Bishops Jaromír-Gebhard (1068–90) and Jindřich (1182–97). The canonical election of bishops and other ecclesiastics was only gradually introduced, against the will of the monarchs.

Vratislav II invested heavily in the Church,[150] but Jaromír-Gebhard began a campaign against his decision in 1063 to restore the ancient Moravian diocese, with its seat in Olomouc. The ecclesiastical separation of Moravia radically diminished the power of the bishops of Prague.[151] Jaromír-Gebhard invaded Olomouc, and also produced a document that purported to show the extent of his own diocese when it fell under the charge of St Vojtěch-Adalbert. The size of the original Prague bishopric was wildly enlarged, being said to include not only Bohemia and Moravia but also western Slovakia and southern Poland, along with Lesser Poland and large parts of Silesia. The bishop relied on these claims to persuade the participants of a synod called at Mainz in the spring of 1086. Emperor Henry IV even included it in a special privilege.[152] His authority reinforced, Jaromir-Gebhard questioned his subordination to Vratislav II and began to claim suzerainty over the duke. He even ignored his brother's royal coronation on 15 June 1086, which was conducted instead by Archbishop Egilbert of Trier.

Rulers were involved in a dispute over the continued use of a 'double liturgy' (in Latin and Slavonic). When Duke Spytihněv II expelled all monks from Sázava in 1056, the community survived in exile in Hungary before being recalled to Sázava in 1061 by Vratislav II. Bishop Jaromir-Gebhard opposed this. In 1089 Vratislav II, as the newly crowned king, tried unsuccessfully to gain papal approval for the use of the Slavonic liturgy. In 1095, the last Slavonic abbot Božetěch was expelled and the monastery was soon reconsecrated under the Latin rite.

Duke Břetislav II returned to the old tradition of appointing foreigners and nominated his German chaplain, Herman, a decision that was approved by Emperor Henry IV during Easter 1099 in Regensburg. Vladislav I's German wife Richeza promoted the Schwabian monk Meinhard[153] to the bishopric in Prague. Among

[150] Z. Hledíková, 'Das Studium von mittelalterlichen kirchlichen Korporationen in Böhmen und Mähren', *Quaestiones Medii Aevi Novae* 2 (1997), 61–9.

[151] V. Medek, *Osudy moravské církve do konce 14. století, I díl dějin olomoucké arcidiecéze* (Prague, 1971).

[152] *CDB* I, 92–5, no. 86.

[153] Meinhard came from the monastery of Zwiefalen, which had been founded by the duchess's Berg family.

other foreign bishops of Prague were in 1169 Gotpold, former abbot of the Cistercian monastery at Sedlec, and Queen Judith's relative, Frederick.

The Church flourished in Moravia under Bishop Jindřich Zdík. Bishop Zdík implemented a broad programme of reforms across the diocese. In 1131 he moved the cathedral from its former seat at the church of St Peter to St Václav's in the castle of Olomouc. In 1142 he supported the elected Duke Vladislav II against his numerous relatives. He declared the Moravian dukes anathema after they had showed their support for the opposite faction by depriving the bishop of his landed possessions. Despite papal support and a military expedition led by Vladislav II in 1143, the bishop was not able to return to Olomouc immediately, but only after two years of mediation by the papal legate, Cardinal Guido. Still, some of the dukes resisted and in 1145 Jindřich Zdík survived a serious attempt on his life. Pope Eugenius III laid another anathema on the Moravian dukes and an interdict on their churches. Before his death in 1150, Zdík exempted the inhabitants of his diocese from all services and taxes due to the Moravian rulers.

Jindřich Břetislav of Přemyslid dynasty became bishop of Prague in 1182. This grandson of King Vladislav II was educated in Paris and had proved himself to be a capable administrator. In 1193 he also became duke. This unusual situation in which the highest political and ecclesiastical offices were united under the control of one man lasted until his death in 1197. Then Vladislav III's chaplain Daniel Milik became bishop despite protests from the Bohemian clergy, defensive of their independence from secular power. They sent a complaint to the pope accusing the new bishop of having been unjustly elected and of having committed several crimes. But the traditional right of Bohemian rulers to decide on the bishop's appointment was not threatened. Přemysl Otakar I also received, together with a hereditary royal title, the right of investiture and control over the Bohemian and Moravian bishops. The royal right to investiture was confirmed by Frederick II's 'Golden Bull of Sicily' in 1212 and lasted until the end of the dynasty.

## *Poland*

The strong connection of the Polish Church administration with the ducal administrative system is revealed by the network of first bishopric sees. Established in 1000, the Polish Church province was divided into bishoprics consistent with territories of provinces or regions of the Piast realm discussed by later sources: Pomerania, Silesia and Greater and Lesser Poland. It was no accident that when the Piast government fell in 1038–9, the Church administration system was swept away by pagan reaction or by elite rebellion. It seems probable that the co-operation of provincial bishops was important for the enactment of the internal policies of the Piasts, especially before the network of *comites provinciae* and castellans was established in the twelfth century. It is no wonder that during the eleventh century external contacts of local churches were subordinated to the control of the monarchs. The strong tradition of ducal control over the Church did not weaken during the first wave of 'Gregorian reforms'. Although he actively supported Pope Gregory VII against Emperor Henry IV, Duke Bolesław II the Bold saw it as an element of his own policy. Thus, he opposed anything and anyone threatening to diminish his ducal, and from 1076, royal authority. Therefore in 1079 he ordered the execution of Bishop Stanisław of Cracow on the grounds of treason. But, although royal authority was respected, it had its limits. Nobles did not accept the execution and expelled the king. A ruler had to obey rules, including those dealing with religion and the Church. When Bolesław III the Wrymouth sentenced his older half-brother Zbigniew to be blinded and thus broke his word, he had to cleanse himself in the eyes of his people through accepting the humiliation of an ecclesiastical penance. The duke took part in penitent pilgrimages to Hungary and to St Vojtěch-Adalbert's tomb in Gniezno from 1112 to 1113. Only then did the archbishop and other bishops, during Easter, officially announce him free of guilt and capable of ruling.

Despite the subdivision of Poland and the subsequent disintegration of the realm's centralized administrative infrastructure after Bolesław's death in 1138, the Polish Church not only survived but even flourished. This success was also dependent on the new function of the bishops as supporters of political claims made by various provincial dukes. In 1146 Archbishop Jakub of Żnin declared an anathema on the senior duke Władysław II the Exile, which might have contributed to his final defeat. During the second half of the twelfth century bishops were still close allies of 'their' local dukes but they were no longer subordinated to the ruler to the extent they had been previously. Near the end of the century their position strengthened. First, they were seen as natural leaders of local noble factions.

Second, in cases of major importance they could count on the support of the whole Polish Church structure and on papal authority. This provoked two diametrically opposed reactions from rulers. Some tried to save their traditional position and fought against any attempt of Church officials to act independently, which brought long periods of conflict, rarely won by dukes. Bolesław I the Tall of Silesia querelled with his son, Jarosław, bishop of Wrocław, over the latter's decisions but generally had to accept them. The majority of rulers tried to adjust to the situation and actively co-operated with bishops, gaining acceptance for their reign. The best example of this behaviour was Kazimierz the Just who, after taking the ducal seat in Cracow, at the expense of his older brother Mieszko III the Old actively sought the acceptance of Polish bishops. Legally, his behaviour was rebellion (see Chapter 3). But with the agreement of the Polish Church his deeds were accepted. In return he rewarded the Church with liberties during the meeting in Łęczyca in 1180. This opened a new chapter in relations between Polish dukes and Church officials: the latter were no longer strictly dependent on rulers, or at least fought fiercely not to be. But the process of their gaining independence lasted until the end of the thirteenth century.

From the end of the twelfth century ecclesiastics tried to free their institutions from strong ducal supervision. This became possible due to the weakening of the rulers' political position caused by long-lasting conflicts between members of the Piast dynasty. They had to rely on allies among influential subjects, both nobles and higher clergy. Without the support of their authority in local societies and resources no one could hold power for long. Additionally the Polish Church was increasingly entangled in relations with mighty knightly families. The latter founded many churches and monasteries, but also their members, in much larger numbers than before, acquired the highest Church dignities in Poland. As a result they supported or at least fully accepted the ecclesiastical stuggle for liberty. In 1180 the duke of Cracow, Kazimierz the Just, gave up several services traditionally owed by clergy: the ducal right to confiscate a deceased bishop's property (*ius spolii*) and the right of free transport for the ducal retinue during its journey through Church estates (*podwody*). He did this in exchange for political support during his wars with Mieszko III the Old. Led by his example, other dukes soon issued privileges for clergy of their churches. The most important appeared in 1210 during the meeting in Borzykowa. Three allied dukes – Leszek the White of

Cracow, his brother Conrad I of Mazovia and Władysław Odonic of Greater Poland – consented to the free election of bishops and other main Church officials and gave up their *ius spolii*. This privilege, although it was not valid for the whole of Poland – Silesia in particular was still ruled by more traditionally oriented dukes – was a milestone in building the clergy's separate position. Alone among ducal subjects, they had the right freely to choose their leader according to their own laws. Another element of this process was the continuous effort of several bishops during the thirteenth century to build their own territorial power equal in every aspect to that of dukes. The most spectacular success was that of bishops of Wrocław. In 1201 Duke Henryk I the Bearded granted them as hereditary the vast and compact territory of old castellan districts of Nysa and Otmuchów (which had been in hands of Jarosław, uncle of Henry I and bishop of Wrocław, until his death). After a series of conflicts with the rulers of Silesia, in 1290 the bishops also obtained the privilege to have full economic and legal liberty over that territory. Soon they were known as 'dukes of Nysa and Otmuchów'.[154]

The long-lasting subdivision of Poland among rival members of the Piast dynasty served to reinforce the institution of the Church, which promoted changes already introduced elsewhere in Europe: in 1197, the papal legate Pietro of Capua demanded that all marriages be conducted in churches and that priests remain celibate across Polish lands. Soon the obligation to baptize all children was also introduced. The struggle was mostly led by Archbishop Henryk Kietlicz (1199–1219) who argued strongly in favour of the free election of bishops, the exemption of the Church from civil jurisdiction and an end to private ownership of churches. He was supported by Innocent III (1198–1216). The first election of a bishop by a cathedral chapter took

[154] Wolfgang Irgang, '"Libertas Ecclesiae" und landesherrliche Gewalt. Vergleich zwischen dem Reich und Polen', in *Das Reich und Polen. Paralellen, Interaktionen und Formen der Akkulturation im Hohen und Späten Mittelalter*, ed. Alexander Patschovsky and Thomas Wünsch (Stuttgart, 2003), 93–118; Thomas Wünsch, 'Ius commune in Schlesien. Das Beispiel des kanonischen Rechts 13.–15. Jahrhunderts', in *Lux Romana w Europie Środkowej ze szczególnym uwzględnieniem Śląska*, ed. Antoni Barciak (Katowice, 2001), 109–27; Wünsch, 'Territorial dung zwischen Polen, Böhmen und dem deutschen Reich. Das Breslauaer Bistumsland vom 12.–16. Jh.', in *Geschichte des christlichen Lebens im schlesischen Raum*, ed. Joachim Köhler and Reiner Bendel (Münster, 2002), vol. I, 199–264.

place in Wrocław in 1201, and the *privilegium fori* was granted by the synod of Borzykowa in 1210/11. All of these privileges were again confirmed by a summit at Wolborz in 1215, at which inhabitants of the Church's lands were also declared exempt from civil jurisdiction and taxes. In 1217 the first known provincial synod was convened in Kamień while, in 1231, privileges of immunity were granted to the bishoprics of Płock and Poznań; the latter could even issue its own coins. The archbishoprics of Gniezno and Cracow received substantial jurisdictional and economic privileges in 1234 and 1254 respectively.

By the end of the thirteenth century, the Polish Church played a leading role in attempts to restore the monarchy. Its territorial organization had remained constant for a long time, cutting across the shifting borders of different principalities. The organization of the Church had remained centralized and was reinforced as a result of the reforms imposed by Pope Innocent III. Its institutions formed an effective infrastructure and communication network across an otherwise divided country. The canonization of Bishop Stanisław in 1254 offered a fresh ideological impetus in the Church's attempts to spearhead the unification of the country. The Dominican Vincent of Kielcza claimed in the middle of the thirteenth century that the subdivision of Poland was punishment for the part played by King Bolesław II in Stanisław's death during 1079, but this 'penance' would come to an end and that the country would be reunited, just as the mutilated body of the bishop was miraculously restored to a state of wholeness.

## *Hungary*

Hungarian rulers selected candidates to be elected as prelates, and headed mixed synods which issued ecclesiastical legislation. Prelates played crucial roles in the royal council, in diplomacy as chancellors and envoys, and in the political life of the realm.

Institutional structures did not suffice; ecclesiastical personnel had to be introduced into the realm after conversion. During the first phase of establishing ecclesiastical structures, in the reign of István, the clergy almost exclusively consisted of foreigners. The names of some survive and provide an indication of the variety of their origins: for example, the Frankish or Lombard Bishop Bonipert of Pécs (1009–36); his cleric Hilduin from Chartres or Reims; Liedvin (Leodvin) from Lotharingia, bishop of Bihar in the middle of the eleventh century; the hermits Zoerard and Benedict, perhaps from Poland or Istria; the hermit Gunther from Niederaltaich, a frequent visitor at the royal court; and Bishop Gerard from Venice. The recruitment of locals started quickly: there is evidence of a native cleric who rose to a high ecclesiastical position already in the middle of the eleventh century, Mór, bishop of Pécs.

Foreigners continued to play a role as clerics in Hungary. Bertalan, bishop of Pécs, was from Burgundy; Raynaldus, bishop of Transylvania, from Normandy; Berthold, archbishop of Kalocsa, and János, bishop of Bosnia, were German; Robert, chancellor of the king, bishop of Veszprém, then archbishop of Esztergom, was from Liège. Yet by the late eleventh and early twelfth centuries even legislation expressed suspicion of foreign clerics: newcomers were to be allowed to fill clerical offices in the kingdom only if they had a letter proving their status, or if their background could be verified; otherwise, they were to be expelled.[155]

From the second half of the twelfth century, Hungarian students started to attend universities abroad, especially Paris. During the thirteenth century the favoured destination became Bologna, to study law. The names of hundreds of students who attended universities in western Europe are known from the late twelfth and thirteenth centuries. Occasionally, more detailed information about Hungarian students appears in the sources, for example concerning one student, Bethlehem, who died leaving behind no debts and was praised for his piety. Many of those who attended universities then filled high ecclesiastical positions in the realm and played important roles at the royal chancery.[156]

155 Szabolcs Anzelm Szuromi, 'Fulbert et Bonipert: les relations entre deux évêques au XI siècle', in *Fulbert de Chartres, précurseur de l'Europe médiévale?*, ed. Michel Rouche (Paris, 2008), 55–62; Előd Nemerkényi, 'Latin grammar in the cathedral school: Fulbert of Chartres, Bonipert of Pécs, and the way of a lost Priscian manuscript', *Quidditas* 22 (2001), 39–54; László Koszta, 'Eremiten im Königreich Ungarn des 11. Jahrhunderts', in *Central European Charterhouses in the Family of the Carthusian Order*, ed. Martin Homza (Salzburg, 2008), 67–82; László Koszta, 'Un prélat français de Hongrie: Bertalan, évêque de Pécs (1219–1251)', *Cahiers d'études hongroises* 8 (1996), 71–96; *Legenda SS. Zoerardi et Benedicti*, ed. I. Madzsar, SRH 2, 347–61; Bak *et al.*, eds., *Laws*, 26, c. 3; 63, c. 21.

156 József Laszlovszky, 'Nicholaus clericus: a Hungarian student at Oxford University in the twelfth century', *Journal of Medieval History* 14 (1988), 217–31; Laszlovszky, 'Hungarian university peregrinatio to Western Europe in the second half of the twelfth century', in *Universitas Budensis 1395–1995: International Conference for the*

Historians used to accept the testimony of Martinus Polonus and Cardinal Boso's *Gesta Romanorum Pontificum* (both accounts were written substantially later than the events they describe) that King Kálmán renounced his right of investiture, and dated this to the council of Guastalla in 1106 (supposedly in exchange for papal acquiescence to the incorporation of Croatia in the Hungarian kingdom). They noted, however, that renunciations of the ruler's rights over ecclesiastics recurred on the part of later Hungarian kings up to 1169. The authenticity of the alleged renunciation at Guastalla has now been seriously questioned. In the thirteenth century, the regulation of investiture in Hungary in theory upheld canonical election, but the rights of the ruler as patron included the ability to nominate the candidate; he also had to agree to the result of the election before the papal confirmation of the prelate-elect was sought. In practice, this perpetuated royal influence over the choice of prelates. Rulers continued to influence elections, and in some cases to exert their power over recalcitrant prelates. Kings sometimes confiscated estates from ecclesiastical institutions in retaliation for political opposition: for example, András II seized some from the archbishopric of Esztergom, and Béla IV from the bishopric of Veszprém. At times they even deposed prelates who opposed them, as Béla III did with Archbishop András of Kalocsa; he was later reinstated through papal pressure.[157]

Whereas in the early period we mainly hear of co-operation between clerics and rulers, with the penetration of Gregorian ideas into Hungary, and an increasing knowledge of canon law acquired through studying abroad, some high-ranking ecclesiastics came into open conflict with the ruler. Prelates also chose sides in struggles for the throne. Lukács, bishop of Eger, then from 1158 to 1181 archbishop of Esztergom, who had studied in Paris, clashed with several

*History of Universities on the Occasion of the 600th Anniversary of the Foundation of the University of Buda*, ed. László Szögi and Júlia Varga (Budapest, 1997), 51–61; Péter Sárközy, 'Links to Europe: Hungarian students at Italian universities in the thirteenth–eighteenth centuries,' in *Universitas Budensis*, 135–41.

157 Kornél Szovák, 'The relations between Hungary and the popes in the twelfth century', in *A Thousand Years of Christianity*, 41–6 (the Hungarian version in *Magyarország és a Szentszék kapcsolatának 1000 éve*, ed. István Zombori (Budapest, 1996), 21–46, includes notes); László Solymosi, 'The situation of the Church in Hungary and the papal hegemony (thirteenth century)', in *A Thousand Years of Christianity*, 47–52; László Mezey, 'Ungarn und Europa im 12. Jahrhundert. Kirche und Kultur zwischen Ost und West', in Theodor Mayer, ed., *Probleme des 12 Jahrhunderts. Reichenau-Vorträge 1965–1967* (Stuttgart, 1968), 255–72.

rulers. He excommunicated István III for using ecclesiastical resources; he refused to crown László II, who dethroned István III, and then excommunicated him when the archbishop of Kalocsa crowned him. The king imprisoned Lukács, but after László's death the archbishop similarly refused to crown László's younger brother István IV. Finally, he also maintained the same attitude towards Béla III, in spite of papal intervention on the king's side; finally Béla received papal permission to be crowned by the archbishop of Kalocsa. The reason that time was Béla's gift of a mantle to the archbishop's envoy, branded simony by Lukács; according to some historians, this was an excuse and Lukács's real objections were connected to his fear of Béla's Byzantine orientation. Archbishop Robert of Esztergom used the interdict to force András II to agree to uphold ecclesiastical rights. Lodomer, archbishop of Esztergom, became the most determined enemy of King László IV (Ladislas) over the issue of ecclesiastical revenues and the treatment of immigrant pagan Cumans (detailed in Chapter 7).

## RELATIONS BETWEEN POPES AND RULERS

### *Bohemia*

From the start, not only dukes' policy but also the Bohemian Church were closely connected with the Empire. The first missionaries came from Bavaria and supervision over the Christianization process was in hands of a bishop of Regensburg. Duke Boleslav I asked Pope John XIII for the creation a separate bishopric, but only his son, Boleslav II, succeeded. The role of the pope was not decisive. For long decades, no information suggests any direct relations between the Czech dynasty and the papal court in Rome, even *c.* 1000 when Hungarian and Polish rulers were actively searching for direct connections with Holy See. For Bohemian dukes a pope was a distant and not especially important actor in their policies. Indeed, the pope would not oppose imperial interests to favour a ruler whose Church was subordinated to one of the imperial archbishops: in 1039, the pope did not support the elevation of Prague as the seat of the Church province and the idea of a Prague archbishopric was deferred for 350 years.[158]

[158] Barbara Krzemieńska, *Boj knížete Břetislava I: o upravnění českého státu (1039–1041)* (Prague, 1974), 16–40; Wienfried Baumann, 'Heinrich III. gegen Břetislav I. Der Kampf von 1040 im Grenzwald und sein literariches Echo', *Beiträge zur Geschichte im Landkreis Cham* 1 (1984), 25–37.

The situation changed in the second half of the eleventh century as a result of clashes between the reforming papacy and the emperors. Popes looked for allies even in remote places of Christian Europe. Spytihněv I took advantage of the situation and during Emperor Henry IV's minority co-operated with Rome closely enough to gain a mitre from Pope Nicholas II *c.* 1059–60. The meaning of this privilege is unclear. Only a short entry in Cardinal Deusdedit's registy book contains this information.[159] Perhaps it was a sign of Spytihněv's special dignity, not royal but still above a duke's. Moreover, the mitre was a sign closely related to Rome, originally a symbol of Roman patriciate, and in the Church a liturgical ornament of bishops. Certainly, the Bohemian duke successfully broke the imperial monopoly of relations with Rome to strengthen his position inside and outside Bohemia. The Papal Curia continued to consider Bohemian rulers as valuable allies against emperors. Vratislav II succeeded in renewing and then confirming the privilege of having a mitre from Popes Alexander II (1061–73) and Gregory VII (in 1073). The political situation changed with the royal coronation of Vratislav II in 1086, resulting from his service during Henry IV's fights against Pope Gregory VII and Saxon opposition; the mitre lost its significance.[160]

During the twelfth century relations between Rome and Bohemian elites strengthened as a result of conflicts between the papacy and the Empire. Duke Vladislav II (1140–72) fought in 1142 with the opposition, led by the Moravian duke Konrád II Ota and succeeded only with the support of Emperor Conrad's army, but could not definitively subordinate the Moravian duke. The papal legate, Cardinal Guido, arrived to mediate between fighting sides. Such as intervention was necessary also because Bishop Jindřich Zdík of Olomouc – who opposed the Moravian duke Konrád II Ota and supported Duke Vladislav II of Prague – had to leave his bishopric. The legate was successful: Vladislav and Konrád became reconciled, Bishop Zdík returned to his see and peace was re-established thanks to papal authority, not imperial force. Cardinal Guido also visited the Bohemian and Moravian dioceses with the aim of enforcing strict observation of canonical rules. He forbade priestly marriage and

[159] *CDB* I, no. 57, p. 60.

[160] Josef Žemlička, 'Mitra českých knížat', *Sborník Společnosti přátel starožitností* 3 (1992), 17–22.

reordered the cathedral chapters of Prague and Olomouc. In Prague he promoted the rebuilding of St George's church after it sustained damage from a fire in 1142.[161] Yet papal authority was not respected for long. In 1145 Konrád II Ota tried to imprison Bishop Jindřich Zdík, which started another phase of Konrád's conflict with the Prague duke Vladislav. Vladislav looked to the imperial court for support. In 1158 he received the royal title from the emperor without the active participation of the pope.

Papal authority among Czechs had ambiguous character not solely in political matters. On the one hand they respected papal teaching and accepted his legates' actions against numerous phenomena in the Bohemian Church that were unacceptable to Rome. For example, the papal legate Peter of Capua contributed at the end of the twelfth century to the deposition of abbots of Sazáva and Břevnov. But on the other hand such obedience had its limits. Jindřich Břetislav, bishop of Prague (from 1182) and duke of Bohemia (1193–7), during long years of domestic struggle, sought political support at both the imperial and the papal court. In 1197 the papal legate Cardinal Peter of Capua arrived in Prague to show papal acceptance of Jindřich's reign, but at the same time to reform the Bohemian clergy. He failed. When during a ceremony of new priests' ordination he demanded that the newly ordained take a vow of chastity, they not only angrily refused but also beat him nearly to death. Local tradition had more authority than papal orders.[162]

Growing papal authority among Czechs also weakened ducal authority, coinciding with other socio-political processes. Magnates and knights observed that not only the emperor but also the pope would not accept several actions by dukes. Papal authority could be invoked to support a bishop or clergy in conflicts with a ruler of Prague. In addition, relations with the Papal Court became a game in which both dukes and knights participated on almost equal terms. For example, King Přemysl Otakar I persuaded Bishop Daniel Milik in 1198 to accept the king's divorce and remarriage to the daughter of King Béla III of Hungary, Konstancie (Constance). Adelaide, divorced after twenty-one years of marriage on the pretext that she was too closely

[161] For Guido's story, see *CDB* I, no. 135, pp. 136–8; Peter Hilsch, *Die Bischöfe von Prag in der frühen Stauferzeit. Ihre Stellung zwischen Reichs- und Landesgewalt von Daniel I. (1148–1167) bis Heinrich (1182–1197)* (Munich, 1969), 234–7.

[162] *Letopis Jarlocha*, 510–12; *Hilsch, Die Bischöfe von Prag*, 205–16.

related to Přemysl, complained to the pope. At first Innocent III did not accept Přemysl's marriage to Constance, and investigated its legitimacy for years, declining to raise the status of the Prague see to the level of archbishopric. In 1203 Innocent III issued a charter adressed specifically to 'Suppanis Boemie' – the aristocracy of the Czech knighthood. He thanked them for their strong support for the papal legate during his mission, with a papal warning for the Czech duke. Also Honorius III stressed in his political practice that Czech magnates were separate agents in Bohemia. Around 1217 the pope issued two charters with more or less the same content – exhortations to maintain fidelity towards Rome. The first was sent to King Přemysl Otakar I, the second to specific members of the Czech aristocracy, mentioned by name, and all other *suppanis* with the clear suggestion that their fidelity to Rome was appreciated as much as the king's. At the end of the twelfth century and beginning of the thirteenth Bohemian relations with the Roman Curia ceased to be a ducal monopoly.[163]

Until 1215 the relations of the king with the clergy were less problematic and followed patterns well known from earlier centuries. But after the Fourth Lateran Council, Bishop Ondřej (Andrew), former chancellor of King Přemysl Otakar I, closely co-operating with Pope Innocent III, began a campaign against the traditional place of the Church in the Přemyslid realm. Acting in correspondence with ideas officially proclaimed during the council, he required full ecclesiastical economic and judicial liberty from the king. Thus a long conflict started between the king and the bishop, entailing an ecclesiastical interdict and the bishop's exile. Přemysl Otakar I distributed liberties for specific institutions and estates as his predecessors had, but for a long time he refused to issue a universal privilege for clergy. In the end, papal pressure in a specific political context, the struggle to ensure succession for Přemysl's son, Václav I, prevailed. Although the bishop never returned to Prague from exile (he died in 1223), the king in 1221 accepted an agreement dictated by a papal legate. In the charter he freed the Church of Prague and its subjects from all royal dues and most judicial duties.[164] That coincided with growing

[163] *CDB* II, ed. Gustav Friedrich (Prague, 1912), no. 36, p. 33 (Innocent III), no. 135, p. 125 and no. 136, 125–6 (Honorius III).

[164] *CDB* II, no. 217, pp. 203–5. See also nos. 209–10, 214–16, pp. 193–6, 199–203.

pressure from papal officials on the Bohemian clergy to accept and to act according to the law of the Roman Church. Although it was not easy – even for Bishop Ondřej during the debate with the king in 1221 – common law and economic privilege for the clergy built a framework for the relative separateness of the group among Bohemian society.

## *Poland*

Close relations between the Piast rulers and the papacy began during the reign of Mieszko I,[165] who placed his realm under the tutelage of St Peter, i.e. the Apostolic See, around 992.[166] This included a formal agreement to send annual tribute to Rome, an obligation that continued even after the establishment of a Polish archbishopric in 1000. The tradition of special bonds connecting the papal and Piast courts was of great importance for the first Polish rulers. While Bolesław I, the oldest son and heir of Mieszko I, was not mentioned in his father's donation to St Peter, it was officially proclaimed soon after his death that a lock of his hair had been sent to the pope when he was a child. The connection to the Holy See was confirmed by Bruno of Querfurt when he called Bolesław a *tributarius* of St Peter in his letter to Henry II.[167] Peter was also presented as one of greatest patrons of the early Piast realm. Bolesław I was so closely linked to ecclesiastical circles in Italy that he sent his son to be a monk in Ravenna in a hermitage under the guidance of St Romuald. Doubtless, Bolesław maintained these relations as part of the political game with and within the Empire. Bolesław the Brave used his relations also in more direct way and complained to the pope that Henry II was hindering his attempts to send tribute owed to St Peter.[168]

[165] For a synthesis on relations between clergymen and Piast dukes, see Dobosz, *Monarchia*.

[166] Bruno of Querfurt, *Epistola*, 103.

[167] *Epistola Brunonis*; on Bolesław I the Brave's epitaph, mentioning the sending to Rome of the lock of hair, see Józef Birkenmajer, 'Epitafium Bolesława Chrobrego (próba ustalenia tekstu)', in *Munera philologica Ludovico Ćwikliński oblata* (Poznań, 1936), 347–70, and Brygida Kürbis, 'Epitafium Bolesława Chrobrego: analiza literacka i historyczna', in Kürbis, *Na progach historii*, vol. II, *O świadectwach do dziejów kultury Polski średniowiecznej* (Poznań, 2001), 243–82; Wiszewski, 'Dagome iudex et Ote senatrix'.

[168] Thietmar of Merseburg VI.92.

After the crisis of 1038–9, these relations weakened. No trace exists of a papal intervention in the interest of Kazimierz the Restorer when in 1039 Břetislav I robbed the archbishopric of Gniezno of its relics of St Vojtěch-Adalbert, the Five Martyred Brothers and Radim-Gaudentius. The rebuilding of the Polish Church was carried out by Kazimierz with the support of the clergy from the German part of the Empire, especially the Rhineland, but not from Italy. Bolesław II, renewed the payment of Peter's pence and actively supported papal policy against Emperor Henry IV. As a result he was given a royal crown by the pope in 1076. But his successor, Władysław Herman, was a dutiful ally of the emperor. We know nothing about his relations with Rome, although he was active as the Church benefactor.[169]

Relations with Rome became closer after the ascension of Bolesław III. Between 1102 and 1106, when he fought against his brother Zbigniew, Bolesław was especially keen to maintain warm relations with the Papal Curia. Around 1103 he sent one of his newly created bishops, Baldwin of Cracow, to Rome to obtain a papal benediction. He also succeeded in obtaining a dispensation from Pope Paschal II to marry (c. 1103) his close relative, Zbysława. Papal authority was used by Bolesław to strengthen and stabilize his position; in turn, he had to make concessions to Roman authority. He supported the papal legate Gwalo, bishop of Beauvais, who in 1103 called a synod of the Gniezno province and deposed two bishops. For Bolesław, co-operation with the papacy was crucial for neutralizing the political influence of Archbishop Martin of Gniezno. The latter supported the duke's brother and opponent, Zbigniew. One can assume that Archbishop Martin, nominated by Władysław Herman, represented the pro-imperial orientation in the Polish Church. But after Bolesław's victory in wars with his brother and the German king Henry V, Martin had to follow Bolesław and his policy and support the pope. A visible sign of the change was when a Paschal II issued privilege to the archbishop of Gniezno to wear the pallium.[170]

The political background of Bolesław III's relationship with Rome was also clear decades later, when he supported another legate, Gilles

[169] Teresa Dunin-Wąsowicz, 'Saint Gilles a Polska we wczesnym średniowieczu', *Archeologia Polski* 16 (1971), 651–65.

[170] Jadwiga Karwasińska, 'Archiepiscopus Poloniae – Archiepiscopus Gnesnensis: o adresacie bulli Paschalisa II', *Studia Źródłoznawcze* 28 (1983), 41–50.

of Tusculum. Gilles in 1124–6 forced Polish clergy to accept the legislation of the Lateran Council and reformed the administrative structure of the Polish Church (creating the bishopric of Lubusz and recreating the bishopric of Kruszwica, plans of create bishopric(s) for Pomerania in Wolin and/or Szczecin). The duke needed papal support at the time for his endavours to Christianize newly conquered Pomerania and subordinate the Church there to the power of the Gniezno archbishop. While Otto of Bamberg at least symbolically converted all of Pomerania in 1124–8, the dioecesan organization of the territory was not finished until the late 1130s and became a point of debate between Bolesław III and the imperial Church. Bolesław III's policy of expansion drew him into conflict with Germany/ Saxony and provoked a diplomatic offensive by the Magdeburg archbishop, Norbert. The latter, seizing on the duke's decision in 1130 to support the anti-pope Anaclet II, resurrected the former claims of the Magdeburg see. Consequently in 1131 Pope Innocent II resubordinated the Polish dioceses to Magdeburg, prompting Norbert to visit Rome in 1133 for confirmation of the decision. The archbishop's death in 1134, along with Bolesław III's decision to acknowledge the authority of the pope in 1135, resulted in the restoration of Gniezno's metropolitan status. In 1136 the Polish archbishopric received a bull of protection from Innocent II.[171]

The pragmatic dimension of the relationship with the papacy can be seen during the wars between Bolesław III's oldest son, Władysław, and his younger brothers. After Władysław's expulsion and deposition in 1146, he tried to restore his power with military help from Emperor Conrad II, but without success. Then he turned to Rome, and in 1148 Pope Eugene III ordered both the Polish Church and the dukes to accept the authority of Władysław. But although the pope sent his

[171] Helmut Beumann, 'Die päpstliche Schisma von 1130, Lothar III. und die Metropolitanrechte von Magdeburg und Hamburg –Bremen in Polen und Dänmark', in Beumann, *Wissenschaft von Mittelalter. Ausgewählte Aufsätze* (Cologne and Vienna, 1972), 478–500; Jürgen Petersohn, *Die südliche Ostseeraum im kirchlich-politischen Kräftsspiel des Rechis, Polens und Dänmarks vom 10. bis 13. Jahrhundert. Mission – Kirchenorganisation – Kultpolitik* (Cologne and Vienna, 1979); Petersohn, 'Gründung, Vorgeschichite und Frühzeit des pommerschen Bistums', *Baltische Studien* n.s. 78 (1992), 7–16; Stanisław Rosik, *Conversio gentis Pomeranorum: studium świadectwa o wydarzeniu (XII wiek)* (Wrocław, 2010). On relations between Bolesław III and the Church in 1133–6, see Dobosz, *Monarchia i możni*, 222–6 (with further literature).

legate, Guido of Crema, to Poland with his bull, and the legate sternly warned the archbishop and bishops to be obedient to Rome, neither Church dignitaries nor dukes cared much for the papal orders. The Piast dukes defeated imperial intervention and papal threats were ineffective.

Relations declined even further in 1160: Bishop Werner of Płock persuaded the Polish Church to acknowledge the anti-pope, Victor IV, following the lead of Emperor Frederick Barbarossa. The decision to support the next three anti-popes caused a lasting crisis in Poland's relationship with Rome until 1177, when Emperor Frederick I was reconciled with Pope Alexander III. From that time, the role played by the papacy in political conflicts between Piast dukes started to grow. Ambitious dukes who wanted to elevate their position among relatives needed the support of both papal and local Church authority, and therefore accepted a change in position of the Church in Polish society. At a summit in Łęczyca, convened in 1180, eight Polish bishops along with noblemen, acting as representatives of the provinces, accepted the political authority of Duke Kazimierz II the Just, who expelled his older brother, Mieszko III, from the country against the traditional law of succession. In turn Kazimierz agreed to exempt the Church from some services due to princes. This decision was confirmed by Pope Alexander III, who became the guarantor of political order in Poland alongside Emperor Frederick I.[172]

This situation remained fairly stable in the twelfth century, although the position of the pope strengthened gradually in relations with the Piast dukes. Over the next century, the popes supported Polish Church dignitaries in their constant endeavours to free the clergy from the rulers' supervision. Popes' legal opinions sometimes created politically awkward situations. In 1210 Innocent III restored the seniority principle in succession. That meant the deposition of Duke Leszek the White, the most favourable to Church reform, from the throne in Cracow. It passed to Mieszko, duke of Opole, who would then be succeeded by Władysław Spindleshanks, duke of Poznań and an enemy of Church reforms. This papal intervention caused conflict between the Piast dukes, and led to swift political

[172] For a commentary on and edited version of the Łęczyca charter, see Aleksander Gieysztor, 'Nad statutem łęczyckim 1180 r.: odnaleziony oryginał bulli Aleksandra III z 1181 r.', in *Księga pamiątkowa 150-lecia Archiwum Głównego Akt Dawnych* (Warsaw, 1958), 181–207.

action organized by the Gniezno archbishop, Władysław Kietlicz, a strong supporter of the reforms. As a result, Innocent III's bull was revoked, and Leszek the White was restored to power over Cracow and his relatives with ecclesiastical support.

During the twelfth and the first half of the thirteenth century the nature of Piast–papal relations changed compared to their tenth and eleventh-century history. Dukes tended to use papal authority as an additional argument in their political games thanks to the support of the dignitaries of their local church. The papacy's role was at first equal to, then in the thirteenth century even stronger than, that of the emperor as an intermediary and the highest authority – at least formally – for Polish political life. In the middle of the thirteenth century the Roman Curia developed a concept of 'direct subordination' (*immediata subiectio*) to describe the relationship of Poland to the papacy. The idea was rooted historically in the tributes paid by Mieszko I and Bolesław the Brave, continued later under the name of Peter's Pence. The model was widely accepted as part of a necessary process to reconstruct Poland's political unity, thereby offsetting the power of its neighbours.

## *Hungary*

Relations with the papacy were not always as harmonious as they are represented in traditional Hungarian historiography, which argued that a special relationship was established between István I and Pope Sylvester II and continued under their successors. Reference to this 'special relationship', however, first appeared during the pontificate of Pope Gregory VII and served contemporary political aims. In a letter in 1074, the pope claimed that István had offered the realm with all rights and power to St Peter. It was probably as a counter-argument that the author of the *Legenda Maior* of István invented the story of István offering the realm to the Virgin Mary. Hungarian rulers took sides in papal–imperial power struggles. Their views on royal power as well as *Realpolitik* dictated their choices. László I first backed Victor III and Urban II against the imperial candidate Clement III, but later, as part of his alliance with Henry IV, he chose the anti-pope over Urban II. Kálmán, whose younger brother Álmos tried to gain the throne with German help, was more accommodating towards the papacy, but at the same time commissioned Hartvic's *Life* of István, which protected royal rights over the church against papal claims.

Papal legates travelled through Hungary, as in 1112 and 1115, when they were engaged on anti-imperial business. During the twelfth century, papal legates also started to be sent to Hungary in connection with the ecclesiastical affairs of the kingdom, such as the election of the archbishop of Kalocsa in 1168/9, a conflict between the abbot of Pannonhalma and the bishop of Győr in 1184–6, and the rights of the bishopric of Pécs in 1190. During the schism starting in 1159, Géza II equivocated between the two popes until the autumn of 1161, when he chose to side with Alexander III. Béla III supported the pope in his conflicts with Frederick Barbarossa, although he did clash with Alexander III over both the deposition of the archbishop of Kalocsa and the election to the archbishopric of Split (1180).

Papal and royal interests could coincide in expansionary efforts linked to missionary enterprise, for example, against the Bogomils of Bosnia from the end of the twelfth century, and against Galich and Cumania in the thirteenth. Yet such situations also led to clashes; King Imre imprisoned a papal legate sent to Bulgaria when the pope recognized the Bulgarian ruler, thus failing to support Hungarian plans for overlordship linked to attempts to Catholicize the Bulgars. From the 1190s, ecclesiastical institutions from the realm increasingly asked for papal confirmation of their privileges, and started to refer their conflicts to the papal court. During the thirteenth century, papal legates also intervened in political matters: in 1200 to bring about peace between the king and his rebellious brother; in 1263 between the king and his son; in the late thirteenth century in the conflict between the king and the archbishop over the treatment of the Cumans. Pope Honorius III was involved in justifying the policy of reclaiming royal donations, and later a papal legate was involved in enforcing the articles of the Golden Bull (see Chapter 7). Papal envoys were also involved in negotiations between rulers of Hungary and Přemysl Otakar II of Bohemia.[173]

[173] Gerics, *Egyház, állam*; James Ross Sweeney, 'Gregory VII, the reform program and the Hungarian Church at the end of the eleventh century', in *Studi Gregoriani per la storia della 'Libertas ecclesiae'*, vol. XIV, ed. Alfons M. Stickler, *La riforma Gregoriana e l'Europa*, vol. II, *Comunicazioni* (Rome, 1991), 265–76; Sweeney, 'Papal–Hungarian relations during the pontificate of Innocent III, 1198–1216', Ph.D. dissertation, Cornell University, 1971; Sweeney, '"Summa Potestas Post Deum": papal "Dilectio" and Hungarian "Devotio" in the reign of Innocent III', in *The Man of Many Devices*, 492–8; Sweeney, 'Innocent III, canon law, and papal

The first known papal letter concerning Hungary was written by Gregory VII in 1074. From that time on, hundreds of papal letters survive from the period in originals or copies. Some formulas from papal letters were taken over into royal letters and prelates' letters from the late twelfth century. Papal practices also influenced the method of transcribing charters by inserting the entire text into the new charter and by the practice of keeping registers at *loca credibilia*.[174]

## WRITTEN CULTURE

Literacy was introduced in all three countries with Christianity.[175] No evidence of indigenous script exists in Bohemia and Poland; runic script had existed among the Hungarians, but writing was not widely used. While in Bohemia, Latin and vernacular literacy developed in parallel, Latin predominated in Hungary and Poland.[176]

### *Bohemia*

Bohemian elites from the beginnings of the Přemyslid realm probably had contact with both Latin and vernacular writing. This was an inheritance from Great Moravian culture but one should not overestimate the presence of Slavonic literacy in tenth- and eleventh-century Bohemia. Liturgy was the privileged way of transmitting

judges delegate in Hungary', in *Popes, Teachers, and Canon Law in the Middle Ages*, ed. Sweeney and Stanley A. Chodorow (Ithaca, NY, 1989), 26–52; Sweeney, 'Innocent III and the Esztergom election dispute: the historical background of the decretale "Bone Memorie II" (X.I.5.4)', *Archivum Historiae Pontificiae* 15 (1977), 113–37; Sweeney, 'The decretal Intellecto and the Hungarian Golden Bull of 1222', in *Album Elemér Mályusz* (Brussels, 1976), 89–96; Sweeney, 'Innocent III, Hungary and the Bulgarian coronation: a study in medieval papal diplomacy', *Church History* 42 (1973), 320–34.

174 László Solymosi, 'Der Einfluß der päpstlichen Kanzlei auf das ungarische Urkundenwesen bis 1250', in *Papsturkunde und europäisches Urkundenwesen. Studien zu einer formalen und rechtlichen Kohärenz vom 11. bis 15. Jahrhundert*, ed. Peter Herde and Hermann Jakobs (Cologne, 1999), 87–96.

175 Adamska and Mostert, eds., *The Development of Literate Mentalities*; Előd Nemerkényi, 'The formation of Latin literacy in medieval Hungary', *Mittellateinisches Jahrbuch* 41 (2006), 417–21; Solymosi, 'Die Entwicklung der Schriftlichkeit'; Solymosi, *Írásbeliség*.

176 For recent literature concerning the beginnings of literacy among western Slavs, see Wojciech Mrozowicz, 'Początki kultury pisma na Słowiańszczyźnie Zachodniej', in *Słowiańszczyzna w tworzeniu Europy (X–XIII/XIV w.)*, ed. Stanisław Rosik (Wrocław, 2008), 29–42.

literacy. The first Slavonic texts known from Bohemian manuscripts were written in the eleventh century but transmitted in Latin liturgical compilations.[177] With the exception of the abbey of Sázava no other ecclesiastical centre of a Slavonic liturgy is known. It is impossible to tell how many Slavonic manuscripts were in use before the Sázava abbey was destroyed in 1095, and the Slavonic liturgy disappeared in Bohemia, at least until 1346. The abbey's scriptorium is thought to have been the most important centre of manuscript production in eleventh-century Bohemia. Yet the volume of production and the ratio of Latin to Slavonic texts is unclear.[178]

*Legenda Christiani* narrates that the duke and future saint Václav was taught to read – or at least to understand – liturgical books or prayers; this is perhaps a *topos* rather than reliable information about the past.[179] Certainly not all members of the Přemyslid dynasty read psalters. But the casual character of the story in the *Legenda* suggests that for the ecclesiastical elites it was natural that virtuous rulers of Bohemia would be able to read. It is almost certain that these remarks concerned reading Latin. Even if the presence of Slavonic literacy in Bohemia was much stronger than is represented nowadays, the domination of Latin was still out of the question. The first liturgical books arrived from Benedictine scriptoria of Bavaria and Saxony, and until the end of the twelfth century only a few were written in Bohemia. Nevertheless, some were commissioned by Bohemian Church officials or royal dignitaries. The very high quality of several manuscripts suggests the recipients' appreciation of the beauty of books. This is equally true of their intellectual content. For example, at the time of Vratislav II's coronation (1085), precious books were ordered in unknown abbeys in the Rhineland or Bavaria (most likely connected with the scriptorium of St Emmeram abbey in Regensburg). Among

177 Radoslav Večerka, 'Kyjevské listy jako reprezentant staroslověnštiny velkomoravského typu', *Přednášky a besedy z 27. běhu LŠSS [Letní školy slovanských studií]* 2 (1994), 49–52; 'The Prague glagolitic fragments' (no. 11.01.07.a), p. 89, and 'The Kiev folios' (no. 09.03.03), p. 74, both in Wieczorek and Hinz, eds., *Europe's Centre: Catalogue*.

178 Marie Bláhová, 'Cyrilometodějská tradice v českých zemích ve středověku', in *Środkowoeuropejskie dziedzictwo cyrylo-metodiańskie*, 134–50; Bláhová, 'Sázaver Geschichtsschreibung', in *Der heilige Prokop, Böhmen und Mitteleuropa*, 185–204. See also the works of Emilie Bláhová, Dušan Třeštík and others cited in the section 'Liturgy and saints' (pp. 361–73).

179 *Kristiánova legenda. Život a umučení svatého Václava a jeho báby svaté Ludmily*, ed. Jan Ludvikovský (Prague, 1978), chap. III.

them, the most interesting is the *Codex Vyssegradensis* written in gold, presenting in miniatures the highest sacral authority of the king (including the first known representation of the Tree of Jesse). In the second half of the eleventh century several other painted manuscripts were brought to Bohemia, all prepared in leading manuscript centres of the Empire. That was the case of *Evangeliarium Zabrdovicense*, made in the 1060s–70s, probably in Freising at the bishopric court or in the cloister of Tegernsee. Probably at the same time and in the same place the manuscript of *Apocalypse of St Vitius* (or *St Vitus's Codex*) was prepared. All these manuscripts were stored in Prague cathedral or Vyšehrad collegiate libraries. Other ecclesiastical centres used books of a more pragmatic character. This change happened mostly during the thirteenth century.[180]

Unlike in Poland (see below) the first, local hagiographical work was written early. *Legenda Christiani* was probably composed *c.* 994 by a member of the Bohemian clergy (as some historians argue, of

[180] Pavel [Pavol] Černý, *Evangeliář zábrdovický a Svatovítská apokalypsa* (Prague, 2004); Anežka Merhautová and Pavel Spunar, *Kodex vyšehradský: korunovační evangelistář prvního českého krále* (Prague, 2006). For detailed studies, see: Černý, 'Evangeliář zábrdovický – nově identifikovaná památka "bavorské malířské školy"', in *Problematika historických a vzácných knižních fondů Čech, Moravy a Slezska* (Olomouc, 1997), 5–21; Černý, 'Kodex vyšehradský, "korunovační" charakter jeho iluminované výzdoby a některé aspekty "politické teologie" 11. století', in *Královský Vyšehrad*, vol. II, *Sborník příspěvků ke křesťanskému miléniu a k posvěcení nových zvonů na kapitulním chrámu sv. Petra a Pavla* (Prague, 2001), 33–56; Hana J. Hlaváčková, 'Ostrovský žaltář: Pražská Kapitulní knihovna, A 57/1', in *1000 let kláštera na Ostrově (999–1999)* (Prague, 2003), 121–32; Zdeňka Hledíková, 'Kodex Reg. lat. 14 – Evangeliář sv. Václava nebo sv. Vojtěcha?', in *In omnibus caritas: K poctě devadesátých narozenin prof. ThDr. Jaroslava Kadlece* (Prague, 2002), 203–32; Hledíková, 'Nejstarší břevnovský rukopis', in *Milénium břevnovského kláštera (993–1993)* (Prague, 1993), 41–52; Martina Pippal, 'The influence of southern German scriptoria on their eastern and northern neighbours', in Wieczorek and Hinz, eds., *Europe's Centre: Hanbook*, 559–62. For a guide to manuscript fonds of central Czech libraries, see Pavel Brodský, Marie Hradilová, Stanislav Petr and Marie Tošnerová, *Průvodce po rukopisných fondech v České republice*, vol. IV, *Rukopisné fondy centrálních a církevních knihoven v České republice*, ed. Marie Tošnerová (Prague, 2004). On manuscript and old printed book collections in Bohemia in general, see Anežka Baďurová, 'Historické knižní fondy v České republice a současný stav jejich knihovnického zpracování', *Sborník archivních prací* 53, 2 (2003), 641–84. On the history of books in Czech, see a collection of articles by Ivan Hlaváček, *Knihy a knihovny v českém středověku (studie k jejich dějinám do husitství)* (Prague, 2005); and on the late medieval period, see Josef Krása, *České iluminované rukopisy 13./16. Století*, ed. Karel Stejskal, Petr Wittlich and Rostislav Švácha (Prague, 1990).

Přemyslid origin).[181] Yet that was the exception. Written stories were created and memorized mainly outside Bohemia before they were imported.[182] The next complex literary work originating in Bohemia, one deeply rooted in the oral tradition of Czech and narrative schemes popular among Slavs and others, Cosmas of Prague's *Chronicle of the Czechs*, was written in the first half of the twelfth century, probably between 1119 and 1125.[183] This work contextualized varied stories about the Czech past for the first time, and for centuries served as a general pattern for all other historiographers, although they did not necessarly derive inspiration and information from the Chronicle.[184]

Cosmas of Prague related that Břetislav I during his expedition against Poland issued laws regulating relations between the Church, the ducal administration and all inhabitants of his realm.[185] Historians argued that Cosmas was reliable and stressed that this law was the first written juridical document in Bohemia. Yet no trace of such a charter before Cosmas's chronicle is known. Therefore we can only state that it is possible that some kind of record was made of a ducal oral declaration, notes, that after almost a century, enriched by tradition, Cosmas incorporated. But, if we rely on sources, we have to deduce that until the second half of the twelfth century rulers' law-making and -enforcement were based on the spoken rather than written word.

181 See above, 'Liturgy and saints' (pp. 361–73), and Dušan Třeštík, 'Christian the monk, brother of Boleslav II', in Wieczorek and Hinz, eds., *Europe's Centre: Handbook*, 270–1; Třeštik, 'Přemyslovec Krystián', *Archologické Rozchledy* 51 (1999), 602–13; David Kalhous, 'Kristiánova legenda a počátky českého politického myšlení', ph.D. dissertation, Masaryk University, Brno, 2005 (is.muni.cz/th/12320/ff_d/Disertace.pdf).

182 An outline of the history of Czech medieval historiography can be found in Marie Bláhová, 'Dějepisectví v českých zemích přemyslovského období', in *Przemyslidzi i Piastowie – twórcy i gospodarze średniowiecznych monarchii*, ed. Józef Dobosz (Poznań, 2006), 107–39.

183 Dušan Třeštík, *Kosmova kronika: studie k počátkům českeho dějepisectvi a politického myslení* (Prague, 1968); literature in Western languages is listed by Lisa Wolverton, 'Introduction', in Cosmas of Prague, *The Chronicle of the Czechs*, 3–17; see also Marie Bláhová, 'Verschriftlichte Mündlichkeit in der Böhmischen Chronik des Domherrn Cosmas von Prag', in Adamska and Mostert, eds., *The Development of Literate Mentalities*, 323–42.

184 Marie Bláhová, 'Die Hofgeschichtsschreibung am böhmischen Herrscherhof im Mittelalter', in *Die Hofgeschichtsschreibung im mittelalterlichen Europa*, ed. Jarosław Wenta and Rudolf Schieffer (Toruń, 2006), 51–72.

185 Cosmas II.4, 86–8.

The pragmatic use of writing in tenth–twelfth-century Bohemia is poorly attested by the sources. Epitaphs may be situated on the verge between sacral and pragmatic writing, although they were written probably no earlier than the middle of the eleventh century and appeared in larger numbers in the twelfth.[186] The first ducal charter for the ecclesiastical chapter of Litomeřyce, likely prepared by clergymen from the collegiate church, was issued in 1057. But that only shows – as in other countries – that the Church was the driving force in including the written instruments into the local legal system. The first written set of laws was issued in 1189 by Duke Konrád II Ota (see Chapter 4). From this point on, a new period of pragmatic literacy started in Bohemia, when written words gradually gained more validity than spoken ones.[187] The final success of this process was evident no earlier than in the fourteenth century, when the new society of peasants and townspeople with their own rights and need for writing communications emerged and then fully dominated Bohemian society.

## *Poland*

We know next to nothing about the first imported manuscripts. It is certain that dukes knew the value of written communication and were ready both to accept writing and to order records to be made in their name. It is highly probable that some kind of letter or charter was written for envoys sent by Mieszko I and Oda to Rome with a request for St Peter's protection over their realm. But the content of this request is known to us only from the register called *the Dagome iudex*, inserted into a manuscript of the papal chancery. By whom and where

[186] Martin Lutovský, *Hroby knížat: kapitoly z českých dějin a hrobové archeologie* (Prague, 1997); Marie Bláhová, 'Vier Epitaphe aus den böhmischen mittelalterlichen Chroniken und Annalen', in *De litteris, manuscriptis, inscriptionibus Festschrift zum 65. Geburtstag von Walter Koch*, ed. Theo Kölzer, Franz-Albrecht Bornschlegel, Christian Friedl and Georg Vogeler (Vienna, Cologne and Weimar, 2007), 271–8.

[187] Jan Bistrický, 'Übersicht über das Urkundenwesen der böhmischen Herrscher bis zum Jahre 1197', in *Typologie der Königsurkunden. Kolloquium der Commission Internationale de Diplomatique in Olmütz*, ed. Bistrický (Olmütz, 1998), 227–40; Marie Bláhová, 'Počátky kodifikace zemského práva v Čechách', in *Kultura prawna w Europie Środkowej*, ed. Antoni Barciak (Katowice, 2006), 74–84.

the original message was written are debated.[188] According to Thietmar of Merseburg, Bolesław the Brave also used written letters for official communications. But once again, the supposed letters, as for example to the emperor of Byzantium, do not survive. Thietmar also recounted that Bolesław ordered clergymen to read penitential books for him. Historians suggested that he did so because he himself did not read or write. The letter of Mathilda, duchess of Lotharingia, to King Mieszko II (*c.* 1028), Bolesław II's son, states that he used not only vernacular and Latin, but also Greek to praise the Lord.[189] Some historians claimed on that basis that Mieszko read and possibly wrote Latin and Greek. That is one possibility, but it is equally possible that like his father he just repeated prayers in these languages.[190] The so-called Prayers of Gertrude, supposedly composed or written down by Gertrude (*c.* 1025–1108), Mieszko II's daughter and grand duke of Kiev, Izyaslav I's wife, are similarly disputable. The prayers were inserted into *Psalterium Egberti*, a manuscript probably brought to Poland from the Empire by Richenza/Richenza, the wife of Mieszko II, and given to Gertrude on the occasion of her marriage. The prayers were written in Latin obviously for Gertrude's private use, and some of them were formulated as composed by herself. That led historians to suppose that she both composed them and wrote them down.[191]

The Bohemian Boleslav I's political influence in Poland led to the institution and flowering of the cults of St Vojtěch-Adalbert and the Five Martyred Brothers. As a guest in Poland, Bishop Bruno of Querfurt possibly wrote there one version of the *Vita* of Vojtěch-Adalbert and *Vita Quinque Fratrum*. But the impact of these text on Polish culture at the time was limited. Historians argue that at the

188 Victor Wolf von Glanvell, *Die Kanonessammlung des Kardinals Deusdedit*, vol. I, *Die Kanonessammlung selbst* (Paderborn, 1905; 2nd edn, Aalen, 1967), lib. III, cap. 199, 359; Charlotte Warnke, 'Ursachen und Voraussetzungen der Schenkung Polens an den heiligen Petrus', in *Europa Slavica – Europa Orientalis*, 127–77. The Polish literature has been presented revently by Gerard Labuda, 'Stan dyskusji nad dokumentem "Dagome iudex" i państwem "Schinesghe"', in *Civitas Schinesghe cum pertinentiis*, ed. Wojciech Chudziak (Toruń, 2003), 9–17.

189 Kürbis, *Epistola Mathildis Suevae*, 49–83.

190 Adamska, 'The introduction of writing in Central Europe'.

191 *Modlitwy księżnej Gertrudy z Psałterza Egberta z kalendarzem*, ed. Małgorzata H. Malewicz and Brygida Kürbis (Cracow, 2002); Brygida Kürbis, 'Die Gertrudianischen Gebete im Psalterium Egberti. Ein Beitrag zur Geschichte der Frömmigkeit im 11. Jahrhundert', in *Europa Slavica – Europa Orientalis*, 248–61.

court of Bolesław I, or Mieszko II, one more hagiographical work concerning St Vojtěch-Adalbert was written, the book mentioned a century later by Anonymous in his chronicle as *Liber de passione martyris*. That is only a hypothesis and the true nature of this *Book of the Martyrdom* is unclear.[192] It is still unknown whether historiographical sources were written in Poland before 1038/9. Some research has suggested that perhaps at the court of Bolesław I, and apparently at the court of Mieszko II, someone wrote the first annalistic notes concerning the Piast family and the Polish Church in the margins of tables of the dates of Easter. These were taken out of Poland by Břetislav I in 1038/9 and stimulated the development of Bohemian annalistic writing. But others see the process in quite opposite way: Polish annalistic writing developed on the basis of Bohemian annalistic notes and the first annals were written in Poland in Cracow, during the reign of Kazimierz the Restorer. Detailed information concerning the day of birth of Kazimierz, completely unique in Polish annals, and relatively rich genealogical material concerning his family suggest that influence in both directions was possible. The ancient annals could be written by Richeza's (Kazimierz's mother) entourage and then taken to Bohemia. There its content was enriched by notes of Czech provenance and this new form began the new Polish annalistic tradition at the court of Kazimierz the Restorer in Cracow.[193]

All this, however, is hypothetical. The first surviving manuscripts and letters come from the times of Kazimierz's son, Władysław. In 1086 Duke Władysław Herman issued a letter for the Bamberg cathedral. The original is most probably the oldest surviving document written in Poland. At almost the same moment, between 1085 and 1092, Bishop Lambert of Cracow, called also Suła, issued a letter

[192] Vita II; *Vita quinque fratrum*, 7–84; Jadwiga Karwasińska, *Święty Wojciech. Wybór pism* (Warsaw, 1996); Jerzy Strzelczyk, 'Einleitung', in *Heiligenleben zur deutsch-slawischen Geschichte. Adalbert von Prag und Otto von Bamberg*, ed. Lorenz Weinrich, in collaboration with Jerzy Strzelczyk, *Ausgewählte Quellen zur deutschen Geschichte des Mittelalters* (Darmstadt, 2005), 3–26; and Jürgen Hoffmann, *Vita Adalberti. Früheste Textüberlieferungen der Lebensgeschichte Adalberts von Prag* (Essen, 2005) (on Vojtěch-Adalbert's first *vita*).

[193] Tomasz Jurek, 'Początki polskiej annalistyki', in *Nihil superfluum esse: studia z dziejów średniowiecza ofiarowane Jadwidze Krzyżaniakowej*, ed. Jerzy Strzelczyk and Józef Dobosz (Poznań, 2000), 129–46; Marzena Matla-Kozłowska, 'Kwesita zależności polskiego i czeskiego rocznikarstwa (od drugiej połowy XI do połowy XIII wieku)', *Studia Źródłoznawcze* 43 (2005), 27–52.

to the Bohemian king Vratislav II. Władysław Herman highly valued the use of writing for promoting his majesty. The duke donated three precious manuscripts, written with golden ink and enriched with numerous illuminations, to Polish Church institutions. He gave the Płock bishopric chapter the *Book of Gospels from Płock* or *Pułtusk Golden Codex* and to the archbishopric chapter of Gniezno the *Codex Aureus Gnesnensis* or *Gniezno Golden Codex*.[194] The *Codex Aureus Gnesnens* and perhaps *Codex Aureus Pultaviensis* were even prepared in the same scriptorium as the *Codex Vyssegradensis* (see above), ordered by King Vratislav II.

The first libraries appeared at the same time, when the first evidence of the activity of local scriptoria appears. In 1101 the first inventory of the Cracow bishopric chapter library and treasury was written, and it was followed by a second inventory of the library in 1110. If in the first one only five codices were mentioned, in 1110 no fewer than fifty-three were present in the Cracow library. It is unlikely that over the course of nine years forty-eight new manuscripts were brought to Cracow; more probably the difference was a result of more thorough recording. But even that is significant: it was no longer only precious manuscripts that were worth acknowledging as items in the treasury, but also less valuable pieces that were important tools of work for the clergy. Among these fifty-three codices, twenty-six were prepared for liturgical purposes, but there were also juridical manuscripts, a copy of the encyclopedia by Isidore of Seville and several literary works and textbooks for learning Latin.[195] If the number of volumes is not impressive, the library is at least similar to west European cathedral libraries as far as the themes and purposes of books are concerned. All or almost all of these manuscripts were imported. Short annalistic notes and other practical pieces – inventories or necrological annotations – were added to imported liturgical manuscripts. No earlier than around the middle of the twelfth century, the first longer pieces of writing were composed in the Polish scriptoria, added to existing

[194] Aleksander Gieysztor, 'Symboles de la royauté en Pologne: un groupe de manuscrits du XIe et du début du XIIe siècle', *Comptes rendus. Académie des Inscriptions et Belles-Lettres* 1 (1990), 128–37.

[195] MPH I, 376–8; Lech Kalinowski, 'Najstarsze inwentarze skarbca katedry krakowskiej jako źródło do dziejów sztuki w Polsce', in *Cultus et cognitio: studia z dziejów średniowiecznej kultury*, ed. Stefan K. Kuczyński, Tadeusz Lalik, Tadeusz Rosłanowski, Henryk Samsonowicz, Stanisław Trawkowski and Tadeusz Wasilewski (Warsaw, 1976), 217–31.

manuscripts. One example is the short *Płock Notes of Miracles* composed *c.* 1148 and added to the Płock Bible imported from western countries.[196] The first literary works prepared in the Piast realm had a historiographical character: the Chronicle of Anonymous written *c.* 1108/9 and the *Cronica Polonorum* of Master Vincent written at the turn of the twelfth and thirteenth centuries. The latter was held in the Cracow chapter library as a separate volume and was without doubt written in one of Lesser Poland's scriptoria. But whether Anonymous's Chronicle was preserved in separate manuscripts, or within a bigger collection of historiographical works, is a mystery. The first preserved copies of the chronicle come from the fifteenth century.[197]

Although the first letters of the duke and bishops were written in Poland at the end of the eleventh century, the more regular use of pragmatic writing started in the second half of the twelfth century. This was strictly connected with the growing need of Church institutions for written proof of land ownership. And although the ducal chancery functioned from the reign of Bolesław III the Wrymouth (1102–38), almost all ducal charters were prepared in Benedictine and Cistercian monasteries and in (archi)episcopal scriptoria. Only after a charter was written did the duke or his official check its content and approve a ducal seal to be hung on it. A real development of ducal chanceries took place in the thirteenth century, when ducal writers and chancery officials slowly but irreversibly monopolized the process of issuing rulers' charters. At the end of the thirteenth century the first city chanceries appeared, but their activity was still insignificant as was frequency of issuing knights' and townsmen's private letters or charters. This would change during the fourteenth century.[198]

196 Zofia Kozłowska-Budkowa, 'Płockie zapiski o cudach z r. 1148', *Kwartalnik Historyczny* 44 (1930), 341–8.

197 *Codex Aureus Gnesnensis. Facsimile* (Warsaw, 1988, 2nd edn, 2004), with English introduction by Tadeusz Dobrzeniecki and Aleksander Gieysztor; on Anonymous's Chronicle, see the introduction to *Gesta Principum Polonorum*, tr. Knoll and Schaer, 2007.

198 Anna Adamska, '"From Memory to Written Record" in the periphery of medieval Latinitas: the case of Poland in the eleventh and twelfth century', in *Charters and the Use of the Written Word in Medieval Society*, ed. K. Heidecker (Turnhout, 2000), 83–100; Adamska, 'The Ecclesiastical Chanceleries in Medieval Poland as Intellectual Centres', *Quaestiones Medii Aevii Novae* 10 (2005), 171–98. For more bibliography, see Adamska, 'La bibliographie de la diplômatique polonaise 1956–1996', *Archiv für Diplomatik* 44 (1998), 275–336.

### *Hungary*

Only a few runic words on objects have been found in Hungary, rather than lengthy texts, and scholars disagree over the reading of these: in one case, according to one scholar the short inscription is in Turkic, according to another in Hungarian. It has been argued that the use of runic writing was restricted to a small segment of the population; it was certainly never used for administrative and legislative purposes, unlike the newly introduced Latin.[199] The first surviving texts in the vernacular – ecclesiastical texts – date from the late twelfth century in Hungary. The first vernacular texts there were tied to the pastoral role of the church: a burial speech and oration, and a prayer to the Virgin Mary.[200] Yet the use of vernacular writing did not become widespread until the fourteenth and fifteenth centuries. Greek was also used at times, an example of which remained in the transcript of the foundation charter of the monastery of Veszprémvölgy, but Latin dominated. During the eleventh century, many genres of Latin texts started to be produced in Hungary: charters, saints' lives, liturgy and according to some scholars a chronicle (which does not survive). The population at large, however, remained illiterate; there is no evidence of correspondence or other signs of literacy beyond ecclesiastical circles.

Latin written culture was a fundamental cornerstone of ecclesiastical life. Legislation prescribed that bishops supply books to churches; royal gifts of books, especially to monasteries, were also numerous. At ecclesiastical centres, books were copied, so that by the end of the eleventh century local production replaced imported books as the primary means of acquisition. Carolingian minuscules and from the thirteenth century Gothic cursive script was used. Around 1092 László I founded the bishopric of Zagreb; three of its liturgical books (of the type normally possessed by bishoprics) survive: a Benedictionale, the gift of the archbishop of Esztergom; a Sacramentary, which came from a Benedictine abbey; and the *Agenda pontificalis*, containing the rituals performed by the prelate, donated by the bishop of Győr. Two other codices survive that are indicative of the book culture of the early Hungarian Church. The Evangelistary of Szelepcsény, written at the

[199] György Györffy and János Harmatta, 'Rovásírásunk az eurázsiai írásfejlődés tükrében', in Kovács and Veszprémy, eds., *Honfoglalás és nyelvészet*, 145–62; 'The Székely Runiform Script', in Róna-Tas, *Hungarians and Europe*, 437–44.

[200] Loránd Benkő, *Az Árpád-kor magyar nyelvű szövegemlékei* (Budapest, 1980).

end of the eleventh century, perhaps for the archbishopric of Esztergom, was based on a model from the Rhone–Lotharingian region. The *Codex Albensis* contained liturgical songs.[201]

Three book-lists provide information on the use of books in Benedictine monasteries; such books were read to the monks, used for private study and employed in the monastic school. Around 1093, a charter listed the items in the library of the abbey of Pannonhalma, the most significant Benedictine abbey. This includes 80 books, each of which contained more than one work; in total, there were between 200 and 250 works. About half of these were liturgical books, such as evangelistaries, lectionaries and hymn-books. Other works included two copies of the Rule with commentary, Cassianus's *Collationes patrum*, the *Vitae patrum* (attributed to St Jerome), the second book of Gregory the Great's *Dialogues*, his *Liber Regulae pastoralis* and commentaries on Job, the *Life of St Martin* by Sulpicius Severus, lives of saints, writings of St Augustine, St Isidore's *Etymologies*, Cicero's *Against Catiline*, Lucanus's *Pharsalia*, Donatus's grammar and sayings attributed to Cato. Later charters contain what scholars argue are authentic late-eleventh-century book-lists of two other Benedictine abbeys, Pécsvárad and Bakonybél. The former contains thirty-five books, mostly liturgical, the latter eighty-four books, including a Gospel written with golden letters and two with silver letters. Concerning the possessions of smaller family monasteries, few indications remain: the Bible of Admont, produced in the 1130s, used to belong to the monastery of Csatár, but the lay patron pawned it and was unable to redeem it. The Cistercian monastery of Egres was founded from Pontigny, whose book-lists mention 'in Hungary' next to eight volumes, including works by Church fathers, Anselm and Yvo of Chartres.[202]

[201] N. Berend *et al.*, 'The kingdom of Hungary', 336; László N. Szelestei, ed., *Tanulmányok a középkori magyarországi könyvkultúráról* (Budapest, 1989), and n. 140 in this chapter.

[202] Nemerkényi, *Latin Classics*, chap. 4 ('The monastic school'); Előd Nemerkényi, 'Cathedral libraries in medieval Hungary', *Library History* 20 (2004), 7–17; Előd Nemerkényi, 'Latin classics in medieval libraries: Hungary in the eleventh century', *Acta Antiqua Academiae Scientiarum Hungaricae* 43 (2003), 243–56; Tünde Wehli, *Az Admonti biblia: Wien, ÖNB, Cod. s. n. 2701–2* (Budapest, 1977); Takács, ed., *Paradisum plantavit*, 75–9, 598–600; László Veszprémy, 'La biblioteca nell'inventario della fine del secolo undicesimo (1093–1095)', in *Mille anni di storia dell'arciabbazia di Pannonhalma*, ed. József Pál and Ádám Somorjai (Rome, 1997), 83–99.

Hungarian monasteries and ecclesiastical centres fostered the production of works. Bishop Mór of Pécs, who wrote the *Life* of two hermits, Zoerard and Benedict, had been a monk, then the abbot, at Pannonhalma. It has been suggested that the anonymous author of the *Life* of Imre was also connected to the abbey. The Venetian Cerbanus translated from Greek into Latin both Maximus Confessor's *De caritate*, dedicating it to David, the abbot of Pannonhalma between 1130 and 1151, and parts of Johannes Damascenus's work. The *Pray Codex*, was also the product of a Hungarian (probably Benedictine) scriptorium in 1192–5. The *Codex* contains a Sacramentary, synodal decisions, the earliest Hungarian annals and the first vernacular text. The immigrant cleric Gerard wrote a commentary on parts of the Book of Daniel, as well as a collection of homilies, of which only the conclusion survives.[203]

The first letter written by a Hungarian prelate, of which we known the contents, dates from 1161, by Archbishop Lukács of Esztergom (1158–81) to the archbishop of Salzburg. Although synodal legislation from the end of the eleventh century required that prelates use writing if they communicated with other prelates or excommunicated someone, if such written documents were produced, as these served immediate needs, they were not preserved. Prelates also participated in the issuing of royal charters from the first decades of the eleventh century, then wrote foundation or donation charters on behalf of laymen, but started to issue charters under their own seals, in their own name only, in the late twelfth century. The first extant charter by a Hungarian prelate is from 1183. Numerous charters survive from the thirteenth century: about three-quarters concern beneficiaries who were ecclesiastics or ecclesiastical institutions, and the remaining one-quarter of the recipients were laypeople. The first bishops' seals to survive are from the early thirteenth century.[204]

The ecclesiastical sphere in many ways was not clearly separated from the activities of laypeople, and this was especially true in the provision of written documents. Writing, whether or not to benefit

[203] István Kapitánffy, 'Cerbanus e la sua traduzione di San Massimo', in *Mille anni di storia dell'arciabbazia di Pannonhalma*, ed. József Pál and Ádám Somorjai (Rome, 1997), 101–20; Nemerkényi, *Latin Classics*, ch. 2.

[204] László Solymosi, 'Chartes archiépiscopales et épiscopales en Hongrie avant 1250', in *Die Diplomatik der Bischofsurkunde vor 1250*, ed. Christoph Haidacher and Werner Köfler (Innsbruck, 1995), 159–77.

ecclesiastical institutions, remained the domain of ecclesiastics in the period. Apart from ecclesiastical institutions, the royal court was a significant centre of writing. Commissioning saints' lives, a mirror for princes (the *Admonitions* to István's son) and histories, it also contained the royal chapel, the first centre for legal literacy in Hungary. During the reign of Béla III, an independent chancery, under a chancellor, developed from the chapel, which issued charters. Clerics trained in Paris played a key role there. Béla also expressed his wish for every matter discussed in his presence to be recorded in writing, although it is not known whether there was any attempt to carry this out. Béla IV tried to establish written petitions at the royal court but was forced to retract that requirement in 1267 due to pressure from the nobility.

The most important historical work tied to the interests of the dynasty was the Hungarian Chronicle. Its date of composition is debated: some historians claim it is from as early as the second half of the eleventh century, but more argue for an early-twelfth-century origin (under the reign of Kálmán). In any case, later authors did not simply add new material to update the text, but rewrote it several times according to then-current political needs; none of these versions is extant today. Scholars have tried to identify the various layers of the chronicle that survives in two fourteenth-century versions, based on the internal contradictions of the text as well as some surviving fragments of what were probably earlier versions, embedded in other texts. In the twelfth century, the chronicle was rewritten at least twice, first during either the reign of Géza II (1141–62) or István III (1162–72), second during that of Béla III (1172–96) (or perhaps András II (1205–35)). The first revision was connected to the ascension of the Álmos branch of the dynasty to the throne. As the ruling kings descended from Álmos's son Béla II (who had been blinded by King Kálmán), the chronicler created a negative description of Kálmán. Subsequent rewritings were also in the service of legitimizing particular rulers or promoting political goals.[205]

[205] Gyula Kristó, *Magyar Historiográfia I: történetírás a középkori Magyarországon* (Budapest, 2002); Kristó, *A történeti irodalom Magyarországon a kezdetektől 1241-ig* (Budapest, 1994); Gábor Thorockay, 'A magyar krónikairodalom kezdeteiről', in *Aktualitások a magyar középkorkutatásban: in memoriam Kristó Gyula (1939–2004)*, ed. Márta Font, Tamás Fedeles and Gergely Kiss (Pécs, 2010), 23–31; Elemér Mályusz, 'La chancellerie royale et la rédaction des chroniques dans la Hongrie médiévale', *Le Moyen Âge* 75 (1969), 51–86, 219–54; László Veszprémy,

Royal charters were increasingly important instruments of government. In Hungary the first charters were produced during the reign of King István I, but none of the original charters survives. Of nine Latin and one Greek charters attributed to the first king that are extant in transcripts and copies, six are later forgeries, and three are interpolated. The first charter that survives in an interpolated version is from 1002 (1001 according to another view). The earliest charters show similarities to charters of Emperor Otto III; based on these similarities scholars have concluded that Chancellor Heribert's unknown scribe 'C' moved to the Hungarian court and wrote them. The first extant charter to survive is the foundation charter of the Abbey of Tihany (1055). This resembles Lotharingian charters.

Although the production of charters was at first associated with the royal court, already during the second half of the eleventh century nobles began to have their donations to ecclesiastical institutions put into writing. The first private charter – the foundation charter of a monastery – to survive was issued in 1061. It is thought to have been formulated by the local bishop (of Veszprém) and was not sealed. Wills of laypeople started to be recorded in writing as well. Around 1090, private charters sealed with a royal seal appeared. The use of writing spread in the eleventh century, presumably on ecclesiastical initiative: charters were written by clerics and recorded ecclesiastical rights and possessions. Thereafter, writing occupied an increasingly important social, as well as administrative and juridical, function. From the twelfth century fifty-nine original charters survive; until the middle of the century all charters benefited ecclesiastical institutions. From that time, charters for laypeople as beneficiaries were issued as well. The first charter concerning exclusively lay parties dates from 1192. Thousands of royal and non-royal charters were issued during the thirteenth century. Medieval royal charters often included a lengthy descriptive narrative of the events that were being rewarded. This has been explained by a desire to secure possessions, or as the continuation of pre-literate oral epic forms of transmitting the deeds of heroes.[206]

'Historical past and political present in the Latin chronicles of Hungary (twelfth–thirteenth centuries)', in *The Medieval Chronicle: Proceedings of the 1st International Conference on the Medieval Chronicle, Driebergen/Utrecht, 13–16 July 1996*, ed. Erik S. Kooper (Amsterdam, 1999), 260–8.

206 Györffy, *Diplomata Hungariae*; Györffy, 'Die ungarischen Königsurkunden bis 1200'; László Veszprémy, 'Chronicles in charters: historical narratives (narrationes) in charters as substitutes for chronicles in Hungary', in *The Medieval Chronicle III*.

Until the middle of the twelfth century, donations and legal decisions in disputed cases were put into writing if the beneficiary requested it. It was possible to obtain a royal seal for private charters by taking the text to the royal chapel, where it was reformulated, if necessary, and sealed. Alternatively, an ecclesiastical institution was asked to issue an unsealed charter. Private charters in the eleventh and beginning of the twelfth centuries could simply list witnesses as a means of authentication. Most charters were authenticated as chirographs from the first half of the twelfth century on (the text was recorded twice on the same parchment, which was then cut in two across letters or signs). This form continued even with the increasing use of seals, until the middle of the thirteenth century, when it became rare. Royal seals disappeared from private charters in the late twelfth century; with the development of the royal chancery the form and authentication of royal charters were regularized, and recipients no longer participated in having the charter made. Private charters came to be produced by *loca credibilia* (see Chapter 7).[207]

*Proceedings of the 3rd International Conference on the Medieval Chronicle. Doorn/Utrecht 12–17 July 2002*, ed. Erik S. Kooper (Amsterdam, 2004), 184–99; Imre Szentpétery and Iván Borsa, eds., *Az Árpád-házi királyok okleveleinek kritikai jegyzéke/Regesta regum stirpis Arpadianae critico diplomatica,* 3 vols. (Budapest, 1923–87).

207 Solymosi, *Írásbeliség*, 193–215; Solymosi, 'Die Anfänge der weltlichen Gerichtsbarkeit'; Iván Borsa and György Györffy, 'Actes privés, "Locus credibilis" et notariat dans la Hongrie médiévale', in *Notariado público y documento privado: de los origines al siglo XIV. Actas del VII. Congreso Internacional de Diplomática Valencia, 1986*, 2 vols. (Valencia, 1989), vol. II, 941–9; Tamás Fedeles and Irén Bilkei, eds., *Loca credibilia: hiteleshelyek a középkori Magyarországon* (Pécs, 2009).

# 7

# NEW DEVELOPMENTS OF THE THIRTEENTH CENTURY

Radical transformations from the end of the twelfth century meant that, in many respects, there was discontinuity between the history of the eleventh and twelfth centuries on the one hand, and of that of the thirteenth on the other. The thirteenth century was a period of great tension between rulers and the nobility, of the devastating Mongol invasion and of innovations and new beginnings. In Hungary and Poland, the power of the nobility was on the rise, leading to political fragmentation, whereas, in contrast, in Bohemia the ruler acquired the royal title. The Mongols invaded all three countries and with the exception of Bohemia defeated the local rulers in battle. The extent of the devastation they caused in each country is open to debate. Social and economic changes included the more widespread use of writing in administration and legal cases; the development of towns and monetization; and an increase in the role of immigrants.

The growing number of settlers arriving from German-speaking lands – townsmen, peasants, knights – together with the increasing attractiveness of German courtly culture for elites triggered both co-operation and conflicts between locals and newcomers. Yet the new culture that emerged from the meeting of different traditions was much more important than conflicts. Benefits for rulers were especially significant. Chartered towns with fortifications and a new organizational form (communes), and their resulting standing as communities in relation to rulers, were the visible sign of change. Castellanization, the process of building castles as residences for knights, not just for royal administration, was another such sign. In the countryside, new spatial organization was introduced by western immigrants and widely adapted by local landowners in the second half of the thirteenth century. Social, legal and economic organization also affected the system of power. Instead of orally transmitted rights, written and commonly accepted laws and privileges became the norm.

## KINGS AND NOBLES

Political dynamics were shaped by the interaction of the nobility and the rulers. Despite similarities in the need to balance the interests of the nobles and the dynasty, the three polities displayed divergent trends: on the one hand towards growing noble power and fragmentation in Hungary and Poland and, on the other, towards increasing stability and a permanent royal title in Bohemia.

### *Bohemia*

In Bohemia, after many decades of upheaval, political stability was achieved by Přemysl Otakar I (duke of Prague, 1192–3 and 1197–8, king of Bohemia, 1198–1230). A hereditary royal crown granted in 1212 might be seen as a symbol of new political order. But more important was the reinforcement of internal power structures. An unprecedented level of co-operation between two brothers – Přemysl Otakar I as senior ruler and Vladislav Jindřich as the margrave of Moravia – contributed to internal political stabilization. All male members of Moravian Přemyslid line died or were expelled in the two first decades of the thirteenth century and their hereditary lands were incorporated into the domains of Přemysl Otakar I and Vladislav Jindřich. For the first time for more than a hundred years, power over Bohemia and Moravia was in hands of closely co-operating rulers from one family.

Peace, however, was not complete. Přemysl Otakar I participated in political conflicts in the Empire, and as a result reached an unprecedented political position there. He was no longer a lowly duke from the eastern borderlands of the Empire, but one of the leading figures in imperial policy. Přemysl Otakar I actively participated in political conflicts in the Empire. He manoeuvred between the competing factions associated with German rulers and the papacy. Soon after he had been crowned by King Philip of Swabia in 1198, he switched allegiance and supported King Otto IV of Brunswick, who rewarded Přemysl by recrowning him at Merseburg on 24 August 1203 and declaring the royal title to have hereditary status. Philip of Swabia quickly decreed that the coronation he performed five years previously was now void, and appointed the junior prince Děpolt III as the new duke of Bohemia. These actions forced Přemysl Otakar I back within Philip's camp, just as the political situation in Germany had begun to favour the Staufs. Accordingly, Philip withdrew his appointment of Děpolt III.

One condition of the arrangement between Philip and Přemysl was that the Bohemian king's divorced wife Adelaide should return to Prague, although this did not mean that the Hungarian princess Constance was expelled. The 'returning' wife spent a year in Bohemia before she was sent home in 1205, a decision that she again questioned. Adelaide's complaints help to explain why Otto IV's political ally, the reformer Pope Innocent III, was hesitant to accept the political promotion of Přemysl Otakar I. In 1202 the pope even attempted to rescind the king's divorce and his subsequent marriage to Constance. However, political expediency demanded that, in 1207, the Church formally recognize both the king's royal status and his marriage. Even so, Prague was not elevated to an archbishopric despite the king's wishes.[1]

In November 1211, Přemysl Otakar I was among the electors who elected Frederick II king of Germany. The new status of Bohemian rulers was acknowledged by Emperor Frederick II in the Golden Bull of Sicily (September 1212). This privilege recognized the status of the Přemyslids as *Reichsfürsten* with a hereditary royal title. Přemysl Otakar I appointed his son Václav as his only successor. To ensure a smooth succession, Václav I was crowned 'co-king' in 1228, two years before his father's death in 1230. The old ruler wanted to control the political situation in the kingdom almost until his last days. In time, the rule of primogeniture was constantly applied within the Přemyslid dynasty.[2]

After Přemysl Otakar I's death his son, Václav I (1228–53), took power but not without a fight. His brother, margrave of Moravia,

[1] Wojciech Iwańczak, 'Innocent III and Bohemia', in *Innocenzo III. Urbs et orbis. Atti del Congresso Internazionale (Roma, 9–15 settembre 1998)*, ed. Andrea Sommerlechner, vol. II (Rome, 2003), 1200–12.

[2] Josef Žemlička, *Přemysl Otakar I: panovník, stát a česká společnost na prachu vrcholného feudalismu* (Prague, 1990).

Přemysl, questioned his authority. Although Margrave Přemysl (1228–39) was defeated in 1231, he continued to resist until he was expelled in 1237. He returned but his power was diminished while the king's increased. After the margrave's death a son of Václav I, Vladislav, was nominated as the margrave of Moravia and co-operated with his father. But after Vladislav's death in 1247, and after his brother, Přemysl Otakar (II) (1253–78), became the ruler of Moravia, peace ended. The young duke rebelled against his father the same year and was acknowledged by the nobles as a 'young king', the traditional title of co-rulers and future heirs during the reign of their father. Václav I did not accept the usurpation and in 1248 defeated his son. Nevertheless, he did not deny the title of Moravian margrave's title to Přemysl Otakar (II), who also remained heir presumptive of the kingdom. On Václav's death in 1253, Přemysl Otakar (II) as the only living member of the dynasty was elected ruler of Bohemia and Moravia.[3]

Although the centre of power in Bohemia was clearly located at the king's court and the royal family did not need to fight with other branches of the dynasty, this did not prevent deep internal conflicts between kings and their sons or brothers. Young members of the family fought to gain power earlier or to prove to their supporters their bravery and aptitude for power. These dynastic tensions decreased in the second half of the thirteenth century because Přemysl Otakar II had only one legitimate son, Václav (II), who was choosen to inherit, and was crowned co-ruler in 1271, seven years before his father's death. The only possible competitor, the illegitimate son of King Přemysl and his close ally, Mikulaš, could not inherit the royal crown. In 1260, the pope acknowledged Mikulaš's hereditary right, with the exception of the crown. He therefore became duke of Olomouc in 1269. During the reign of his half-brother, King Václav II, Mikulaš remained loyal and as a result became governor in Lesser Poland as well as, after the royal coronation of Václav as the king of Poland in 1300, his *capitaneus* in the whole Polish kingdom. The only son of Václav II, Václav III (1305–6), followed his uncle and never openly questioned his father, always co-operating with him. In contrast to the twelfth century, the dignity of Bohemian

[3] Stanislav Barta, 'Smiření otca se synem: uzavřeni sporu krále Václavá I s makrabetem Přemyslem roku 1249', in *Ritual smiřeni: konflikt a jeho řešení ve stredoveku*, ed. Martin Nodl and Martin Wihoda (Brno, 2008), 101–8.

rulers, the power of royal administration and the well-organized royal army were not reduced by rebellion. This resulted from a balanced coexistence of the strong political central power and an equally strong tendency of the nobles to free themselves from it.[4]

Political changes in relations between dukes and nobles were directly connected to the implantation of western knightly culture. Although the strongest influence came from the Empire, Czech knights were also acquainted with it during their military expeditions to Rome and participation in crusades to the Holy Land. These mixed impulses were supported and altered by royal cultural policy. Přemyslid kings, acting as *Reichsfürsten* abroad, tried to establish a new cultural landscape at home. The royal court in Prague and royal officials with their entourages disseminated new trends among nobles to strengthen, or impose new forms of, relations between rulers and their representatives and subjects, even privileged ones, that were desired by kings. These cultural changes were accepted so far as they were in common with the knights' desire to expand their liberties and to show their domination over local society. Historians stress the slow evolution of traditional culture, rather than revolutionary change. Noble heraldry started at the begininng of the thirteenth century; new knightly ceremonies and means of ostentation (like tournaments) were observed from the second quarter of the century. At the same time kings started to replace the wooden fortification of traditional strongholds and courts with constructions of stone, castles and palaces. Menacing royal fortresses built in the new style were clear symbols of the ruler's invincible power.[5]

Yet after 1241, when the king feared for the kingdom's security, he accepted that not only the king, but also the mightiest nobles would reside in their own, stone-built seats. Paradoxically, they were quite often constructed not in the regions devoid of royal protection, but

[4] Jörg K. Hoensch, *Přemysl Otakar II. von Böhmen. Der goldene König* (Graz, Vienna and Cologne, 1989).

[5] Dana Dvořáčková-Malá, 'Dvorská kultura přemyslovského období: nástin problematiky a možnosti výzkumu', *Mediaevalia Historica Bohemica* 12, 1 (2009), 9–43; Dvořáčková-Malá, 'Dvorský ceremoniál, rituály a komunikace v dobovém kontextu', in *Dvory a rezidence ve středověku*, vol. III, *Všední a sváteční život na středověkých dvorech* (Prague, 2009), 33–55; Dvořáčková-Malá, 'Der Herrscherhof im Mittelalter Struktur, Raum und Repräsentation', *Historica* 14 (2010), 59–90; Dvořáčková-Malá, 'K modelu středověkého panovnického dvora jako sociálního system', *Český Časopis Historický* 107, 2 (2009), 309–35.

near royal fortresses. Nobles did not think about possible fights with warriors from abroad. They tried *hic et nunc* to compete with and control royal administration. All mighty families wanted their own castles or seats made of stone. Their number was growing and they were built in much more varied locations. If traditionally and according to the logic of war they were located on hills or even just in a dominant position in the lowlands, at the end of the thirteenth century some were built simply in villages. Not so exclusive as they were in the middle of the century, representative buildings of stone played an informational rather than military role. Nevertheless, during the thirteenth century, step by step, nobles emulated royal features of propaganda of power. But did their real position change too?

According to traditional historiography, the situation of the nobility changed drastically during the thirteenth century. In the eleventh and twelfth centuries, warriors and powerful allies of the ruler were at the same time paid officials of a duke or a king. They had no hereditary estates, nor subjects who could pay dues. All revenues and lands were just given by a ruler to knights as a temporary benefice for their service. This changed at the turn of the twelfth and thirteenth centuries when the aspirations of nobles grew while at the same time the traditional system of royal administration disappeared. Simultanously, rulers gave liberties to the Church, even minting rights, which clearly emphasized the growing margin of the bishops' independence from royal power.[6] Using these new rights, bishops could try to build their own region's power modelled on the position of Church dignitaries in the Empire. The most influential Czech families among the king's allies also tried to acquire similar privileges. As a result, wealthy and powerful landowning families originated from the highest ranking *benefitiarii* of dukes. Conflicts between two groups of nobles – dignitaries and warriors living as *benefitiarii regis* on the one hand and landowners on the other – led to a broader struggle between King Václav I and his son Přemysl Otakar II. The latter had as his supporters members of benefitium-system elites. When he was defeated, the old system definitively ended. After taking power, Přemysl Otakar II supported nobles, extended their privileges and

[6] Jiří Sejbal, 'The minting rights of the Bishops of Olomouc in the thirteenth century', in *Moneta mediaevalis: studia numizmatyczne i historyczne ofiarowane Profesorowi Stanislawowi Suchodolskiemu w 65. rocznice urodzin* (Warsaw, 2002), 309–25.

enlarged their hereditary fortunes. He created the *zemsky sud* (*iusticium terre*, *colloquium generalis*, land's court) with powers replacing those of the old ducal court over warriors. At first the land's court functioned as a court of appeal for clergy and nobles in civil cases. But then it became the institution where cases between the king or his administration and nobles were judged. During the last decades of the thirteenth century it changed its character once again and functioned as the highest representative of the nobility, controlling law-making and royal policy. Nobles gained more and more power at the expense of the royal administration, and at the end of the thirteenth century they held so-called *dominium generale* over the kingdom, and left for the king *dominium speciale* (current issues, including those concerning towns and the Church). Royal administration lost its powers thanks to a series of liberties gained by nobles. The latter judged their servants and were judged by peers without royal intervention. Historians have coined the term 'privatized state', meaning that state administration had no real significance for internal affairs governed by elites.[7]

This analysis has been severely criticized in recent years by younger Czech medievalists. Historical ideas about the eleventh and twelfth centuries (see Chapter 5) deeply influenced a vision of the thirteenth century. Once traditional ideas about the earlier period were revised (proving the existence of noble landholding and ecclesiastical foundations), this entailed the reconsideration of thirteenth-century trends. The growing number of wealthy estate-holders in the thirteenth century would be hard to deny. Their presence, however, was not a revolution but part of a long process. That is clearly attested by the development of the foundation activity of Czech nobles. It started in the second half of the eleventh century as donations of small portions of land, then evolved during the twelfth century into the foundation of medium-sized monasteries founded by wealthy noble families. From the turn of the century, and continuing during the entire thirteenth century, founding a monastery in the middle of large, family estates was common among the Czech nobility, and a gesture of display of power.[8]

More disputable are the origin and place of the land's court among thirteenth-century institutions of the Kingdom of Bohemia. It is not

[7] Josef Žemlička, 'České 13. století: "privatizace" státu', *Český Časopis Historický* 101, 3 (2005), 509–40.

[8] For a detailed analysis, see Pauk, *Działalność fundacyjna*.

certain whether the court was created by kings in the thirteenth century. Rather, it had been a constant element of law and order in Czech society since its roots in the tenth and eleventh centuries. Its members as well as subjects were always estate-holders and its remit was traditional case law concerning estate-holding, -inheritance or -creation. This hypothesis was intricately tied to the belief that no ducal law-making existed in tenth to twelfth-century Bohemia, because law was created during meetings of freemen, then nobles (*colloquia*). Therefore King Václav II's attempt to establish written norms of law by royal order was questioned by all nobles. The mightiest of the nobility tried to control royal policy concerning the internal order of the Bohemian kingdom. During the whole thirteenth century, members of the land's court were the highest royal officials of Prague. The king constantly led the court, although sometimes he passed the presidency to one of his allies. There is no doubt that near the end of the thirteenth century land's court members were representatives of the highest nobility's interests, but at the same time the court was part of the royal administration.

According to younger Czech medievalists it is hardly possible to talk about a privatized state at the end of the thirteenth century, or to describe the whole century as a period of revolutionary change in the relations between nobles and rulers. Unquestionably, noble influence on royal policy was stronger than before, and kings gave up part of their powers to estate-holders (*liberties*). Yet this was not a drastic change; the mightiest nobles had always had strong influence on rulers' policy. The thirteenth century instead is simply the first time when a relative abundance of charters and narrative sources makes it possible to understand this influence. An analysis of litigation between King Václav II and nobles about estates also showed clearly that the king did not give up his rights lightly. He acted exactly according to the traditional law of the land. Even when his opponent was a mighty official or one of his own faithful allies, the monarch did not relinquish his rights to a disputed property. He clearly acted as the monarch, restrained by law and traditional customs but not by private interests of nobles. Therefore it is hard to interpret the whole political and juridical situation in the kingdom as the aforementioned division of power into two parts (*dominium generale* and *speciale*) with one of them taken by the highest nobility.[9]

[9] Libor Jan, 'Dominium generale a dominium speciale – jeden mýtus česke historiografie', in *Z pomocných věd historických*, vol. XVI, *Inter laurum et olivam*, ed. Jiří Šouša

Even if one agreed with the new paradigm of the place played by Czech nobles in the Přemyslid realm, several changes did occur during the thirteenth century. One of the most important was the appearance of written oaths of fidelity to the king made by all the highest members of the Czech nobility during the reign of Václav II. Before his ascension there is no trace of such oaths. Historians suggested that allegiance to a king was pledged orally earlier. Yet charters from the reign of Václav II are the first to suggest the existence of such a ritual and their wording follows western patterns closely. It is almost certain that long before Václav's reign knights and especially royal officials were connected to their superior by bonds of fidelity and protection. But it was during his reign that western patterns for the first time influenced so evidently the organization of relations between the ruler and his nobles. They also influenced relations between mighty nobles or Church institutions and less wealthy knights who obtained a role of *ministeriali* at the side of their superiors. The royal court implemented new forms of social and legal ties between subjects, and changed the old ones to the king's advantage. During the second half of the thirteenth century kings tried to establish and strengthen control over Czech nobles in every possible way. Rulers equally used traditional law and their position in relations with newly established dependent groups to accentuate their dominant position in every part of social life in the kingdom. This was in accordance with the cultural policy of rulers, who – like Václav II since 1290 – consciously made courts a centre of western culture, even if that was not commonly accepted by more traditionally oriented nobles.[10]

Although they promoted change in social life, in the thirteenth century Czech rulers were relatively rarely bothered by open mutiny from their subjects. Rather, both sides tried to co-operate for mutual profit. On the one hand royal power was still dependent on knights' personal service in royal administration and army, and on dues paid by nobles. On the other hand, nobles possessing estates as their main source of income had to be careful about taking part in conflicts. They

and Ivana Ebelova (Acta Universitatis Carolinae. Philosophica et historica, 1–2/ 2002 (Prague, 2007)), 645–52; Jan, *Václav II*, 163–256.

[10] Marcin Rafał Pauk, 'Der böhmische Adel im 13. Jahrhundert. Zwischen Herrschaftsbildung und Gemeinschaftsgefühl', in *Böhmen und seine Nachbarn in den Přemyslidenzeit*, ed. Ivan Hlaváček and Alexander Patschovsky (Ostfildern, 2011), 247–88.

could lose their revenues and nobody would take care of their families, especially if they rebelled against royal authority. All this was outweighed by threats against independence or current status. During the 1260s King Přemysl Otakar II tried to establish royal control over southern Bohemia. As part of this policy, he founded in this region the royal chartered town Česke Budějovice and royal abbey Trnova (then Zlota Koruna). But members of the Vitkovce clan, dominant over the territory since the end of the twelfth century, took this as both an offence and a threat to their social position. They therefore tried to undermine the royal institutions. Eventually, they rebelled against the king in 1276 together with one of the most influential Czech clans, the lords of Rýzomburk, and other knightly families from Styria and Austria. The king, who was at war with Rudolf of Habsburg, had to sign a peace treaty to return to Bohemia. Rebels accused him of violating traditional laws and claimed that this justified their disobedience. The king suppressed the rebellion violently. Several mighty conspirators were killed or detained in custody. Others fled to Rudolf of Habsburg. Not only royal domination but also the right to establish new forms of co-operation in society were confirmed.

Přemysl Otakar II as well as his son, Václav II, were assertive when nobles tried to belittle their dignity or their competence. Václav's father died when his son was a minor. When he came of age at twelve in 1283, he was placed under the informal care of Záviš of Falkenštejn of the Vitkovce clan, the partner and soon the second husband of the queen-widow, Václav's mother, Kunhuta. For several years Záviš was the most influential person in Bohemia, and the young king accepted this. Záviš maintained his position even after Kunhuta's death in 1285. Václav II allowed him to marry Erzsébet, the sister of the king of Hungary, to ensure the political alliance between Bohemia and Hungary. But during Záviš's prolonged stay in Hungary, the Prague court became dominated by his opponents. The young king started to support knightly clans hostile to the Vitkovce in general and Záviš in particular. The magnate had to remain at his stronghold in Svojanov. In 1289 he invited the king to take part in a banquet celebrating his newborn son. Although Václav accepted the invitation, he ordered Záviš's detention. Then the king tried to force him to return estates and other assets which he had received as Kunhuta's dowry. The Vitkovce rebelled, but according to chronicles in 1290 the king's uncle, Mikuláš, the duke of Opava, warned the warriors defending

Vitkovce fortresses that he would kill his prisoner if they did not surrender. When the commandant of the Hluboká stronghold refused, Záviš was decapitated. The king defeated the Vitkovce clan and established his strong personal authority.[11]

## *Poland*

The death of Mieszko III the Old, Bolesław III the Wrymouth's last living son, on 13 March 1202 definitively ended the practice of succession according to seniority in Poland and sparked a period of more complex political play there. Although Cracow was still recognized as the informal capital and the seat for any potential 'duke-*princeps*', from the reign of Kazimierz II the Just (1176–97) not only the Piast dukes, but also the nobles of Lesser Poland, came to be seen as a decisive force in providing power over Cracow. Their factions supported different rulers for the throne. Excluding Cracow, the other principalities became hereditary to different branches of the dynasty, starting with each son of Bolesław III (Silesia went to the descendants of Władysław II; Greater Poland to those of Mieszko III; Masovia and Kuyavia to those of Bolesław IV, then Kazimierz II the Just) and in some instances led to territorial subdivisions. The realm ultimately became divided into regions with different dynasties of rulers, administrative traditions, legal systems, coins and even ethnicities (with different proportions of the non-Slavic population in different regions). The political integrity of the realm had become an illusion. No common external policy existed; local princes entered into their own political and military alliances with the Empire, Bohemia, Rus' and Denmark.

Yet rulers possessing Cracow tried to establish some control, even if only honorary, over their relatives. In 1202 parts of the Cracow nobility and Church hierarchy supported the ducal claims of Kazimierz II's son, Leszek I the White. Leszek launched a serious effort to rule as senior duke and he achieved some success in curbing the activities of local dukes. Nevertheless, Leszek's superior status was questioned by his own brothers and cousins. The death of Leszek the

11 Libor Jan, 'Domací šlechtičká opozice a přemyslovšti králové 13. veku', in *Ritual smiřeni*, 85–100; Jan, 'Proces se Zavišem a promeny královské vlády v letech 1289–1290', *Český Časopis Historický* 103 (2005), 1–40; Josef Žemlička, 'Transformation of the dukedom of "the Bohemians" into the Kingdom of Bohemia', in *Political Culture in Central Europe*, vol. I, 47–64.

White in 1227 prompted a new period of instability, as the elites – secular and spiritual – played a major and active role in fights between the provincial dukes. In Greater Poland the two Władysławs (Spindleshanks and his nephew Odonic (1207–39)) fought from 1227 to 1231 for exclusive control over central Poland. In Masovia, Konrad I (1194–1247) extended his territory by 1229 through the annexation of the Sieradz and Łęczyca lands belonging to Leszek I's widow; the Silesian duke Henryk I the Bearded attempted to subordinate Lesser Poland, encountering resistance from Konrád I of Masovia. Henryk I the Bearded (1234) of Silesia, the oldest male in the Piast family, held the upper hand in the realm from 1233. He ruled over half of Poland (Silesia, Opole, Lesser Poland and southern Greater Poland) and his authority was more or less willingly accepted by weaker relatives. After his death in 1238, his son Henryk II the Pious (1238–41) tried to assume his father's power. But the dukes of Opole (between Silesia and Cracow) and Sandomierz freed themselves from Henryk's control and allied with his enemies. His position in relations with nobles of Lesser Poland, or even Silesia, was nothing like his father's. He fought hard to re-establish his authority as the senior ruler in Poland, which was finally acknowledged by the papacy but not by Polish dukes and nobles. He was killed in 1241 during the Mongol invasion.

After 1241, most Silesian dukes changed their political horizon. They focused on fights for domination over Silesia, a region divided into four duchies in the middle of the thirteenth century, and fourteen by the end of the century. The Silesian Piasts strengthened their political relations with the Czech kings, who were treated as protectors by most of the weaker rulers. The same role was played by Hungarian kings for the dukes of Lesser Poland. On the whole of Polish territory political relations between all Piast rulers concentrated on building the biggest possible sphere of domination in relations with other dukes. During the late thirteenth century one finds attempts to reverse the gradual decline of ducal and elite political status by appealing to the symbolic unity of the realm. The common name and dynastic tradition and the Gniezno archbishopric all served as reminders of a glorious past. In addition, most inhabitants of Piast duchies shared a common culture and judicial traditions, as well as the holy patronage of St Vojtěch-Adalbert. This conceptual framework was acknowledged abroad, where speaking of a 'Polish Kingdom' was fairly common. In reality, however, the monarchy had been displaced by a polyarchy in which local dukes challenged each other in order to gain as much power as possible.

Conflicts were exacerbated even more at the end of thirteenth century, when Henryk IV the Righteous of Wrocław united Silesia and Lesser Poland under his authority and – probably imitating the Bohemian system – tried to gain a royal crown. He died of poison in 1290, but his plans were not forgotten. In 1295, after assuming power over Gdańsk and Eastern Pomerania (1294), Przemysł II of Greater Poland was crowned king of Poland. His authority was acknowledged only by the dukes of Kuyavia and Masowia. Silesian dukes refused to accept his dignity as superior to theirs, and the nobles of Lesser Poland elected the Czech king Václav II as their ruler. In 1296, Przemysł II was assassinated, which started a long period of wars for domination over Poland between Václav II, Władysław Łokietek (1275–1333), duke of Kuyavia, and Henry I (III) of Głogów (Silesia) (1273–1309). At first it was Václav who succeeded and was crowned in 1300. But in the end Władysław won, and after the death of Václav III in 1306 he established sole rule over the majority of the old Piast lands (Greater and Lesser Poland, Kuyavia and Eastern Pomerania). He was crowned in 1320, and from then the Kingdom of Poland became a stable political entity.

In short, the political history of Poland during the thirteenth century was that of permanent, costly conflict between Piast dukes attempting to maintain their position as independent rulers, or to dominate their relatives. All dukes had to participate and to gather enough resources to confront not only other Piast rulers but also their foreign allies. Resources included not simply money or land but above all authority among elites and the latter's co-operation. From the middle of the thirteenth century, dukes of small or sometimes tiny duchies were obliged to rely on strong support of their subjects. Here lay the cause of the rapid changes in thirteenth-century Polish society, among them changes in royal–noble relations. These were closely connected with broader issues: implementing western patterns of rule by Piast dukes (territorialization of power), migration of lower-ranking German knights towards the east, new legislative directions (the beginnings of liberty and of states) and an evolving economy (increasing monetization, the emergence of towns and rural colonization). Dukes supported the new trends because they might strengthen ducal position. In the long term, however, most rulers were weakened, due to the political situation: elites – at first knights, in Silesia soon also townsmen – had to be won over, and for that Piasts had to give up much of their privileged social position.

In all Piast duchies, dukes still had the final decision on all transactions made by knights concerning land or rents. Rulers without any formal limitations decided the most important economic and legal issues (duties, liberties, the creation of new villages and recreation of old ones as chartered villages) as well as political ones (declaration of war, marriages, alliances). Yet from 1180 one can observe the growing role of *wiece* (in Latin *colloquia*) in local policy. These conventions of the knights of a duchy or land had no formal influence on ducal policy. But as the majority of most important political decisions known to us were declared during these meetings through charters, historians assumed that nobles, whose highest elite testified in charters, had an informal right to control the legality of a ruler's decision. The weaker the position of a ruler, the more often he announced his decisions in public.[12]

The sacral character of power during the first half of the thirteenth century was stressed by the alone dukes (such as Henryk I the Bearded), resisting pressure by the reformed clergy to relinquish the right to control the local Church. Most dukes, motivated by political need, gave up such control. Consequently, they issued liberties for the clergy, but soon they were pressed to do so for nobles as well. It was detrimental to ducal status that dukes consciously and deliberately violated political custom by introducing more direct violence into their interactions. In the 1230s, Duke Konrád I of Masovia ordered his knights to abduct his relative the ruling duke, Henryk I the Bearded, and a duchess, the widowed Grzymisława, with her minor son (Bolesław IV the Chaste (1232–79)). In both cases knights and nobles tried to free their dukes (although in official Silesian ducal historiography, Henryk's family are given the most credit). This was a major change from the situation at the end of the twelfth century, when a knight's attempt to engage the opposing duke in personal combat during the battle on Mozgawa River was considered a severe crime.

[12] Antoni Barciak, 'Tage und Debatte im Beisein des Herzogs in Polen. Zur Funktionsweise von Tagen (wiece) des 13. Jahrhunderts', in *Ritualisierung politischer Willensbildung. Polen und Deutschland im hohen und späten Mittelalter*, ed. Wojciech Fałkowski (Wiesbaden, 2010), 67–78; Tomasz Jurek, 'Ritual und Technik der sozialen Kommunikation zwischen Landesherren und Gesellschaft in Polen im 13. Jahrhundert', in *Ritualisierung politischer Willensbildung*, 101–26.

At the end of the thirteenth century dukes accepted even treason: in at least one case, knights abducted their own lord and handed him over to another, a relative of the first (e.g. Henryk V the Fat of Wrocław and Legnica was kidnapped by his own knights in 1293 and handed over to Henryk I (III) of Głogów). Dukes did not hesitate to break their own oaths to force their relatives to take oaths of fidelity. In 1280 Henryk IV Probus organized a convention of dukes attended by Przemysł II of Greater Poland, Henryk V the Fat and Henryk I (III) of Głogów. As they arrived he imprisoned them, and forced them to give him land (Przemysł II) or take oaths of fidelity (both Silesian dukes). Such ducal behaviour was widely known by nobles. The brutality of ducal power was also visible in relations with subjects. In 1239 Konrad I of Masovia sentenced Jan Czapla, his own chancellor and canon of Płock cathedral, to death. Jan was tortured and hanged publicly, near the cathedral. Less deadly but nonetheless violent measures of political pressure were used by other dukes. In 1257 Bolesław Rogatka, duke of Legnica (1241–78), kidnapped the bishop of Wrocław, Thomas I, and imprisoned him in the castle of Wleń. In 1283 Henryk IV Probus expelled Thomas II, bishop of Wrocław, from the latter's own lands and organized a knightly tournament in the capital of the bishop's duchy, Nysa.

The weakening position of Piast dukes was closely related to the growing subdivision of Poland. It continued apace as nine principalities in 1250 gave way to nineteen around 1280. Eleven of these nineteen were small Silesian principalities. Each duke established his own court with offices mirroring patterns used by powerful rulers. The later Piast dukes also used court offices to strengthen their position among elites. But while mighty dukes in the past had operated in a much larger perspective of the whole of Poland, when dealing with nobles and their factions, the younger and more numerous generation of rulers, fighting among themselves for rulership over smaller duchies, had to choose their knightly allies among local landowners. The latter supported their rulers in exchange for concessions, among them liberties and participation in duchies' government. If a duke denied them privileges or pursued political goals different from those accepted by nobles, or was even expected to do so in the near future, he would be deposed, expelled or not allowed to be enthroned despite legally succeeding according to the will of his predecessor. When Henryk IV Probus died in 1290 in his testament he chose the duke of Głogów, Henryk I (III), as his sucessor in the duchy of

Wrocław. But the nobility refused to accept the new duke, afraid that he would continue the hectic activity of his predecessor. Therefore, they acclaimed Henryk V the Fat as their ruler. Yet when the same Henryk V sentenced to death one of his knights, Pakosław, who was guilty without any doubt, the deceased's son, Lutek Pakosławic, kindnapped the duke in revenge (1293). The traitor and his allies had to leave the duchy of Wrocław. But the noble participants in the conspiracy were never punished. They settled down in their new patron's duchy of Głogów, were given landed properties, and after a peace agreement between the dukes in conflict all of them freely sold their estates in the duchy of Wrocław.

Noble position was also strengthened by administrative reforms commonly pursued by Piasts in the thirteenth century. The system of provinces administered by *comites* was completely unsuitable when (1) a province became divided into several duchies; (2) dukes needed closer surveillance over their smaller realms and incomes generated by them; or (3) local nobles wanted new administrative structures, which might more clearly display their position both at court and in the realm. A network of castellan districts was therefore created, with a castellan as the main ducal representative and a range of smaller officials dependent on him as well as judges (*iudices castri*), stewards (*villici*) and *tribuni* as military deputies. The origin of the system is a subject of discussion among historians. The traditional hypothesis is that it emerged on the basis of the districts linked to the fortresses of the old Piast realm. The newer concept stresses the system's resemblance to that created reforms in the Empire, where from the end of the twelfth century burgraves' districts with burgraves as royal deputies played quite a similar role. According to the latter concept the emergence of castellans might be another step in the much wider process of the modernization of the Piast realm on the German model. Regardless of which hypothesis one accepts, the castellan system, created to strengthen ducal position, was in fact one more element contributing to the local nobility's hierarchization, and the formalization of its growing importance in duchies' government. Although castellan offices never became hereditary, they were used by noble families both as a sign of social status and as a way to join the highest elite of the land.

The only office higher than castellan was that of palatine. Its position varied in different regions. In Silesian duchies the office of palatine disappeared, almost completely replaced by *camerarius*. In other regions the office of palatine survived at first as the highest dignity at each ducal court. When the divisions of regions into smaller duchies progressed, consequently the number of palatines grew. Typically, from the middle of the thirteenth century the palatine's office ceased to be connected with the ducal court and started to be related to a land. Even if a duchy ceased to exit as a separate entity, and was incorporated into a larger unit, the office of palatine survived. Therefore in Lesser Poland palatines of Cracow and Sandomierz coexisted although from 1242 only one ruler governed both duchies as duke of Cracow. Once again an office, which started as a part of ducal administrative system, became a part of wider, social hierarchy of local nobles.

The growing number of foreign knights invited into the realm by dukes and the spread of western knightly culture were among the factors modifying relations between dukes and nobles during the thirteenth century. Since the war between sons of Henryk II the Pious for domination over Silesia (1248–51) Piast dukes, who needed strong military support, had encouraged immigration of more lowly knights from the Empire. In Silesia these migrants were so numerous and their culture so attractive for locals that during the fourteenth century almost the whole of the knightly elite became Germanized. In other regions of Piast Poland, where the position of nobles in relation to dukes was stronger, the scale of knightly migration was smaller and knightly elites were more traditionally oriented. Nevertheless, cultural changes were visible everywhere: familiy residences changed into countryside castles or strongholds, knights took part in tournaments organized by dukes and noble heraldry was born. This also changed relations with rulers along patterns more similar to west European ones. Yet, apart from Silesia, strong differences still remained in family structure (big clans rather than families as basic units of social order), and a lack of formal bonds of knights as duke's vassals. The traditional ethics of knightly duties to a ruler bound together with allodial character of noble land ownership allowed little room for the spread of vassalage. It appeared in larger numbers only in ecclesiastical institutions, especially at bishops' courts and tied to rich abbeys. The social position of Church dignitaries and institutions originating in the struggle for independence from dukes and secular patrons was relatively novel; these new actors needed innovative solutions to build their own sphere of domination among local elites. The Piast dukes had still the advantage of tradition, the antiquity of their power. Therefore, although changes in relations between rulers and dukes were profound, they were almost always publicly presented as part of an old tradition. This creates problems for modern historians, trying to disentangle new elements from traditional ones in thirteenth-century social life.[13]

## *Hungary*

The thirteenth century has been called the century of the Golden Bulls by a modern historian, pinpointing the charters granted to the nobility in Hungary as the most significant development of the period.[14] The growth of noble power was certainly one of the key changes of the century, and it occurred at the expense of the king's authority. Nobles emerged as a status group in the thirteenth century, based on the criteria of landownership (of an *allodium*), a status as a warrior, and the gaining of liberties from 1222 onwards. Other groups had a status between nobles and peasants: freemen who inherited the obligation to fight for a lord and oversee his domains, such as castle warriors and warriors on ecclesiastical domains.

Dynastic rivalry created favourable conditions for the nobility's accumulation of power, as they could back one of two protagonists during most of the century. Thus András (Andrew) (II), the brother of King Imre (Emeric), revolted against his brother and secured Croatia and Dalmatia for himself as prince in 1197–8; despite this concession, fighting between the brothers flared up again in the following years. Béla (IV), eldest son of András II, in turn had to be crowned king in 1214 due to pressure from nobles, and received Croatia and Slavonia as prince of Slavonia in 1220. Béla IV himself was then in prolonged conflict and even civil war with his son István (V). The latter was prince of Transylvania, and briefly prince of Styria, but after the loss of that territory in 1262 István forced the king to confer the title 'younger king'

[13] For a social history, but one focusing on local traditions and institutions, see Piotr Górecki, *Economy, Society and Lordship in Medieval Poland, 1100–1250* (New York, 1992); Górecki, *Parishes, Tithes and Society in Earlier Medieval Poland, ca. 1100–1250* (Philadelphia, 1983); Górecki, 'Words, Concepts and Phenomena: Knighthood, Lordship and the Early Polish Nobility, c. 1100–1350', in *Nobles and Nobility in Medieval Europe: Concepts, Origins, Transformations*, ed. Anne Duggan (London, 2000), 115–55.

[14] Gyula Kristó, *Az aranybullák évszázada* (Budapest, 1976).

on him, as well as granting him the government of the eastern part of the realm (east of the Danube), splitting royal power in the kingdom. István had a parallel royal court, governed his areas as a sovereign ruler and conducted his own foreign policy. Hostilities and even open war did not cease between the two kings for the rest of Béla's rule.[15]

The first half of the thirteenth century was characterized by the continually renewed conflict between nobles and king as well as between those groups that ultimately became the lesser and greater nobility. The elite claimed descent from illustrious ancestors, be they Hungarian or real or alleged immigrants in the early period of the realm. By the early thirteenth century, they started using the denomination *de genere* and the name of the illustrious person they regarded as the ancestor of the lineage. The chronicler Simon of Kéza around 1285 wrote of more than 100 such kindreds.[16] They started to use their own coat of arms, founded monasteries that became the burial places of members of the lineage, and kept estates within the lineage. In addition, typical names recurred over generations within each lineage. A handful of the elite families participated in the royal council, in the government of the realm. They did not represent the nobility or even the barons; it was the king who selected them. The emergence of the lesser nobility was a complex process. Some impoverished freemen voluntarily joined the service of lay or ecclesiastical lords after the Mongol invasion of 1241–2; the king eventually ruled that these decisions were irreversible. Thus, some lost their status and even their freedom. Others, who were formerly castle warriors and *servientes regis*, servants of the king, were becoming part of the nobility. The latter's servitude to the king distinguished and elevated them above those who served other lords. Some descended from free warriors, others were elevated by the king. Eventually, they formed the majority of the nobility. They did not participate in the government of the kingdom, although they were gaining importance at a local level.[17]

In the early thirteenth century, the balance of power shifted decisively towards the nobility. Whereas traditionally Hungary's kings

[15] Jenő Szűcs, *Az utolsó Árpádok* (Budapest, 1993); Attila Zsoldos, *Családi ügy: IV. Béla és István ifjabb király viszálya az 1260-as években* (Budapest, 2007).

[16] Veszprémy and Schaer, ed. and tr., *Simon of Kéza*, 158–9.

[17] Fügedi, *Kings, Bishops*; Rady, *Nobility*; Erik Fügedi and János M. Bak, 'Fremde Ritter im mittelalterlichen Ungarn', *Quaestiones Medii Aevi Novae* 3 (1998), 3–18.

were the greatest landowners in the kingdom and drew significant revenues in kind and in money from their estates, King András II instituted the donation in perpetuity of royal domains to nobles on a large scale, including castle lands and entire counties.[18] The revenues from these lands now also went to their new owners. Whereas exceptionally from the last decade of the twelfth century entire counties were donated by kings, these were always peripheral lands. András started the systematic policy of giving away large areas of royal lands in core areas in perpetuity, together with their revenues and the rights of jurisdiction. This benefited prelates and leading lay royal officials. It contributed to the emergence of an elite within the nobility, around twenty families holding high offices in the realm (the term 'baron' first appeared in 1217 to describe them).

For example, one family, the Szentgyörgyi of the Hont-Pázmány lineage received around fifteen estates in about as many years from the king in the early thirteenth century. They became lords of enormous areas of land in several parts of the realm. Another important member of the elite, Nicholas of the Csák lineage, held about forty *praedia* in the 1230s. In comparison, a few pieces of data on the possessions of freemen outside the elite signal that they held one to three *praedia*. Landowners also began to consolidate their previously scattered landholdings into large territorial units in order to establish large estates. The barons thereby also built territorial lordships. One possible reason for the change in royal policy (called 'new dispositions' in one of András's charters) was to ensure the military service of mounted knights. Because the lands of the *udvornici* (*udvarnokföldek*) that had earlier been donated by kings no longer existed in surplus, and no new lands could be acquired through expansion, the only lands the king could donate were castle lands; but this led to the significant loss of royal revenues.[19]

To compensate for the loss of royal estates, András's treasurer Dénes (Denis), son of Ampod, attempted to introduce a system based on monetary revenues. In 1217 extraordinary taxation (*collecta*, *exactio*) is first mentioned in Hungary; it became a regular tax, exacted in coins. The eightieth, a tax on international trade, was also introduced.

[18] Árpád Nógrády, '"Magistratus et comitatus *tenentibus*". II. András kormányzati rendszerének kérdéséhez', *Századok* 129 (1995), 157–94; Gyula Kristó, 'II. András király "új intézkedései"', *Századok* 135 (2001), 251–300.

[19] Barta and Barta, 'Royal finance'.

Revenues also accrued from the yearly exchange of coins, since minting was a royal monopoly. Royal revenues from minting, salt mining and customs duties were farmed out to individuals who collected them. One indication about the unpopularity of the system was that eventually András's son and successor Béla IV had Dénes blinded.

The high nobility (called aristocracy or barons by modern historians) were not simply accumulating landed property and high positions of political power. They also scored a victory against the royal court on the question of how positions of power should be conferred. Queen Gertrude of the family of the margraves of Andechs-Meran was seen as a source of undue influence over the king, to the benefit of her German entourage and other German noble immigrants. Emblematic in this respect was the rise of her brother Berthold to the point where he simultaneously held the positions of archbishop of Kalocsa (despite not having reached the required canonical age and knowledge, and the initial papal rejection of his appointment), *ban* of Croatia and voivode of Transylvania. A conspiracy to assassinate the queen and members of her entourage was successful in 1213 and, although one of the assassins was executed, most of the conspirators were not punished. Berthold was deprived of his secular positions although he kept his see, and the high nobility increasingly gained control of effective political power. They built up large and increasingly consolidated landed estates and their own following of warriors, which eventually gave them political power independent of the king.[20]

The discontent of the groups merging into the lower nobility – including the *servientes regis* as well as the castle warriors – against the barons grew parallel to the latter's acquisition of lands and power. The former not only did not benefit from royal land grants, but their status was also threatened by the growing power of the barons. A revolt by some of the nobles (who had significant political power under King

[20] György Székely, 'Gertrud királyné, Szent Erzsébet anyja: egy politikai gyilkosság és elhúzódó megtorlása', *Turul* 81 (2008), 1–9; Tamás Körmendi, 'A Gertrúd királyné elleni merénylet a külhoni elbeszélő forrásokban', *Történelmi szemle* 51 (2009), 155–94; Wolfgang Schüle, 'Erzbischof Johann von Esztergom und der Mord an Königin Gertrud 1213', in *Proceedings of the Thirteenth International Congress of Medieval Canon Law: Esztergom, 3–8 August*, ed. Péter Erdő and Szabolcs Anzelm Szuromi (Vatican City, 2010), 651–60.

Imre, but who were sidelined or ignored by András II) and the *servientes regis* forced the king to agree to the Golden Bull in 1222 (so named from the pendant golden royal seal). Although the Bull is often compared to the English Magna Carta, the similarities are in fact superficial. The Bull purported to restore liberties granted by St István that had diminished since his times. It set out safeguards against the king injuring the interests of the nobility, for example, limiting the influence that could be given to foreigners at court and prohibiting the farming out of royal revenues, promising the administration of such revenues to members of the nobility. It contained detailed regulations on judicial issues and against abuses of power by royal officials.

About a third of the articles of the Bull concerned the rights of the *servientes regis*, who eventually became the lower nobility. It prohibited the 'destruction' of *servientes regis* to benefit barons. That is, barons were not to gain the lands of and jurisdiction and authority over the *servientes regis*, who belonged firmly under the power of the king. It exempted them from royal tax, brought them uniformly under the jurisdiction of the king (or his representative, the count palatine) and made military service obligatory only if the kingdom was attacked; otherwise the king had to pay for their participation in the army.

Finally, the Bull contained a famous clause granting the right of resistance to the nobles and prelates if the king did not keep the promises made within it. It was renewed in 1231, granting additional privileges to prelates, and replacing the nobles' right of resistance with the sanction that the archbishop of Esztergom was to excommunicate any king who failed to honour the articles. The Golden Bull of 1222 was copied and confirmed in the fourteenth century. Another bull was granted in 1267, now specifically to the *servientes regis* and this time explicitly equating them with nobles. Whereas earlier the *servientes regis* had received privileges as the allies of members of the higher nobility or prelates, now they pressed for their own rights. These were partially a renewal of several articles of the Golden Bull, clearly disregarded in practice after 1222: the new decree reinforced that nobles were not to pay any type of tax to the king and were not to be forced to participate in non-defensive wars. New demands were also included: a yearly congregation of representatives of the nobility to correct any abuses and the return to their previous status of royal castle and *udvarnok* lands which the king had given to free settlers. By the last third of the century, a socially and legally (although not economically) unified nobility had emerged.[21]

King Béla IV tried to turn the tide and reinforce royal power. His decision to have the chairs of high-ranking nobles burnt at the royal council symbolized his policies in this respect: only the king could sit; all others were to stand in his presence. Béla saw the restoration of royal lands as the key to buttressing royal power. Already during his father's lifetime, in the years prior to 1231, he attempted to prevent donation of royal lands in perpetuity. As king, he confiscated lands donated by his father and restored their status as royal lands. Moreover, he ordered a review of claims to various other landed possessions as well. The Mongol invasion of 1241–2 put an end to his endeavours in this direction. In order to restore the kingdom and fortify it against possible future attacks, after the invasion, royal prerogatives continued to be granted to nobles, including the right to build stone castles. He also started to grant royal lands and peoples to nobles, to enable them both to build fortresses and to equip warriors as heavy cavalry for the royal army. The dissolution of the royal castle-land system (*várispánság*) continued at a more rapid pace from the 1260s.

Nobles took part in and benefited from the civil wars between Béla IV and his son István (Stephen) V in the 1260s. Nobles could back either king even if they lived in the section of the realm assigned to the other ruler, and thus received grants of land to retain or gain their adherence. The punishment of unfaithful or suspect barons, entailing the spoliation of lands, sowed the seeds of anarchy. After István's accession to sole rule in 1270, baronial parties started fighting each other. In 1272, István's young son László (Ladislas) (IV) was taken prisoner by a baron, probably trying to force the division of power between the king and his son and guarantee his own political ascendancy through controlling the minor co-ruler. The king died soon thereafter and László IV inherited the throne at the

[21] Jenő Szűcs, 'Az 1267. évi dekrétum háttere: Szempontok a köznemesség kialakulásához', in *Mályusz Elemér emlékkönyv: Társadalom-és művelődéstörténeti tanulmányok*, ed. Éva H. Balázs, Erik Fügedi and Ferenc Maksay (Budapest, 1984), 341–94; Attila Zsoldos, 'Az 1267. évi dekrétum és politikatörténeti háttere (IV. Béla és Ifjabb István király viszályának utolsó fejezete)', *Századok* 141 (2007), 803–42; József Gerics, 'Von den Universi Servientes Regis bis zu der Universitas Nobilium Regni Hungariae', in *Album Elemér Mályusz*, 97–108; James Ross Sweeney, 'The decretal Intellecto'; Bak *et al.*, eds., *Laws*, 34–43.

age of ten. Two rival baronial groups, the Csák and Héder lineages, fought for power, leading to anarchy. The king tried to establish an alternative power base, relying on the nomadic and to a large extent pagan Cumans who had immigrated into the kingdom and from whom he descended on his mother's side. This led to clashes with the Church, and increasing anarchy. By the late thirteenth century, noble power was manifest in disobedience and resistance to the king. This became more marked after László's death in 1290, during the reign of András III, when barons rebelled almost every year against him. It culminated after his death (1301) in a period called the era of the kinglets or oligarchs, when several of the highest-ranking nobles (barons) effectively carved out *de facto* independent territories for themselves. This came to an end only when the Angevins came to power in Hungary and Charles Robert broke the power of the barons through a series of military confrontations, threats and promises (between 1301 and the 1320s). The thirteenth-century rise of the nobility sowed the seeds of fourteenth- and fifteenth-century mechanisms whereby kings relied on the lower nobility against the barons, which led to the rise of members of the lower nobility and in turn created new conflicts with the kings.[22]

Linked to the shifting balance of power towards the nobility, the nobility's concept of itself and its political institutions developed. Already in the early part of the thirteenth century, while the royal chancery emphasized that the *servientes regis* owed service to the king, they themselves were underlining their free status, and increasingly used the word noble (*nobilis*) within the counties, blurring the lines between the status of the elite, who held very large estates and descended from illustrious ancestors, and the free smallholders. Royal counties now started to become the organizational bases of the nobility. Common action within the counties strengthened the feeling of belonging to the same group for *servientes regis* as well as for the barons. From 1232, there is evidence of corporate noble organizations within counties. They had elected judges to oversee the litigation of nobles within the county. In the 1267 decree, the king recognized that the *servientes regis* were nobles. From that time, the *ispán* of the county, a royal official (one of the barons), exercised judicial power together with the elected judges of the nobility at the request of the king. The county, from being a unit

[22] Szűcs, *Az utolsó Árpádok*; N. Berend, *At the Gate of Christendom*, 171–83.

in the service of royal power, was thus transformed into an institution of the nobility, and this form of organization soon spread to the whole realm. As early as 1270 the royal coronation oath included promises to safeguard the interests of the (lower) nobility. The first diet was held in 1277; an assembly was gathered with barons, representatives of the nobles and of the Cumans. From then on, such assemblies of the realm (parliaments) were called increasingly frequently.[23]

Noble identity was also linked to a number of chronicles. The *Gesta Hungarorum* of the so-called Hungarian Anonymous (*c.* 1200) set out to justify the acquisition of estates by the nobility of the author's own days. He depicted the conquest of Hungary, claiming to demonstrate how the ancestors of the nobles of his own time conquered areas which they then received by royal grant. The author in fact invented most of his stories based on the practices of his own period and on folk etymologies of placenames. It is possible that the now lost version of the *Gesta Ungarorum* by Master Ákos (late thirteenth century) presented all aristocratic families as taking part in the conquest of the land, their role almost equal to that of the ruling dynasty. Simon of Kéza's *Gesta Hungarorum* (*c.* 1285) went much further. He represented the viewpoint of the lower nobility, applying the theory of *communitas* to the Hungarian past. He depicted the whole nobility as one political body, with the lower nobility sharing in the exercise of political power. According to this view, it is the community that holds real power, and elects the king.[24]

## EXTERNAL AFFAIRS AND EXPANSION

The expansion of power and territory remained an aim of rulers, and led to repeated warfare, but rarely resulted in long-term gains.

[23] Erik Fügedi, 'Kinship and privilege: the social system of medieval Hungarian nobility as defined in customary law', in *Nobilities in Central and Eastern Europe: Kinship, Property and Privilege*, ed. János M. Bak (Krems, 1994), 55–75; György Bónis, *Hűbériség és rendiség a középkori magyar jogban* (Budapest, 2003); József Gerics, *A korai rendiség Európában és Magyarországon* (Budapest, 1987); Szűcs, 'Az 1267. évi dekrétum'; Rady, *Nobility*.

[24] Kristó, *Történetírás*; Jenő Szűcs, 'Theoretical elements in Master Simon of Kéza's Gesta Hungarorum (1282–1285)', in Veszprémy and Schaer, ed. and tr., *Simon of Kéza*, xxix–cii.

### *Bohemia*

From the reign of Václav I the One-Eyed (1230–53), Bohemian expansionary efforts focused on Austria. Václav, married to Kunhuta, daughter of the late King Philip of Swabia, had bad relations with the Babenbergs and conducted attacks against Austria, supported by the Hungarians. His younger brother Přemysl, margrave of Moravia from 1225, allied with the Austrian margrave Frederick the Quarrelsome. In 1236 Emperor Frederick II incorporated Austria and Styria within the domain of the Staufs and, the following year, encouraged Václav I to invade Austria and seize Vienna. In the absence of the king, Přemysl tried to separate Moravia from Bohemia. Facing such a danger, Václav I helped Frederick the Quarrelsome to regain control of Austria and Styria. Přemysl was defeated and escaped to Hungary, where he died. In 1240 the chaotic situation in the empire led the Bohemian king to invade Austria again.

In 1246 Austro-Bohemian tension abated with the marriage of the margrave's sister Gertrude to Václav's son and heir, Vladislav. After the death of Emperor Frederick II in 1250, the Bohemians once more attempted military action against the Austrian margraviate. This resulted in a compromise: Přemysl Otakar was elected margrave on 21 November 1258 but the 28-year-old was to marry the 46-year-old Duchess Margaret. Přemysl Otakar II (1253–78) inherited a realm that was both united and strong, and added to it the Austrian margraviate. His kingdom was now the largest part of the Empire and the Přemyslids were the only rulers holding a hereditary royal title in the Empire. The range of his power diminished to a minor extent in 1254, when a papal legate negotiated with Hungary a confirmation of Bohemia's rights over Austria on condition of subjugating Styria to King Béla IV.

In 1259 the Styrian nobles asked Přemysl to free them from Hungarian rule, provoking a long war in which the Bohemians were supported by two Silesian princes: Henryk V the Fat of Wrocław and Legnica and Władysław of Opole. The resubordination of Styria allowed the king to divorce the childless Margaret Babenberg in 1260. A peace treaty was agreed in Vienna in March 1261, reinforced by an inter-dynastic marriage: Přemysl even before the formal approval of his divorce from Pope Urban IV (received on 20 April 1262), by 25 October 1261 married Béla IV's granddaughter, Kunhuta.

After his royal coronation (1261), Přemysl Otakar II did not engage in conflicts over the next decade, apart from a minor attack on Bavaria

(1262) and another Prussian episode (in the winter of 1267/68). In 1268 the childless prince Ulrik of Karnten declared Přemysl Otakar II his successor and, during the following year, Karnten and Kraina were subordinated to the Bohemian governor of Styria.

This period of peace came to an end when Béla IV of Hungary died in May 1270. A Hungarian plundering expedition into Austria provoked Bohemian retaliation and following two victories in May 1271, Přemysl Otakar II secured written guarantees for his suzerainty over Kraina, Karnten and Styria. The Bohemian king saw the regency by Queen Erzsébet, (Elizabeth) the Cuman, following István's death on 1 August 1272 as an opportunity to expand his domain into western Hungary. His successful invasion was halted, however, with Rudolf of Habsburg's election as German king on 29 September 1273. One year later a summit of electors from the Empire demanded from Přemysl Otakar II not only that he withdraw his administration from Kraina, Karnten, Styria and Austria but also that he swear allegiance for Bohemia and Moravia. The Bohemian ruler's inaction meant that on 15 May 1275 the Hoftag in Augsburg formally deprived Přemysl Otakar II of the Bohemian and Moravian fiefs. After a German army invaded Austria in September 1276, the Bohemian king asked for peace. On 26 November, near Vienna, he paid a humiliating homage to King Rudolf so that the German would return to him all of his territorial possessions. Rudolf stipulated that Přemysl's son, Václav, was to marry Rudolf's daughter Judith (endowed with northern Austria). This decrease of status provoked Přemysl Otakar II to renew military conflict in July 1278. It ended with a decisive battle on 26 August at Moravske Pole/Suche Kruty/Dürnkrut, where Přemysl Otakar II was killed.[25]

Václav II's (1283–1305) political activity was restrained by his ally, Rudolf of Habsburg, king of the Romans, whose daughter Gutta became Václav's wife. The mighty ally strengthened Václav's position both in the Empire (in quarrels with Otto of Brandenburg) and in Bohemia, but closed the possibility of expanding his power in the

[25] Marie 'Bláhová, 'Böhmen in der Politik Rudolfs von Habsburg', in *Rudolf von Habsburg 1273–1291* (Cologne, Weimar and Vienna, 1993), 59–78; Ivan Hlaváček, 'Die Aufenthalte Rudolfs I. in Böhmen und Mähren aus verwaltungs- und rechtsgeschichtlicher Sicht', in *Rudolf von Habsburg 1273–1291*, 80–5; Libor Jan, 'Das Zeitalter der Gewalt und der freundschaftlichen Kontakte. Gemeinsame Wurzeln des tschechisch-österreichischen Raumes in Mitteleuropa', in *Tschechen und Österreicher. Gemeinsame Geschichte, gemeinsame Zukunft* (Vienna, 2006), 31–41.

traditional direction, Austria, which was ruled by the Habsburgs. A more promising field of expansion lay to the north: the divided Piast state, especially Silesia which was historically and personally – by inter-dynastic marriages – connected with Bohemia. In 1289 Duke Kazimierz of Bytom (Upper Silesia) pledged an oath of fidelity to the king, but more importantly, after the death of Henryk IV the Righteous in 1290 the king announced his rights to the duchy of Cracow. Although Przemysł II of Greater Poland was heir to Cracow, the Czech king did not relinquish his plans. He won the alliance of the Silesian dukes reigning Opole and Cieszyn, and was accepted by several nobles of the region. Finally Przemysł II, under the pressure of war with Václav, and immersed in Pomeranian policy, accepted the king's proposition and passed him his rights over Lesser Poland. After a brief war with Kuyavian duke Władysław, Václav was enthroned. After Przemysł II's death in 1296, Václav through a series of treaties and military expeditions in 1299 overwhelmed all lands reigned by Władysław of Kuyavia: the major part of Greater Poland, Pomerania and Kuyavia. After that he married a daughter of deceased king, Elizabeth, and with strong support from the Polish Church and the nobles of Greater Poland was crowned king of Poland in 1300.[26]

## *Poland*

During the thirteenth century, the majority of Piast rulers reigning in small duchies had no means of expansion. Instead, they focused on maintaining their power. Only the most powerful dukes – those of Greater Poland, Cracow, Wrocław and Mazovia – were involved in broader foreign policy, usually looking for mighty allies to help in quarrels with other Piast dukes. Even Henryk I the Bearded, duke of Silesia, whose daughter was engaged *c.* 1207–8 to Otto, palatine of Bavaria, and whose wife, Hedwig, was of the powerful Andechs family of imperial counts, did not intervene directly in the imperial political scene. His son, Henryk II the Pious, during his short reign (1238–41) actively participated in political struggles between Pope Gregory IX and Emperor Frederick II. His reasons, however, were

[26] On political factions, see Robert Antonín, *Zahraníční polítíka krále Václava II. v letech 1283–1300* (Brno, 2009); Irena Prokopová, 'Guta Habsburská – česká královna a její dvůr', *Muzejní a vlastivědná práce: Časopis Společnosti přátel starožitností* 43 (113), 4 (2005), 189–211.

tied to internal affairs: he tried to gain suzerainty over all Poland. With strong papal support he began to try to impose his authority over his numerous relatives, but this came to nothing when he was killed in 1241. During the second half of the thirteenth century even the mightiest Piast dukes were only allies of crowned rulers, mostly kings of Bohemia (dukes of Silesia since 1254) and kings of Hungary (dukes of Lesser and Greater Poland). With their troops they took part in battles between both kings as at Groissenbrunn in 1260, where Bolesław I of Lesser Poland fought under the command of Béla IV of Hungary and Silesian dukes supported the Bohemian king Přemysl Otakar II. Throughout the thirteenth century only a few Piast dukes had enough power and skill to try to establish their own policy, not just to seize opportunities as they appeared. The loss of international importance was the price successors of Bolesław III the Wrymouth paid for the multiplication of duchies and lack of any coherent power structure.[27]

Even in such an unfavourable situation, the Piasts pursued expansionary policies along their eastern border. There were two possible fields of expansion or political control: Rus', a region which had become subdivided into duchies ruled by Rurikevich dynasty, and the pagan lands of the north-eastern region. Even here it is hard to find traces of a long-lasting, coherent policy of all the Piast dukes. Following the lead of his father, Kazimierz I the Just, Leszek I the White, duke of Cracow, engaged in the conflicts ravaging the lands of Rus'. In 1205, having joined forces with his brother Konrad I of Masovia, he defeated the invading army of the prince of Galich, Roman, near Zawichost. In the following year Leszek prepared a retaliatory expedition. His ambitions were stifled by Hungarian intervention. Later he agreed with King András II to divide their respective spheres of interest in the east.

This success might have alarmed Konrad I of Masovia, who sought to strengthen his relations with Rus' princes in 1207 by marrying Agafia, the daughter of Svyatoslav Andrei Igorevich, prince of Siewierz and Przemyśl.[28] When Leszek I laid siege to Galich in 1214, supported by Hungarian troops, he ordered that Konrad's father-in-law be hanged along with his two brothers, Roman and

[27] Tomasz Jurek, 'Der Einfluss Böhmens auf das geteilte Polens im 13. Jahrhundert', in *Böhmen und seine Nachbarn*, 161–202.

[28] Agafia went on to bear ten children.

Rostislav. The duke also brought under his control the lands of Lubaczów and Przemyśl, although this proved short-lived. A fresh Polish–Hungarian conflict meant that Leszek had to relinquish his most recent gains in the east by 1215. In time a delicate balance of power was achieved, and there was even a joint Polish–Hungarian expedition to Volyn in 1221. However, this venture and Leszek's next expedition in 1227 both failed. With Leszek's sudden death, Piast expansion towards Rus' stopped. The dukes of Cracow chose to strengthen their alliances with Hungarian kings, rather than fight for uncertain results, especially after 1240–1 when the Mongols became the superiors of Rus' princes. Moreover, the Piast dukes had to defend their lands against expansion. Besides fights in 1241 and smaller attacks, Leszek II the Black (1279–88), duke of Cracow and Sandomierz, at the battle of Goślice in 1280 defeated an invasion by the prince of Galich, Lev Danilovich, who was supported by Lithuanian and Mongol troops. In 1283 he defeated the first serious plundering expedition launched by the Lithuanians; in 1287 another Mongol raid devastated the region.

Eastern Pomerania and the pagan lands of the Prussians and the Yatvingians were areas where the Piasts tried to establish or revive their influence over the course of the thirteenth century. One of Leszek I's concerns in the first quarter of the thirteenth century was to restore Piast authority over the Baltic coast, and in particular over the important Vistula estuary. In 1217 he journeyed to Eastern Pomerania, where he put an end to Danish influence, re-established his political suzerainty and confirmed the legality of the rule of Duke Sventopelk (who originated from the local nobility). In both 1222 and 1223 Leszek also organized crusades to the north-east against the pagan Prussians.

Northern pagan lands were especially dangerous for the security of inhabitants of Mazovia, Kuyavia and Greater Poland. The principality of Mazovia suffered especially from frequent raids plundering its north-eastern neighbours, the pagan Prussians and Yatvingians. Innocent III called international crusades in 1219 and 1222, but these failed to curb the activities of the Balts. Therefore Konrad of Mazovia followed the example of the former canon of Bremen, Albert, who founded the Order of the Sword, a military order comprising poor German knights for the most part, to build a Christian enclave among the pagan peoples. Konrad established the Dobrzyń Brotherhood in 1224 to fight against Prussians. At the same time the Polish Church restarted its missionary activity, particularly among the pagan Prussians. In 1216 a priest named Christian was consecrated as the 'missionary bishop' in Prussia. At first he was 'endowed' with the Chełm (Kulm) land, which was separate from the Płock diocese, but over the next few years Christian received several papal privileges granting him full rights over the converted Prussians. This strategy was supported by the dukes who organized crusades against the Prussians with the approval of the papacy.

Yet the Dobrzyń Brotherhood, as well as a standing knightly guard organized by all prominent Piast dukes (of Silesia, Mazovia and Greater and Lesser Poland) to defend the northern borders, proved insufficient. Small, poorly commanded military units were unable to secure a long border against pagan raids. In these circumstances, Konrad of Mazovia in accordance with and with the help of other Piast dukes, especially Henryk I the Bearded, in 1225 invited the Teutonic Knights to attend to his northern frontier. Their Grand Master, Herman von Salza (1209–39), managed his relations with both the Empire and the papacy while looking to exploit opportunities for territorial gain. Their expulsion from Hungary made them open to the offer from Poland, although Herman von Salza proceeded more cautiously. Before their arrival in 1230, the Grand Master had Konrad's donation of the Chełmno land from 1228 confirmed by Emperor Frederick II and by the pope, who also promised him ownership of all lands to be gained from the pagans.

The experience gained by the knights through operating in the Holy Land and Transylvania served them well when organizing a systematic territorial expansion along the Vistula River and then eastwards along the Baltic coast, building castles at locations such as Kwidzyń, Elbląg and Frombork before moving inland. At the beginning their activity was eagerly supported by their formal lord, the Mazovian duke Konrad. The crusade called in 1234 involved several Polish dukes as well as knights from Germany, including the margrave of Meissen. The victorious campaign resulted in a significant enlargement of the Order's territory.

It soon became fashionable for west European knights to travel to the region and take part in battles with the Prussians. The Bohemian king Přemysl Otakar II arrived there in 1255, marked by the name of one of the new towns, *Königsberg* (in Polish – *Krolewiec*, in Lithuanian – *Memel* and in Russian – *Kaliningrad*). The Teutonic Knights did not, however, limit their expansion in the direction of

Prussia, seeking also to open a corridor to the Baltic coast through Pomerania. During gruelling wars between 1241 and 1253, with the support of forces from Poland, they managed to conquer much of the east Pomeranian duchy of Sventopelk. The growing power of the Teutonic Order worried the Roman Curia, which sought to maintain papal sovereignty over their lands. In 1243, the papal legate William of Modena divided a conquered Prussia into bishoprics; in 1245 these were all subordinated to the newly established archbishopric of Riga. This solution was later undone by the Teutonic Knights, who incoporated all four Prussian capitularies at Chełmno, Pomezania, Sambia and Kurland within the Teutonic Order, subordinating the bishops to the Grand Masters.

In the north-west, Pomeranian principalities were conquered by Denmark. King Valdemar II the Victorious (duke of Schleswig 1183–1216, king of Denmark 1202–41) subordinated all lands along the southern and eastern coasts of the Baltic Sea, from the territory of Obodrites all the way to Estonia, with the exception of the Prussian coast. In 1227, the north German dukes defeated Valdemar II at Bornhöved. The sudden political vacuum led the Brandenburgian margraves of the Ascanian dynasty to annex the Polish land of Lubusz between 1248 and 1250 and to subordinate completely the west Pomeranian princes in 1250. They also conquered a 'corridor' between Pomerania and Greater Poland, converting these lands into the 'Neumark' (*marchia nova*) and edging closer towards the Vistula estuary as well as the important port of Gdańsk. Their expansion was halted by the duke of Greater Poland, Bolesław I the Pious, who in 1272 drove the Brandenburgians out of Gdańsk. After that, the rulers of the Ascanian dynasty concentrated on reinforcing their earlier territorial gains. In 1287 the formerly Polish diocese of Lubusz/Lebus was included in the Magdeburg archbishopric's extensive programme of settling people from German lands in Western Pomerania. Several towns were established near old centres such as Kołobrzeg/Kolberg; older towns received charters with the new laws, including Szczecin. Almost all of the clergy present there was German. Piast dukes lost their influence over this part of Pomerania. Yet thanks to the policy of Duke Bolesław I the Pious and Przemysł II, rulers of Greater Poland gained strong alliance with Mściwój II of Gdańsk. After long years of almost unbroken co-operation, the Pomeranian duke bequeathed the duchy to Przemysł II in his testament. Przemysł II took power there in 1294, and was therefore crowned king of

Poland in 1295. Although he died a year later, ties remained unbroken and the subsequent Polish kings – Václav II (1300–5) and Václav III (1305–6) – were also entitled to rule Eastern Pomerania (also called Gdańsk Pomerania), along with the duke of united Poland, Władysław I Łokietek, from 1306.

The Lithuanians, united under the rule of Duke Mindaugas (1219–63), became a serious challenge to Rus'ian, Polish and German neighbours. In 1260, with Yatvingian support, he raided the Polish and Rus'ian frontiers. In 1262 he also invaded Mazovia and killed Duke Siemowit in Jazdów (today situated within Warsaw), resulting in an alliance between the Mazovians and Duke Daniel of Galich. In 1264 the allied army defeated the Yatvingians at Zawichost and their lands were subsequently colonized by Polish and Volhynian settlers to form the province of Podlasie.

Near the end of the century Duke Henryk IV Probus of Silesia tried to revive Polish engagement in Bohemia. Between 1267 and 1271 the duke had been at the court of Přemysl Otakar II, his uncle and protector. After the latter's death Henry tried to bring the young son of the deceased ruler, the future king Václav II, under his tutelage. He failed, but still had strong political influence in Bohemia, strong enough that Václav II in 1290 suspected that his enemies from the Vitkovce clan wanted to confer power over Bohemia on the duke of Silesia. Even if that was unrealistic, it shows the substantial political authority of the Piast dukes at the end of the thirteenth century. But the rulers did not have enough resources and, for most, horizons were not wide enough to allow them to conduct a more ambitious foreign policy.[29]

## *Hungary*

Marriage alliances, always significant for dynasties, continued to play an important role in the realm. Marriages of the sons and daughters of Hungary's kings in the thirteenth century created ties to a vast array of dynasties east and west, including those of Aragon, a variety of German lands, Bulgaria, Nicea, Poland, Serbia, Sicily and Bohemia. After the Mongol invasion, Béla IV created a system of alliances through marriages first to the east and north (Galich and Polish

[29] On political struggles between Piasts, see Zientara, *Heinrich der Bärtige*. On main lines of Piast policy, see Eduard Mühle, *Die Piasten, Polen im Mittelalter* (Munich, 2011), 63–73.

princes), and in 1261 with the Czech king Přemysl Otakar II. The most significant marriage alliance in the long term proved to be the one with the Angevins (1269), creating their claim to the throne in the fourteenth century.

Building on earlier endeavours as well as enlarging their sphere of interest, kings tried to expand the realm throughout the thirteenth century. The geographical scope of their interest mostly encompassed the Balkans, Galich and the lands inhabited by the Cumans (the area that later became Moldavia and Wallachia). There may have been a more ambitious project conceived of by King András II; some historians argue that he undertook to go on crusade in 1217 in order to gain the title of Latin emperor. He returned after three months without accomplishing anything.[30] It was easy to find a justification for war against various eastern and southern neighbours, who were either 'schismatics' (that is, Orthodox), 'heretics' (that is, declared to be adhering to errors) or 'pagans' (that is, legitimate targets for missionary work). This expansionary drive took various forms. It included intervention in rivalries between various members or branches of a local dynasty, trying to ensure that the Hungarian king's influence would be perpetuated through the local ruler he backed. King Imre in this way backed Vukan Nemanja to become Grand Župan of Serbia in 1201, but his rival, Vukan's brother Stefan (Stephen), gained the throne soon thereafter. This did not prevent Imre and his successors from using the title 'king of Serbia', without any basis in reality.

Military campaigns could be deployed in aid of a local ruler, or as a way to conquer an area. The evolution from the first type of military intervention to the second is clear in the case of the attempted expansion to the principality of Galich (Galicia, Halych). András II sent and several times personally led armies against Galich between 1205 and 1233 (partly in a Polish alliance; see below). Backing the child Daniel Romanovich of the Rurikid dynasty (who was staying at the Hungarian court) from 1205, András soon assumed the title 'king of Galicia and Lodomeria'. In 1214 András appointed his own

30 Sweeney, 'Hungary in the Crusades'; András Borosy, 'A keresztes háborúk és Magyarország I–II', *Hadtörténelmi Közlemények* 109, 1 (1996), 3–41, and 109, 2 (1996), 11–52; László Veszprémy, 'The crusade of Andrew II, King of Hungary, 1217–1218', *Iacobus* 13/14 (2002), 87–110; József Laszlovszky, Judit Majorossy and József Zsengellér, eds., *Magyarország és a keresztes háborúk* (Máriabesnyő and Gödöllő, 2006).

five-year-old son Kálmán (Coloman) as ruler of Galich, and by 1216 had him crowned king of Galich with papal approval. Kálmán was expelled in 1219. Subsequently András arranged for his third son, Prince András, to rule Galich but, despite new wars, direct Hungarian power over Galich collapsed. Béla IV tried to sustain Hungarian influence through backing Daniel Romanovich as king of Galich.[31] Other examples of attempted expansion include Bulgaria: after earlier thirteenth-century endeavours, István V imposed his authority on Vidin (1266) through several military campaigns and took the title 'king of Bulgaria'. For about a decade after the Mongol invasion, Béla IV also tried to expand the realm westwards. He led several campaigns against Austria, briefly gaining the southern part of Styria (1254). This, however, was soon lost (1261) to the Czech king Otakar II who had also become duke of Austria.

War against heretics and the sending of missions could also be tied to expansion. In the case of Bosnia, this was linked to papal calls for crusade against heretics, and King Imre from 1200 exerted pressure on the Bosnian ruler to acknowledge the Catholic Church. In the 1230s, crusades to Bosnia resulted in the creation of a missionary bishopric. Kálmán, the younger brother of the king, gave military support to missionaries and tried to subjugate Bosnia. Béla IV campaigned in Bosnia in 1244 and 1253. Thereafter he installed the former prince of Chernigov, Rostislav (who had fled to Hungary from the Mongols and married one of Béla's daughters), as duke of Bosnia.[32]

The other area of mission was Cumania, the eastern neighbour of Hungary. The Cumans were Turkic nomads; like other nomadic peoples of the steppe they raided settled neighbours, in this case the kingdom of Hungary. They became a focus of attention in the early thirteenth century. In 1211 King András II settled the Teutonic Knights in Barcaság (Burzenland) to protect the realm against Cuman attacks, and to convert the Cumans. Because of the Knights' attempt to carve out an independent territory, the king expelled them in 1225. The conversion of the Cumans was taken up by the

[31] Font, *Árpád-házi királyok*, 188–232; Márta F. Font, 'On the frontiers of West and East: the Hungarian kingdom and the Galician principality between the eleventh and thirteenth centuries', *Annual of Medieval Studies at CEU Budapest* 6 (2000), 171–80.

[32] Dubravko Lovrenović, 'Modelle ideologischer Ausgrenzung. Ungarn und Bosnien als ideologische Gegner auf der Basis verschiedener Bekenntnisse des Christentums', *Südost-Forschungen* 63/4 (2004/5), 18–55.

Dominicans from Hungary (where a Dominican province had existed since 1221). After initial failures, some of the Cuman leaders became interested in conversion, accepting baptism with their people. This was due to military considerations, as the Cumans needed allies and protection, especially against the Mongols. In 1227 or 1228 a Cuman bishopric was created, with indulgences granted to those who helped construct churches there. That the mission was closely intertwined with expansionary aims is manifest in the royal family's involvement in the process. Prince Béla (the future Béla IV) was present at the baptism of one chieftain, and King András II was the godfather of another. The converted leaders took an oath of fidelity to the king, and in 1233, the king of Hungary adopted the title 'rex Cumanie'. The Mongol attack wiped out the bishopric in 1241. Part of the territory came under Mongol rule, making any further missionary and expansionary plans illusory. Even the area that remained under nominal Hungarian overlordship never became a stable part of the realm and eventually became independent.[33]

Hungarian efforts at expansion were mostly unsuccessful and led to the accumulation of empty 'royal titles' without permanent conquest or even influence. Other lands were soon lost. At the instigation of the Venetians, the crusaders who gathered for the fourth crusade conquered Zadar (Zara) from the Hungarian king in 1204. Even areas that were subjugated for a time and perhaps even served defensive functions (the south-eastern lands) became independent in the fourteenth century.

## THE MONGOL INVASION

The Mongol invasion was a major intrusion of steppe peoples into central Europe. Its exact impact and the scale of the destruction,

[33] Harald Zimmermann, *Der Deutsche Orden im Burzenland. Eine diplomatische Untersuchung* (Cologne, 2000); Zsolt Hunyadi, 'The Teutonic Order in Burzenland (1211–1225): recent reconsiderations', in *L' Ordine Teutonico tra Mediterraneo a Baltico incontri e scontri tra religioni, popoli e cultura; atti del convegno internazionale di studio Bari-Lecce-Brindisi, 14–16 settembre 2006*, eds. Hubert Houben and Kristjan Toomaspoeg (Galatina, 2008), 151–72. For background on the Cuman bishopric, see Petre Diaconu, *Les Coumans au Bas-Danube aux XIe et XIIe siècles* (Bucharest, 1978); István Vásáry, *Cumans and Tatars: Oriental Military in the Pre-Ottoman Balkans, 1185–1365* (Cambridge, 2005); Nora Berend, 'The Mendicant orders and the conversion of pagans in Hungary', in *Alle frontiere della cristianità: i frati mendicanti e l'evangelizzazione tra '200 e '300. Atti del XXVIII Convegno internazionale, Assisi, 12–14 ottobre 2000* (Spoleto, 2001), 253–79.

however, have been debated. It affected Hungary and Poland significantly more than it did Bohemia-Moravia.

## *Hungary*

In spite of expansionary desires, rulers were forced on the defensive by the Mongol invasion of 1241–2. The Mongol attacks reached all three countries, but affected them in unequal measure. Hungary was no stranger to nomad attacks and, although King Béla IV had been receiving news about the Mongols, it seems that the king and his entourage did not realize until it was too late that in the Mongols they were not confronted by a typical nomadic raiding party. The Mongols attacked Hungary in a co-ordinated fashion. The royal army suffered a crushing defeat near Muhi (11 April 1241); most of the political elite died in the battle, but King Béla managed to escape to Trau (Trogir, Dalmatia). A Mongol detachment followed him, but was unable to capture him. The Mongols withdrew of their own accord in March 1242.[34]

Historical controversy surrounds two crucial points. First, did the Mongols intend to invade and subjugate Hungary or not? If they did, why did they withdraw? Second, how much devastation did the Mongols cause? The facts that the Mongols subjugated Rus', that they expressed a belief in a divine mandate to rule the world and that they stayed in Hungary for an extended period may indicate that they intended to continue with their conquest towards the west. Others however argue that there was no intended conquest, simply a punitive expedition against the country for harbouring the Cumans. Yet others believe it was an exploratory expedition to prepare a later conquest; alternatively that there was not enough pasture for the Mongols to sustain a permanent conquest; or that the strength of resistance in the area west of the Danube led to a change in Mongol plans.

Loss of life due to the invasion has been estimated between 15% and 50% of the population. The reason for this huge discrepancy is that the calculations are based on different premises. For example, one historian counted mentions of deserted villages; but others pointed out that villages were not necessarily destroyed with the entire population of

[34] Balázs Nagy, ed., *A Tatárjárás* (Budapest, 2003); Peter Jackson, *The Mongols and the West* (Harlow, 2005), chs. 3–4; János B. Szabó, *A tatárjárás* (Budapest, 2007).

the village dying in the invasion. Villagers may also have moved away to more fertile lands or to towns. Contemporaries described complete devastation by the Mongols massacring everyone after taking a village or town, but in fact different areas of the realm were affected to a different degree: most of the devastation happened in the eastern areas, where the Mongols spent a year, while areas west of the Danube were less affected. Archaeological excavations have uncovered hidden treasures, datable by coins to the period of the invasion. The most numerous such discoveries are from the central parts of the Great Plains, suggesting the greatest destruction there (death preventing the owners from recovering their goods). Moreover, villages with unburied bodies have been uncovered, attesting not only to the invasion's impact, but also to the fact that in these places no subsequent reconstruction and resettlement followed.[35] The aftermath of the invasion may have led to the loss of more lives than the efforts of the Mongols themselves, due to famine and epidemics.

Béla IV initiated many policies linked at least partially to reconstruction and defence. Some were successful, such as urbanization and an acceleration of building stone fortifications, while others failed. For example, although the king installed the Hospitallers in the south-eastern parts of the kingdom in 1247, within a few years the knights left the area. Historians have claimed that significant changes in Hungary were the results of the Mongol invasion: a change in social and economic structures (which had, however, started well before the invasion); a change in the settlement structure of the Great Plains (Alföld) from villages to extensive pasturing of cattle; and an increase in immigration to repopulate the realm. Béla IV certainly recruited settlers, although most of them were not immigrants from far away, but people who migrated from one part of the realm to another, or who came from immediately neighbouring lands. The image of complete devastation also needs to be balanced against the fact that Béla quickly recovered his military might, shown by victories against the Austrian duke to regain border counties occupied by the latter. The most likely explanation is that the western parts of the kingdom, which were the largest and most densely populated, were almost untouched by the effects of the invasion, and constituted the basis

[35] On archaeological research related to the invasion, see Ágnes Ritóok and Éva Garam, eds., *A tatárjárás 1241–42: katalógus* (Budapest, 2007).

for a quick recovery. In its long-term results, the Mongol invasion was most significant in creating an image of fear.[36]

This fear dominated in the relations to the papacy. During the second half of the thirteenth century, kings as well as their enemies often referred to the Mongol threat, or a possible alliance between Hungary's king and the Mongols, entailing the loss of Hungary for western Christendom. Béla IV often used this rhetoric to wrest concessions from the pope, and during the reign of László IV the king's enemies portrayed him as someone ready to use Cumans and Mongols to extirpate the Catholic Church from Hungary.[37]

## *Poland and Bohemia*

Mongol armies attacked Poland at the beginning of 1241. The exact course of the military campaign was debated among historians because of the poor set of sources describing the Mongol raid in Poland and Bohemia. The only detailed account is by Jan Długosz in the fifteenth century, and although many – especially Polish – historians accepted his account, its reliability is now seriously in doubt. One *tümen* of the Mongol army – around 10,000 men at the beginning of the campaign – certainly pillaged Kuyavia, Lesser Poland with Sandomierz and Cracow, and Silesia, where during the battle near Legnica (9 April 1241) the Silesian duke Henryk II the Pious was killed and his army defeated. At least one more battle had taken place in March, probably near the village Chmielnik in Lesser Poland. Here the nobles of the region were defeated. Traditional ideas on the course of the campaign held that invaders first attacked Lesser Poland, sacked Sandomierz and Cracow, then went north towards Kuyavia and, without touching borders of Greater Poland, went back to Lesser Poland and approached Silesia. More recently historians have questioned this scenario. They pointed out that the army would have had problems with supplies if it had marched back and forth on the same route (Lesser Poland–Kuyavia–Lesser Poland). Moreover, it could have easily gone from Kuyavia towards Silesia through the fresh lands of Greater Poland. Much more probably the army first attacked Mazovia and Kuyavia, entering Poland near Lublin, then went south and

[36] Erik Fügedi, *Castle and Society in Medieval Hungary (1000–1437)*, tr. János M. Bak (Budapest, 1986); Hunyadi, *The Hospitallers in the Medieval Kingdom of Hungary*, 39.

[37] N. Berend, *At the Gate of Christendom*, 163–71.

conquered Lesser Poland, and after that headed to Silesia. The immediate effects of the invasion are no clearer than its route. Certainly, the domination of Silesian dukes in Poland definitely ended after the death of Henryk II. Other, non-political consequences are hard to determine. Several important strongholds and cities were burned (Sandomierz, Cracow, probably Wrocław), and memories of the terrible consequences of invasion – empty villages, uncultivated lands – were vivid in thirteenth- and fourteenth-century local historiography in Silesia. But it is impossible precisely to define the extent of losses. Losses caused by the war were without doubt considerable, but one has to remember that the renewal of the Silesian and Lesser Poland economy proceeded quite quickly. After 1241 dozens of villages were re-formed as chartered villages; chartered towns appeared in larger numbers only after the invasion. It would be impossible, even with the help of foreign settlers, to make such reforms without strong local demographics. It seems that the war made movement easier when the traditional structures, but not the demographic potential, were shattered.

Bohemia did not suffer much from the Mongol army. The southern Mongol forces stopped on the Great Hungarian Plains. The northern ones, after pillaging Silesia, went south to join them. The relatively small unit which fought for several months and suffered significant losses in battle did not dare to face the Bohemian king on a battlefield. Because the king blocked the entrance from Silesia to Bohemia with his army, the Mongols crossed the mountains, entered Moravia and surrounded Olomouc. They were expelled from the realm only with the help of the Austrian Babenbergs. Shortly after the invasion, King Václav started to create for western publicity an image of himself as a great warrior and the only brave and wise ruler who defeated the Mongols. He suggested that when Henryk II unwisely started the battle at Legnica, the Bohemian king's reinforcements were only one day from the battlefield. This was transparently not true, as he and his army were still on the territory of Bohemia during the battle. More reliable is the king's narrative that his army entered Silesia after the battle and tried to catch and punish Mongols in Polish lands. Such a strategy would have helped to protect Bohemia and Moravia from Mongol attack, while the risk was nearly nil, considering the invaders' losses resulting from previous battles. But the plan failed. If the hostile army was able to pillage Moravia for a considerable time despite the king's military superiority, this throws a different light on Václav's military achievements in the fight against the Mongols.

## THE ECONOMY AND TOWNS

Urbanization took off in the thirteenth century in all three polities. West European models played a role, but to different degrees and based on different town laws.

### *Bohemia*

Debates about the beginnings of towns in the Přemyslid realm have for years focused on the definition of 'a town' – was a stronghold with a market and several craftsmen a town, a proto-town, an early town or not a town at all? The thirteenth century, however, certainly constitutes a clear dividing line in the existence of craft and commercial centres in Bohemia and Moravia. The appearance of chartered towns was slightly delayed in comparison with Poland, especially Silesia. However, the first attempts to make Prague conform to western town norms in architecture and urban layout were noticeable at the end of the twelfth century. Even if earlier forms of social and economic life were not comparable to a 'proper' town, seven of eighteen of the most important strongholds – the so-called *hradské centra* – in Bohemia were changed into chartered towns during the thirteenth century, mostly during the second half, and the urban layout of four more was close to that typical of chartered towns. For some archaeologists and historians, this signals that towns were built upon older market or administrative centres. This is undeniable, but does not resolve the question of whether towns in Bohemia were a new social and economic phenomenon or simply a step up the development ladder, whose elements had already been present across the land. The problem is the same in the Polish case.

Although differences between strongholds and market settlement on the one hand and western-type towns on the other were insurmountable, the creation of a new settlement type was closely related to using old structures, especially a network of central strongholds. The difference between Poland and Bohemia was that new towns located in an area devoid of previous settlement appeared in larger numbers in Silesia than in Bohemia and Moravia. Přemyslid dukes preferred at first to transform older-type settlements into towns. From the middle of the thirteenth century, especially during the reign of Přemysl Otakar II, towns were established on fallow lands as well.

Nevertheless, the Silesian example played an important role in towns' location in Bohemia and Moravia. The northern part of the margraviate of Moravia was especially strongly influenced by Silesian examples, to such an extent that local towns' law, though derived from Magdeburg, was called 'Leobschützer law', i.e. coming from the Upper Silesian town Leobschütz (Głubczyce). When in Silesia the development of new type of settlement (a network of western-style villages related to a chartered town) was connected with gold-mining activity in the Kaczawa River valley (the first town, Goldberg-Złotoryja appeared at the beginning of the thirteenth century), this inspired in Moravia a new settlement organization in the neighbouring bishop of Wrocław's duchy of Nysa. A gold-miners' village (a town since 1306) called Zuckmantel was situated there, the possession of which was contested between Margrave Vladislav Jindřich and the bishop of Wrocław. Although the margrave did not control the region permanently, he supported the organization of new patterns of rural and urban life. Uničov, a town established through *locatio* circa 1213 (its official charter was issued in 1223), was created by Margrave Vladislav Jindřich near miners' villages, in the valley of the River Oskavá. Similarly, Goldberg was established through *locatio* by Henryk I the Bearded in 1211 (the year the charter was issued).

The mining industry also triggered the establishment of towns in Bohemia: Čáslav and Kolín were located in silver-mining territory, where later, at the end of the thirteenth century, the more famous town of Kutná Hora appeared. But even its earlier cousins were populated by townsmen who mined silver for themselves around 1260 (the year when each town obtained a royal mining privilege). The region's economic power at the very end of the thirteenth century had a stable foundation in the more efficient use of silver ore near Kutná Hora. Annual production at this site reached around thirty tonnes of pure metal, equalling almost half of the output across all of Europe's mines. The region not only became a source of political power of the last Přemyslids, but also created good conditions for unprecedented development of small towns in the vicinity.

Despite the importance of towns in Bohemia, one should not exaggerate the role of mining in their creation and growth. Towns appeared early as market centres with a closely guarded monopoly on trade in food, crops and craft products. From the second half of the thirteenth century such monopolies, together with customs and other dues paid by wandering merchants, were the most reliable income for most new towns. Beer brewing in particular and the monopoly on its sale in town and in the surrounding villages helped establish a durable economy in the towns. Their economies were not stable. To survive, townsmen had to cultivate their own fields not only near but also in towns, and have herds of cattle. Nevertheless, the semi-rural character of smaller towns did not alter their dominant function as centres of trade and more specialized craft production.[38]

From 1250 this new type of exchange centre for locals started not only to dominate the rural landscape but also to change it. In Bohemia, towns needed a more efficient rural economy to survive than traditional villages. And in some places where new-style villages failed to appear in significant numbers, or at all, townspeople themselves tried to improve local conditions by reorganizing their own surrounding areas. The development of a network of towns mostly created economic benefits for the Czech lands, but problems also appeared. Throughout the medieval era, wood was used as a basic building material for houses, craft and trade facilities. As a consequence of the founding of towns, which caused a growth in wood consumption central parts of Bohemia were rapidly deforested. That would become more obvious in the fourteenth century but the roots of the problem started a century earlier.[39]

Similarities between town origins in Silesia and Přemyslid lands are striking. From Silesia, not only settlers, but also their leaders, professional enterpreneurs (*locatores*) arrived, collecting new settlers in the west or in Silesia, organizing the space and social framework for new towns. As in Silesia, they became vogts, leading communities as a ruler's representative. Historians argue that in Moravia a change in the local administrative organization, from strongholds to town circles (*Weichbilds*), took shape as early as in the thirteenth century and under Silesian influence. The southern parts of Moravia were influenced by Austrian patterns, with the *ius emphiteuticum* or *Burgrecht*, which slightly differed from

[38] Jiří Kejř, 'Ursprung und Entwicklung von Stadt- und Marktrecht in Böhmen und Mähren', *Bohemia. Zeitschrift für Geschichte und Kultur der Böhmischen Länder* 31, 2 (1990), 270–82; Kejř, *Die mittelalterlichen Städte in den böhmischen Ländern. Gründung – Verfassung – Entwicklung* (Cologne, 2010).

[39] Jan Klápšte, Zdenek Smetánka and Martin Tomášek, 'The medieval Bohemian town and its hinterland', *Ruralia* 3 (2000) (*Památky Archologické*, Supplementum 14), 294–302.

models in Silesia. A *locator* who became a ruler's representative was called 'judge' (*iudex*) although in the vernacular his title was related to the term 'vogt': 'Vojt, Vojtdink'. Austrian legal terminology became widespread in the whole of Moravia, even in northern parts, where settlement was organized on Silesian patterns.[40]

The thirteenth century was a time of significant growth in town creation in Bohemia and Moravia, connected to the colonization of uncultivated land and the reformation of villages that were already in existence, moving them to a form of self-government. The growing number of rural settlements organized according to western legal patterns, and social and economic customs, relied on towns to maximize profits from reforming the local economy. Specialization of food production and monetization engendered a need for stable exchange, market places and specialized crafts production, which in turn gave rise to new towns. The relatively high productivity of silver-mining contributed to the transformation of the traditional economy. It accelerated the creation of towns near the mines and enabled a fast monetization of the economy. This process started in the twelfth century and was completed during the thirteenth.

Some historians maintain that high profits derived by the Přemyslid kings from silver-mining and coinage enabled their audacious foreign policy and expansion in the territories of Austria, Hungary and Poland. According to estimate based on indirect sources, the total ducal yield from silver-mining ranged from 4,000 to 10,000 kg a year. Equally disputable were hypotheses concerning the total output of silver-mining. The highest proposal is 100,000 kg a year; the more moderate estimate of 75,000 kg is more likely. Although recently some historians have belittled the role of silver, the additional income it provided facilitated wars against the margrave of Austria and the king of Hungary. At the same time, increasing, then stable, amounts of silver obtained from Bohemian mines enabled the implementation of a monetary reform *c.* 1300. King Václav II, for both economic and prestige reasons, ceased production of small deniers that were irregular in weight, and started minting a single precisely defined currency: the grossus pragensis. It was minted at the only mint in Kutná Hora, to enable close control over the production process by royal officials. Its

40 Adrienne Körmendy, *Meliorratio terrae. Vergleichende Untersuchungen über die Siedlungs bewegung im ostlichen Mitteleuropa im 13.–14. Jahrhundert* (Poznań, 1995), 115–120.

weight was set for the whole time of minting at 2.4 grammes, which made the currency's value stable as opposed to that of deniers, which during the whole thirteenth century constantly and unpredictably decreased their weight, quality of alloy and general value. The new currency was modelled on the grossus of Touraine minted by the French king Louis IX from 1266. The quality of the new currency quickly made it very popular, and almost common, in economic transactions made in neighbouring countries. The economic and political success of Václav II's reform influenced other rulers, among them the Silesian and Polish Piasts, to change their own minting customs. But in their case the limited quantity of silver available delayed the process well into the fourteenth century.[41]

What was technological novelty in the twelfth century became commonly used in the next: the heavy plough, the three-field system, mills and horse-treadmills. Their more widespread use made a significant difference between the end of the twelfth and the end of the thirteenth century in the technological landscape of Bohemian villages.[42] New or re-formed settlements densely covered the whole realm and supported urban culture, which was quite new for Bohemian society. Benefits for the owners of towns – these were not only rulers, but also monasteries and other ecclesiastical institutions and nobles – secured their privileged position in society. The question of whether townsmen would mould into the local social and cultural context or remain outside it was resolved only in the following two centuries.[43]

41 Libor Jan, 'Nové poznatky o mincovní reformě krále Václava II.', *Folia Numismatica* 21 (2006–7), 103–16; Věra Němečková, 'Peníze posledních Přemyslovců a počátky české grošové měny', *Folia Numismatica* 21 (2006–7), 91–101. For a popular review of the whole period of the production of Prague grosses (1300–1547), see Jarmila Hásková, 'The Groschien Period', in Jiří Sejbal *et al.*, *Money in the Czech Lands before 1919* (Pacov, 1996), 51–61. About changing early medieval deniers into one-sided and less valuable bracteats minted before grosses, see Roman Zaoral, 'Die Anfänge der Brakteatenwährung in Böhmen', in *XII. Internationaler Numismatischer Kongress Berlin 1997. Akten – Proceedings – Actes*, vol. II (Berlin, 2000), 993–9.

42 Jan Klápšte, 'Studies of structural change in medieval settlement in Bohemia', *Antiquity: A Quarterly Review of Archeology* 65, 247 (1991), 396–405; Josef Janáček, 'Stříbro a ekonomika českých zemi ve 13. Stoleti', *Československý Časopis Historický* 20 (1972), 875–906 (for an estimate of total output, see 880–9); Jan, *Vaclàv II*, 79–118.

43 Josef Žemlička, 'Die Deutschen und die deutschrechtliche Kolonisation Böhmens und Mährens im Mittelalter', in Piskorski, ed., *Historiographical Approaches*, 107–43.

## *Poland*

Throughout the thirteenth century a radical change affected the Piast lands: the appearance of chartered towns founded by rulers, and operating in a network of villages reorganized along western lines. This followed the changes in rural life which started in the second half of the twelfth century in the region of Silesia. Settlers and local peasants organized according to 'German law' (*ius Teutonicum*) were freed from traditional dues to a ruler and were obliged to pay annual rent. If any other service was expected it had to be mentioned in contracts describing conditions under which settlers populated new or newly re-formed villages. For inhabitants of such villages a town was indispensable as a centre for basic monetary exchange, where they sold their products for money. In the old order of rural life, a barter system of exchange dominated, and market villages had sufficed.

At least as important was the fact that production in new villages was more specialized than in traditional rural settlements. They therefore offered much more for the market but their inhabitants also needed more urban craft products than did peasants from nearly self-sufficient local societies. Chartered towns at first proliferated slowly in Poland. Before 1241 only two or three were created, and all were in Silesia (Złotoryja, Środa Śląska, perhaps Wrocław). Chartered towns were new in many respects in Polish society: they formed communities distinct from other social groups, bound together as one subject confronting ducal power, with their own legal basis derived from foreign legal tradition and populated at least at the beginning by immigrants speaking a language different from that of surrounding areas. Rural reform was easier; it did not change the social context so deeply. Both processes accelerated a third: the old economy based on services and dues paid in produce was replaced by a new one, based on monetary circulation. For many social, political and economic reasons the latter was the greatest accomplishment of the thirteenth century in this part of the Europe.[44]

Apart from Silesia, towns appeared in Poland only after 1241. Some researchers have maintained that town creation helped to compensate

[44] Sławomir Gawlas, 'Fürstenherrschaft, Geldwirtschaft und Landesausbau'; Halina Manikowska, 'Melioratio terrae and system transformations on lands to the East of the Odra during the thirteenth century and the late Middle Ages', in *Poteri economici e poteri politici, secc. XIII–XVIII: atti della trentesima settimana di studi, 27 aprile–1 maggio 1998*, ed. Simonetta Cavaciocchi (Florence, 1999), 303–23.

for heavy demographic losses and repopulate the lands that had been devastated by Prussian, Yatvingian and Mongol raids. For these reasons, the immigration of foreign settlers into towns and the countryside was often encouraged. Vast forests were cleared and exploited for their agricultural potential while new urban nodes of economic infrastructure were created. The settlers came mostly from central and eastern Germany but also from as far away as Frisia and the Netherlands. The settlers were encouraged by dukes, bishops, abbots and local aristocracies who granted liberties, which meant that migrating groups were typically organized by entrepreneurs (*locatores*). Such a *locator* in most cases became a hereditary vogt (*advocatus*) who would benefit from economic privileges of the town while at the same time representing the duke. A hereditary vogt was often a duke's vassal and received his title as payment from the duke for his role in a town's creation. Often, a first vogt or his direct heirs sold the dignity with all revenues to another person.

In first decades of a town's existence the vogt's position as an intermediary between a duke and the community was crucial. Supported by representatives of the community (called assessors, *scabini*), he carried out the duke's juridical functions when the latter was absent as well as judging townsmen according to municipal law. The latter was shaped in the main according to Magdeburg law, but soon local variations emerged, and these, being better calibrated for local conditions, dominated (in particular the version observed in Środa Śląska (Neumarkt) was very popular in Poland as *Neumarkter Recht*, but very popular in mountain areas was the version of Magdeburg law composed for Lwówek Śląski (Löwenberg) – *Löwenberger Recht*).[45]

Historians estimated that during the thirteenth century around 130 towns were chartered in Silesia and around 40 in Greater Poland, 30 in Lesser Poland, and nearly 30 in Kuyavia together with Łęczyca and Sieradz lands. Mazovia (four locations) and Gdańsk-Pomerania (five) evolved at a slower pace. Some parts of Poland were considerably Germanicized, such as Lower Silesia, Prussia and Western Pomerania,

[45] Benedykt Zientara, 'Une voie d'ascension sociale aux XII$^{e}$–XIV$^{e}$ siècle: les "locators" en Europe centrale', in *Gerarchie economiche e gerarchie sociali, secoli XII–XVIII: atti della Dodicesima Settimana di Studi, 18–23 Aprile 1980*, ed. Annalisa Guarducci (Florence, 1990), 33–52; Zientara, 'Socio-economic and spatial transformation of Polish towns during the period of location', *Acta Poloniae Historica* 34 (1976), 57–83; Zientara, 'Walloons in Silesia'.

but this has been exaggerated in the historiography because too often the (re)location of a town or a village according to 'German law' was thought to indicate the ethnic identity of its inhabitants. Every case was different and the locations of Wrocław (1242 and 1261), Płock (1237), Poznań (1253) and Cracow (1257) must be considered individually by taking local circumstances into account. This migratory process was advantageous in economic terms because western immigrants brought with them modern agro-technology as well as international trade contacts. All this served to improve the economic base of the region and to instigate further exploration of available lands (*melioratio terrae*). As a result, the effectiveness of agriculture doubled and the population grew from around 1.2 million to 1.8 million.[46]

Although numerous towns appeared in Poland during the thirteenth century, their inhabitants' political rights were embryonic. They were still supervised by the ducal administration through the vogt, and the duke had every right to intervene in economic or social relations in towns. Relatively large cities, such as Wrocław or Cracow, might generate considerable income for their owner, a duke, and their richest inhabitants could be as wealthy as middle-ranking knights. But most of these new communities were only a little wealthier than bigger villages, and the majority of their inhabitants made their living from agriculture, animal husbandry and cattle-breeding.[47] The time of towns would come no earlier than in the fourteenth and first half of the fifteenth century and only in some regions, especially Silesia. Only then would communities buy the office of vogt (both its property and rights) from a town's owners or the temporary holders and transform their self-government into a form of municipal council with a mayor as head of the community elected by its members.

The growing economic and social role of towns for the surrounding villages, together with their relatively strong defensive character (although initially only the largest towns were enclosed by a stone wall), made them ideal for administrative purposes. In the thirteenth century the administrative role of towns slowly emerged and castellan districts – introduced at the beginning of the twelfth century – with

[46] For a critical review, see Jan Piskorski, 'The medieval "colonization of the East" in Polish historiography', in Piskorski, ed., *Historiographical Approaches*, 97–105.

[47] Henryk Samsonowicz, 'Ackerbürgertum im östlichen Mitteleuropa', in *Ackerbürgertum und Stadtwirtschaft. Zu Regionen und Perioden landwirtschaftlich bestimmten Städtewesens im Mittelalter*, ed. Kurt-Ulrich Jäschke (Heilbronn, 2002), 89–97.

ducal castles and strongholds dominated as basic administrative units. With time, towns completely took over the role of faciliators of the exchange of goods and services, and that led to the abandonment of the old castellan system. Ducal representatives were required to oversee taxes, customs and dues collection. This was easier when the administrative centre was located in the centre of exchange, which from the end of the thirteenth century was the town. Therefore in the fourteenth century castellan districts with separate castellan fortresses would be replaced in Silesia by burgraves and by units with centres situated in major towns (*Weichbilds*). The process was less radical in other Piast lands, but appeared in the fourteenth century.[48]

The Baltic coast developed in quite different ways. The Hanseatic League, with its centre at Lübeck, enforced a monopoly on all trans-Baltic trade to Scandinavia and Rus' while also trying to monopolize contacts with England and Flanders. Wolin, Szczecin, Strzałów, Gryfia, Kołobrzeg and Gdańsk formed a chain of co-operating trade centres that dictated the conditions of much of Poland's foreign exchange.

## *Hungary*

The economic structures of the kingdom of Hungary changed during the thirteenth century. Working the land became more important than animal husbandry in this period, although the latter (especially cattle) still played a more significant role than in western Europe at the time. In the eastern part of the realm, extensive agricultural practices dominated. Cultivation was in the process of changing in the first half of the thirteenth century to a regular system of land rotation: rather than using arable land until it became infertile, each piece of land was used only for a set period of time (three, four or five years) and then cultivation moved on to a new piece of land. Thus cultivation rotated between a specific set of fields without becoming a two- or three-field system. The uncultivated land was used for pasture. The asymmetric heavy plough with a mouldboard started to spread in Hungary from

[48] Roman Czaja, 'Städte und Bürgertum in den polnischen Ländern an der Wende vom 13. zum 14. Jahrhundert', in *Rechtsstadtgründungen*, 323–338; Eugen Oskar Kossmann, 'Vom altpolnischen Opole, schlesischen Weichbild und Powiat des Adels', *Zeitschrift für Ostforschung* 42 (1993), 161–94; Walter Kuhn, *Die deutschrechtliche Städte in Schlesien und Polen in der ersten Hälfte des 13. Jahrhunderts* (Marburg am Lahn, 1968) (and earlier in *Zeitschrift für Ostforschung* 15 (1966), 278–337, 457–510, 704–43).

the west from the middle of the thirteenth century. Cereal crop yields changed from about double to about 3–4 times of the grain sowed.[49]

From the early thirteenth century on, new villages were mostly established in an organized manner on the initiative of the king, and from the middle of the century increasingly on large lay and ecclesiastical estates. Only those with large estates could afford to grant privileges to settlers: more favourable conditions, personal freedom, fixed dues in kind or money linked to the land rather than the person, and the right to elect an elder who judged in lesser (i.e. civil, not criminal) cases. Otherwise the settlers remained under the jurisdiction of the lord. Neighbouring Slavs, Vlachs and Germans immigrated, mostly settling lands that had been uninhabited or sparsely inhabited, and local residents moved away from their original areas of settlement to gain privileges. Peripheral, hitherto unoccupied areas were also organized and brought under cultivation on royal initiative from the middle of the century.

The dissolution of the *praedium*-based economic structure began, shifting to peasant farmers on lands owned by lords. Peasant communities shared out plots of land with periodic reassignment of plots to particular households for cultivation, and determined the rhythm of agricultural work for all plots. This was radically new compared to the previous system where the lord retained direct control over his lands (*praedium*) cultivated by means of the labour service of a servile population, using the lord's implements. Dues in kind and even in money increased and came to be tied to the plot rather than to the person, and labour service decreased. On ecclesiastical, royal and large lay (noble) estates the workforce of slaves was increasingly replaced by free peasant households farming lands owned by but not directly controlled by the lord. This change did not characterize medium and small estates, which remained more traditional for longer. By the end of the century, however, the word *praedium* came to mean an estate whose inhabitants had departed. In the second half of the thirteenth century increasingly free peasant tenants (*jobbágy*) with their plots became the basis of agricultural production.[50]

With the increasing differentiation of production, local trade developed especially from the early thirteenth century, although some local markets had emerged for animals (including fish), wine and

[49] Szabó, 'The praedium'. On every aspect of the economy: Kubinyi *et al.*, eds., *Gazdaság*; Székely and Bartha, eds., *Magyarország története*, II, 1012–91.

[50] Bolla, *A jogilag egységes jobbágyságról*; Kristó, *Nichtungarische Völker.*

agricultural products already during the twelfth century. The main items of internal trade were animals and animal products, fish, salt and wine. Whereas until the middle of the twelfth century the king had more or less a monopoly over local markets (in royal seats and *ispáns*' seats), thereafter ecclesiastical and lay lords increasingly gained the right to hold markets. At the same time, dues from markets were also increasingly frequently donated by the king to lords. The reform of customs duties in the late thirteenth century attests to the growth of the mass market, among urban dwellers and peasants, for everyday goods, including basic foodstuffs (cereals, fish, fruit, cheese and so on) and artisanal products. The network of markets at the end of the period consisted of a marketplace every 20–30 km. Inter-regional trade also started to develop, especially in wine and salt. The important wine-producing areas of Szerém and Somogy had their own liquid measurement (*köböl*) already in the early thirteenth century. Some ecclesiastical institutions acquired the privilege of participating in the trade of salt (which was a royal monopoly).

Initially, international trade played a minor role in the kingdom. Grain, wine, live animals, fruit, wood, animal skins, honey, fish, copper and salt were sold to the neighbouring Austrian lands. Imports from abroad consisted mostly of arms and armaments and luxury products (such as certain textiles and spices), all for the elite. One branch of the trade to the Levant passed through Hungary. The settlement of *Latini* (northern French, Walloon and Lotharingian) merchants in the twelfth century was an indicator of the primarily foreign involvement in long-distance trade. During the thirteenth century, a new trade pattern emerged. Western-manufactured products (espcially textiles for the mass market) began to be imported in more significant quantities, while silver mined in Hungary as well as live animals (primarily oxen, pigs and sheep), animal skins, salted fish, grain, wax, honey, copper and to a lesser extent wine and salt were exported. Although foreign merchants still dealt with bringing imports into the realm, local merchants increasingly took over the task of distributing the goods within the kingdom. Silver-mining became radically more productive in the second half of the century, using German miners, financed by associates with capital. New technology allowed the exploitation of silver and other metal from greater depths. By the fourteenth century almost a quarter of Europe's silver production came from Hungary. Customs duties were reformed repeatedly in the second half of the century, and customs duties relating to value rather than volume of trade were introduced.

In the thirteenth century, monetization advanced; slaves, animals and land acquired set values (the usual price of a slave, for example, was 3 marks). Nonetheless, coins were not the sole means of purchase. Thus property could be purchased for a combination of money and animals: for example, one charter records the sale of a *praedium* for 90 *pensae* (a money of account, equivalent to 40 deniers), 16 oxen and 2 horses. Land was frequently pawned for loans, and King András II, who constantly battled against a lack of ready money, often paid off loans with donations of land. On lower social levels, buying and selling or the payment of dues also meant the use of both money and agricultural products and animals. From the end of the twelfth century on, foreign coins, especially the deniers of Friesach, were in use in Hungary. András II started to imitate them, but the silver content of his coins was much lower. Minting also started in the bishopric of Csanád. After 1242, Béla IV restored a stable Hungarian silver currency, and Austrian deniers disappeared from the kingdom. Several new mints were established, and minting was leased out to the *ispán* of the treasury. Regional differences existed in the weight of the monetary units (the mark and its subunits).[51]

Urbanization took off, based on the earlier privileges of immigrant settlers. In Hungary, the 'law of Fehérvár' was the oldest urban privilege, even attributed to István I himself to enhance its prestige. The origin of this urban law lay in the set of privileges issued by István III (1162–72) to the so-called *Latini*, the Walloon settlers of Fehérvár. In the thirteenth century, these privileges were granted to many newly forming urban communities. This set of privileges meant self-government, elected magistrates deciding all law cases (instead of the county's *ispán*); exemption from tolls in the realm; and the free settlement of other 'guests' (*hospites*). In Fehérvár itself urbanization is indicated by the change in terminology between the late twelfth century and the third decade of the thirteenth century. Whereas initially the recipients of the privileges were the *Latini*, in 1237, Béla IV issued privileges for the burghers (*cives*) of Fehérvár. This shows that other settlers apart from the *Latini* already numbered among the citizens.

The writing down of *hospes* privileges, which happened for many different groups including peasants in the kingdom, was not necessarily linked to the foundation of towns. The crucial difference between

[51] László Solymosi, *A földesúri járadékok új rendszere a 13. századi Magyarországon* (Budapest, 1998); Huszár, *Münzkatalog*; Gedai, 'Friesach Denars'.

*hospes* and urban privileges was the granting of immunity to the latter: exemption from the authority of the *ispán*, self-government, the collection by town authorities of a monetary tax for the king, the right to hold a market and collect dues from it, and military service by a set number of soldiers under the royal banner. Town-dwellers received the same status and formed a corporate community (*universitas*, *communitas*). Nonetheless, both medieval sources and modern historians leave ambiguity in the definition of what a town was in medieval Hungary. The vocabulary of medieval sources varies, sometimes not distinguishing between free villages and towns; and historians have pointed out that some settlements that did not possess urban privileges were nonetheless towns based on their economic function and the density of their population.

The 'liberty of the citizens of Fehérvár' became an urban privilege and was granted to communities from the late 1230s onwards, and it was especially in the second half of the century that urbanization flourished. New towns were sometimes created by granting urban privileges to existing settlements. Other towns, including Buda (later to become the capital), were founded on the initiative of the king, for military as well as economic reasons. Walled towns were to be centres of protection and the inhabitants were required to equip soldiers. Towns played key roles on trade routes and as economic centres. In order to retain the loyalty of his barons – who were the *ispán*s of counties and would therefore have lost prestige and revenues if county seats were given urban privileges – Béla IV did not elevate any of the old county centres to urban status. After his death in 1270, however, most of the settlements that received urban privileges were old county centres. By 1300, thirty-two towns possessed urban privileges and, counting those that were towns in terms of economic status without having urban privileges, the number of towns was around fifty. Most were on significant international or internal trade routes, but urbanization did not affect all parts of the realm equally. The eastern and southern areas, except for the borderlands of the kingdom, had very few towns, because of the lack of economic need for their development.[52]

[52] Erik Fügedi, 'La formation des villes et les ordres mendiants en Hongrie', *Annales* 25 (1970), 966–87; Fügedi, 'Die Entstehung des Städtewesens in Ungarn'; Gerevich, ed., *Towns in Medieval Hungary*; Monika Jánosi, Péter Kovács, József Köblös and István Tringli, *Elenchus fontium historiae urbanae Hungariam usque ad annum 1301 tangentium* (Budapest, 1997).

The majority of urban immigration during the thirteenth century consisted of Germans: for example, privileges were granted to them in the towns of Pest in 1244 (restoring lost pre-1241 privileges) and shortly thereafter in Buda. German townspeople are also known to have lived in Nagyszombat (today Trnava, Slovakia) in the early thirteenth century, and in Pozsony (Bratislava, Slovakia) from probably the second half of the century. German law, however, became important only in the fourteenth century, although Podolin (Podolínec, Slovakia), in Szepes county, already had Magdeburg law in 1292. Germans were also important as miners, for example, in the silver and gold mines of Radna (Rodna, Romania) and Beszterce (Bistriţa, Romania) in north Transylvania and in the silver mine of Selmecbánya (Banská Štiavnica, Slovakia) in the first half of the thirteenth century. In Rimabánya (Rimavská Baňa, Slovakia) the archbishop of Kalocsa recruited *hospes* settlers to mine gold in 1268; in Gölnicbánya (Gelnica, Slovakia) (Szepes county) in the middle of the thirteenth century settlers were involved in gold- and silver-mining; and in the early fourteenth century in gold-mining in Aranyosbánya (Baia de Arieş, Romania) (Torda county). Mining became especially important in the fourteenth century.[53]

## SOCIETY

Social categories came to be more legally defined, and the rights of various groups were often put into writing. Immigration also significantly shaped each society, although the origin of immigrants varied.

### *Bohemia*

Social changes that had started in the twelfth century developed fully over the next century. They were connected both to the reorganization of the economy and to the political situation, and created the basis for estates.[54]

[53] András Kubinyi, 'Deutsche und Nicht-Deutsche in den Städten des mittelalterlichen ungarischen Königreiches', in *Verfestigung und Änderung der ethnischen Strukturen im pannonischen Raum im Spätmittelalter. Internationales Kulturhistorisches Symposion Mogersdorf 1994 in Mogersdorf*, ed. Roland Widder (Eisenstadt, 1996), 145–77; Kristó, *Nichtungarische Völker*, 134–5, 140, 147–51, 157–8, 193–5; Derek Keene, Balázs Nagy and Katalin Szende, eds., *Segregation – Integration – Assimilation: Religious and Ethnic Groups in the Medieval Towns of Central and Eastern Europe* (Farnham, 2009).

[54] Jiří Kejř, 'Anfänge der ständischen Verfassung in Böhmen', in *Die Anfänge der ständischen Vertretungen in Preussen und seinen Nachbarländern*, ed. Hertmut Boockmann (Munich, 1992), 177–217.

Although debate among Czech medievalists about the role played by magnates in the thirteenth century is not settled (see above), there is no doubt that noble and royal interests collided. The former wanted to increase their own lands and rights over its inhabitants at the king's expense. If in the eleventh and twelfth centuries knights possessed allodial estates, these were of modest size. But at the end of the twelfth century and during the thirteenth, allodial estates of nobles grew as a result of their taking over royal domains. Parts occupied by knights became hereditary possessions of their family. The mechanism of building allodial estates favoured nobles closely related to the court or at least those holding administrative offices. They were able to increase their property quickly using their position to accumulate royal gifts or to change the character of royal offices' endowment from temporary to hereditary (especially in the case of castellans' offices). Some historians suggest that the scale on which officials and their families took over royal property, which earlier had been a source of income for officials, was massive; the popularity among the highest nobility of the name *župan* (an independent man of high standing), which replaced *comes* (a ruler's official), has been used an indicator of this process.[55]

What united the future nobility were personal freedom and ownership of landed estates of very different size. These bonds were formalized in the second half of the thirteenth century (between 1260 and 1278), when nobles received the right to settle cases concerning their estates at the land court (*zemsky soud*). The rule was established that only inscribing estates in the land register (*zemske desky*, kept at the land's court) proved their owner's membership in the nobility and conferred the right to participate in political councils. Wealth caused growing differentiation between the magnates (*barones*, *proceres*), and the lower nobility (originating from the former *milites secundi ordini* and called *nobiles* or *armigeri*). But despite these differences knights began to form one noble estate, with privileges and liberties slowly freeing them from close control by or dependence on kings and their dignitaries. The first common political action of free landholders took place in 1278 after the death of Přemysl Otakar II and the minority of his son, Václav II. The decisive moment in the formation of a noble estate was the death of Václav III (1306) and the following inter-regnum when nobles, and especially the mightiest

[55] Jan, *Václav II*, 176–87.

who formed the *pany* group (around fifteen of the wealthiest families), dominated the administration.[56]

Kings issued liberties for individuals; the first privileges for the nobility of the kingdom as a whole were recorded in the fourteenth century. Nevertheless, the number of liberties was large enough to destroy the old system of law enforced by castellans as royal deputies. From the middle of the thirteenth century, their activity became redundant in the face of a large number of freed estates. A consequent reform of the system took place in the fourteenth century: a regular network of administrative and judicial districts with capitals in towns appeared. The political and military position of the high- and middle-ranking nobles, together with their economic independence, made the kings' situation difficult. Rulers, who needed both the military and the financial aid of nobles, had to reconcile allowing nobles to realize their own interests with maintaining royal authority and rights in the kingdom. As part of the solution, kings started to create a new group of knights: vassals settled on fiefs situated in royal domains. Although the process was only beginning in the second half of the thirteenth century, it was treated with suspicion by the Czech nobility from the very start.[57]

During the middle of the thirteenth century, Bohemia experienced an increased influx of German settlers, typically across the newly deforested highlands in the Rudavy hills, the Bohemian Forest and both slopes of the Sudeten Mountains. The Austrians encouraged settlement in new lands throughout Moravia and Slovakia. The growing influence of German culture and language was reinforced by royal marriages, resulting in royal courts becoming progressively more 'cosmopolitan'. Indeed, the Bohemian king Václav I, like the Polish duke Henryk IV Probus, wrote respectable German poetry.

[56] Josef Žemlička, 'Ke zrodu vrcholně feudalní "pozemkové" šlechty ve státě Přemyslovců', *Časopis Marice Moravske* 109 (1990), 17–38, stresses the role of changing former royal land estates into allodial and hereditary estates of high nobility – called territorialization – in the destruction in the eleventh and twelfth centuries of the administrative and social system of the Czech monarchy.

[57] Libor Jan, 'Lenní přísahy a přísahy verností na dvoře posledních Přemyslovcu', in *Stát, státnost a rituály přemyslovského veku problémy, názory, otázky*, ed. Martin Wihoda (Brno, 2006), 101–12; Robert Antonín, 'Lenní institut a jeho funkce při smíření v diplomacii Václava II', in *Rituál smíření: konflikt a jeho řešení ve středověku. Sborník příspěvků z konference konané ve dnech 31. května–1. června 2007 v Brně* (Brno, 2008), 109–20; Krzysztof Kowalewski, *Rycerze, włodycy, panosze: ludzie systemu lennego w średniowiecznych Czechach* (Warsaw, 2009), 20–56.

Nobles and high-ranking ecclesiastics copied royal policies of economic reform with the help of both western organizational patterns of social life and newcomers from the west. As the western, mostly German settlers populated Bohemia and Moravia during the process of the transformation of villages and creation of towns, new social groups with rights different from those possessed by Czech peasants (of varied categories) were forming. They differed in both language and customs from the locals and proved relatively hard to assimilate. This easily led to mutual hostility. But sources on conflict between newcomers and locals refer to members of the top of the social order. Czech elites, especially nobles of middling rank, saw the settling of foreigners as endangering their position. Especially during the reign of Přemysl Otakar I, at least part of the Bohemian elite claimed that such a reduction in their status was planned by the king, who endeavoured to reduce the power of local knights.[58]

Apart from linguistic and cultural differences, thirteenth-century peasants in Bohemia differed in their legal status. The number of free landholders, the former *heredes*, diminished from the middle of the twelfth century. Some achieved the status of the lower nobility, while others were relegated to the group of tenants with the right to leave their villages restricted. The third group among village inhabitants consisted of *servientes* – unfree people working in the households of landowners, and their descendants. Although their number diminished in comparison with earlier centuries, while those of tenants and paid workers increased, they were still present and played a significant role among noble estates' workforce. Settlers living in villages reformed or founded according to western laws were personally free and cultivated their own land, but had to pay dues to landowners and help on the lords' private farm like tenants, although to a lesser extent. They were not counted among 'free men' unlike all nobles and *heredes*. According to the law, they fell somewhere between the local unfree or personally dependent peasantry and the *heredes*.[59]

[58] Jan, *Domácí šlechtická opozice*.

[59] Jaroslav Čechura, 'Sedlák', in *Člověk českého středověku* Každodenní život, 14 (Prague, 2002), 436–59; in a context of changes in the land estates property system, see Čechura, 'Zur Grundherrschaftsentwicklung im früh- und hochmittelalterlichen Böhmen', in *Grundherrschaft und bäuerliche Gesellschaft im Hochmittelalter*, ed. Werner Rösener (Göttingen, 1995), 272–93.

The position of townsmen was better, although over the course of the thirteenth century pressure arose to redefine it. All citizens of towns were personally free and paid their taxes to a common urban budget. Dues were paid to the overlord of the town by the vogt and then by the council from these resources. The difference between townsmen and peasants may look subtle but was substantial: citizens of each town formed a separate group and as a group would deal with their lord. On the one hand this unity of citizens was strengthened by local urban law, defined specifically for each town, although shaped according to either Magdeburg, Halle or Silesian urban laws. On the other hand, townsmen were clearly divided into several groups based on their economic status. The most prosperous formed the political elite of the town, with widespread contacts with nobles and the royal administration. Members of this group, sometimes called the patriciate by historians, originated from the first settler groups and were still mobile. Their family relations covered at least several towns over the entire Bohemian and Moravian territory. Members of this group did not rely on one type of income. Along with commerce, they dealt in rents and carried out other financial operations, as well as owning land, although usually near towns and of modest size. At the end of the thirteenth century they were rich and influential enough to strive for equal social status with the nobility. We do not have much information about other groups living in towns. Craftsmen, servants, Jews and different categories of *hospites* were present without doubt and together formed the majority of town populations. A more detailed picture of these groups emerges only in the fourteenth century.[60]

## *Poland*

During the thirteenth century deep social changes in legal, ethnic and cultural character began. A society that had consisted of ducal subjects, diversified only in terms of local customs and different dues paid or services owed to a ruler, was changed into a multi-ethnic society, constituents of social estates. These groups were at first strongly dependent on rulers who guaranteed their existence. Gradually, new villages, towns and knights freed themselves from or reduced the rulers' control and decreased their obedience to traditional law

[60] Jiří Kejř, *Die mittelalterichen Städte in den böhmischen Ländern. Gründung – Verfassung – Entwicklung* (Cologne, 2009).

codes. For years the old order existed alongside the new, but the latter won out in the end.[61]

In electing their own leader, clergymen were followed by townsmen and – on a much lesser scale – peasants from chartered towns and villages. They too lived in separate groups, ruled by their own codes of law. They chose their leaders, or at the beginning at least their representatives in their towns' courts. Townsmen – even earlier than the clergy – obtained the right to be judged mostly according to their own law. The vogts were still ducal representatives but were subject to laws that had been issued for townspeople only. Dukes retained the right to judge only the highest crimes, those subject to capital punishment. By the fifteenth century even these rights were taken over by larger towns' courts after they had purchased the vogt's powers. In time power over towns would be monopolized by a small group of the privileged, wealthiest citizens. They dominated in the council, and their position became hereditary as long as their assets were big enough. Urban society became divided into several smaller groups: apart from citizens and non-citizens, there were also a patriciate – men of power and wealth – and others, mostly craftsmen but also all the remaining inhabitants of different social and legal status. The process started in the thirteenth century, but deeper conflicts become visible over the sources in the next two centuries.[62]

The situation of peasants was very different. Those living in chartered villages usually paid their dues only to the proprietor of the village and were freed from other duties to dukes. They were also personally free. For a time they lived near unfree settlers of different categories but these disappeared during the thirteenth century. Unlike townspeople – for whom Magdeburg law provided the basis of their local constitutions – no trace of legal unification on a larger scale exists

[61] Henryk Samsonowicz, 'Die Stände in Polen', in *Die Anfänge der ständischen Vertretungen*, 159–68.

[62] See above and Henryk Samsonowicz, 'Les origines du patriciate des villes polonaises', *Acta Poloniae Historica* 67 (1993), 5–15; Samsonowicz, 'Wer traf die Entscheidungen in den selbstverwalteten Städten des mittelaterlichen Polen?', in *Rechtsstadtgründungen*, 373–84. The case of one of the first known conflicts between the patriciate of the dominant city and craftsmen from a dependent town has been analysed recently in Stanisław Rosik, 'Zur Genese und Funktion so genannten Neustädte in Schlesien im 13. und 14. Jahrhundert', in *Rechtsstadtgründungen*, 169–79. Henryk Samsonowicz, 'Hierarchies économique et hierarchies sociales dans les villes', in *Gerarchie economiche*, 163–70.

for peasants' living conditions. To reform a village following an example was up to the will of the owner, who usually wanted to have a similar legal situation in all his estates. But each village constituted a case of its own. As a result, when chartered villages dominated the landscape, the differences between peasants' conditions were diminishing. But they never disappeared.

Knights consciously formed a social group by stressing their separateness from the other subjects of the Piasts. The uniqueness of their social position was related to their duties as warriors, which caused the emergence of a specific ethos and legal position. They typically had special rights: the free choice of church where they paid their tithe, and the allodial and hereditary character of landholding. In the thirteenth century, nobles tried to obtain further liberties as clergymen did, but in a different way. Although legally knighthood was not subdivided according to social status or wealth, in reality noble elites gathered at a ruler's court, and those holding courtly dignities were not only more influential and rich but also had higher social standing. Fights among nobles and the lack of formal structures enabling common action led to further divisions. As a result, when dukes issued privileges – for example, the exercise of ducal justice in villages – they did so only for a specific person and in a specific land. Only in harsh political situations did dukes respond to pleas coming from the knighthood represented as a group. Even in those situations, the example of, and perhaps a little pressure from, Church elites was needed. That was the case of Władysław III Spindleshanks who in 1228 during a meeting with local elites in Cienia village officially swore that he would preserve traditional rights of nobles and would avoid unjust actions. In particular, he would not impose new and unjust taxes. He promised this with the consent not only of his nobles, but also of the Church elite.

Group actions were hard to organize for knights, because they did not form a homogeneous group in terms of culture or ethnicity. Western guests invited by rulers at court brought new customs, ideas and languages, and were envied by locals. In Silesia, the guests' culture took deep roots and caused the appearence of a new entity, a nobility making use of the cultural heritage of both Polish and (mostly) German members and predecessors. In other parts of Poland, mutual acculturation did not go so smoothly and provoked several conflicts with 'strangers'. Aversion to foreigners and a growing regional consciousness at the end of the thirteenth and into the fourteenth century put pressure on rulers to ensure a privileged position for locals at court and in administration. That meant the exclusion not of all foreigners, but of knights not connected with regional elites or born in the region.[63]

Deep changes took place in the ethnic character of Polish society as well. In central and eastern parts of the realm, Slavic settlement and culture dominated. But in western and northern regions western culture and different dialects of the German language were abundant. Silesia was an exceptional case in that its townsmen and knights accepted German culture and language as their own throughout the thirteenth and fourteenth centuries. The process took place on a much lesser scale in Greater Poland, but even in Mazovia and Lesser Poland German culture was brought by settlers. Germans, Slavs and small groups of Walloons (known as Romans or *Latini*) and peasants established a typical multi-ethnic substratum of thirteenth-century Polish society.

Political division made differentiation of local and regional cultures and legal particulars easier. As a result, at the end of the thirteenth century Polish society was much more heterogeneous than it had been in previous centuries. But the process also had another side. Since the beginning of the thirteenth century mass evangelization and mass Christianization had created a fairly homogeneous society of believers. In the thirteenth and first half of the fourteenth centuries, more than a thousand new village churches were built against less than hundred during the whole period of tenth to twelfth centuries. Monetization of economy made exchange between local and regional markets easier. Communication and trade did not affect rulers' policy – at least not in the thirteenth century – but they accelerated a development of strong national identity among Poles coexisting with still strong particular, local traditions. Social change, economic and legal liberties and political circumstances turned a society of ducal subjects into one of different social groups, active social agents, who shaped society according to their own needs during tough negotiations with rulers.[64]

[63] Wojciech Iwańczak, 'Political culture of the nobility in late medieval Poland', in *Political Culture in Central Europe*, vol. I, 101–11; Tomasz Jurek, 'Die Migration deutscher Ritter in Polen', in *Das Reich und Polen*, 243–76; Jurek, *Geneza szlachty polskiej*, ch. 5.

[64] On thirteenth-century social and political change, see Piotr Górecki, *A Local Society in Transition: The Henryków Book and Related Documents* (Toronto, 2007), 36–86. On relations between political and economic change, see Gawlas, *O kształt zjednoczonego królestwa*; on ethnic differentiation, see P. Górecki, 'Assimilation,

## *Hungary*

Social change during the century was also significant. Social groups became more precisely and legally defined. While from a legal point of view the nobility emerged as a unified status group, social differentiation led to many free *servientes regis* becoming part of the *familia* of ecclesiastical or lay lords, providing military service. A legally coherent (although economically stratified) nobility as well as a free peasantry emerged. The term *iobagio* changed its meaning. Initially it meant people who fulfilled warrior and administrative functions on royal and ecclesiastical estates. In the later thirteenth century, it came to mean primarily free peasants living under the jurisdiction of lords, holding an inheritable estate whose ultimate owner was the lord; these peasants paid monetary dues in exchange for cultivating the land. This freedom meant that, although they were under the lord's jurisdiction, such peasants could move freely, could hold their plot and even sell it, provided the new owner continued to give the lord his dues; the peasant community regulated agricultural matters.

After the Mongol invasion, inter-related factors led to the amelioration of the economic, social and legal condition of peasants, and the legal recognition of their rights: immigration and especially internal mass migration, the illegal escape of servile populations to find better conditions; great landlords' need for manpower on their lands as part of the 'internal expansion' of cultivation; and the greater significance of production for markets. Whereas prior to the middle of the thirteenth century, perhaps up to 90 per cent of the population of villages were either slaves or bound servile elements, by the end of the century the majority were free, gaining the rights previously belonging to a small segment of the rural population. Others of servile status, characterized by a variety of legal and economic conditions, continued to live on the lands of churches and smallholder lords. Even these lords, however, had to start granting concessions to retain their population. Gradually during the fourteenth century, the remaining servile people merged into the free peasantry.[65]

resistance and ethnic group formation in medieval Poland: a European paradigm?', in *Reich und Polen*, 447–76; for the fourteenth and fifteenth centuries, see Andrzej Janeczek, 'Ethnische Gruppenbildung im spätmittelalterliche Polen', in *Reich und Polen*, 401–46.

65 Jenő Szűcs, 'Megosztott parasztság – egységesülő jobbágyság: a paraszti társadalom átalakulása a 13. században', *Századok* 115 (1981), 3–65, 263–319; Bolla, *A jogilag egységes jobbágyságról*.

Two significant changes affected the nobility. The inheritance of women was ensured through the 'daughters' quarter' in the Golden Bull of 1222. One-quarter of the property was given to the daughters (if there were several, it was distributed among them rather than each receiving one-quarter).[66] In the second half of the century, *familiaritas* developed: as royal power weakened and aristocratic landholding increased, lower-ranking groups, in order to maintain their social status (which had earlier been dependent on royal support), became members of the households of more powerful lords. They provided counsel, administrative and military service in exchange for provisions in kind (sometimes from the revenues of estates they administered on behalf of their lord), or land. Such nobles, however, held their own estates in perpetuity; the bond of *familiaritas* was not inherited, and some *familiares* had the right to change lords.[67]

Different status groups received their own privileges. Of these, two notable examples illustrate the position such groups had in society. The so-called lance-bearers of Szepes (*szepesi lándzsásnemesek*) were originally border-guards in the county of Szepes, who received a charter of privileges in 1243, elevating their status. This gave them autonomy from the county's *ispán*, and the right to pay taxes only when the *servientes regis* had to pay, in exchange for sending one heavily armed warrior for each four families to the royal army. The other group, the Székely (*Siculi*, *Seklers*), whose origin is debated (according to later sources, they first fought in the royal army in 1116), were Hungarian-speakers at least by the modern period. They had settled in Transylvania by the thirteenth century. Their territories were divided into seats: six were in south-east Transylvania, covering one large territory, while the seventh lay in another part of Transylvania. These were administrative and jurisdictional units. A count appointed by the king governed them, and the inhabitants were all freemen. The Székely provided military service in the royal army as light cavalry. Each household owed the king an ox when he was crowned, at his marriage and at the birth of the heir to the throne; otherwise they were exempt from tax.[68]

66 Martyn C. Rady, 'The filial quarter and female inheritance in medieval Hungarian law', in *The Man of Many Devices*, 422–31.

67 Bónis, *Hűbériség*; Rady, *Nobility*, ch. 7.

68 See Chapter 5, n. 3; Paul Niedermaier, ed., *Die Szekler in Siebenbürgen: von der privilegierten Sondergemeinde zur ethnischen Gruppe* (Cologne, 2009).

Privileges in writing were also granted to many immigrant and minority groups for the first time during the thirteenth century. Such groups could be quite small. For example, in 1224, following a dispute, the Pechenegs of one settlement, Árpás, had their rights and obligations put into writing by the count palatine. According to these privileges, those Pechenegs who participated in the army did not owe payment, whereas those who were not in the army paid money. Every three years they all paid taxes on their horses. The palatine's official, the *ispán*, had limited rights to be fed and housed by them during his visits.[69]

More significantly, written privileges were also issued for very large groups or even for the totality of a particular minority group. The Germans (Saxons) of southern Transylvania gained territorial privileges from King András II in 1224 in the so-called *Andreanum*. The king established their duties, such as the payment of tax, military service, and the provision of housing and food for the king and his officials. He also gave them rights: the election of their own officials, and the guarantee that only the king and the *ispán* of Szeben were to have jurisdiction over them. Saxon merchants did not have to pay customs duties in the entire kingdom, and markets in their own territory were not taxed. The charter also created territorial unity, as no outsider was allowed to receive villages or estates in their land. Other German immigrants who settled elsewhere in the kingdom, in other counties and towns, did not automatically have corporate privileges, but various privileges were granted separately to different German groups. For example, Germans in Keresztúr (Hostie, Slovakia), Bars county, paid tithes on wheat according to the German custom according to a charter from 1246: they left it in the fields. Another group of Germans at Korpona (Krupina, Slovakia), Hont county, received privileges in 1244 according to which they could not be judged on the testimony of Hungarians alone – there had to be German witnesses as well.[70]

[69] Kristó, *Nichtungarische Völker*, 129–81. This and the following paragraphs are based on the overview in Nora Berend, 'Immigrants and locals in medieval Hungary: eleventh–thirteenth centuries', in *Grenzräume und Grenzüberschreitungen im Vergleich. Der Osten und der Westen des mittelalterlichen Lateineuropa*, ed. Klaus Herbers and Nikolas Jaspert (Berlin, 2007), 205–18.

[70] Szentpétery and Borsa, *Regesta*, no. 413; Kristó, *Nichtungarische Völker*; László Blazovich, 'Az Andreanum és az erdélyi szászok az etnikai autonómiák rendszerében a középkori Magyarországon', *Erdélyi Múzeum* 3/4 (2005), 5–17, epa.oszk.hu/00900/00979/00307/pdf/002.pdf; Friedrich Müller, ed., *Zur Rechts-*

Jews received privileges from King Béla IV in 1251; the ruler based these privileges on the charter issued by Duke Frederick of Austria in 1244. It is probable that the Jewish elite who moved back and forth between Austria and Hungary had asked the Hungarian king to issue the same privileges they had received in Austria. The protection granted to the Jews was comprehensive, including punishments of Christians for killing or harming Jews, punishment for the rape of Jewish women and the kidnapping of children, legal protection (Jews were not to be condemned on the testimony of Christian witnesses alone, and did not have to take oaths unless the king ordered them to do so) and measures to ensure the safety of synagogues. It also included economic privileges: Jewish merchants were to pay the same customs duties as citizens of the city where the merchants resided, and detailed regulations pertained to money-lending.[71]

Cumans were also settled in the kingdom and their status was regulated in writing. Perhaps in 1239, but in any case prior to the Mongol invasion of 1241, the existing ties between the Hungarian king and the Cumans led to the acceptance into Hungary of a number of Cumans, under their own leader, who were fleeing from the Mongols. King Béla IV saw their potential in providing military power for him. Conflicts with the local population led to accusations that the Cumans were the Mongols' vanguard; their chieftain and his family were massacred on the eve of the Mongol invasion. The Cumans left the kingdom, killing and pillaging on their way. Nonetheless, after the invasion, King Béla invited the Cumans to return. Their baptism and the marriage of a Cuman chieftain's daughter to Béla's son István, during which Cuman leaders swore an oath over a dog cut in two, was meant to guarantee the Cumans' fidelity to the king.

Béla used them in his army in foreign wars, and tried to rely on them even against his own nobility. Yet they sided with his son István V in the war between them. László IV, son of István V and the Cuman chieftain's daughter Erzsébet, ascended the throne as a minor; his rule was plagued by the growth of noble power. He spent increasing amounts of time with the Cumans, preferred a Cuman concubine to his wife and tried to build his power on Cuman support, which alienated the ecclesiastical hierarchy. A papal legate, Philip of Fermo, came to identify the Cumans as the main cause of the problems in the

*und Siedlungsgeschichte der Siebenbürger Sachsen* (Cologne, 1971); Horst Klusch, *Zur Ansiedlung der Siebenburgen Sachsen* (Bucharest and Klausenburg, 2001).

71 N. Berend, *At the Gate of Christendom*, esp. 76–81.

kingdom. Under pressure, in 1279, King László IV regulated the position of the Cumans, who differed significantly from the local population in their beliefs, habits and way of life. The royal charter defined Cuman legal status collectively: they constituted a *universitas* with their own representatives and came under royal jurisdiction. They were all to accept baptism and settle permanently: giving up paganism and a set of social customs was encompassed in the medieval concept of conversion to Christianity. The Cumans eventually revolted and László defeated them in the battle of Hódtó (1282). Cuman resentment finally led to the assassination of the king in 1290. Cuman integration in Hungary was a longer process, ending in the fourteenth and fifteenth centuries.[72]

Royal policies towards non-Christians led to numerous clashes with the papacy over the course of the century. András II repeatedly ignored his promises and oaths not to give power over Christians to non-Christians (Jews and Muslims), that is, public office as mint-masters or collectors of royal revenues. Béla IV and especially László IV were chastised for their policies towards the Cumans. Papal intervention was tied to discontent within the realm by nobles and prelates who saw their own revenues threatened; it was often the archbishop of Esztergom who initiated ecclesiastical reprimands and sanctions against the king. The papacy also interpreted the Hungarian situation in the light of its other preoccupations, for example, turning Hungary's Muslim population into a 'threat' for Christians because of the prevalent concern about the crusades.[73]

## CULTURAL CHANGES AND LITERACY

The significance of literacy increased in the thirteenth century, although it became more widespread in Bohemia than in the other two polities. Chivalry and immigrants to a greater or lesser extent influenced the culture of all three polities.

### *Bohemia*

During the thirteenth century literacy became widespread in the Přemyslid realm in two dimensions: the number of people able to

[72] Pálóczi Horváth, *Pechenegs, Cumans*; N. Berend, *At the Gate of Christendom*.

[73] N. Berend, *At the Gate of Christendom*.

read and write, and the diversity of social groups whose members learned both skills. The latter was caused by the reform of Czech clergy carried on during the first half of the century. Until the beginning of the thirteenth century most disciples at local schools originated from clerical families. Only after celibacy was forced upon Czech clergymen did sons of the nobility and in time townsmen appear in schools. At the same time, the number of schools increased. Besides the oldest, the Prague cathedral school, new ones at the collegiate churches were created (Stará Boleslav, Litoměřice). The role of monasteries in education was meagre not only in the thirteenth but also during earlier centuries. We have no information about external monastic schools with one exception: convents provided education for sons and more often daughters of founders – at least from the royal family.[74] But usually sons and daughters of both royal and noble families were taught at the court or at home. For those who stressed the importance of psalter reading, there was a chance to acquire literacy.[75] Otherwise disciples were trained in social roles determined by their gender. We know nothing about the active internal schools of religious orders. Apart from several historiographical works, there is no other evidence of the intellectual activity of Bohemian monks.

The Prague cathedral school was for a long time the highest educational institution available for the majority of Bohemian clergy. Only a few are known to have attended monastic schools in the Empire. For the first time in 1140, and then from the 1180s, priests – mostly canons of Prague and Vyšehrad, but also of Olomouc chapters – appeared in larger numbers with the title magister. It is possible that the majority of them had university degrees. In the thirteenth century they were mentioned in numerous charters from across Bohemia. They studied mostly in Paris and Bologna, with a few in Padua and Vicenza. At Bologna they were usually included in the German *natio* but sometimes they were numerous enough to create their own *natio*. From the second half of the thirteenth and the beginning of the fourteenth centuries around fifty Czech students are identified among students of Italian universities.[76]

74 *Letopis Vincencia, kanovníka kostela pražkého*, ed. Joseph Emler, in FRB, 2, 420.

75 Queen Gutta educated her maids (*domicellas*) herself: see *Petra Žitavského Kronika Zbraslavská*, ed. J. Emler, FRB, 4 (Prague, 1884), 27.

76 Maria Bláhová, 'Studenten aus den böhmischen Ländern in Italien im Mittelalter. Die Přemyslidische Zeit', *Civis. Studi e Testi* 17, 51 (1993), 157–78.

The cathedral school in Prague flourished under the guidance of its masters, bearing in the thirteenth century the title of scholastic (*scholasticus*). Apart from traditional lectures in theology from the first half of the century, lecturers taught Aristotelian philosophy (*libri naturales*) and rhetoric. In the collegiate school of Vyšehrad, Master Henry of Isern (also called Italicus) propagated study in rhetoric and elements of the law for notaries and administrative officials. This flowering of teaching did not last long and ended during the conflict between Přemysl Otakar II and Rudolf of Habsburg (1273–8) when foreign pupils abandoned Prague. During the thirteenth century, besides the cathedral and chapter schools, the importance of schools of religious orders grew, especially those of the Dominican order. In Prague, the central school (*studium generale*) for the Bohemian province was established in the fourteenth century, at the same time as the Franciscan studium there. Earlier, but also in the fourteenth century, canons regular of St Augustine organized a school for their province in the monastery of St Thomas at the Mala Strána in Prague. During the thirteenth century, the Dominican school in Prague educated not only regular preachers, but also the chronicler and Church official Martin of Opava.[77]

During the thirteenth century, in Bohemian and Moravian towns the demand was still growing for the teaching of reading and writing, skills useful for townsmen dealing with trade and craft but also for those sons of townsmen who planned to make a career in the Church. Practical skills, such as bookkeeping in trade enterprises, were acquired during apprenticeships under the guidance of masters, experienced trades- or craftsmen. But before that, boys were taught the educational basics at parish schools. These schools appeared in Bohemia for the first time in the 1220s. A *magister scholarum* of parish church of Znojmo was mentioned in 1225, and a *scholasticus* appeared at St Peter's church in Brno in 1234. At the end of the century, some bigger towns had more than one school. In Brno, for instance, in 1298 there was a school at St Peter's, whose *rector scolarum* opposed the

[77] Marie Bláhová, 'Das intelektuelle Leben in den böhmischen Ländern unter den lätzten Přemysliden', in *Geistesleben im 13. Jahrhundert*, ed. Jan A. Aaertsen and Andreas Speer (Berlin and New York, 2000), 540–52; Jaroslav Kadlec, 'Die Franziskaner in den böhmischen Ländern und ihre Generalstudium in vorhussitischer Zeit', *Archiv für Kirchengeschichte von Böhmen-Mähren-Schlesien* 8 (1987), 84–91.

existence of another school at St Jacob's church. On a smaller scale, there were schools in Žatec (possibly 1256), Mohelnica (1275), Hlubčice (supposedly 1275), Litoměřice (1298) and Česke Budějovice (1309). But generally, the number of towns' parish schools was rather limited and they were relatively inconsequential. Otherwise their absence from the sources would be hard to explain. The same is true about village parish schools: sources provide no information until the end of the Přemyslid state.[78]

Nevertheless, the spread of administrative literacy changed Bohemian culture, although in the thirteenth century we can observe only the beginning of this process. From the end of the twelfth century the number of charters that were issued not just or even mainly for Church institutions, but more and more often for laymen, mostly nobles, grew steadily. The archives preserved from the largest institutions of the period contain hundreds of charters issued from the eleventh century, but with the majority written in the thirteenth. Apart from charters in both Church and secular institutions (especially newly created towns) of different sizes, many economic, accounting and other types of administrative books were written. During the thirteenth century they were still written in Latin; the next century witnessed the appearance of charters in German and Czech (at the end of the fourteenth century). Kings, who issued hundreds of charters in the thirteenth century, had to secure regular access to a well-prepared workforce and therefore developed a professional chancery. Church institutions lost their monopoly on writing and preparing legal instruments. To meet a wider need to keep records and to allow men educated in different ways to use them for administrative purposes, the vernacular began to be used in these books. Czech and German were used along with Latin in literature. Generally, the use of Czech in literature was connected much more with political life and purposes than religious aims. Libraries were in the hands of clergymen and Church institutions. They did not develop as extensively as chanceries and archives. Most of their fonds consisted of liturgical literature. Only in institutions with adjacent schools did a wider interest in philosophy, rhetoric and history emerge. Even if on

78 Marie Bláhová, 'Artes und Bildung im mittelalterlichen Böhmen (vor der Gründung der Prager Universität)', in *Scientia und Ars im Hoch- und Spätmittelalter (Albert Zimmermann zum 65. Geburtstag)*, ed. Andreas Speer and Ingrid Craemer-Ruegenberg (Berlin and New York, 1994), vol. II, 777–94.

minor scale, the purposes for which reading and writing in Czech were used were similar to those in neighbouring imperial lands.[79]

Changes in elite material culture were linked to German influence. Kings' and nobles' entourages in particular promoted new, courtly patterns of behaviour and ostentation of power. Czech kings hired and hosted many German knights, mostly from the lower-ranking nobility (*ministerials*). Therefore western cultural influences were adapted in Bohemia in forms popular in the Empire. The advantage was that for western neighbours the behaviour of Czech kings and nobility became familiar, broadly understood and accepted.[80]

When Jans der Enikel wrote his *Fürstenbuch* (history of Vienna) in the last quarter of the thirteenth century, he told the story of the war between Václav I and the margrave of Austria. In his description of a battle in 1246 he described the Czech king's knights, both German and Czech, as similar. For him, Václav's magnates, such as Siegfried and Kadolt Waisen of Dürnholz or Wock of Rožemberk from the Vítkovce clan, were prepared and dressed for battle not only exactly as any western knight would be, but in such a dignified way that no one from the entire Empire's nobility could compare with them.[81] For *Minnesängers* of the middle of the thirteenth century, the court of the Přemyslid kings was only slightly less attractive than the emperor's and much more so than the courts of other central European and imperial rulers, including the margrave of Austria and duke of Tirol. Not only literature, but also knightly tournaments, bloomed at the courts of the last Přemyslid kings. Whether this picture is real or imagined by medieval authors is not as important as the fact that Czech rulers consciously imparted to the elite of the Empire the idea that they

[79] Ivan Hlávaček, 'Die Nationalsprachen in den böhmisch-mährischen Stadtkanzleien der vorhussitischen Zeit', in *La language des actes: actes du XIe Congrès Internationale de Diplomatique*', ed. Olivier Guyotjeannin, elec.enc. sorbonne.fr/CID2003/hlavacek.

[80] Libor Jan, 'Počátky turnajů v českých zemích a jejich rozkvět v době Václava II', *Listy Filologické* 128, 1–2 (2005), 1–19.

[81] *Jansen Enikels Fürstenbuch*, MGH, Deutsche Chroniken, 3/2 (Hanover and Leipzig, 1900), 658, vers 3071–p. 660, vers 3117: 'die komen so ritterlichen / daz man in diutchen richen / nindert moht funden han / zwen so wol gewafent man' (about the Waisen brothers) and 'in diutchen richen / im niht moht gelichen' (about Wock). See Anna M. Drabek, 'Die Waisen. Eine niederösterreichisch-mährische Adelsfamilie unter Babenbergen und Přemysliden', *Mitteilungen des Instituts für Österreichische Geschichtsforschung* 74 (1966), 292–332.

and their nobles were part of western elites on equal terms and therefore political players at the same level.[82]

Accommodation to western courtly culture was seen in both the symbolic meaning and architectural shape of royal foundations. One of the most prestigious, the Cistercian monastery Svatá, then Zlota, Koruna (Holy, then Golden, Crown), was founded in 1263 by King Přemysl Otakar II. The church was built in the Gothic style, and the whole foundation symbolized the close relation between royal power and Christ's royal majesty, whose Holy Crown relics were supposedly kept in a special chapel, similar to the Sainte-Chapelle of Paris. Courtly elites, especially the royal family, were responsible for innovations in the Czech cultural landscape. The first monastery of Poor Clares not just in Bohemia, but in all of central Europe, was founded by Anežka (Agnes), the daughter of Přemysl Otakar I in 1231, a year after the first Franciscan house at St Jacob's church was erected by Anežka's brother, King Václav I. The convent church was the first building in Bohemia in the Gothic style. In Moravia, the first monumental building in the new style was also connected with the Přemyslid dynasty, the Cistercian nunnery of Porta Coeli (near Tišnov and Brno), founded around 1233 by Konstancie, widow of Přemysl Otakar I and daughter of the Hungarian king Béla III. Intricately connected with both a new type of piety and courtly culture, the popularity of military orders was widespread in

[82] Hans Joachim Behr, *Literatur als Machtlegitimation. Studien zur Funktion der deutschsprachigen Dichtung am böhmischen Königshof im 13. Jahrhundert* (Munich, 1989); Marie Bláhová, 'Das Bild Přemysl Ottokars II. in der böhmischen Geschichtsschreibung des Mittelalters', in *Böhmisch-österreichische Beziehungen im 13. Jahrhundert. Österreich (einschliesslich Steiermark, Kärnten und Krain) im Grossreichprojekt Ottokars II. Přemysl, König von Böhmen. Vorträge des internationalen Symposions vom 26. bis 27. September 1996 in Znaim* (Prague, 1998), 163–83; Václav Bok, 'Zu dichterichen Aufgaben und Intentionen mittelhochdeutschen Autoren im Dienst der letzten Premyslidenkönige', in *Böhmen und seine Nachbarn*, 437–56; Jörg K. Hoensch, 'Höfische Kultur in Böhmen unter Wenzel I. und Přemysl Otakar II.', in *Aspekte kultureller Integration. Festschrift zu Ehren von Prof. Dr Antonín Meštan*, ed. Karel Mácha and Peter Drews (Munich, 1991), 175–89; Josef Macek, 'Das Turnier im mittelalterlichen Böhmen', in *Das ritterliche Turnier im Mittelalter. Beiträge zu einer vergleichenden Formen- und Verhaltensgeschichte des Rittertums*, ed. Josef Fleckenstein (Göttingen, 1985), 371–89. On relations between the Czech and Austrian nobility. see Marcin Rafał Pauk, 'Nobiles Bohemie – ministeriales Austriae. Kontakte der böhmischen und österreichischen Eliten in der Regierungszeit König Přemysl Ottokar II', in *Tschechen und Österreicher*, 43–53. On tournaments in Bohemia, see Jan, 'Počátky turnaju v českých zemích'.

Bohemia and Moravia. The Order of St John in particular was popular with Czech nobles.[83]

One should beware of looking at Bohemian and Moravian culture from the perspective of the 'innovations of the thirteenth century'. During the entire thirteenth century Czech elites did not produce anything comparable in their building of 'national self-consciousness' to the twelfth-century Chronicle of Cosmas of Prague. At the cathedral chapter of Prague the only annalistic notes that were written were merely a continuation of Cosmas's chronicle. A 'list of kings' may have existed too, but it has not been preserved. More numerous were historiographical works originating in the Bohemian monastic milieu. In the second half of the thirteenth century a *historia fundationis* of Břevnov abbey was perhaps written by monks but it is known from a late, fourteenth-century version added to the Pulkava chronicle. The thirteenth-century version of *fundatio* of the Benedictine cloister in Třebíči was woven into the narrative of Cosmas's Chronicle. Other religious orders' monasteries preserved the memory of their own beginnings. Among the numerous known *fundationes* – in varying degrees of preservation – *Cronica domus Sarensis*, written at the end of the thirteenth century about the Cistercian abbey in Ždar, is the most extensive and complete. The most original work of this period was annals written between 1214 and 1222 by Abbot Jarloch of the Premonstratensian monastery in Milevsko, which narrated political history interwoven with the order's history in 1167–98. Even this work was not written as an independent new narrative but as a continuation of the annals written in the twelfth century by Master Vincent, the canon of Prague. The next wave of historiographical activity took place in the fourteenth century; even then, the two major works dealing with Přemyslid times, the *Chronicle of Zbraslav* and *Dalimil's Chronicle*, built their narratives on stories derived from Cosmas.[84]

[83] Libor Jan, 'Böhmische and mährische Adelige als Förderer und Midglieder der geistlichen Ritterorden', in *The Crusades and Military Orders: Expanding the Frontiers of Medieval Latin Christianity*, ed. Zsolt Hunyadi and József Laszlovszky (Budapest, 2001), 303–17; Martin Wihoda, 'The Přemyslid dynasty and the beginnings of the Teutonic Orders', in *The Crusades and Military Orders*, 337–47; Jiři Kuthan, *Die mittelalterliche Baukunst der Zisterzienser in Böhmen und in Mähren* (Munich, 1982).

[84] Marie Bláhová *et al.*, ed. and tr., *Kronika tak řečeneho Dalimila* (Prague, 2005); Bláhová, 'Dějepisectví v českých zemích přemyslovského obdobi', Bláhová, 'Offiziele Geschichtsschreibung in den mittelalterlichen böhmischen Ländern',

In the first half of the thirteenth century a local style (or styles), traditionally called Romanesque by art historians, dominated in art, including the monumental residential houses of Prague townsmen. Its creative influence is visible in the *Codex Gigas*. Around 1229 Benedictine monks from Podlažice compiled a 640-page collection of texts, in a manuscript of 920 millimetres high and 505 millimetres wide. It is illustrated with beautiful Romanesque initials and pictures, like the well-known image of the devil from page 290, which is 500 millimetres high.[85] In the second quarter of the century the *Sedlecký antifonář* was written for Cistercian nuns, illustrated with high-quality miniatures. They were especially interesting as they reflected strong eastern Byzantine influences on Romanesque art in the Empire. A widespread use of the Gothic style in architecture began after the middle of the thirteenth century, and in decorative and plastic arts during the last quarter of the thirteenth and into the fourteenth century. Royal courts, especially those of Přemysl Otakar II and Václav II, played a decisive role in propagating innovations in art, but in addition the local high nobility and several Church institutions (Cistercian abbeys, and the Prague and Vyšehrad chapters) were also important for the development of new stylistic trends, new forms of religiosity and a perception of the wider world propagated through art.[86]

in *Die Geschichtsschreibung in Mitteleuropa. Projekte und Forschungsprobleme*, ed. Jarosław Wenta (Toruń, 1999), 21–40.

85 Kamil Boldan, Michal Dragoun, Dušan Foltýn, Jindřich Marek and Zdeněk Uhlíř, *Codex Gigas – Ďáblova Bible. Tajemství největší knihy světa. Publikace vydaná u příležitosti konání stejnojmenné výstavy v Galerii Klementinum* (Prague, 2007).

86 Anežka Merhautová, *Raně středověká architektura v Čechách* (Prague, 1971); Jiří Kuthan, *Česká architektura v době posledních Přemyslovců: města – hrady – kláštery – kostely* (Vimperk, 1994); Kuthan, *Přemysl Ottokar II. König, Bauherr und Mäzen. Höfische Kunst um die Mitte des 13. Jahrhunderts* (Vienna, Cologne and Weimar, 1996); Klárá Benešovská, Zdeněk Drogoun, Tomáš Durdik and Petr Chotěboř, *Architektura románská* (Prague, 2001); Klárá Benešovská, Tomáš Durdik and Petr Chotěboř, *Architektura gotická* (Prague, 2001); Klára Benešovská, 'The royal house in Brno and its chapels / Královský dům v Brně a jeho kaple', in *Court Chapels of the High and Late Middle Ages and Their Artistic Decoration / Dvorské kaple vrcholného a pozdního středověku a jejich umělecká výázdoba* (Prague, 2003), 185–93, 426–30; Krása, *České iluminované rukopisy 13./16. století*; Jiří Kuthan, 'Architektura 13. století v českých zemích jako historický a sociální fenomén', in *Splendor et Gloria Regni Bohemiae: umělecké dílo jako projev vladařské reprezentace a symbol státní identity* (Prague, 2007), 207–34; Zuzana Kulová and Michaela Bäumová, *Item plures et alios libros: knihy kláštera Teplá ve fondech Národní knihovny České republiky* (Prague, 2009); Kuthan, 'Der böhmische und polnische König Wenzel II. (1271–1305) als

## *Poland*

When after the Fourth Lateran Council a regular network of parishes started to be established, this provided the basis for educational acceleration in the Piast duchies. The chronology and scale of parish school activity still are open questions. It seems probable that the numbers of pupils educated in parochial schools should not be exaggerated. During the whole thirteenth century the number of schools was much smaller than the number of parishes. Even in rich cities such as Wrocław and Cracow this type of school emerged only in the second half of the thirteenth century. Sometimes they were contested by cathedral chapters, as rivals of the cathedral schools which traditionally had a monopoly of education. This prevented the emergence of a parochial school in Poznań. Yet these educational establishments in rural or small-town parishes did not appear on a massive scale. The process was just beginning, and change on a major scale did not become visible until the fourteenth century.

This did not exclude a growing appreciation of and need for education. Writing and reading were needed by merchants and representatives of ducal administration – at least in chanceries and by secretaries at law courts. Rapidly growing in comparison with earlier centuries, the number of charters during the thirteenth century also shows the widespread acceptance of writing for practical uses. This was necessitated by new legal procedures, which diminished the role of the spoken word in trials and stressed the value of writing. The whole process did not develop in a regular pattern over the territory of Poland. The most significant proliferation of written instruments took place in Silesia, where chanceries of dukes produced one or two charters per year during the ruler's lifetime at the beginning of the century and four to five at its end. The chancery of the bishop of Wrocław started with an average of one charter every two years (mostly prepared in monastic scriptoria) but finished with ten or more written in the chancery at the end of the thirteenth century. In other parts of Poland, the starting point resembled that in Silesia but at the end of century the gap had grown huge. Greater and Lesser Poland's

Gründer, Bauherr und Auftraggeber von Kunstwerken', in *Sedlec: historie, architektura a umělecká tvorba sedleckého kláštera ve středoevropském kontextu kolem roku 1300 a 1700. Mezinárodní sympozium, Kutná Hora 18.–20. září 2008 / Sedletz. Geschichte, Architektur und Kunstschaffen im Sedletzer Kloster im mitteleuropäischen Kontext um die Jahre 1300 und 1700. Internationales Symposium, Kuttenberg 18.–20. September 2008* (Prague, 2009), 39–69.

ecclesiastical chanceries still produced no more than one to two charters a year. Two causes seem probable: Silesia had the most urbanized landscape and the highest ratio of foreign newcomers (peasants, townsmen, knights), whose culture influenced society deeply.[87]

The century, or more precisely its second half, was a 'golden age' of hagiography. In Silesia at least two *vitae* – *maius et minus* – of St Hedwig were written around the year of her canonization (1267) and were transmitted along with an extensive list of miracles. The possible existence of an earlier *vita* is known only from brief notes in *Vita maior*. In Lesser Poland, the *vitae* of Bishop Stanisław of Cracow (d. 1079) were written for his canonization in 1252. They were prepared, as was Hedwiga's, in two versions – *maior* and *minor*. Their author, Wincenty of Kielcza, was a Dominican friar, secretary to the bishop of Cracow and canon at the cathedral chapter. He composed also the first well-known liturgical hymn written by a Pole: 'Gaude mater Polonia', dedicated to the memory of St Stanisław. At the end of the thirteenth century or the beginning of the fourteenth, two more *vitae* of duchesses were written. Although they were not officially declared to be saints, they were worshipped in nunneries that had been established thanks to their efforts. Salomea, the daughter of Leszek the White of Cracow, was the wife of Duke Kálmán of Hungary. After his death in 1241 she returned to Cracow, took the veil as a Poor Clare and with the support of her brother, Duke Bolesław IV, founded a new convent in Zawichost, later transferred to Skała. She died in 1268. Her younger companion, Kinga, daughter of Béla IV, king of Hungary, and wife of Duke Bolesław IV the Chaste of Cracow, founded the convent of Poor Clares in Stary Sącz.

The holy duchesses' *vitae* propagated the same ideal of female aristocratic ascetic life that was present in the *vita* of St Hedwig. This ideal became popular among the elites of Poland, although it was imported from abroad (Germany, Bohemia and Hungary), as two other examples demonstrate. In the second half of the thirteenth century a *vita* of Anna, wife of Henryk II the Pious of Wrocław, sister of the Czech king Přemysl Otakar I, was written. She founded a convent of Poor Clares in Wrocław, and was portrayed in her *vita* as a humble imitator of the piety embodied in St Hedwig. Less is known

[87] Rościsław Żerelik, *Kancelaria biskupów wrocławskich do 1301 roku* (Wrocław, 1991).

about Jolenta (Helena), another daughter of King Béla IV, wife of Bolesław the Pious of Greater Poland. After her husband's death (1279) she settled in the convent of Poor Clares in Gniezno, where she died *c.* 1298 in the odour of sanctity, although her *vita* was composed in the seventeenth century. This appreciation for female sanctity was new in Polish culture and was doubtless connected to strong influences that reshaped tradition in accordance with new trends of piety and western court culture.[88]

Not only hagiography, but also historiography prospered in thirteenth-century Poland. The chronicle of Master Vincent Kadłubek written in Lesser Poland at the turn of the twelfth and thirteenth centuries, was a starting point for many regional versions of the history of the Piasts and their duchies. In Silesia, the *Cronica Silesiaco-Polona* was written *c.* 1290, in while Greater Poland the *Cronica Polonorum* in its first redaction was created *c.* 1295. In Lesser Poland extensive annalistic notes in the Annals of the *Cracow cathedral chapter* complemented and continued Master Vincent's book. Annalistic activity was extremely popular during the thirteenth century in Silesia. Cistercian monasteries in Lubiąż, Kamieniec and Krzeszów as well as the city of Wrocław and many others patronized the creation of new annals. No fewer than a dozen of them – written in the thirteenth century – are known. In Greater Poland *Annals of the Poznań cathedral chapter* was also composed. In Lesser Poland, the annals of Cracow cathedral chapter were continued, and Franciscan annals in Cracow were written. Catalogues of Church dignitaries, mostly bishops, were created for pragmatic reasons. The oldest of these in Poland was written in Silesia: the *Chorus Vratislaviensis* before the middle of the thirteenth century. Soon similar compositions appeared in Greater and Lesser Poland. In the monastic scriptorium of Henryków (Silesia) another type of partly historiographical, partly pragmatic, writing appeared. Two abbots, both called Peter, composed the *Henryków Book*, describing the history of the abbey's land estate creation, but

88 Joseph Gottschalk, 'Der historische Wert der Legenda maior de beate Hedwigi', *Archiv für schlesische Kirchengeschichte* 20 (1962), 84–125; Gottschalk, *St Hedwig, Herzogin von Schlesien* (Cologne, 1964); Halina Manikowska, 'Zwischen Askesis und Modestia. Buss und Armutsideale in polnischen, böhmischen und ungarischen Hofkreisen im 13. Jahrhundert', *Acta Poloniae Historica* 47 (1983), 33–53; Aleksandra Witkowska, 'The thirteenth-century "Miracula" of St Stanislaus, Bishop of Kraków', in *Procès du cannonisation au Moyen Âge / Medieval canonisation process. Aspects juridiques et religieux*, ed. Gábor Klaniczay (Rome, 2004), 149–63.

including historiographical information and additional descriptions of local customs, social relations and economic practices of the population of thirteenth-century Silesia.[89]

Local culture changed, but not because west European culture was unconditionally attractive. The Piast dukes, especially those of Silesia and Greater Poland, at the beginning of the thirteenth century tried to establish privileged connections with western neighbours, and needed a common code of communication: courtly culture. Thus the process of acculturation was accelerated by legal and economic changes bound up with the growing presence of newcomers. On territories and in social groups where their presence and authority were not dominant, local culture evolved but did not lose its integrity and specificity. In other cases – as of Silesian knights and townsmen – acculturation became complete and a new culture, with a domination of German elements, was born. Regardless of the degree of change, several elements were present on the entire Polish territory: knightly heraldry was born and followed by escutcheons of institutions (towns, duchies, bishoprics, monasteries); nobles with their rural residences changed the local landscape; although Latin still dominated in charters and literature, vernacular language started to grow in importance and in the fourteenth century appeared as a second official language (in particular the local dialect of German in Silesia; in other parts of Poland the use of Polish was restricted to literature and unofficial writings); and rituals, gestures and customs observed and clothes worn in western Europe became popular (such as knights' tournaments and their weaponry and the clothing of the nobility, clergy and townsmen). The picture is completed by elements of new religiosity, the swift acceptance of new religious orders, especially Franciscans and Dominicans, an unprecedented role for female religiosity and influence of women saints in society, new religious practices such as – for

[89] Piotr Górecki, *A Local Society*; Wojciech Drelicharz, 'Richtungen in der Entwicklung der kleinpolnischen Annalistik im 13.–15. Jahrhundert', in *Die Geschichtsschreibung in Mitteleuropa*, 53–72; Wojciech Mrozowicz, 'Kataloge der Breslauer Bischöfe. Überlegungen über alte und die Möglichkeiten neuer Editionsansätze', in *Quellen kirchlicher Provenienz: neue Editionsvorhaben und aktuelle EDV-projekte. Editionswissenschaftliche Kolloquium*, ed. Helmut Flachenecker and Janusz Tandecki (Toruń, 2011), 59–70; Mrozowicz, 'Chronica Polonorum', in *Encyclopedia of the Medieval Chronicle*, ed. Graeme Dunphy *et al.*, vol. I (Leiden and Boston, 2010), 395; Mrozowicz, 'Mittelalterliche Annalistik in Schlesien. Ein Beitrag zur neuen Ausgabe', *Questiones Medii Aevi Novae* 6 (2001), 277–96.

example – public, ostentatious alms-giving, active participation in institutional care for the sick, and strongly emotional forms of cult of new saints, popular not only among elites.[90]

The new culture and new piety needed a new architectural framework. During eleventh and twelfth centuries official buildings, secular as well as Church, were designed in diverse styles now commonly called Romanesque. Their architects copied different types of monuments built in different local traditions, and the effect is very far from a coherent style. The introduction and spread of new, Gothic forms were revolutionary, and were not always accepted. In Silesia Henryk I the Bearded accepted Gothic forms for the Cistercian convent in Trzebnica he founded in 1202. But his own residences in Wrocław and Legnica were built in a much more conservative style. This was not a coincidence. The Gothic style was introduced in Poland by Cistercian monks whose builders copied the styles of Burgundian abbeys. The first Polish examples appeared in Lesser Poland, in Cistercian monasteries of Koprzywnica and Jędrzejów. Both complexes were planned and built by Master Simon of San Gagliano Abbey in northern Italy. Such purity of form did not last long, and Silesian abbeys in Trzebnica (nuns) and Henryków (Cistercian monks) were much more individually constructed. The influence of the new style on local investors was at first not very impressive. Even if they became accustomed to the new forms of spatial, architectural language, the investors saw them as appropriate for religious orders or buildings; only later did secular investors introduce it into their own forms of architectural expression. That changed especially after the introduction of mendicant houses in towns in the middle of the thirteenth century. Their churches, although designed with pragmatic purposes, were aesthetically impressive. Even more importantly, they were open to those looking for spiritual help. Nobles and the poor alike grew accustomed to the new artistic

[90] Wojciech Iwańczak, 'Höfische Kultur und ritterliche Lebensformen in Polen vor dem Hintergrund der europäischen Entwicklung', in *Reich und Polen*, 277–300; Tomasz Jurek, 'Die Urkundensprache im mittelalterlichen Schlesien', in *La langue des actes*: elec.enc.sorbonne.fr/CID2003/jurek; Maciej Michalski, *Kobiety i świętość w żywotach trzynastowiecznych świętych księżnych polskich* (Poznań, 2004); Tomas Wünsch, 'Kulturbeziehungen zwischen Polen und Reich im Mittelalter', in *Reich und Polen*, 357–400; Aleksandra Witkowsa, 'Il mutamenti del XIII secolo (1198–1320)', in *Storia del christianesimo in Polonia*, ed. Jerzy Kłoczowski (Bologna, 1980), 91–113.

language. This was reinforced by support for the new style, raising the prestige of founders, in realms and cities and for social groups recognized by Poles as cultural centres (as was Prague Bohemia) or trendsetters (the Bohemia and Hungarian royal courts). During the second half of the thirteenth century Piast dukes and their subjects accepted this novelty fully and started to use elements of it in their own residences. In this period new foundations supported by dukes and secular potentates were usually built in Gothic form. The best example might be the collegiate church of St Cross in Wrocław, founded by Duke Henryk IV Probus (d. 1290). The same duke rebuilt his residence in Wrocław in the new style. But to see Gothic realization on bigger scale one had to wait for the fourteenth and fifteenth centuries when town halls (Wrocław) or market halls (Cracow) were built by rich townsmen.[91]

## *Hungary*

Significant changes characterized the kingdom of Hungary's cultural and religious life as well (see also Chapter 6). During the twelfth and thirteenth centuries, around 200–300 Hungarian clerics attended university in western Europe. Most completed the liberal arts course only, although some went on to study theology. From the 1260s, an increasing number of clerics studied abroad, and, instead of Paris, most frequented Bologna to study law, so that from 1265 Hungarians formed a *natio* there. Eighty Hungarian students have been identified between 1221 and 1301. The most important patron of such students from the 1240s on was the king; many ecclesiastics who studied abroad already had positions and benefices in the realm that financed their education. On their return, they served the king in leading positions at the court and in prelacies. Representative of the new educated ecclesiastical elite was Muthmer, the queen's chancellor. In his will in 1273, he listed a Bible, a missal, a book of the lives of saints, a preaching manual, Gratian's *Decretum*, Gregory IX's Decretals, Peter Lombard's *Sentences* and Peter Comestor's *Historia scholastica*. Another cleric and royal notary listed eighteen books in his will of 1277, including works of Roman and canon law. By the end of the

91 Paul Crossley, *Gothic Architecture in the Reign of Kasimir the Great: Church Architecture in Lesser Poland 1320–1380* (Cracow, 1985); Teresa Mroczko, Marian Arszyński and Andrzej Włodarek, *Architektura gotycka w Polsce*, vols. I–III (Warsaw, 1995).

thirteenth century, the more significant of the twenty-eight collegiate and fourteen cathedral chapters became centres of learning, with their schools and libraries, although their main means of book acquisition was through donations and testaments of bishops and members of the chapters, rather than through purchase. The cathedral chapter of Veszprém was the centre of the teaching of law.[92]

Literacy became more widespread in the thirteenth century and its role more significant in society. Symptomatic of the new rise of literacy is the growth in the number of royal charters. While from the eleventh and twelfth centuries 198 royal charters survive or are known from copies or references, the number from the thirteenth century alone is 4,221. Charters became significant as a means of proof of ownership. King Béla IV even tried (but failed) to introduce to court written petitions, based on the model of the papal chancery. The royal chancery developed into an office, with a chancellor and court notaries. In the second half of the century specialization emerged within the chancery. Gothic cursive script, formulas and significant uniformization were introduced. In charters from 1207 onwards, the dating was uniformly according to *annus regni* (year of reign). Ecclesiastical institutions also modernized the way they kept important charters, and started to use cartularies. The oldest known cartulary was compiled *c.* 1240 at the abbey of Pannonhalma and contains copies of sixty charters (*Liber ruber*).[93]

[92] Endre Veress, *Matricula et acta Hungarorum in universitatibus Italiae studentium* (Budapest, 1915); György Bónis, *A jogtudó értelmiség a középkori Nyugat- és Közép-Európában* (Budapest, 1972); Péter Sárközy, 'Links to Europe: Hungarian students at Italian universities in the thirteenth–eighteenth centuries', in *Universitas Budensis 1395–1995. International Conference for the History of Universities on the Occasion of the 600th Anniversary of the Foundation of the University of Buda*, ed. László Szögi and Júlia Varga (Budapest, 1997), 135–41; Csaba Csapodi, András Tóth and Miklós Vértesy, *Magyar könyvtártörténet* (Budapest, 1987), ch. 1; Edit Madas and István Monok, *A könyvkultúra Magyarországon a kezdetektől 1800-ig* (Budapest, 2003).

[93] Solymosi, *Írásbeliség*; László Veszprémy, 'Chronicles in charters: historical narratives (narrationes) in charters as substitutes for chronicles in Hungary', *The Medieval Chronicle III: Proceedings of the 3rd International Conference on the Medieval Chronicle. Doorn/Utrecht 12–17 July 2002*, ed. Erik S. Kooper (Amsterdam, 2004), 184–99; László Veszprémy, 'The birth of a structured literacy in Hungary', in Adamska and Mostert, eds., *The Development of Literate Mentalities*, 163–81; Gábor Sarbak, 'A pannonhalmi Liber ruber', in *Mons Sacer 996–1996 (Pannonhalma 1000 éve)*, ed. Imre Takács, 3 vols. (Pannonhalma, 1996), vol. I, 401–21.

Even more significant for the spread of written documents was the growth of non-royal charters. Laypeople now wanted to have their rights, possessions and significant donations or purchases recorded in charters. Instead of notaries, in Hungary this service was provided by the *loca credibilia* (*hiteleshely*). Chapters and larger monasteries exercised this function. They also participated in juridical procedures as witnesses. From the thirteenth century, their services were widely required; about eighty ecclesiastical institutions functioned as *loca credibilia* during that century. From the existing practice of larger ecclesiastical institutions, the *loca credibilia* adopted the custom of safeguarding a copy of the charters they issued; in this way registers emerged. With the development of these registers, chirographs were used less and less often. From the thirteenth century, the *loca credibilia* also started using seals to authenticate the charters they issued: the first-known such charter is from 1201. By the 1230s, seals were widely used to authenticate charters. The inscriptions of the earliest seals identified them as the seal of the patron saint of the institution. These seals existed before they were used to seal charters: their function was to seal the bandages on the hands of those who undertook the ordeal by hot iron. These seals were soon changed to a new type, the seal of the chapter (representing the community). Many institutions never possessed the first type of seal, and only acquired a seal because of their function as *loca credibilia*.[94]

Legal procedures developed, linked to the growth of literacy as well as to social changes. For example, from the 1230s it was the seller who had the financial responsibility in case a third person sued for the estate that had been sold. Specialization started in the royal judicial process. The former *udvarispán* became a judge at the royal court (and held the *iudex curiae regiae* title from *c.* 1230). He could judge anyone at the court, but could not start legal proceedings when he was outside the court. At the king's request, the count palatine, the 'court judge' (*iudex curiae*, *országbíró*), the vice-palatine and *vice-iudex curiae* as well as various members of the court could also act as judges.

94 Fedeles and Bilkei, eds., *Loca credibilia*; Tamás Kőfalvi, 'Places of authentication (loca credibilia)', *Chronica: Annual of the Institute of History University of Szeged* 2 (2002), 27–38; Zsolt Hunyadi, 'Administering the law: Hungary's local credibilia', in *Custom and Law in Central Europe*, ed. Martyn Rady, Centre for European Legal Studies Occasional Papers No. 6 (Cambridge, 2003), 25–35.

Requirements became more complex and were linked to writing. In 1231, a law prohibited the *poroszló* from acting alone (see Chapter 4): the chapter or convent had to send a witness, and written reports had to be produced for each case. From the early thirteenth century every legal act started to be recorded in charters. The count palatine and other judges issued sealed charters. Written notes were also used to facilitate the process of judgement. The portion of the Register of Várad that has survived records almost 400 cases in less than thirty years (1208–35); it shows the volume of business at places of ordeal.[95]

Historical writing also flourished in the thirteenth century.[96] Although the first chronicle may have been written in the late eleventh or early twelfth century, the first surviving chronicle is from around 1200, and during the thirteenth century several more chronicle versions were written, of which one survives. Hypotheses about the lost thirteenth-century versions were constructed based on the existing fourteenth-century chronicle composition (like hypotheses about the earlier chronicle version; see Chapter 6). These chronicles or *gesta* ('deeds') record the – often invented – history of the Hungarians. Their focus is the origins and deeds of the ruling dynasty and the people. The choice of genre was much more restricted than in western Europe: no universal chronicles, monastic chronicles, or urban or family histories were written.

There is some disagreement over how many continuators worked on the lost thirteenth-century chronicle version, and on the authorship of some of the elements incorporated into existing *gesta* and the surviving fourteenth-century chronicle. Whether it is the work of one man or several consecutively, it was probably during the thirteenth century that a history of the pagan past was added to the *gesta*. And although it is debated whether Simon of Kéza composed or adapted the list of immigrant nobles, the list was certainly written in the late thirteenth century. Scholars drew attention to the similarities between the style of the *gesta* and the style of charters written at the royal court. Many of the ecclesiastics who worked on the *gesta* served as royal scribes.

95 Solymosi and Szovák, eds., *Regestrum Varadinense*.

96 Kristó, *Tőrténetírás*; László Veszprémy, 'Historical past and political present'.

The first surviving *Gesta Hungarorum*, of the so-called Hungarian Anonymous, is entirely different from the other historical texts.[97] It is entirely about the pagan past of the Hungarians, especially the conquest of the land of Hungary. According to most historians the *gesta* was written around 1200, although some maintain that it is from the middle of the thirteenth century (the only surviving manuscript dates from that time, but this is a copy and not the original). The author could not be identified; the only certainty is that he was a notary of King Béla (according to most scholars, Béla III). In his *gesta*, the Scythians, the alleged ancestors of the Hungarians, appear as fearsome warriors, rather than as the loathsome barbarians of west European sources. He named Magog as the ancestor of both Attila the Hun and the Hungarians. As discussed above, the anonymous author also championed the rights of the elite. In order to justify the nobility's right to its estates, he depicted the ancestors of the nobles of his own times conquering the land and then receiving a royal grant of their possessions. According to one opinion, Master Ákos was the author of one version of the *Gesta Ungarorum* in the late thirteenth century, prior to Simon of Kéza, and he emphasized that all aristocratic families took part in the conquest of the land.

Master Simon of Kéza's *Gesta Hungarorum*, written between 1282 and 1285, is a reworking of an earlier version of the *gesta*.[98] The court cleric of László IV, perhaps of unfree origin, he fully developed the theory of Hungarian descent from the Huns. Attila and his empire now appeared as the ancestors of the Hungarians, a prestigious ancestry to match Trojan and other origins claimed for other peoples at the time. Since now the first part of the *gesta* consisted of the history of the Huns, the Hungarian conquest was presented as the reclaiming of a land that was theirs by heritage. In the second part, the history of the Hungarians, Simon wrote of the deeds of kings and the nobility. He divided the latter into descendants of the conquerors and those of immigrant nobles. He also invented an explanation for the existence of unfree Hungarians: they were descendants of those who committed a crime against the *communitas* and were therefore deprived of their liberty.

[97] Martyn Rady and László Veszprémy, eds., tr., *Anonymus and Master Roger. Anonymi Bele Regis Notarii Gesta Hungarorum / Anonymous, Notary of King Bela, The Deeds of the Hungarians* (Budapest, 2010).

[98] Veszprémy and Schaer, ed. and tr., *Simon of Kéza.*

Gothic art appeared in the realm, and several churches were reconstructed in the new style. One outstanding piece of work from that period was the Porta Speciosa, the southern portal of the abbey church of Pannonhalma. Monasteries of various noble lineages were also built or added to in the same style that characterized buildings associated with the royal court. Stylistic influences have been traced to Reims and Bamberg. Along with chivalric ideals and heavy armour, royal seals and a variety of jewellery attest to French influence. At the same time, late Romanesque and early Gothic styles continued in architecture and wall-paintings.[99]

Wacław/Václav II (1300–5), king of Bohemia, was crowned king of Poland in 1300 at Gniezno by Archbishop Jakub Świnka, and king of Hungary in 1301. However, the symbolic 'unification' of the three countries that form the subject of this book under one Přemyslid ruler did not last long. The death of the king on 21 June 1305 was followed by the murder of his only son, Václav III, on 8 August 1306, leaving all three realms without an obvious successor. The fourteenth century brought major political changes. A strong monarchy was established in both Hungary and Poland, and Poland was once again reunited. The local dynasties died out and the new kings often had more far-reaching ambitions. Bohemia became the centre of the German Empire, an earlier attempt having failed in the thirteenth century, but this succeeded in a different way and under a different dynasty in the fourteenth. The Jagiellonian dynasty in the fifteenth century once again briefly united all three central European realms. Coming together only to move apart again continued to be a pattern of the region's history for centuries to come.

99 Marosi, *Die Anfänge der Gotik in Ungarn.*

# SELECT BIBLIOGRAPHY

For further bibliography, please consult the notes.

Abbreviations:

FRB – Fontes Rerum Bohemicarum
KDWp – *Kodeks dyplomatyczny Wielkopolski / Codex Diplomaticus Maioris Poloniae*, vol. I, ed. Ignacy Zakrzewski (Poznań, 1877)
KMTL – Gyula Kristó, Pál Engel and Ferenc Makk, *Korai Magyar Történeti Lexikon: 9.–14. század*, Budapest, 1994
MGH – Monumenta Germaniae Historica
MPH – Monumenta Poloniae Historica / Pomniki Dziejowe Polski
SRG – Scriptores rerum Germanicarum
SRH – *Scriptores Rerum Hungaricarum*, ed. Imre Szentpétery, 2 vols., Budapest, 1937–8, repr. Budapest, 1999
NS – Nova Series
s.n. – series nova

## PRIMARY SOURCES

*Annales Altahenses Maiores*, ed. E. Von Oefele, MGH, SRG, 20, Hanover, 1891.

Bak, János M., György Bónis, James Ross Sweeney, eds. and trs., *The Laws of the Medieval Kingdom of Hungary*, vol. I, *1000–1301*, Bakersfield, CA, 1989.

*Chronici Hungarici compositio saeculi XIV*, ed. Alexander [Sándor] Domanovszky, in *SRH*, vol. I, 217–505; Eng. tr. and facsimile, Dezső Dercsényi, ed., *The Hungarian Illuminated Chronicle*, Budapest, 1969.

*Codex diplomaticus et epistolaris Regni Bohemiae*, vol. I, ed. Gustav Friedrich, Prague, 1904–7; vol. V, fasc. 1, ed. Jindřich Šebánek, Sáša Dušková, Prague, 1974.

Constantine Porphyrogenitus, *De administrando imperio*, ed. Gyula Moravcsik, tr. R. J. H. Jenkins, new rev. edn, Washington, DC, 1967.

*Cosmae pragensis chronica boemorum*, ed. Bertold Bretholz, MGH SRG, n.s. 2, Berlin, 1923; Eng. tr. Cosmas of Prague, *The Chronicle of the Czechs*, tr. Lisa Wolverton, Washington, DC, 2009.

*Die Conversio Bagoariorum et Carantanorum und der Brief des Erzbischofs Theotmar von Salzburg*, ed. Fritz Lošek, MGH Studien und Texte, Hanover, 1997.

Dobszay, László and Gábor Prószéky, eds., *Corpus Antiphonalium Officii, Ecclesiarum Centralis Europae: A Preliminary Report*, tr. Erzsébet Mészáros, Budapest, 1988.

Dörrie, Heinrich, *Drei Texte zur Geschichte der Ungarn und Mongolen. Die Missionsreisen des fr. Iulianus O. P. ins Ural-Gebiet (1234/5) und nach Rußland (1237) und der Bericht des Erzbischofs Peter über die Tartaren*, Nachrichten der Akademie der Wissenschaften in Göttingen aus dem Jahre 1956. Philologisch-Historische Klasse, Göttingen, 1956, 126–202.

*Epistola Brunonis ad Henricum regem*, ed. Jadwiga Karwasińska, MPH, s.n., 4/3, 85–106, Warsaw, 1973.

Falvy, Zoltán and László Mezey, eds., *Codex Albensis. Ein Antiphonar aus dem 12. Jahrhundert*, Budapest and Graz, 1963.

*Galli Anonymi Chronicae et Gesta ducum sive principum Polonorum*, ed. K. Maleczyński, MPH, s.n., 2, Cracow, 1952; Eng. tr. Paul W. Knoll and Frank Schaer, eds., tr., *Gesta Principum Polonorum: The Deeds of the Princes of the Poles*, corrected reprint, Budapest, 2007.

Glanvell, Victor Wolf von, *Die Kanonessammlung des Kardinals Deusdedit*. vol. I, *Die Kanonessammlung selbst*, Aalen, 1967, repr. Paderborn, 1905.

Györffy, György, *Diplomata Hungariae Antiquissima*, vol. I, *1000–1131*, Budapest, 1992.

Huszár, Lajos, *Münzkatalog Ungarn von 1000 bis heute*, Budapest, 1979.

Kantor, Marvin, *Medieval Slavic Lives of Saints and Princes*, Ann Arbor, 1983.

*Kronika tak řečeneho Dalimila*, ed. and tr. Marie Blahová *et al.*, Prague, 2005.

*Legenda Christiani. Vita et passio sancti Venceslai et sanctae Ludmile ave eius / Kristiánova legenda život a umučení svatého Václava a jeho báby svaté Ludmily*, ed. Jan Ludvikovský, Prague, 1978.

*Legenda Sancti Gerhardi episcopi*, ed. Emericus Madzsar, in *SRH*, vol. II, 461–506.

*Legenda S. Stephani regis ab Hartvico episcopo conscripta*, ed. Emma Bartoniek, in *SRH*, vol. II, 401–40; Eng. tr. with introduction, Nora Berend, 'Hartvic, *Life of King Stephen of Hungary*', in *Medieval Hagiography: An Anthology*, ed. Thomas Head, New York, 2000, 375–98.

*Legenda S. Stephani regis maior*, ed. Emma Bartoniek, in *SRH*, vol. II, 377–92.

*Legenda S. Stephani regis minor*, ed. Emma Bartoniek, in *SRH*, vol. II, 393–400.

*Letopis Jarlocha, opata kláštera milevského*, in FRB, 2, ed. Joseph Emler, 461–516, Prague, 1874.

*Letopis Vincencia, kanovníka kostela pražkého*, ed. Joseph Emler, FRB, 2, Prague, 1875.

*Menander Protector. Historiae Fragmenta*, tr. and ed. R. C. Blockley, Liverpool, 1985.

*Ottonis et Rahewini Gesta Friderici I. imperatoris*, ed. G. Waitz, MGH SRG, Hanover, 1912; Eng. tr., Charles Christopher Mierow, *Otto of Freising and His Continuator, Rahewin: The Deeds of Frederick Barbarossa*, Toronto, 1994.

*P. Magistri, qui Anonymus dicitur, Gesta Hungarorum*, ed. Aemilius [Emil] Jakubovich, in *SRH*, vol. I, 13–117, Eng. tr. Martyn Rady and László Veszprémy, *Anonymus and Master Roger. Anonymi Bele Regis Notarii Gesta Hungarorum / Anonymus, Notary of King Bela, The Deeds of the Hungarians*, Budapest, 2010.

Žitavského, Petra, *Kronika Zbraslavská*, ed. J. Emler, FRB, 4, Prague, 1884.

Réthy, László, *Corpus Nummorum Hungariae I*, Budapest, 1899, repr. 1982.

*S. Adalberti Pragensis episcopi et martyris vita altera auctore Brunoni Querfurtensi*, ed. Jadwiga Karwasińska, MPH, s.n., vol. 4/2, 1–69, Warsaw, 1969.

Scheiber, Alexander, *Jewish Inscriptions in Hungary from the Third Century to 1686*, Budapest, 1983.

*Simonis de Kéza, Gesta Hungarorum*, ed. Alexander [Sándor] Domanovszky, in *SRH*, vol. I, 129–94; Eng. tr., László Veszprémy and Frank Schaer, eds. and tr., *Simonis de Kéza Gesta Hungarorum – Simon of Kéza, The Deeds of the Hungarians*, Budapest, 1999.

Solymosi, László and Kornél Szovák, eds., *Regestrum Varadinense (1208–1235): Ritvs explorandae veritatis, qvo Hvngarica Natio in dirimendis controuersijs ante annos trecentos & quadraginta vsa est, & eius testimonia plurima, in sacrario sumi temple Varadien. reperta. Colosuarij 1550*, Budapest, 2009.

Spitzer, Shlomo J. and Géza Komoróczy, eds. and tr., *Héber kútforrások Magyarország és a magyarországi zsidóság történetéhez a kezdetektől 1686-ig*, Budapest, 2003.

Szentpétery, Imre and Iván Borsa, *Regesta regum stirpis Arpadianae critico-diplomatica / Az Árpád-házi királyok okleveleinek kritikai jegyzéke*, 4 vols., Budapest, 1923–87.

*Thietmari Merseburgensis episcopi chronicon*, ed. Robert Holtzmann, MGH SRG, n.s. 9, Berlin, 1935; ed. W. Trillmich, Ausgewählte Quellen zur deutschen Geschichte des Mittelalters 9, Berlin, 1957; Eng. tr., David A. Warner, *Ottonian Germany: The Chronicon of Thietmar of Merseburg*, Manchester, 2001.

*Vita et passio S. Wencezlai et S. Ludmilae, ave eius*, ed. Jaroslav Ludvikowský, Prague, 1978.

*Vita quinque fratrum eremitarum [seu] Vita uel passio Benedicti et Iohannis sociorumque suorum auctore Brunone Quesrfurtensi*, ed. Jadwiga Karwasińska, MPH, s.n., 4/3, 7–84, Warsaw, 1973.

*Widukindi monachi Corbeiensis rerum gestarum saxonicarum*, ed. Paul Hirsch, MGH SRG, 60, Hanover, 1935.

## SECONDARY LITERATURE

Adamska, Anna, 'La bibliographie de la diplômatique polonaise 1956–1996', *Archiv für Diplomatik* 44 (1998): 275–336.

'The ecclesiastical chanceleries in medieval Poland as intellectual centres', *Quaestiones Medii Aevii Novae* 10 (2005): 171–98.

'"From Memory to Written Record" in the periphery of medieval *Latinitas*: the case of Poland in the eleventh and twelfth century', in *Charters and the Use of the Written Word in Medieval Society*, ed. K. Heidecker, Turnhout, 2000, 83–100.

'The introduction of writing in central Europe (Poland, Hungary and Bohemia)', in *The New Approaches to Medieval Communication*, ed. Marco Mostert, Turnhout, 1999, 165–90.

Adamska, Anna and Marco Mostert, eds., *The Development of Literate Mentalities in East Central Europe*, Turnhout, 2004.

Althoff, Gerd, 'Symbolische Kommunikation zwischen Piasten und Ottonen', in *Polen und Deutschland vor 1000 Jahren. Die Berliner Tagung über den 'Akt von Gnesen'*, ed. Michael Borgolte, Berlin, 2002, 303–7.

Altmann, Julianna *et al.*, *Medium Regni: Medieval Hungarian Royal Seats*, Budapest, 1999.

Antoniewicz, Włodzimierz, 'Znaczenie odkryć w Wiślicy', *Silesia Antiqua*, 10 (1968): 105–15.

Antonín, Robert, *Zahraníční polítíka krále Václava II. v letech 1283–1300*, Brno, 2009.

*Archeologie pravěkých Čech*, vols. I–VIII, Prague, 2007–8 (vol. II, Slavomil Vencl and Jan Fridrich, *Paleolit a mezolit*; III, Ivan Pavlů and Marie Zápotocká, *Neolit*; IV, Miroslav Dobeš, Evžen Neustupný, Jan Turek and Milan Zápotocký, *Eneolit*; V, Luboš Jiráň, *Doba bronzová*; VI, Natalie Venclová and Petr Drda, *Doba halštatská*; VII, Natalie Venclová and Petr Drda, *Doba laténská*; VIII, Vladimír Salač and Eduard Droberjar, *Doba římská a stěhování národů*).

Bálint, Csanád, *Die Archäologie der Steppe*, Vienna and Cologne, 1989.

Barciak, Antoni, 'Tage und Debatte im Beisein des Herzogs in Polen. Zur Funktionsweise von Tagen (wiece) des 13. Jahrhunderts', in *Ritualisierung politischer Willensbildung. Polen und Deutschland im hohen und späten Mittelalter*, ed. Wojciech Fałkowski, Wiesbaden, 2010, 67–78.

Barford, Paul, *The Early Slavs*, London, 2001.

Bartha, Antal, *Hungarian Society in the Ninth and Tenth Centuries*, Budapest, 1975.

Bartosiewicz, László, 'Animal husbandry and medieval settlement in Hungary: a review', *Beiträge zur Mittelalterarchäologie in Österreich* 15 (1999): 139–55.

Baumann, Wienfried, 'Heinrich III. gegen Břetislav I. Der Kampf von 1040 im Grenzwald und sein literariches Echo', *Beiträge zur Geschichte im Landkreis Cham* 1 (1984): 25–37.

Behr, Hans Joachim, *Literatur als Machtlegitimation. Studien zur Funktion der deutschsprachigen Dichtung am böhmischen Königshof im 13. Jahrhundert*, Munich, 1989.

Benešovska, Klára, Tomáš Durdík, Petr Chotěbor and Zdeněk Dragoun, *Architecture of the Romanesque*, Ten centuries of architecture, Prague, 2001.

Benkő, Elek, 'Pilgerzeichenforschung und Pilgerzeichenüberlieferung in Ungarn und in Siebenbürgen', in *Das Zeichen am Hut im Mittelalter. Europäische Reisemarkierungen*, ed. Hartmut Kühne, Lothar Lambacher and Konrad Vanja, Frankfurt am Main, 2008, 167–84.

Berend, Nora, *At the Gate of Christendom: Jews, Muslims and 'Pagans' in Medieval Hungary, c. 1000–c. 1300*, Cambridge, 2001.

ed., *The Expansion of Central Europe*, Farnham, 2013.

Berend, Nora, József Laszlovszky and Béla Zsolt Szakács, 'The kingdom of Hungary', in *Christianization and the Rise of Christian Monarchy: Scandinavia, Central Europe and Rus'* c. *900–1200*, ed. Nora Berend, Cambridge, 2007, 319–68.

Bistrický, Jan, 'Übersicht über das Urkundenwesen der böhmischen Herrscher bis zum Jahre 1197', in *Typologie der Königsurkunden. Kolloquium der Commission Internationale de Diplomatique in Olmütz*, ed. Bishický, Olomouc, 1998, 227–40.

Bláhová, Emilie, 'Literarische Beziehungen zwischen dem Sázava-Kloster und der Kiever Rus'', in *Der heilige Prokop, Böhmen und Mitteleuropa. Internationales Symposium Benešov–Sázava 24.–26. September 2003*, Prague, 2005, 237–53.

Bláhová, Marie, 'Artes und Bildung im mittelalterlichen Böhmen (vor der Gründung der Prager Universität)', in *Scientia und Ars im Hoch- und Spätmittelalter (Albert Zimmermann zum 65. Geburtstag)*, ed. Andreas Speer and Ingrid Craemer-Ruegenberg, Berlin and New York, 1994, vol. II, 777–94.

'Böhmen in der Politik Rudolfs von Habsburg', in *Rudolf von Habsburg 1273–1291*, Cologne, Weimar and Vienna, 1993, 59–78.

'Die Hofgeschichtsschreibung am böhmischen Herrscherhof im Mittelalter', in *Die Hofgeschichtsschreibung im mittelalterlichen Europa*, ed. Jarosław Wenta and Rudolf Schieffer, Toruń, 2006, 51–72.

'Das intelektuelle Leben in den böhmischen Ländern unter den lätzten Přemysliden', in *Geistesleben im 13. Jahrhundert*, ed. Jan A. Aaertsen and Andreas Speer, Berlin and New York, 2000, 540–52.

'Offiziele Geschichtsschreibung in den mittelalterlichen böhmischen Ländern', in *Die Geschichtsschreibung in Mitteleuropa. Projekte und Forschungsprobleme*, ed. Jarosław Wenta, Toruń, 1999, 21–40.

'Studenten aus den böhmischen Ländern in Italien im Mittelalter. Die Přemyslidische Zeit', *Civis. Studi e testi* 17, 51 (1993), 157–78.

'Vier Epitaphe aus den böhmischen mittelalterlichen Chroniken und Annalen', in *De litteris, manuscriptis, inscriptionibus ... Festschrift zum 65. Geburtstag von Walter Koch*, ed. Theo Kölzer, Franz-Albrecht Bornschlegel, Christian Friedl and Georg Vogeler, Vienna, Cologne and Weimar, 2007, 271–78.

'Verschriftlichte Mündlichkeit in der Böhmischen Chronik des Domherrn Cosmas von Prag', in Adamska and Mostert, eds., *The Development of Literate Mentalities*, 323–42.

Borgolte, Michael, ed., *Polen und Deutschland vor 1000 Jahren. Die Berliner Tagung über den 'Akt von Gnesen'*, Berlin, 2002.

Bowlus, Charles R., *Franks, Moravians, and Magyars: The Struggle for the Middle Danube 788–907*, Philadelphia, 1995.

Brather, Sebastian, *Archäologie der westlichen Slawen. Siedlung, Wirtschaft und Gesellschaft im früh- und hochmittelalterlichen Ostmitteleuropa*, Berlin, 2001.

Brauer, Michael, Pavlína Rychterová and Martin Wihoda, 'Kolonisation und Akkulturation im Mittelalter: vergleichende europäische und regionale Perspektiven. Einleitung', in *Die mittelalterliche Kolonisation: vergleichende Untersuchungen; studentische Arbeiten aus dem internationalen Seminar, veranstaltet in Prag vom 7. bis 11. März 2005*, ed. Michael Brauer, Prague, 2009, 7–20.

Buko, Andrzej, *The Archeology of Early Medieval Poland: Discoveries – Hypotheses – Interpretations*, Leiden and Boston, 2008.

Čechura, Jaroslav, 'Zur Grundherrschaftsentwicklung im früh- und hochmittelalterlichen Böhmen', in *Grundherrschaft und bäuerliche Gesellschaft im Hochmittelalter*, ed. Werner Rösener, Göttingen, 1995, 272–93.

Černý, Pavel [Pavol], *Evangeliář zábrdovický a Svatovítská apokalypsa*, Prague, 2004.

'Kodex vyšehradský, "korunovační" charakter jeho iluminované výzdoby a některé aspekty "politické teologie" 11. století', in *Královský Vyšehrad*, vol. II, *Sborník příspěvků ke křesťanskému miléniu a k posvěcení nových zvonů na kapitulním chrámu sv. Petra a Pavla*, Prague, 2001, 33–56.

Csernus, Sándor and Klára Korompay, eds., *Les Hongrois et l'Europe: conquête et intégration*, Paris and Szeged, 1999.

Curta, Florin, *The Making of the Slavs: History and Archaeology of the Lower Danube Region c. 500–700*, Cambridge, 2001.

Dalewski, Zbigniew, 'Begräbnis des Herrschers. Ritual und Streit um die Thronfolge in Polen des früheren Mittelalters', *Frühmittelalterliche Studien* 43 (2009): 327–48.

*Ritual and Politics: Writing the History of a Dynastic Conflict in Medieval Poland*, Leiden, 2008.

'Um 1055. Was Herrscher taten, wenn sie viele Söhne hatten – zum Beispiel im Osten Europas', in *Die Macht des Königs. Herrschaft in Europa vom Frühmittelalter bis in die Neuzeit*, ed. Bernhard Jüssen, Munich, 2005, 125–37.

'"Vivat princeps in eternum": sacrality of ducal power in Poland in the earlier Middle Ages', in *Monotheistic Kingship: The Medieval Variants*, ed. Aziz Al-Azmeh, Budapest, 2004, 215–30.

Derwich, Marek, 'Les deux fondations de l'abbaye de Lubiń dans le cadre de l'implantation de monachisme bénédictin en Pologne (moitié de XIe–fin du XIIe siècle)', *Le Moyen Âge* 108 (2002): 9–24.

'Die Prämonstratensenorden im mittelalterlichen Polen. Seine Rolle in Kirche und Gesellschaft', in *Studien zum Prämonstratensenorden*, ed. Irene Crusius and Helmut Flachenecker, Göttingen, 2003, 311–47.

Dragoun, Zdeňek, 'Romanesque Prague and new archaeological discoveries', in *Prague and Bohemia: Medieval Art, Architecture and Cultural Exchange in Central Europe*, ed. Zoë Opačić, British Archaeological Association Conference Transactions 32, Leeds, 2009, 34–47.

Dvořáčková-Malá, Dana, 'Dvorská kultura přemyslovského období: nástin problematiky a možnosti výzkumu', *Mediaevalia Historica Bohemica* 12, 1 (2009): 9–43.

Engel, Pál, *The Realm of St Stephen: A History of Medieval Hungary 895–1526*, London, 2001.

Fedeles, Tamás and Irén Bilkei, eds., *Loca credibilia: hiteleshelyek a középkori Magyarországon*, Pécs, 2009.

Fiala, Zdenek, 'Die Organisation der Kirche in Přemyslidenstaat des 10.–13. Jahrhundert', in *Siedlung und Verfassung Böhmens in der Frühzeit*, ed. František Graus and Herbert Ludat, Wiesbaden, 1967, 133–43.

Font, Márta F., 'Politische Beziehungen zwischen Ungarn und der Kiever Rus' im 12. Jahrhundert', *Ungarn Jahrbuch* 18 (1990): 1–18.

*Im Spannungsfeld der christlichen Großmächte. Mittel- und Osteuropa im 10.-12. Jahrhundert*, tr. Tibor Schäfer, Herne, 2008.

Fried, Johannes, *Otto III. und Boleslav Chrobry. Das Widmungsbild des Aachener Evangeliars, der 'Akt von Gnesen' und das frühe polnische und ungarische Königtum*, Stuttgart, 1989.

Frolík, Jan, 'Hroby Přemyslovskych knižat na Pražskem Hrade', in *Castrum Pragense*, vol. I, Prague, 2005, 25–46.

Frolík, Jan, Marshall Joseph Becker and Jitka Petříčková, *Nejstarši sakrálni architektura Pražského hradu: Výpověd archeologických pramenů, Castrum Pragense*, vol. III, Prague, 2000.

Fügedi, Erik, *Castle and Society in Medieval Hungary (1000–1437)*, tr. János M. Bak, Budapest, 1986.

*Kings, Bishops, Nobles and Burghers in Medieval Hungary*, ed. János M. Bak, London, 1986.

Garipzanov, Ildar, Patrick Geary and Przemysław Urbańczyk, eds., *Franks, Northmen, and Slavs: Identities and State Formation in Early Medieval Europe*, Turnhout, 2008.

Gawlas, Sławomir, 'Fürstenherrschaft, Geldwirtschaft und Landesausbau. Zur Modernisierungsprozess im piastischen Polen', in *Rechtsstadtgründungen im mittelalterlichen Polen*, ed. Eduard Mühle, Cologne, 2011, 13–76.

'Der hl. Adalbert als Landespatron und die frühe Nationenbildung bei den Polen', in *Polen und Deutschland vor 1000 Jahren. Die Berliner Tagung über den Akt von Gnesen*, ed. Benjamin Scheller, Europa im Mittelalter, Abhandlungen und Beiträge zur historischen Komparatistik, 5, Berlin, 2002, 193–233.

*O kształt zjednoczonego królestwa: niemieckie władztwo terytorialne a geneza społecznoustrojowej odrębności Polski*, Warsaw, 1996.

'Polen: eine Ständegesellschaft an der Peripherie des lateinischen Europa', in *Europa im späten Mittelalter. Politik – Gesellschaft – Kultur*, ed. Rainer

Christoph Schwinges, Christian Hesse and Peter Moraw, Historische Zeitschrift – Beihefte n.s. 40, Munich, 2006, 237–61.

'Die Probleme des Lehnswesens und Feudalismus aus polnischer Sicht', in *Das europäische Mittelalter im Spannungsfeld des Vergleichs. Zwanzig internationale Beiträge zu Praxis, Problemen und Perspektiven der historischen Komparatistik*, ed. Michael Borgolte and Ralf Lusiardi, Berlin, 2001, 97–123.

'Die zentrale Funktion der Städte in Ostmitteleuropa in der Zeit des Landesausbaus', in *Städtelandschaften im Ostseeraum im Mittelalter und in der frühen Neuzeit*, eds. Roman Czaja and Carsten Jahnke, Toruń, 2009, 9–28.

Geary, Patrick J., *The Myth of Nations: The Medieval Origins of Europe*, Princeton, 2002.

Gedai, István, *Die Friesacher Münze im Alpen-Adria-Raum*, Graz, 1996.

Gerevich, László, ed., *Towns in Medieval Hungary*, Boulder, CO, 1990.

Gerics, József, 'Von den Universi Servientes Regis bis zu der Universitas Nobilium Regni Hungariae', *Album Elemér Mályusz*, Brussels, 1976, 97–108.

Gieysztor, Aleksander [Alexander], *L'Europe nouvelle autour de l'An Mil: la papauté, l'empire et les 'nouveaux venus2019*, Rome, 1997.

'Les Juifs et leur activité économique en Europe Orientale', in *Gli ebrei nell'alto medioevo*, Settimane di studio del centro italiano di studi sull'alto medioevo, 26/1, Spoleto, 1980, 498–528.

'Politische Heilige im hochmittelalterlichen Polen und Böhmen', in *Politik und Heiligenverehrung im Hochmittelalter*, ed. Jürgen Petersohn, Sigmaringen, 1994, 325–41.

'Sanctus et gloriosissimus martyr Christi Adalbertus: un état et une église missionaires aux alentours de l'an Mille', in *La conversione al Cristianesimo nell'Europa dell'alto medioevo*, Settimane di Studi del Centro Italiano di Studi sull'Alto Medioevo, 14, Spoleto, 1967, 611–47.

'Symboles de la royauté en Pologne: un groupe de manuscrits du XIe et du début du XIIe siècle', *Comptes rendus: Académie des Inscriptions et Belles-Lettres* 1 (1990): 128–37.

Gillett, Andrew, ed., *On Barbarian Identity: Critical Approaches to Ethnicity in the Early Middle Ages*, Turnhout, 2002.

Göckenjan, Hansgerd, *Hilfsvölker und Grenzwächter im Mittelalterlichen Ungarn*, Wiesbaden, 1972.

*Ungarn, Türken und Mongolen. Kleine Schriften von Hansgerd Göckenjan*, ed. Michael Knüppel and Eberhard Winkler, Wiesbaden, 2007.

Gołąb, Zbigniew, *The Origins of the Slavs: A Linguist's View*, Columbus, OH, 1992.

Goliński, Mateusz, 'Jews in medieval Legnica: their location in municipal areas', in *Jews in Silesia*, ed. Marcin Wodziński and Janusz Spyra, Cracow, 2001, 17–32.

Górecki, Piotr, 'Assimilation, resistance and ethnic group formation in medieval Poland: a European paradigm?', in *Das Reich und Polen. Parallelen,*

*Interaktionen und Formen der Akkulturation im hohen und späten Mittelalter*, ed. Thomas Wünsch and Alexander Patschovsky, Vorträge und Forschungen 59, Ostfildern, 2003, 447–76.

*Economy, Society and Lordship in Medieval Poland, 1100–1250*, New York, 1992.

*A Local Society in Transition: The Henryków Book and Related Documents*, Toronto, 2007.

*Parishes, Tithes and Society in Earlier Medieval Poland, ca. 1100–1250*, Philadelphia, 1983.

'Words, concepts and phenomena: knighthood, lordship and the early Polish nobility, c. 1100–1350', in *Nobles and Nobility in Medieval Europe: Concepts, Origins, Transformations*, ed. Anne Duggan, London, 2000, 115–55.

Górecki, Piotr and Nancy Van Deusen, eds., *Central and Eastern Europe in the Middle Ages: A Cultural History*, London and New York, 2009.

Görich, Knut, *Friedrich Barbarossa. Biographie*, Munich, 2011.

Graus, František, 'Slovanská liturgie a pisemnictvi v přemyslovských Čechách 10. století', *Československý Časopis Historický* 14 (1966): 473–95.

Grudziński, Tadeusz, *Boleslaus the Bold and Bishop Stanislaus: The Story of a Conflict*, Warsaw, 1985.

Gumowski, Marian, *Hebräische Münzen im mittelalterlichen Polen*, Graz, 1975.

Györffy, György, *King Saint Stephen of Hungary*, Highland Lakes, NJ, 1994.

Gyulai, Ferenc, *Archaeobotany in Hungary: Seed, Fruit, Food and Beverage Remains in the Carpathian Basin from the Neolithic to the Late Middle Ages*, Budapest, 2010.

Hanak, Walter K., 'Saint Procopius, the Sázava monastery and the Byzantine–Slavonic legacy: Some reconsiderations', *Byzantina et slavica cracoviensia* 1 (1991): 71–80.

Hásková, Jarmila, *Česká mince doby románské*, Cheb, 1975.

'The Groschien period', in Jiří Sejbal *et al.*, *Money in the Czech Lands before 1919*, Pacov, 1996, 51–61.

Higounet, Charles, *Les Allemands en Europe centrale et orientale au Moyen Âge*, Paris, 1989.

Hilsch, Peter, *Die Bischöfe von Prag in der frühen Stauferzeit. Ihre Stellung zwischen Reichs- und Landesgewalt von Daniel I. (1148–1167) bis Heinrich (1182–1197)*, Munich, 1969.

'Die Juden in Böhmen und Mähren im Mittelalter und die ersten Privilegien (bis zum Ende des 13. Jahrhunderts)', in *Die Juden in den Böhmischen Ländern. Vorträge der Tagung des Collegium Carolinum in Bad Wiessee vom 27. bis 29. November 1981*, ed. Ferdinand Seibt, Munich, 1983, 13–26.

Hlaváček, Ivan, 'Die Aufenthalte Rudolfs I. in Böhmen und Mähren aus verwaltungs und rechtsgeschichtlicher Sicht', in *Rudolf von Habsburg 1273–1291*, Cologne, Weimar and Vienna, 1993, 80–5.

'Böhmisch-österreichischen Nachbarschaft bis zu den Anfängen Přemysl II.', in *Böhmisch-österreichische Beziehungen im 13. Jahrhundert. Österreich (einschliesslich Steiermark, Kärnten und Krain) in Grossreichsprojekt Ottokars II. Přemysl, König von Böhmen*, Prague, 1998, 11–23.

*Knihy a knihovny v českém středověku (studie k jejich dějinám do husitství)*, Prague, 2005.

Hledíková, Zdenka, 'Das Studium von mittelalterlichen kirchlichen Korporationen in Böhmen und Mähren', *Quaestiones Medii Aevi Novae* 2 (1997): 61–9.

'Úcta sv. Ludmily mezi 12. a 14. stoletím a její formování v klášteře sv. Jiří na Pražském hradě', in *Nomine Liudmilam: sborník prací k poctě svaté Ludmily/Nomine Liudmilam: Collection of Works in Honour of St Ludmila*, Mělník, 2006, 41–53.

Hoensch, Jörg K., 'Höfische Kultur in Böhmen unter Wenzel I. und Přemysl Otakar II.', in *Aspekte kultureller Integration. Festschrift zu Ehren von Prof. Dr Antonín Meštan*, eds. Karel Mácha and Peter Drews, Munich, 1991, 175–89.

*Přemysl Otakar II. von Böhmen. Der goldene König*, Graz, Vienna and Cologne, 1989.

Hoffmann, Jürgen, *Vita Adalberti. Früheste Textüberlieferungen der Lebensgeschichte Adalberts von Prag*, Essen, 2005.

Holtzman, Robert, 'Über den Polenfeldzug Friedrich Barbarossas vom Jahre 1157 und die Begründung schlesischer Herzogthümer', *Zeitschrift des Vereins für Geschichte Schlesiens* 56 (1922): 42–55.

Hrdlička, Ladislav, 'The archeological study of the historical centre of Prague: 1969–1993', in *25 Years of Archeological Research in Bohemia*, Prague, 1994 (*Památky Archologické*, Supplementum 1), 174–84.

Hunyadi, Zsolt, *The Hospitallers in the Medieval Kingdom of Hungary c. 1150–1387*, Budapest, 2010.

'Maiores, optimates, nobiles: semantic questions in the early history of the Hungarian nobility', *Annual of Medieval Studies at the CEU 1996/1997* (1998): 204–11.

'The Teutonic Order in Burzenland (1211–1225): recent reconsiderations', in *L'Ordine Teutonico tra Mediterraneo e Baltico: incontri e scontri tra religioni, popoli e cultura; atti del convegno internazionale di studio Bari-Lecce-Brindisi, 14–16 settembre*, ed. Hubert Houben and Kristjan Toomaspoeg, Galatina, 2008, 151–72.

Irgang, Wolfgang, '"Libertas Ecclesiae" und landesherrliche Gewalt. Vergleich zwischen dem Reich und Polen', in *Das Reich und Polen. Paralellen, Interaktionen und Formen der Akkulturation im hohen und späten Mittelalter*, eds. Alexander Patschovsky and Thomas Wünsch, Stuttgart, 2003, 93–118.

Iwańczak, Wojciech, 'Innocent III and Bohemia', in *Innocenzo III. Urbs et orbis. Atti del Congresso Internazionale (Roma, 9–15 settembre 1998)*, ed. Andrea Sommerlechner, vol. II, Rome, 2003, 1200–12.

'Political culture of the nobility in late medieval Poland', in *Political Culture in Central Europe, Tenth–Twentieth Century*, vol. I, *Middle Ages and Early Modern Era*, ed. Halina Manikowska and Jaroslav Pánek, Prague, 2005, 101–11.

Jan, Libor, 'Die Anfänge der Pfarrorganisation in Böhmen und Mähren', in *Pfarreien im Mittelalter. Deutschland, Polen, Tschechien und Ungarn im*

*Vergleich*, eds. Nathalie Kruppa and Leszek Zygner, Veröffentlichungen des Max-Planck-Instituts für Geschichte, 238, Göttingen, 2008, 183–99.

'Böhmische and mährische Adelige als Förderer und Midglieder der geistlichen Ritterorden', in *The Crusades and Military Orders: Expanding the Frontiers of Medieval Latin Christianity*, ed. Zsolt Hunyadi and József Laszlovszky, Budapest, 2001, 303–17.

*Česka moravská šlechta ve 13. a 14. stoleti: otazky zrodu a kontinuity*, Brno, 2011.

'Hereditas, výsluha, kastelánie: nekolik poznámek k terminologii a metodologii současné historiografie přemyslovského období', *Časopis Matice Moravske* 128 (2009): 461–72.

'Několik postřehů k vývoji panovnické komory, soudů a správy země', in *Pocta Janu Janákovi: předsedovi Matice moravské, profesoru Masarykovy univerzity věnují k sedmdesátinám jeho přátelé a žáci*, ed. Bronislav Chocholác, Brno, 2002, 75–83.

'K počátkum ceské šlechty: družina, beneficium, pozemkové vlastnictví', in *Šlechta, moc a reprezentace ve středověku*, ed. Martin Nodl and Martin Wihoda, Prague, 2007, 45–52.

'Skryty půvab "středoevropského modelu"', *Český Časopis Historický* 105, 4 (2007): 873–902.

*Václav II. a struktury panovnické moci*, Brno, 2006.

'Das Zeitalter der Gewalt und der freundschaftlichen Kontakte. Gemeinsame Wurzeln des tschechisch-österreichischen Raumes in Mitteleuropa', in *Tschechen und Österreicher*, 31–41.

'Zrod zemského soudu v Čechách'. In *Kultura prawna w Europie Środkowej*, ed. Antoni Barciak, Katowice, 2006, 74–84.

Janáček, Josef, 'Stříbro a ekonomika českých zemi ve 13. stoleti', *Československý Časopis Historický* 20 (1972): 875–906.

Janeczek, Andrzej, 'Ethnische Gruppenbildung im spätmittelalterliche Polen', in *Das Reich und Polen. Parallelen, Interaktionen und Formen der Akkulturation im hohen und späten Mittelalter*, ed. Alexander Patschovsky and Thomas Wünsch, Vorträge und Forschungen 59, Ostfildern, 2003, 401–46.

Jilek, Heinrich, 'Die Wenzels- und Ludmila-Legenden des 10. und 11. Jahrhunderts (Neuere Froschungsergbnisse)', *Zeitschrift für Ostforschung* 24 (1975): 79–148.

Jurek, Tomasz, 'Der Einfluss Böhmens auf das geteilte Polens im 13. Jahrhundert', in *Böhmen und seine Nachbarn in den Přemyslidenzeit*, ed. Ivan Hlaváček and Alexander Patschovsky, Ostfildern, 2011, 161–202.

'Fremde Ritter im mittelalterlichen Polen', *Questiones Medii Aevi Novae* 3 (1998): 19–49.

'Geneza szlachty polskiej', in *Šlechta, moc a reprezentace ve středověku*, ed. Martin Nodl and Martin Wihoda, Prague, 2007, 63–140.

'Ritual und Technik der sozialen Kommunikation zwischen Landesherren und Gesellschaft in Polen im 13. Jahrhundert', in *Ritualisierung politischer Willensbildung. Polen und Deutschland im hohen und späten Mittelalter*, ed. Wojciech Fałkowski, Wiesbaden, 2010, 101–26.

Justová, Jarmila, 'The bailay of the ducal residence at Libice-nad-Cidlinou and its hinterland', in *Archeology in Bohemia 1986–1990*, Prague, 1991, 140–5.

Kadlec, Jaroslav, 'Die Franziskaner in den böhmischen Ländern und ihre Generalstudium in vorhussitischer Zeit', *Archiv für Kirchengeschichte von Böhmen-Mähren-Schlesien* 8 (1987): 84–91.

'Der heilige Prokop', in *Tausend Jahre Benediktiner in den Klöstern Břevnov, Braunau und Rohr im Auftrag der Abteien Břevnov und Braunau in Rohr*, St Ottilien, 1993, 309–24.

Kajmakamova, Milijana V., M. Salamon and Malgorzata Smorag Rózycka, ed., *Byzantium, New Peoples, New Powers: The Byzantino-Slav Contact Zone, from the Ninth to the Fifteenth Century*, Cracow, 2007.

Kalandra, Zaviš, *České pohanství*, Prague, 1947.

Kalhous, David, *České země za prvních Přemyslovců v 10.–12. století*, Prague, 2011.

'Slovanské písemnictví a liturgie 10. a 11. věku', *Český Časopis Historický* 108, 1(2010): 1–33.

Karwasińska, Jadwiga, *Święty Wojciech: wybór pism*, Warsaw, 1996.

Kavka, František, 'Die Städte Böhmens und Mährens zur Zeit des Přmysliden Staates', in *Die Städte Mitteleuropas im 12. und 13. Jahrhundert*, ed. Wilhelm Rausch, Linz, 1963, 137–53.

Kejř, Jiří, 'Böhmen und das Reich unter Friedrich I', in *Friedrich Barbarossa. Handlungsspielräume und Wirkungsweisen des staufischen Kaisers*, ed. Arnold Haverkamp, Sigmaringen, 1992, 241–89.

'Böhmen zur Zeit Friedrich Barbarossas', in *Kaiser Friedrich Barbarossa. Landesausbau – Aspekte seiner Politik – Wirkung*, eds. Bernhard Töpfer and Evamaria Engel, Weimar, 1994, 101–13.

*Die mittelalterlichen Städte in den böhmischen Ländern. Gründung – Verfassung – Entwicklung*, Cologne, 2010.

'Ursprung und Entwicklung von Stadt- und Marktrecht in Böhmen und Mähren', *Bohemia. Zeitschrift für Geschichte und Kultur der Böhmischen Länder* 31, 2 (1990): 270–82.

'Zwei Studien über die Anfänge der Städteverfassung in den böhmischen Ländern', *Historica* 16 (1969): 81–142.

Kiss, Gergely, 'Contribution à l'évolution des chapitres dans la Hongrie médiévale', *Specimina Nova Pars Prima: Sectio mediaevalis* 1 (2001): 107–19.

'The exemption of the royal Benedictine monasteries in Hungary in the eleventh-thirteenth centuries', *Specimina Nova Pars Prima Sectio Mediaevalis* 2 (2003): 25–63.

'Les influences de l'Église orthodoxe en Hongrie aux Xe–XIIIe siècles', *Specimina Nova Pars Prima Sectio Mediaevalis* 4 (2007): 51–71.

Klaniczay, Gábor, *Holy Rulers and Blessed Princesses: Dynastic Cults in Medieval Central Europe*, tr. Éva Pálmai, Cambridge, 2002.

Klápště, Jan. 'Studies of structural change in medieval settlement in Bohemia', *Antiquity* 65, 247 (1991): 396–405.

Klápště, Jan and Zdeněk Smetánka, 'The archeology of medieval villages in Bohemia and Moravia (Czech Republic)', *Ruralia* 1 (1996) (*Památky Archologické*, Supplementum 5): 331–8.

'The settlement pattern within the medieval landscape near Kostelec nad Černými lesy (Central Bohemia)', *Ruralia* 2 (1999) (*Památky Archologické*, Supplementum 11): 226–36.

Klápšte, Jan, Zdenek Smetánka and Martin Tomášek, 'The medieval Bohemian town and its hinterland', *Ruralia* 3 (2000) (*Památky Archologické*, Supplementum 14): 294–302.

Kłoczowski, Jerzy, 'Les paroisses en Bohême, en Hongrie et en Pologne (XI–XIII siècles)', in *Le istituzioni ecclesiastiche della 'Societas Christiana' dei secoli XI–XII: diocesi, pievi e parocchie. Atti della sesta settimana internazionale di studio Milano, 1–7 settembre 1974*, Milan, 1977, 187–98 (Miscellanea del Centro di Studi Medioevali 8).

Kłoczowski, Jerzy and Hubert Łaszkiewicz, eds., *East-Central Europe in European History: Themes and Debates*, Lublin, 2009.

Kobusiewicz, Michał, ed., *Pradzieje Wielkopolski od epoki kamienia do średniowiecza*, Poznań, 2008.

Kőfalvi, Tamás, 'Places of authentication (loca credibilia)', *Chronica: Annual of the Institute of History University of Szeged* 2 (2002): 27–38.

Kossmann, Eugen Oskar, 'Vom altpolnischen Opole, schlesischen Weichbild und Powiat des Adels', *Zeitschrift für Ostforschung* 42 (1993): 161–94.

Koszta, László, 'Die Domkapitel und ihre Domherren bis Anfang des 12. Jahrhunderts in Ungarn', in *The Man of Many Devices, Who Wandered Full Many Ways . . . Festschrift in Honor of János M. Bak*, ed. Balázs Nagy and Marcell Sebők, Budapest, 1999, 478–91.

'Die Gründung von Zisterzienserklöstern in Ungarn 1142–1270', *Ungarn Jahrbuch* 23 (1997): 65–80.

Kovács, László, ed., *Honfoglalás és régészet*, Budapest, 1994.

'Muslimische Münzen im Karpatenbecken des 10. Jahrhundert', *Antaeus* 29–30 (2008): 479–533.

'Die zwischen 1000 und 1141 verborgene Hortfunde des Karpatenbeckens', *Acta Archaeologica Academiae Scientiarum Hungaricae* 59 (2008): 429–55.

Kovács, László and László Veszprémy, eds., *A Honfoglaláskor írott forrásai*, Budapest, 1996.

Kovács, Tibor and István Bardoly, eds., *The Coronation Mantle of the Hungarian Kings*, Budapest, 2005.

Kowalewski, Krzysztof, *Rycerze, włodycy, panosze: ludzie systemu lennego w średniowiecznych Czechach*, Warsaw, 2009.

Kowalska, Zofia, 'Die grosspolnischen und schlesischen Judenschutzbriefe des 13. Jahrhunderts im Verhältnis zu den Privilegien Kaiser Friedrichs II (1238) und Herzog Friedrichs II von Österreich (1244). Filiation der Dokumente und inhaltliche Analyse', *Zeitschrift für Ostmitteleuropa Forschung* 47 (1998): 1–20.

Krása, Josef, *České iluminované rukopisy 13./16. století*, ed. Karel Stejskal, Petr Wittlich and Rostislav Švácha, Prague, 1990.

Kristó, Gyula, *Early Transylvania (895–1324)*, Budapest, 2003.

*Histoire de la Hongrie médiévale: le temps des Arpads*, tr. Chantal Philippe, Rennes, 2001.

*Hungarian History in the Ninth Century*, tr. Gy. Novák and E. Kelly, Szeged, 1996.

*Magyar Historiográfia I: történetírás a középkori Magyarországon*, Budapest, 2002.

*Nichtungarische Völker im mittelalterlichen Ungarn*, tr. Tibor Schäfer, Herne, 2008.

Kristó, Gyula, Pál Engel and András Kubinyi, eds., *Historische Demographie Ungarns (896–1996)*, tr. Tibor Schäfer, Herne, 2007.

Kristó, Gyula, Pál Engel and Ferenc Makk, *Korai Magyar Történeti Lexikon: 9.–14. század*, Budapest, 1994.

Kristó, Gyula and Ferenc Makk, *Die Ersten Könige Ungarns. Die Herrscher der Arpaden-dynastie*, tr. Tibor Schäfer, Herne, 1999.

Krumphanzlová, Zdenka, '*Der Ritus der slawischen Skelttfriedhöfe der mittleren und jüngeren Burgwallzeit in Böhmen*', *Památky Archeologické* 57 (1966): 277–327.

Krzemieńska, Barbara L., *Boj knížete Břetislava I. o upravnění českého státu (1039–1041)*, Prague, 1974.

*Břetislav I. Čechy a středni Evropa v prvé poloviné XI století*, Prague, 1999.

'Břetislav II. Pokus o charakteristiku osbnosti panovnika', *Československy Časopis Historický* 35 (1987): 722–31.

Krzemieńska, Barbara and Dušan Třeštík, 'Hospodářské základy raně středověkého státu ve střední Evropě (Čechy, Polsko, Uhry v 10. a 11. století)', *Hospodářské dějiny / Economic history. Praha, Ústav československých a světových dějin Československé akademie věd* 1 (1978): 149–230.

'Zur Problematik der Dienstleute im frühmittelalterlichen Böhmen', in *Siedlung und Verfassung Böhmens in der Frühzeit*, ed. František Graus and Herbert Ludat, Wiesbaden, 1967, 70–98.

Kubinyi, András, József Laszlovszky and Péter Szabó, eds., *Gazdaság és gazdálkodás a középkori Magyarországon: gazdaságtörténet, anyagi kultúra, régészet*, Budapest, 2008.

Kuhn, Walter, *Die deutschrechtliche Städte in Schlesien und Polen in der ersten Hälfte des 13. Jahrhunderts*, Marburg am Lahn, 1968.

Kürbis, Brygida, 'Gertrudianischen Gebete im Psalterium Egberti. Ein Beitrag zur Geschichte der Frömmigkeit im 11. Jahrhundert', in *Europa Slavica – Europa Orientalis. Festschrift für Herbert Ludat zum 70. Geburtstag*, eds. Klaus-Detlev Grothusen and Klaus Zernack, Berlin, 1980, 248–61.

'Epitafium Bolesława Chrobrego: analiza literacka i historyczna', in Kürbis, *Na progach historii*, vol. II, *O świadectwach do dziejów kultury Polski średniowiecznej*, Poznań, 2001, 243–82.

ed., *Kodeks Matyldy: księga obrzędów z kartami dedykacyjnymi*, Cracow, 2000.

Kurnatowska, Zofia, 'Ostrów Lednicki in the early Middle Ages', in *Polish Lands at the Turn of the First and the Second Millennium*, ed. Przemysław Urbańczyk, Warsaw, 2004, 167–84.

'The stronghold in Gniezno in the light of older and more recent studies', in *Polish Lands at the Turn of the First and the Second Millennium*, ed. Przemysław Urbańczyk, Warsaw, 2004, 185–206.

Kuthan, Jiři, 'Der böhmische und polnische König Wenzel II. (1271–1305) als Gründer, Bauherr und Auftraggeber von Kunstwerken', in *Sedlec: historie, architektura a umělecká tvorba sedleckého kláštera ve středoevropském kontextu kolem roku 1300 a 1700. Mezinárodní sympozium, Kutná Hora 18.–20. září 2008. / Sedletz. Geschichte, Architektur und Kunstschaffen im Sedletzer Kloster im mitteleuropäischen Kontext um die Jahre 1300 und 1700. Internationales Symposium, Kuttenberg 18–20. September 2008*, Prague, 2009, 39–69.

*Die mittelalterliche Baukunst der Zisterzienser in Böhmen und in Mähren*, Munich, 1982.

*Přemysl Ottokar II. König, Bauherr und Mäzen. Höfische Kunst um die Mitte des 13. Jahrhunderts*, Vienna, Cologne and Weimar, 1996.

Labuda, Gerard, 'Die Gründung der Metropolitanorganisation der polnischen Kirche auf der Synode in Gnesen am 9. und 10. März 1000', *Acta Poloniae Historica* 84 (2001): 5–30.

*Mieszko II król Polski (1025–1034): czas przełomu w dziejach państwa polskiego*, Poznań, 2008.

'O stosunkach prawnopublicznych między Polską a Niemcami w połowie XII w. (Merseburg 1135, Kaina 1146, Krzyszkowo 1157)', *Czasopismo Prawno-Historyczne* 25 (1973): 25–58.

*Studia nad początkami państwa polskiego*. vol. II, Poznań, 1988.

Lalik, Tadeusz, 'Märkte des 12. Jahrhunderts in Polen', in *L'artisanat et la vie urbaine en Pologne médiévale*, ed. Aleksander Gieysztor and Tadeusz Rosłanowski, Ergon 3, Kwartalnik Historii Kultury Materialnej 10 (1962), 3, Warsaw 1962, 364–7.

Lasota-Moskalewska, Alicja, 'Polish medieval farming in the light [of] archeozoology', *Questiones Medii Aevi Novae* 9 (2004): 205–16.

Laszlovszky, József, 'Hungarian university peregrinatio to western Europe in the second half of the twelfth century', in *Universitas Budensis 1395–1995: International Conference for the History of Universities on the Occasion of the 600th Anniversary of the Foundation of the University of Buda*, ed. László Szögi and Júlia Varga, Budapest, 1997, 51–61.

Leciejewicz, Lech, 'Die sozialen Eliten im frühpiastischen Polen', in *Die frühmittelalterliche Elite bei den Völkern des östlichen Mitteleuropas (mit einem speziellen Blick auf die großmährische Problematik). Materialien der internationalen Fachkonferenz, Mikulčice, 25.–26.5.2004*, ed. Pavel Kouril, Brno, 2005, 353–8.

Łowmiański, Henryk, *Początki Polski*, vols. I–VI, Warsaw, 1963–85.

'The problem of the origins of the Polish state in recent historical research', *Questiones Medii Aevi* 1 (1977): 33–70.

Lübke, Christian, *Arbeit und Wirtschaft im östlichen Mitteleuropa. Die Spezialisierung menschlicher Tätigkeit im Spiegel der hochmittelalterlichen Toponymie in den Herrschaftsgebieten von Piasten, Premysliden und Arpaden*, Stuttgart, 1991.

'Ethnic Diversity in East Central Europe and the beginnings of the economic change in the High Middle Ages', in *Movimientos, migratorios, asentamientos y expansion: siglos VIII–XI*, Pamplona, 2008, 289–304.

'Multiethnizität und Stadt als Faktoren gesellschaftlicher und staatlicher Entwicklung im östlichen Europa', in *Burg – Burgstadt – Stadt. Zur Genese mittelalterlicher nichtagrarischer Zentren in Ostmitteleuropa*, ed. Hans Brachmann, Berlin, 1995, 36–50.

*Regesten zur Geschichte der Slawen an Elbe und Oder (vom Jahr 900 an)*, vols. I–V, Berlin, 1984–88.

'Das Reich von Kiev als Faktor der Beziehungen zwischen Deutschland und Polen (10.–11. Jahrhundert)', in *Mittelalter – eines oder viele? / Średniowiecze – jedno czy wiele?*, ed. Sławomir Moździoch, Wojciech Mrozowicz and Stanisław Rosik, Wrocław, 2010, 127–39.

Ludat, Hermann, *An Elbe und Oder von das Jahr 1000*, Cologne and Vienna, 1971.

Macek, Josef, 'Das Turnier im mittelalterlichen Böhmen', in *Das ritterliche Turnier im Mittelalter. Beiträge zu einer vergleichenden Formen- und Verhaltensgeschichte des Rittertums*, ed. Josef Fleckenstein, Göttingen, 1985, 371–89.

Machilek, Franz, 'Die Adalbertsverehrung in Böhmen im Mittelalter', in *Adalbert von Prag: Brückenbauer zwischen dem Osten und Westen Europas*, Baden-Baden, 1997, 163–83.

Magocsi, Paul Robert, *Historical Atlas of East Central Europe*, Seattle, 1993.

Makk, Ferenc, *The Árpáds and the Comneni: Political Relations between Hungary and Byzantium in the Twelfth Century*, Budapest, 1989.

*Ungarische Außenpolitik (896–1196)*, Herne, 1999.

Makkai, László and András Mócsy, eds., *History of Transylvania*, vol. I, Boulder, CO, 2001.

Maleczyński, Karol, Maria Bielińska and Antoni Gąsiorowski, *Dyplomatyka polska wieków średnich*, Warsaw, 1971.

Manikowska, Halina, 'Melioratio terrae and system transformations on lands to the east of the Odra during the thirteenth century and the late Middle Ages', in *Poteri economici e poteri politici, secc. XIII–XVIII: atti della trentesima settimana di studi, 27 aprile–1 maggio 1998*, ed. Simonetta Cavaciocchi, Florence, 1999, 303–23.

Marcantonio, Angela, *The Uralic Language Family: Facts, Myths and Statistics*, Oxford, 2002.

Mareš, Franz Wenzel, 'Die slavische Liturgie in Böhmen zur Zeit der Gründung der Prager Bistums', in *Millennium dioecesis Pragensis 973–1973. Beiträge zur Kirchengeschichte Mitteleuropas im 9.–11. Jahrhundert. Tausend Jahre Prager Bistum*, ed. Franz Zagiba, Annales Instituti Slavici 8, Vienna, 1974, 95–110.

Mařík, Jan, 'The Slavniks and Saxony', in *Der Wandel um 1000. Beiträge der Sektion zur Slavischen Frühgeschichte der 18. Jahrestagung des Mittel- und*

*Ostdeutschen Verbandes für Altertumsforschung in Greifswald, 23. bis 27. März 2009*, ed. Felix Biermann, Thomas Kersting and Anne Klammt, Greifswald, 2011, 191–7.

Marosi, Ernő, *Die Anfänge der Gotik in Ungarn. Esztergom in der Kunst des 12.–13. Jahrhunderts*, Budapest, 1984.

Mašek, Michal, Petr Sommer and Josef Žemlička, *Vladislav II. Druhý král z Přemyslova rodu. K 850. výročí jeho korunovace*, Prague, 2009.

Matla, Marzena, *Pierwsi Przemyślidzi i ich państwo (od X do połowy XI wieku): ekspansja terytorialna i jej polityczne uwarunkowania*, Poznań, 2008.

Mende, Balázs Gusztáv, ed., *Research on the Prehistory of the Hungarians: A Review*, Varia Archaeologica Hungarica 18, Budapest, 2005.

Merhautová, Anežka and Pavel Spunar, *Kodex vyšehradský: korunovační evangelistář prvního českého krále*, Prague, 2006.

Merhautová-Livorová, Anežka, *Bazilika sv. Jiří na pražském hradě*, Prague, 1972.

Michałowski, Roman, 'La christianisation de la Pologne aux X$_e$–XII$_e$ siècles', in *Clovis. Histoire et memoire. Actes du Colloque International d'Histoire de Reims du 19 au 25 septembre 1996*, ed. Michel Rouche, vol. II, Paris, 1997, 419–34.

'Christianisation of political culture in Poland in the tenth and the early eleventh century', in *Political Culture in Central Europe (Tenth–Twentieth century)*, vol. I, *Middle Ages and Early Modern Era*, ed. Halina Manikowska and Jaroslav Pánek, Prague, 2005, 31–40.

'Christianisation of the Piast monarchy in the tenth and eleventh centuries', *Acta Poloniae Historica* 101 (2010): 5–35.

'The nine-week Lent in Boleslaus the Brave's Poland: a study of the first Piasts' "religious policy"', *Acta Poloniae Historica* 89 (2004): 5–50.

*Zjazd gnieźnieński: religijne przesłani powstania arcybiskupstwa gnieźnieńskiego*, Wrocław, 2005.

Mishin, Dmitrij, 'Ibrahim ibn-Ya'qub al-Turtushi's account of the Slavs from the middle of the tenth century', *Annual of Medieval Studies at the CEU, 1994–1995* (1996): 184–99.

*Modlitwy księżnej Gertrudy z Psałterza Egberta z kalendarzem*, ed. Małgorzata H. Malewicz and Brygida Kürbis, Cracow, 2002.

Modzelewski, Karol, 'Comites, principes, nobiles: the structure of ruling class as reflected in the terminology used by Gallus Anonymous', in *The Polish Nobility in the Middle Ages: Anthology*, ed. Antoni Gąsiorowski, Wrocław, 1984, 177–206.

'La division autarchique du travail à l'échelle d'un État: l'organisation "ministériale" en Pologne médiévale', *Annales: Économies, Sociétés, Civilisation* 19, 6 (1964): 1125–38.

*L'Europe des barbares: Germains et slaves face aux héritiers de Rome*, Paris, 2006 (Italian version, *L'Europa dei barbari: le culture tribali di fronte alla cultura romano-cristiana*, Turin, 2008).

'L'organisation de l'opole (vicinia) dans la Pologne des Piasts', *Acta Poloniae Historica* 57 (1988): 43–76.

'L'organizzazione delle Stato polacco nei secoli X–XIII: la società e le strutture del potere', in *Gli slavi occidentali e meridionali nell'alto medioevo.* vol. II, Settimane del Centro italiano di studi sull'alto medioevo, 30, Spoleto, 1983, 557–96.

'Le système des villages de "ministeriales" dans l'organisation économique de l'État polonais aux Xe–XIIIe siècles', *Fasciculi Historici* 9 (1977): 21–8.

'Servi, heredes, ascripticii: la conditio paysanne aux yeux du groupe dirigeant en Pologne médievale', *Questiones Medii Aevi* 4 (1990): 45–69.

'The system of the ius ducale and the idea of feudalism (comments on the earliest class society in medieval Poland)', *Questiones Medii Aevi* 1 (1977): 71–99.

'Le système du ius ducale en Pologne et le concept de féodalisme', *Annales Économies, Sociétés, Civilisation* 37, 1 (1982): 164–82.

'Thing und Acht. Zu vergleichenden Studien der germanischen und slawischen Stammesverfassung', in *Leges-Gentes-Regna. Zur Rolle von germanischen Rechtsgewohnheiten und lateinischer Schriftstradition bei der Ausbildung der frühmittelalterlichen Rechtskultur*, eds. Gerhard Dilcher and Eva-Marie Distler, Berlin, 2006, 79–89.

Molenda, Danuta, 'Die Beteiligung fremder Fachleute im Erzbergbau im mittelalterlichen Polen', *Questiones Medii Aevi Novae* 3 (1998): 177–204.

'Mining town in Central–Eastern Europe in feudal times: problem outline', *Acta Poloniae Historica* 34 (1976): 165–88.

'Der polnische Bleibergbau und seine Bedeutung für den europäischen Bleimarkt vom 12. bis 17. Jahrhundert', in *Montanwirtschaft Mitteleuropas vom 12. bis 17. Jahrhundert. Forschungsprobleme: Stand, Wege und Aufgabe der Forschung*, ed. Werner Kroker and Ekkehard Westermann, Bochum, 1984, 187–98.

Moravcsik, Gyula, *Byzantium and the Magyars*, Budapest, 1970.

Moszyński, Leszek, *Die vorchristliche Religion der Slaven im Lichte der slawischen Sprachwissenschaft*, Cologne, Weimar and Vienna, 1992.

Moździoch, Sławomir, 'Die frühstädtischen Siedlungskomplexe und Lokationsstädte in Schlesien im 12.–13. Jh. (Änderungen der Raumstruktur im Lichte der archäologischen Quellen)', in *Hausbau und Raumstruktur früher Städte in Ostmitteleuropa*, ed. Hansjürgen Brachmann (Památky Archologické,. Supplementum 6), Prague, 1996, 87–100.

'Das mittelalterliche Dorf in Polen im Lichte der archäologischen Forschung', *Ruralia* 1 (1996) (*Památky Archologické*, Supplementum 5): 282–93.

*Organizacja gospodarcza państwa wczesnopiastowskiego na Śląsku: studium archeologiczne*, Wrocław, Warsaw and Cracow, 1990.

'The origins of the medieval Polish towns', *Archaeologia Polona* 32 (1994): 129–53.

'Vorformen der Stadtentwicklung im südlichen Polen in 11.–12. Jh', in *Actes du XIIe Congres International des Sciences Préhistoriques et Protohistoriques*, Bratislava, 1993, 185–91.

Mrozowicz, Wojciech, 'Mittelalterliche Annalistik in Schlesien. Ein Beitrag zur neuen Ausgabe', *Questiones Medii Aevi Novae* 6 (2001): 277–96.

Mühle, Eduard, *Die Piasten, Polen im Mittelalter*, Munich, 2011.

Nagy, Balázs, ed., *A Tatárjárás*, Budapest, 2003.

Nemerkényi, Előd, *Latin Classics in Medieval Hungary: Eleventh Century*, Budapest, 2004.

Nestupný, Evžen, ed., *Space in Prehistoric Bohemia*, Prague, 1998.

Pálóczi Horváth, András, *Pechenegs, Cumans, Iasians: Steppe Peoples in Medieval Hungary*, Budapest, 1989.

Panzram, Bernhard, *Die schlesischen Archidiakonate und Archipresbyteriate bis zur Mitte des 14. Jahrhunderts*, Breslau, 1937.

Paramonova, Maria Y., 'Heiligkeit und Verwandschaft. Die dynastische Motive in den lateinischen Wenzelslegenden und den Legenden der Boris und Gleb', in *Fonctions sociales et politiques du culte des saints dans les sociétiés de rite grec et latin au Moyen Age et á l'epoque modern: Approche comparative*, ed. Marek Derwich and Michail Dmitriev, Wrocław, 1999, 433–55.

Paszkiewicz, Borys, 'Beginning of the Polish provincial coinage: some remarks', in *Peníze v promenách casu / Money in Metamorphosis of Time / Geld im Wandel der Zeit*, vol. IV, Ostrava, 2007, 21–40.

Pauk, Marcin Rafał, 'Der böhmische Adel im 13. Jahrhundert. Zwischen Herrschaftsbildung und Gemeinschaftsgefühl', in *Böhmen und seine Nachbarn in den Přemyslidenzeit*, ed. Ivan Hlaváček and Alexander Patschovsky, Ostfildern, 2011, 247–88.

*Działalność fundacyjna możnowładztwa czeskiego i jej uwarunkowania społeczne (XI–XIII wiek)*, Cracow, 2000.

Petersohn, Jürgen, *Die südliche Ostseeraum im kirchlich-politischen Kräftsspiel des Rechis, Polens und Dänmarks vom 10. bis 13. Jahrhundert. Mission – Kirchenorganisation – Kultpolitik*, Cologne and Vienna, 1979.

Petráček, Tomáš, *Fenomén darovaných lidí v českých zemích 11.–12. století: k poznání hospodářských a sociálních dějin českých zemí v době knížecí*, Prague, 2003.

Piekalski, Jerzy, *Von Köln nach Krakau. Der topographische Wandel früher Städte*, Berlin, 2001.

Piendl, Max, 'Böhmen und die Grafen von Bogen', *Bohemia* 3 (1962), 137–49.

Piskorski, Jan M., ed., *Pommern im Wandel der Zeiten*, Szczecin, 1999.

ed., *Historiographical Approaches to Medieval Colonization of East Central Europe*, Boulder, CO, 2002.

Pleszczyński, Andrzej, 'Miejsca władzy w Czechach w X–XII wieku: zarys modelu przestrzennego centrum wczesnośredniowiecznej wspólnoty, jego geneza i charakter ideowy', in *Sedes regni principales. Materiały z konferencji. Sandomierz 20–21 października 1997*, ed. Barbara Trelińska, Sandomierz, 1999, 81–94.

*Vyšehra: rezidence českých panovníků. Studie o rezidenci panovníka raného středověku na příkladu českého Vyšehradu*, Prague, 2002.

Plisiecki, Piotr, 'The parochial network and the tithes system in the medieval diocese Cracow', in *Pfarreien im Mittelalter. Deutschland, Polen, Tschechien und Ungarn im Vergleich*, eds. Nathalie Kruppa and Leszek Zygner, Veröffentlichungen des Max-Planck-Instituts für Geschichte, 238, Göttingen, 2008, 223–34.

Polakovič, Daniel, 'Medieval Hebrew inscriptions in Cheb (Eger)', *Judaica Bohemiae* 42 (2006): 5–52.

Prinz, Friedrich, 'Das Reich, Bayern, Böhmen und Österreich: Grundzüge einer historischen Nachbarschaft. Einige Vorüberlegungen', in Prinz, *Nation und Heimat. Beiträge zur böhmischen und sudetendeutschen Geschichte*, Munich, 2003, 50–68.

Prinzig, Günter and Maciej Salamon, eds., *Byzanz und Ostmitteleuropa 950–1453. Beiträge zu einer table-ronde des XIX International Congress of Byzantine Studies, Copenhagen 1996*, Wiesbaden, 1999.

Profantová, Nad'a, *Kněžna Ludmila: vládkyně a světice, zakladatelka dynastie*, Prague, 1996.

Radó, Polycarpus, *Libri liturgici manuscripti bibliothecarum Hungariae et limitropharum regionum*, Budapest, 1973.

Rady, Martyn, ed., *Custom and Law in Central Europe*, Centre for European Legal Studies Occasional Papers No. 6, Cambridge, 2003.

*Nobility, Land and Service in Medieval Hungary*, Basingstoke, 2000.

Rajman, Jerzy, 'The origin of Polish Premonstratensian Circary', *Analecta Praemonstratensia* 66 (1990): 203–19.

Richter, Miroslav, 'Zur ältesten Geschichte der Stadt Prag', in *Frühgeschichte der europäischen Stadt. Voraussetzungen und Grundlagen*, eds. Hans Jürgen Brachmann and Joachim Herrmann, Berlin, 1991, 174–79.

Róna-Tas, András, *Hungarians and Europe in the Early Middle Ages: An Introduction to Early Hungarian History*, Budapest, 1999.

Rosik, Stanisław, *Conversio gentis Pomeranorum: studium świadectwa o wydarzeniu (XII wiek)*, Wrocław, 2010.

'Zur Genese und Funktion so genannten Neustädte in Schlesien im 13. und 14. Jahrhundert', in *Rechtsstadtgründungen im mittelalterlichen Polen*, ed. Eduard Mühle, Cologne, 2011, 169–79.

Rydzewski, Jacek, ed., *Pradzieje i wczesne średniowiecze Małopolski: przewodnik po wystawie, katalog zabytków/Prehistory and Early Middle Ages of Little Poland: Exhibition Guide and Catalogue*, Cracow, 2005.

Sadek, Vladimír, 'Medieval Jewish scholars in Prague', *Review of the Society for the History of Czechoslovak Jews* 5 (1992–3): 135–49.

Samsonowicz, Agnieszka, *Łowiectwo w państwie Piastów i Jagiellonów*, Wrocław, 1990.

'The right to hunt in medieval Poland', *Fasciculi Archeologiae Historicae* 21 (2008): 65–70.

Samsonowicz, Henryk, 'Ackerbürgertum im östlichen Mitteleuropa' – in *Ackerbürgertum und Stadtwirtschaft. Zu Regionen und Perioden landwirtschaftlich bestimmten Städtewesens im Mittelalter*, ed. Kurt-Ulrich Jäschke, Heilbronn, 2002, 89–97.

'Les origines du patriciate des villes polonaises', *Acta Poloniae Historica* 67 (1993): 5–15.

'Wer traf die Entscheidungen in den selbstverwalteten Städten des mittelaterlichen Polen?', in *Rechtsstadtgründungen im mittelalterlichen Polen*, ed. Eduard Mühle, Cologne, 2011, 373–84.

Seibt, Ferdinand, 'Der heilige Herzog Wenzel', in *Lebensbilder zur Geschichte der böhmischen Länder*, vol. IV, Munich and Vienna, 1981, 9–21.

Sejbal, Jiří, 'The minting rights of the bishops of Olomouc in the thirteen century', in *Moneta mediaevalis: studia numizmatyczne i historyczne ofiarowane Profesorowi Stanisławowi Suchodolskiemu w 65. rocznicę urodzin*, Warsaw, 2002, 309–25.

Sellier, André and Jean Sellier, *Atlas des peuples d'Europe Centrale*, new edn, Paris, 1995.

Siama, Monika, *La mythologie chrétienne en Pologne du haut moyen âge: le cas de saint Adalbert*, Grenoble, 2009.

Sikorski, Dariusz A., *Kościół w Polsce za Mieszka I i Bolesława Chrobrego: rozważania nad granicami poznania historycznego*, Poznań, 2010.

Sinor, Denis, *Inner Asia and Its Contacts with Medieval Europe*, London, 1977.

Słupecki, Leszek, *Slavonic Pagan Sanctuaries*, Warsaw, 1994.

Smetánka, Zdeněk, *Legenda o Ostojovi: archeologie obyčejného života*, 2nd edn, Prague, 2010.

Sobiesiak, Joanna, *Bolesław II Przemyślida: dynasta i jego państwo*, Cracow, 2006.

Solymosi, László, 'Die Eigenarten der Urkundenausstellung des Stuhlweißenburger Kapitels in der Arpadenzeit', in *Im Gedächtnis der Kirche neu erwachen: Studien zur Geschichte des Christentums in Mittel- und Osteuropa. Festgabe für Gabriel Adriányi zum 65. Geburtstag*, ed. Reimund Haas, Karl Josef Rivinius and Hermann-Josef Scheidgen, Cologne, Weimar and Vienna, 2000, 479–94.

'Die Entwicklung der Schriftlichkeit im Königreich Ungarn vom 11. bis zum 13. Jahrhundert', in *Schriftkultur zwischen Donau und Adria bis zum 13. Jahrhundert. Akten der Akademie Friesach 'Stadt und Kultur im Mittelalter', Friesach (Kärnten), 11.–15. September 2002*, ed. Reinhard Härtel, Klagenfurt, 2008, 483–526.

'Die Gesellschaft um die erste Jahrtausendwende in Ungarn', in *The First Millennium of Hungary in Europe*, ed. Klára Papp, János Barta, Attila Bárány and Attila Györkös, Debrecen, 2002, 38–48.

Sommer, Petr, 'Der beginnende böhmische Staat und seine Heiligen', *Questiones Medii Aevii Novae* 14 (2009): 41–54.

'Early mediaeval monasteries in Bohemia', in *25 Years of Archaeological Research in Bohemia* (*Památky archeologické*, Supplémentum 1), Prague, 1994, 206–11.

'Die gegenwärtige tschechische kirchliche Archäologie', in *Kirchenarchäologie heute. Fragestellungen – Methoden – Ergebnisse*, ed. Niklot Krohn, Darmstadt, 2010, 544–60.

'Heidnische und christiliche Normen im Konflikt. Die Vorstellungswelt der böhmischen Gesellschaft im frühen Mittelalter', in *Prozesse der Normbildung und Normveränderung im mittelalterlichen Europa*, eds. Doris Ruhe and Karl-Heinz Spieß, Stuttgart, 2000, 161–86.

'Der heilige Prokop und sein Kult im Mittelalter', in *Die Heiligen und ihr Kult im Mittelalter*, Prague, 2010, 275–97.

'Procession in early medieval Bohemia', in *Wallfahrten in der europäischen Kultur/ Pilgrimage in European Culture*, eds. Daniel Doležal and Hartmut Kühne, Frankfurt, 2006, 167–76.

'Sázava und böhmische Klöster des 11. Jahrhunderts', in *Der heilige Prokop, Böhmen und Mitteleuropa. Internationales Symposium Benešov–Sázava 24.–26. September 2003*, ed. Petr Sommer, Prague, 2005, 151–71.

Sommer, Petr, Dušan Třeštík, Josef Žemlička and Zoë Opačić, 'Bohemia and Moravia', in *Christianization and the Rise of Christian Monarchy: Scandinavia, Central Europe and Rus'* c. *900–1200*, ed. Nora Berend, Cambridge, 2007, 214–62.

Strzelczyk, Jerzy, 'Die Bedeutung der Gründung des Erzbitums Gnesen und die Schaffung einer kirchlichen Organisation für die Ausformung einer "kirchlichen Kulturlandschaft"', *Siedlungsforschung* 20 (2002): 41–64.

'Einleitung', in *Heiligenleben zur deutsch-slawischen Geschichte. Adalbert von Prag und Otto von Bamberg*, eds. Lorenz Weinrich and Jerzy Strzelczyk, Ausgewählte Quellen zur deutschen Geschichte des Mittelalters, Darmstadt, 2005, 3–26.

'Die Rolle Böhmens und St. Adalberts für die Westorientierung Polens', in *Adalbert von Prag – Brückenbauer zwischen dem Osten und Westen Europas*, Baden-Baden, 1997, 141–62.

Suchodolski, Stanisław, 'Hatte die Münzprägung im Mittelalter einen Einfluß auf die politischen Ereignisse in Polen gehabt?', *Numismatische Zeitschrift* 103 (1995): 57–66.

*Początki mennictwa w Europie Środkowej, Wschodniej i Północnej*, Wrocław, 1971.

Sweeney, James Ross, 'Hungary in the Crusades, 1169–1218', *International History Review* 3 (1981): 467–81.

'Innocent III, canon law, and papal judges delegate in Hungary', in *Popes, Teachers, and Canon Law in the Middle Ages*, ed. James Ross Sweeney and Stanley A. Chodorow, Ithaca, NY, 1989, 26–52.

Świechowski, Zygmunt, *Katalog architektury romańskiej w Polsce*, Warsaw, 2009.

Szűcs, Jenő, 'Theoretical elements in Master Simon of Kéza's Gesta Hungarorum (1282–1285)', in *Simonis de Kéza Gesta Hungarorum – Simon of Kéza, The Deeds of the Hungarians*, ed. and tr. László Veszprémy and Frank Schaer, Budapest, 1999, xxix–cii.

Szymański, Józef, *Kanonikat świecki w Małopolsce od końca XI do połowy XIII w*, Lublin, 1995.

Takács, Imre, ed., *Paradisum plantavit: Bencés monostorok a középkori Magyarországon / Benedictine Monasteries in Medieval Hungary*, Pannonhalma, 2001.

Takács, Miklós, 'Handwerkliche Produktion in den dörflichen Siedlungen im árpádenzeitlichen Ungarn (10.–13. Jahrhundert)', in *Arts and Crafts in Medieval Rural Environment*, ed. Jan Klápště and Petr Sommer, *Ruralia* 6, Turnhout, 2007, 53–70.

Tiplic, Ioan Marian, *Transylvania in the Early Middle Ages (Seventh–Thirteenth Century)*, Gundelsheim, 2006.

Tóth, Endre and Károly Szelényi, *The Holy Crown of Hungary: Kings and Coronations*, Budapest, 1999.

Tóth, Sándor László, 'Princes and dignitaries in the ninth–tenth century Magyar tribal federation', *Chronica: Annual of the Institute of History, University of Szeged* 3 (2003): 21–36.

Trawkowski, Stanisław, 'Die Rolle der deutschen Dorfkolonisation und des deutschen Rechtes in Polen im 13. Jahrhundert', in *Die deutsche Ostsiedlung des Mittelalters als Problem der Europäischen Geschichte*, Sigmaringen, 1975, 349–68.

'Heredes im frühpiastischen Polen', in *Europa Slavica – Europa Orientalis. Festschrift für Herbert Ludat zum 70. Geburtstag*, ed. Klaus-Detlev Grothusen and Klaus Zernack, Berlin, 1980, 262–85.

Třeštík, Dušan, *Kosmova kronika: studie k počátkům českeho dějepisectvi a politického myslení*, Prague, 1968.

*Mýty kmene Čechů: tři studie ke 'starým povéstem českým'*, Prague, 2003.

*Počátky Přemyslovců: vstup Čechů do dějin (530–935)*, Prague, 1997.

'Slavische Liturgie und Schrifttum in Böhmen des 10. Jahrhunderts. Vorstellungen und Wirklichkeit', in *Der heilige Prokop, Böhmen und Mitteleuropa. Internationales Symposium Benešov–Sázava 24.–26. September 2003*, ed. Petr Sommer, Prague, 2005, 205–36.

'Von Svatopluk zu Bolesław Chrobry. Die Entstehung Mitteleuropas aus der Kraft des Tatsächlichen und aus einer Idee', in *The Neighbours of Poland in the Tenth Century*, ed. Przemysław Urbańczyk, Warsaw, 2000, 111–46.

*Tschechen und Österreicher. Gemeinsame Geschichte, gemeinsame Zukunft.* Vienna, 2006.

Tyszkiewicz, Lech, 'Die slawische Burgenorganisation und ihre Umgestaltung in das mittelalterliche Kastellaneisystem Oberschlesiens', in *Stadtgeschichte Oberschlesiens. Studien zur städtischen Entwicklung und Kultur einer ostmitteleuropäischen Region vom Mittelalter bis zum Vorabend der Industrialisierung*, ed. Thomas Wünsch, Berlin, 1995, 9–24.

Urbańczyk, Przemysław, ed., *Early Christianity in Central and East Europe*, Warsaw, 1997.

'Foreign leaders in early Slavic societies', in *Integration und Herrschaft. Ethnische Identitäten und Soziale Organisation im Frühmittelalter*, ed. Walter Pohl and Max Diesenberger, Vienna, 2002, 215–67.

ed., *Origins of Central Europe*, Warsaw, 1997.

'Political circumstances reflected in post-war Polish archaeology', *Public Archaeology* (2000): 49–56.

'Slavic and Christian identities during transition to the Polish Statehood', in *Franks, Northmen and Slavs*, ed. Garipzanov *et al.*, 205–22.

*Trudne początki Polski*, Wrocław, 2008.

'Who named Poland?', in *Mittelalter – Eines oder viele?*, eds. Sławomir Moździoch, Wojciech Mrozowicz and Stanisław Rosik, Wrocław, 2010, 167–82.

*Władza i polityka we wczesnym średniowieczu*, Wrocław, 2000.

Urbańczyk, Przemysław and Stanisław Rosik, 'The kingdom of Poland, with an appendix on Polabia and Pomerania between paganism and Christianity', in *Christianization and the Rise of Christian Monarchy: Scandinavia, Central Europe and Rus'* c. *900–1200*, ed. Nora Berend, Cambridge, 2007, 263–318.

Vaníček, Vratislav, 'Sakralita české panovnické hodnosti, dynastie Přemyslovců a Vyšehradu v proměnách Christianizace a středověké modernizace', in *Královský Vyšehrad*, vol. III, Prague, 2007, 20–37.

'Šlechta a český stát za vlády Přemyslovcu: K formování ideologie české šlechty od 11. do početku 14. století', *Folia Historica Bohemica* 12 (1988): 65–107.

*Soběslav I: Přemyslovci v kontextu evropských dějin v letech 1092–1140*, Prague, 2007.

'Sociální mentalita ceské šlechty: urozenost, rytírství, reprezentace. (Obecné souvislosti, pojetí družiny, "modernizacní" trend)', in *Šlechta, moc a reprezentace ve středověku*, ed. Martin Nodl and Martin Wihoda, Prague, 2007, 141–88.

Varga, Gábor, *Ungarn und das Reich vom 10. bis zum 13. Jahrhundert. Das Herrscherhaus der Árpáden zwischen Anlehnung und Emanzipation*, Munich, 2003.

Vašica, Josef, *Literární památky epochy velkomoravské 863–885*, 2nd edn, Prague, 1996.

Vélimský, Tomáš, 'K problematice rané kolonizace 12. stoleti v Českém středohoří a vzniku feudální pozemkové držby', *Medievalia Historia Bohemica* 4 (1995): 81–101.

Vepřek, Miroslav, 'Církevněslovanské modlitvy českého původu: prieres en slavon d'origine tcheque', *Slavia* 77, 1–3 (2008): 221–30.

Veszprémy, László, 'Chronicles in charters: historical narratives (narrationes) in charters as substitutes for chronicles in Hungary', in *The Medieval Chronicle III: Proceedings of the 3rd International Conference on the Medieval Chronicle. Doorn/Utrecht 12–17 July 2002*, ed. Erik S. Kooper, Amsterdam, 2004, 184–99.

'Historical past and political present in the Latin chronicles of Hungary (twelfth–thirteenth centuries)', in *The Medieval Chronicle: Proceedings of the 1st International Conference on the Medieval Chronicle, Driebergen/ Utrecht, 13–16 July 1996*, ed. Erik S. Kooper, Amsterdam, 1999, 260–8.

'The invented eleventh century of Hungary', in *The Neighbours of Poland in the eleventh Century*, ed. Przemysław Urbańczyk, Warsaw, 2002, 137–54.

ed., *Szent István és az államalapítás*, Budapest, 2002.

Veszprémy, László and Béla K. Király, eds., *A Millennium of Hungarian Military History*, Boulder, CO, 2002.

Veszprémy, László, Tünde Wehli and József Hapák, *The Book of the Illuminated Chronicle*, Budapest, 2009.

Visy, Zsolt, ed., *Hungarian Archaeology at the Turn of the Millennium*, Budapest, 2003.

Warnke, Charlotte, 'Ursachen und Voraussetzungen der Schenkung Polens an den heiligen Petrus', in *Europa Slavica – Europa Orientalis. Festschrift für Herbert Ludat zum 70. Geburtstag*, ed. Klaus-Detlev Grothusen and Klaus Zernack, Berlin, 1980, 127–77.

Wasilewski, Tadeusz, 'Poland's administrative structure in early Piast times: *castra* ruled by *comites* as centres of provinces and territorial administration', *Acta Poloniae Historica* 44 (1981), 5–31.

Wieczorek, Alfried and Hans-Martin Hinz, eds., *Europe's Centre around AD 1000: Catalogue*, Stuttgart, 2000.

eds., *Europe's Centre around AD 1000: Handbook*, Stuttgart, 2000.

Wihoda, Martin, 'Das Sázava Kloster in ideologischen Koordinaten der böhmischen Geschichte des 11. Jahrhunderts', in *Der heilige Prokop, Böhmen und Mitteleuropa Internationales Symposium Benešov – Sázava 24.–26. September 2003*, ed. Petr Sommer, Prague, 2005, 257–71.

'Testament knížete Břetislava', in *Saga moravskych Přemyslovcu: život na Morave od XI. do pocatku XIV. stoleti. Sbornik a katalog vystavy poradane Vlastivednym muzeem v Olomouci a Muzeem mesta Brna k 700. vyroci tragicke smrti Vaclava III., posledniho českeho krale z dynastie Přemyslovcu. Olomouc, Přemyslovsky palac, 20. dubna az 6. srpna 2006, Brno, Hrad Spilberk, 14. zari 2006 az 21. ledna 2007*, ed. Renata Fikova, Olomouc, 2006, 33–50.

*Zlatá bulla sicilská: podivuhodný příběh ve vrstvách paměti*, Prague, 2006.

Wiśniowski, Eugeniusz, *Parafie w średniowiecznej Polsce: struktura i funkcje społeczne*. Lublin, 2004.

Wiszewski, Przemysław, 'At the beginnings of the Piast dynastic tradition: the ancestors of Mieszko in the "Chronicle" of Gallus Anonymus', *Quaestiones Medii Aevi Novae* 9 (2004): 153–82.

'Dagome iudex et Ote senatrix: on the place of the Polish ruler in the aristocratic circle of the Holy Roman Empire at the close of the tenth century', in *Potestas et communitas. Interdisziplinäre Beiträge zu Wesen und Darstellung von Herrschaftsverhältnissen im Mittelalter östlich der Elbe / Interdisciplinary Studies of the Constitution and Demonstration of Power Relations in the Middle Ages East of the Elbe*, ed. Aleksander Paroń, Sébastien Rossignol, Bartłomiej Sz. Szmoniewski and Grisza Vercamer, Wrocław and Warsaw, 2010, 111–23.

*Domus Bolezlai: Values and Social Identity in Dynastic Traditions of Medieval Poland (c. 966–1138)*, East Central and Eastern Europe in the Middle Ages, 450–1450, 9, Leiden and Boston, 2010.

Wolfinger, Lucas, 'Politische Handeln mit dem hl. Adalbert von Prag. Mittelalterliche Vorstellungen von einer civitas sancta', *Mitteilungen des Instituts für Österreichische Geschichtsforschung* 114 (2006): 219–50.

Wolfram, Herwig, *Conversio Bagoariorum et Carantanorum. Das Weissbuch der Salzburger Kirche über die Erfolgreiche Mission in Karantanien und Pannonien*, Vienna and Cologne, 1979.

*Salzburg, Bayern, Österreich. Die Conversio Bagoariorum et Carantanorum und die Quellen ihrer Zeit*, Vienna and Munich, 1995.

Wolverton, Lisa, *Hastening toward Prague: Power and Society in the Medieval Czech Lands*, Philadelphia, 2001.

Wünsch, Thomas, 'Ius commune in Schlesien. Das Beispiel des kanonischen Rechts 13.–15. Jahrhunderts', in *Lux Romana w Europie Środkowej ze szczególnym uwzględnieniem Śląska*, ed. Antoni Barciak, Katowice, 2001, 109–27.

'Kulturbeziehungen zwischen Polen und Reich im Mittelalter', in *Das Reich und Polen. Parallelen, Interaktionen und Formen der Akkulturation im hohen und späten Mittelalter*, ed. Thomas Wünsch and Alexander Patschovsky, Vorträge und Forschungen 59, Ostfildern, 2003, 357–400.

'Territorialbildung zwischen Polen, Böhmen und dem deutschen Reich. Das Breslauer Bistumsland vom 12.–16. Jh.', in *Geschichte des christlichen Lebens im schlesischen Raum*, ed. Joachim Köhler and Reiner Bendel, vol. I, Münster, 2002, 199–264.

Zagiba, Franz, '"Krleš" und "Christe keinado" bei der Begrüssung Thietmars als ersten Bischof von Pragom Jahr 1076 [sic]', in *Millennium dioecesis Pragensis, 973–1973. Beiträge zur Kirchengeschichte Mitteleuropas im 9.–11. Jahrhundert*, ed. Franz Zagiba, Annales Instituti Slavici 8, Vienna, 1974, 119–26.

Zagorhidi, Czigany B., 'Les couvents de la province dominicaine hongroise au XIIIème siècle', in *Dominikanie w środkowej Europie w XIII–XV wieku. Aktywność duszpasterska i kultura intelektualna*, eds. J. Kłoczowski and J. A. Spież, Poznań, 2002, 285–92.

Zaoral, Roman, 'Die Anfänge der Brakteatenwährung in Böhmen', in *XII. Internationaler Numismatischer Kongress Berlin 1997. Akten – Proceedings – Actes*, vol. II, Berlin, 2000, 993–9.

Zaremska, Hanna, 'Statut Bolesława Pobożnego dla Żydów: uwagi w sprawie genezy', *Roczniki Dziejów Społecznych i Gospodarczych* 64 (2004): 107–34.

*Żydzi w średniowiecznej Europie Środkowej*, Poznań, 2005.

*Żydzi w średniowiecznej Polsce: gmina krakowska*, Warsaw, 2011.

Zemek, Metodej, 'Das Olmützer Domkapitel. Seine Entstehung und Entwicklung bis 1600', *Archiv für Kirchengeschichte von Böhmen-Mähren-Schlesien* 9 (1988): 66–86.

Žemlička, Josef, *Čechy v době knížecí (1034–1198)*, Prague, 1997.

'České 13. století: "privatizace" státu', *Český časopis historický* 101, 3 (2005): 509–40.

'K ústrojí přemyslovského státu: Čechy a Morava jako zeme, království, markrabství', *Česky Časopis Historický* 108 (2010): 361–405.

'Leitmeritz (Litoměřice) als Beispiel eines frühmittelalterlichen Burgerzentrums Böhmens', in *Burg – Burgstadt – Stadt. Zur Genese mittelalterlicher nichtagrarischer Zemtren in Ostmitteleuropa*, ed. Hans Brachmann, Berlin, 1995, 256–64.

*Přemysl Otakar I: panovnik, stát a česká společnost na prachu vrcholného feudalismu*, Prague, 1990.

'Das Reich der bömischen Boleslavs und die Krise an der Jahrthausendwende. Zur Charakteristik der frühen Staaten in Mitteleuropa', *Archeologické Rozhledy* 47 (1995): 267–78.

*Rod Přemyslovců na rozhrani 10. a 11. stoleti*, Prague, 2000.

'Transformation of the dukedom of "the Bohemians" into the Kingdom of Bohemia', in *Political Culture in Central Europe, Tenth-Twentieth Century*, vol. I, *Middle Ages and Early Modern Era*, ed. Halina Manikowska and Jaroslav Pánek, Prague, 2005, 47–64.

Zernack, Klaus, 'Zum Problem der nationalen Identität in Ostmitteleuropa', in *Nationales Bewußtsein und kollektive Identität*, ed. Helmut Berding, Frankfurt am Main, 1994, 176–88.

Zientara, Benedykt, *Heinrich der Bärtige und seine Zeit. Politik und Gesellschaft im mittelalterlichen Schlesien*, Munich, 2002.

'Socio-economic and spatial transformation of Polish towns during the Period of Location', *Acta Poloniae Historica* 34 (1976): 57–83.

'Une voie d'ascension sociale aux XIIe–XIVe siècle: les "locatores" en Europe centrale', in *Gerarchie economiche e gerarchie sociali, secoli XII–XVIII: atti della Dodicesima Settimana di Studi, 18–23 aprile 1980*, ed. Annalisa Guarducci, Florence, 1990, 33–52.

'Walloons in Silesia in the twelfth and thirteenth centuries', *Quaestiones Medii Aevi* 2 (1981): 127–50.

Zimmermann, Harald, *Der Deutsche Orden im Burzenland. Eine diplomatische Untersuchung*, Cologne, 2000.

*Der Deutsche Orden in Siebenbürgen. Eine diplomatische Untersuchung*, Cologne and Weimar, 2011.

*Siebenbürgen und seine Hospites Theutonici. Vorträge und Forschungen zur südostdeutschen Geschichte. Festgabe zum 70. Geburtstag*, ed. Konrad Gündisch, Cologne, 1996.

Zimonyi, István, *Muszlim források a honfoglalás előtti magyarokról: a Ǧayhānī-hagyomány magyar fejezete*, Budapest, 2005; German tr., *Muslimische Quellen über die Ungarn vor der Landnahme. Das ungarische Kapitel der Ǧaihânî-Tradition*, Herne, 2006.

Zoll-Adamikowa, Helena, 'Zum Beginn der Köperbestattung bei den Westslawen', in *Rom und Byzanz im Norden. Mission und Glaubenswechsel im Ostseeraum während des 8–14. Jahrhunderts*, vol. II, ed. Michael Müller-Wille, Mainz and Stuttgart, 1998, 227–38.

Zsoldos, Attila, *Az Árpádok és asszonyaik: a királynéi intézmény az Árpádok korában*, Budapest, 2005.

ed., *Saint Stephen and His Country. A Newborn Kingdom in Central Europe: Hungary*, Budapest, 2001.

Zygner, Leszek, 'Die Pfarrei im mittelalterlichen Polen. Ein Forschungsüberblick', in *Pfarreien im Mittelalter. Deutschland, Polen, Tschechien und Ungarn im Vergleich*, eds. Nathalie Kruppa and Leszek Zygner, Veröffentlichungen des Max-Planck-Instituts für Geschichte, 238, Göttingen, 2008, 67–82.

# INDEX